Hague-Zagreb Essays 4
on the law of international trade

Session 1981 Eernewoude

HAGUE-ZAGREB ESSAYS 4

ON THE LAW OF INTERNATIONAL TRADE

international sales
standard forms - general conditions
the sole distributor
international arbitration - national adjudication

edited by

C.C.A. VOSKUIL AND J.A. WADE

SPRINGER-SCIENCE+BUSINESS MEDIA, B.V.

Interuniversitair Instituut voor Internationaal Recht T.M.C. Asser Instituut
20-22 Alexanderstraat, The Hague

The T.M.C. Asser Instituut was founded in 1965 by the Dutch universities offering courses in international law to promote education and research in the fields of law covered by the departments of the Institute: Private International Law, including International Commercial Arbitration, Public International Law and Law of the European Communities. The Institute discharges this task by the establishment and management of documentation and research projects, in some instances in co-operation with non-Dutch or international organisations, by the dissemination of information deriving therefrom and by publication of monographs and series. In addition, the Institute participates in the editing of the Yearbook Commercial Arbitration and in the editing and publishing of, *inter alia,* the Netherlands International Law Review and the Netherlands Yearbook of International Law.

Institute Address: Alexanderstraat 20-22, The Hague
Postbox : 30461, 2500 GL The Hague
Telephone : (0)70 - 63 09 00
Telex : 34273 asser nl

ISBN 978-94-015-1189-6 ISBN 978-94-015-1187-2 (eBook)
DOI 10.1007/978-94-015-1187-2

Originally published by Martinus Nijhoff, The Hague in 1983
Softcover reprint of the hardcover 1st edition 1983

Springer-Science+Business Media, B.V.

PREFACE

The present publication of reports and discussions stems from the fourth Session of the Hague-Zagreb Colloquium, held at Eernewoude, in the Netherlands. The preceding three Sessions were held at Stubiče Toplice, in Yugoslavia (1974), Zeist, in the Netherlands (1976) and, again in Yugoslavia, at Opatija (1978).

The fourth Session was originally planned for May 1980. On the eve of the meeting, the then President of the Socialist Federal Republic of Yugoslavia, the late Marshall J.B. Tito, passed away. On hearing the news of the Marshall's death, the Organizing Committee of the Hague-Zagreb Colloquium immediately decided that the Session should not then be held. The postponement lasted, in fact, a whole year: the fourth Session was convened at Eernewoude in May 1981.

For the Eernewoude Session the formula that had produced such excellent results in the previous conferences was maintained. Four topics of international trade law were thoroughly discussed on the basis of reports submitted by scholars from the various legal systems represented at the conference. Apart from the Yugoslav and Dutch participants, scholars from the United Kingdom, the Federal Republic of Germany, Belgium and Norway took part in the discussions, be it in the capacity of reporter, of chairman or as expert in the field covered by the Colloquium: the law of international trade.

A student competition had again been organised and the members of the winning teams from Yugoslavia and from the Netherlands were among the participants. The papers they had submitted were discussed in a special meeting.

Significant financial support was once again kindly provided by the Yugoslav and Dutch Governments under the terms of the Cultural Treaty concluded between the two countries.

The Presidency of the Colloquium is in the hands of Professor Ž. Matić, at the time Dean of the Faculty of Law of Zagreb University and Dr. C.C.A. Voskuil, Director of the T.M.C. Asser Institute for International and European Community Law, the Hague. The latter presided over the Eernewoude Session.

The Colloquium was privileged to welcome to its fourth Session Dr. Ch. M.J.A. Moons, at that time Vice-President of the Dutch Supreme Court, the *Hoge Raad der Nederlanden*, as its honorary guest, and was honoured by the presence during part of the Session of H.E. M. Šumonja, at that time Ambassador of the Socialist Federal Republic of Yugoslavia to the Netherlands.

We wish again to extend our gratitude to the Governments of Yugoslavia and the Netherlands for the invaluable support rendered under the Cultural Treaty.

Similarly we would like to express our gratitude to the reporters, the chairmen and all other participants, as well as to the staff-members of our Institutes who, once again, made such a splendid effort in organizing the Eernewoude Session and preparing the present volume.

C.C.A. Voskuil Z. Matić

CONTENTS*

* for detailed tables of contents see each report

PARTICIPANTS*

Eernewoude Session, 12 - 15 May 1981

Praesidium:

C.C.A. VOSKUIL, Director, T.M.C. Asser Instituut, The Hague
Z. MATIĆ, Professor and Dean of the Faculty of Law, University of Zagreb

Honorary Guest:

Ch. M.J.A. MOONS, Vice-President of the *Hoge Raad der Nederlanden,* The Hague

Guests:

Yugoslavia

His Excellency M. ŠUMONJA, Ambassador of the Socialist Federal Republic of Yugoslavia, The Hague
N. FILIPOVIĆ, Professor, Faculty of Law, University of Zagreb

Norway

P. LØDRUP, Professor, Institute for Private Law, University of Oslo

The Netherlands

P.J. VERDAM, Member of the *Raad van State,* President of the Board, T.M.C. Asser Instituut, The Hague
J.J.H. POP, Mayor of the City of Franeker

Chairmen of Sessions*:

H. DUINTJER TEBBENS, Head of Department, T.M.C. Asser Instituut, The Hague
V. FILIPOVIĆ, Professor, Faculty of Law, University of Zagreb
P. ŠARČEVIĆ, Professor, Faculty of Law, University of Rijeka
CLIVE M. SCHMITTHOFF, Professor, City University, London

Reporters*:

J. BARBIĆ, Professor, Faculty of Law, University of Zagreb
U. DROBNIG, Professor, Director, Max Planck Institute, Hamburg
A. GOLDŠTAJN, Professor, Faculty of Law, University of Zagreb
H. VAN HOUTTE, Professor, Faculty of Law, University of Louvain
Ž. MATIĆ, Professor and Dean of the Faculty of Law, University of Zagreb
P. ŠARČEVIĆ, Professor, Faculty of Law, University of Rijeka
F.J.A. VAN DER VELDEN, Lecturer, Faculty of Law, University of Utrecht
J.A. WADE, Deputy Director, T.M.C. Asser Instituut, The Hague
J.L. YELLAND, Barrister at Law, Lecturer, Queen Mary College, University of London

Student Reporters*:

V. CRNIĆ, University of Rijeka
E.C.N. DE LÉON, University of Amsterdam
T.Th. STERNFELD, University of Amsterdam
V. TOMLJENOVIĆ, University of Rijeka

* Listed in alphabetical order

Participants*:

E. VAN AERDE-VAN LEEUWEN, Research Officer, T.M.C. Asser Instituut, The Hague
D. DRAŽANČIĆ, dipl. jur., Research Assistent, Faculty of Law, University of Zagreb
L. ERADES, Vice-President of the *Arrondissementsrechtbank,* Rotterdam
R.E. EVERARD, Research Officer, T.M.C. Asser Instituut, The Hague
H.U. JESSURUN D'OLIVEIRA, Professor, Faculty of Law, University of Amsterdam
E. LISSONE, Company lawyer, Hunter Douglas N.V., Rotterdam
H. MEIJERS, Professor, Faculty of Law, University of Amsterdam
D. MITROVIĆ, Professor, Faculty of Political Sciences, University of Belgrade
E. PALLUA, Scientific Counsellor, Adriatic Institute of the Yugoslav Academy of Science and Arts, Zagreb
K. SAJKO, Professor, Faculty of Law, University of Zagreb
J.P. VERHEUL, Professor, Faculty of Law, University of Leyden

Organization and Secretariat:

G.J. DE ROODE, Institute Manager, T.M.C. Asser Instituut, The Hague
G.D. LEE-HEEMSKERK, Secretary to the Director, T.M.C. Asser Instituut, The Hague
P.A. SCHREGARDUS, Research Assistant, T.M.C. Asser Instituut, The Hague

* Listed in alphabetical order

LIST OF DOCUMENTS ANNEXED

Conventions and Treaties

National Legislation

Yugoslavia

Judicial Decisions

Belgium

The Netherlands

LIST OF ABBREVIATIONS

AAe	Ars Aequi (The Netherlands)
AC	Appeal Cases
ACLOT	Act on Civil Liability for Oiltankers
ADSp	Allgemeine Deutsche Spediteurbedingungen
AGB	Allgemeine Geschäftsbedingungen
AGBGB	Gesetz zur Regelung des Rechts der Allgemeinen Geschäftsbedingungen (West-Germany)
AJCL	American Journal of Comparative Law
AJIL	American Journal of International Law
AK	Asser Private International Law Card Index (T.M.C.Asser Institute)
ALAMAR	Latin American Association of Shipowners
All ER	All England Law Reports
AMC	American Maritime Cases
AWD	Aussenwirtschaftsdienst des Betriebs-Beraters (West-Germany; since 1975: RIW)
BB	Der Betriebs-Berater (West-Germany)
Ber D Ges VR	Berichte der Deutschen Gesellschaft für Völkerrecht (West-Germany)
BG	Bundesgericht (Switzerland)
BGB	Bürgerliches Gesetzbuch (West-Germany)
BGBl	Bundes Gesetzblatt (West-Germany)
BGE	Entscheidungen des Bundesgerichts (Switzerland)
BGH	Bundesgerichtshof (West-Germany)
BGHZ	Entscheidungen des Bundesgerichtshofes in Zivilsachen (West-Germany)
BW	Burgerlijk Wetboek (Netherlands)
BYIL	British Yearbook of International Law
Car & P	Carrington & Payne's Law Reports (England)
CC	Civil Code
CCPr	Code of Civil Procedure
Ch, Ch D	Chancery Division (England)
CIM	Convention Internationale concernant le Transport des Marchandises par Chemins de Fer
CISG	United Nations Convention on Contracts for the International Sale of Goods, Vienna, 1980
CJS	Corpus Juris Secundum
C Jud	Code Judiciaire (Belgium)
CLC	International Convention on Civil Liability for Oil Pollution Damage
CLJ	The Cambridge Law Journal (England)
Clunet	Journal du Droit International (France)
CMI	Comité Maritime International
CMLR	Common Market Law Review
CMR	Convention relative au contract de transport international de marchandises par route
COGSA	Carriage of Goods by Sea Act
Col LR	Columbia Law Review
COLREG	Convention on the International Regulations for Preventing Collisions at Sea

Comm C	Commercial Code
Corn LR	Cornell Law Review
CPrC	Code de Procédure Civile
CPrCComm	Code de Procédure Civile et Commerciale (France)
CRISTAL	Contract Regarding an Interim Supplement to Tanker Liability for Oil Pollution
D, Dall	Recueil Dalloz - Sirey (France)
DB	Der Betrieb (West Germany)
DMF	Droit Maritime Français
Dow & Cl	Dow & Clarke's Law Reports (England)
EAG	see EKG
E & B	Ellis & Blackburn's Law Reports (England)
ECC	European Contract for Coffee
ECE	Economic Commission for Europe
ECR	European Court Reports
EEC	European Economic Community
EGBGB	Einführungsgesetz zum Bürgerliches Gesetzbuch (West-Germany)
EKG	Einheitliches Gesetz über den Abschluss von Internationalen Kaufverträgen über Bewegliche Sachen (West Germany)
ENEA	European Nuclear Energy Agency
Euratom	The European Atomic Energy Community
F	Federal Reporter (USA)
FRG	Federal Republic of Germany
FTC	Federal Trade Commission (USA)
Gaz Pal	La Gazette du Palais
GDR	German Democratic Republic
GMT	Greenwich Mean Time
GRT	Gross Registered Ton
H & N	Hurlstone & Norman's Law Reports (England)
Hans RGZ	Hanseatische Rechts- und Gerichtszeitschrift (West-Germany)
Harv LR	Harvard Law Review
HC Deb	Hansard: Reports of Debates House of Commons (England)
HGB	Handelsgesetzbuch (West-Germany)
HR	Hoge Raad der Nederlanden
IAEA	International Atomic Energy Agency
ICC	International Chamber of Commerce
ICJRep	International Court of Justice, Reports of Judgments, Advisory Opinions and Orders
ICLQ	International and Comparative Law Quarterly (England)
ICNT	Informal Composite Negotiating Text
IFC	International Convention on the Establishment of an International Fund for Compensation for Oil Pollution Damage
ILA	International Law Association
ILM	International Legal Materials (USA)
ILR	International Law Reports
IMC	International Maritime Committee
IMCO	Intergovernmental Maritime Consultative Organization
IMF	International Monetary Fund
IPRax	Praxis des Internationalen Privat- und Verfahrensrecht (West-Germany)
JBL, JBusL	Journal of Business Law (England)
JCB	Jurisprudence Commerciale de Belgique

JUGPOL	Agreement between the *Yugoslav* and *Polish* Economic Councils on the general conditions of contracts involving the delivery of goods (1971)
JW	Juristische Wochenschrift (West-Germany)
KB	Law Reports King's Bench Division (England)
Ktg	Kantongerecht (Netherlands)
Law Com	Law Commission (England)
LG	Landgericht (West-Germany)
LJPM & A	Law Journal Reports (Probate, Matrimonial and Admiralty) (England)
LJQB	Law Journal Queen's Bench (England)
Lloyd's Rep	Lloyd's List Law Reports (England)
LMCLQ	Lloyd's Maritime and Commercial Law Quarterly (England)
LQR	Law Quarterly Review (England)
LRHL	Law Reports House of Lords (England)
LRRP	Reports of Restrictive Practices Cases (England)
LT	Law Times (England)
MLR	The Modern Law Review (England)
MR	Master of the Rolls
NILR	Netherlands International Law Review
NJ	Nederlandse Jurisprudentie (Netherlands)
NJB	Nederlands Juristenblad (Netherlands)
NJW	Neue Juristische Wochenschrift (West-Germany)
NTIR	Nederlands Tijdschrift voor Internationaal Recht (see NILR)
NYIL	Netherlands Yearbook of International Law
NYULR	New York University Law Review
OECD	Organization for Economic Cooperation and Development
OJ	Official Journal of the European Communities
OLG	Oberlandesgericht (West-Germany)
P & I	Protection and Indemnity
PCIJ	Permanent Court of Justice
QB, QBD	Law Reports Queen's Bench Division (England)
QBD	Law Reports (Queen's Bench Division)
RabelsZ	Rabels Zeitschrift für ausländisches und internationales Privatrecht (West-Germany)
Rb	Arrondissementsrechtbank (Netherlands)
Rec Cours	Receuil des Cours (Academie de Droit International: Collected Courses of the Hague Academy of International Law)
Rev Arb	Revue D'Arbitrage (France)
Rev Crit	Revue Critique de Droit International Privé (France)
Rev Trim de droit commun	Revue trimestrielle de droit commun (France)
RCZ	Entscheidungen des Reichsgerichts, Zivilsachen (West-Germany)
RIW	Recht der Internationalen Wirtschaft (West-Germany; until 1975: AWD)
RTR	Road Traffic Reports (England)
RW	Rechtskundig Weekblad (Belgium)
SDR	Special Drawing Rights
SEW	Sociaal Economische Wetgeving (Netherlands)
SFRY	Socialist Federal Republic of Yugoslavia
SI	Statutory Instruments (England)

S & S	Schip en Schade (Netherlands)
Stb	Staatsblad van het Koninkrijk der Nederlanden
TexLR	Texas Law Review
TIR	Transport International Routier
TLR	Times Law Reports (England)
TOVALOP	Tanker Owners Voluntary Agreement Concerning Liability for Oil Pollution
Trb	Tractatenblad van het Koninkrijk der Nederlanden
Trib comm	Tribunal de commerce (Belgium)
UCC	Uniform Commercial Code
U Chicago LR	University of Chicago Law Review
ULFIS	Uniform Law on the Formation of Contracts for the International Sale of Goods, The Hague, 1964
ULIS	Uniform Law on the International Sale of Goods, The Hague, 1964
UN	United Nations
UNCITRAL	United Nations Committee on International Trade Law
UNCLOS	United Nations Conference on the Law of the Sea
UNCTAD	United Nations Conference on Trade and Development
UNECAFE	United Nations Economic Commission for Asia and the Far East
UNECE	United Nations Economic Commission for Europe
UNEP	United Nations Environment Programme
UNIDROIT	International Institute for the Unification of Private Law (Rome)
UNTS	United Nations Treaty Series
U Pa LR	University of Pennsylvania Law Review
USC	United States Codes
VersR	Versicherungsrecht (West-Germany)
VRS	Verkehrsrechtsammlung (West-Germany)
W	Weekblad van het Recht (Netherlands)
WLR	Weekly Law Reports (England)
WM	Wohnungswirtschaft und Mietrecht (West-Germany)
WPNR	Weekblad voor Privaatrecht, Notarisambt en Registratie (Netherlands)
WvK	Wetboek van Koophandel (Netherlands)
ZaÖRV	Zeitschrift für ausländisches öffentliches Recht und Völkerrecht (West-Germany)
ZfRvgl	Zeitschrift für Rechtsvergleichung (West-Germany)
ZfVgl Rechtswiss	Zeitschrift für vergleichende Rechtswissenschaft (West-Germany)
ZHR	Zeitschrift für das gesammte Handelsrecht und Wirtschaftsrecht (West-Germany)
ZPO	Zivilprozessordnung (West-Germany)

INTERNATIONAL SALES

UNIFORM LAW ON THE INTERNATIONAL SALE OF GOODS, UNIFORM LAW ON THE FORMATION OF CONTRACTS FOR THE INTERNATIONAL SALE OF GOODS (1964) AND UNITED NATIONS CONVENTION ON CONTRACTS FOR THE INTERNATIONAL SALE OF GOODS (1980)

by Jaksa Barbić

1. INTRODUCTION

Fourteen years after the adoption of the Hague Uniform Laws, the United Nations Commission on International Trade Law (UNCITRAL) drew up a Draft Convention on the International Sale of Goods. The Draft Convention was the result of several years of work by a Working Group of 14 States, which made a revision of the Uniform Law on the International Sale of Goods (ULIS) and the Uniform Law on the Formation of Contracts for the International Sale of Goods (ULFIS), and unified both revised texts into a single Convention. The Convention was adopted at the United Nations International Conference held in Vienna in 1980.

The Convention has introduced numerous changes in the Hague Uniform Laws. When comparing the relevant texts one gains the impression that the intention was to simplify the formulations contained in the Hague Uniform Laws. As a result, the new text has been shortened by a third, and is, in consequence, in some places less precise. In certain matters the changes have brought about some improvements the need for which was pointed out in the critiques levelled at some formulations contained in the Uniform Laws. The Convention is, however, in good part an expression of a compromise not only between formulations stemming from the continental and common law legal systems, but also of the demands voiced by the developing countries. Because of this, the new text contains in some instances hybrid solutions intended to adjust as much as possible differing conceptions and differing interests. As a result, the original intention of the drafters of the Convention was not fulfilled in some places. Instead of a simplification that should facilitate the application of the Convention in practice, such half-way and compromise solutions could, in my opinion, cause difficulties in their implementation.

For illustration's sake, only a few of such changes made in the Convention are discussed in the present paper.

2. APPLICATION OF CONFLICT OF LAWS

The first significant difference between the Convention and ULIS and ULFIS relates to the application of the rules of private international law. The intention of both ULIS and ULFIS was for the rules of private international law to be excluded for the purpose of the application of these laws, the only exception being when otherwise specified by these laws (Art. 2 ULIS and Art. 1, para. 9 ULFIS). In line with this, they deal with objective criteria governing their application. This is understandable since these are the only conditions required for their application. The Convention has abandoned these criteria.

The Convention, ULIS and ULFIS have in this respect only one common point of departure, notably the one according to which they all apply to contracts of sale of goods between parties whose places of business are in different States (Art. 1, para. 1 of both laws and the Convention) while they fundamentally differ with respect to additional requirements. ULIS and ULFIS elaborate in Art. 1, para. 1 additional requirements for application, insisting always on acts that take place in the territories of different States (carriage of goods from the territory of one State to the territory of another; effecting of the acts constituting the offer and the acceptance in the territories of different States; delivery of the goods in the territory of a State other than that within whose territory the acts constituting the offer and the acceptance are effected). The Convention contains a different solution. It demands that "different States" should be Contracting States, or that the rules of private international law lead to the application of the law of a Contracting State (Art. 1, para. 1, subparas. (a) and (b)).

The rationale for laying down such conditions for the application of the Convention is for the Convention to become in the ratifying countries municipal law applicable to contracts for the international sale of goods whenever the law of these countries is applied. Consequently, although the rules of private international law refer to the law of a particular country, the Convention which it has ratified will apply instead of its law otherwise applicable to internal contracts for the sale of goods, even if a contract is involved between parties whose places of business are in different States, but where one of such countries is not a Contracting State. It is not necessary for goods to be carried from the territory of one State to the territory of another, nor for acts in connection with the formation of the contract to be effected in the territories of different States. This means that the Convention may also be applied when all this takes place in the territory of only one country which may, but need not, be a Contracting State. It is essential for the parties to have their places of business in different States.

Furthermore, the Convention may also be applied when parties whose places of business are in different States, but one of which or even both of them are not Contracting States, stipulate the application of the law of a third country which has ratified the Convention. If they have not expressly stipulated in the contract the application of the law applied in a third country to internal contracts for the sale of goods, it should be presumed that the law applied in that country to the contracts for the international sale of goods, i.e., the Convention, has been stipulated. This is so because even when the applicable law is stipulated, if this is properly done, the rules of private international law apply, i.e., the rule on party autonomy.

Considered in this way, the sphere of application of the Convention has been expanded relative to ULIS and ULFIS. In this way the application of municipal substantive law regulating internal contracts to international contracts for the sale of goods has been narrowed. For even the Convention does not entirely preclude the taking into account of municipal law regarding contracts for the international sale of goods, as can be seen, for example, in the cases provided for in Articles 6, 12 and 28. In view of this, it can be said that the formulation proposed contributes more to the unification of the law of the international sale of goods than do ULIS and ULFIS. Countries which ratify the Convention will in this way have introduced duality in the regulation of contracts for domestic and international sale of goods.

However, the application of the rules of private international law, with all the problems their application brings, is not excluded. Non-interference in the application of the rules of private international law is a more realistic stand than the one adopted in this respect in ULIS and ULFIS.

In this connection it should be noted that although the application of the rules of private international law makes possible more extensive application of the uniform law contained in the Convention, it nevertheless allows the application of non-unified municipal law. For it should be noted that the Convention in Art. 7, para. 2 contains the provision incorporated in ULIS whereby questions concerning matters governed by this law which are not expressly settled therein shall be settled in conformity with the general principles on which this law is based (ULIS Art. 17). This is in line with the stand explicitly expressed in ULIS where exclusion of the rules of private international law in connection with its application, and the wish solely to apply unified law to contracts for the international sale of goods is expressed.

This is, however, not always possible consistently to achieve in practice, because there are questions which are not regulated by this law and which cannot be settled in conformity with the general principles on which ULIS is based. Some of these are explicitly cited in ULIS itself (Art. 8), but to this should be added cases where certain cogent rules of municipal law must be applied. In addition, there may be situations in which questions concerning matters governed by ULIS which are no expressly settled therein cannot be settled in conformity with the general principles on which this law is based. In such cases the question arises as to whether, notwithstanding the provision of Article 17 of ULIS, resort will have to be made to solutions provided in municipal law, which would thus be indirectly applied. The obligation nevertheless remains primarily to seek a solution in conformity with the general principles on which ULIS is based, and also to apply other sources of the law of international trade. Thus, the question remains open as to the possibility of applying municipal law since, because of the formulations it contains, it is not always suitable to be applied to contracts for the international sale of goods.

Therefore, a more realistic stand prevailed by inserting in Art. 7, para. 2 of the Convention the provision that in the absence of the general principles on which the Convention is based questions concerning matters governed by the Convention which are not expressly settled in it are to be settled in conformity with the law applicable by virtue of the rules of private international law.

By providing for its application in cases when the rules of private international law lead to the application of the law of a Contracting State (Art. 1, para. 1, subpara. (b)), the Convention in fact precludes the application of the municipal law of this State which applies to internal contracts of sale of goods with respect to those questions which are settled in the Convention. Since the rules of private international law are the basis for the application of substantive law, the municipal law governing contracts for the internal sale of goods which is indicated by these rules will apply on the basis of the Convention to questions not settled in it. According to the provision corresponding to the one contained in Art. 17 of ULIS, account will nevertheless have to be taken of the international character of contracts to which municipal law applies, and of the suitability of the formulations of municipal law for filling in the gaps in such contracts.

Even though the Convention thus offers broader possibilities for applying the Convention, it should nevertheless be noted that the requirements to be met according to Art. 1, para. 2 for it to be concluded that the parties have their places of business in different States, have to some extent a restrictive character. For it is not enough for the parties really to have their places of business in different States, since it is demanded that at least one of the subjective requirements cited there be fulfilled. Thus, this fact must appear from the contract or from any dealings between, or from information disclosed by, the parties at any time before or at the conclusion of the contract. In practice this will most frequently be the case, especially when the formation of a contract in writing is involved, but a situation where the Convention is not applicable is also possible, if the parties have their places of business in different States.

This additional requirement for it to be concluded that the parties have their places of business in different States was most likely aimed at the parties being from the outset certain as to the application of the Convention. But in this way a subjective element has been added to the requirements for its application, which could in practice sometimes lead to uncertainty. For it should be noted that in cases where the Convention is not applicable, a municipal law must be applied. As a rule, there will be no difficulties if the requirement that the places of business are in different States appears from the contract or from any dealings between the parties, but difficulties might arise in deciding when it can be considered that this appears from informations disclosed by the parties. Is it in such a case necessary for a party himself to disclose such information to the other party, or is it sufficient for the party to learn of this in some other way? It would be in the interest of legal security and the unification of the law of the international sale of goods for this requirement, since it is already contained in the Convention, to be interpreted in a broader sense, i.e., that it is also fulfilled by the fact that it is known to the parties that the places of business are in different States, instead of insisting that one party must disclose this to the other. This would be in line with the principle contained in the Convention whereby in the interpretation and application of the provisions of the Convention, regard is to be had to its international character and to the need to promote uniformity and the observation of good faith in international trade (Art. 7, para. 1). This can, however, cause difficulties in proving whether or not the fact was known that the parties had their places of business in different States, especially because it should be considered that this requirement was fulfilled only if this was known to all contracting parties.

The same difficulty in proving this circumstance may arise if a party has more than one place of business. In such a case the place of business is that which has the closest relationship to the contract and its performance, having regard to the circumstances known to or contemplated by the parties at any time before or at the conclusion of the contract (Art. 10, subpara. (a) of the Convention). Consequently, here, too, a subjective requirement has been adopted which must be fulfilled by all contracting parties, the objective existence of the closest relationship to the contract and its performance not being sufficient.

Although this is not explicitly provided for in Art. 1, para. 1 of the Convention, the Convention has nevertheless settled the dilemma as to the moment when the parties must have had their places of business in different States. For the purposes of the Convention, this should be at the moment of the conclusion of the contract. This appears from the provisions according to which the aforesaid special subjective requirement for the application of the Convention (i.e., that this fact appear either from the contract or from any dealings between, or from information disclosed by, the parties) must be fulfilled at any time before or at the conclusion of the contract (Art. 1, para. 2 in fine), and that in the event that a party has more than one place of business, the closest relationship to the contract and its performance is assessed having regard to the circumstances known to or contemplated by the parties at any time before or at the conclusion of the contract (Art. 10, subpara. (a)). It is evident that this special subjective requirement can be met by the time required only if up to that moment the places of business were in different States. A subsequent change in the places of business could not have an influence on the application of the Convention. Since the Convention also regulates the formation of contracts, relevant questions should be governed by the Convention if the requirements for its application had been met before the formation of the contract.

3. DELIMITATION OF SALE CONTRACTS

Another significant change in the provisions regulating the application of the Convention was made by the introduction of an additional provision supplementing the provisions of ULIS and ULFIS which regulate the delimitation of contracts for the sale of goods and other similar contracts.

These laws provide for such delimitation only with respect to who supplies and in what measure the materials for the manufacture of goods which have to be supplied (ULIS, Art. 6; ULFIS, Art. 1, para. 7). This kind of delimitation is not sufficient nor precise enough, especially with respect to the subject-matter of contracts for work, for it does not cover cases in which the party who orders the goods does not supply necessary material at all but it is nevertheless not a contract of sale of goods but a contract for work. Because of this, such delimitation does not exclude the application of municipal law when it is necessary to determine the legal nature of contracts for the sale of goods and to distinguish such contracts from other related contracts. And this delimitation is essential for the application of ULIS and ULFIS.

The Convention has retained this criterion as contained in these laws, but has added to it one more which primarily applies. According to this additional criterion, the Convention does not apply to contracts in which the preponderant part of the obligations of the seller consists in the supply of labour or other services (Art. 3, para. 2). Consequently, account should be taken of the fact that according to the Convention contracts in which the proponderant part of the obligations of the seller consists in the supply of labour or other services are not considered as being contracts for the sale of goods. This is the essential criterion for distinguishing contracts for the sale of goods from related contracts. In this way the need has been removed for the purpose of determining the application of the Convention to ascertain the nature of contracts according to legal rules outside the Convention. This approach is simpler and more reliable than ascertaining the nature of contracts according to the rules of municipal laws applicable to internal contracts, because they differ in this respect. In this way this significant improvement contributes to the creation of uniform criteria for the application of the Convention.

4. INTERPRETATION AND APPLICATION

An innovation relative to the present regulation of international contracts for the sale of goods is seen in the formulation contained in the Convention regarding the interpretation and application of the Convention. In order to promote uniformity in the application of the Convention, the Convention lays down the rule according to which regard is to be had to its international character and to the need to promote uniformity and the observance of good faith in international trade (Art. 7, para. 1). This rule in fact relates to two things: (a) uniformity of the rules applicable to international contracts for the sale of goods; and (b) observation of good faith in international trade.

Since according to the Convention it applies when the rules of private international law lead to the application of the law of a Contracting State, it was necessary to lay down an interpretative rule according to which regard is to be had to the international character of the Convention in the interpretation and application of its provisions. If the Convention is a constituent part of the law of the country indicated by the rules of private interantional law, this is necessary to prevent individual notions and formulations of the Convention from being given the content and meaning they have in the municipal law applicable to internal contracts for the sale of goods. In this way, in deciding conflicts arising from contracts for the international sale of goods, municipal courts are also called upon in applying the Convention to depart from the positions based on their municipal law which differ from the uniform rules of international trade. This should also be taken into consideration when municipal law is applied to contracts for the international sale of goods. A different attitude, would call into question the purpose of the adoption of the Convention, viz. the unification of the law of the international sale of goods. The existence of a uniform text is not sufficient to establish uniformity in practice. This is why uniformity in application is also demanded. It is another question how effectively to achieve uniformity in practice. Because of this, in addition to direct instructions contained in the Convention, it would be necessary to ensure efficacious monitoring of its application in practice and find a way of making the information collected accessible to all those concerned.

The fact that the Convention has accepted good faith as a principle to which regard should be paid in international trade, should be considered as being positive. However, the question whether or not this has been done in the most appropriate way is open to discussion. The good faith provision of the Convention is not directly addressed to parties to contracts of sale of goods, as is done in municipal legal provisions in which the principle of good faith is widely accepted. These demand from parties respect for this principle at the formation and in the performance of contracts. In the Convention this principle is linked to the interpretation and application of the text of the Convention so that the parties, to which it should be actually addressed, are only indirectly referred to.

The above-cited rule of the Convention imposes such interpretation and application of the Convention as give due regard to the need to promote the observance of good faith. Consequently, the purpose of this provision is to ensure the observance of good faith in international trade, so that this might be better expressed in a separate provision addressed directly to the contracting parties. This is all the more so since the application of this principle will give rise to varied interpretation with respect to its content, because in addition to laying down a general rule, the content of this principle cannot be defined in greater detail. This is, after all, not really necessary since practice to date has shown that views are clearly formed in connection with individual cases. It could be even said that the generalization of this principle is advantageous for its application.

5. OBSERVANCE OF USAGES

The Convention has introduced significant changes in relation to ULIS in connection with the observance of usages. Both texts provide that the parties shall be bound by the usages which they have expressly or impliedly made applicable to their contract and by any practices which they have established between themselves, even though this is textually not expressed by them in the same way. The difference primarily relates to when it can be considered that the parties have impliedly made a usage applicable to their contract. ULIS (Art. 9) does not contain any detailed provisions thereon and only specifies two ways in which the parties may make usages applicable to their contract.

In contrast to ULIS, the Convention separately defines requirements that must be met in concluding that the parties have impliedly made a usage applicable to their contract and its performance. Thus, it is demanded (a) that the parties knew or ought to have known the usage, (b) that the usage is widely known in international trade, and (c) that the usage is regularly observed by the parties in contracts of the type involved in the particular trade concerned (Art. 9, para. 2).

From the fact that requirements are only made in connection with implied application of usages, it could be concluded that such requirements are not demanded when the parties have expressly made a usage applicable to their contract. In this way only the introductory provision of the Convention concerning the application of usages would apply, i.e., that the parties are bound by any usage to which they have agreed (Art. 9, para. 1). Consequently, the parties can agree to be bound by any usage they have selected, regardless of whether a universal international, regional international, municipal, local, general or special usage is involved.

In this connection the question primarily arises whether the Convention requires for the implied application of usages the fulfilment of all three requirements laid down in it, or only one of them. According to the wording used, it should be assumed that the application of usages demands the fulfilment of all the three requirements. The first of these is of a subjective and the second and third of an objective nature. It is evident that in this way the application of usages is narrowed and confined to international trade transactions. In this respect ULIS is more in favour of the application of usages because, in addition to noting that the parties can make themselves bound by any usage which they have expressly or impliedly made applicable to their contract, it does not pose any additional requirement for their making a selection of usages. What is more, Art. 9, subpara. 2 of this law contains an exclusively objective formulation concerning the application of usages, i.e., it only states that the parties shall be bound by usages which reasonable persons in the same situation as the parties usually consider to be applicable to their contract.

Do the requirements thus defined in the Convention leave room for tacit application of municipal usages? The Convention demands that the usage is widely known in international trade, which in other words means that such usage is international in character. Here it is not decisive whether such usage has become international because a municipal usage is involved which is applied in international trade so that it has become widely known in it, or one that international practice has turned into an international usage. What does it actually mean that a usage is widely known in international trade? What criteria should be applied to judge whether a usage is widely known? Does it mean that it is universally known, or is it sufficient for it to be widely known in international trade in a particular region of the world? All these are questions which will pose themselves in the application of the above-cited provision of the Convention.

In view of the requirement that a usage is regularly observed by the parties in contracts of the type in the particular trade concerned, there is no doubt that the formulation "widely known in international trade" is not solely confined to general usages. Consequently, special usages – usages of a particular trade – will be tacitly applied, but this does not exclude the application of general usages if they are regularly observed by the parties in contracts of the type involved in the particular trade concerned.

If these two criteria are linked together, and according to the Convention they should be thus applied, then it can logically be concluded that it would be sufficient for a usage to be widely known in international trade within a particular trade. Its application need not be broader, but the observation of usages more widely known is not excluded.

It seems that the formulation contained in ULIS is better. This law does not lay down so many requirements, so that, understandably, not so many questions appear in the application of the appropriate legal provision which is clearly and well-defined. In particular, there is no subjective requirement for the parties to have known or ought to have known the usage, which requirement , in addition to the above-mentioned differentiation of usages, is an additional restriction on application. When parties are involved who professionally take part in trade transactions, this does not constitute a great problem, because for such parties it can be more easily presumed that the requirement has been fulfilled that they ought to have known the usage for which the previous two requirements have been met. In assessing when it should be considered that the parties ought to have known the usage, it should be deemed that this subjective requirement is met if reasonable persons in the same situations as the parties usually consider a usage to be applicable to their contract. This is in fact an objective criterion taken from ULIS which is based on the average conduct of persons within a particular trade, so that by this very fact it is a criterion decisive for determining when it should be concluded that the parties ought to have known the usage. In this way the criterion contained in ULIS is indirectly applied in assessing whether one of the requirements of the Convention is met, even though this criterion is not expressly mentioned in the Convention.

The Convention refers in several places to the observance of usages and, which is understandable, it does not directly specify whether international or national usages are meant. Thus, according to Art. 8, para. 3, in laying down rules for the interpretation of statements made by and other conduct of a party, it is necessary, among others, to take into consideration usages in determining the intent of a party or the understanding a reasonable person would have thereof in the same circumstances. In regulating the way the acceptance of an offer may be indicated, Art. 18, para. 3 specifies, among other possibilities, that if by virtue of usage the offeree may indicate assent by performing an act, such as one relating to the dispatch of goods or payment of the price, without notice to the offeror, the acceptance is effective at the moment the act is performed provided that the act is performed within the period of time laid down in this Article. Art. 32, para. 2 regulates the obligation of the seller when he is bound to arrange for the carriage of the goods. In this case he must make such contracts as are necessary for the carriage to the place agreed by means of transportation which are appropriate in the circumstances and according to the usual terms for such transportation. As regards determination of the conformity of goods, Art. 35, para. 2 of the Convention gives a negative definition, i.e., it specifies when the goods do not conform with the contract. Thus, it is, among others, specified that except where otherwise agreed the goods do not conform with the contract unless they are fit for the purpose for which goods of the same description would ordinarily be used even if they are contained or packaged in the manner usual for such goods.

What usages apply in assessing whether or not acts have been performed that can be considered as acceptance of an offer? What usages should one refer to in determining what are usual terms for the transportation of the goods? It is evident that usages will be decisive for determining the purpose for which goods of the same description would ordinarily be used, and will be so for determining the usual manner in which such goods are contained or packaged. What usages should we take into consideration in such cases?

The question of the selection of usages to be applied in the above cases is especially interesting in view of the fact that according to the Convention tacit submission to usages requires, *inter alia,* that they are widely known in international trade. In this connection the question arises whether the cases in which the

Convention itself refers to the application of usages fall under the criteria mentioned in Art. 9 or outside it. In other words, is this a matter of implied applicability of usages, or that a municipal usage observed in a particular place applies, especially in cases where the Convention applies because the rules of private international law lead to the application of the law of a Contracting State. Should one insist on the application of international usages in connection with the packaging of the goods, or in connection with determining whether or not the goods are fit for the purposes for which goods of the same description would ordinarily be used even when the goods are delivered to the same country in which the seller is, i.e., when they do not cross the state border and should be used in the same country? These examples evidently show that it will not always be easy generally to preclude the application of municipal usages, so that from this viewpoint, too, the formulation contained in ULIS seems to be better.

Nor does the Convention contain a provision on the relationship between usages and the provisions of the Convention. ULIS lays down a rule according to which in the event of conflict with this law, the usages shall prevail unless otherwise agreed by the parties (Art. 9, para. 2). This provision has not entered into the Convention, which creates a dilemma as to whether this means that according to the Convention usages are no longer given priority, or that this question should be considered as not being regulated in the Convention, so that it must be settled by recourse to other sources. The omission of the afore-cited provision does not mean that the provisions of the Convention are given priority over usages, because in this respect the Convention has not settled anything. This should be considered as being a question which the Convention has not settled, which means that an answer will have to be sought in the municipal law applicable according to the rules of private international law. In giving the answer to this question regard is to be had to the fact that by its legal nature the usage is an implied will of the parties and that the provisions of the Convention, subject to Art. 12, are of a non-mandatory character. Incorporation of a relevant solution into the Convention would provide greater legal security. If to this is added what has been said about the dilemma in connection with the application of international (universal or regional) and municipal usages, and about whether criteria concerning implied application of usages are also observed when the Convention in certain places refers to the observance of usages, one is apt to conclude that the Convention has brought about considerable uncertainty regarding the observance of usages.

A shortcoming of the Convention is also seen in that it does not contain the provision laid down in Art. 9, para. 3 of ULIS, and Art. 13, para. 2 of ULFIS, notably: "where expressions, provisions or forms of contract commonly used in commercial practice are employed, they shall be interpreted according to the meaning usually given to them in the trade concerned". The rule laid down in the Convention regarding the interpretation and application of the Convention cannot replace the above provision of the Uniform Laws, because it is directly aimed at the interpretation of the Convention's provisions. What can, however, be significant is the view contained in it regarding the need to promote uniformity and observance of good faith in international trade. Since the view taken in ULIS and ULFIS is a rational solution, and since it stimulates uniformity in international trade, the omission of the formulation contained in these laws does not mean that this rule regarding interpretation cannot be applied to the contract regime laid down by the Convention. A different attitude would not be rational and would not be conductive to the needs of international trade.

6. FORMATION OF THE CONTRACT

The Convention seems to have introduced a change in relation to ULFIS regarding the minimum content the parties should agree upon for a contract for the sale of goods to be formed. The change introduced has adopted a conception according to which it is sufficient for a contract to be valid that the parties have agreed on the goods and the price to be paid. In defining in the first sentence of Art. 14, para. 1 what an offer should contain in order to be valid (in this respect there are no differences from the provision contained in Art. 4, para. 1 of ULFIS), the Convention specifies in the second sentence that a proposal is sufficiently definite if it indicates the goods and expressly or implicitly fixes or makes provisions for determining the quantity and the price. Accordingly, a proposal which with respect to the price did not contain what is laid down in the above provision would not be a proposal for concluding a contract. Such details as to when a proposal should be considered sufficiently definite are not provided for in ULFIS.

Such a conclusion regarding the essential elements of contracts about which the parties must agree is, however, called into question in view of the provision of Art. 55 of the Convention, which lays down the obligation of the buyer to pay the price if it is not stated in the contract or at least ascertainable. There are differences between ULIS and the Convention in this respect. According to Art. 57 of ULIS,

"where a contract has been concluded but does not state a price or make provision for the determination of the price, the buyer shall be bound to pay the price generally charged by the seller at the time of the conclusion of the contract".

In Art. 55 of the Convention the following rule is laid down:

"Where a contract has been validly concluded but does not expressly or implicitly fix or make provision for determining the price, the parties are considered, in the absence of any indication to the contrary, to have impliedly made reference to the price generally charged at the time of the conclusion of the contract for such goods sold under comparable circumstances in the trade concerned".

The above cited provisions of the Convention are contradictory. If the essential requirement for a valid offer, without which no contract can be concluded, is that the contract at least implicitly makes provision for determining the price, then there is no place in the Convention for the provision regulating the price the buyer must pay if the price is not ascertainable form the contract. This latter provision would only fit in if the Convention did not take the view that a statement which did not at least implicitly make provision for determining the price was not a proposal for concluding a contract. One of these provisions has no place in the Convention.

Even such a solution provided in Art. 55 of the Convention is not fully unobjectionable. It specifies the time at which the price generally prevailing should be taken into consideration (the time of the conclusion of the contract), but it does not specify the place in which the price should be ascertained. The reference to the price generally charged at the time of the conclusion of the contract is only provided. The Convention no longer contains the rule of Art. 57 of ULIS that the price generally charged by the seller is to be taken into account. Such a provision was provided in the Draft Convention and even if it had been accepted in the Convention difficulties might have appeared. If the price generally charged by the seller was taken into account, it would perhaps be logical to take into account the price generally prevailing the place of business of the seller at the time of the conclusion of the contract. However, even here difficulties might appear. First of all, the seller can have several places of business. In such a case it would be possible to take into account the place of business, which is otherwise according to the Convention decisive for determining the applicability of the Convention. Should, in case the parties know that the goods will be dispatched from a particular place of business of the seller or from another place where the goods are located, such place be taken into account? Should instead the price generally prevailing in the place of delivery of the goods be applied?

In precising in the Convention the price generally charged at the time of the conclusion of the contract reference is made to the comparable circumstances in the trade concerned. It leads to the application of an objective criterion and not to the subjective one as it was foreseen in the Draft Convention. In determining the price in the trade concerned there could be difficulties linked to the place where such a price exists, while it would be often impossible to take into account the price in the trade concerned which exists all over the world. Therefore, the formulation contained in the Convention regarding the claiming of damages if the contract is avoided speaks in favour of the solution that this would be the price generally prevailing in the place of delivery of the goods in the trade concerned. According to Art. 76, para. 2 of the Convention, in assessing damages, the current price, i.e., the current price prevailing at the place where delivery of the goods should have been made is taken into account or, if there is no current price at that place, the price at such other place as serves as a reasonable substitute, making due allowance for differences in the cost of transporting the goods. Should the idea of the place of delivery accepted in this Article be applied? In any case, it would be better if this uncertainty was eliminated by making a more definite formulation in the Convention.

In the Draft Convention changes in relation to ULIS and ULFIS were proposed according to which the formation of a contract, or the existence of certain significant rights of a contracting party, was tied to the fulfilment of special subjective requirements on the part of the other contracting party. This solution might have given rise to difficulties in practice so that the proposed changes were not fully inserted in the final text of the Convention. Instead of this the solutions given in ULIS and ULFIS are in a way even improved.

In regulating the formation of contracts, the makers of the Draft Convention were guided by the wish to mitigate the rule adopted in ULFIS according to which a reply to an offer which purports to be an acceptance but which contains additional or different terms which do not materially alter the terms of the offer shall constitute an acceptance unless the offeror promptly objects to the discrepancy (Art. 7, para. 2). This rule will in practice be a source of insecurity between the parties as to whether or not the contract has been formed at all. The Draft, therefore, proposed a supplement which would, however, not obviate difficulties that might be caused by the above rule.

First of all, legal security has been increased, but not satisfactorily, by enumerating cases when additional or different terms of acceptance are considered to alter the terms of the offer materially, because the enumeration is only *exampli gratia.* These are, *inter alia,* the terms relating to the price, payment, quality and quantity of goods, place and time of delivery, extent of one party's liability to the other, or the settlement of disputes. This was foreseen in the Draft and now is accepted in the Convention in Art. 19, para. 3. On the other hand, not even additional or different terms relating to those enumerated will be considered to alter the terms of the offer materially unless the offeror by virtue of the offer or the particular circumstances of the case has reason to believe they are acceptable to the offeror (Art. 17, para. 3 of the Draft Convention). This subjective requirement was rejected so that it does not exist in the Convention.

If the intention had been to diminish the insecurity caused by the rule taken over from ULFIS, a better result would have been achieved if the cases where it is considered that additional or different terms materially alter the terms of the offer had been enumerated in full. In such a case the offeror would be sure that in the cases cited he would not need to object to any discrepancy without undue delay in order to prevent the formation of a contract whose content deviated from the one contained in his offer. Instead of this, the Convention primarily cites cases, but only by way of example, where the offeror need not object to the discrepancy. In the Draft Convention the said additional subjective requirement was laid down. The need to meet this subjective requirement too would not in fact eliminate party insecurity as to whether the contract has been formed or not, but would rather introduce a criterion which would make the situation more complicated than it was.

First of all, it would be necessary to proceed from the fact that the offeror also has his own idea of what is acceptable to him. Since he otherwise does not need to react in order to prevent the formation of a contract because of additional or different terms which alter the terms of his offer materially, in deciding whether or not to do this, he cannot solely rely on his comprehension of the acceptability of changes and additions. This is so because what is decisive in only what the offeree has reason to believe would be acceptable to the offeror. A simpler solution would be, in view of the adoption of the criterion of acceptability, to leave it to the offeror alone to decide whether or not to object to the discrepancy. Since this is a case when additional or different terms alter the terms of the offer materially, it should be left to the offeror, provided he considers such terms acceptable, to state that he agrees to such terms and thus to make possible the formation of the contract. In this way the judgment as to what is acceptable to the offeror would be transferred to the offeree. The offeror would be placed in a situation where the formation of the contract is made dependent on whether the additional or different terms are acceptable to him but according to the judgment of the offeree, i.e., of the party who initiates the change, and not on the party to whom such changes should be acceptable and who should in fact express his opinion thereon.

This would be, however, to some extent mitigated by the enumeration of the grounds on which the offeree should base his judgment. Such judgment may derive from the offer or from the particular circumstances of the case. In spite of this, major problems would arise. First of all, at what moment should particular circumstances of the case exist? Is this the moment when the offeror sends his offer, when it reaches the offeree, or when the offeree sends his acceptance, or when such acceptance reaches the offeror? It seems that this, as a rule, could not be before the moment the offeror sends his offer, even though in some cases it would be possible also to take into consideration the circumstances which prevailed before that. Nor could this be after the moment when the acceptance of an offer becomes effective, and this means when it reaches the offeror (Art. 16, para. 2 of the Draft Convention). This latter moment is significant, because it is otherwise the moment of the formation of the contract so that the circumstances prevailing after it could no longer be taken into consideration. According to the Draft Convention such assessment can be made either on the basis of the offer or on the basis of the particular circumstances of the case, even though, if this criterion were to be taken into account, it would have been logical to have used the formulation necessitating the fulfilment of all these requirements.

As assessment of this kind would in this way be rendered difficult in conditions under which international trade is evolving today, owing to economic instability, in particular frequent and sometimes sudden changes in prices for individual goods, their availability on the international market, rate of exchange fluctuations, etc. In addition, account should be taken of differences that might occur between the terms of sale on the international market where the Convention should be applied and the terms of sale under which business transactions are performed on internal markets and governed by municipal law. Such transactions often precede or follow contracts for the international sale of goods.

This is one more reason why this criterion was not incorporated into the Convention. This criterion, especially under the above-mentioned conditions, would tend to increase differences in the parties' interpretation of the acceptability of additional or different terms of the acceptance of an offer, and thereby also their uncertainty as to whether a contract has been formed or not. In the event of a dispute a retrospective judgment by a court or arbitration would not be easy, because it would be reduced to assessing the justifiability of the offeree's idea about the existence of a subjective characteristic on the side of the offeror. In this connection it should be reckoned in practice with the possibility of the court or arbitration resorting to the objectification of criteria they apply in ascertaining whether or not the offeree had reason to believe that additional and different terms were acceptable to the offeror, relying on reasonable conduct in such situations. As assessment thus made, although it might sometimes in practice be the only way out, would open up possibilities for moving still further away from what the offeror considers as acceptable, because the court only examines the assessment of the offeree, and whether or not additional or different terms are really acceptable to the offeror.

In view of this formulation as was proposed in the Draft Convention, the only security for the offeror would be to refuse to ascertain whether additional or different terms alter the terms of the offer materially and, if he does not wish to be bound by the contract, to object to the discrepancy without undue delay. The criteria laid down in this provision were too unreliable to give the parties security regarding the existence of the contract. The more realistic stand prevailed and in Art. 19 of the Convention there is no longer the subjective criterion mentioned above. The enumeration of the cases when additional or different terms of acceptance are considered to alter the terms of the offer materially is practically the only change made in the rule contained in Art. 7 of ULFIS. It is a pity that the above-mentioned cases are not enumerated in full because it would be a greater contribution to the security of the contracting parties. However, it must be added that even a chance for reaching better results is missed enumeration made *exampli gratia* means certain improvement in relation to ULIS.

7. FUNDAMENTAL BREACH

The Convention has retained fundamental breach of contract as a requirement bearing on the realization of certain rights of the parties (e.g., cases cited in Art. 46, para. 2; Art. 51, para. 2; Art. 64, para. 1, subpara. (a); Art. 49, para. 1, subpara. (a); Art. 73, paras. 1 and 2). In this way the Convention has retained the differentiation of breaches of contract by intensity, which could not be considered as being positive for practice. In determining what is a fundamental breach of contract, the Convention fundamentally differs from ULIS. According to ULIS, a breach of contract is regarded as fundamental wherever the party in breach knew, or ought to have known, at the time of the conclusion of the contract, that a reasonable person in the same situation as the other party would not have entered into the contract if he had foreseen the breach and its effects (Art. 10). The Convention defines a fundamental breach of contract as a breach committed by one of the parties if it results in such detriment to the other party as substantially to deprive him of what he is entitled to expect under the contract, unless the party in breach did not foresee and a reasonable person of the same kind in the same circumstances would not have foreseen such a result (Art. 25). In the Draft Convention a fundamental breach of contract was defined as a breach committed by one of the parties if it results in substantial detriment to the other party unless the party in breach did not foresee and had no reason to foresee such result

(Art. 23). In comparison with the Draft Convention and ULIS the Convention shows that the rule, which is a combination of the rules dealing with this matter contained in ULIS and in the Draft Convention, is accepted.

The basic difference between ULIS and the Convention lies in that it is no longer required to assess a breach of contract that has occurred during its implementation according to the criteria of a reasonable person, considered retrospectively to the moment of the conclusion of the contract. This criterion will be difficult to apply in practice because it contains a number of hypothetical elements. Nor has the Convention's revised criteria for a fundamental breach of contract made the situation better for practice, since difficulties will now appear with respect to other questions.

Instead of the hypothetical will of a reasonable person, in the way it was stated in ULIS for determining the fundamental breach of the contract the Convention has introduced an objective criterion, viz. substantial detriment to the other party resulting from a breach of contract. Substantial detriment is defined as such a detriment which deprives the other party of what he is entitled to expect under the contract. In this connection the question arises as to what should be considered to be substantial detriment. What criteria should be applied for determining it? Should the economic strength of the party harmed by the breach be taken into account, or is this circumstance of no significance? Is the ratio of what the parties are obliged to do under the contract of any significance here? What benefit which the party affected by detriment has expected from this transaction has to be taken into account? All these questions will have to be answered in the implementation of this provision, which will, however, in practice cause fewer difficulties than the formulation contained in ULIS. The assessment of the existence of substantial detriment will depend on the circumstances of individual cases. In this connection it will be necessary to apply an objective criterion without taking into account the economic strength of the harmed party. The acceptance of the tests of a reasonable person means a contribution to such objectivisation of the relevant criteria. A guideline for such assessment could be provided by the benefit which is regularly expected from the proper performance of such transaction in the particular trade. A criterion could, therefore, be sought in the extent to which such benefit has been diminished due to the breach of contract. The fact that the party in breach knew of the special circumstances of that particular transaction should also be taken into consideration.

Still greater difficulties might arise through the application of the subjective requirement for a fundamental breach of contract. For, if a breach results in substantial detriment to the other party, this does not of itself mean that the breach is fundamental if the party in breach did not foresee and a reasonable person of the same kind in the same circumstances would not have foreseen such a result. What is positive here is that, in contrast to ULIS, this subjective requirement is not strictly tied to the moment of the conclusion of the contract. This separation from an objective firmly determined moment has, however, not removed difficulties that might arise in the application of this requirement.

First of all, must the party in breach know that substantial detriment to the other party has occurred? According to the above-cited provision of the Convention, this seems not to be required. It is only required that the party in breach foresaw and a reasonable person of the same kind in the same circumstances would have foreseen such a result of his breach. The question as to at what moment this subjective requirement must be fulfilled is not settled either. From the wording used in the Convention one might conclude that this is the moment when the breach of contract was made. In some instances it will be easy to determine this moment, for example, in the event of non-fulfilment of the contract within the stipulated period of time. Both parties learn of the breach at the same moment. However, this is not so simple for example when goods are delivered which with respect to quality do not correspond to what was ordered. What should in this case be decisive: the moment at which the seller completed the last acts of delivery, the moment of the passing of the risk to the buyer, because the seller is liable for the lack of conformity existing at that time, or the moment when according to the regular course of things the buyer would have the right to resort to a remedy because of a fundamental breach of contract?

In deciding which of these moments is decisive, regard should be given to the fact that the prime principle of the law of contracts is *pacts sunt servanda,* and that the party in breach violates by his conduct this principle to the detriment of the other party and should therefore bear the consequences thereof. The party harmed by the breach of contract should be given maximum assistance, since this would contribute to strengthening the contractual discipline of the parties. The subjective requirement introduced in the Convention favours the party in breach, so that for the above reason it should be flexibly interpreted. The party in breach bears the onus of proving that he did not foresee and that a reasonable person of the same kind in the same circumstances would not have foreseen such a result of the breach of contract. Linking this subjective requirement to the time before the injured party had learned of the breach could lead to speculations on the part of the party in breach and to his careless conduct in performing his obligations, and would also be contrary to the principle of the observance of good faith in international trade. Setting this moment too far away from the moment the party in breach committed the acts of breach would, on the other hand, enable the other party to behave in a speculative way. Therefore, the moment of the existence of the subjective requirement according to the circumstances of the case could be moved up to not later than the moment when in the regular course of things the other party had the right to resort to a remedy because of a fundamental breach of contract.

The introduction of such a subjective requirement renders difficult the position of the party harmed by a breach of contract, and diminishes the significance of the improvement made in relation to ULIS by the introduction of an objective requirement regarding subsantial detriment. Thanks to the acceptance of the objective test of a reasonable person this diminishing of such improvement is not so significant as at first sight would appear to be the case. For the party harmed by a breach of contract to decide to make use of his right because of a fundamental breach of contract it is not sufficient that substantial detriment has occurred for such party must take account of whether the party in breach foresaw and a reasonable person of the same kind in the same circumstances would have foreseen such a result. This conclusion is not affected by the fact that the party in breach must prove that he did not foresee and a reasonable person of the same kind in the same circumstances would not have foreseen such a result of the breach committed.

To illustrate this, we can take the case where the buyer decides to declare the contract avoided due to a breach of contract made by the seller. The buyer may declare the contract avoided without previously fixing an additional period of time of reasonable length for performance by the seller of his obligations if the failure by the seller to perform any of his obligations under the contract and the Convention amounts to a fundamental breach of contract (Art. 49, para. 1, subpara. (a)). When a breach is not fundamental, the party has to fix an additional period of time of reasonable length for performance by the seller of this obligations and may declare the contract avoided if the seller has not delivered the goods within this period of time or has declared that he will not deliver within the fixed period (Art. 49, para. 1, subpara. (b)). If the buyer who has suffered substantial detriment as a result of a breach of contract made by the seller declares the contract avoided believing that a fundamental breach of contract was made by the seller and therefore does not fix an additional period of time for performance by the seller of his obligations, he runs the risk of the avoidance of the contract not being valid. For, in the event of a dispute, the seller may be able to prove that he did not foresee and that a reasonable person of the same kind in the same circumstances would not have foreseen that his breach of contract would result in substantial detriment to the buyer. For the buyer it is difficult to ascertain with certainty whether or not the subjective requirement has been fulfilled by the seller. His situation would be made easier if for ascertaining the existence of substantial detriment resort were made only to the objective criterion determining the extent of loss of the benefit which is otherwise regularly to be expected from the proper performance of such transaction in the particular trade. However, it must be said that when merchants are involved, it can be presumed with good reason that the seller must have foreseen such a result of his breach of contract. This emerges also from the application of the criterion of a reasonable person. This, however, would not obviate difficulties arising from the application of the subjective criterion accepted in the Convention.

It would be more in the interest of legal security if the Convention accepted only the objective criterion regarding substantial detriment caused to the contracting party affected by a breach of contract. Since a differentiation of the gravity of a breach of contract has been accepted, difficulties in applying the rules on fundamental breach would in this way be considerably lessened.

LAW APPLICABLE TO INTERNATIONAL SALES HAGUE CONVENTIONS AND YUGOSLAV PRIVATE INTERNATIONAL LAW

by Zeljko Matić

1. THE LAW APPLICABLE TO CONSUMER SALES (New Developments in the Hague Conference on Private International Law)*

The Fourteenth Session of the Hague Conference on Private International Law, held from 6th - 25th October 1980, has prepared the rules on the law applicable to consumer sales, which rules are somewhat different from those presented in the Preliminary Draft Convention of 1979, which is discussed shortly in the report below.

The question whether these new rules should be included in the future general convention on sales, or should be the subject-matter of a separate convention on the law applicable to consumer sales, ought to be set aside for the purposes of these additional remarks, because it relates to matters of the law of international treaties and was not finally decided during the XIVth Session. We shall, therefore, limit this addition to questions of the concept of consumer sales and of the law applicable to them, i.e., basically to the questions dealt with in our earlier report.

1.1 The Hague Convention on the Law Applicable to International Sales of 1955

Twenty years after entering into force the Hague Convention of 1955 [1] has been subjected to an attempt to exclude from its scope of application so-called "consumer sales". It was thought that the choice of law rules of the Convention do not regulate that type of sale in a satisfactory manner, and that it is necessary to develop a set of new rules which would take into account the constantly growing consumer protection which has forced changes in the traditional law of contracts in countries with a liberal economy and developed industry.[2]

The delegates to the Thirteenth Session of the Hague Conference expressed the desirability of studying that problem and of a Protocol to amend the Convention of 1955. The Netherlands Standing Committee concurred and decided to include this item on the agenda of the Fourteenth Session to be held in October 1980. It formed the Special Commission of experts, who after two meetings in 1979 presented the Preliminary Draft Convention on the Law Applicable to Certain Consumer Sales.[3]

The provisions of the Hague Convention of 1955, as well as problems raised in theory with regard to its rules, are well known. Therefore, we shall not deal with them in this report, but shall rather confine our considerations to the problem of consumer sales with a short survey of Yugoslav Private International Law rules which could apply to international sales in general.

* Developments resulting from the establishment of the 1980 Draft have been added to this paper by means of a smaller lettertype. For text see Annex 7.

1. The text of the Convention is reproduced in Annex 5.

2. Pélichet, *Mémoire sur les ventes aux consummateurs,* Conférence de La Haye de d.i.p., Doc. prél. No. 1, March 1979, p. 2.

3. The text of the Preliminary Draft is reproduced in Annex 6.

1.2 Law Applicable to Consumer Sales (Some Basic Characteristics of the Preliminary Draft Convention of 1979)

The Preliminary Draft Convention deviates from the Hague Convention of 1955 in several respects: it limits its scope to consumer sales only, it restricts the role of the autonomy of the parties, it broadens the role of the mandatory provisions of the law of the habitual residence of the buyer, and it discards the applicability of the law of the habitual residence of the seller as a subsidiary applicable law in cases where there was no valid choice of law by the parties to the contract.[4]

1.2.1 Concept of consumer sales

Article 1 section 1 of the Preliminary Draft defines consumer sales as sales where, "the seller acts in the course of his business or profession and the buyer is a consumer". This definition has to be enlarged and amended by the concepts of "consumer" and "buyer" which are defined in Article 2. The consumer is, "a natural or legal person who, in the particular case, does not act primarily in the course of his business or profession". This definition is not the same as the one in the UNCITRAL Draft Article 2 letter a, because the Special Commission preferred to develop its own definition. The emphasis in the definition of "consumer" is on two terms: *"primarily"* and *"in the particular case".* The first is intended to solve the so-called "mixed" cases where a professional buys a specific good for both professional and personal use. The predominance of personal use of the buyer would include a particular sale in the scope of the future convention, and on the contrary, if the object was intended for professional use predominantly, it will have the opposite effect. The decision in a particular case might be a difficult one for the judge or for the arbitrator, therefore the Preliminary Draft Convention establishes a presumption in Article 2 section 2 that a buyer is generally a consumer in sales within the scope of the convention, which presumption can be challenged by the seller who has to prove that, "the buyer was acting primarily in the course of a business or profession, or that the seller reasonably so believed".

The Preliminary Draft does not cover all consumer sales (it says expressly that its scope are "certain" consumer sales), and the situations which it regulates are stated in Article 3. The first two situations (under nos. 1 and 2) represent cases where the seller has come to the buyer's country to negotiate the contract or has received the order in that country. The other two situations (under nos. 3 and 4) deal with cases where the buyer was somehow provoked by the seller to enter into the contract of sale. If the buyer, without any incentive on the part of the seller concludes a sale in the country of the seller's habitual residence, the Conven-

4. For detailed analysis see, *Pélichet,* op.cit., and Report by von Mehren, *Law applicable to certain consumer sales,* Hague Conference on PIL, Preliminary Document No. 2 of October 1979.

tion would not apply. The same would be true in case of section 4, when the buyer travelled from the country other than that of his habitual residence.

Article 1 of the Preliminary Draft Convention further differs from the Hague Convention of 1955 in two respects. It excludes from its scope of application certain specific types of sales (auctions, sales authorized by judicial authority or by way of execution, sales of securities or other legal instruments, or sales on commodity or other exchanges) which were within the scope of application of the Convention of 1955. The reasons for the exclusion of these sales are that they are seldom within the scope of "consumer sales", as defined in Article 3, and some of them are usually subject to special regulations. On the other hand, as consumers today frequently buy small boats and small airplanes, the sale of ships, boats and airplanes are included in the Preliminary Draft, if they fall in the category of "consumer sales". The Convention of 1955, on the contrary, excluded from its scope of application sales of ships and registered boats and aircrafts.

The question was raised whether the loans and other extensions of credit, made in connection with consumer sales, should be included in the scope of the Preliminary Draft. Agreement was not reached in the Special Commission and the matter was referred to the Special Commission dealing with the future work of the Conference.[5]

1.2.1 Concept of consumer sales (1980 Draft)

Article 1 section 1 of the 1980 Draft which defines, together with Article 2 and Article 3, the concept of consumer sale, differs in wording from Article 1 section 1 and Article 2 letter a. of the Preliminary Draft of 1979.

The new definition of consumer sale is closer, although not identical with the UNCITRAL Convention on contracts for the international sale of goods, and it provides that the Convention shall apply, "to *certain* contracts for the international sale of goods bought *primarily for personal, family and household use,* where the seller acts in the course of his business of profession and where at any time before the contract was entered into, he *knew or ought to have known* that the goods were being bought *primarily* for any such use."

As can be seen from this text the new Draft has combined the essence of Article 1 section 1 and Article 2 of the previous Draft and some elements of the UNCITRAL Convention (Art. 2). The main elements of the definition (combined in Artt. 1, 2, 3 and 5) are the following:

1. seller acts in the course of his business or profession;
2. buyer (consumer) buys goods primarily for a personal, family or household use;
3. seller knew or ought to have known at any time before the contract was concluded, that the goods were being bought primarily for a personal, family or household use of the buyer (the burden of proof to the contrary rests with the seller - Art. 3);
4. the Convention applies only to *certain* consumer sales, as defined in Article 5, excluding in particular so called "normal" sales in the seller's country or another country, which sales occurred without the seller's initiative;

5. von Mehren, op.cit., p. 18.

5. to the contracts of sale are affiliated contracts in which the goods have to be manufactured or produced by a supplier (seller) who is to furnish a substantial part of the necessary materials (Art. 1 sect. 3).

We have discussed in our earlier report the term *"primarily"* with regard to the buyer's use of the goods and shall therefore avoid repetition here.

Finally, it has to be noted that the provision of Article 1 section 2 of the 1979 Draft has been put separately (with additions which do not change the essence) in the new Article 4 of the 1980 Draft.

1.2.2 Autonomy of the parties

The Preliminary Draft Convention substantially restricts the role of the parties' autonomy for consumer sales in Article 4. The Special Commission was almost equally divided into two groups of experts: the one favouring the total elimination of the autonomy of the parties, the other permitting the parties' choice subject to the application of mandatory rules of the law of the country in which the buyer habitually resides, whenever these rules are more favourable to the buyer than the mandatory rules of the chosen law.[6] The differences were not settled during the sessions of the Special Commission, therefore the whole of Article 4 is in brackets in the text of the Preliminary Draft.

Article 4 section 2 of the Preliminary Draft differs considerably from the provision of Article 2 section 2 of the Convention of 1955. Instead of the implied choice of law by the parties, which has "unambiguously" *(indubitablement)* to result from the terms and provisions of the contract, the choice of law for consumer sales must be *express and in writing.* The fear of the superior legal skill of the economically stronger and more ingenious seller has undoubtedly influenced the experts to adopt that attitude, especially in the view that "stipulations for governing law were more problematical in consumer sales".[7]

It is interesting to note that the experts were not unanimous in favour of the chosen law as the one which should govern questions relating to the consent of the parties as to the choice of the applicable law. Therefore, the whole provision of section 3 of Article 4 is put in double brackets.

1.2.2 Autonomy of the parties (1980 Draft)

The delegates to the XIVth Session decided in favour of the inclusion of the autonomy of the parties (the provision on autonomy in Art. 4 of the 1979 Draft was put into brackets as a whole). Article 6 does not differ from the provisions of the earlier Article 4 except in section 3 which refers to the question of the law applicable to the existence, validity and form of the consent of the parties to the choice of law.

6. von Mehren, op.cit., p. 26-27.
7. von Mehren, op.cit., p. 28.

1.2.3 Objective connecting factor

The Preliminary Draft Convention adopts in Article 5 the premise that the consumer who is purchasing consumer goods must be protected against the economic and legal power of the seller. Therefore, it is justifiable to adopt the law of the habitual residence of the buyer as the subsidiary applicable law.[8] This solution is different from the one in Article 3 section 1 of the 1955 Convention. The Special Commission has rejected the approach that the consumer should be given an option between the law of his habitual residence and the law of the seller's habitual residence. The reasons were that such an option would lead to greater complications, and that the consumer can hardly complain if he receives the same protection that his law gives him in cases of purely internal local sales.[9]

1.2.3. Objective connecting factor (1980 Draft)

Contrary to the provisions of the 1979 Draft and Article 2 section 3 of the Hague Convention of 1955 the law applicable to that question is the internal law of the consumer's habitual residence at the time the order was given, i.e., the law which is the subsidiary applicable law according to Article 7 of the new Draft.

As well as the 1955 Convention, the Preliminary Draft Convention excludes the possibility of *renvoi.* In all other respects, except for minor differences in the terms of Article 6, the Preliminary Draft follows the lines of the 1955 Convention.

It will be interesting to follow the future progress of the Draft and compare its present provisions with the ones finally adopted in the Plenary Session of the Hague Conference this year.

1.2.4. Scope of the applicable law (1980 Draft)

There is a new provision in Article 8 defining the scope of the applicable law, which did not exist either in the earlier Draft or in the 1955 Convention. The provision does not limit the scope of the applicable law exclusively to the matters mentioned in it, but constitutes a very useful clarification of possible ambiguities with regard to the matters which are expressly mentioned.

8. Pélichet, op.cit., p. 46; von Mehren, op.cit., p. 30.
9. von Mehren, op.cit., p. 30.

2. YUGOSLAV PRIVATE INTERNATIONAL LAW: CHOICE OF LAW RULES IN INTERNATIONAL SALES

2.1 Choice of Law Rules Concerning Contracts in Yugoslav Law

2.1.1 Internal and International Sources of Law

Before the Second World War there were several legal systems in force on the territory of Yugoslavia, which had different choice of law rules applicable to contracts: General Civil Code (Austrian),[10] Serbian Civil Code of 1844, General Civil Code of Montenegro of 1880 and Hungarian customary law in force in some parts of Croatia (Medjimurje) and in the province of Vojvodina. These laws were stripped of their formal legal force by the Act of Non-validity of Statutory Legal Rules enacted before April 6, 1941, but could be applied as general rules of law, unless the application of their provisions would be contrary to the constitutional system of the new Yugoslavia and the principles of that system. However, the question of their applicability or non-applicability is today a matter of purely historical interest.

The present Yugoslav law has no general rules concerning choice of law for contracts that have an international character, and particularly not rules for international sales of goods. It is necessary, therefore, to try to derive those rules by analogy from the existing statutory rules which deal with similar situations, i.e., with contracts of maritime and inland navigation, carriage of passengers and goods by air, some bilateral treaties concluded between Yugoslavia and other countries (e.g., with Poland), two multilateral conventions (European Convention on International Commercial Arbitration of 1961 and Convention on the Settlement of Investment Disputes between States and Nationals of Other States of 1965, which have both been ratified by Yugoslavia), and possibly by anticipation of the Draft of the Act concerning Private International Law and Procedure of 1974, with the presumption that its final version shall not change from the existing one.[11] Some indications on the scope of validity of the principle of autonomy can be found also in the Act concerning obligations of 1978, but the choice of law rules of that Act relate primarily to interlocal conflicts and are not representative of the general trend in Yugoslav private international law.[12] There are not many judicial decisions which could give us a valuable lead towards the answer to the question: what law is applicable to contractual relations? There is, however, one particular decision of the Supreme Economic Court (No. SL 93/65-3 of June 18, 1965)[13] which could enlighten us on two crucial questions: whether autonomy of the par-

10. The Austrian General Civil Code was in force in Croatia from 1853, but without the changes enacted in 1915, 1916 and 1917, which were in force in some other parts of Yugoslavia (e.g., in Bosnia and Herzegovina, and a part of Croatia: Dalmatia).

11. The relevant texts of new Yugoslav Laws and the text of the Draft of the Act concerning Private International Law and Procedure are translated in Annexes 1, 2 and 4.

12. The relevant text is translated in Annex 3.

13. Published in, Pak, *Zbirka propisa i sudskih odluka medjunarodnog privatnog prava,* (1971) pp. 350-357.

ties is a generally adopted principle for the choice of law rules concerning contracts, and what law is to be applied in the absence of the parties' choice. To those two questions the abovementioned decision gives us an answer by following the system of rules set down in the Act concerning Contracts for Use of Sea-Going Vessels of 1959, which was later without important changes transferred into the new Act concerning Maritime and Inland Navigation of 1977. The decision considers the autonomy of the parties as a general principle of private international law for contractual relations having an international element, and affirms the idea of applicability of the law most closely connected with the contract as a subsidiary choice of law rule in cases where the parties' choice is absent.

The question to be answered is: what can be deduced from the sources of Yugoslav law as an answer to the question what law is applicable to international sales of goods?

2.1.2 Autonomy of Parties (Subjective Connecting Factor)

Autonomy of the parties is considered as a primary connecting factor for contracts with an international element in the following provisions:

- Article 1000 of the Act concerning Maritime and Inland Navigation (as well as in Art. 1008 of the same Act for contracts of building, repair and adaptation of vessels, and in Art. 1009 for insurance contracts);
- Article 223 of the Act concerning Obligations and Basic Real Rights in Air Navigation (as well as in Art. 225 of the same Act for insurance contracts);
- Articles 1101 and 1105 of the Act concerning Obligations (under proviso that the Act deals primarily with interlocal conflicts);
- Article 19 of the Draft of the Act concerning Private International Law and Procedure;
- Article VII of the European Convention on International Commercial Arbitration; and
- Article 42 of the Convention on the Settlement of Investment Disputes between States and Nationals of Other States.

From these provisions it can with fair certainty be assumed that Yugoslav law adopts the principle of autonomy of the parties for contracts with international elements, and consequently for international sales. There are, however, some questions which are still left open.

2.1.2.1 The parties' duty to choose the law having connection with their contract

The question is a controversial one in legal doctrine, but the majority of Yugoslav authors advocate the unlimited right of the parties to choose whatever law they deem appropriate for their contractual relations.[14] As a further argument can

14. That view is expressed by, Katičić, *Ogledi o medjunarodnom privatnom pravu* (1971) p. 228; Cigoj, *Mednarodno zasebno pravo*, Vol. I (1977) p. 58; Sajko, *Mjerodavno pravo za zakljucenje ugovora sa stranim partnerima* (Novi Sad 1979) p. 395, Matić, in Goldštajn/Barbić/

be put forward the fact that such a limitation is not mentioned in either of the provisions of the existing Yugoslav laws in force, nor in the Draft of the Act concerning Private International Law and Procedure. This militates for the general non-existence of such a limitation on the parties' autonomy, apart from the pragmatic reasons against it, which are well-known and need not necessarily be repeated here.

2.1.2.2 The 'implied' choice of law

All Yugoslav laws in force and the Draft of the Act concerning Private International Law and Procedure provide for both "explicit" and "implied" choice of law by the parties. There are, however, some differences in the texts as to the limits of the judges' freedom in ascertaining whether or not the parties have tacitly chosen the applicable law. The Act concerning Maritime and Inland Navigation does not use (in Art. 1002) the words "without doubt", which can be found in Article 224 of the Act concerning Obligations and Basic Real Rights in Air Navigation, and in Article 19 of the Draft of the Act concerning PIL and Procedure. The latter two were obviously influenced by the idea of the Hague Convention of 1955, not limiting, however, the scope of the judge's investigation into the parties' possible "intent" to the contract itself, but allowing him to take into consideration all the circumstances of the particular case.

The discrepancy between those texts emphasizes the need for clarification of this question in future judicial practice. Of course, the matter could be easily settled, at least for cases of international sales, by simple enacting the Act concerning PIL and Procedure with the text of the 1974 Draft. There were, however, some doubts recently raised in the Committee of Experts, which was revising the 1974 Draft, with regard to the question of "implied" choice of the parties. Some of the experts have advocated the adoption of only express choice of law by the parties. That solution would follow the idea put forward in the Preliminary Draft Convention on the Law Applicable to Consumer Sales of 1979 of the Hague Conference. It should, however, be kept in mind that the reasons that militate for such a limitation in consumer sales are not necessarily appropriate for other, commercial, sales and for contracts in general.

2.1.2.3 Choice of two or several laws applicable to a contract (splitting of laws)

The problem of a choice of two or several laws applicable to the same contract has been extensively discussed in legal doctrine and the purposes of this report do not require a repetition of the arguments put forward *pro* and *contra.*

Yugoslav laws concerning maritime and air navigation do in certain cases allow the application of two laws to the different parts of the same contract (the law chosen by parties and the law most closely connected with the contract: compare the texts of Art. 1102 and Art. 224 of the abovementioned Laws). Opinions

---

Vedris/Matić, *Obvezno pravo,* Vol. I (1979) pp. 369-371.

in Yugoslav theory are not unanimous. Katičić [15] mentions that an extensive interpretation of the text would grant the parties the possibility of a choice of several laws, and Sajko [16] is in favour of such an interpretation. The author of this report is against such an interpretation [17], considering that the *a posteriori* possibility of application of the law most closely connected with the contract in cases where the law chosen by the parties cannot be applied (because that law has no provision for a specific kind of contractual relation or question that has arisen, or if the application of the chosen law would lead to a result incompatible with public policy - *ordre public*), does not mean that the parties have the right to choose two or several law *a priori*, i.e., at the time of contracting. The further argument against such a right of the parties is the fact that by creating a 'mosaic' of applicable laws the parties could disturb the balance of rights and interests which underlies every system of rules of a particular "civilized" legal system. Such a 'mosaic' would be mostly in favour of some skilled and less honest party, and furthermore, by a choice of several laws for different rights and obligations, the parties would provide for the application of a "law" that does not, as such, exist in any country.

It should be noted that the Hague Convention of 1955, as well as the new Preliminary Draft Convention of 1979, does not allow a choice of several laws for one contract, but that the Draft Convention on the Law Applicable to Contractual Obligations of the Commission of the European Communities (Art. 3 sect. 1) seems to adopt the different solution.

2.1.2.4 Change in the substantive rules of the chosen law

There is no provision in Yugoslav law for the case when the law chosen by the parties has changed its substantive rules regulating contractual relations, between the time of contracting and the time of judicial or arbitral proceedings. This question is open to interpretation.

2.1.2.5 Subsequent choice of law and the change of the chosen law

There are no provisions on these questions in Yugoslav law, but it could be argued, both from the text and because of the reasons underlying the principle of autonomy, that the parties should not be limited in time in making their choice, nor in being able to change their mind later, at least if such a subsequent choice or later change of the applicable law does not prejudice the rights of third persons which have been acquired in the meantime.[18]

15. Katičić, op.cit., p. 230; and in, *Medjunarodno privatno pravo,* (1976) p. 159.
16. Sajko, op.cit., pp. 396-397 and 400.
17. Matić, op.cit., pp. 375-377.
18. That solution is adopted in Swiss Draft Act on PIL (1978) in Article 119.

2.1.3 Objective Connecting Factors

Yugoslav laws, apart from the Act concerning Obligations (Art. 1101 and Art. 1105), which is not primarily concerned with "international" contracts, provide for the application of the law most closely connected with the contract in cases of absence of a valid parties' choice of the applicable law. There are, however, differences in the provisions of these laws. The Act concerning Obligations and Basic Real Rights in Air Navigation (Art. 224) adopts the presumption that the law of the domicile or seat of the air carrier is the most closely connected law, unless particular reasons indicate the contrary. The same idea is adopted in the Draft of the Act concerning PIL and Procedure of 1974 (Art. 20). On the other hand, the Act concerning Maritime and Inland Navigation (Art. 1002) does not contain such a presumption. It seems that the problem is still partly open in the Committee of Experts who are revising the Draft of 1974. One group of experts, which represents the majority, favours the system of the Draft of 1974 and of the Act concerning Air Navigation. The other group favours a strict system of objective connecting factors, without reference to the law most closely connected with the contract. The third group would only depart from the strictly defined objective factors if particular reasons in the case indicate that it would be more appropriate to apply some other law. So the question is still unsolved.

2.2 Draft Act concerning Private International Law and Procedure (1974), and dilemmas

The Draft of 1974 follows the basic solution of other Yugoslav laws in maritime and air navigation, leaning towards the solution adopted in the Act concerning Obligations and Basic Real Rights in Air Navigation (1977) in questions of "implied" choice of law, and of objective connecting factors. It accepts partly the ideas behind the Hague Convention of 1955, but does not provide for special rules concerning consumer sales.

During the discussions in the Committee of Experts since the publication of the Draft in 1974, the following dilemmas have arisen:

a) the problem of "implied" choice of law, which problem has been mentioned above;

b) the problem of the law most closely connected with the contract as a subsidiary applicable law, and the opposite solution of a more strict determination of objective connecting factors, which problem has also already been mentioned;

c) the question which objective connecting factor to adopt, either with the presumption that it in principle points to the law most closely connected with the international sale, or without that presumption, as a single connecting factor.

As far as the last problem is concerned, the Draft of 1974 provides for application of the law of the domicile, or seat, of the seller at the time when he received the offer, unless the offer was received in the place where the buyer was domiciled or had its seat. In that case the buyer's law would apply. These rules were criticized for various reasons. One of the reasons was that this rule favours the application of the law of the seller in the great majority of cases. The opposite view was also expressed, i.e., that the buyer's law should be eliminated entirely as a possible applicable law. The second reason for criticism was that the term "offer" is ambiguous (the Hague Convention of 1955 and the Draft on Consumer Sales of 1979 use the term "order", as a fact defining the relevant time), and that it could lead to difficulties of characterization in particular cases.

No other acceptable solutions were, however, proposed, and the return to the traditional rules of the *lex loci contractus* or *lex loci solutionis* is obviously out of place. So the question is still open.

ANNEX 1

ACT CONCERNING MARITIME AND INLAND NAVIGATION
(Službeni list SFRJ No. 22 of April 22, 1977)

Article 1000

Contracts concerning relations in navigation are governed by the law chosen by the parties.

Article 1001

As an exception from the provision in Article 1000, this Act is applicable to contracts for the employment of ships:
1) in the case of the operator's liability for damage to, shortage or loss of cargo, regulated by provisions of this Act, the application of which cannot be excluded by agreement of the contracting parties, if the port of loading or that of destination is in a SFR of Yugoslavia;
2) when the passenger would be put in a worse position by applying the provisions of another law than by applying the provisions of this Act.

An agreement concluded contrary to the provisions of s. 1 of this Article has no legal effect.

Article 1002

If it is impossible to apply the law chosen by the parties to the contract for the employment of ships, either to the whole contract or to some relation deriving from the contract, or, if the parties have not explicitly chosen the applicable law, and their intention as to the law to be applied cannot be ascertained even from the circumstances of the case, the contract or the contractual relation is governed by the law with which it is most closely connected.

If it is impossible to ascertain the law which is most closely connected with contracts for the employment of ships, the following apply:
1) the law of the place where the contract was concluded – to the main rights and obligations of contracting parties;
2) the operator's national law – if the contract for carriage of passengers of goods is concluded on the basis of the general terms established in advance by the operator;
3) provisions of this Act – to the contract of towage.

To the manner of performance of collateral rights and obligations of the contracting parties (the way of loading and delivering of cargo, the computation of lay time and demurrage time, the way of paying freight, and similar), in cases mentioned in s. 2 of this Article the law of the place where those acts have been performed, or where they should have been performed, applies.

ANNEX 2

ACT CONCERNING OBLIGATIONS AND BASIC REAL RIGHTS IN AIR NAVIGATION
(Službeni list SFRJ No. 22 of April 22, 1977)

Article 223

Provisions of this Act concerning contracts of carriage of passengers and goods do not apply if the parties have contracted for the application of some other specific law.

As an exception from s. 1 of this Article the provisions of this Act concerning contracts of employment of aircrafts apply obligatorily:

1) when both parties – employer of the aircraft and carrier – are natural or legal persons domiciled or having a seat in a SFR of Yugoslavia, and the airport of departure or that of destination is in a SFR of Yugoslavia;
2) if the application of another law would violate the provisions of this Act which cannot be excluded or changed, and the airport of departure or that of destination is in a SFR of Yugoslavia;
3) when the passenger would be put, by application of another law, in a worse position than by applying the provisions of this Act.

An agreement concluded contrary to the provisions of s. 2 of this Article has no legal effect.

Article 224

If it is impossible to apply the law chosen by the parties, to the whole contract or to some relation deriving from the contract, or, if the parties have not explicitly chosen the applicable law, and their intention as to the law to be applied cannot without doubt be ascertained even from the circumstances of the case, the contract or the contractual relation is governed by the law with which it is most closely connected.

Unless particular reasons indicate to the contrary, to the main rights and obligations applies, as the most closely connected, the law of a state where, at the time of conclusion of the contract, the carrier had his domicile or his seat.

To the collateral rights and collateral obligations (the way of acceptance or delivery of the goods or the way of paying freight and similar) the law where these acts have been performed, or where they should have been performed, applies.

ANNEX 3

ACT CONCERNING OBLIGATIONS
(Službeni list SFRJ No. 29 of May 26, 1978)

The law applying to obligations arising from contracts.

Article 1101

(1) The law governing the rights and duties arising from a contract is the law of the republic or the autonomous province which the parties have chosen.
(2) If the parties have not chosen the applicable law, the law to be applied is the law of the republic or the autonomous province in whose territory the contract was concluded.

Obligations which have arisen outside the SFRJ.

Article 1105

The law governing rights and duties which have not originated in the territory of the SFRJ, if the parties have not chosen the applicable law, is the law of the republic or the autonomous province in whose territory those rights and duties are performed, but, if the rights and duties are performed in the territory of several republics or autonomous provinces or are performed outside the SFRJ, the applicable law is the law of the republic or the autonomous province which has the closest connection with the contract or the other obligation.

ANNEX 4

ACT CONCERNING PRIVATE INTERNATIONAL LAW AND PROCEDURE
(Draft of 1974)

Contracts

Article 19

(1) Contractual relations are governed by the law chosen by the parties. That law applies if the choice was done explicitly or if it follows without doubt from the circumstances of the case.
(2) Contracts concerning immovables are governed by the law of the place where they are situated.

Article 20

(1) In the absence of a choice of the applicable law, the contract is governed by the law with which it is most closely connected.
(2) Unless particular reasons indicate to the contrary, it is to be assumed that the following apply:

a) to the sale of corporeal movable goods – the law of the domicile or of the seat of the seller at the time of the acceptance of the offer; but if the offer was accepted in the place where the buyer is domiciled or has its seat – the law of that place;
b) . . .
c) . . . etc.

[TRADUCTION – TRANSLATION]

No. 7411. CONVENTION ON THE LAW APPLICABLE TO INTERNATIONAL SALES OF GOODS. DONE AT THE HAGUE, ON 15 JUNE 1955

The States signatory to this Convention;

Desiring to establish common provisions concerning the law applicable to sales of goods;

Have resolved to conclude a Convention for this purpose and have agreed on the following provisions:

Article premier

This Convention shall apply to international sales of goods.

It shall not apply to sales of securities, to sales of ships and of registered boats or aircraft, or to sales upon judicial order or by way of execution. It shall apply to sales based on documents.

For the purposes of this Convention, contracts to deliver goods to be manufactured or produced shall be placed on the same footing as sales, provided the party who assumes delivery is to furnish the necessary raw materials for their manufacture or production.

The mere declaration of the parties, relative to the application of a law or the competence of a judge or arbitrator, shall not be sufficient to confer upon a sale the international character provided for in the first paragraph of this article.

Article 2

A sale shall be governed by the domestic law of the country designated by the Contracting Parties.

[1] In accordance with article 9, the Convention came into force on 1 September 1964, the sixtieth day after the date of deposit of the fifth instrument of ratification. The instruments of ratification of the following States were deposited with the Netherlands Government on the dates indicated:

State	*Date of Deposit*	*Date of entry into force*
Italy	17 March 1958	1 September 1964
Belgium	19 October 1962	1 September 1964
France	30 July 1963	1 September 1964

Denmark	3 July	1964	1 September 1964
Finland	3 July	1964	1 September 1964
Norway	3 July	1964	1 September 1964
Sweden	8 July	1964	6 September 1964

Such designation must be contained in an express clause, or unambiguously result from the provisions of the contract.

Conditions affecting the consent of the parties to the law declared applicable shall be determined by such law.

Article 3

In default of a law declared applicable by the parties under the conditions provided in the preceding article, a sale shall be governed by the domestic law of the country in which the vendor has his habitual residence at the time when he receives the order. If the order is received by an establishment of the vendor, the sale shall be governed by the domestic law of the country in which the establishment is situated.

Nevertheless, a sale shall be governed by the domestic law of the country in which the purchaser has his habitual residence, or in which he has the establishment that has given the order, if the order has been received in such country, whether by the vendor or by his representative, agent or commercial traveller.

In case of a sale at an exchange or at a public auction, the sale shall be governed by the domestic law of the country in which the exchange is situated or the auction takes place.

Article 4

In the absence of an express clause to the contrary, the domestic law of the country in which inspection of goods delivered pursuant to a sale is to take place shall apply in respect of the form in which and the periods within which the inspection must take place, the notifications concerning the inspection and the measures to be taken in case of refusal of the goods.

Article 5

This Convention shall not apply to:

1. The capacity of the parties;
2. The form of the contract;
3. The transfer of ownership, provided that the various obligations of the parties, and especially those relating to risks, shall be subject to the law applicable to the sale pursuant to this Convention;
4. The effects of the sale as regards all persons other than the parties.

Article 6

In each of the Contracting States, the application of the law determined by this Convention may be excluded on a ground of public policy.

Article 7

The Contracting States have agreed to incorporate the provisions of articles 1-6 of this Convention in the national law of their respective countries.

Article 8

This Convention shall be open for signature by the States represented at the seventh session of The Hague Conference on Private International Law.

It shall be ratified, and the instruments of ratification shall be deposited with the Ministry of Foreign Affairs of the Netherlands.

A record shall be made of each deposit of instruments of ratification, a certified copy of which shall be transmitted through the diplomatic channel to each of the signatory States.

Article 9

This Convention shall enter into force on the sixtieth day following the deposit of the fifth instrument of ratification in accordance with the provisions of article 8, second paragraph.

For each signatory State subsequently ratifying the Convention, it shall enter into force on the sixtieth day following the date of deposit of the instrument of ratification of that State.

Article 10

This Convention shall apply to the metropolitan territories of the Contracting States as a matter of course.

If a Contracting State wishes the Convention to be applicable to all its other territories, or to those of its other territories for the international relations of which it is responsible, it shall give notice of its intention in this regard by an instrument which shall be deposited with the Ministry of Foreign Affairs of the Netherlands. The latter shall transmit through the diplomatic channel a certified copy thereof to each of the Contracting States. The Convention shall enter into force as regards such territories on the sixtieth day following the date of deposit of the above-mentioned instrument of notification.

It is understood that the notification provided for in the second paragraph of this article shall not take effect until after the entry into force of the Convention pursuant to article 9, first paragraph.

Article 11

Any State not represented at the seventh session of The Hague Conference on Private International Law may accede to this Convention. A State desiring to accede shall give notice of its intention by an instrument which shall be deposited with the Ministry of Foreign Affairs of the Netherlands. The latter shall transmit through the diplomatic channel a certified copy thereof to each of the Contracting States. The Convention shall enter into force as regards the acceding State on the sixtieth day following the date of deposit of the instrument of accession.

It is understood that the deposit of the instrument of accession may not take place until after the entry into force of the Convention pursuant to article 9, first paragraph.

Article 12

This Convention shall have a duration of five years from the date specified in article 9, first paragraph. This period shall begin to run as from that date even for the States which ratify or accede to the Convention subsequently.

The Convention shall be renewed by tacit agreement for successive periods of five years unless it is denounced.

Notice of denunciation must be given, at least six months before the expiration of the period, to the Ministry of Foreign Affairs of the Netherlands, which shall notify all the other Contracting States thereof.

The denunciation may be limited to the territories, or to certain of the territories, specified in a notification made pursuant to article 10, second paragraph.

The denunciation shall have effect only as regards the State effecting it. The Convention shall remain in force for the other Contracting States.

In WITNESS WHEREOF, the undersigned, duly authorized by their respective Governments, have signed the present Convention.

DONE at The Hague, on 15 June 1955, in a single copy, which shall be deposited in the archives of the Government of the Netherlands and of which a certified copy shall be transmitted, through the diplomatic channel, to each of the States represented at the seventh session of The Hague Conference on Private International Law.

For the Federal Republic of Germany:

For Austria;

For Belgium:

VAN DER STRATEN
[1 August 1955]

ANNEX 6

PRELIMINARY DRAFT CONVENTION ON THE LAW APPLICABLE TO CERTAIN CONSUMER SALES

adopted by the Special Commission on June 29th, 1979

Article 1

This Convention shall apply to certain international sales of goods, including sales based on documents, where the seller acts in the course of his business of profession and the buyer is a consumer.

The Convention shall not apply to auctions, sales authorized by judicial authorities or by way of execution, sales of securities or other legal instruments, or sales on commodity or other exchanges.

For the purposes of this Convention, contracts to deliver goods to be manufactured or produced shall be considered as sales, provided the supplier is to furnish the necessary materials or parts.

The declaration of the parties relative to choice of law or the jurisdiction of a judge or arbitrator is not by itself sufficient to confer upon a sale an international character.

Article 2

A "consumer" is a natural or legal person who, in the particular case, does not act primarily in the course of his business or profession.

A buyer shall be considered a consumer unless the seller establishes that the buyer was acting primarily in the course of a business or profession, or that the seller reasonably so believed.

Article 3

The Convention shall apply where –

1 the negotiations for the sale were mainly conducted in the country in which the consumer then had his habitual residence and the consumer there took the steps necessary on his part for the conclusion of the contract;

2 the seller or his representative, agent or commercial traveller received the order in the country in which the consumer then had his habitual residence;

3 the order was preceded by a specific invitation addressed to the consumer in the country in which he had his habitual residence, or by advertising or other

marketing activities undertaken in, or directed to, that country, and the consumer there took the steps necessary on his part for the conclusion of the contract; or

4 the consumer travelled from the country in which he had his habitual residence to another country and there gave his order, provided that the consumer's journey was directly or indirectly arranged by the seller for the purpose of inducing the consumer to buy.

[*Article 4*

The internal law chosen by the parties shall govern a sale to which this Convention applies. However, a choice of law made by the parties shall in no case deprive the consumer of the protection afforded by the mandatory rules of the internal law of the country in which he had his habitual residence at the time the order was given.

The choice of the applicable law must be express and in writing.

[Questions relating to the consent of the parties as to the choice of the applicable law shall be governed by that law.]]

Article 5

[In the absence of a choice of law by the parties,] the internal law of the country in which the consumer had his habitual residence at the time the order was given shall govern a sale to which this Convention applies.

Article 6

The formal requirements for sales to which this Convention applies shall be governed by the law specified in the preceding Articles.

Article 7

This Convention shall not apply to –

1 the capacity of the parties;

2 the effects of the sale as regards any person other than the parties.

Article 8

The application of a law specified by the Convention may be refused only where such application would be manifestly incompatible with public policy *(ordre public)*.

ANNEX 7

[CONVENTION] ON THE LAW APPLICABLE TO CERTAIN CONSUMER SALES

Article 1

This Convention shall apply to certain contracts for the international sale of goods bought primarily for personal, family or household use, where the seller acts in the course of his business or profession and where at any time before the contract was entered into, he knew or ought to have know that the goods were being bought primarily for any such use.

The declaration of the parties relative to choice of law or the jurisdiction of a court or arbitrator is not by itself sufficient to confer upon a contract of sale an international character.

For the purpose of this Convention, contracts to supply goods to be manucfactured or produced shall be considered as contracts of sale, provided that the supplier is to furnish a substantial part of the necessary materials.

Article 2

For the purpose of this Convention, a person who buys goods primarily for a personal, family or household use, is hereinafter referred to as the consumer.

Article 3

It is for the seller to show that he neither knew nor ought to have known that the goods were being bought primarily for personal, family or household use.

Article 4

The Convention shall not apply to sales -

a by auction;
b by way of execution or otherwise by authority of law;
c of stocks, shares, investment securities, negotiable instruments or money;
d on commodity or other exchanges.

Article 5

The Convention shall apply only in the following cases –

1 the negotiations for the sale were conducted mainly in the country in which the consumer then had his habitual residence and the consumer there took the steps necessary on his part for the conclusion of the contract:

2 the seller or his representative, agent or commercial traveller received the order in the country in which the consumer then had his habitual residence;

3 the order was preceded by a specific invitation addressed to the consumer in the country of his habitual residence, or by advertising or other marketing activities

undertaken in, or directed to, that country, and the consumer there took the steps necessary on his part for the conclusion of the contract;

4 the consumer travelled from the country of his habitual residence to another country and there gave his order provided that the consumer's journey was directly or indirectly arranged by the seller for the purpose of inducing the consumer to buy.

Article 6

The internal law chosen by the parties shall govern a contract to which the Convention applies. However, a choice of law made by the parties shall in no case deprive the consumer of the protection afforded by the mandatory rules of the internal law of the country in which he had his habitual residence at the time the order was given.

The choice of law must be express and in writing.

Questions relating to the existence, validity and form of the consent of the parties to the choice of law shall be determined in accordance with the internal law of the country in which the consumer had his habitual residence at the time the order was given.

Article 7

In the absence of a choice of law by the parties, the internal law of the country in which the consumer had his habitual residence at the time the order was given shall govern a contract to which the Convention applies.

Article 8

The law applicable to a contract pursuant to Article 6, paragraph 1, or Article 7 shall govern in particular –

a the form of the contract;
b the existence and validity of the contract;
c the interpretation of the contract;
d the consequences of non-performance of the contract, including the assessment of damages; however, a court need not give relief that would not be given under its own law in a similar case.

Article 9

Articles 6 and 7 shall not apply to –

a the capacity of the parties;
b the effects of the contract as regards any person other than the parties.

Article 10

The application of a law specified by the Convention may be refused only where such application would be manifestly incompatible with public policy *(ordre public)*.

THE LAW OF INTERNATIONAL SALES: THE HAGUE CONVENTIONS 1964 AND THE UNCITRAL UNIFORM SALES CODE 1980 – SOME MAIN ITEMS COMPARED

by F.J.A. van der Velden

1. INTRODUCTION

1.1. Codification of uniform private law

For many centuries the great diversity of existing legal systems and the uncertainty of the applicability of a particular system in a given case have stimulated legislators, institutions and individuals to seek harmonization and unification.

In the recent wave of international harmonization and unification of private (and especially commercial) law which began at the end of the 19th century and which is still growing, two approaches are of great importance: the international unification of conflict of laws rules on the one hand, and the creation of uniform laws on the other. The unification of private international law has had a very real character since the foundation of the Hague Conference on Private International Law, which has resulted in a considerable number of conventions on the subject, following the first meeting in 1893 under the presidency of T.M.C. Asser.[1] The wish to unify substantive law materialised in 1926 in the establishment, under the auspices of the League of Nations, of the International Institute for the Unification of Private Law (UNIDROIT) in Rome [2] and, in 1966, in the establishment of the United Nations Commission on International Trade law (UNCITRAL).[3]

The main concern of both UNIDROIT and UNCITRAL is the law of international sale. In June 1964, a UNIDROIT draft of a Uniform law on the International Sale of Goods (ULIS) and a draft of a Uniform Law on the Formation of Contracts for the International Sale of Goods (ULFIS) were adopted by a diplomatic conference, and came into force in August 1972. In March 1980 in Vienna, a diplomatic conference was held in order to discuss a draft Convention on Contracts for the International Sale of Goods ("United Nations Convention on Contracts for the International Sale of Goods" (CISG)). The draft was made by UNCITRAL and designed to improve, and to promote thereby, the Hague Conventions on international sales contracts.

In this paper we will describe the main innovations brought into the field of international sales law by ULIS and ULFIS and compare these innovations with the UNCITRAL convention. By doing so, we hope to be able to discover a common core of established international uniform sales law rules.

1. See, Voskuil, *L'Esprit d'Internationalité* (La Haye 1968).
2. See, Matteucci, "UNIDROIT, The First Fifty Years", *Revue de Droit Uniforme* (1976) p. 15.
3. *Uncitral Yearbook* I (1968-1970) p. 5; Honnold, "The United Nations Commission on International Trade Law: Mission and Methods", AJCL (1979) p. 201 at p. 211 n. 33.

1.2. Unification of the law of international sales

The unification of the law on international sales began in 1929 with an initiative from Ernst Rabel, founder and director of the Kaiser Wilhelm Institut für ausländisches und internationales Privatrecht in Berlin. Rabel came up with the idea of investigating the possibility of creating a world-wide uniform sales law by UNIDROIT, the newly created International Institute for the Unification of Private Law. In the preface to his book *Das Recht des Warenkaufs,* which was to a certain extent the academic precursor of what in 1964 became the Uniform Law on International Sales (ULIS), Rabel wrote:

"At the beginning of our work stood the question if and to what extent the law of sale is fit to be uniformly enacted in all countries of the world." [4]

The history of the ULIS codification is well known. After a first draft had been examined by the Member States of UNIDROIT in 1939, the so-called Rome Draft was ready to be discussed at a diplomatic conference. However, World War II intervened, and not only temporarily stopped this UNIDROIT project, but what was more important, changed international commercial practice to such an extent that a complete revision of the Rome Draft was necessary. After a diplomatic conference in 1951, two subsequent commissions were created, one for the preparation of a Uniform Sales Law and another for a Uniform Law on the Formation of International Sales. The Commissions drew up, with intermediate drafts in 1956, the 1963 Drafts of the Uniform Law on the International Sale of Goods (ULIS) and the Uniform Law on the Formation of Contracts for the International Sale of Goods (ULFIS).[5] Both drafts were adopted by the diplomatic

4. Rabel, *Das Recht des Warenkaufs* (Berlin 1936, reprint Berlin 1957) p. V.

5. Tunc, "The Two Hague Conventions of 1st July 1964", in *Diplomatic Conference on the Unification of Law Governing the International Sale of Goods, The Hague,* Part I Records, pp. 355-191 at p. 359 (Hereafter: *Commentary*). It is useful to quote from the testimony given by Tunc on the intention of the draftsmen of ULIS:

"It is not unprofitable to draw attention now to the basic ideas which guided the proceedings of the Special Commission as well as those of the Conference. In their effort to achieve unification, the draftsmen of the Uniform Law have never made a concession on some part of the Law or particular rule to some national law in exchange for corresponding concessions. The Uniform Law is less a work of compromise than a work of choice and creation. The draftsmen have been guided by municipal institutions whenever these seem intrinsically good and likely to effect an improvement in international relationships. On every point, they have sought what seems to them to be the best in the experience of different countries. On numerous problems, however, they have felt compelled to innovate or to override municipal law. If the Uniform Law is a work of compromise, it is so to the extent that its draftsmen have constantly sought to balance the rights of the buyer and the seller and to modify where necessary those concepts which were good in themselves but which favoured too greatly one or other of the parties. If it was necessary to override municipal practices in order to achieve uniformity, there is good reason to think that the law forms a body of rules which it would be to the advantage of all to see generally adopted."

conference held in the Hague (the Netherlands) from 2 to 25 april 1964 [6] (amendments, while numerous, were mostly of minor importance). Twenty-eight States participated in the 1964 Conference, four were represented by observers. It must, therefore, have been disillusioning to many people to see that it was not until 1972 that five States, the number required to bring the conventions into operation, had ratified.

At the present time nine States – Belgium, Gambia, West Germany, Israel, Italy, Luxembourg, the Netherlands, San Marino, and the United Kingdom – have adopted ULIS and ULFIS.[7]

2. MAIN PRINCIPLES OF ULIS AND ULFIS

Unifying and codifying international sales law as done in ULIS and ULFIS raises numerous problems. The differences between the various domestic sales law systems were enormous both in principle and in technical elaboration. Similarly, in international commerce there was no unanimity or uniformity. On many points the draftsmen of both uniform sales laws had to struggle through an almost overwhelming flow of legal problems in search of solutions.

Four [8], or even five [9], solutions can be said to be fundamental and original:

1. the definition of international sales to be governed by the Uniform Laws;
2. the determination of the scope of operation of the laws;
3. the non-mandatory character;
4. the "reasonable person" criterion; and
5. the system of remedies for the violation of an obligation.

2.1. International sales: definition, applicability

ULIS only relates to contracts of sale that are international in character within the meaning of Article 1 ULIS. In this Article the adjective "international" is defined as having a double meaning, a subjective one, concerning the parties to the contract, and an objective one, concerning the contract of sale itself.

The subjective criterion requires that the contracting parties have their places of business, or, in the absence of such a place, their habitual residence, in dif-

6. ULIS is printed in, Tractatenblad (1964) no. 117, ULFIS in, Tractatenblad (1964) no. 118. Texts of the Conventions. Records and Documents of the 1964 Conference are published by Staatsuitgeverij, Christoffel Plantijnstraat, The Hague.

7. States can adopt ULIS and ULFIS with several restrictions, laid down in Art. II-V of ULIS and in the same Artt. of ULFIS. The number of restrictions, and their actual use by almost all Contracting States (Belgium (IV), FRG (III), Gambia (III, V), Italy (IV), Luxembourg (IV), Netherlands (III), UK (III, V) makes the applicability of the Uniform Laws uncertain and gives broad opportunities for forum shopping: see, Van der Velden, *De Eenvormige Koopwetten van 1964* (Deventer 1979) p. 269.

8. Tunc, *Commentary*, p. 361.

9. Although Tunc refers in his enumeration to four fundamental solutions, at least the criterion of "reasonable person" has to be added to them.

ferent States, regardless of whether these States are either by ratification or accession parties to the ULIS/ULFIS Convention. The nationality of the parties is of no importance and is completely disregarded.

The objective criterion requires that either the acts constituting offer and acceptance are effected in different States, or that the goods [10] are sold during international transport or are to be transported internationally, or that the acts of offer and acceptance are made in a State other than the State of the place of delivery. Once the circumstances of the sale comply with this definition, ULIS and ULFIS apply.

The world-wide applicability of ULIS/ULFIS can be restricted by a contracting State. Article III of the ULIS and ULFIS Conventions permits Contracting States to restrict the subjective criterion of applicability, at the time of their adherence or accession, to parties who have their places of business in States that are members of these conventions. Many Contracting States have made this restriction.[11]

Relevant to the question of applicability of ULIS/ULFIS is Article 4 ULIS. This Article states that the parties to a sales contract that is international in the objective sense, but lacks the subjective criterion of internationality, can choose ULIS/ULFIS as the law of the contract on one condition, i.e., that the ULIS/ULFIS rules do not derogate from the mandatory provisions of the national law that would have been applicable had no choice been made.[12]

2.2. Scope of ULIS and ULFIS (Art. 8 ULIS)

ULIS and ULFIS govern only the rights and duties of the contracting parties and the rules concerning the formation of an international sale. As Article 8 stipulates, the Uniform Laws shall not be concerned with the validity of the contract or of its provisions, or of any usage, nor with the effect which the contract may have on property.

The exclusions in Article 8 are counterbalanced by the rules of interpretation and completion in Article 17, which state that, "questions concerning matters governed by the present law which are not expressly settled therein shall be settled in conformity with the general principles on which the present law is based".[13]

10. Restrictions as to the meaning of "goods" are made in Art. 5, and as to the meaning of "sale", in Art. 6 ULIS.

11. FRG, Gambia, the Netherlands, San Marino and the UK.

12. Compare: EEC Convention on the Law Applicable to Contractual Obligations, Rome 1980, Art. 3.5.3.

13. For example, the principles of good faith, reasonableness, non-abuse of rights or unjust enrichment, informal character of communications and *de minimus non curat praetor,* can be deduced from the ULIS/ULFIS text and its history. See Dölle, *Kommentar zum einheitlichen Kaufrecht: das Haager Kaufrechtsübereinkommen von 1 Juli 1964,* bearbeitet von Ernst von Caemmerer (Munich 1976), p. 130; Van der Velden, op.cit., p. 54.

2.3. Non-mandatory character of ULIS and ULFIS

The Uniform Laws of 1964 are strictly of a non-mandatory character. The parties to the contract may exclude the Uniform Laws. They may otherwise be set aside by international practice by which the parties are bound.[14] The parties may entirely or partially exclude the applicability of the Uniform Laws; the exclusion may be express or implied. With an express exclusion, be it in writing or oral, the parties' knowledge of it may be assumed. Implied exclusions are not so straightforward. An exclusion is not only to be implied if the parties, without express exclusion, conclude a contract of a special type, so that the contract is partly or wholly governed by corresponding usages, but also if the parties substitute for the ULIS or ULFIS rules any other rules which they consider more appropriate.

The possibility of a partial exclusion (express or implied) of ULIS/ULFIS, as provided for in Article 3 ULIS, has created several uncertainties. The partial exclusion could be the consequence of a partial insertion into the contract of a given domestic law. The co-existence of two laws applicable to different parts of one contract (*dépeçage*) is not universally accepted. It is excluded, for example, in the Hague Convention on the Law applicable to International Sales of Goods (1955).[15] ULIS, on the other hand, accepts *dépeçage.*[16]

Parties can also partly replace ULIS provisions by contract clauses. In this case the question has to be answered whether ULIS, even as regards the subjects contractually settled, remains the law of the contract, and thus still rules the interpretation and the remedies in case of non-performance of that contractual clause.

A second unsolved exclusion problem in ULIS/ULFIS is that of an international sales contract which contains a choice of law clause declaring applicable the law of a State that is a party to the ULIS/ULFIS conventions. See, e.g., *Landgericht Landshut* ((FRG) 14-7-1976 NJW p. 2033), where it was decided that ULIS was applicable to a German-Dutch international sale contract even though the contract declared German law applicable. Such a statement did not, in the court's opinion, exclude ULIS. This interpretation of Article 3 ULIS has to be welcomed. It breathes the spirit of uniform law and pays tribute to the Preamble to the ULIS Convention, which expresses the desire of the signatory States to establish a uniform law for the sale of goods.

2.4. Reasonable person

One of the general principles of uniform sales law is the "reasonable man" criterion.[17] International contracts of sale require a strictly objective approach

14. Art. 3 ULIS; art. 2 ULFIS; Art. 9.5.2. ULIS.
15. *Recueil des Conventions de la Haye*, ed. Permanent Bureau of the Conference, The Hague; dépeçage is accepted in the EEC Convention 1980, see, *supra* n. 11.
16. Art. 2 ULIS.
17. See, *supra* n. 13.

by uniform law to the rights and duties of the parties. This objective approach in ULIS is laid down in the criterion "a reasonable person in the same situation", a criterion still more explicit in its French translation: "personne raisonable de même qualité placée dans la même situation (de cette partie ou de l'autre partie)".[18] Regarding this paraphrase, the reasonable person principle contains three elements:

1. the reasonable person;
2. possession of the specialist qualifications generally to be expected of a person in the situation in question; and
3. the same circumstances as the party involved.[19]

The concept of a "reasonable person" is hard to define, and seems to connote not only a sufficiently intelligent, skilled and careful member of society but also an ethical standard of behaviour so that he must also be judicious and fair.[20] In view of the words, "de même qualité", this reasonable person standard has to be defined in terms of the professional group or commercial branch in question, e.g., merchant or non-merchant, merchant in a special branch or otherwise, international merchant, merchant in basic commodities or in industrial products. Strictly personal qualifications such as age or sex are not intended.

The second refinement of the reasonable person standard, "placée dans la même situation", is the implementation of the concrete circumstances of the party in question. This refinement concerns only the objective circumstances of that party and not his personal situation. So, e.g., the kind of contract, the circumstances (time and place) of its conclusion and its performance are also to be considered as subject to the reasonable person standard.

2.5. System of remedies

ULIS provided its own system of remedies in case of breach of any of the obligations created by the contract of sale, be it the obligations of the seller to deliver the goods in the quality and quantity contracted for, at the place and the time parties arranged, or the obligations of the buyer to pay the price and take delivery.

Not every non-performance of the contract is a breach of contract. The non-performing party who can prove that his non-performance was due to circumstances which, according to the intention of the parties or to reasonable standards, he was not bound to take into account, to avoid or to overcome, is not in breach of the contract.[21] Of the totality of breaches of contract, those which are unimportant will not be taken into consideration, in accordance with the legal maxim, *de minimis non curat praetor.*

18. Artt. 9.5.2., 10, 13 ULIS; Art. 13 ULFIS.
19. Graveson-Cohn-Graveson, *The Uniform Laws on International Sales Act 1967* (London 1968), p. 59.
20. Dölle(-Reinhardt), *supra* n. 13, p. 71.
21. Art. 74 ULIS.

As to the breaches of contract that can be remedied, the ULIS remedy system distinguishes between breaches that are fundamental and breaches that are not. A breach of contract is fundamental whenever the party in breach knew or ought to have known, at the time of the conclusion of the contract, that a reasonable person would not have entered into the contract if he had foreseen the breach and its effects.[22] The ULIS definition of fundamental breach tries to balance the interest of both parties and to exclude all subjective criteria.

The remedies which the Uniform Law gives for a fundamental breach are specific performance on the one hand, and avoidance of the contract on the other, while either may be accompanied by damages. The claimant has to make his choice within a proper (sometimes short, sometimes reasonable) period, otherwise, in case of non-delivery or non-payment, the contract will be *ipso facto* avoided. In the case of a part-delivery or non-conformity of the goods delivered, or of any of the other obligations of the party in breach, the claimant loses his right of avoidance if not properly protested.[23] *Ipso facto* avoidance will not take place if the party in breach fulfils his duty within the period in which the claimant has to make his decision. Should the claimant require performance and it is not forthcoming within a reasonable time, then the claimant can declare the contract void or – in some cases [24] reduce the price of the sale proportionally.

Independent of the fundamental breach criterion, Article 28 ULIS provides that a non-performance of delivery at the appointed time always amounts to a fundamental breach of the contract, whenever a price for such goods is quoted on a market where the buyer can obtain them.

If the breach of contract does not amount to a fundamental breach, then the party in breach retains the right to perform his duties; the injured party can claim only damages, and in some cases, a price reduction. Yet, the claimant has the right to impose on the seller an additional period of performance. If the party in breach fails to perform his obligation within this additional period, his breach will amount to a fundamental breach, and brings with it the abovementioned remedies of avoidance, specific performance and damages.

This general system has one important exception. Commercial usage can oblige the claimant to re-purchase or to resell goods in place of those contracted for. If this re-purchase or resale is reasonably possible, the contract shall be *ipso facto* avoided as from the moment such a purchase or resale should be effected.[25] The claimant under a duty to re-purchase or resell can only demand damages

22. Art. 10 ULIS. For further discussion of the concept of fundamental breach, see, *infra*, n. 5.5.6.

23. Non-delivery: Artt. 26, 30; non-payment: Art. 62; part-delivery: Art. 45; non-conformity: Art. 43; other obligations: Art. 51 (handing over of documents); Art. 52 (transfer of property); Art. 55 (other obligations of seller); Art. 66 (acceptance of delivery); Art. 70 (other obligations of buyer).

24. Art. 46 ULIS.

25 Art. 25; art. 61(2) ULIS.

under Article 82 et seq. Reference should be made to the fact that the claimant may exercise his rights without previous summons for performance, contrary to the practice in several civil law systems. A second point is that no party in breach is entitled to apply to a court or an arbitrator to grant a period of delay.[26]

This, in its outline, simple and easy-to-handle system of remedies has, in ULIS, been worked out for not less than nine different species of breach, each with its own particular variations. These nine species are: breach in time of delivery, breach in place of delivery, non-conformity of the goods delivered, breach in handing over documents, non-transfer of property, breach of other obligations of the seller, breach of payment, breach in taking delivery, breach of other obligations of the buyer.[27]

The detailed elaboration of the basic system of ULIS remedies, although well considered and perfected, is in practice too complicated, and, therefore, not perspicuous or manageable enough to serve international commerce between States with enormous legal, social and economic differences.

3. UNCITRAL CONVENTION ON THE INTERNATIONAL SALE OF GOODS

3.1. History

The Diplomatic Convention which accepted the UNIDROIT drafts of ULIS and ULFIS in 1964, did not end the discussions on the most suitable codification of international sales law. To involve the UN in the development of an international trade law, the UN General Assembly, on 17 December 1966, decided to create the "United Nations Commission on International Trade Law (UNCITRAL)"

In its first meeting, on 29 January 1968, UNCITRAL gave priority to unification of the rules of international sales, international payment and commercial arbitration. As to international sales, UNCITRAL decided not to work out completely new legislation but to re-examine ULIS and ULFIS in order to make both globally acceptable. After several redrafts, the Commission at its tenth and eleventh plenary meetings, in June 1977 and June 1978, adopted the draft Convention on Contracts for the International Sale of Goods. On the recommendation of the UNCITRAL Commission, the General Assembly of the UN submitted this draft Convention for consideration to a Conference of Plenipotentiaries, which took place in Vienna in March-April, 1980.

Many reasons have been proposed as answers to the question why ULIS and ULFIS have had so little succes. Did ULIS and ULFIS need to be modified to make them more acceptable to countries of different legal, economic or social systems? [28] Was it "lack of clarity", resulting, in part, from inadequate parti-

26. Art. 24(3); Art. 64 ULIS.
27. See, *supra* n. 23.
28. *Uncitral Yearbook* I, p. 99. An example of the concerns of the third world countries shown during the Vienna Conference is given by Perrott, "The Vienna Convention

cipation in the drafting process by representatives of different backgrounds? [29] Did ULIS, in resolving the differences between national laws, pay too little attention to commercial practices? [30] Was ULIS too complicated [31] or outdated in many of its provisions? [32] Or were the divergences between common law and civil law the principal stumbling-block in preparing uniform rules for the international contract of sale, and were the 1964 Conventions essentially the product of the civil law tradition of Western Europe? [33]

To treat this question in our own way we will now discuss the extent to which CISG has, in general, adhered to, amended or deleted the various items in ULIS and ULFIS mentioned above.

3.2. CISG and the main principles of ULIS and ULFIS

As already mentioned, ULIS introduced to the legal world of international trade a set of rules that were original and several of which were also fundamental. Of these, the five main items were:

1. the definition of international sale;
2. the determination of the scope of operation of the Uniform Law;
3. the non-mandatory character;
4. the objective standard; and
5. the system of remedies.

3.3. International sale: definition, applicability

The CISG definition of the internationality of an international sale [34] has only one subjective criterion, laid down in Article 1. This is: do the parties to

---

1980 on Contracts for the International Sale of Goods", *International Contract Law and Finance Review* (1980) p. 577 at p. 582.

29. Honnold, "The Draft Convention on Contracts for the International Sale of Goods: an Overview", AJCL (1979), p. 223 at p. 225, Roth, "The Passing of Risk". AJCL (1979) p. 291 at p. 294.

30. Farnsworth, "Unification of Sales Law in the Regional and International Level", in, *Aspects of Comparative Commercial Law*. The USSR did not participate in the drafting of either uniform law, nor in the Hague Conference 1964. The USA only participated in the Hague Conference, but its participation was very positive. Of the Eastern European countries, only two (Hungary and Bulgaria) participated. The non-Western legal systems were represented only by semi-Western countries (Egypt, Turkey, Japan), the third world countries were represented by South American countries (Colombia, and the observers Argentina, Mexico and Venezuela) and by Yugoslavia.

31. Honnold, loc.cit., *supra* n. 29, at p. 229, Meyer, "Uncitral en het nieuwe verdrag inzake de internationale handelskoop", NJB 1980, p. 1021. The many different reservations Contracting States can make under the ULIS/ULFIS Conventions seriously disturbs the applicability system of these uniform laws.

32. Meyer, loc.cit., p. 1024.

33. Eörsi, "Problems of Unifying Law on the Formation of Contracts for the International Sale of Goods", AJCL (1979), p. 311 at p. 316; Honnold, loc.cit., *supra* n. 29, at p. 225.

34. CISG, like ULIS, only relates to sales with an international character, a restriction unknown in other conventions on commercial law subjects, like the Geneva Conventions

the contract of the sale of goods have their places of business, or – in the absence of a place of business – their habitual residences, in different States? Lacking the objective criterion as found in ULIS it was necessary, in order to make parties aware of the international character of the contract, and thereby of the possibility of the applicability of CISG, to require that the presence of this subjective criterion be known by each party, at least at the conclusion of the contract.

As compared with ULIS, an improvement is made as to the place of business. Article 10 CISG indicates which place of business is to be taken into account if a party to the contract has more than one place of business in more than one State.

The applicability of CISG to international sales is governed by two rules. CISG must be applied if the places of business of the parties are in two different Contracting States; it must also be applied if the rules of private international law refer to the law of a Contracting State. The first of these two rules creates a sphere of application to which international lawyers are accustomed, and probably represents a lesson learned from the ULIS Convention. Under that Convention many of the adopting States have made the Article III restriction as to the worldwide application of ULIS and, therefore, ULIS is mostly applicable if the parties have their places of business in Contracting States.[35] The second rule of applicability of CISG resembles an article added by the Dutch legislature to the Dutch ULIS Act, which states that ULIS is applicable as Dutch law to an international sale if any rule of private international law refers to Dutch law. The introduction of this second rule of applicability removed the necessity for a special provision for cases where the parties choose CISG as the law of the contract (cf. Art. 4 ULIS).

3.3.1. Restrictions: consumer protection, product liability

Not all international sales answering the definition of Article 1 CISG are governed by this law.

---

of 1930 and 1931 on negotiable instruments, which conventions apply to all international and domestic bills of sale and cheques. The restriction to "international" sales has its advantages, but at the same time it also has disadvantages. The head of the legal department of a Dutch-British oil company declared that as long as different legal regimes existed between international and domestic sales, his company would oblige its salesmen to contract only under a choice of law clause declaring Dutch law applicable. The reason was simple: these people, although not trained in the law, were technically skilled, and were well trained to apply one system of contract. To burden these persons with the duty of applying different legal systems in different (international and domestic) situations involved too much risk for the company.

35. The only possible restriction a Contracting State can make concerning the applicability of CISG is given in Art. 96. By introducing the restriction into the uniform sales law by operation of Art. 12 CISG, it will now be applied uniformly by all competent *fora;* see, Honnold, loc.cit., *supra* n. 29, at p. 227 n. 29. The Art. III restriction has been adopted by Gambia, FRG, Netherlands, San Marino and UK.

Article 2 CISG, like Article 5 ULIS, excludes the sale of some categories of goods such as ships, securities and electricity, and some special types of sale, such as those by auction and by authority of law. Special attention has to be given to Article 2 subsection a and Article 5.

In Article 2 subsection, a CISG bars application in the case of consumer sales.[36] This explicit exclusion, unknown in ULIS/ULFIS, must be welcomed. On the one hand, while international travel makes consumer sales a large proportion of international selling, parties to a consumer sale are not usually aware of the applicability of any international sales convention. On the other hand, the various ways in which consumers are, or are not, protected by their national laws, depends too much on the domestic socio-economic situation to make the establishment of a uniform rule possible.

Article 5, a provision not present in the 1978 CISG draft, and introduced at the Vienna Conference, excludes the applicability of CISG in cases of liability of the seller for death or personal injury caused by the goods. Here again, the better protection given to injured persons by national product liability laws is recognised. Both exclusions are surely an improvement to international sales law.

3.4. Scope of the uniform sales law; interpretation, completion

With ULIS and ULFIS, CISG only governs the formation of international sale contracts and the rights and duties of the seller and the buyer. In Article 4 in particular, CISG excludes claims concerning the validity of the contract or property rights.[37]

Within the ambit of Article 4, the interpretation and completion of CISG raises problems. If the Uniform Law does not contain an explicit solution for a legal problem, Article 7 requires that the provisions of CISG be interpreted and applied with regard to the international character of the situation and to the need to promote uniformity and the observance of good faith in international trade.

However, since CISG, in contrast to ULIS, contains no provision stating that the rules of private international law are excluded in international sale contracts, one can question whether cases not covered are to be decided by way of com-

36. The lack of a uniform definition of consumer sale is obvious. The Art. 2 CISG definition is not identical to the one used in the EEC 1980 Convention, *supra* n. 11, nor to the one used in the revision of the Hague Sales Convention 1955. The EEC Convention gives priority to consumer protection rules in case of the delivery of goods to a person for a use that is not in the course of his business or profession. The Sales Convention 1955, revision, will apply to contracts for the international sale of goods bought primarily for personal, family or household use, where the seller acts in the course of his business or profession.

37. The explicit regulation in Art. 42 of the duty of the seller to deliver goods which are free from rights or claims based on industrial property is also new. (For Art. 4 CISG see, Art. 8 ULIS).

pletion of the Uniform Law, in conformity with the general principles on which it is based, or should be decided by the national law designated by private international law in non-conventional international sales.[38] The answer was not given in the 1978 CISG draft, but only at the 1980 Vienna Conference. In the second section of Article 7, a provision is introduced that completion of the Uniform Law has to be done in conformity with the general principles on which CISG is based and, in the absence of such principles, in conformity with the national law indicated by private international law. This addition to Article 7 has an ambiguous quality. It obliges judges and arbitrators, used to a restrictive interpretation of statute law, and those who are anti-uniformists, to apply CISG in a broader way, by using at least an historical, analogical and systematic interpretation; yet, it hinders uniformists from applying section 1 of Article 7 in an all-embracing way. The uniformists' interpretation of section 1, Article 7 explaining the word "interpretation" in its liberal sense, so that it also encompasses completion, was, in appearance, the interpretation intended by the 1978 CISG draftsmen. The Article 7, section 1 provision can also (without the restriction of of s. 2) be found in other UNCITRAL uniform laws (i.e., the Hamburg Rules) and was beyond any doubt intended to be the link to bind the uniform laws to what might have become the *lex mercatoria moderna.* It created the possibility of applying through CISG general principles of uniform law developed in other branches of international commerce. Now, by the introduction of section 2, the meaning of "interpretation" is restricted to "explanation of the words and sentences used." However, it is still unclear whether section 2 will contribute to the creation of a uniform international standard of legal norms and principles in the way in which section 1 did. Another consequence of the restriction of the meaning of section 1 is that the "good faith observance" of this provision is no longer a source of law, but has become a mere means of explanation.

3.5. Non-mandatory character

CISG, like ULIS and ULFIS, is of a non-mandatory character, with the same consequences as discussed in paragraph 2.3 above: parties can, and usages may, exclude the application of the Uniform Law. However, in CISG one exception is made. A Contracting State may at the time of signature, ratification or accession make a declaration as referred to in Article 96. This Article allows a Contracting State to require a contract of sale (or its modification or abrogation or any indication of intention to create legal obligations) to be made in writing, where any party has his place of business in that Contracting State. This declaration not only creates obligations of a public international law character, but it becomes, by operation of Article 12 CISG, part of the uniform sales law.

38. Huber, "Der UNCITRAL-Entwurff eines Ubereinkommens über internationale Warenkaufverträge", RabelsZ 43 (1979) p. 413 at p. 422; Bonell, "Some critical reflection on the new Uncitral draft Convention on international sale", *Uniform Law Review* (1978) II, p. 2.

The almost unlimited non-mandatory character of CISG is somewhat surprising. If CISG is to promote international trade by uniform law, as is stated in the considerations of the CISG Convention, and if uniform law is to replace municipal law, it is arguable that at least some provisions of CISG must have a compulsory character. There is, for example, no reason for allowing the provision of Article 7 section 1 CISG (interpretation of international sale contracts in conformity with the need to promote uniformity and according to the good faith standard in international trade) to be substituted by a national legal system merely by the parties' intent, when their contract is an international one.

3.6. Objective standard

In its attempt to determine the rights and duties of the parties to the contract, CISG has not explicitly adhered to the simple and strictly objective criterion of the reasonable person as used in ULIS, Article 13 CISG offers several definitions of what is, in essence, the "reasonable man" criterion. For example, by Article 9 section 2 (comparable with Art. 9 s. 2 ULIS) parties are, unless otherwise agreed, considered bound by, "a usage of which the parties knew or ought to have known and which in international trade is widely known to, and regularly observed by, parties to contracts of the type involved in the particular trade concerned". And Article 65 (comparable with Art. 74 ULIS) exempts a party from liability for non-performance, "if he proves that the failure was due to an impediment beyond his control and that he could not reasonably be expected to have taken the impediment into account at the time of the conclusion of the contract or to have avoided or overcome it or its consequences". A direct reference to the reasonable person criterion used in ULIS is introduced in Article 8 section 2: ". . . a reasonable person of the same kind as the other party would have had in the same circumstances. . ." and in Article 25: ". . . unless the party in breach did not foresee and a reasonable person of the same kind in the same circumstances would not have foreseen . . .".[39] Through this last definition, it becomes possible, in the light of an Article 7 interpretation, to introduce this Article 25 criterion into those provisions, regarding the facts which, "the party knew (discovered, foresaw, etc.) or ought to have known (discovered, foreseen)". [40] The same criterion can be applied to those provisions which demand "reasonable" behaviour (reliance, expectance, mitigation) [41], or in any other way make use of the adjective "reasonable" (time, delay, measures, expenses, excuse, etc.).[42]

39. This description of "reasonable person" is better than the one given in the English text of ULIS; the French text of ULIS distinguishes kind (*qualité*) and circumstance (*dans la situation de l'autre partie*) while the English text only speaks of "situation".

40. Arts. 2, 9, 38, 49, 64, 68; 39 (discovered), 43 (was aware), 74 (forsaw), 79 (knew) CISG.

41. Artt. 26 and 35 (reliance); 60 and 79 (expectance) CISG.

42. See, *supra*, section 2.4.

3.6.1. Objective standard: exception

The only questionable phrase relating to the measure of objectivity, is, the one that, as in ULIS Article 36 and 40, obliges to consider the facts of which the party "knew or could not have been unaware".[43] Here, a more subjective criterion than "the reasonable man" probably has to be applied, as, when this special formula is used, good faith urges the party concerned to use the greatest vigilance possible in his personal situation.[44]

3.7. System of remedies

In CISG, two series of remedies are elaborated, one of them governing all the species of non-performance by the seller, one governing all the non-performances of the buyer. Both series are based on one simple system of remedies which, in principle, hardly differs from the ULIS system described above. The system of remedies differentiates between breaches that are, and breaches that are not, fundamental. Fundamental breaches are breaches by one party which result in detriment to the other party, so as substantially to deprive him of what he is entitled to expect, unless the party in breach did not foresee, and a reasonable person of the same kind in the same circumstances would not have foreseen, such a result.[45] All breaches give a right to the remedies of performance (or repair of the goods delivered) and – in addition to other remedies or not – to the remedy of damages. All breaches also give the right to fix an additional period of time for performance. The sale price may be reduced. Added to these remedies, fundamental breaches give right to avoid the contract, or to ask for substitution of the defective goods. The right to avoid the contract also exists when an additonal period of time for performance is given in the case of non-delivery, if the seller does not deliver within this additional period. Under CISG, no arbitrator or judge has the right to grant to the party in breach a period of delay during which performance remains possible, and the other party is temporarily excluded from his remedies.

When comparing the ULIS and the CISG system of remedies, several interesting points can be noted.

3.7.1. Fundamental and non-fundamental breaches; avoidance

CISG has maintained the ULIS division between fundamental and non-fundamental breaches. In cases of breach, performance and damages can always be claimed. Fundamental breaches give the right of avoidance of the contract (in ULIS often an *ipso facto* avoidance, in CISG always a declared avoidance) and non-fundamental breaches give the right to fix an additional period of

43. Artt. 35, 40, 42 CISG.
44. See, Tunc, *Commentary* to ULIS/ULFIS Artt. 36, 40, p. 356 et seq.
45. Art. 25 CISG.

time for performance. The consequence of non-performance within the additional period is in ULIS [46] a fundamental breach, while in CISG [47] only a non-delivery (non-payment) within the additional period set after a non-delivery (non-payment) will result in the right of avoidance (although it is possible that any non-fundamental breach after the passage of the additional period would be considered a fundamental breach).[48] A consequence of this restricted interpretation of "additional period of time for performance" in CISG is that in the case of delivery of goods that do not conform to the contract, the seller has to await his co-contractor's convenience and can claim damages as long as the breach of performance is not fundamental.[49] CISG undoubtedly complicates the consequences of the additional period.

In ULIS, avoidance of the contract can be caused by operation of law (*ipso facto* avoidance) or by a declaration of the claimant. The *ipso facto* avoidance is intended for sales where time and place of delivery or payment are of the essence of the contract [50], and for sales where the claimant, according to usage or to contract, has the duty to effect a replacement sale or a replacement purchase.[51] In ULIS, declarations concerning *non-ipso-facto* avoidances have sometimes to be made promptly, sometimes within a reasonable period after the breach or after a given event.[52]

CISG jettisoned the concept of automatic avoidance because it led to uncertainty as to the continued existence of the contract; in ULIS the contract can come to an end without both parties being aware of that fact. In CISG the contract still exists without doubt if the claimant has not sent a notice declaring the avoidance of the contract.[53] CISG also deleted the different approaches to the periods in which a declaration of avoidance has to be made, and only refers to a reasonable time. Although the use of different periods of declaration was well considered and carefully systematised in ULIS, it complicated the system of remedies considerably. For greater certainty and better practicability, CISG simplified the complex remedy system of ULIS.

The removal of two provisions from ULIS that correspond to international commercial usage and simplify the elaborated ULIS system of remedies in many sales is both remarkable and regrettable. Articles 25 and 61 section 2 ULIS state that if it is in conformity with usage and reasonably possible for the

46 Art. 26 ULIS.

47. The declaration of avoidance must have been duly (by appropriate means of communication, sufficiently stamped letter, etc.) sent to the other party, although it need not to be received by this party. See, Art. 25 CISG.

48. Artt. 27, 44 ULIS.

49. Artt. 49, 64 CISG.

50. Meyer, loc.cit., p. 1029, informs us that at the Vienna Conference of 1980 the great majority of delegations held the view that the mere passing of time could not create fundamental breach.

51. Huber, loc.cit., p. 487, Michida, "Cancellation of Contract", AJCL (1979) p. 279 at p. 287 et seq.

52. Artt. 25, 61 ULIS.

53. Farnsworth, "Damages and Specific Relief", AJCL (1979) p. 247 at AmJCL 1979, p. 250; Secretariat's Commentary, *supra* n. 5, p. 123.

buyer (seller) to purchase (or resell) goods to replace those to which the contract was related, he has no right to require performance; on the contrary, the contract is avoided as from the time the purchase (resale) should have been effected. A consequence of the setting aside of these Articles is that the claimant even if he can purchase or resell the goods contracted for elsewhere immediately, has to declare the contract void in cases of fundamental breach, and to wait for performance in non-fundamental breaches, in spite of the fact that "time is money".[54]

Article 28 ULIS states that whenever a price for the goods is quoted on a market where the buyer can obtain them, e.g., when the contract was for the delivery of commodities, agricultural seeds and the like, the failure to deliver the goods at the date fixed shall amount to a fundamental breach of the contract. This Article is also deleted. The possibility of speculation (not unusual in this branch of trading: speculation was the very reason for the adoption of Article 28) was in the case of an Article 28 sale stopped by the *ipso facto* avoidance of Article 26 ULIS. Although the CISG definition of fundamental breach (see, Art. 25) opens the possibility of declaring the contract avoided in the case of a non-observance of the time fixed for delivery of commodities, the advantages of the "hard and fast" rule of Article 28 ULIS are obviously missing from the CISG remedy system.[55]

In its remedies system, CISG makes more room for the seller to make up deficiencies in, or to remedy non-conformities of, the goods. A comparison of Articles 44 ULIS and 49 CISG illustrates the differences. ULIS has a clear rule: the seller can always exercise these rights, unless his breach of contract is fundamental (or has become fundamental by non-performance within the additional period of time). In cases of fundamental breach the seller is at the buyer's mercy. CISG in Article 49 section 2, gives a less passive position to the seller. The seller himself can propose an additional period of time for performance, and ask the buyer to agree or not with his proposal for performance. If the buyer does not answer within a reasonable time, the seller may perform within the time indicated in his proposal. During that period of time, the buyer is barred from any remedy that is inconsistent with performance.

3.7.2. Fundamental breach: definition

One of the major differences between ULIS and CISG is the way in which the "fundamental breach" is defined. A breach is of a fundamental nature if contract or usage so declare. In the absence of such clear determinants, the law has to give a rule of interpretation.

In ULIS a breach of contract is fundamental, "whenever the party in breach knew or ought to have known, at the time of the conclusion of the contract, that a reasonable person in the same situation as the other party would not

54. Contract and usage can reintroduce the repurchase/resale obligation..
55. Huber, loc.cit., p. 486; Michida, loc.cit., p. 286; Meyer, loc.cit., p. 1027.

have entered into the contract, if he had foreseen the breach and its effects".[56] This definition is an objective one: the measure of fundamentality is to be decided according to the "reasonable man" criterion. The deficiency of the definition comes from the *ex post facto* reasoning that is to be effected, in that one has to establish that the party in breach ought to have known what is in a reasonable man's mind at the time of the conclusion of the contract. This is almost impossible. As Graveson [57] puts it:

"In times of a buyer's market it would seem that any breach of the seller is fundamental: in such times no reasonable buyer will buy from a seller if he foresees that there will be even the slightest breach; he can buy from any other seller and will undoubtedly do so; of this fact every seller is or ought to be aware. In times of a seller's market the opposite will be true: few breaches will seem fundamental because reasonable buyers will try to take what they get. If there has been a change between the time of the conclusion of the contract and the breach and the buyer's market has turned into a seller's market or *vice versa,* the matter becomes highly complex".[58]

To overcome the *ex post facto* reasoning necessary in the Article 10 ULIS definition, the British and Dutch Governments, at the 1964 Diplomatic Conference [59] where ULIS was finally framed, proposed a new and quite simple formula, in which objective criteria were to be judged according to the time of the occurence of the breach of contract. This proposal read: "A breach of contract shall be deemed to be fundamental, wherever the performance of the contract is, by reason of the breach, rendered radically different from that for which the parties contracted".

As several authors [60] have remarked, Article 10 ULIS has a clear meaning in spite of its complicated wording; a breach is fundamental if it results in the disappearance of any interest on the part of the other party in carrying out the contract and if that consequence was known or ought to have been known by the party in breach.

CISG, in its 1978 draft, proposed an almost new definition of fundamental breach. In view of the long discussions that finally led to the wording of the ULIS breach criterion, and taking into account the various detailed commentaries on its formula by lawyers of different legal systems [61], the CISG draft contained

56. In the 1956 and 1963 drafts of ULIS, fundamental breach (then Art. 15) was defined as follows: "A breach of the contract shall be deemed to be fundamental whereever the party knew or ought to have known, at the time the contract was made, that the other party would not have contracted had he foreseen that such a breach would occur", 1964 Conference, Part 2, Documents, p. 9 (1956 ULIS draft), p. 214 (1963 ULIS draft), *supra*, n. 5.

57. Graveson-Cohn-Graveson, op.cit, p. 55.

58. See, the example given by Michida, loc.cit., p. 279.

59. 1964 Conference, Part 2, Documents, p. 274, *supra* n. 5.

60. Graveson-Cohn-Graveson, op.cit., p. 57, Mertens-Rehbinder, *Internationales Kaufrecht, Kommentar zu den Einheitlichen Kaufgesetzen* (Frankfurt a/M 1975) p. 129, Dölle, op.cit., p. 51; Huber, loc.cit., p. 462.

61. See, *supra* n. 60; Huber, loc.cit., p. 462 n. 79.

an unexpected and surprising definition of fundamental breach. Article 23 CISG 1978 draft states:

"A breach committed by one of the parties is fundamental if it results in substantial detriment to the other party, unless the party in breach did not foresee and had no reason to foresee such a result."

This definition of fundamental breach, intended to replace the sophisticated Article 10 ULIS text with an easy-to-handle phrase, was not very successful. It focused only on breaches that resulted in a detriment, and only those breaches which resulted in a substantial detriment were fundamental. In this 1978 definition not much was left of the relationship between the ULIS fundamental breach concept and the Scandinavian legal doctrine upon which it was based.[62] After thorough discussion, the Vienna Conference reached a somewhat more acceptable definition – a compromise with those discontented with the draft provision. This new definition (Art. 25 CISG) reads:

"A breach of contract committed by one of the parties is fundamental if it results in such detriment to the other party as substantially to deprive him of what he is entitled to expect under the contract, unless the party in breach did not foresee and a reasonable person of the same kind in the same circumstances would not have foreseen such a result."

The improvements in this definition as compared with the 1978 one are clear. The meaning of "substantial", as clarified, relates now only to the rights of the other party in the contract. The rather subjective ruling of foreseeability is replaced by the strictly objective one used by ULIS (see *supra* section 3.6.) and, now, Article 25 expressly refers to the rights which the party not in breach was entitled to expect under the contract. Therefore, the foreseeability of the fundamental character of the breach is no longer time-tabled as it was in ULIS; it is restricted only by the possible expectations of the other party at the time of the conclusion of the contract. Not withstanding these improvements, Article 25 holds the possibility of many different interpretations. First, the meaning of detriment.

Detriment is hardly a term of art. It is rarely used in (international) legal terminology. Is detriment damage or loss, or damage and loss? Is consequential damage/loss included, or has detriment to be interpreted in a specific way now that a "damage is damage, loss is loss" interpretation is not ruled out.[63]

A paraphrase of detriment, acceptable for international use could, in my opinion, be the one given by the Corpus Iuris Secundum, namely:

62. See, Dölle (-Huber), *supra*, n. 13, p. 57.

63. N.Y. Court in, Schwimmer *v.* Air France (1976) 14 Avi 17; 466, cited in, Fothergill *v.* Monarch Airlines [1980] 3 WLR 209 (HL). For damage and loss, see Art. 66 CISG.

". . . in its technical use has been said that the detriment need not be real and need not involve actual loss, nor does it necessarily refer to material disadvantage to the party suffering it, but means a legal detriment as distinguished from a detriment in fact and has been defined as giving up something which one had the right to keep, or doing something which he had the right not to do." [64]

Secondly, "substantial" is an adjective, as uncertain as "fundamental" itself, and, therefore, creates a somewhat circular definition. The concept "fundamental breach", the keystone of the CISG remedy system, is unfamiliar to countries and persons who are not part of or educated in the Anglo-American legal system, and it varies in the countries and persons who are.[65] Therefore, a universal consensus on the meaning of fundamental breach is necessary. One may, however, doubt whether the Article 25 CISG definition will be the guideline needed.

3.7.3. ULIS and CISG remedies: motivating options

If we compare the system of remedies of ULIS and CISG as we did in the preceding paragraphs, it is clear that alongside the many similarities some remarkable differences exist. These differences are closely related to the options, either legislative, political, economic or social, that the draftsmen of each code could have had in mind.

3.7.3.1. *Legislative option*

In the legislative option, the choice is between a codification that aims at a simple system of remedies, suitable for the most usual type of contract, leaving aside all other types, and a codification that covers at least the various main types of contracts for the sale of goods.

Two main types can be distinguished. On the one hand, there is the sale on the market of bulk and staple goods, where basic commodities, agricultural seeds and the like, which are replaceable and of an average quality, are dealt with and openly obtainable, and where the price of the goods is quoted openly. On the other hand, there are the sales of industrial products, where prices are settled by dealing between seller and buyer and quality is an important part of the dealing, while time is less important.[66]

Each market requires its own, special regulation in a uniform codification of international sales. The staple market is less interested in the conformity of the goods to the contract (the goods only need to be of an average quality) than in a quick and prompt delivery and payment of price. Prices on these markets and for such goods are daily quoted. These prices will rise and fall from day to day according to the supply and demand on the market. Each delay in performance

64. C.J.S. Volume 26a, p. 984.
65. E.g., the different opinions on fundamental breach of Lords Denning, Wilberforce and Diplock, see, Photo Productions *v.* Securicor [1980] 1 All ER 556.
66. Dölle, op.cit., p. 230.

can thus create a difference between the price contracted for and the quoted market price. If prices fall, the buyer will no longer be interested in the goods bought, now that he is able to obtain the same goods for a lower price, while the seller will get less for his goods if, at the end, the buyer refuses to pay and he has then to resell the goods. If prices rise the positions of buyer and seller are reversed. In staple markets, therefore, trading is risky, and invites speculation if parties must wait for performance after the time contracted for. Damages could compensate, but are in practice difficult to enforce and of a secondary interest to the claimant. Therefore, in the usages of staple markets, time is of the essence, so that an immediate avoidance of the contract after delay can clear any uncertainty.

The industrial products scene, on the contrary, is usually not interested in a fixed date of delivery but in delivery itself, and especially in the conformity of the goods to the terms of the contract. Usually the seller is still entitled to perform his obligations even if he is later than the agreed time for performance. In the case of defective performance, he has the right to replace or repair the goods if he can do so within a reasonable time. The buyer can only force the seller to fulfil his duty by fixing an additional period for performance, unless the contrary is agreed or self evident from the circumstances, as, e.g., the well-known example of the delivery of Christmas turkeys after Christmas.[67]

The CISG has deleted those ULIS provisions that, (a) focused on short time avoidance in case of breach, (b) declared the non-delivery of goods, the prices of which were quoted on a market accessible to the buyer, to be a fundamental breach, and (c) declared the contract avoided if usage obliged a party to repurchase or resell the goods in case of non-performance by the other party. In this respect the CISG will be of little importance to contractors in commodity sales. They have to shelter, as they used to, behind their own standard-form contracts.

3.7.3.2. *Economic option*

A second option is an economic one. Here we have to distinghuish between legal systems meant to serve the free enterprise society and those serving a society with a planned economy. A free enterprise system considers it good for its society if its resources are, at any moment, allocated and reallocated by their possessors whenever economic efficiency is served by such action. The duty created by contract to dispose the goods in a fixed way can frustrate an economically more desirable destination. To avoid frustrating its own objectives, a free enterprise society will therefore allow any reallocation, although it constitutes a breach of contract, and, at the same time, grant redress to the injured party by awarding damages according to his expectations.

67. Michida, loc.cit., p. 282.

"Since reallocation through breach will not make the injured party worse off as long as his expectations are protected . . . , and will, by hypothesis, make the party in breach better off, it is in society's interest that the contract be broken and the resources reallocated." [68]

A society with a planned economy will, on the contrary, try to urge the parties to the contract to fulfil their duties in order to realize the exigencies of the economic plan. In such an economic system, specific performance prevails as a remedy for a breach of contract. Only the promisee is able, under certain circumstances, to waive the right of specific relief and accept damages in exchange.

These two economic models and their legal/conceptual consequences are, in practice, and especially in international practice, less antagonistic. Free enterprise is bridled in almost all countries by governmental measures, and States with planned economies seem, on the international level, to be well aware of the advantages a free economy can produce. The restrictions CISG laid on the right to avoid the contract seem to be based on the opinion that avoidance is economically wasteful.[69]

3.7.3.3. *Socio-political option*

A third option is of a socio-political kind. Here the question is: has a worldwide uniform law to be constructed as if the parties to the contract were equal, ignoring the differences between East and West, industrialized and developing countries, between North and South, or must uniform law recognize these differences and, by defending the weaker, create greater equality. As, e.g., Michida states:

"In worldwide transactions, efficient communication and storage facilities for the preservation of goods are not always guaranteed. At seaports where adequate storage facilities do not exist one may see piles of industrial products on the ground exposed to the weather. These conditions intensify the harshness that results from immediate cancellation by buyer or seller. On the other hand, in countries like the United States, where merchants enjoy efficient systems of communication, preservation storage and transportation, a rule permitting immediate cancellation for any sort of breach can be less hard." [70]

The position of the Third World countries directly influenced the preparations of and the discussions during the Vienna conference. The New Interna-

68. Farnsworth, AJCL (1979) p. 248.
69. Farnsworth, "Legal Remedies for Breach of Contract", Co LR (1970) p. 1145.
70. Michida, loc.cit., pp. 280-282. Other data in the socio-political sphere, like acquaintance with one of the official languages of the international sales law codifications and with its legal background (as a means of interpretation), are also to be taken into account. The ULIS and ULFIS conventions permitted Contracting States to introduce translations of the uniform laws into their domestic law. The advantages of a translation outweighed the disadvantages created by differences in translations.

tional Economic Order discussions in the United Nations thus contributed to the final text of CISG. The identification of the Third World countries with the buyer's position is particularly noteworthy and understandable. Developing countries are, as sellers of commodities, confronted with a powerful world market of buyers, and, as buyers of industrial products, they encounter the know-how and economic power of their co-contractor. The less stringent ruling on remedies in the case of a commodities sale, and the need, at the least, for an implicitly fixable price for the goods, are examples of the concern the Vienna Conference had for the position of these countries.[71]

Other options can possibly be added to these three.

Although it is clear that these options have played their role in the lawmaking process of CISG, they cannot be judged right or wrong by lawyers only. Economists, economic geographers, experts on development problems and many other specialists must give their opinions and make their contributions. Only after multi-disciplinary research can a verdict of this kind be given.

4. CONCLUSION

To arrive at a conclusion from our comparison of some main items of the 1964 Uniform Laws on the international sale of goods and their counterparts in the Uncitral Convention is only partially feasible.

1. CISG retains and improves on most of the achievements made by ULIS/ ULFIS. Its applicability to international sales between parties both of whom have their places of business in Contracting States, or one of whom has his place of business in a Contracting State and private international law rules declares the law of that State applicable, is surely an improvement, as is the exclusion of consumer sales and product liability. The general scope of CISG remains the same, i.e., it governs the formation of an international sale contract and the obligations arising from that contract, as ULFIS and ULIS do. The explicit introduction of private international law, which possibly restrains the creation of a *lex mercatoria moderna*, is regrettable. CISG also maintains (with the exception of Art. 12) the strictly non-mandatory character of the Uniform Law. Even the CISG system of remedies for breach of contract is, in its principles, based on the division ULIS made between fundamental and non-fundamental breaches. The legal system of international sales law created by ULIS has thus been stabilized by CISG.

2. CISG simplified the system of remedies. The sophisticated and thereby complicated divisions of the ULIS remedies system, where almost each obligation has, in case of breach, its own variation of the general system of remedies, is reduced in CISG to two kinds of remedies: one for breaches by the seller and one for breaches by the buyer.

71. Meyer, loc.cit., pp. 1024, 1027.

3. The system of remedies given in CISG has its clear deficiencies. The very restricted right to declare the contract avoided introduced by CISG will, too often, especially in commodities sales, force the contracting parties to replace the statutory provisions by contractual agreements. On the other hand, the right to correct a part-delivery or a non-conformity of the goods by replacing or repairing the defective goods has been extended. What is unclear, is the crucial definition of "fundamental breach", as it is uncertain and circular.

4. If, however, we try to see the CISG draft in the light of the purposes Uncitral had in mind when it decided to revise ULIS and ULFIS, conclusions are hard to find. A codification of the law of international sales "capable of wider acceptance (than ULIS and ULFIS) by countries of different legal, social and economic systems" cannot be judged only by its legal consistency. Only by co-operation between lawyers and economists, geographers and development specialists can CISG be examined as to its suitability for these purposes. Such an examination has not yet been made.

5. Nevertheless, the chances of success of the CISG Convention seem to have a fertile basis. Some forty-nine, Western and Eastern, Northern and Southern developed and developing countries have signed the Final Act.[72] Many of these States also seem to be willing to sign the CISG Convention itself.

72. Perrot, loc.cit., p. 577.

CONCORDANCE: ULIS and ULFIS (1964) with CISG (1980)

UNIFORM LAW ON THE INTERNATIONAL SALE OF GOODS

Chapter 1
Sphere of application of the law

Article 1

1. The present Law shall apply to contracts of sale of goods entered into by parties whose places of business are in the territories of different States, in each of the following cases:

(*a*) where the contract involves the sale of goods which are at the time of conclusion of the contract in the course of carriage or will be carried from the territory of one State to the territory of another;

(*b*) where the acts constituting the offer and the acceptance have been effected in the territories of different States;

(*c*) where delivery of the goods is to be made in the territory of a State other than that within whose territory the acts constituting the offer and the acceptance have been effected.

2. Where a party to the contract does not have a place of business, reference shall be made to his habitual residence.

3. The application of the present Law shall not depend on the nationality of the parties.

4. In the case of contracts by correspondence, offer and acceptance shall be considered to have been effected in the territory of the same State only if the letters, telegrams or other documentary communications which contain them have been sent and received in the territory of that State.

5. For the purpose of determining whether the parties have their places of business or habitual residences in "different States", any two or more States shall not be considered to be "different States" if a valid declaration to that effect made under Article II of the Convention dated the 1st day of July 1964 relating to a Uniform Law on the International Sale of Goods is in force in respect of them.

UNITED NATIONS CONVENTION ON CONTRACTS FOR THE INTERNATIONAL SALE OF GOODS

PART I
SPHERE OF APPLICATION AND GENERAL PROVISIONS

Chapter 1
Sphere of application

Article 1

1. This Convention applies to contracts of sale of goods between parties whose places of business are in different States:
a) when the States are Contracting States; or
b) when the rules of private international law lead to the application of the law of a Contracting State.

2. The fact that the parties have their places of business in different States is to be disregarded whenever this fact does not appear either from the contract or from any dealings between, or from information disclosed by the parties at any time before or at the conclusion of the contract.

3. Neither the nationality of the parties nor the civil or commercial character of the parties or of the contract is to be taken into consideration in determining the application of this Convention.

(Art. 2 CISG → Art. 5 ULIS)

Article 2

Rules of private international law shall be excluded for the purposes of the application of the present Law, subject to any provision to the contrary in the said Law.

Article 3

The parties to a contract of sale shall be free to exclude the application thereto of the present Law either entirely or partially. Such exclusion may be express or implied.

Article 4

The present Law shall also apply where it has been chosen as the law of the contract by the parties, whether or not their places of business or their habitual residences are in different States and whether or not such States are Parties to the Convention dated the 1st day of July 1964 relating to a Uniform Law on the International Sale of Goods, to the extent that it does not affect the application of any mandatory provisions of Law which would have been applicable if the parties had not chosen the Uniform Law.

Article 5

1. The present Law shall not apply to sales:
(*a*) of stocks, shares, investment securities, negotiable instruments or money;
(*b*) of any ship, vessel or aircraft, which is or will be subject to registration;
(*c*) of electricity;
(*d*) by authority of law or on execution or distress.

2. The present Law shall not affect the application of any mandatory provision of national law for the protection of a party to a contract which contemplates the purchase of goods by that party by payment of the price by instalments.

Article 10

For the purposes of this Convention:
a) if a party has more than one place of business, the place of business is that which has the closest relationship to the contract and its performance, having regard to the circumstances known to or contemplated by the parties at any time before or at the conclusion of the contract;
b) if a party does not have a place of business, reference is to be made to his habitual residence

(Art. 11 CISG → Art. 15 ULIS)

(deleted)

Article 6

The parties may exclude the application of this Convention or, subject to article 12, derogate from or vary the effect of any of its provisions.

(Art. 7 CISG → Art. 17 ULIS)

(deleted)

Article 2

This Convention does not apply to sales:
a) of goods bought for personal, family or household use, unless the seller, at any time before or at the conclusion of the contract, neither knew nor ought to have known that the goods were bought for any such use;
b) by auction;
c) on execution or otherwise by authority of law;
d) of stocks, shares, investment securities, negotiable instruments or money;
e) of ships, vessels, hovercraft or aircraft;
f) of electricity.

Article 6

Contracts for the supply of goods to be manufactured or produced shall be considered to be sales within the meaning of the present Law, unless the party who orders the goods undertakes to supply an essential and substantial part of the materials necessary for such manufacture or production.

Article 7

The present Law shall apply to sales regardless of the commercial or civil character of the parties or of the contracts.

Article 8

The present Law shall govern only the obligations of the seller and the buyer arising from a contract of sale. In particular, the present Law shall not, except as otherwise expressly provided therein, be concerned with the formation of the contract, nor with the effect which the contract may have on the property in the goods sold, nor with the validity of the contract or of any of its provisions or of any usage.

Chapter II
General provisions

Article 9

1. The parties shall be bound by any usage which they expressly or impliedly made applicable to their contract and by any practices which they have established between themselves.

2. They shall also be bound by usages which reasonable persons in the same situation as the parties usually consider to be applicable to their contract. In the event of conflict with the present Law, the usages shall prevail unless otherwise agreed by the parties.

(Art. 3 CISG → Art. 6 ULIS)

Article 5

This Convention does not apply to the liability of the seller for death or personal injury caused by the goods to any person.

(Art. 6 CISG → Art. 3 ULIS)

Article 3

1. Contracts for the supply of goods to be manufactured or produced are to be considered sales unless the party who orders the goods undertakes to supply a substantial part of the materials necessary for such manufacture or production.
2. This Convention does not apply to contracts in which the preponderant part of the obligations of the party who furnishes the goods consists in the supply of labour or other services.

(see, Art. 1 (3) CISG → Art. 1 ULIS)

Article 4

This Convention governs only the formation of the contract of sale and the rights and obligations of the seller and the buyer arising from such a contract. In particular, except as otherwise expressly provided in the Convention, it is not concerned with:
a) the validity of the contract or of any of its provisions or of any usage;
b) the effect which the contract may have on the property in the goods sold.

(Art. 5 CISG → Art. 5 ULIS)

Article 9

1. The parties are bound by any usage to which they have agreed and by any practices which they have established between themselves.
2. The parties are considered, unless otherwise agreed, to have impliedly made applicable to their contract or its formation a usage of which the parties knew or ought to have known and which in international trade is widely known to, and regularly observed by, parties to contracts of the type involved in the particular trade concerned.

3. Where expression, provisions or forms of contract commonly used in commercial practice are employed, they shall be interpreted according to the meaning usually given to them in the trade concerned.

Article 10

For the purposes of the present Law, a breach of contract shall be regarded as fundamental wherever the party in breach knew, or ought to have known, at the time of the conclusion of the contract, that a reasonable person in the same situation as the other party would not have entered into the contract if he had foreseen the breach and its effects.

Article 11

Where under the present Law an act is required to be performed "promptly", it shall be performed within as short a period as possible, in the circumstances, from the moment when the act could reasonably be performed.

Article 12

For the purposes of the present Law, the expression "current price" means a price based upon an official market quotation, or, in the absence of such a quotation, upon those factors which, according to the usage of the market, serve to determine the price.

Article 13

For the purposes of the present Law, the expression "a party knew or ought to have known", or any similar expression, refers to what should have been known to a reasonable person in the same situation.

Article 14

Communications provided for by the present Law shall be made by the means usual in the circumstances.

(Art. 10 CISG → Art. 1 ULIS)

PART III
SALE OF GOODS

Chapter I
General provisions

Article 25

A breach of contract committed by one of the parties is fundamental if it results in such detriment to the other party as substantially to deprive him of what he is entitled to expect under the contract, unless the party in breach did not foresee and a reasonable person of the same kind in the same circumstances would not have foreseen such a result.

(Art. 26 CISG → Art. 14 ULIS)

(deleted)

(deleted)

(deleted)

Article 27

Unless otherwise expressly provided in this Part of the Convention, if any notice, request or other communication is given or made by a party in accordance with this Part and by means appropriate in the circumstances, a delay or error in the transmission of the communication or its failure to arrive does not deprive that party of the right to rely on the communication.

Article 15

A contract of sale need not be evidenced by writing and shall not be subject to any other requirements as to form. In particular, it may be proved by means of witnesses.

Article 16

Where under the provisions of the present Law one party to a contract of sale is entitled to require performance of any obligation by the other party, a court shall not be bound to enter or enforce a judgment providing for specific performance except in accordance with the provisions of Article VII of the Convention dated the 1st day of July 1964 relating to a Uniform Law on the International Sale of Goods.

Article 26

A declaration of avoidance of the contract is effective only if made by notice to the other party.

(Art. 28 CISG → Art. 16 ULIS)

Article 11

A contract of sale need not be concluded in or evidenced by writing and is not subject to any other requirement as to form. It may be proved by any means, including witnesses.

Article 12

Any provision of article 11, article 29 or Part II * of this Convention that allows a contract of sale or its modification or termination by agreement or any offer, acceptance or other indication of intention to be made in any form other than in writing does not apply where any party has his place of business in a Contracting State which has made a declaration under article 96 of this Convention. The parties may not derogate from or vary the effect of this article.**

Article 13

For the purposes of this Convention 'writing' includes telegram and telex.

(Art. 14 CISG → Art. 4 ULFIS)

Article 29

1. A contract may be modified or terminated by the mere agreement of the parties.
2. A contract in writing which contains a provision requiring any modification or termination by agreement to be in writing may not be otherwise modified or terminated by agreement. However, a party may be precluded by his conduct from asserting such a provision to the extent that the other party has relied on that conduct.

Article 28

If, in accordance with the provisions of this Convention, one party is entitled to require performance of any obligation by the other party, a court is not bound to enter a judgement for specific performance unless the court would do so under its own law in respect of similar contracts of sale not governed by this Convention.

---

* artt. 14-24

** art. 96 is printed at the end of this Annex.

Article 17

Questions concerning matters governed by the present Law which are not expressly settled therein shall be settled in conformity with the general principles on which the present Law is based.

Chapter III
Obligations of the seller

Article 18

The seller shall effect delivery of the goods, hand over any documents relating thereto and transfer the property in the goods, as required by the contract and the present Law.

Section I. Delivery of the Goods

Article 19

1. Delivery consists in the handing over of goods which conform with the contract.

2. Where the contract of sale involves carriage of the goods and no other place for delivery has been agreed upon, delivery shall be effected by handing over the goods to the carrier for transmission to the buyer.

(Art. 30 CISG → Art. 18 ULIS)

Chapter II
General Provisions

Article 7

1. In the interpretation of this Convention, regard is to be had to its international character and to the need to promote uniformity in its application and the observance of good faith in international trade.
2. Questions concerning matters governed by this Convention which are not expressly settled in it are to be settled in conformity with the general principles on which it is based or, in the absence of such principles, in conformity with the law applicable by virtue of the rules of private international law.

Article 8

1. For the purposes of this Convention statements made by and other conduct of a party are to be interpreted according to his intent where the other party knew or could not have been unaware what that intent was.
2. If the preceding paragraph is not applicable, statements made by and other conduct of a party are to be interpreted according to the understanding that a reasonable person of the same kind as the other party would have had in the same circumstances.
3. In determining the intent of a party or the understanding a reasonable person would have had, due consideration is to be given to all relevant circumstances of the case including the negotiations, any practices which the parties have established between themselves, usages and any subsequent conduct of the parties.

(Art. 9 CISG → Art. 9 ULIS)

Chapter II
Obligations of the seller

Article 30

The seller must deliver the goods, hand over any documents relating to them and transfer the property in the goods, as required by the contract and this Convention.

Section I. Delivery of the goods and handing over of documents

Article 31

If the seller is not bound to deliver the goods at any other particular place, his obligation to deliver consists:
a) if the contract of sale involves carriage of the goods – in handing the goods over to the first carrier for transmission to the buyer;

3. Where the goods handed over to the carrier are not clearly appropriated to performance of the contract by being marked with an address or by some other means, the seller shall, in addition to handing over the goods, send to the buyer notice of the consignment and, if necessary, some document specifying the goods.

b) if, in cases not within the preceding subparagraph, the contract relates to specific goods, or unidentified goods to be drawn from a specific stock or to be manufactured or produced, and at the time of the conclusion of the contract the parties knew that the goods were at, or were to be manufactured or produced at, a particular place – in placing the goods at the buyer's disposal at the place;
c) in other cases – in placing the goods at the buyer's disposal at the place where the seller had his place of business at the time of the conclusion of the contract.

Article 32

1. If the seller, in accordance with the contract or this Convention, hands the goods over to a carrier and if the goods are not clearly identified to the contract by markings on the goods, by shipping documents or otherwise, the seller must give the buyer notice of the consignment specifying the goods.
2. If the seller is bound to arrange for carriage of the goods, he must make such contracts as are necessary for carriage to the place fixed by means of transportation appropriate in the circumstances and according to the usual terms for such transportation.
3. If the seller is not bound to effect insurance in respect of the carriage of the goods, he must, at the buyer's request, provide him with all available information necessary to enable him to effect such insurance.

Sub-section 1
Obligations of the seller as regards the date and place of delivery

A. Date of delivery

Article 20

Where the parties have agreed upon a date for delivery or where such date is fixed by usage, the seller shall, without the need for any other formality, be bound to deliver the goods at that date, provided that the date thus fixed is determined or determinable by the calendar or is fixed in relation to a definite event, the date of which can be ascertained by the parties.

Article 33

The seller must deliver the goods:
a) if a date is fixed by or determinable from the contract, on that date;
b) if a period of time is fixed by or determinable from the contract, at any time within that period unless circumstances indicate that the buyer is to choose a date; or
c) in any other case, within a reasonable time after the conclusion of the contract.

(Art. 34 CISG → Art. 50 ULIS)

Article 21

Where by agreement of the parties or by usage delivery shall be effected within a certain period (such as a particular month or season), the seller may fix the precise date of delivery, unless the circumstances indicate that the fixing of the date was reserved to the buyer.

(see, Art. 33 CISG)

Article 22

(see, Art. 33 CISG)

Where the date of delivery has not been determined in accordance with the provisions of Articles 20 or 21, the seller shall be bound to deliver the goods within a reasonable time after the conclusion of the contract, regard being had to the nature of the goods and to the circumstances.

B. Place of delivery

Article 23

1. Where the contract of sale does not involve carriage of the goods, the seller shall deliver the goods at the place where he carried on business at the time of the conclusion of the contract, or, in the absence of a place of business, at his habitual residence.

(see, Art. 31 (b) CISG → Art. 19 ULIS)

2. If the sale relates to specific goods and the parties knew that the goods were at a certain place at the time of the conclusion of the contract, the seller shall deliver the goods at that place. The same rule shall apply if the goods sold are unascertained goods to be taken from a specified stock or if they are to be manufactured or produced at a place known to the parties at the time of the conclusion of the contract.

(see, Art. 31 (c) CISG → Art. 19 ULIS)

C. Remedies for the seller's failure to perform his obligations as regards the date and place of delivery

Article 24

1. Where the seller fails to perform his obligations as regards the date or the place of delivery, the buyer may, as provided in Articles 25 to 32:
   (*a*) require performance of the contract by the seller;
   (*b*) declare the contract avoided.

(see, Art. 45 CISG → Art. 41 ULIS)

2. The buyer may also claim damages as provided in Article 82 or in Articles 84 to 87.

3. In no case shall the seller be entitled to apply to a court or arbitral tribunal to grant him a period of grace.

Article 25

The buyer shall not be entitled to require performance of the contract by the seller, if it is in conformity with usage and reasonably possible for the buyer to purchase goods to replace those to which the contract relates. In this case the contract shall be *ipso facto* avoided as from the time when such purchase should be effected.

(deleted)

(a) Remedies as regards the date of delivery

Article 26	
1. Where the failure to deliver the goods at the date fixed amounts to a fundamental breach of the contract, the buyer may either require performance by the seller or declare the contract avoided. He shall inform the seller of his decision within a reasonable time; otherwise the contract shall be *ipso facto* avoided.	(see, Art. 45 CISG → Art. 41 ULIS)
2. If the seller requests the buyer to make known his decision under paragraph 1 of this Article and the buyer does not comply promptly, the contract shall be *ipso facto* avoided.	
3. If the seller has effected delivery before the buyer has made known his decision under paragraph 1 of this Article and the buyer does not exercise promptly his right to declare the contract avoided, the contract cannot be avoided.	
4. Where the buyer has chosen performance of the contract and does not obtain it within a reasonable time, he may declare the contract avoided.	
Article 27	
1. Where failure to deliver the goods at the date fixed does not amount to a fundamental breach of the contract, the seller shall retain the right to effect delivery and the buyer shall retain the right to require performance of the contract by the seller.	(see, Art. 45 CISG → Art. 41 ULIS)
2. The buyer may however grant the seller an additional period of time of reasonable length. Failure to deliver within this period shall amount to a fundamental breach of the contract.	(see, Art. 47 CISG → Art. 44 ULIS)
Article 28	
Failure to deliver the goods at the date fixed shall amount to a fundamental breach of the contract whenever a price for such goods is quoted on a market where the buyer can obtain them.	(deleted)
Article 29	**Article 32**
Where the seller tenders delivery of the goods before the date fixed, the buyer may accept or reject delivery; if he accepts, he may reserve the right to claim damages in accordance with Article 82.	1. If the seller delivers the goods before the date fixed, the buyer may take delivery or refuse to take delivery. 2. If the seller delivers a quantity of goods greater than that provided for in the contract, the buyer may take delivery or refuse to take delivery of the excess quantity. If the buyer takes delivery of all or part of the excess quantity, he must pay for it at the contract rate. (Art. 53 CISG → Art. 56 ULIS)

(b) Remedies as regards the place of delivery

Article 30

1. Where failure to deliver the goods at the place fixed amounts to a fundamental breach of the contract, and failure to deliver the goods at the date fixed would also amount to a fundamental breach, the buyer may either require performance of the contract by the seller or declare the contract avoided. The buyer shall inform the seller of his decision within a reasonable time; otherwise the contract shall be *ipso facto* avoided.

(see, Art. 45 CISG → Art. 41 ULIS)

2. If the seller requests the buyer to make known his decision under paragraph 1 of this Article and the buyer does not comply promptly, the contract shall be *ipso facto* avoided.

3. If the seller has transported the goods to the place fixed before the buyer has made known his decision under paragraph 1 of this Article and the buyer does not exercise promptly his right to declare the contract avoided, the contract cannot be avoided.

Article 31

1. In cases not provided for in Article 30, the seller shall retain the right to effect delivery at the place fixed and the buyer shall retain the right to require performance of the contract by the seller.

(idem.)

2. The buyer may however grant the seller an additional period of time of reasonable length. Failure to deliver within this period at the place fixed shall amount to a fundamental breach of the contract.

Article 32

1. If delivery is to be effected by handing over the goods to a carrier and the goods have been handed over at a place other than that fixed, the buyer may declare the contract avoided, whenever the failure to deliver the goods at the place fixed amounts to a fundamental breach of the contract. He shall lose this right if he has not promptly declared the contract avoided.

(idem.)

2. The buyer shall have the same right, in the circumstances and on the conditions provided in paragraph 1 of this Article, if the goods have been despatched to some place other than that fixed.

3. If despatch from a place or to a place other than that fixed does not amount to a fundamental breach of the contract, the buyer may only claim damages in accordance with Article 82.

Sub-section 2

Obligations of the seller as regards the conformity of the goods

A. Lack of conformity

Article 33

1. The seller shall not have fulfilled his obligation to deliver the goods where he has handed over:

(*a*) part only of the goods sold or a larger or a smaller quantity of the goods than he contracted to sell;
(*b*) goods which are not those to which the contract relates or goods of a different kind;
(*c*) goods which lack the qualities of a sample or model which the seller has handed over or sent to the buyer, unless the seller has submitted it without any express or implied undertaking that the goods would conform therewith;
(*d*) goods which do not possess the qualities necessary for their ordinary or commercial use;
(*e*) goods which do not possess the qualities for some particular purpose expressly or impliedly contemplated by the contract;
(*f*) in general, goods which do not possess the qualities and characteristics expressly or impliedly contemplated by the contract.

2. No difference in quantity, lack of part of the goods or absence of any quality or characteristic shall be taken into consideration where it is not material.

Article 34

In the case to which Article 33 relates, the rights conferred on the buyer by the present Law exclude all other remedies based on lack of conformity of the goods.

Article 35

1. Whether the goods are in conformity with the contract shall be determined by their condition at the time when risk passes. However, if risk does not pass because of a declaration of avoidance of the contract or of a demand for other goods in replacement, the conformity of the goods with the contract shall be determined by their condition at the time when risk would have passed had they been in conformity with the contract.

2. The seller shall be liable for the consequences of any lack of conformity occurring after the time fixed in paragraph 1 of this Article if it was due to an act of the seller or of a person for whose conduct he is responsible.

Section II. Conformity of the goods and third party claims

Article 35

1. The seller must deliver goods which are of the quantity, quality and description required by the contract and which are contained or packaged in the manner required by the contract.
2. Except where the parties have agreed otherwise, the goods do not conform with the contract unless they:
a) are fit for the purposes for which goods of the same description would ordinarily be used;
b) are fit for any particular purpose expressly or impliedly made known to the seller at the time of the conclusion of the contract, except where the circumstances show that the buyer did not rely, or that it was unreasonable for him to rely, on the seller's skill and judgment;
c) possess the qualities of goods which the seller has held out to the buyer as a sample or model;
d) are contained or packaged in the manner usual for such goods or, where there is no such manner, in a manner adequate to preserve and protect the goods.
3. The seller is not liable under subparagraph (a) to (d) of the preceding paragraph for any lack of conformity of the goods if at the time of the conclusion of the contract the buyer knew or could not have been unaware of such lack of conformity.

(deleted)

Article 36

1. The seller is liable in accordance with the contract and this Convention for any lack of conformity which exists at the time when the risk passes to the buyer, even though the lack of conformity becomes apparent only after that time.
2. The seller is also liable for any lack of conformity which occurs after the time indicated in the preceding paragraph and which is due to a breach of any of his obligations, including a breach of any guarantee that for a period of time the goods will remain fit for their ordinary purpose or for some particular purpose or will retain specified qualities or characteristics.

Article 36

The seller shall not be liable for the consequences of any lack of conformity of the kind referred to in sub-paragraphs (*d*), (*e*) or (*f*) of paragraph 1 of Article 33, if at the time of the conclusion of the contract the buyer knew, or could not have been unaware of, such lack of conformity.

(see, Art. 35 CISG → Art. 33 ULIS)

Article 37

If the seller has handed over goods before the date fixed for delivery he may, up to that date, deliver any missing part or quantity of the goods or deliver other goods which are in conformity with the contract or remedy any defects in the goods handed over, provided that the exercise of this right does not cause the buyer either unreasonable inconvenience or unreasonable expense.

Article 37

If the seller has delivered goods before the date for delivery, he may, up to that date, deliver any missing part or make up any deficiency in the quantity of the goods delivered, or deliver goods in replacement of any non-conforming goods delivered or remedy any lack of conformity in the goods delivered, provided that the exercise of this right does not cause the buyer unreasonable inconvenience or unreasonable expense. However, the buyer retains any right to claim damages as provided for in this Convention.

B. Ascertainment and notification of lack of conformity

Article 38

1. The buyer shall examine the goods, or cause them to be examined, promptly.
2. In case of carriage of the goods the buyer shall examine them at the place of destination.
3. If the goods are redespatched by the buyer without transhipment and the seller knew or ought to have known, at the time when the contract was concluded, of the possibility of such redespatch, examination of the goods may be deferred until they arrive at the new destination.
4. The methods of examination shall be governed by the agreement of the parties or, in the absence of such agreement, by the law or usage of the place where the examination is to be effected.

Article 38

1. The buyer must examine the goods, or cause them to be examined, within as short a period as is practicable in the circumstances.
2. If the contract involves carriage of the goods, examination may be deferred until after the goods have arrived at their destination.
3. If the goods are redirected in transit or redispatched by the buyer without a reasonable opportunity for examination by him and at the time of the conclusion of the contract the seller knew or ought to have known of the possibility of such redirection or redispatch, examination may be deferred until after the goods have arrived at the new destination.

Article 39

1. The buyer shall lose the right to rely on a lack of conformity of the goods if he has not given the seller notice thereof promptly after he has discovered the lack of conformity or ought to have discovered it. If a defect which could not have been revealed by the examination of the goods provided for in Article 38 is found later, the buyer may nonetheless rely on that defect, provided that he gives the seller notice thereof promptly after its discovery. In any event, the buyer shall lose the right to rely on a lack of conformity of the goods if he has not given notice thereof to the seller within a period of two years from the date on which the goods were handed over, unless the lack of conformity constituted a breach of a guarantee covering a longer period.

2. In giving notice to the seller of any lack of conformity, the buyer shall specify its nature and invite the seller to examine the goods or to cause them to be examined by his agent.

Article 39

1. The buyer loses the right to rely on a lack of conformity of the goods if he does not give notice to the seller specifying the nature of the lack of conformity within a reasonable time after he has discovered it or ought to have discovered it.
2. In any event, the buyer loses the right to rely on a lack of conformity of the goods if he does not give the seller notice thereof at the latest within a period of two years from the date on which the goods were actually handed over to the buyer, unless this time-limit is inconsistent with a contractual period of guarantee.

3. Where any notice referred to in paragraph 1 of this Article has been sent by letter, telegram or other appropriate means, the fact that such notice is delayed or fails to arrive at its destination shall not deprive the buyer of the right to rely thereon.

Article 40

The seller shall not be entitled to rely on the provisions of Articles 38 and 39 if the lack of conformity relates to facts of which he knew, or of which he could not have been unaware, and which he did not disclose.

C. Remedies for lack of conformity

Article 41

1. Where the buyer has given due notice to the seller of the failure of the goods to conform with the contract, the buyer may, as provided in Articles 42 to 46:
(*a*) require performance of the contract by the seller:
(*b*) declare the contract avoided;
(*c*) reduce the price.

2. The buyer may also claim damages as provided in Article 82 or in Articles 84 to 87.

Article 42

1. The buyer may require the seller to perform the contract:
(*a*) if the sale relates to goods to be produced or manufactured by the seller, by remedying defects in the goods, provided the seller is in a position to remedy the defects;
(*b*) if the sale relates to specific goods, by delivering the goods to which the contract refers or the missing part thereof;
(*c*) if the sale relates to unascertained goods, by delivering other goods which are in conformity with the contract or by delivering the missing part or quantity, except where the purchase of goods in replacement is in conformity with usage and reasonably possible.

2. If the buyer does not obtain performance of the contract by the seller within a reasonable time, he shall retain the rights provided in Articles 43 to 46.

Article 40

The seller is not entitled to rely on the provisions of articles 38 and 39 if the lack of conformity relates to facts of which he knew or could not have been unaware and which he did not disclose to the buyer.

(Art. 41 CISG → Art. 52 ULIS)

Section III. Remedies for breach of contract by the seller

Article 45

1. If the seller fails to perform any of his obligations under the contract of this Convention, the buyer may:
a) exercise the rights provided in articles 46 to 52;
b) claim damages as provided in articles 74 to 77.
2. The buyer is not deprived of any right he may have to claim damages by exercising his right to other remedies.
3. No period of grace may be granted to the seller by a court or arbitral tribunal when the buyer resorts to a remedy for breach of contract.

Article 46

1. The buyer may require performance by the seller of his obligation unless the buyer has resorted to a remedy which is inconsistent with this requirement.
2. If the goods do not conform with the contract the buyer may require delivery of substitute goods only if the lack of conformity constitutes a fundamental breach of contract and a request for substitute goods is made either in conjunction with notice given under article 39 or within a reasonable time thereafter.
3. If the goods do not conform with the contract, the buyer may require the seller to remedy the lack of conformity by repair, unless this is unreasonable having regard to all the circumstances. A request for repair must be made either in conjunction with notice given under article 39 or within a reasonable time thereafter.

(Art. 47 CISG → Art. 44 ULIS)

Article 43

The buyer may declare the contract avoided if the failure of the goods to conform to the contract and also the failure to deliver on the date fixed amount to fundamental breaches of the contract. The buyer shall lose his right to declare the contract avoided if he does not exercise it promptly after giving the seller notice of the lack of conformity or, in the case to which paragraph 2 of Article 42 applies, after the expiration of the period referred to in that paragraph.

Article 49

1. The buyer may declare the contract avoided:
a) if the failure by the seller to perform any of his obligations under the contract or this Convention amounts to a fundamental breach of contract; or
b) in case of non-delivery, if the seller does not deliver the goods within the additional period of time fixed by the buyer in accordance with paragraph (1) of article 47 or declares that he will not deliver within the period so fixed.
2. However, in cases where the seller has delivered the goods, the buyer loses the right to declare the contract avoided unless he does so:
a) in respect of late delivery, within a reasonable time after he has become aware that delivery has been made;
b) in respect of any breach other than late delivery, within a reasonable time;
(i) after he knew or ought to have known of the breach;
(ii) after the expiration of any additional period of time fixed by the buyer in accordance with paragraph (1) of article 47, or after the seller has declared that he will not perform his obligations within such an additional period; or
(iii) after the expiration of any additional period of time indicated by the seller in accordance with paragraph (2) of article 48, or after the buyer has declared that he will not accept performance.

(Art. 50 CISG → Art. 46 ULIS)

Article 44

1. In cases not provided for in Article 43, the seller shall retain, after the date fixed for the delivery of the goods, the right to deliver any missing part or quantity of the goods or to deliver other goods which are in conformity with the contract or to remedy any defect in the goods handed over, provided that the exercise of this right does not cause the buyer either unreasonable inconvenience or unreasonable expense.

2. The buyer may however fix an additional period of time of reasonable length for the further delivery or for the remedying of the defect. If at the expiration of the additional period the seller has not delivered the goods or remedied the defect, the buyer may choose between requiring the performance of the contract or reducing the price in accordance with Article 46 or, provided that he does so promptly, declare the contract avoided.

Article 48

1. Subject to article 49, the seller may, even after the date for delivery, remedy at his own expense any failure to perform his obligations, if he can do so without unreasonable delay and without causing the buyer unreasonable inconvenience or uncertainty of reimbursement by the seller of expenses advanced by the buyer. However, the buyer retains any right to claim damages as provided for in this Convention.
2. If the seller requests the buyer to make known whether he will accept performance and the buyer does not comply with the request within a reasonable time, the seller may perform within the time indicated in his request. The buyer may not, during that period of time, resort to any remedy which is inconsistent with performance by the seller.
3. A notice by the seller that he will perform within a specified period of time is assumed to include a request, under the preceding paragraph, that the buyer make known his decision.
4. A request or notice by the seller under paragraph (2) or (3) of this article is not effective unless received by the buyer.

	Article 47 **1. The buyer may fix an additional period of time of reasonable length for performance by the seller of his obligations.** **2. Unless the buyer has received notice from the seller that he will not perform within the period so fixed, the buyer may not, during that period, resort to any remedy for breach of contract. However, the buyer is not deprived thereby of any right he may have to claim damages for delay in performance.** **(Art. 49 CISG → Art. 43 ULIS).**
Article 45 1. Where the seller has handed over part only of the goods or an insufficient quantity or where part only of the goods handed over is in conformity with the contract, the provisions of Articles 43 and 44 shall apply in respect of the part or quantity which is missing or which does not conform with the contract. 2. The buyer may declare the contract avoided in its entirety only if the failure to effect delivery completely and in conformity with the contract amounts to a fundamental breach of the contract.	**Article 51** **1. If the seller delivers only a part of the goods or if only a part of the goods delivered is in conformity with the contract, articles 46 to 50 apply in respect of the part which is missing or which does not conform.** **2. The buyer may declare the contract avoided in its entirety only if the failure to make delivery completely or in conformity with the contract amounts to a fundamental breach of the contract.** **(Art. 52 CISG → Art. 29 ULIS)**
Article 46 Where the seller has proffered to the buyer a quantity of unascertained goods greater than that provided for in the contract, the buyer may reject or accept the same proportion as the value of the goods at the time of the conclusion of the contract has been diminished because of their lack of conformity with the contract.	**Article 50** **If the goods do not conform with the contract and whether or not the price has already been paid, the buyer may reduce the price in the same proportion as the value that the goods actually delivered had at the time of the delivery bears to the value that conforming goods would have had at that time. However, if the seller remedies any failure to perform his obligations in accordance with article 37 or article 48 or if the buyer refuses to accept performance by the seller in accordance with those articles, the buyer may not reduce the price.** **(Art. 51 CISG → Art. 45 ULIS)**
Article 47 Where the seller has proffered to the buyer a quantity of unascertained goods greater than that provided for in the contract, the buyer may reject or accept the excess quantity. If the buyer rejects the excess quantity, the seller shall be liable only for damages in accordance with Article 82. If the buyer accepts the whole or part of the excess quantity, he shall pay for it at the contract rate.	**(see, Art. 52 (2) CISG → Art. 29 ULIS)**
Article 48 The buyer may exercise the rights provided in Articles 43 to 46, even before the time fixed for delivery, if it is clear that goods which would be handed over would not be in conformity with the contract.	**(see, Art. 72 CISG → Art. 76 ULIS)**

Article 49

1. The buyer shall lose his right to rely on lack of conformity with the contract at the expiration of a period of one year after he has given notice as provided in Article 39, unless he has been prevented from exercising his right because of fraud on the part of the seller.

2. After the expiration of this period, the buyer shall not be entitled to rely on the lack of conformity, even by way of defence to an action. Nevertheless, if the buyer has not paid for the goods and provided that he has given due notice of the lack of conformity promptly, as provided in Article 39, he may advance as a defence to a claim for payment of the price a claim for a reduction in the price or for damages.

(deleted; see UN Convention on the Limitation Period 1974, artt. 8 and 25)

Section II. Handing Over of Documents

Article 50

Where the seller is bound to hand over to the buyer any documents relating to the goods, he shall do so at the time and place fixed by the contract or by usage.

Article 34

If the seller is bound to hand over documents relating to the goods, he must hand them over at the time and place and in the form required by the contract. If the seller has handed over documents before that time, he may, up to that time, cure any lack of conformity in the documents, if the exercise of this right does nct cause the buyer unreasonable inconvenience or unreasonable expense. However, the buyer retains any right to claim damages as provided for in this Convention.

(Art. 35 CISG → Art. 33 ULIS)

Article 51

If the seller fails to hand over documents as provided in Article 50 at the time and place fixed or if he hands over documents which are not in conformity with those which he was bound to hand over, the buyer shall have the same rights as those provided under Articles 24 to 32 or under Articles 41 to 49, as the case may be.

(see, Art. 34 CISG)

Section III. Transfer of Property

Article 52

1. Where the goods are subject to a right or claim of a third person, the buyer, unless he agreed to take the goods subject to such right or claim, shall notify the seller of such right or claim, unless the seller already knows thereof, and request that the goods should be freed therefrom within a reasonable time or that other goods free from all rights and claims of third persons be delivered to him by the seller.

Article 41

The seller must deliver goods which are free from any right or claim of a third party, unless the buyer agreed to take the goods subject to that right or claim. However, if such right or claim is based on industrial property or other intellectual property, the seller's obligation is governed by article 42.

2. If the seller complies with a request made under paragraph 1 of this Article and the buyer nevertheless suffers a loss, the buyer may claim damages in accordance with Article 82.

3. If the seller fails to comply with a request made under paragraph 1 of this Article and a fundamental breach of the contract results thereby, the buyer may declare the contract avoided and claim damages in accordance with Articles 84 to 87. If the buyer does not declare the contract avoided or if there is no fundamental breach of the contract, the buyer shall have the right to claim damages in accordance with Article 82.

4. The buyer shall lose his right to declare the contract avoided if he fails to act in accordance with paragraph 1 of this Article within a reasonable time from the moment when he became aware or ought to have become aware of the right or claim of the third person in respect of the goods.

Article 53

The rights conferred on the buyer by Article 52 exclude all other remedies based on the fact that the seller has failed to perform his obligation to transfer the property in the goods or that the goods are subject to a right or claim of a third person.

Article 42

1. The seller must deliver goods which are free from any right or claim of a third party based on industrial property or other intellectual property, of which at the time of the conclusion of the contract the seller knew or could not have been unaware, provided that the right or claim is based on industrial property or other intellectual property:

a) under the law of the State where the goods will be resold or otherwise used, if it was contemplated by the parties at the time of the conclusions of the contract that the goods would be resold or otherwise used in that State; or

b) in any other case, under the law of the State where the buyer has his place of business.

2. The obligation of the seller under the preceding paragraph does not extend to cases where:

a) at the time of the conclusion of the contract the buyer knew or could not have been unaware of the right or claim; or

b) the right or claim results from the seller's compliance with technical drawings, designs, formulae or other such specifications furnished by the buyer.

Article 43

1. The buyer loses the right to rely on the provisions of article 41 or article 42 if he does not give notice to the seller specifying the nature of the right or claim of the third party within a reasonable time after he has become aware or ought to have become aware of the right or claim.

Section IV. Other Obligations of the Seller

Article 54

1. If the seller is bound to despatch the goods to the buyer, he shall make, in the usual way and on the usual terms, such contracts as are necessary for the carriage of the goods to the place fixed.

2. If the seller is not bound by the contract to effect insurance in respect of the carriage of the goods, he shall provide the buyer, at his request, with all information necessary to enable him to effect such insurance.

Article 55

1. If the seller fails to perform any obligation other than those referred to in Articles 20 to 53, the buyer may:

(*a*) where such failure amounts to a fundamental breach of the contract, declare the contract avoided, provided that he does so promptly, and claim damages in accordance with Articles 84 to 87, or

(*b*) in any other case, claim damages in accordance with Article 82.

2. The buyer may also require performance by the seller of his obligation, unless the contract is avoided.

Chapter IV
Obligations of the buyer

Article 56

The buyer shall pay the price for the goods and take delivery of them as required by the contract and the present Law.

2. The seller is not entitled to rely on the provision of the preceding paragraph if he knew of the right or claim of the third party and the nature of it.

Article 44

Notwithstanding the provisions of paragraph (1) of article 39 and paragraph (1) of article 43, the buyer may reduce the price in accordance with article 50 or claim damages, except for loss of profit, if he has a reasonable excuse for his failure to give the required notice.

(Art. 45 CISG → Art. 41 ULIS)

(see, Art. 32 (2) CISG → Art. 19 ULIS)

(see, Art. 32 (3) CISG → Art. 19 ULIS)

(see, Art. 45 CISG → Art. 41 ULIS)

Chapter III
Obligations of the buyer

Article 53

The buyer must pay the price for the goods and take delivery of them as required by the contract and this Convention.

Section I. Payment of the Price

Article 57

Where a contract has been concluded but does not state a price or make provision for the determination of the price, the buyer shall be bound to pay the price generally charged by the seller at the time of the conclusion of the contract.

Article 58

Where the price is fixed according to the weight of the goods, it shall, in case of doubt, be determined by the net weight.

B. Place and date of payment

Article 59

1. The buyer shall pay the price to the seller at the seller's place of business or, if he does not have a place of business, at his habitual residence, or, where the payment is to be made against the handing over of the goods or of documents, at the place where such handing over takes place.

2. Where, in consequence of a change in the place of business or habitual residence of the seller subsequent to the conclusion of the contract, the expenses incidental to payment are increased, such increase shall be borne by the seller.

Article 60

Where the parties have agreed upon a date for the payment of the price or where such date is fixed by usage, the buyer shall, without the need for any other formality, pay the price at that date.

Section I. Payment of the price

Article 54

The buyer's obligation to pay the price includes taking such steps and complying with such formalities as may be required under the contract or any laws and regulations to enable payment to be made.

Article 55

Where a contract has been validly concluded but does not expressly or implicitly fix or make provision for determining the price, the parties are considered, in the absence of any indication to the contrary, to have impliedly made reference to the price generally charged at the time of the conclusion of the contract for such goods sold under comparable circumstances in the trade concerned.

Article 56

If the price is fixed according to the weight of the goods, in case of doubt it is to be determined by the net weight.

Article 57

1. If the buyer is not bound to pay the price at any other particular place, he must pay it to the seller:
a) at the seller's place of business; or
b) if the payment is to be made against the handing over of the goods or of documents, at the place where the handing over takes place.
2. The seller must bear any increase in the expenses incidental to payment which is caused by a change in his place of business subsequent to the conclusion of the contract.

(Art. 58 CISG → Art. 71 ULIS)

Article 59

The buyer must pay the price on the date fixed by or determinable from the contract and this Convention without the need for any request or compliance with any formality on the part of the seller.

C. Remedies for non-payment	
Article 61	
1. If the buyer fails to pay the price in accordance with the contract and with the present Law, the seller may require the buyer to perform his obligation.	(see, Art. 61 CISG → Art. 70 ULIS)
2. The seller shall not be entitled to require payment of the price by the buyer if it is in conformity with usage and reasonably possible for the seller to resell the goods. In that case the contract shall be *ipso facto* avoided as from the time when such resale should be effected.	(deleted)
Article 62	
1. Where the failure to pay the price at the date fixed amounts to a fundamental breach of the contract, the seller may either require the buyer to pay the price or declare the contract avoided. He shall inform the buyer of his decision within a reasonable time; otherwise the contract shall be *ipso facto* avoided.	(see, Art. 61 CISG → Art. 70 ULIS)
2. Where the failure to pay the price at the date fixed does not amount to a fundamental breach of the contract, the seller may grant to the buyer an additional period of time of reasonable length. If the buyer has not paid the price at the expiration of the additional period, the seller may either require the payment of the price by the buyer or, provided that he does so promptly, declare the contract avoided.	
Article 63	
1. Where the contract is avoided because of failure to pay the price, the seller shall have the right to claim damages in accordance with Articles 84 to 87.	(idem.)
2. Where the contract is not avoided, the seller shall have the right to claim damages in accordance with Articles 82 and 83.	
Article 64	
In no case shall the buyer be entitled to apply to a court or arbitral tribunal to grant him a period of grace for the payment of the price.	(see, Art. 61 CISG → Art. 70 ULIS)
Section II. Taking Delivery	Section II. Taking delivery
Article 65	Article 60
Taking delivery consists in the buyer's doing all such acts as are necessary in order to enable the seller to hand over the goods and actually taking them over.	The buyer's obligation to take delivery consists: a) in doing all the acts which could reasonable be expected of him in order to enable the seller to make delivery; and b) in taking over the goods.
	(Art. 61 CISG → Art. 70 ULIS)

Article 66	
1. Where the buyer's failure to take delivery of the goods in accordance with the contract amounts to a fundamental breach of the contract or gives the seller good grounds for fearing that the buyer will not pay the price, the seller may declare the contract avoided.	**(see, Art. 64 CISG → Art. 70 ULIS)**
2. Where the failure to take delivery of the goods does not amount to a fundamental breach of the contract, the seller may grant to the buyer an additional period of time of reasonable length. If the buyer has not taken delivery of the goods at the expiration of the additional period, the seller may declare the contract avoided, provided that he does so promptly.	**(see, Art. 63 CISG → Art. 70 ULIS)**
Article 67	**Article 65**
1. If the contract reserves to the buyer the right subsequently to determine the form, measurement or other features of the goods (sale by specification) and he fails to make such specification either on the date expressly or impliedly agreed upon or within a reasonable time after receipt of a request from the seller, the seller may declare the contract avoided, provided that he does so promptly, or make the specification himself in accordance with the requirements of the buyer in so far as these are known to him.	**1. If under the contract the buyer is to specify the form, measurement or other features of the goods and he fails to make such specification either on the date agreed upon or within a reasonable time after receipt of a request from the seller, the seller may, without prejudice to any other rights he may have, make the specification himself in accordance with the requirements of the buyer that may be known to him.**
2. If the seller makes the specification himself, he shall inform the buyer of the details thereof and shall fix a reasonable period of time within which the buyer may submit a different specification. If the buyer fails to do so the specification made by the seller shall be binding.	**2. If the seller makes the specification himself, he must inform the buyer of the details thereof and must fix a reasonable time within which the buyer may make a different specification. If, after receipt of such a communication, the buyer fails to do so within the time so fixed, the specification made by the seller is binding.**
	(Art. 66 CISG → Art. 96 ULIS)
Article 68	
1. Where the contract is avoided because of the failure of the buyer to accept delivery of the goods or to make a specification, the seller shall have the right to claim damages in accordance with Articles 84 to 87.	**(see, Art. 61 CISG → Art. 70 ULIS)**
2. Where the contract is not avoided, the seller shall have the right to claim damages in accordance with Article 82.	
Section III. Other Obligations of the Buyer	
Article 69	
The buyer shall take the steps provided for in the contract, by usage or by laws and regulations in force, for the purpose of making provision for or guaranteeing payment of the price, such as the acceptance of a bill of exchange, the opening of a documentary credit or the giving of a banker's guarantee.	**(see, Art. 54 CISG → Art. 57 ULIS)**

Article 70

1. If the buyer fails to perform any obligation other than those referred to in Sections I and II of this Chapter, the seller may:

(*a*) where such failure amounts to a fundamental breach of the contract, declare the contract avoided, provided that he does so promptly, and claim damages in accordance with Articles 84 to 87; or

(*b*) in any other case, claim damages in accordance with Article 82.

2. The seller may also require performance by the buyer of his obligation, unless the contract is avoided.

Section III. Remedies for breach of contract by the buyer

Article 61

1. If the buyer fails to perform any of his obligations under the contract or this Convention, the seller may:
a) exercise the rights provided in articles 62 to 65;
b) claim damages as provided in articles 74 to 77.
2. The seller is not deprived of any right he may have to claim damages by exercising his right to other remedies.
3. No period of grace may be granted to the buyer by a court or arbitral tribunal when the seller resorts to a remedy for breach of contract.

Article 62

The seller may require the buyer to pay the price, take delivery or perform his other obligations, unless the seller has resorted to a remedy which is inconsistent with this requirement.

Article 63

1. The seller may fix an additional period of time of reasonable length for performance by the buyer of his obligations.
2. Unless the seller has received notice from the buyer that he will not perform within the period so fixed, the seller may not, during that period, resort to any remedy for breach of contract. However, the seller is not deprived thereby of any right he may have to claim damages for delay in performance.

Article 64

1. The seller may declare the contract avoided:
a) if the failure by the buyer to perform any of his obligations under the contract or this Convention amounts to a fundamental breach of contract; or
b) if the buyer does not, within the additional period of time fixed by the seller in accordance with paragraph (1) of article 63, perform his obligation to pay the price or take delivery of the goods, or if he declares that he will not do so within the period so fixed.

2. However, in cases where the buyer has paid the price, the seller loses the right to declare the contract avoided unless he does so:

a) in respect of late performance by the buyer, before the seller has become aware that performance has been rendered; or

b) in respect of any breach other than late performance by the buyer, within a reasonable time:

(i) after the seller knew or ought to have known of the breach; or

(ii) after the expiration of any additional period of time fixed by the seller in accordance with paragraph (1) of article 63, or after the buyer has declared that he will not perform his obligations within such an additional period.

(Art. 65 CISG → Art. 67 ULIS)

Provisions common to the obligations of the seller and of the buyer

Section I. Concurrence between Delivery of the Goods and Payment of the Price

Article 71

Except as otherwise provided in Article 72, delivery of the goods and payment of the price shall be concurrent conditions. Nevertheless, the buyer shall not be obliged to pay the price until he has had an opportunity to examine the goods.

Article 58

1. If the buyer is not bound to pay the price at any other specific time, he must pay it when the seller places either the goods or documents controlling their disposition at the buyer's disposal in accordance with the contract and this Convention. The seller may make such payment a condition for handing over the goods or documents.
2. If the contract involves carriage of the goods, the seller may dispatch the goods on terms whereby the goods, or documents controlling their disposition, will not be handed over to the buyer except against payment of the price.
3. The buyer is not bound to pay the price until he has had an opportunity to examine the goods, unless the procedures for delivery or payment agreed upon by the parties are inconsistent with his having such an opportunity.

(Art. 59 CISG → Art. 60 ULIS)

Article 72

1. Where the contract involves carriage of the goods and where delivery is, by virtue of paragraph 2 of Article 19, effected by handing over the goods to the carrier, the seller may either postpone despatch of the goods until he receives payment or proceed to despatch them on terms that reserve to himself the right of disposal of the goods during transit. In the latter case, he may require that the goods shall not be handed over to the buyer at the place of destination except against payment of the price and the buyer shall not be bound to pay the price until he has had an opportunity to examine the goods.

(see, Art. 58 CISG)

2. Nevertheless, when the contract requires payment against documents, the buyer shall not be entitled to refuse payment of the price on the ground that he has not had the opportunity to examine the goods.

Article 73

1. Each party may suspend the performance of his obligations whenever, after the conclusion of the contract, the economic situation of the other party appears to have become so difficult that there is good reason to fear that he will not perform a material part of his obligations.

2. If the seller has already despatched the goods before the economic situation of the buyer described in paragraph 1 of this Article becomes evident, he may prevent the handing over of the goods to the buyer even if the latter holds a document which entitles him to obtain them.

3. Nevertheless, the seller shall not be entitled to prevent the handing over of the goods if they are claimed by a third person who is a lawful holder of a document which entitles him to obtain the goods unless the document contains a reservation concerning the effects of its transfer or unless the seller can prove that the holder of the documents, when he acquired it, knowingly acted to the detriment of the seller.

Section II. Exemptions

Article 74

1. Where one of the parties has not performed one of his obligations, he shall not be liable for such non-performance if he can prove that it was due to circumstances which, according to the intention of the parties at the time of the conclusion of the contract, he was not bound to take into account or to avoid or to overcome; in the absence of any expression of the intention of the parties, regard shall be had to what reasonable persons in the same situation would have intended.

2. Where the circumstances which gave rise to the non-performance of the obligation constituted only a temporary impediment to performance, the party in default shall nevertheless be permanently relieved of his obligation if, by reason of the delay, performance would be so radically changed as to amount to the performance of an obligation quite different from that contemplated by the contract.

Chapter V
Provisions common to the obligations of the seller and of the buyer

Section I. Anticipatory breach and instalment contracts

Article 71

1. A party may suspend the performance of his obligations if, after the conclusion of the contract, it becomes apparent that the other party will not perform a substantial part of his obligations as a result of:
a) a serious deficiency in his ability to perform or in his creditworthiness; or
b) his conduct in preparing to perform or in performing the contract.
2. If the seller has already dispatched the goods before the grounds described in the preceding paragraph become evident, he may prevent the handing over of the goods to the buyer even though the buyer holds a document which entitles him to obtain them. The present paragraph relates only to the rights in the goods as between the buyer and the seller.
3. A party suspending performance, whether before or after dispatch of the goods, must immediately give notice of the suspension to the other party and must continue with performance if the other provides adequate assurance of his performance.

(Art. 72 CISG → Art. 76 ULIS)

Section IV. Exemptions

Article 79

1. A party is not liable for a failure to perform any of his obligations if he proves that the failure was due to an impediment beyond his control and that he could not reasonably be expected to have taken the impediment into account at the time of the conclusion of the contract or to have avoided or overcome it or its consequences.
2. If the party's failure is due to the failure by a third person whom he has engaged to perform the whole or a part of the contract, that party is exempt from liability only if:
a) he is exempt under the preceding paragraph; and
b) the person whom he has so engaged would be so exempt if the provisions of that paragraph were applied to him.
3. The exemption provided by this article has effect for the period during which the inpediment exists.

3. The relief provided by this Article for one of the parties shall not exclude the avoidance of the contract under some other provision of the present Law or deprive the other party of any right which he has under the present Law to reduce the price, unless the circumstances which entitled the first party to relief were caused by the act of the other party or of some person for whose conduct he was responsible.

Section III. Supplementary Rules Concerning the Avoidance of the Contract.

A. Supplementary grounds for avoidance

Article 75

1. Where, in the case of contracts for delivery of goods by instalments, by reason of any failure by one party to perform any of his obligations under the contract in respect of any instalment, the other party has good reason to fear failure of performance in respect of future instalments, he may declare the contract avoided for the future, provided that he does so promptly.

2. The buyer may also, provided that he does so promptly, declare the contract avoided in respect of future deliveries or in respect of deliveries already made or both, if by reason of their interdependence such deliveries would be worthless to him.

Article 76

Where prior to the date fixed for performance of the contract it is clear that one of the parties will commit a fundamental breach of the contract, the other party shall have the right to declare the contract avoided.

4. The party who fails to perform must give notice to the other party of the inpediment and its effect on his ability to perform. If the notice is not received by the other party within a reasonable time after the party who fails to perform knew or ought to have known of the impediment, he is liable for damages resulting from such non-receipt.
5. Nothing in this article prevents either party from exercising any right other than to claim damages under this Convention.

Article 80

A party may not rely on a failure of the other party to perform, to the extent that such failure was caused by the first party's act or omission.

(Art. 81 CISG → Art. 78 ULIS)

Article 73

1. In the case of a contract for delivery of goods by instalments, if the failure of one party to perform any of his obligations in respect of any instalment constitutes a fundamental breach of contract with respect to that instalment, the other party may declare the contract avoided with respect to that instalment.
2. If one party's failure to perform any of his obligations in respect of any instalment gives the other party good grounds to conclude that a fundamental breach of contract will occur with respect to future instalments, he may declare the contract avoided for the future, provided that he does so within a reasonable time.
3. A buyer who declares the contract avoided in respect of any delivery may, at the same time, declare it avoided in respect of deliveries already made or of future deliveries if, by reason of their interdependence, those deliveries could not be used for the purpose contemplated by the parties at the time of the conclusion of the contract.

(Art. 74 CISG → Art. 82 ULIS)

Article 72

1. If prior to the date for performance of the contract it is clear that one of the parties will commit a fundamental breach of contract, the other party may declare the contract avoided.
2. If time allows, the party intending to declare the contract avoided must give reasonable notice to the other party in order to permit him to provide adequate assurance of his performance.

	3. The requirements of the preceding paragraph do not apply if the other party has declared that he will not perform his obligations.
	(Art. 73 CISG → Art. 75 ULIS)
Article 77 Where the contract has been avoided under Article 75 or Article 76, the party declaring the contract avoided may claim damages in accordance with Articles 84 to 87.	(see, Art. 61 CISG → Art. 70 ULIS)
B. Effects of avoidance Article 78 1. Avoidance of the contract releases both parties from their obligations thereunder, subject to any damages which may be due. 2. If one party has performed the contract either wholly or in part, he may claim the return of whatever he has supplied or paid under the contract. If both parties are required to make restitution, they shall do so concurrently.	Section V. Effects of avoidance Article 81 1. Avoidance of the contract releases both parties from their obligations under it, subject to any damages which may be due. Avoidance does not affect any provision of the contract for the settlement of disputes or any other provision of the contract governing the rights and obligations of the parties consequent upon the avoidance of the contract. 2. A party who has performed the contract either wholly or in part may claim restitution from the other party of whatever the first party has supplied or paid under the contract. If both parties are bound to make restitution, they must do so concurrently.
Article 79 1. The buyer shall lose his right to declare the contract avoided where it is impossible for him to return the goods in the condition in which he received them. 2. Nevertheless, the buyer may declare the contract avoided: (*a*) if the goods or part of the goods have perished or deteriorated as a result of the defect which justifies the avoidance; (*b*) if the goods or part of the goods have perished or deteriorated as a result of the examination prescribed in Article 38; (*c*) if part of the goods have been consumed or transformed by the buyer in the course or normal use before the lack of conformity with the contract was discovered; (*d*) if the impossibility of returning the goods or of returning them in the condition in which they were received is not due to the act of the buyer or of some other person for whose conduct he is responsible; (*e*) if the deterioration or transformation of the goods is unimportant.	Article 82 1. The buyer loses the right to declare the contract avoided or to require the seller to deliver substitute goods if it is impossible for him to make restitution of the goods substantially in the condition in which he received them. 2. The preceding paragraph does not apply: a) if the impossibility of making restitution of the goods or making restitution of the goods substantially in the condition in which the buyer received them is not due to his act or omission; b) if the goods or part of the goods have perished or deteriorated as a result of the examination provided for in article 38; or c) if the goods or part of the goods have been sold in the normal course of business or have been consumed or transformed by the buyer in the course of normal use before he discovered or ought to have discovered the lack of conformity.

Article 80

The buyer who has lost the right to declare the contract avoided by virtue of Article 79 shall retain all the other rights conferred on him by the present Law.

Article 81

1. Where the seller is under an obligation to refund the price, he shall also be liable for the interest thereon at the rate fixed by Article 83, as from the date of payment.

2. The buyer shall be liable to account to the seller for all benefits which he has derived from the goods or part of them, as the case may be:

(*a*) where he is under an obligation to return the goods or part of them, or
(*b*) where it is impossible for him to return the goods or part of them, but the contract is nevertheless avoided.

Section IV. Supplementary Rules Concerning Damages

A. Damages where the contract is not avoided

Article 82

Where the contract is not avoided, damages for a breach of contract by one party shall consist of a sum equal to the loss, including loss of profit, suffered by the other party. Such damages shall not exceed the loss which the party in breach ought to have foreseen at the time of the conclusion of the contract, in the light of the facts and matters which then were known or ought to have been known to him, as a possible consequence of the breach of the contract.

Article 83

Where the breach of contract consists of delay in the payment of the price, the seller shall in any event be entitled to interest on such sum as is in arrear at a rate equal to the official discount rate in the country where he has his place of business or, if he has no place of business, his habitual residence, plus 1 %.

Article 83

A buyer who has lost the right to declare the contract avoided or to require the seller to deliver substitute goods in accordance with article 82 retains all other remedies under the contract and this Convention.

Article 84

1. If the seller is bound to refund the price, he must also pay interest on it, from the date on which the price was paid.
2. The buyer must account to the seller for all benefits which he has derived from the goods or part of them:
a) if he must take restitution of the goods or part of them; or
b) if it is impossible for him to make restitution of all or part of the goods or to make restitution of all or part of the goods substantially in the condition in which he received them, but he has nevertheless declared the contract avoided or required the seller to deliver substitute goods.

(Art. 85 CISG – Art. 91 ULIS)

Section II. Damages

Article 74

Damages for breach of contract by one party consist of a sum equal to the loss, including loss of profit, suffered by the other party as a consequence of the breach. Such damages may not exceed the loss which the party in breach foresaw or ought to have foreseen at the time of the conclusion of the contract, in the light of the facts and matters of which he then knew or ought to have known, as a possible consequence of the breach of contract.

(Art. 75 CISG → Art. 85 ULIS)

Section III. Interest

Article 78

If a party fails to pay the price or any other sum that is in arrears, the other party is entitled to interest on it, without prejudice to any claim for damages recoverable under article 74.

(Art. 79 CISG → Art. 74 ULIS)

B. Damages where the contract is avoided	
Article 84 1. In case of avoidance of the contract, where there is a current price for the goods, damages shall be equal to the difference between the price fixed by the contract and the current price on the date on which the contract is avoided. 2. In calculating the amount of damages under paragraph 1 of this Article, the current price to be taken into account shall be that prevailing in the market in which the transaction took place or, if there is no such current price or if its application is inappropriate, the price in a market which serves as a reasonable substitute, making due allowance for differences in the cost of transporting the goods.	**Article 76** 1. If the contract is avoided and there is a current price for the goods, the party claiming damages may, if he has not made a purchase or resale under article 75, recover the difference between the price fixed by the contract and the current price at the time of avoidance as well as any further damages recoverable under article 74. If, however the party claiming damages has avoided the contract after taking over the goods, the current price at the time of such taking over shall be applied instead of the current price at the time of avoidance. 2. For the purposes of the preceding paragraph, the current price is the price prevailing at the place where delivery of the goods should have been made or, if there is no current price at that place, the price at such other place as serves as a reasonable substitute, making due allowance for differences in the cost of transporting the goods. (Art. 77 CISG → Art. 88 ULIS)
Article 85 If the buyer has bought goods in replacement or the seller has resold goods in a reasonable manner, he may recover the difference between the contract price and the price paid for the goods bought in replacement or that obtained by the resale.	**Article 75** If the contract is avoided and if, in a reasonable manner and within a reasonable time after avoidance, the buyer has bought goods in replacement or the seller has resold the goods, the party claiming damages may recover the difference between the contract price and the price in the substitute transaction as well as any further damages recoverable under article 74. (Art. 76 CISG → Art. 84 ULIS)
Article 86 The damages referred to in Articles 84 and 85 may be increased by the amount of any reasonable expenses incurred as a result of the breach or up to the amount of any loss, including loss of profit, which should have been foreseen by the party in breach, at the time of the conclusion of the contract, in the light of the facts and matters which were known or ought to have been known to him, as a possible consequence of the breach of the contract.	(see, Artt. 75 and 76 CISG)
Article 87 If there is no current price for the goods, damages shall be calculated on the same basis as that provided in Article 82.	(see, Art. 76 (2) CISG)
C. General provisions concerning damages	
Article 88 The party who relies on a breach of the contract shall adopt all reasonable measures to mitigate the loss resulting from the breach. If he fails to adopt such mesures, the party in breach may claim a reduction in the damages.	**Article 77** A party who relies on a breach of contract must take such measures as are reasonable in the circumstances to mitigate the loss, including loss of profit, resulting from the breach. If he fails to take such measures, the party in

Article 89

In case of fraud, damages shall be determined by the rules applicable in respect of contracts of sale not governed by the present Law.

Section V. Expenses

Article 90

The expenses of delivery shall be borne by the seller; all expenses after delivery shall be borne by the buyer.

Section VI. Preservation of the Goods

Article 91

Where the buyer is in delay in taking delivery of the goods or in paying the price, the seller shall take reasonable steps to preserve the goods; he shall have the right to retain them until he has been reimbursed his reasonable expenses by the buyer.

Article 92

1. Where the goods have been received by the buyer, he shall take reasonable steps to preserve them if he intends to reject them; he shall have the right to retain them until he has been reimbursed his reasonable expenses by the seller.

2. Where goods despatched to the buyer have been put at his disposal at their place of destination and he exercises the right to reject them, he shall be bound to take possession of them on behalf of the seller, provided that this may be done without payment of the price and without unreasonable inconvenience or unreasonable expense. This provision shall not apply where the seller or a person authorised to take charge of the goods on his behalf is present at such destination.

Article 93

The party who is under an obligation to take steps to preserve the goods may deposit them in the warehouse of a third person at the expense of the other party provided that the expense incurred is not unreasonable.

breach may claim a reduction in the damages in the amount by which the loss should have been mitigated.

(deleted)

(deleted)

Section VI. Preservation of the goods

Article 85

If the buyer is in delay in taking delivery of the goods or, where payment of the price and delivery of the goods are to be made concurrently, if he fails to pay the price, and the seller is either in possession of the goods or otherwise able to control their disposition, the seller must take such steps as are reasonable in the circumstances to preserve them. He is entitled to retain them until he has been reimbursed his reasonable expenses by the buyer.

Article 86

1. If the buyer has received the goods and intends to exercise any right under the contract or this Convention to reject them, he must take such steps to preserve them as are reasonable in the circumstances. He is entitled to retain them until he has been reimbursed his reasonable expenses by the seller.
2. If goods dispatched to the buyer have been placed at his disposal at their destination and he exercises the right to reject them, he must take possession of them on behalf of the seller, provided that this can be done without payment of the price and without unreasonable inconvenience or unreasonable expense. This provision does not apply if the seller or a person authorized to take charge of the goods on his behalf is present at the destination. If the buyer takes possession of the goods under this paragraph, his rights and obligations are governed by the preceding paragraph.

Article 87

A party who is bound to take steps to preserve the goods may deposit them in a warehouse of a third person at the expense of the other party provided that the expense incurred is not unreasonable.

Article 94

1. The party who, in the cases to which Articles 91 and 92 apply, is under an obligation to take steps to preserve the goods may sell them by any appropriate means, provided that there has been unreasonable delay by the other party in accepting them or taking them back or in paying the cost of preservation and provided that due notice has been given to the other party of the intention to sell.

2. The party selling the goods shall have the right to retain out of the proceeds of sale an amount equal to the reasonable costs of preserving the goods and of selling them and shall transmit the balance to the other party.

Article 95

Where, in the cases to which Articles 91 and 92 apply, the goods are subject to loss or rapid deterioration or their preservation would involve unreasonable expense, the party under the duty to preserve them is bound to sell them in accordance with Article 94.

Chapter VI

Passing of the Risk

Article 96

Where the risk has passed to the buyer, he shall pay the price notwithstanding the loss or deterioration of the goods, unless this is due to the act of the seller or of some other person for whose conduct the seller is responsible.

Article 97

1. The risk shall pass to the buyer when delivery of the goods is effected in accordance with the provisions of the contract and the present Law.

2. In the case of the handing over of goods which are not in conformity with the contract, the risk shall pass to the buyer from the moment when the handing over has, apart from the lack of conformity, been effected in accordance with the provisions of the contract and of the present Law, where the buyer has neither declared the contract avoided nor required goods in replacement.

Article 88

1. A party who is bound to preserve the goods in accordance with article 85 or 86 may sell them, by any appropriate means if there has been an unreasonable delay by the other party in taking possession of the goods or in taking them back or in paying the price or the cost of preservation, provided that reasonable notice of the intention to sell has been given to the other party.
2. If the goods are subject to rapid deterioration or their preservation would involve unreasonable expense, a party who is bound to preserve the goods in accordance with article 85 or 86 must take reasonable measures to sell them. To the extent possible he must give notice to the other party of his intention to sell.
3. A party selling the goods has the right to retain out of the proceeds of sale an amount equal to the reasonable expenses of preserving the goods and of selling them. He must account to the other party for the balance.

Chapter IV

Passing of risk

Article 66

Loss of or damage to the goods after the risk has passed to the buyer does not discharge him from his obligation to pay the price, unless the loss or damage is due to an act or omission of the seller.

Article 67

1. If the contract of sale involves carriage of the goods and the seller is not bound to hand them over at a particular place, the risk passes to the buyer when the goods are handed over to the first carrier for transmission to the buyer in accordance with the contract of sale. If the seller is bound to hand the goods over to a carrier at a particular place, the risk does not pass to the buyer until the goods are handed over to the carrier at that place. The fact that the seller is authorized to retain documents controlling the disposition of the goods does not affect the passage of the risk.
2. Nevertheless, the risk does not pass to the buyer until the goods are clearly identified to the contract, whether by markings on the goods, by shipping documents, by notice given to the buyer or otherwise.

(Art. 68 CISG → Art. 99 ULIS)

Article 98

1. Where the handing over of the goods is delayed owing to the breach of an obligation of the buyer, the risk shall pass to the buyer as from the last date when, apart from such breach, the handing over could have been made in accordance with the contract.

2. Where the contract relates to a sale of unascertained goods, dely on the part of the buyer shall cause the risk to pass only when the seller has set aside goods manifestly appropriated to the contract and has notified the buyer that this has been done.

3. Where unascertained goods are of such a kind that the seller cannot set aside a part of them until the buyer takes delivery, it shall be sufficient for the seller to do all acts necessary to enable the buyer to take delivery.

Article 69

1. In cases not within articles 67 and 68, the risk passes to the buyer when he takes over the goods or, if he does not do so in due time, from the time when the goods are placed at his disposal and he commits a breach of contract by failing to take delivery.
2. However, if the buyer is bound to take over the goods at a place other than a place of business of the seller, the risk passes when delivery is due and the buyer is aware of the fact that the goods are placed at his disposal at that place.
3. If the contract relates to goods not then identified, the goods are considered not to be placed at the disposal of the buyer until they are clearly identified to the contract.

Article 99

1. Where the sale is of goods in transit by sea, the risk shall be borne by the buyer as from the time at which the goods were handed over to the carrier.
2. Where the seller, at the time of the conclusion of the contract, knew or ought to have known that the goods had been lost or had deteriorated, the risk shall remain with him until the time of the conclusion of the contract.

Article 68

The risk in respect of goods sold in transit passes to the buyer from the time of the conclusion of the contract. However, if the circumstances so indicate, the risk is assumed by the buyer from the time the goods were handed over to the carrier who issued the documents embodying the contract of carriage. Nevertheless, if at the time of the conclusion of the contract of sale the seller knew or ought to have known that the goods had been lost or damaged and did not disclose this to the buyer, the loss or damage is at the risk of the seller.

Article 70

If the seller has committed a fundamental breach of contract, articles 67, 68 and 69 do not impair the remedies available to the buyer on account of the breach.

(Art. 71 CISG → Art. 73 ULIS)

Article 100

If, in a case to which paragraph 3 of Article 19 applies, the seller, at the time of sending the notice or other document referred to in that paragraph, knew or ought to have known that the goods had been lost or had deteriorated after they were handed over to the carrier, the risk shall remain with the seller until the time of sending such notice or document.

(see, Art. 79 (2) CISG → Art. 97 ULIS)

Article 101

The passing of the risk shall not necessarily be determined by the provisions of the contract concerning expenses.

(deleted)

UNIFORM LAW ON THE FORMATION OF CONTRACTS FOR THE INTERNATIONAL SALE OF GOODS

(Annex I) **Article 1** (see, Art. 1 CISG)

1. The present Law shall apply to the formation of contracts of sale of goods entered into by parties whose places of business are in the territories of different States, in each of the following cases:

(*a*) where the offer or the reply relates to goods which are in the course of carriage or will be carried from the territory of one State to the territory of another;
(*b*) where the acts constituting the offer and the acceptance are effected in the territories of different States;
(*c*) where delivery of the goods is to be made in the territory of a State other than that within whose territory the acts constituting the offer and the acceptance are effected.

2. Where a party does not have a place of business, reference shall be made to his habitual residence.

3. The application of the present Law shall not depend on the nationality of the parties.

4. Offer and acceptance shall be considered to be effected in the territory of the same State only if the letters, telegrams or other documentary communications which contain them are sent and received in the territory of that State.

5. For the purpose of determining whether the parties have their places of business or habitual residences in "different States", any two or more States shall not be considered to be "different States" if a valid declaration to that effect made under Article II of the Convention dated the 1st day of July 1964 relating to a Uniform Law on the Formation of Contract for the International Sale of Goods is in force in respect of them.

6. The present Law shall not apply to the formation of contracts of sale:

(*a*) of stocks, shares, investment securities, negotiable instruments or money;
(*b*) of any ship, vessel or aircraft, which is or will be subject to registration;
(*c*) of electricity;
(*d*) by authority of law or on execution or distress.

7. Contracts for the supply of goods to be manufactured or produced shall be considered to be sales within the meaning of the present Law, unless the party who orders the goods undertakes to supply an essential and substantial part of the materials necessary for such manufacture or production.

8. The present Law shall apply regardless of the commercial or civil character of the parties or of the contracts to be concluded.

9. Rules of private international law shall be excluded for the purpose of the application of the present Law, subject to any provision to the contrary in the said Law.

(Annex II) Article 1

The present Law shall apply to the formation of contracts of sale of goods which, if they were concluded, would be governed by the Uniform Law on the International Sale of Goods.

(This annexed Art. 1 ULFIS relates to Art. 1 ULIS, and is meant for States introducing both uniform laws).

(Annex I) Article 2

1. The provisions of the following Articles shall apply except to the extent that it appears from the preliminary negotiations, the offer, the reply, the practices which the parties have established between themselves or usage, that other rules apply.

2. However, a term of the offer stipulating that silence shall amount to acceptance is invalid.

(see, Art. 6 CISG → Art. 3 ULIS)

Article 3

An offer or an acceptance need not be evidenced by writing and shall not be subject to any other requirement as to form. In particular, they may be proved by means of witnesses.

(see, Art. 11 CISG → Art. 15 ULIS)

Article 4

1. The communication which one person addresses to one or more specific persons with the object of concluding a contract of sale shall not constitute an offer unless it is sufficiently definite to permit the conclusion of the contract by acceptance and indicates the intention of the offeror to be bound.

2. This communication may be interpreted by reference to and supplemented by the preliminary negotiations, any practices which the parties have established between themselves, usage and any applicable legal rules for contracts of sale.

PART II
FORMATION OF THE CONTRACT

Article 14

1. A proposal for concluding a contract addressed to one or more specific persons constitutes an offer if it is sufficiently definite and indicates the intention of the offeror to be bound in case of acceptance. A proposal is sufficiently definite if it indicates the goods and expressly or implicitly fixes or makes provision for determining the quantity and the price.
2. A proposal other than one addressed to one or more specific persons is to be considered merely as an invitation to make offers, unless the contrary is clearly indicated by the person making the proposal.

(Art. 4 (2) ULIS: see Art. 9 CISG → Art. 9 ULIS)

(Annex II) Article 4

1. The communication which one person addresses to one or more specific persons with the object of concluding a contract of sale shall not constitute an offer unless it is sufficiently definite to permit the conclusion of the contract by acceptance and indicates the intention of the offeror to be bound.

2. This communication may be interpreted by reference to and supplemented by the preliminary negotiations, any practices which the parties have established between themselves, usage and the provisions of the Uniform Law on the International Sale of Goods.

(This annexed Art. 4 ULFIS is meant for States introducing both uniform Laws).

(Annex I)

Article 5

1. The offer shall not bind the offeror until it has been communicated to the offeree; it shall lapse if its withdrawal is communicated to the offeree before or at the same time as the offer.

2. After an offer has been communicated to the offeree it can be revoked unless the revocation is not made in good faith or in conformity with fair dealing or unless the offer states a fixed time for acceptance or otherwise indicates that it is firm or irrevocable.

3. An indication that the offer is firm or irrevocable may be express or implied from the circumstances, the preliminary negotiations, any practices which the parties have established between themselves or usage.

4. A revocation of an offer shall only have effect if it has been communicated to the offeree before he has despatched his acceptance or has done any act treated as acceptance under paragraph 2 of Article 6.

Article 15

1. An offer becomes effective when it reaches the offeree.
2. An offer, even if it is irrevocable, may be withdrawn if the withdrawal reaches the offeree before or at the same time as the offer.

Article 16

1. Until a contract is concluded an offer may be revoked if the revocation reaches the offeree before he has dispatched an acceptance.
2. However, an offer cannot be revoked:
a) if it indicates, whether by stating a fixed time for acceptance or otherwise, that it is irrevocable; or
b) if it was reasonable for the offeree to rely on the offer as being irrevocable and the offeree has acted in reliance on the offer.

Article 17

An offer, even if it is irrevocable, is terminated when a rejection reaches the offeror.

(Art. 18 CISG → Art. 8 ULFIS)

Article 6

1. Acceptance of an offer consists of a declaration communicated by any means whatsoever to the offeror.

2. Acceptance may also consist of the despatch of the goods or of the price or of any other act which may be considered to be equivalent to the declaration referred to in paragraph I of this Article either by virtue of the offer or as a result of practices which the parties have established between themselves or usage.

(see, Art. 18 CISG)

Article 7

1. An acceptance containing additions, limitations or other modifications shall be a rejection of the offer and shall constitute a counter-offer.

2. However, a reply to an offer which purports to be an acceptance but which contains additional or different terms which do not materially alter the terms of the offer shall constitute an acceptance unless the offeror promptly objects to the discrepancy; if he does not so object, the terms of the contract shall be the terms of the offer with the modifications contained in the acceptance.

Article 8

1. A declaration of acceptance of an offer shall have effect only if it is communicated to the offeror within the time he has fixed or, if no such time is fixed, within a reasonable time, due account being taken of the circumstances of the transaction, including the rapidity of the means of communication employed by the offeror, and usage. In the case of an oral offer, the acceptance shall be immediate, if the circumstances do not show that the offeree shall have time for reflection.

2. If a time for acceptance is fixed by an offeror in a letter or in a telegram, it shall be presumed to begin to run from the day the letter was dated or the hour of the day the telegram was handed in for despatch.

3. If an acceptance consists of an act referred to in paragraph 2 of Article 6, the act shall have effect only if it is done within the period laid down in paragraph I of the present Article.

Article 19

1. A reply to an offer which purports to be an acceptance but contains additions, limitations or other modifications is a rejection of the offer and constitutes a counter-offer.

2. However, a reply to an offer which purports to be an acceptance but contains additional or different terms which do not materially alter the terms of the offer constitutes an acceptance, unless the offeror, without undue delay, objects orally to the discrepancy or dispatches a notice to that effect. If he does not so object, the terms of the contract are the terms of the offer with the modifications contained in the acceptance.

3. Additional or different terms relating, among other things, to the price, payment, quality and quantity of the goods, place and time of delivery, extent of one party's liability to the other or the settlement of disputes are considered to alter the terms of the offer materially.

(Art. 20 CISG → Art. 8 ULFIS)

Article 18

1. A statement made by or other conduct of the offeree indicating assent to an offer is an acceptance. Silence or inactivity does not in itself amount to acceptance.

2. An acceptance of an offer becomes effective at the moment the indication of assent reaches the offeror. An acceptance is not effective if the indication of assent does not reach the offeror within the time he has fixed or, if no time is fixed, within a reasonable time, due account being taken of the circumstances of the transaction, including the rapidity of the means of communication employed by the offeror. An oral offer must be accepted immediately unless the circumstances indicate otherwise.

3. However, if, by virtue of the offer or as a result of practices which the parties have established between themselves or of usage, the offeree may indicate assent by performing an act, such as one relating to the dispatch of the goods or payment of the price, without notice to the offeror, the acceptance is effective at the moment the act is performed, provided that the act is performed within the period of time laid down in the preceding paragraph.

Article 20

1. A period of time for acceptance fixed by the offeror in a telegram or a letter begins to run from the moment the telegram is handed in for dispatch or from the date shown on the letter or, if no such date is shown, from the date shown on the envelope. A period of time for acceptance fixed by the offeror by telephone, telex or other means of instantaneous communication, begins to run from the moment that the offer reaches the offeree.

(Annex II)

Article 9

1. If the acceptance is late, the offeror may nevertheless consider it to have arrived in due time on condition that he promptly so informs the acceptor orally or by despatch of a notice.

2. If however the acceptance is communicated late, it shall be considered to have been communicated in due time, if the letter or document which contains the acceptance shows that it has been sent in such circumstances that if its transmission had been normal it would have been communicated in due time; this provision shall not however apply if the offeror has promptly informed the acceptor orally or by despatch of a notice that he considers his offer as having lapsed.

Article 10

An acceptance cannot be revoked except by a revocation which is communicated to the offeror before or at the same time as the acceptance.

Article 11

The formation of the contract is not affected by the death of one of the parties or by his becoming incapable of contracting before acceptance unless the contrary results from the intention of the parties, usage or the nature of the transaction.

Article 12

1. For the purposes of the present Law, the expression "to be communicated" means to be delivered at the address of the person to whom the communication is directed.

2. Communications provided for by the present Law shall be made by the means usual in the circumstances.

2. Official holidays or non-business days occurring during the period for acceptance are included in calculating the period. However, if a notice of acceptance cannot be delivered at the address of the offeror on the last day of the period because that day falls on an official holiday or a non-business day at the place of business of the offeror, the period is extended until the first business day which follows.

Article 21

1. A late acceptance is nevertheless effective as an acceptance if without delay the offeror orally so informs the offeree or dispatches a notice to that effect.
2. If a letter or other writing containing a late acceptance shows that it has been sent in such circumstances that if its transmission had been normal it would have reached the offeror in due time, the late acceptance is effective as an acceptance unless, without dealy, the offeror orally informs the offeree that he considers his offer as having lapsed or dispatches a notice to that effect.

Article 22

An acceptance may be withdrawn if the withdrawal reaches the offeror before or at the same time as the acceptance would have become effective.

Article 23

A contract is concluded at the moment when an acceptance of an offer becomes effective in accordance with the provisions of this Convention.

Article 24

For the purposes of this Part of the Convention, an offer, declaration of acceptance or any other indication of intention 'reaches' the addressee when it is made orally to him or delivered by any other means to him personally, to his place of business or mailing address or, if he does not have a place of business or mailing address, to his habitual residence.

(Art. 25 CISG → Art. 10 ULIS)

Article 13

1. Usage means any practice or method of dealing, which reasonable persons in the same situation as the parties, usually consider to be applicable to the formation of their contract.

2. Where expressions, provisions or forms of contract commonly used in commercial practice are employed, they shall be interpreted according to the meaning usually given to them in the trade concerned.

(see, Art. 9 CISG → Art. 9 ULIS)

Article 96

A Contracting State whose legislation requires contracts of sale to be concluded in or evidenced by writing may at any time make a declaration in accordance with article 12 that any provision of article 11, article 29, or Part II of this Convention, that allows a contract of sale or its modification or termination by agreement or any offer, acceptance, or other indication of intention to be made in any form other than in writing, does not apply where any party has his place of business in that State.

INTERNATIONAL SALES: DISCUSSIONS

The Colloquium was opened by Dr. Voskuil. In his address of welcome he thanked the governments of the Netherlands and of Yugoslavia, whose generosity and understanding had again made it possible for the Cultural Treaty between the two countries to serve as the vehicle for the present session of the Colloquium. Welcoming the reporters and participants, in particular those who were participating for the first time, he wished also to draw particular attention to the welcome presence of Professor Schmitthoff, whose wisdom and learning had already enhanced the two previous sessions, and of Professor Lødrup, whose participation represented an innovative Scandinavian contribution. Professor Matić having replied, the chair was taken by Dr. Duintjer Tebbens, who proposed that attention should be directed initially to uniform sales law and subsequently to conflict of laws. Accordingly, he invited Dr. van der Velden to introduce his paper, to be followed by Professor Barbic.

1. UNIFORM SALES LAW

1.1 Introduction

Dr. van der Velden explained that the approach adopted in his paper was one of comparison of the principal features of the Vienna Convention and those of the Hague Conventions. An underlying and most significant distinction lay in the fact, or perhaps the belief, that the Vienna Diplomatic Conference represented the most farreaching attempt to date to establish a code of uniform law governing international sales that would be acceptable not only to states of the Common Law and civil law traditions but also to states of widely differing economic structure and stages of development. Whether this belief was justified would be borne out by events. Certainly the Vienna Conference made a number of changes to the system embodied in ULIS and ULFIS, both minor and major. Particular changes could be seen to be the result of pressure or insistence on the part of representatives of particular systems, both legal and economic. Some were clearly more favourable to certain groups than to others, e.g., the provisons contained in Articles 12, 14, 35, 55, 59, 68. After a systematic review of a number of changes that could be viewed as favourable to particular groups, the reporter turned to the wider issue of whether the Vienna Convention should be viewed as an improvement generally on the Hague Conventions, concluding in favour of its general acceptance as a truly international uniform law for international sales.

Professor Barbić agreed that the Vienna Conference had proceeded from the basis of the Hague rules and had introduced alterations in order to produce an overall simplification of the system with a view to obtaining more widespread acceptance. Clearly, however, the result, particularly that embodied in the Draft Convention, represented a compromise between several groups that would raise significant problems. Some of these had been reduced by improvements that had subsequently been introduced and which were contained in the final version of the Convention. This is so with regard, for example, to formation and the over-emphasis in the Draft on subjective requirements. The present Article 19 has substantially modified this, although the new construction raises its own problems. Similarly with regard to fundamental breach. Replacing the Draft's subjective approach with the objective test of reasonableness was undoubtedly sensible, although it is likely to be defeated by the practice of inserting special clauses in the contract.

1.2 Scope of the 1980 Convention

In his introduction Professor Barbić drew attention also to a particular problem subsumed under Article 1 paragraph 2 which introduces an exception to the scope rule embodied in the first paragraph of Article 1, the result of which is that the Convention governs contracts of sale concluded between parties with places of business in different States being Contracting States or when conflicts rules lead to application of the law of a contracting State, unless the fact of divergence of place of business is not apparent from the contract or any dealings between or information disclosed by the parties at or prior to contracting. What, however, of the situation where, otherwise than through these three stipulated means of knowledge, the parties are aware that their places of business are not in the same State? It was suggested that this apparent difficulty could be resolved in favour of application of the Convention by resort to the principle of good faith, itself expressly stipulated as a tool of interpretation in Article 7, paragraph 1.

A matter also falling under paragraph 1 of Article 1 was the question whether reference there to rules of conflict of laws (para. 1 (b)) was also a reference to the widely accepted rule of party autonomy? In particular, would a choice of law clause stipulating the law of a third country, which was a Contracting State, be a reference to that country's internal law to the exclusion of the Convention or would the Convention be applicable. Several German and Dutch courts had adopted the latter approach in similar circumstances arising in connection with the Hague Conventions and the general view was that this was the right approach: that if the parties did not want the Convention to apply they should either incorporate specific provisions of that country's law into their contract or otherwise by clear reference specify for application of that law to the exclusion of the Convention.

It was pointed out that a power to exclude the application of the Convention or to vary or derogate from any of its provisions, with one exception (Art. 12), was expressly given to the parties under Article 6. Accepting that use would be made of this faculty, which would weaken the practical effect of the Convention, regret was expressed that also the scope of the Convention was limited in the way laid down in Article 1 and that a wider operation, like that adopted recently in the Hamburg Rules, had not been achieved. The failure to do so would lead inevitably to several regimes existing, to the detriment of uniform rules applying in international trade. Nevertheless, it was necessary to accept the present inability to achieve such uniformity, as experience with the Hague Rules had demonstrated, where extensive use had been made of the reservations provided by Articles III, IV and V ULIS. Regrettably, however, this failure also encouraged use of the freedom to exclude a Convention's applicability to the extent that unfamiliarity with and uncertainty as to national judicial interpretation and application of a new law was considered good reason to wait and see. Paradoxically, the more frequent and consistent the use of the exclusion clause the longer the uncertainty existed: Article 3 ULIS and Article 6 CISG were to this extent contrary to the spirit of the uniform laws. This would be exacerbated if national courts were to interprete Article 6 as impliedly giving the parties the freedom to exclude by implication the application of the Convention ("The parties may exclude . . . or . . . *derogate from* or vary"), a freedom expressly contained in Article 3.

1.3 **Rules of interpretation: Article 7 CISG**

The chairman moved the discussion to Article 7 Vienna Convention, which enjoined reference to be made to the three precepts of the international character of the convention, the need to promote its uniform application and observance of good faith in international trade.

As a means of ensuring compliance with the first two precepts it was accepted as desirable that reference should be made to previous decisions and practices of courts and arbitrators, both at home and in other countries. Experience of the Warsaw Convention, for example, showed the extent of divergence in air-transport liability, so much so that in the '60's there was even talk of a conference to draft a law on interpretation of the Warsaw Convention. The practical difficulties associated with divergent national interpretations rendered the matter far from being an academic or idealistic one. It was not, however, a problem that readily lent itself to an easy or simple solution. Even the ultimate of a central court with supervisory jurisdiction over the Convention would not obviate all difficulties, as experience within the Common Market has shown. In the case of the Vienna Convention, with its pretensions to world-wide applicability, such a notion is inherently non-feasible. At a more practical level there remained difficulties relating to accessibility of foreign decisions, language barriers and lack of understanding as to such factors as procedural law and inarticulated modes of thought that underpin judicial decision-making. Certainly academic institutions and lawyers could do something to alleviate lack of materials, as was being done, but it was also necessary to encourage the appropriate party, which in some countries would be the judge, in other the bar, particularly in this instance in those countries, e.g., England, where foreign law must be pleaded in evidence, to use such materials. Nor was it possible to deny the existence on occasion of nationalist trends in judicial decision-making to accomodate uniform law to domestic concepts, including those of economic importance. On the other hand, there are many examples where reference has meaningfully been made to decisions of foreign courts, generally, however, to those of a similar 'family' or legal tradition.

1.4 Usages

Under the Chairman's guidance, and with reference to the introduction of Professor Barbić, the discussion turned to Article 9 Vienna Convention, in particular paragraph 2, whereby the parties impliedly incorporate a usage into their contract given certain conditions: of which they knew or ought to have known, which in international trade is widely known to, and regularly observed by, parties to such contracts in the particular trade concerned.

The formulation adopted in the Convention gave rise to a number of questions as to the scope of the Article. The requirement is that the particular usage must be widely known in international trade, but the critera for assessing this are unstipulated. Must it be universally known, which would appear to be unreasonably stringent, or merely widely known in a particular region.

Further, the international character of the Convention resides in the parties having a place of business in different States and not in any requirement of border-crossing of goods. How is one to reconcile the requirement of knowledge in international trade circles to an inter-State trade or transaction. Or, if one assumes for the sake of the argument that Article 9 is not confined to "international" usages relevant to the particular type of trade and contract, is it sufficient that the usage is a "general" usage. And what is one to do about "national" usages including usages adopted into national law where the Convention is applicable to the parties' contract. Recalling that the concept of incorporation of usage was not confined solely to Article 9 but appeared directly in Article 8 paragraph 3 and Article 18 paragraph 3, and arguably indirectly in Article 32 paragraph 2 and Article 35 paragraph 2(a) and (d), it was argued that Article 7 also applied here in that where the Convention was applicable to the contract the third precept of paragraph 1 of the observance of good faith and the requirement of paragraph 2 that gaps in the Convention are to be settled in conformity with the general principles underlying it would require upholding the applicability of usages that ought reasonably to be held as falling within the spirit of Article 9.

5. CONFLICT OF LAWS

5.1 Introduction

The Chairman resumed the discussions by calling upon Professor Matić to introduce his paper dealing with the Hague Conventions on conflict of laws and with the recent Yugoslav Law on Private International Law. Professor Matić wished to draw attention to one specific problem, that of the extent of autonomy of the parties and in particular the influence of mandatory rules on the proposition of absolute freedom of choice of law. In this connection the recent Convention of Rome on Contractual Obligations was of particular importance. The principle of freedom on the parties to choose the applicable law was there enshined in Article 3. This freedom was, however, to be viewed subject to the restrictions also laid down in the Convention, namely, in Article 3 paragraph 3 and in Article 7. In this latter case it was of interest to note that although the Convention gave Contracting

States the power to make a reservation specifically excluding the application of Article 7 paragraph 1 (see Art. 22 para. 1 (a)), no such power is mentioned for paragraph 2, which by implication cannot be excluded, either by Contracting States or by the parties. The result of these provisions would seem to indicate a clear trend away from allowing the parties an almost unrestricted freedom in choosing the law applicable to their contract. It may be interesting to see whether this trend is furthered in the pending work of the Hague Conference on Private International Law, where several of the delegates involved in drafting the 1980 Contractual Obligations Convention would be involved in revising the 1955 Hague Convention on sales.

5.2 Choice of law

The Chairman, having drawn the attention of the participants to the fact that the text of the 1980 Convention on Contractual Obligations was to be found annexed to the report of Mr. Wade, invited discussion on the question whether the trend indicated by Professor Matić towards restricting party autonomy was to be welcomed or deplored.

In the discussions that followed there was a consensus in favour of restricting the parties' freedom, although doubt was expressed as to whether it was accurate to speak of an innovative trend. Rather, it was stated, the particular provisions in question of the 1980 Convention could well be viewed as only the legislative expression of well-established rules, or at least judicial approaches, of the conflict of laws. Thus Article 3 paragraph 3 mirrors the view that if the contract is exclusively connected with one law, which would be the law objectively applicable, and the parties seek to exclude its operation by designating another, that choice is vulnerable to attack as being in bad faith. Similarly, when one turns to Article 7 paragraph one, judicial authority can be found that reflects the approach adopted there. Although it was true that the codifications of private international law in Austria, Hungary, Poland and the German Democratic Republic did not include provisions as to the applicability of foreign mandatory rules, nevertheless, court practice was less formal in its approach to such matters.

Certainly the provision had been the subject of criticism, principally due to the fact that it seeks to bring in the provisions of a law that would not otherwise be the governing law (whereas Article 3 paragraph 3 is intended to safeguard provisions of the law that would otherwise be applicable) and consequently will not find favour everywhere. Hence the possibility granted by Article 22 of excluding Article 7 paragraph 1 by entering a reservation. Nevertheless, doubts as to its advisability as a rule ought not to be mingled with its "innovative" nature for its roots may be traced back to common private international law. Having said this, it would seem that there could be no intrinsic objection to letting the provision stand in the Convention and declining to make use of the Article 22 reservation. This viewpoint was supported. It was pointed out, on an admittedly somewhat abstract level, that where a number of countries constituted an identifiable group, certainly regionally but perhaps also politically and economically, such as the EEC or the CMEA, it was desirable in the interests of international cooperation that the courts of one country should take into account the mandatory provisions of another country with which the contract has a close connection, even at the cost of infringing the freedom of the parties to designate their own chosen law. On a practical level, widespread acceptance of such an approach would more effectively combat the situation of divergent results in litigation depending on the country where the dispute was adjudicated. It was also pointed out, however, that the detractors of Article 7 paragraph 1 seemed to pay insufficient attention to the fact that the court was merely given the faculty to take into account only mandatory provisions of another law. It was not compelled to apply them. The provision was drafted in very open terms and could even be regarded as little more than a pious exhortation, lip service to the idea of international cooperation. Nor should it be overlooked that the determination of what constituted a close connection remained with the court. It was not difficult to imagine a court construing the facts in a way that would render Article 7 paragraph 1 inapplicable to the case in hand. Its retention in the Convention would not appear to necessitate any substantive change of approach in practical terms. The purport of Article 7 paragraph 1, it was stated, was really little more than to provide a base in what is admittedly an important codification of contract law on an international level for bringing in, where desirable, reference to foreign mandatory provisions that had a claim to be considered in the decision to be handed down in the case.

Article 3 was similarly founded in ordinary conflict of laws and, it was stated, addressed itself to the problem of what might be termed the unconnected choice of law. This was a problem, at least a theoretical one, that was as old as the initial acceptance of party autonomy. It seems to have been generally agreed in many countries that a choice of law that was not bonâ fide could be struck down, in other words, in those cases where a foreign law was chosen in order to evade provisions that would otherwise have been applicable. This is clearly encompassed by Article 3 paragraph 3 in that the fact of the choice of such other law "shall not . . . prejudice" the application of such applicable provisions. The wording of the Article might appear to leave open also the view, accepted in some countries, that the choice should stand, even at the cost of such mandatory provisions, where the choice was not done with a view to evasion but for other commercially acceptable reasons. And this could be of particular importance when the case involved both commercial interests, where the parties' autonomy might be regarded as deserving of protection, and consumer interests, where the mandatory provisions might be expected to have precedence in the interest of protecting the weaker party. Of course, where the object of the contract rendered it a consumer contract then the Rome Convention and the recent chapter of the Hague Convention gave priority to the interests of the consumer.

The discussions were concluded with an examination of the extent to which Article 7 paragraph 1 could be viewed as incorporating the notion of *depeçage.* The general view was that this technique was not present in the minds of the drafters of the Convention but that it could be resorted to as a means of splitting up the contract to allow for the application of foreign mandatory rules. Another view was that *depeçage* was not appropriate in the context of the Convention, and that the problems associated with freedom of the parties to choose the governing law and the extent of applicability of mandatory rules, could be viewed in another light. Namely, that the first task of the court is to ascertain the existence of an agreement between the parties as to a choice of law, including the question to what extent the parties are free to choose a law other than the law objectively applicable, and that the second task is to determine what is the material scope of the law so chosen, to what extent is it effective against provisions that would otherwise be applicable or enter into consideration.

The Chairman, having expressed his particular thanks to the reporters and to the participants for an informative and lively discussion of the complex issues that had arisen, drew the sitting to a close.

STANDARD FORMS – GENERAL CONDITIONS

STANDARD FORMS AND GENERAL CONDITIONS IN INTERNATIONAL TRADE; DUTCH, GERMAN AND UNIFORM LAW

by U. Drobnig

1. INTRODUCTION

1.1. Terms of reference

I shall briefly attempt to define my terms of reference.

Standard Forms and General Conditions are two different forms of a single phenomenon. They both have one negative feature in common: their fixed and printed terms are not the result of mutual negotiations between two contracting parties; rather, they have been elaborated and printed by one of the parties for use in his contracting business with as many partners as possible. The other party has, as a rule, no choice but to accept them *in toto* if he wants to make the deal; or to reject them and lose the deal. Only in transactions of considerable volume will the recipient of printed Standard Forms or General Conditions, provided he has sufficient bargaining power, insist on negotiating amending clauses; or he will send his own General Conditions and thus open the famous battle of the forms.

Strictly speaking, there is one difference of considerable consequence between General Conditions and Standard Forms. The latter take the form of a (pre-printed) contract, leaving a few blanks for the insertion of individual *additional* terms; if these are filled in and the form is signed, this is a complete contract. General conditions, on the other hand, take the form of a closed code of contract terms; they do not leave room for individual terms. The contract itself, therefore, must be established separately, in a special space or on a separate sheet.

Bills of lading furnish an example illustrating the difference. Frequently, bills of lading are issued in two forms, a short form and a long form. The short form is a form contract because it contains blanks which must be filled in and signed. One of the printed clauses of the short form refers to the terms and conditions of the long form; the latter contains general conditions.

If the General Conditions are to become part of the contract, it is therefore necessary to provide for their incorporation. In practice, this incorporation raises major difficulties, and since General Conditions are much more common than Standard Forms, we will devote primary attention to them.

The above distinction between Standard Forms and General Conditions, although clearly supported by international practice [1] and national writers [2], is not always observed; the two terms are frequently used interchangeably. Even statutes such as the German Act on General Conditions of 1976 [3] do so if they intend to apply

1. The UN Economic Commission for Europe has prepared both General Conditions and and Standard Forms of Contract; the line of demarcation is precisely that drawn in the text, see, Benjamin, "The ECE General Conditions and Standard Forms of Contract" (1961) JBusL 113-131, at p. 122.

2. Hondius, *Standaardvoorwaarden* (1978) pp. 67-68; Schmidt-Salzer, *Allgemeine Geschäftsbedingungen*, 2nd ed. (1977) B. 2, B. 54-60.

3. *Gesetz zur Regelung des Rechts der Allgemeinen Geschäftsbedingungen (AGB-Gesetz)* of 9 December 1976, BGBl. I 3317: English Translation in Silberberg, ed., *Gesetz der Allgemeinen Geschäftsbedingungen in der Bundesrepublik Deutschland / The German Standard Contracts Act* (1979).

the same rules to both classes of documents.[4] However, in order to avoid confusion it is suggested to observe here the distinction between the two terms.

Somewhat contrary to the tradition of the Hague-Zagreb Colloquium, I propose to deal with Dutch as well as German law. As a German, I am more familiar with the latter, and I am probably not expected to hide this. In addition, I shall do my best to present also the Dutch situation as completely as possible. Fortunately from an academic point of view, the two legal systems are rather different so that it will be possible to bring out some contrasts.

1.2. Factual Importance

The factual importance of contracting under standard forms and general conditions can for both countries hardly be overestimated. Both producers and merchants have recourse to printed documents setting out crucial terms and conditions of the contracts they intend to conclude.

There are two major reasons for the widespread use of printed forms and conditions. First, the desire to simplify and rationalise the contracting process by excluding crucial terms from having to be negotiated. Second, the desire to impose, by such exclusion, those crucial terms upon the other party without the trouble of having to obtain or perhaps even to 'purchase' its specific consent.

This double and largely overlapping purpose is technically best achieved if printed general conditions are not even introduced into the contracting process, i.e., if they are not sent to the other party (for standard form contracts, of course, this saving device is not applicable, see *supra*, section 1.1.). Notice is then often replaced by a mere reference to the general conditions, leaving it to the other party to ask for them if he desires to see them. Somtimes not even such express reference is made.

In international trade the recourse to standard contracts and general conditions is even more frequent and important than in purely national transactions. Especially the trade in raw materials and agricultural products, ocean shipping, air transport, but also shipbuilding and freight forwarding are almost regularly subjected to standard contracts or to general conditions.[5] An important additional motive here is that in this way the uncertainties about the applicable conflict of laws rule and about the provisions of the applicable national contract law can be largely, although not completely, avoided.

1.3. Two major legal problems

There are essentially two major legal problems with which courts and writers and eventually also legislators are confronted everywhere. These are: first, the in-

4. § 1 para. 1, sent. 2. Confirming the point made in the text, the rules on the incorporation of General Conditions (§ 2) are held to be inapplicable to Standard Form Contracts (*Formularverträge*) and to be applicable only to General Conditions proper, see, *Münchener Kommentar zum Bürgerlichen Gesetzbuch* (-Kötz) I (1979) § 2 AGBG no. 6.

5. See the copious references in Hondius, op.cit., pp. 36-61.

corporation of general conditions (not standard forms) into a contract; and, second, the validity of the individual terms of standard forms and general conditions.

We shall essentially limit our inquiry to the treatment of these problems in border-crossing transactions.[6] For these, the incidence of special national legislation is limited so far. Such legislation is planned, but does not yet exist in the Netherlands.[7] And the relevant German Act is essentially limited to transactions with a consumer.[8] However, the general clause in paragraph 9 of the Act also applies to commercial transactions. It is predicated on the idea that terms in General Conditions which, contrary to the requirements of good faith, "place the other party at an undue disadvantage" are void. An undue disadvantage shall be presumed if a term (1) "is incompatible with the fundamental principles of the statutory provision from which it deviates, or (2) restricts fundamental rights or duties inherent in the nature of the contract to such a degree as to jeopardise its object." International transactions are, as a rule, commercial transactions, as is borne out by the decided cases. Yet, occasionally, even consumers may be involved, so that some attention must be reserved for their special problems.

2. INCORPORATION OF GENERAL CONDITIONS

2.1. The issue

The issue of incorporation may arise in different contexts, so that it is necessary to narrow and define it.

I propose to exclude:

1. Jurisdiction and arbitration clauses, since procedural rules may establish special requirements for them.[9] These special procedural rules and all judicial and literary pronouncements on their application will here be excluded.

2. The same applies with regard to the relevance of forms or conditions for the choice of law. This may be based either upon an express choice of law clause in the printed forms or conditions; or it may be derived implicitly from their individual substantive terms.

6. In one respect we shall go beyond this limit: we shall include transactions concluded by foreigners in the Netherlands or in Germany because, although not bordercrossing, such contracts are of an international character.

7. Verburgh, "Naar een wet op de standaardvoorwaarden . . .", NJBl. 1979, 528, at pp. 530, 531; Van de Sande Bakhuijzen, "Kontrole op standaardvoorwaarden", WPNR 1979, 281.

8. § 24, sent. 1 of the Act (*supra* n. 3) excludes the application of the most important provisions, i.e., § 2 on incorporation and §§ 10 - 12 on the invalidity of specific clauses, as against a merchant.

9. The most obvious illustration is Art. 17, para. 1 of the EEC Convention on Jurisdiction and the Enforcement of Judgments in Civil and Commercial Matters of 27 September 1968.

3. Also excluded are the special conflict of laws provisions of the recent German Act of 1976 because they only apply to the international contracts of German consumers.

It goes without saying that incorporation poses no problems where the ordinary process of contracting has been observed. Consequently, standard forms as contrasted to general conditions can be excluded here altogether (see *supra*, section 1.1.). And even general conditions will only be covered where they have not been explicitly accepted by the other party; however, lack of such explicit acceptance is the rule.

I may thus specify the issue with which we shall deal as follows: under which circumstances are non-negotiated general conditions – apart from their jurisdiction and arbitration clauses – incorporated into an international commercial contract?

Answers to this question will be discussed on two levels, namely, on that of uniform substantive law and on that of conflict of laws, national and uniform.

2.2. **Uniform substantive law**

There are now two instruments of uniform substantive law which are relevant for our purposes: the Uniform Law on the Formation of International Sales Contracts of 1964 (ULFIS) and the new UN Convention on Contracts for the International Sale of Goods, signed in April 1980 in Vienna (CISG). Part II of this Convention deals with the formation of international sales contracts, following closely the corresponding rules of the Uniform Formation Law of 1964. Since the latter has been in force for a number of years and has attracted judicial and academic interpretation which will be relevant also for understanding the new Convention of 1980, I shall deal with both in historical sequence.

2.2.1. Uniform Law on the Formation of International Sales Contracts, 1964 (ULFIS)

This Uniform Law is in force in the Netherlands and in Germany and in seven other countries.[10]

Since the Uniform Formation Law does not specifically regulate the incorporation of general conditions into international sales contracts, our particular issue is covered by its general rules. These general rules open at least two, but in fact probably three, major avenues for the incorporation of general conditions into international sales contracts (*infra* paras. 1-3).

10. Convention relating to a Uniform Law on the Formation of Contracts for the International Sale of Goods of 1 July 1964 (trilingual text in Zweigert/Kropholler, *Sources of International Uniform Law*, I (1971) E 138, F 138, G 138). The uniform law is now in force, although subject to varying reservations, in nine countries: Belgium, Gambia, Germany (Fed. Rep.), Israel, Italy, Luxembourg, the Netherlands, San Marino, and the United Kingdom.

1. The first is through the traditional interplay of offer and acceptance [11] – a method which we had intended not to discuss here. However, there is one provision of the Uniform Law which, though not in terms, yet according to its drafting history may be relevant. According to Article 7, paragraph 2, a purported acceptance of an offer with additional or different terms "which do not materially alter the terms of the offer shall constitute an acceptance" unless the offeror objects; the contract is then concluded according to the modifying terms of the acceptance.

This provision was intended to cover, *inter alia,* the situation where the offeree in sending his acceptance of the offer, adds his own general conditions.[12] Apparently it was thought that these general conditions should not be regarded as a material alteration of the offer and that therefore a contract would be formed, including the conditions, unless the offeror objects.

If this had indeed been the intention of the drafters, it has found small favour with either the writers or the courts. Dutch and German commentators rightly assume that, as a rule, the offeree's general conditions are a material deviation from the terms of the offer [13], and in a Dutch-German case a court has followed suit without engaging in a detailed comparison between the two documents.[14] However, even a material deviation from the offer that is not expressly accepted by the offeror does not necessarily preclude the formation of a contract: the deviating acceptance is a counteroffer (Art. 7, para. 1) which may be accepted impliedly, e.g., by the offeror's delivery or payment (Art. 6, para. 2).[15]

Of course, there may be specific situations in which the offeree's general conditions do not constitute a material deviation from the offer.[16] They will then be incorporated into the contract, unless the offeror objects (Art. 7, para. 2) – as with any other immaterial deviations from the offer.

2. The second general method of incorporating general conditions is one peculiar to commercial transactions – through a course of dealing which the parties have established between themselves.[17] By such a practice also the general conditions of a contracting party may be incorporated into the contract,

11. Art. 4, para. 1, Art. 6, para. 1.

12. Mertens/Rehbinder, *Internationales Kaufrecht* (1975) Art. 7 EAG no. 5; Schlechtriem, *Einheitliches Kaufrecht – wissenschaftliches Modell oder praxisnahe Regelung?* (1978) p. 60; see also, Dölle (-Schlechtriem), *Kommentar zum Einheitlichen Kaufrecht* (1976) Art. 7 EAG no. 18.

13. Van der Velden, *De eenvormige Koopwetten* (1979) p. 252; Mertens/Rehbinder, op.cit., Art. 7 EAG no. 9; Grüter, "Die Auftragsbestätigung nach einheitlichem Kaufrecht", RIW 1975, 611-616, at p. 613; Schlechtriem, "Die Kollision von Standardbedingungen nach BGB und einheitlichem Kaufabschlussgesetz", BB 1974, 1309-1311, at p. 1311; similarly, Dölle (-Schlechtriem) op.cit., Art. 7 EAG no. 20.

14. LG Landshut 14 July 1976, NJW 1977, 2033, RIW 1977, 427.

15. LG Landshut, ibid.; see also, Dölle (-Schlechtriem), op.cit., Art. 7 EAG no. 19.

16. Illustrations in Schlechtriem, op.cit., *supra* n. 12, pp. 62-63.

17. Art. 4, para. 2.

even if they have not been sent to the other party nor has the author even referred to them.[18]

A recent Dutch-German case may serve as an illustration. A Dutch roof layer had, since 1970, regularly bought insulating panels from a German producer. The latter had always confirmed in writing the Dutch buyer's telex orders. In these letters of confirmation, the German seller expressly referred to his general conditions which were reprinted on the back of the letter. The Dutch buyer never objected. The parties had followed the same course in concluding, in 1975, the contracts which later gave rise to controversy. In both instances, the German courts held, although on different grounds, that the German seller's general conditions had been incorporated into the contract in dispute.[19] The appellate court assumed a course of dealing incorporating the seller's general conditions, established between the parties by regular, frequent transactions during five years [20] – rightly under the circumstances, it is submitted.[21]

The minimum contact for establishing a course of dealing is probably established if the controversial transaction is preceded by at least three other transactions between the parties.[22]

3. A third method of incorporating general conditions is not expressly regulated in the Uniform Law, but nevertheless has been demanded in both countries: express reference by the author to his general conditions, provided these are known or easily accessible to the other party.[23] In my view, actual knowledge by the other party and nothing less should be required.[24] For the Uniform Law proceeds from the general rules on formation of contract and does not establish any special, more liberal rules for general conditions – for good reasons in view of the very different national backgrounds. In the interest of the necessary uniformity, the interpretation of the Uniform Law must not be influenced by the very frequent recourse to general conditions in two particular countries, such as Germany and the Netherlands.

18. See, Van der Velden, op.cit., p. 252; Dölle (-Schlechtriem), op.cit., Art. 4 EAG no. 35; also, Mertens/Rehbinder, op.cit., Art. 4 EAG no. 18 and Hausmann, "Stillschweigender Ausschluss der Einheitlichen Kaufgesetze durch Allgemeine Geschäftsbedingungen", RIW/AWD 1977, 186-196, at p. 193.

19. An interim decision of the first instance court is based on the implied acceptance of a counter-offer, *supra* n. 14-15.

20. OLG München 12 August 1977, WM 1977, 1361 (incomplete publications also in IPRspr. 1977 no. 20 and NJW 1978, 499).

21. See also, Rb. Alkmaar 15 June 1978, AK 11235 for a Dutch-Italian case, applying Dutch law instead of the Uniform Formation Law.

22. OLG Stuttgart 24 July 1979, RIW 1980, 365 in interpreting Art. 17 of the EEC Convention on Jurisdiction, *supra* n. 9.

23. Dölle (-Schlechtriem) op.cit., Art. 4 EAG no. 14; these authors are somewhat more liberal in no. 16 by requiring an effort of the recipient to obtain the conditions from their author.

24. Drobnig, "Allgemeine Geschäfstbedingungen im Internationalen Handelsverkehr", *Festschrift Mann* (1977), pp. 591-615 at p. 613; cf. also Reithmann (-Martiny), *Internationales Vertragsrecht*, 3rd ed. (1980) no. 301, p. 263.

4. Apart from the three methods of incorporation just mentioned, *other ways are not available.* In particular, under the Uniform Law general conditions can no longer become part of the contract by mere reference if the other party merely ought to, but does not in fact know of them.[25] *A fortiori* general conditions are irrelevant if their author does not even bother to refer to them. If silence under the law at the offeree's place of business means consent, this must not be qualified as a "usage" which would therefore prevail.[26] This would mix up law and usage, indirectly re-introduce conflict of laws rules and destroy the uniformity which the Uniform Law had achieved.[27]

5. One particular and rather frequent case requires special consideration – the famous "battle of the forms". Both parties, the offeror as well as the offeree, effectively refer to their respective general conditions which contain more or less contradictory terms. To complicate matters, both these general conditions are nowadays often especially equipped for the battle – by a "defensive" clause expressly refusing acceptance of any general conditions which may have been or may in the future be sent by the other contracting party; and insisting on exclusive application of the author's own conditions.

Thus the issue is no longer – as heretofore – whether the conditions of one of the parties have been incorporated into the contract. Rather it is, whether any, and if so, which of the two conflicting sets of conditions do prevail. Of course, the answer to the two questions may be furnished by a practice which the parties have established between themselves.[28] But what is the solution if such a practice has not been established? In the Netherlands, Hondius tends to think that according to Article 7 ULFIS those general conditions prevail which were sent (or received) last.[29] However, Van der Velden has correctly pointed out that Article 7 does not cover this case. He himself is here inclined to deny the formation of a contract.[30] I would adopt the same position.

A different solution would apply if both parties have started to perform the contract or have otherwise indicated that they regard the contract as concluded, in spite of their conflicting general conditions. In this situation it is clear that the parties have impliedly confirmed the contract.[31] The only doubtful point can be whether in this case the general conditions of the two parties are com-

25. Mertens/Rehbinder, op.cit., Art. 4 EAG no. 18; Nörenberg, "Internationale Verträge und Allgemeine Geschäftsbedingungen", NJW 1978, 1082-1087 at p. 1084. But *contra* Van der Velden, op.cit., p. 252: it suffices if the offeree "may reasonably be deemed to know".

26. This argument has been propounded by Graveson/Cohn/Graveson, *The Uniform Laws on International Sales Act 1967* (1968) p. 112.

27. Similarly Cigoj, "International Sales: Formation of Contract", (1976) 23 NILR 257 at p. 269; see also, Dölle (-Schlechtriem), op.cit., Art. 13 EAG no. 8, 10.

28. Art. 2, para. 1; see, Van der Velden, op.cit., p. 252; Dölle (-Schlechtriem), op.cit., Art. 2 EAG no. 35.

29. Hondius, op.cit., pp. 423-424.

30. Van der Velden, op.cit., p. 252. Of the same opinion is probably Dölle (-Schlechtriem) op.cit., Art. 6 EAG no. 20.

31. Van der Velden, op.cit., pp. 252-253 (but he erroneously invokes the authority of Hondius for this proposition). The author bases his result upon "good faith". Germany:

pletely to be disregarded [32] or whether they should not rather apply in so far as they are reconcilable with each other.[33] In the interest of party autonomy (Art. 2, para. 1), the latter solution would seem to be justified.

6. In Germany the further question arises as to the relationship between the Uniform Formation Law and the German Act on General Conditions.[34] German authors agree that the Uniform Law, although earlier, has precedence on the ground that the uniform rules are to be regarded as a special and therefore prevailing regulation.[35] Prevailing opinion would therefore disregard the special provisions of the German Act relating to the incorporation of general conditions into an international contract covered by the Uniform Law.[36] But according to a minority view, all problems of control of validity of terms, whether by way of special rules on incorporation, against surprising clauses, for narrow interpretation, or formalities or by outright control, are outside the scope of the Uniform Formation Law and are therefore fully governed by the German Act.[37] I personally do not think it permissible to narrow the scope of uniform legislation by "requalifying" controversial issues under a functional approach. Legal security and the principle of *pacta sunt servanda* would be imperiled if the technique used by ULFIS to delimit its scope of application, i.e., conclusion of contract, could be recast into a problem of substantive validity and thereby the scope of the Uniform Law be narrowed.

2.2.2. UN Convention on Contracts for the International Sale of Goods of April 1980 [38]

This convention has in substance largely adopted the corresponding rules of the Uniform Formation Law of 1964.

However, the Convention contains two new rules which are relevant in the present context. ULFIS Article 6(2) had said that an offer may be accepted not only by an express declaration but also by an act of the offeree. The new

Schlechtriem, op.cit., *supra* n. 13), p. 1311; Dölle (-Schlechtriem), op.cit., Art. 7 EAG no. 20; Mertens/Rehbinder, op.cit., Art. 7 EAG no. 9, Art. 4 EAG no. 19, Art. 2 EAG no. 4. This corresponds to the position in internal German law: see, BGH 9 February 1977, WM 1977, 451, 452; 10 June 1974, BB 1974, 1136; 26 September 1973, BGHZ 61, 282, 288-289; OLG Köln 19 March 1980, WM 1980, 905.

32. Thus van der Velden, ibid.

33. Thus, perhaps, Dölle (-Schlechtriem), *supra* n. 31.

34. *Supra* n. 3.

35. Drobnig, loc.cit., p. 615; Stoll, "Internationalprivatrechtliche Probleme bei der Verwendung Allgemeiner Geschäftsbedingungen", *Festschrift Beitzke* (1979) 759-785, at pp. 780-781 with references; Hausmann, "Zum teilweisen Ausschluss der Einheitlichen Kaufgesetze durch Allgemiene Geschäftsbedingungen", WM 1980, 726-737, at p. 730; Hübner, "Allgemeine Geschäftsbedingungen und internationales Privatrecht", NJW 1980, 2601-2607, at p. 2607.

36. See references in preceding note; also, Hausmann, loc.cit., ibid., at pp. 729, 730-731, 732.

37. See especially, Stoll, loc.cit., at pp. 781-783 with references; Landfermann, "AGB-Gesetz und Auslandsgeschäfte", RIW 1977, 445-453, at pp. 451-452.

38. English text in NJB 1980, 1033. See Part II (Art. 14-24).

Convention generalises the equivalence of statement and conduct in Article 18(1) sentence 1. However, it also qualifies it by a sentence (the second) incorporating a new rule: "Silence or inactivity does not in itself amount to acceptance". This new sentence reinforces the argument that the incorporation of general conditions can only be achieved by observing the general rules on the formation of contract which require assent by the other party to the first party's general conditions (see *supra* section 2.2.1. paras. 1-4).

ULFIS Article 7 on a qualified acceptance has been adopted almost literally by the new Convention Article 19(1)-(2). However, an additional third paragraph is new. It clarifies the meaning of additional terms, "which do not materially alter the terms of the offer" (para. 2) by enumerating a number of points which "are considered to alter the terms of the offer materially" (para. 3). Among these are the extent of one party's liability to the other and the settlement of disputes. These clauses are typically contained in general conditions. Thus the new Convention confirms the point made as to ULFIS Article 7(2) that – contrary to the drafter's intention – an acceptance to which the offeree's general conditions are added will usually amount to a counter-offer (see *supra* section 2.2.1. para. 1).

With respect to the "battle of forms", the new Convention does not indicate a solution. One German author has ventured the opinion that this is to be regarded as a case of open dissensus which, being a problem of validity, falls outside the Convention.[39] I cannot share this opinion since conclusion of contract and not validity is involved so that a solution must be found within the four corners of the Convention itself (see Art. 7(2)).

One must regret that the new Convention has also abstained from regulating specifically the various problems about the incorporation of general conditions.[40]

2.3. National Conflict of Laws

1. The issue. In so far as uniform legislation (i.e., at present the Uniform Formation Law) is not applicable, a conflict of laws problem arises: which national legal system should determine whether the requirements for effective incorporation of general conditions have been met? The legal systems involved are usually those at the seller's and at the buyer's business residence as well as the law governing the contract. The question presupposes that these legal systems have developed different rules on the question – an assumption that is, generally speaking, correct.[41]

In the Netherlands and in Germany, there are two, or rather three, major approaches to the problem: *lex fori, lex contractus,* and the law at the recipient's business residence (*infra* paras. 2-4).

39. Huber, "Der UNCITRAL-Entwurf eines Übereinkommens über internationale Warenkaufverträge", RabelsZ 45 (1979) 413-526, at p. 445.

40. Huber, ibid., at p. 446 n. 56 tends to think that this problem is not yet ripe for uniform legislation.

41. See the broad comparative survey in Hondius, op.cit., at p. 139-214; see also, Sandrock, *Handbuch der Internationalen Vertragsgestaltung* (1980) I 291-337.

2. The *lex fori* is usually applied not on the basis of a deliberate choice of law consideration, but without any reflection, as the court's natural law. Examples are furnished both by Dutch [42] and by German courts.[43] Under the circumstances, these voices do not really count.

3. The *lex contractus* is applied with differing degrees of consciousness and definiteness.

In Germany, an early decision held that German law as the *lex contractus* automatically implied the application of the German party's general conditions, in view of their normative character.[44] This view, however, has been refuted authoritatively.[45]

In some cases the courts had raised and answered the question of the law applicable to the contract. When it came to examine the incorporation of one party's general conditions, that problem was solved under the same law. Illustrations for this method are again to be found in both countries.[46] Although with a slight reservation, these decisions may well be attributed to the *lex contractus*-principle.

Several German courts based their application of the *lex contractus* on the rules of conflict of laws in general, but without assigning a specific reason.[47] However, they probably meant to say the same as that which one court at least clearly spelt out: the *lex contractus* is applicable because the incorporation of general conditions is an aspect of the formation of the contract.[48]

42. See recently, HR 9 December 1977, NJ 1978 no. 187 with note G.J.S., S&S 1978 no. 23; Rb. Rotterdam 2 November 1979, S&S 1981 no. 7; Rb. Alkmaar 15 June 1978, AK no. 11 235; Rb. Dordrecht 30 October 1974, NJ 1975 no. 156; Rb. Amsterdam 14 February 1973, NJ 1974 no. 28; probably also, Ktg. Amsterdam 9 December 1966, NJ 1968 no. 241, noted by De Winter, WPNR 1971, 384.

43. BGH 12 July 1974, WM 1974, 1118, NJW 1974, 2177; OLG München 20 March 1975, RIW/AWD 1976, 447; OLG München/Augsburg 4 April 1974, NJW 1974, 2181; OLG Düsseldorf 2 November 1973, IPRspr. 1973 no. 136, AWD 1974, 103; OLG Bremen 22 June 1973, WM 1973, 987, IPRspr. 1973 no. 8; OLG Hamburg 19 March 1971, IPRspr. 1971 no. 23, AWD 1971, 188.

44. LG München I 14 August 1952, VRS 5, 346 with respect to the General German Freight Forwarders Conditions, obviously influenced by conceptions prevailing during the Third Reich.

45. BGH 4 February 1963, WM 1963, 456, 457, IPRspr. 1962/63 no. 25; Helm in *Grosskommentar zum Handelsgesetzbuch V,* 3rd ed. (1973) §§ 407 - 409 HGB no. 17.

46. *Netherlands:* Hof Amsterdam 17 December 1976, S&S 1977 no. 94; Rb. Rotterdam 16 May 1980, S&S 1980 no. 114; Rb. Rotterdam 4 December 1978, S&S 1979, no. 37; Rb. Rotterdam 17 December 1968, S&S 1969 no. 56; Rb. Breda 2 January 1962, NJ 1962 no. 381; Rb. Rotterdam 19 February 1954, NJ 1955 no. 62, apparently approved by Kollewijn, *Tien Jaren Nederlandse Rechtspraak Internationaal Privaatrecht 1954-1963* (1966) p. 250. *Germany*: e.g., BGH 10 March 1971, VersR 1971, 619, IPRspr. 1971 no. 21b; BGH 2 October 1970, VersR 1971, 123, IPRspr. 1970 no. 29; 9 February 1970, WM 1970, 552; see already, RG 14 December 1928, Hans.RGZ 1928 B 86, 87-89, JW 1929, 662, RGZ 123, 97, 98-100.

47. BGH 13 July 1973, WM 1973, 1238, IPRspr. 1973 no. 25; OLG München 30 October 1973, VersR 1975, 129, 130; OLG München 9 May 1973, IPRspr. 1973 no. 24, NJW 1973, 1560.

48. LG Zweibrücken 5 March 1974, NJW 1974, 1060.

The formation of the contract is subject to the law governing the contract, assuming that it has been concluded. This rule is, indeed, generally recognised both in the Netherlands [49] and in Germany.[50] Some Dutch authors expressly extend this rule to cover also the incorporation of general conditions.[51] However, differences exist as to the scope and generality of this rule. It seems to be accepted much more broadly in the Netherlands; in Germany, on the other hand, more reservations have been expressed and exceptions made, in the past as in the present.

4. The (partly differing) alternatives to the *lex contractus* proposed in Germany have one objective in common: it appears to be unfair to judge certain situations which arise during the negotiating process, as being governed by a legal system (i.e., the *lex contractus*) which the parties at that particular period of time had not yet determined and could not otherwise know. How can the recipient of a communication know whether a specific document received constitutes an offer; whether it is binding upon the offeror; and whether his silence may constitute an acceptance – when the choice of law clause proposed by the sender has not yet been accepted by the recipient; or when, before acceptance, the elements of the contract which permit one to determine its proper law – in the absence of a choice of law clause – have not yet been settled? The focus thus is clearly upon the situation of the recipient of the communication, the offeree. And the questions which he may raise at this moment are typically submitted to counsel, not to a court.

Views on a special treatment of the so-called pre-consensual period have therefore been put forward first by various German writers, such as Zitelmann and Frankenstein, Neuner and Wahl, Lewald and Raape, Ferid and Kegel.[52] They were practically unanimous in suggesting a new connecting point: relevant should be the law of the domicil (or of the business residence) of the person making a declaration (an offer, an acceptance, etc.). Some authors regard this connecting point alone as relevant, while others propose to combine it with the *lex contractus.* There was much less unanimity with regard to the scope of application of the new rule: whether a communication is an offer; whether the offer is binding; whether it lapses after a certain time; whether silence means acceptance: any

49. There is not much direct authority, apparently because the matter is uncontroversial, see, Lemaire, *Nederlands Internationaal Privaatrecht* (1968) p. 242. However, van Brakel, *Grondslagen en Beginselen van Nederlands Internationaal Privaatrecht,* 3rd ed. (1952) pp. 227-228 regards the rule set out in the text as based on a circular reasoning. In his view offer and acceptance are each subject to the law of the respective place of declaration (at p. 229).

50. Soergel/Siebert (-Kegel), *Kommentar zum Bürgerlichen Gesetzbuch VII,* 10th ed. (1970) no. 307 preceding Art. 7 EGBGB; Staudinger (-Firsching), *Kommentar zum Bürgerlichen Gesetzbuch. Internationales Privatrecht Ib. Internationales Schuldrecht I,* 10th/11th ed. (1978) nos. 154-157, 444 preceding Art. 12 EGBGB with many references; Reithmann (-Martiny) op.cit., no. 94 with references.

51. Blaauwendraad, "De Loi Scrivener", SEW 12 (1979) 760-769, at p. 769, probably also van Rooij, WPNR 1977, 293-297, at p. 294.

52. A convenient survey of these opinions in Staudinger (-Firsching), op.cit., no. 154.

single or any combination of these problesm was submitted to the law of the person making a declaration. Some thought that even defects of consent such as mistake should be brought under the special rule.[53]

The German courts, however, were clinging to the *lex contractus*, with very few exceptions.[54]

In 1971, the picture changed all of a sudden. In that year, two divisions of the Federal Supreme Court expressed the opinion that in answering the question whether general conditions of a German offeror have been (impliedly) accepted by the foreign offeree not only the *lex contractus* must be taken into account, but also the *lex domicilii* of the foreign offeree.[55] "One cannot regard without more a party's attitude as a declaration of intention, if the party itself according to its domestic law did not need to count upon such an interpretation." [56] Several lower courts have followed this reasoning.[57] In all these cases the foreign offeree had not expressly agreed to the German offeror's reference to his general conditions; and since that silence did not amount to consensus under the offeree's *lex domicilii*, whereas it normally would under German law, the courts held that the German offeror's general conditions were not incorporated into the contract.

Later, the courts have somewhat limited the special rule: the *lex contractus* applies to the incorporation of general conditions if the foreign contracting party was not justified in relying upon his own law "in view of the circumstances surrounding the conclusion of the contract", especially if the contract is concluded in Germany.[58] In fact, the issue in these cases was a different one: foreign freight forwarders had sent goods to German freight forwarders for delivery in Germany. When controversies arose the German freight forwarders invoked the General German Forwarding Conditions. The courts, applying German law as the *lex contractus*, sustained this view on the ground that even foreigners must know that these Conditions are generally applied by all German freight forwarders.[59]
The issue therefore is no longer whether silence means acceptance of general conditions, but whether these, although not even referred to by the German party, have been incorporated into the contract. Is it equitable to submit this question

53. Reference is made again to the survey by Staudinger (-Firsching) ibid.

54. See the instructive survey of cases in Staudinger (Firsching), ibid., no. 155.

55. BGH 18 June 1971, WM 1971, 987, 988, NJW 1971, 2126, 2127 (with critical note Schmidt-Salzer and approving note Pleyer/Ungnade, NJW 1972, 681), JR 1972, 25 with critical note Kolhosser, IPRspr. 1971 no. 5; BGH 22 September 1971, BGHZ 57, 72, 77, IPRspr. 1971 no. 133.

56. BHG 22 September 1971, ibid.

57. OLG Nürnberg 11 October 1973, AWD 1974, 405 with approving note Linke, IPRspr. 1973 no. 12 A; LG Darmstadt 5 April 1977, RIW 1977, 498; LG Zweibrücken 5 March 1974, NJW 1974, 1060; LG Mainz 10 December 1971, IPRspr. 1971 no. 135, AWD 1972, 298 with approving note Ebsen/Jayme.

58. BGH 13 July 1973, WM 1973, 1238, 1240, IPRspr. 1973 no. 25.

59. BGH 13 July 1973, ibid.; OLG Frankfurt 23 April 1980, RIW 1980, 666, 667; OLG Frankfurt 16 January 1979, RIW 1979, 278. However, in the last case, decisive weight was apparently attached to the fact that both parties had pleaded on the basis of the German party's Conditions.

to the *lex contractus,* if that differs, as it did in these cases, from the foreign party's *lex domicilii?*

A subsequent decision of the Federal Supreme Court has developed further this analysis. In this case, a foreign enterprise, apparently for the first time, had charged a German freight forwarder who later invoked his Conditions, which had not been communicated or even referred to. The court distinguished this from the preceding case, requiring, as a rule, vis-à-vis a foreign non-expert an express reference. But whether that party's silence then amounts to acceptance, is subject to its domiciliary law.[60]

As one would expect, German writers in general approve of the new judicial trend since it is in line with earlier writings on the treatment of the preconsensual period of contracting. This is supported primarily by the meaning to be attached to silence upon receiving either the text of the offeror's general condition or a reference to them.[61]

However, it should be extended *a fortiori* to the case where conditions are neither sent nor even referred to.[62] So far, German courts have applied to this aspect of incorporation the *lex contractus,* yet without reflection. But in applying German law as the law governing the contract they have taken into account the special situation of the foreign contracting party. Thus foreign freight forwarders, especially those from the neighbouring countries, are supposed to know that their German colleagues do not do business except on the basis of their General German Freight Forwarders Conditions.[63] But the contrary rule applies

60. BGH 7 July 1976, WM 1976, 1311, NJW 1976, 2075 with critical note Buchmüller in NJW 1977, 501, IPRspr. 1976 no. 8.

61. Buchmüller, ibid; Drobnig, loc.cit., at pp. 604-606; Ebsen/Jayme, loc.cit., Ferid, *Zum Abschluss von Auslandsverträgen* (1954) pp. 40, 41, 42; Hausmann, loc.cit., *supra* n. 18, at p. 192; Hepting, "Die ADSp. im internationalen Speditionsverkehr", AWD 1975, 457-464, at pp. 461-464; Hübner, loc.cit., at. p. 2606; Jayme, "Allgemeine Geschäftsbedingungen und internationales Privatrecht", ZHR 142 (1978) 105-123, at pp. 121-122; idem, "Kollisionsrecht und Bankgeschäfte mit Auslandsberührung", *Untersuchungen über das Spar-, Giro- und Kreditwesen 14* (1977) 19, 38; Kolhosser, loc.cit.; Kronke, "Zur Verwendung von Allgemeinen Geschäftsbedingungen im Verkehr mit Auslandsberührung", NJW 1977, 992-993; Löwe/Graf Westphalen/Trinkner (-Graf Westphalen), *Kommentar zum Gesetz zur Regelung des Rechts der Allgemeninen Geschäftsbedingungen* (1977) § 2 AGBG Anhang nos. 5-8, 10; Reithmann (-Martiny), op.cit., nos. 105, 107; Sandrock, op.cit., I 262-273; Schmidt-Salzer, op.cit., *supra* n. 2, D. 104; Schmitz, "Haftungsausschlussklauseln in allgemeinen Geschäfstbedingungen nach englischem und internationalem Privatrecht", *Schriften zum Internationalen Recht 8* (1977) pp. 74-79, 81-83; Schütze, "Allgemeine Geschäftsbedingungen bei Auslandsgeschäften", DB 1978, 2301-2306, at p. 2301; Spellenberg, *Geschäftsstatut und Vollmacht im internationalen Privatrecht,* (1979) pp. 233-238.

62. Drobnig, loc.cit., at pp. 606-608; Schmidt-Salzer, op.cit., *supra* n. 2, D. 104 p. 114; perhaps also Jayme, ZHR 142 (1978) 121 since he intends to deal with the special connecting factor for "offer and acceptance" of general conditions, though without elaborating. Reithmann (-Martiny), op.cit., 104 would apply to this issue the domiciliary law of the author of the general conditions(!).

63. See *supra* at nn. 58-60; further: OLG München 30 October 1974, VersR 1975, 129; OLG München 9 May 1973, *supra* n. 47; LG Hamburg 14 June 1968, IPRspr. 1968/69 no. 42; LG Frankfurt 24 June 1955, VRS 10, 343; see also BGH 2 October 1970, *supra* n. 46; and BGH 12 July 1974, *supra* n. 43.

if a German freight forwarder is charged by a foreign non-expert of the trade [64], unless the latter for special reasons in fact has or ought to have the relevant knowledge.[65] However, should one really leave to the future *lex contractus,* which is not yet established during the negotiations, the question whether it may have developed special rules designed to protect a foreign contracting party against the imposition of unknown general conditions, not even referred to by their author or user? It would seem to me that the implied incorporation of the offeror's general conditions into his offer must be as much subject to the domiciliary law of the recipient of this offer as their acceptance. This rule would facilitate the task of the courts. They would no longer have to apply the *lex contractus* to the first phase and the offeree's domiciliary law to the second phase of incorporation of general conditions, as they have done in the past, with the almost unavoidable confusion resulting from this complicated operation.[66]

While it may be said that the majority of German writers today advocate recourse to the offeree's domiciliary law, this opinion is not unanimous. There are some recent and strong advocates of the *lex contractus.* These rely mainly on the following three arguments: (1) any splitting-off of individual elements of the formation of contract disrupts the context of the subject-matter; (2) the rules on the incorporation of general conditions and those on their control (which are undoubtedly subject to the *lex contractus,* see *infra* section 3) supplement each other and, on the international level, even overlap, so that they should be subjected to the same legal system; (3) the social need which had inspired the new doctrine can better be satisfied by applying the substantive rules of the (future) *lex contractus* which must and can pay due regard to the peculiar situation of a foreign contracting party.[67] However, at least one of the dissenters says expressly that in forming the proper substantive rule the foreigner's domiciliary law must be duly taken into account.[68] This brings us back full circle!

5. Choice of law clauses in general conditions may pose special problems.

Thus the one of the two major German dissenters (*supra* para. 4 *in fine*) who would refer the incorporation of general conditions to substantive law is consistent in proposing a special rule for the incorporation of choice of law clauses in general conditions; this is to be a special substantive rule of conflict of laws.[69]

64. BGH 7 July 1976, *supra* n. 60; OLG Saarbrücken 22 July 1953, IPRspr. 1952/53 no. 39, NJW 1953, 1832.

65. BGH 10 March 1971, *supra* n. 46; OLG Hamburg 19 March 1971, *supra* n. 43. See generally on these cases, Sandrock, op.cit., I 288-290.

66. See *supra* text to nn. 58-60. Such confusion is noticeable especially in OLG Frankfurt 16 January 1979, *supra* n. 59, where the introduction of general conditions by the German offeree was submitted to the criterion for their acceptance, i.e., to the German party's domiciliary law.

67. Especially Stoll, loc.cit., at pp. 763-767; Linke, "Sonderanknüpfung der Willenserklärung? ", ZvglRwiss. 79 (1980) 1-58; see also Ungnade, "Die Geltung von Allgemeinen Geschäftsbedingungen der Kreditinstitute im Verkehr mit dem Ausland", WM 1973, 1130-1133, at pp. 1132-1133.

68. Linke, ibid., at pp. 45-46.

69. Stoll, loc.cit., at pp. 767-772. The clause proposed by the author at pp. 772 is so complicated as to defy translation; it is also so extremely vague as to be unworkable.

A faint Dutch analogy is to be found in the discussion on the law governing the formation of a choice of law clause, whether or not contained in general conditions. Some writers tend to rely, in this case, on the personal law of each contracting party.[70] A recent case dealt with the question whether the choice of law clause contained in the Dutch buyer's general conditions was binding upon the French seller. The appellate court did not apply the *lex contractus* (which was Dutch according to the choice of law clause and French in its absence). Rather it held that according to Dutch private international law a choice of law clause must be clear and unambiguous; that this requirement was not fulfilled by a clause in Dutch printed on the back of an order confirmation, which was filled in English, without referring to the general conditions on the back. The choice of law clause was therefore invalid, and French law governed the contract.[71]

Prevailing opinion does not adopt the distinction. It would apply to the incorporation of these choice of law clauses the same rules as to that of general conditions generally.[72]

A complication arises if the "battle of forms" relates to contradictory choice of law clauses inserted by each party into its general conditions. Apparently no court so far has been confronted with this dilemma. In my view the Gordian knot must be cut by applying the newly developing rule of substantive law (*supra* section 2.2.1. para. 5) also on the level of conflict of laws. While this may be a dogmatic heresy, it can be justified by the relatively broad acceptance which the new rule has gained among several leading legal systems. If both parties start to perform the contract, they ratify it in spite of the conflicting choice of law clauses proposed by them. These clauses, therefore, cancel each other. Because of the lack of an effective choice of law by the parties, the law governing the contract must therefore be determined on an objective basis. The conflict between the other contradictory terms of the two parties' general conditions must then be resolved on the basis of the *lex contractus* thus found, except if the incorporation of the general conditions is at issue.

2.4. EEC Convention on the Law Applicable to Contractual Obligations, 1980

This convention was signed on 19 June 1980 by seven of the nine Member States of the European Community; the signatures of Denmark and the United Kingdom hopefully will follow.[73]

70. Especially Kollewijn, *Handelingen der Nederlandsche Juristen Vereeniging* 77 (1947) I 2, pp. 109-110; see also de Winter, WPNR 1971, 384, and Haak, "Preadvies: Internationaal overeenkomstenrecht", *Mededelingen van de Nederlandse Vereniging voor Internationaal Recht,* no. 71 (1975) at pp. 49-51, 65-66, who expresses sympathy for the domiciliary law, but has a slight preference for the *lex contractus.*

71. Hof 's-Hertogenbosch 18 March 1975, NJ 1976 no. 200.

72. Reithmann (-Martiny), op.cit., no. 92 with references.

73. O.J. EEC 1980 L 266; explanatory report by Giuliano/Lagarde, *Report on the Convention on the law applicable to contractual obligations,* ibid., 1980 C 282. In the meantime, Denmark and the United Kingdom have in fact signed the convention.

Article 8, paragraph 1 lays down the generally recognised rule that the formation of a contract is subject to that *lex contractus* which would govern the contract if it had been effectively concluded. Paragraph 2 then adds the following exception:

"Nevertheless a party may rely upon the law of the country in which he has his habitual residence to establish that he did not consent if it appears from the circumstances that it would not be reasonable to determine the effect of his conduct in accordance with the law specified in the preceding paragraph."

According to its terms, the provision covers conduct both of the offeror and of the offeree. The drafting history also makes clear that any conduct, including silence is covered. Further, the provision makes it clear that the law of one party's habitual residence can be invoked merely to negate consent of that party which the hypothetical *lex contractus* would establish [74]; Article 8, paragraph 2 only creates a veto power. Finally, the rule also applies to the formation of a choice of law clause.[75]

Obviously, Article 8, paragraph 2 has been strongly influenced by the German rule explained before (*supra* section 2.3.). Its interpretation will therefore be aided by the analysis of the German caselaw and legal theory. It would seem that most of the problems arising from the incorporation of general conditions without the other party's express consent can be settled satisfactorily on the basis of that provision.

3. VALIDITY OF TERMS

On the national level, the control of the contents of general conditions is an important instrument for restricting their effects. The relative importance of rules on incorporation and of rules on the validity of terms differs from country to country. While in the Netherlands both methods do not appear to be used very often and with great success [76], in Germany clearly the emphasis is on the control of terms.[77]

For international transactions, on the other hand, the picture almost reverses. In Germany, so far, cases dealing with the incorporation of general conditions by far outweigh those very few ones dealing with validity of terms; also two Dutch cases touch at least upon the issue. Nevertheless, since the legal problems involved in this latter issue appear to be rather simple, we shall devote but small attention to the control of terms.

74. See Giuliano/Lagarde, ibid., *ad* Art. 8, sub (2).
75. Art. 3, para. 4 on the choice of law clause refers, *inter alia,* to Art. 8.
76. See Hondius, "Preadvies: Naar een wettelijke regeling van algemene voorwaarden", *Handelingen der Nederlandse Juristen Vereniging* (1979) I 1, pp. 91-290, at pp. 119-120, 122-123.
77. Only two provisions of the German Act of 1976, *supra* n. 3, deal with incorporation (§§ 2 and 3), whereas 15 clauses (some of them very detailed) relate to the control of terms (§§ 8-22). The relative weight of the two methods was the same in German court practice before 1976.

A uniform regulation does not exist. The Uniform Sales Law expressly disclaims to govern "the validity of the contract or of any of its provisions" (Art. 8 sentence 1). This disclaimer covers, *inter alia*, the validity of general conditions.[78] The validity of terms in general conditions is therefore subject to the applicable national law, to be determined according to the principles of the conflict of laws.

The position is the same under the UN Convention on Contracts for the International Sale of Goods of 1980; Article 4, litt. (a) follows closely the corresponding provision in ULIS Article 8, sentence 1.

According to general conflict of laws rules, the control of terms in general conditions is subject to the *lex contractus.* This rule has been expressly recognized by writers in Germany [79] and there is some authority for it in Dutch decisions.[80] Of course, the forum's public policy clause may intervene.[81]

The EEC Convention of 1980 expressly confirms that the validity of any term of a contract is governed by the (hypothetical) *lex contractus* (Art. 8, para. 1).

78. Van der Velden, op.cit., at p. 253; Mertens/Rehbinder, op.cit., Art. 3 EKG no. 19-21, Art. 8 EKG no. 29; Dölle (-Herber), op.cit., *supra* n. 12, Art. 8 EKG no. 6, Dölle (-Stoll), op.cit., *supra* n. 12, Art. 74 EKG no. 145; Hausmann, loc.cit., *supra* n. 18, at p. 194.

79. Reithmann (-Martiny), op.cit., no. 109-110; Stoll, loc.cit., at pp. 760; 763; Mertens/ Rehbinder, op.cit., Art. 8 EKG no. 30; implicitly also Dölle (-Herber), ibid., Art. 2 EKG no. 11, Art. 8 EKG no. 1.

Stoll favours a different solution for general conditions supplementing an international sales contract which is subject to the Uniform Sales Law. In view of the protective purposes of rules on the control of terms he advocates application of the domiciliary law of the party who is confronted with general conditions, see Dölle (-Stoll) ibid., Art. 74 EKG no. 147. This view contrasts with his subsequent pronounced disinclination against the taking into account of the same law in connection with the incorporation of general conditions, see *supra* at n. 35, pp. 763-767 and 772-773.

Dölle (Schlechtriem) op.cit., Art. 4 EAG no. 35, is of the opinion that general conditions that have been incorporated by way of preliminary negotiations or prior practices of the parties are not subject to the control of terms. There is no basis for such an immunity.

80. Hof Amsterdam 17 December 1976, S&S 1977 no. 94 at pp. 253, 255 (validity of Dutch shiprepairer's general conditions maintained, probably according to the Dutch *lex contractus*); Nederlandse Bond van Belanghebbenden bij de Handel in Oliën en Vetten en Oliezaden, Arbitraal vonnis in hoger beroep 8 April 1971, NJ 1972 no. 114 (invalidity of clause in Dutch seller's general conditions, apparently on the basis of Dutch law, probably being the *lex contractus).*

81. See BGH 3 February 1966, WM 1966, 450, IPRspr. 1966/67 no. 1: validity of exculpatory clauses in Dutch general conditions for inland navigation bills of lading examined and affirmed.

STANDARD FORMS AND GENERAL CONDITIONS

by Petar Šarčević

1. INTRODUCTION

The Act of Obligations [1] of the Socialist Federal Republic of Yugoslavia, which came into force on 1 October 1978 could not avoid dealing with a field as important as standard forms and general conditions.[2] Articles 142-144 and Article 100 of the Act of Obligations regulate this subject-matter.

Since the special rules governing the use of standard forms and general conditions differ from country to country, we shall first briefly describe the Yugoslav substantive rules governing their use in domestic and international commercial transactions. The second part of the paper deals with some of the conflict of laws problems arising from the use of standard forms and general conditions in international commercial contracts.

2. YUGOSLAV RULES ON STANDARD FORMS AND GENERAL CONDITIONS

As in other legal systems, the terminology on this subject-matter is rather inconsistent in Yugoslav legal theory.[3] Moreover, the Act of Obligations (hereafter referred to as the Act) does not define the terms "standard forms" and "general conditions" as does, for example, the West German Law on Standard Forms of Contract (LSFC).[4] Article 142 I of the Act states that the "general conditions set forth by one of the parties to the contract can either be a part of a standard contract or be referred to in the contract itself. They supplement the special conditions determined by the contracting parties in the same contract and, as a rule, are binding, just as these are."

2.1. Conditions Governing the incorporation of General Conditions into Contracts

In order for general conditions to be incorporated into contracts, it is necessary that the parties to the contract have reached an agreement to this end. According

1. Published in the Official Gazette of the Socialist Federal Republic of Yugoslavia No. 29/1978.

2. Parts of this subject-matter were previously regulated in Usages No. 32 and 33 of the General Usages of Trade, published in the Official Gazette of the Federal People's Republic of Yugoslavia, No. 15/1954.

3. See, Goldštajn, Privredno ugovorno pravo *(Commercial Contract Law)*, Zagreb 1965, p. 142. Professor Goldštajn uses the terms *opći uvjeti poslovanje (general conditions of business)* and *tipski ugovori (standard form contracts)*. Cf. J. Vilus who uses the term *opšti uslovi formularnih ugovora (general conditions of standard contracts)*, which, in her opinion, unifies the general conditions and standard contracts as general conditions which are formulated and printed in advance for standardized situations and become an integral part of the contract if the parties explicitly or tacitly refer to them: Opšti uslovi formularnih ugovora *(General Conditions of Standard Contracts)*, Belgrade 1976, p. 25.

4. *Gesetz zur Regelung der Allgemeinen Geschäftsbedingungen*, which came into force on 1 April 1977.

to Article 142 III of the Act, the general conditions of such a said contract are binding on a party if it knew them or should have known them at the time the contract was concluded. The only rule contained in the Act which aids in determining under which conditions it is to be assumed that the party should have known the general conditions, is contained in Article 142 II. According to this Article, the general conditions have to be made public in the usual manner. Another guideline which could eventually be applied appears in the former regulations on this subject-matter in The General Usages of Trade. Usage 32 IV provides that a party should have known the general conditions in question if they had been supplied to that party prior to the conclusion of the contract.[5]

The basic rule stated above does not apply, however, in cases where the contracting parties regularly do business with one another. In such cases, once the parties have used the general conditions incorporated in a particular contract, these conditions will also be binding on them in their later transactions even though the parties do not expressly refer to them in later contracts.[6] If they do not wish to have the usual general conditions apply to a specific contract, they are required to issue a special statement.[7]

2.2. Validity of Individual Agreements

If individual agreements differ from the general conditions, the question arises as to which are to be given priority. In this case, the Act adopts the same solution set forth in Articles 1342 I of the Italian Civil Code of 1942 and Article 4 of the West German LSFC, i.e., it favours individual agreements over the general conditions of contract (Article 142 I). As a result, the general conditions are to be applied only if they are not contrary to the provisions contained in the individual agreements. Thus, the general conditions of contract assume the role of a supplement in cases where the parties have concluded individual agreements.

2.3. Invalidity of Individual Clauses

It is well known that the general conditions of contract were created, *inter alia,* in order to speed up the closing of business deals and, in addition, to standard-

5. It can be expected that the provisions of Usage No. 32 will continue to be applied in the practice since they provide solutions to specific questions which are not regulated by the Act and, at the same time, are not contrary to the regulations of the Act. According to Art. 1107 of the Act, usages are not to be applied to relations that are regulated by the Act itself: V. Kapor, Primena običaja i uzansi po Zakonu o obligacionim odnosima ("The Application of Customs and Usages in accordance with the Act of Obligations"), in *Anali Pravnog fakulteta u Beogradu,* No. 3-5/1978, pp. 342-345. In this sense, the Supreme Court of Croatia stated that insurance rules are binding on the insured only if they were actually supplied to him. If the insurance rules were not given to the insured (the party to the insurance contract), the restricted coverage set down in the rules cannot be applied. Legal opinion, Session 3/80 of 6 June 1980, published in *Pregled sudske prakse* No. 17/80, p. 67.

6. J. Vilus, Opšti uslovi kod formularnih ugovora ("General Conditions in Standard Contracts") in *Ugovorno i odštetno pravo po Zakonu o obligacionim odnosima,* published by Republički sekretarijat za pravosudje i opštu upravu, Belgrade 1979, p. 230.

7. Ibid., pp. 230-231.

ize the conditions and thus facilitate their being carried out. Along with these advantages, however, they also brought disadvantages, the most significant of which is the fact that they contain clauses which can enable the offeror (usually the seller or supplier) to limit its liability, to cancel contracts, to set terms that are difficult for the offeree to meet, etc.

In comparative legislation one can find varying approaches to this problem. On the one hand, these clauses can be enumerated in advance and declared invalid, as for example in Article 15 of the Israeli Law on Standard Contracts of 1964, Article 1341 I of the Italian Civil Code which contains *clausole onerose o vessatorie,* and Articles 8-11 of the German LSFC in which *unwirksame Klauseln* are listed.

On the other hand, the Act presents two general criteria in Article 143, according to which individual clauses contained in the general conditions of contract can by declared invalid: by reference to 1) the purpose of the contract and 2) good business practices. Article 143 reads as follows:

> 1) Provisions on general conditions which are contrary to the very purpose of a concluded contract or to good business practices are invalid even if the general conditions therein have been approved by the competent authorities.
> 2) The court can reject the application of individual provisions on general conditions which deprive the other party of the right to objection, or those on the grounds of which the party loses rights laid down in the contract or terms, or those which are otherwise unjust or overly stringent.

Immediately the question arises as to how the courts are to decide which provisions are contrary to the purpose of the contract. Judicial practice cannot yet provide us with the answer due to the short period of time that has elapsed since the Act has come into force. In theory it has been pointed out that this provision should be interpreted teleologically, i.e., one must attempt to understand the purpose of the contract in question, namely, the common goal of the contracting parties.[8] This also leads to problems as the Act contains no rules governing cases where such a common goal cannot be ascertained.[9]

The other criterion – using good business practices as a guideline for judging which terms of the contract can be declared invalid – also poses problems. Article 21 of the Act speaks about the application of good business practices; however, the term itself is not defined. In Yugoslav theory, good business practices are regarded as certain social norms which are not legally sanctioned but nevertheless are present in the general consciousness of society.[10] As a rule, these practices are

8. Ibid., p. 234.

9. Professor Goldštajn emphasizes that it is necessary to define "standard form contracts" as a good business man would: op.cit., *supra* n. 3. In connection with this, one should keep Art. 99 of the Act in mind which reads as follows: "1) Contract provisions are to be applied in the way specified therein; 2) When interpreting disputed provisions, one should not adhere to the literal meaning of the words but should examine the common goal of the parties and interpret the provisions in accordance with the principles of the law of obligations set forth in this Act."

10. S. Perović, Obligaciono pravo I *(The Law of Obligations I),* Belgrade 1973, p. 98.

not codified; if codified, they are then referred to as usages.[11] In the past, Yugoslav courts have often applied the principles of good business practices when deciding whether clauses in standard forms that exclude or limit the liability of a party should be declared invalid. In such cases they have maintained that a violation of good business practices is at the same time a violation of the existing legal system.[12]

The provisions of the Act apply to the general conditions used not only in commercial transactions but also in merchant-consumer relations.[13] Since a much stronger control should be provided in favour of persons dealing as consumers, it can be expected that this will lead to different interpretations of the provisions cited above.[14] Such a practice is not uncommon. In England, for example, the courts make a distinction between consumer and non-consumer sales when interpreting provisions for controls over standard forms of contract. "If the buyer does not deal as a consumer (in England), liability for the seller's basic obligations as to description, quality etc. can be excluded or restricted by reference to a contract term, but only in so far as the term satisfies the requirement of reasonableness."[15]

2.4. The Principle in dubio contra proferentem

Assuming that the offeree has less bargaining power than the offeror, Yugoslav legislation protects the offeree by requiring that the courts interpret unclear provisions in his favour. Article 100 of the Act states:

In a case in which a contract has been entered into under conditions printed in advance or the contract has been prepared in another manner and proposed by one of the contracting parties, unclear provisions of the said contract are to be interpreted in favour of the other party.

In addition, the courts are required to interpret provisions and make decisions in accordance with the basic principles for obligatory relations set forth in the Act, e.g., the principle of equality in Article 11, the principle of good faith in Article 12, etc., which also apply to contractual relations involving general conditions and standard forms.

In this context it should be mentioned that Article 144 of the Act provides additional protection for consumers. This protection is also regulated in Article 143 of the Federal Constitution and Article 23 of the Associated Labour Act. Accord-

11. B. Vizner, Komentar Zakona o obveznim odnosima *(Commentary on the Act of Obligations)*, Vol. I, Zagreb 1978, p. 103. A list of the codified usages is given. See, P. Šarčević on the question whether custom can become part of positive law: "The Notion of Positive Law" in *Yugoslav Reports for the Tenth International Congress of Comparative Law* (Budapest), Belgrade 1978, pp. 9-11.

12. For example, the unpublished judgment of the Rijeka County Commercial Court P-630/77 - 13 of 8 March 1978. See also J. Vilus, *supra* n. 3, pp. 235-236.

13. See A. Goldštajn, Prolegomena Zakonu o obveznim odnosima ("Prolegomenon to the Act of Obligations"), in *Obvezno pravo*, ed. A. Goldštajn, Vol. I, Zagreb 1978, p. 7.

14. J. Vilus, op. cit., *supra* n. 3, p. 229.

15. G. Borrie, "Legislative and Administrative Controls over Standard Forms of Contract in England", Journal of Business Law, 1978, p. 318.

ing to Article 23 of this latter Act, organisations of associated labour which produce or sell goods or perform services for direct consumption must co-operate and enter into agreements with all interested parties through their associations and self-managing communities of interest.[16] If they have once adopted the general conditions of a particular contract, according to Article 144 these conditions automatically become a part of all individual contracts relating to these deliveries or services.

2.5. The Question of Judicial Review

Generally speaking, the control provided by the courts is repressive.[17] Thus, if a court took a stand against a particular general condition, it would be declared invalid; however, this process would probably take a long time. As a result, the question has emerged in Yugoslav doctrine as to whether the general conditions could also be subjected to the control of the constitutional courts.[18] The reasoning behind this judicial review was based on the fact that the control of the constitutional courts is preventive and at the same time binding *erga omnes.*[19] After considering the matter, however, the constitutional courts have ruled that they have no jurisdiction over this subject-matter. They reasoned that general conditions and standard forms cannot be regarded as a part of the general acts of a basic organisation of associated labour, neither from the viewpoint of material law nor from that of status regulations.[20]

3. STANDARD FORMS AND GENERAL CONDITIONS IN INTERNATIONAL COMMERCIAL TRANSACTIONS

This part of our report deals with conflict of laws problems arising from interna-

16. Art. 23 III of the Associated Labour Act reads as follows: "Organs of management in organizations of associated labour in the sphere of production and/or sale of goods and services for direct consumption shall be bound, in conformity with law, at the request of consumers' organizations to conclude self-management agreements regulating their mutual relations, rights and obligations regarding regular and adequate supply of specific products, proper performances of services, determination of prices of products and services and consumers' sharing in income realized, due account being taken of the development of these activities, consumer needs, the provision of necessary reserves and of other questions of common concern", *The Associated Labour Act,* edition of the Secretariat of Information of the SFR of Yugoslavia Assembly, translated by M. Pavičić, Belgrade 1977, pp. 57-58.

17. According to official comments, Para. 2-302 of the US Uniform Commercial Code has a similar purpose: "This section is intended to make it possible for the court to police explicitly against contracts or clauses which they find to be unconscionable. In the past such policing has been accomplished by adverse construction of language, by manipulation of the rules of offer and acceptance or by determination that the clause is contrary to public policy or to the purpose of the contract." Uniform Commercial Code, official text, West Publishing Co., 1978, p. 62.

18. See, A. Goldštajn, Opći uvjeti poslovanja ("General Conditions of Business), in *Opći uvjeti poslovanja* II, ed. A. Goldštajn, Zagreb 1970, pp. 13-14.

19. Ibid., p. 13.

20. Ibid., p. 14.

tional commercial contracts in which the general conditions are either referred to or have become an integral part of the contract itself. We shall restrict our discussion to the following choice of law questions: which law is to be applied in determining how and when the general conditions become part of an international contract? Which law is to be applied in ascertaining whether the general conditions are an integral part of the contract if they have been sent together with the offer to the other party in a language that this party does not command or in a language other than that of the contract? We shall also consider the question of the silent party, i.e., does a party's silence mean that it accepts the general conditions and what law governs this particular question? Finally, the question arises as to what law governs the criteria for judging which individual clauses appearing in the text of general conditions and standard forms can be declared invalid. Other questions such as how to establish the choice of the proper law in the general conditions themselves, etc., cannot be included in the scope of this paper.

3.1. Brief Description of the Sources of the Yugoslav Conflict of Laws Rules Applying to Commercial Contracts

Between World Wars I and II there was no unified law of obligations and corresponding conflict of laws rules for the territory of Yugoslavia. Instead, the following laws and in one case customary law were applied depending on the legal region in question: the Austrian Civil Code of 1811,[21] the Serbian Civil Code of 1844, the General Code of Property of 1888 for Montenegro and the Hungarian customary law for one section of Croatia (Medjimurje) and Vojvodina.

Today, rules governing the determination of the proper law of a contract have still not been regulated in entirety in the present Yugoslav legislation. Thus, in accordance with Article 4 of the Law on Invalidity of Legal Provisions Enacted Before 6 April 1941 and During the Enemy Occupation,[22] it would be possible to apply the conflict of laws rules contained in the earlier legislations mentioned above if the relations in question are not regulated by existing legislation and the rules to be applied are not contrary to the Constitution and other laws presently in force. On the other hand, since these rules are out-dated, in theory [23] it is emphasized that these conflict of laws rules should not be applied in cases in-

21. The Austrian Civil Code of 1811 was effective in Croatia and Slavonia. In Slovenia and Dalmatia it was in force with changes enacted in 1914, 1915 and 1916.

22. The Official Gazette of the Federal People's Republic of Yugoslavia No. 86/1946 – final text of 23 October 1946. According to Art. 4 II of the said law, individual legal relations contained in former legislation can be applied if the relations to be settled are not regulated by existing legislation and if such legal regulations are not contrary to the Constitution and other existing laws enacted by the competent authorities of the new State. Decisions and other acts, however, cannot be based directly on these legal regulations.

23. N. Katičić, Odredjivanje mjerodavnog zakona za trgovačke kupoprodajne ugovore u pravu SFR Jugoslavije ("Yugoslav Choice of Laws Rules Applicable to Commercial Sales Contracts") in *Ogledi o medjunarodnom privatnom pravu,* Zagreb 1971, pp. 217-218, 230. Ž. Matić, Obveznopravni odnosi s medjunarodnim, medjurepubličkim i medjupokrajinskim obilježjem ("Obligations with International and/or Interlocal Element"), in Obvezno pravo I *(The Law of Obligations I)*, ed. A. Goldštajn, Zagreb 1979, 2nd ed., pp. 353-354, 361. K. Sajko, Odredjivanje mjerodavnog prava za ugovore o privrednoj suradnji s inozemnim partnerima ("Determining the

volving contractual relations as they are no longer adequate for the needs of contemporary commercial trade.[24]

As a result, one must turn to special laws such as the Law on Sea and Inland Navigation [25] and the Law on Obligatory and Business Relations in Air Navigation [26] which contain rules for determining the proper law of a contract in these respective fields. Consequently, the view prevails in Yugoslav doctrine that these conflict of laws rules should be extended by analogy to other contractual relations.[27] In addition, the Draft Law on Private International Law and Procedure of 1974 [28] can also be used as a guideline for determining the proper law of a contract. It is assumed, namely, that the future Law on Private International Law and Procedure will adopt basically the same solutions set forth in the Draft Law.[29]

In the scope of this paper we cannot enumerate the bilateral agreements between Yugoslavia and other countries that contain provisions relevant to obligatory relations. It should, however, be mentioned that the Yugoslav Economic Council has reached agreements with representatives of the East German (1969), the Polish (1971) and the Soviet (1977) Economic Councils on the general conditions of contracts involving the delivery of goods. Nevertheless, the contracting parties must expressly agree to the use of these conditions by signing a written agreement or by referring to them in the contract. Otherwise, they will not be considered an integral part of the contract.[30] These general conditions contain, *inter alia,* the agreement that the proper law for all questions not expressly regulated by the said conditions is to be the national law of the seller.

As for multilateral agreements, Yugoslavia is not a Party to the Hague Conventions on the International Sale of Goods and the New York Convention on the Enforcement of Foreign Arbitration Awards of 1958. On the other hand, it has ratified the European Convention of 1961 on International Trade Arbitration [31] and the Washington Convention on the Settlement of Investment Disputes between States and Citizens of other Countries of 1965.[32]

3.2. The Incorporation of General Conditions into International Contracts

The rules of the Act governing the incorporation of general conditions into contracts are to be applied to international contracts only if the proper law of

---

Proper Law for Contracts on Commercial Cooperation with Foreign Partners"), in Zaključivanje ugovora s inostranim partnerom *(Concluding Contracts with Foreign Partners),* ed. T. Varadi, Novi Sad 1979, pp. 390-391.

24. Ž. Matić, op.cit., p. 353.
25. Official Gazette of the SFR of Yugoslavia No. 22/1977.
26. Ibid.,
27. See, Ž. Matić, op.cit., p. 362.
28. Published in Prinosi, No. 7, Zagreb 1974, p. 81.
29. Ž. Matić, op. cit. p. 362.
30. For example, in decision No. T-149/74-79 of 3 November 1977, in which the Foreign Trade Arbitration applied the general conditions JUGPOL 1971.
31. Supplement to the Official Gazette of the SFR of Yugoslavia No. 7/1967.
32. Supplement to the Official Gazette of the SFR of Yugoslavia No. 12/1963.

the contract is Yugoslav law.[33] According to the conflict rules on contractual relations, the primary connecting factor for the choice of law in contractual relations is party autonomy. The will of the parties is to be respected if it is explicitly expressed or if it can be deduced from the behaviour of the parties that they had had the application of a specific law in mind (tacit choice of law).[34]

In the absence of a choice of law, the subsidiary law of the contract will be the law of the country with which it is most closely connected. If relevant circumstances do not point to another law, according to the proposed Draft Law the proper law is to be the law of the place of the seller's domicile or seat at the time the offer was accepted; if the offer was accepted at the place where the buyer has his domicile or seat, then the law of this place.[35]

If one aspect of a contract is governed by the law of a particular country, this does not necessarily mean that this law is to be the proper law of the entire contract.[36] Thus, the particular questions raised in the instant proceedings must be dealt with individually.

According to Yugoslav theory, the question as to whether the acceptance of a particular contract implies at the same time agreement to the general conditions therein is governed by the proper law of the contract.[37] It should be pointed out that this applies to situations where the contract has been entered into either by express or tacit acceptance. As far as our knowledge of Yugoslav court decisions is concerned, the courts have held that the general conditions are part of a given contract without separately treating the question of the incorporation of the general conditions into the contract.

Although the following example is not the most appropriate, it nevertheless illustrates problems related to the incorporation of general conditions into international contracts. In this particular dispute involving a Czechoslovak plaintiff and a Yugoslav defendant, the court had to decide whether the general conditions referred to in the contract were valid. Namely, one of the contract clauses stated that the remaining conditions of contract were set forth in a document entitled "The General Conditions of Sales and Payment." The controversy arose over the question as to which "General Conditions of Sales and Payment" had been referred to in the said clause. While the plaintiff claimed that the general conditions in question were his own, which he, however, had neglected to send to the defendant, the latter maintained that the conditions referred to in the contract were "The

33. According to Art. 31 of the Act, a contract is concluded the moment the offeror receives the statement of the offeree that his offer has been accepted. The contract is considered to have been concluded at the place where the offeror has his seat, i.e., domicile, at the moment he made the offer. See also, *supra*, section 2.1., on the rules on the incorporation of general conditions into contracts. See J. Vilus, op.cit., *supra* n. 3., p. 225.

34. Z. Matić, op.cit., p. 373; K. Sajko, op.cit., pp. 392-396.

35. Art. 20 of the Draft Law. According to Jezdić and Pak, this conflict of laws rule should not be applied if the seller and buyer have the same nationality or are citizens of the same country. In such a case the *lex nacionalis* or the *lex patriae* should be applied: Jezdić-Pak, Medjunarodno privatno pravo III *(Private International Law* III), Belgrade 1973, p. 133.

36. North, in Cheshire's *Private International Law,* London 1974, pp. 201-202.

37. B. Eisner, Medjunarodno privatno pravo I *(Private International Law* I), Zagreb 1953, p. 221.

General Conditions for the Delivery of Goods" laid down by the Council for Mutual Economic Assistance.

The court rejected the arguments of both the plaintiff and defendant, thus ruling out the validity of both sets of general conditions. Since both parties were professional dealers in foreign trade transactions, the court ruled that they were obliged to express themselves in precise terminology. Furthermore, it stated that the parties to a contract are obliged to indicate exactly which general conditions are being referred to in a contract.[38]

3.3. Language Risk

The question arises as to whether general conditions which have been sent to the other party in a language that this party does not command or in a language other than that of the negotiations, can be considered part of the contract.[39] In German judicial practice [40] and doctrine,[41] the view has emerged that in such cases the general conditions cannot be regarded as an integral part of the contract. In order to be incorporated into the contract, they must be sent to the other party in the same language used during the negotiations or in his native language. If the party proposing the general conditions fails to comply with this rule, he is liable for the consequences. The same applies to contractual relations between merchants in Germany, and similar tendencies can be detected in American judicial practice in cases involving adhesion contracts concluded by parties with unequal bargaining power.[42]

Since Yugoslav courts have seldom had to judge cases involving this problem, we are forced to cite a court decision of the Supreme Commercial Court of Croatia which does not involve general conditions but nevertheless illustrates the problem of language risk. Contrary to the view upheld by the German courts, the Supreme Court of Croatia maintained that parties which sign contracts without having first read all the documents and/or without having any unclear statements interpreted, do so at their own risk, regardless of the language in which the documents are written. Consequently, the Yugoslav court rejected the plain-

38. Unpublished judgment of the Subotica County Commercial Court P - 333/74 of 5 December 1974.

39. See, E. Jayme's detailed article on language risk, "Sprachrisiko und Internationales Privatrecht beim Bankverkehr mit ausländischen Kunden", in *Recht und Wirtschaft in Geschichte und Gegenwart,* Festschrift für Johannes Bärmann, Munich 1975, pp. 509-522.

40. For example, decision No. 16 U 68/73 of 2 November 1979 of the Oberlandesgericht Düsseldorf, published in *Aussenwirtschaftsdienst des Betriebs-Beraters* No. 2/1974, pp. 103-104.

41. U. Drobnig, "Allgemeine Geschäftsbedingungen im internationalen Handelsverkehr", in *Internationales Recht und Wirtschaftsordnung,* Festschrift für F.A. Mann, Munich 1977, p. 606. E. Jayme, "Allgemeine Geschäftsbedingungen und Internationales Privatrecht", in ZHR No. 142/1978, pp. 121-122.

42. See, A.J. Ehrenzweig-E. Jayme, *Private International Law,* Vol. III Special Part, Leyden 1977, pp. 22, 45-48.

tiff's objection that the disputed settlement he had signed was written in a language other than that of the former negotiations.[43]

The court did not rule on the conflict of laws problems in this case. According to Yugoslav theory, the proper law of the contract governs these questions.[44] In such cases where Yugoslav law is the proper law of the contract, it is necessary to consult the provisions of the Act relating to offer and acceptance, the effect of an alleged mistake, the conclusion of the contract, etc.

3.4. Tacit Incorporation of General Conditions into Contracts

According to the substantive rules mentioned above,[45] the general conditions can become part of a contract by either the tacit or express agreement of the parties. This brings us to the question of which law is to govern the tacit acceptance of general conditions.

In Yugoslav theory, Eisner [46] has emphasized that silence should be governed by the proper law of the contract. In Germany, on the other hand, there is a strong tendency towards posing the question as to whether the silence of a foreign buyer can be interpreted as his tacit acceptance of the given general conditions to be governed by the law of the *lex domicili* of the buyer, not by the proper law of the contract. As has been pointed out, silence is not equated with acceptance in all countries.[47] In fact, it can mean the very opposite. Therefore, it is reasoned that it would be unjust to demand that the act or, in this case, a non-act, of a party be interpreted differently than it would be in its own country. Thus, it follows that in cases where the buyer has remained silent, the tacit incorporation of the general conditions into the contract should be governed by the law of its business residence.[48]

43. The plaintiff, a Yugoslav citizen who was the captain of a ship belonging to a foreign shipowner, was injured while working on board. After expiration of his sick leave he signed a settlement written in Italian. The court rejected his argument that his contract of embarkment was in English and that English was the language that by tacit agreement was to be used by the parties. The fact that the plaintiff had signed his employment contract with the defendant in English and that both parties used English when conversing with one another had no effect on the plaintiff's signing the disputed settlement and the fact that he was obliged to read the document carefully before signing it. No. III-S1-1879/75-2 of 15 October 1975, published in Inozemno i medjunarodno privatno pravo *(Foreign and Private International Law)*, ed. A. Goldštajn, prepared by Barbić, No. 6 in Informator No. 2337 of 26 June 1976, pp. 10-11.

44. B. Eisner, op.cit., p. 221; see also D. Mitrović, Ugovor o prodaji s inozemnim elementom ("The Sales Contract with Foreign Element"), in Enciklopedija imovinskog prava i prava udruženog rada, *(Encyclopedia of Property Law and Law of Associated Labour)*, Vol. II, Belgrade 1978, p. 73.

45. See, *supra*, section 2.1.

46. B. Eisner, op.cit., p. 22.

47. See C.T. Ebenroth, "Das kaufmännische Bestätigungsschreiben im internationalen Handelsverkehr", *Zeitschrift für Vergleichende Rechtswissenschaft* 3/1978, p. 161.

48. U. Drobnig, "Standard Form Contracts in International Commercial Transactions", NILR, 1979, p. 189. See arguments against such an approach by H. Limke, "Sonderanknüpfung der Willenserklärung? ", *Zeitschrift für Vergleichende Rechtswissenschaft* 1980 p. 1 – specially pp. 23-26.

As for Yugoslav judicial practice, it is too early to predict if this view will be adopted, although, in our opinion, it is certainly justified.

3.5. Invalidity of Individual Clauses

It has already been pointed out that general conditions and standard forms sometimes contain clauses which are unfair to the other party.[49] If a particular clause, having been challenged by this party, is declared by the court to be invalid, this has no effect on the validity of the contract as a whole. This practice, however, could lead to the appearance of gaps. Regarding international transactions, we are of the opinion that such gaps should be filled with the rules contained in the proper law of the contract. If, on the other hand, the majority of clauses of the general conditions of a particular contract were to be declared invalid, no supplementary rules whatsoever should be taken into consideration.[50]

As to the question of how the individual clauses in foreign general conditions and standard forms are to be controlled, according to Eisner the control of clauses limiting or excluding liability is governed by the proper law of the contract.[51] Exceptions occur in cases where the imperative provisions of a national law that is otherwise not the proper law of the contract must be applied.[52]

Furthermore, the proper law of the contract should be applied when determining which acts are contrary to the purpose of particular contracts or to good business practices. It should, however, be added that the place where a contract is to be fulfilled can also be important in certain cases. If specific acts designated in the contract are prohibited at the place of fulfilment, these acts should be judged in accordance with the *lex loci solutionis.*[53]

In Yugoslav theory, the view was previously accepted that this question should be governed only by the proper law of the contract. On the contrary, it seems to be more justifiable that in such cases the *lex loci solutionis* should be taken into consideration as well.

49. In Decision No. Sl 969/58 of 16 December 1958, the Supreme Commercial Court ruled that the invalidity of a particular clause referring to a monopoly did not effect the validity of the contract as a whole. Published in Zbirka sudskih odluka *(Collection of Court Decisions),* Vol. III - 3, Decision 578. See also Decision 81 2767/70 in Sudska praksa privrednih sudova u sporovima organizacija udruženog rada *(Judicial Practice of the Commercial Courts in Cases involving Organisations of Associated Labour),* prepared by B. Kašanin and D. Veljković, Belgrade 1975, pp. 293-294; see also D. Martiny, in, Reihmann, *Internationales Vertragsrecht,* Cologne, 1972, p. 75.

50. For example, Decisions Nos. Sl 369/72 and 382/73 of the Supreme Commercial Court, published in: Sudska praksa . . ., op.cit., pp. 197-199. In the same sense: Decision No. VIII ZR 151/66 of 11 November 1968 of the German BGH, published in *Entscheidungen des BGH,* Vol. 51, Cologne-Berlin 1969, pp. 55-60.

51. B. Eisner, op.cit., p. 222. D. Mitrović, Klauzule neodgovornosti u trgovačkoj kupoprodaji sa stranim elementom *(Clauses Excluding Liability in Commercial Sales with Foreign Element),* Belgrade 1966, p. 133.

52. D. Mitrović, op.cit., pp. 133-139.

53. D. Martiny, op.cit., p. 75.

4. CONCLUSION

The use of general conditions and standard forms in international commercial transactions is continually gaining in importance. In view of the perils to which the contracting parties are subjected through their use of general conditions and standard forms, new solutions must be found to protect the "freedom to contract" from becoming a "freedom to adhere".[54] The differences in the substantive rules on the international level will surely not be eliminated in the near future. Therefore, it is all the more important to intensify our search for adequate conflict of law rules.

54. A. Ehrenzweig, "Adhesion Contracts in the Conflict of Laws", ColLR, 1953, p. 1090.

STANDARD FORMS AND GENERAL CONDITIONS: DISCUSSIONS

The Chair was taken by Professor Vilipović, who proposed that the ensuing discussions might usefully follow the thrust of the papers that had been presented and concentrate more on general conditions than on standard forms. In this light it would be necessary to pay particular attention to incorporation of general conditions into the contract with reference to uniform substantive law and to national conflict of laws, and then to consider the question of the validity or invalidity of individual terms, both of general conditions and of standard forms. He then invited Professors Drobnig and Sarčević to introduce their papers.

1. INTRODUCTION

Professor Drobnig prefaced his remarks with the observation that he had attempted in his paper to take into account Dutch law pertaining to the subject-matter, and had not restricted himself exclusively to German law.

Adopting the approach proposed by the Chairman, Professor Drobnig agreed that the emphasis in practice appeared to be on incorporation rather than on validity, certainly on an international level where control over general conditions is almost exclusively exercised with respect to incorporation into the contract. When one adopts a comparative approach and turns to national substantive law, one sees that certain legal systems, such as the French and Italian, employ incorporation as a kind of control device. Other legal systems, however, concentrate on the validity of the contents of the contract, or alleged contents, as the principal means of control. When dealing with a problem of incorporation one could employ the method of turning first to uniform law to see if there are any provisions of ULFIS or the Vienna Convention that would be applicable to the transnational case. Neither of these is directly relevant in the sense that they contain provisions expressly dealing with incorporation. They do, however, specify rules relating to formation of the contract and these provisions oblige one to have recourse to the traditional mechanism of offer and acceptance. This allows for the possibility of finding for incorporation as a result of the establishment of a practice of the parties where the facts would support such a conclusion. An alternative, which is not free of doubt, is where the author of the general conditions makes reference to them but the other party does not respond or react to that reference. Personally, he considered it be doubtful whether such could be sufficient to support incorporation into the contract.

If uniform law is not applicable in the concrete case, one must turn to the conflict of laws, in the first place to national law and ultimately to the Rome Convention on Contractual Obligations 1980. National caselaw, which is not over-abundant, reveals a strong tendency to resort also to the traditional problem of establishing *consensus ad idem* and identifying acceptance of the offer, and its contents. Thus, incorporation of general conditions is seen as a question of formation, which is governed by the *lex contractus,* the proper law of the contract. In the case of non-reaction or silence, the German courts have recently turned to a new solution, that of referring to the place of the offeree to whom the conditions have been offered and who keeps silent. Silence can, of course, mean different things under different legal systems. Under German law it generally has a positive connotation amounting to an affirmative reaction whereas in many if not most other legal systems silence connotes a negative response. In order to reconcile this difference the German courts have chosen to refer to the law of the offeree, with consequent disadvantage to the incorporation of German general conditions. When one turns to validity, one finds that there is no international regulation. The Hague and Vienna Conventions excluded validity of terms from their ambits with the consequence that one falls back on national conflict of laws, where there is unanimity that this issue falls for determination by reference to the *lex contractus.*

Professor Sarčević explained that according to Yugoslav law it is necessary in order for general conditions to be incorporated into the contract that the parties reach agreement to this end. This entails that the accepting party must know, or should have known, of the general conditions at the time the contract was concluded. A particular concern that has arisen in the last twenty years or more has been the task of protecting the party with less bargaining power. To this end assistance has been found, e.g., in reliance on the *contra proferentum* rule. The Obligations Act now declares invalid clauses that are contrary to the purpose of the contract and contrary to good business practices. It is the task, consequently, of the courts to apply these principles to particular cases, a task which is to be accomplished, at least according to current doctrine, by resort to the teleological method of interpretation.

This question of invalid clauses raises, however, the problem of gaps in the contract and the issue of filling them. This leads to the problem of what is the situation where a large number of clauses are declared to be invalid. In the absence of a choice of law by the parties the contract will be governed by the law of the country with which it is most closely connected. Where relevant circumstances do not indicate another country the governing law will be that of the place of the seller's domicile or place of business at the time the offer was accepted. According to Yugoslav theory, the question whether acceptance of the contract implies also agreement to general conditions is governed by the proper law of the contract, a viewpoint that has so far not been the subject of separate adjudication by the courts. The proper law similarly governs the question of what acts are contrary to the purpose of the contract or to good business practices. This governing law is, however, subject in some cases to the application of imperative provisions.

A related problem to the subject under discussion is that of language risk *(sprachrisiko),* which occurs when general conditions are in a language that the allegedly agreeing contract partner does not command, or which is not the language of negotiation. It appears that Yugoslav courts have seldom been confronted with this matter. There remains also the issue of silence of the offeree in regard to general conditions.

2. INCORPORATION

It was agreed that the issue of actual incorporation could raise particularly difficult problems, not merely theoretical, that is, how should particular matters be characterised in order that issues of fact could be resolved, but also in severely practical terms. This was clearly so in the case of a battle of forms, where each party submitted his own general conditions to the other, which conditions were in conflict with those of the other party, and then claimed that his own had been incorporated to the exclusion of the other's. Even if this were to be treated as an issue of formation of the contract and approached on the basis of offer and acceptance, nevertheless very real practical difficulties of reconciling the factually irreconcilable remained, which the judge was nevertheless obliged to resolve. Nevertheless, such resolution, it was also agreed, had to be attained, possibly by making use of the *ex post facto* approach of determining the intention of the parties at the moment of formation in the light of their subsequent conduct and performance of the contract. The situation to be avoided was that of declaring the parties not to have been *ad idem,* more particularly where there had been performance or partial performance of the contract. Other cases could be approached in a not dissimilar way. Thus use could be made of taking the practice of the parties into account and not necessarily restricting this to the practice between the parties to the contract. Thus, in one instance an arbitrator was faced with the situation that a Dutch seller of chemical substances had clearly referred to his general conditions but had not transmitted them to the German buyer, who regularly traded on the Dutch market. The arbitrator held that the previous experience of the buyer on the Dutch market had put him into the position where he should have made enquiry of the reference to the general conditions, for such must have been met previously. In this instance resort was had to the domestic concept of "stendig gebruikelijk beding", namely, a term customarily used in a particular trade or commercial activity and which is presumed to be known to others active in the same trade, in this case including also foreigners.

2.1 Usages

The above was seen as not inherently different to the approach adopted in many countries whereby if one contracts with a party known to be active in a particular field, which is also known to be a field in which activities are generally regulated, then one is taken to have contracted on the basis that such regulations will be applicable. This is the case with, for example, freight forwarders in England and Norway and is supported by caselaw to that effect. In West Germany this approach also holds time but there the distinction is drawn between freight forwarders, including non-Germans, in their mutual relations and others, including also merchants. The former are taken to be bound on the basis of prior or assumed knowledge, the latter not necessarily. On the other hand, even where the 'reasonable' rule of imputing usage was applicable this would not necessarily be determinative where the conditions are unusual. In such a case it is necessary that the other party's attention be drawn expressly to such clauses. This is supported by English case-law; for example, where a French importer of goods brought action against his Swiss insurer, it was held that a clause conferring jurisdiction exclusively on a small and obscure local court in Switzerland was unreasonable to the extent that the condition was only contained in the floating policy covering all shipments generally and not in the certificate of insurance.

2.2 Silence

A related problem is that which arises when one party refers, either directly by transmission or indirectly by reference, to its general conditions and the other party does not respond. Attention was drawn to a recent arbitral award rendered between an American seller and a Norwegian buyer where the arbitrator accepted that the modern trend in such cases is not to regard a person bound by an alleged agreement (the issue turned on the arbitration agreement) simply on the ground that he had not responded in writing to a confirmation sent by the other party unless the internal law of the domicile, place of residence or of business of that person accords that effect to silence. Attention was also drawn to the terms of Article 8 paragraph 2 Contractual Obligations Convention whereby a person is allowed to rely on the law of his habitual residence to rebut a finding of consent according to the law that would otherwise govern the existence and material validity of a contract term.

2.3 Language risk

It was pointed out that the issue of silence, at least factually, was also present in the context of another problem, that of *sprachrisiko,* or language risk. This would arise, for example, where the negotiations are conducted in a third language such as English or French, which might also be the language of the contract, and the seller's general conditions are sent or there is a reference to them in his native language, e.g., German, of which the buyer has no understanding. Should such general conditons be regarded as incorporated into the contract? Similarly, where a foreign worker with imperfect mastery of the language of the country where he now lives obtains a bank loan, is he bound by the bank's conditions where it is clear that he cannot understand them?

This problem was capable of being approached in different ways. One could regard it as a particular aspect of the incorporation of general conditions, in which connection it often arises, and adopt the view that where there are particular rules pertinent to incorporation, those rules would likewise govern this aspect of that general problem. Another approach is to say that it is but another aspect of the basic problem of formation and should be governed by the law applicable to formation, that is, the proper law of the contract. Of course, this latter approach would support the finding that a foreign worker, e.g., a Turk or Yugoslav resident in Germany would be bound by German banking conditions, even if he could not understand them, by application of the proper law of the contract, a situation that may rightly be regarded as harsh and even inequitable. On the other hand, in the case of international contracts, incorporation of 'incomprehensible' general conditions is likely to be defeated by a finding that the proper law of the contract is not the law of the country from which the conditions have originated, subject, of course, to any question of usages. Such an approach had been endorsed by the Dutch Supreme Court in a case involving an agency incorporated in Kuwait and a Dutch shipyard. The latter had transmitted the contract in English. Its letter heading contained a reference in Dutch to the applicability to the contract of its own general conditions, which were also in Dutch. The Supreme Court overruled the finding of the lower courts that such reference was sufficient for incorporation in the absence of objection and held that it was necessary in such a case to examine the particular facts and decide whether there had been real consensus as to formation. In practice it is not uncommon to find that companies that trade internationally also have their general conditions available in another language, often English as being a widely used international language. In international cases it may be thought sufficient that the general conditions are sent or at least referred to in such international language (even perhaps where the language of negotiation and contract is another language?). This is supportable by reference to a decision of the Norwegian Supreme Court of some twenty years ago. Two Norwegian technicians, having worked in Argentina for a number of years, returned to Norway and transhipped their belongings on board a Norwegian ship. The goods having been damaged they claimed damages from the Norwegian company, only to be met by an exemption clause referred to in English on their tickets. The court held that despite the preponderance of connecting factors with Norway, it was reasonable to expect persons of such an educational standing to understand English and the likely effect of such a clause.

On the basis of the discussion it was suggested that a fair and reasonable test of practical and general application would be that the party wishing to see incorporation of his own general conditions must ensure that they, or at least any reference to them, be in a language which renders them, or their existance communicable to the other party. Naturally this would not *per se* solve the problem of the battle of forms where both parties satisfied the test.

3. VALIDITY

Reference was made to recent legislation of a number of countries whose effect is, either directly or indirectly, to limit the operation of general conditions. This is the case in West Germany, Norway, Sweden, the United Kingdom and Yugoslavia.

The emphasis on protecting the consumer has been very strong. Thus, the distinction drawn in West Germany between *Kaufmann – nich Kafleute* means that it is now almost impossible for, e.g., a Dutch company to export its products to Germany based on its own sales conditions where there is a close connection between the transaction and the German consumer, for the transaction will be caught by the legislation and the general conditions must give way to the protective legislation. In the United Kingdom similar protective legislation will oust general conditions unless the transaction qualifies as an international supply contract or, where it is not, the conditions satisfy the test of reasonableness. This latter approach has also been adopted in Norway and Sweden where it is provided in the legislation on contracts that conditions that lead to unreasonable results to one of the parties can be declared null and void. It was explained that this power to avoid is more extensive than the similar provision in the Yugoslav Obligations Act, which declares invalid clauses that are contrary to the purpose of the contract and contrary to good business practices (or, on another view of the provision, to good business usages). The Scandinavian provision contemplates not only extant clauses agreed upon at formation of the contract but also aims at alleviating unreasonable results arising later upon performance, It was noted that English caselaw had recently arrived at a similar result but then on the basis of the parties' original intention at the time of concluding the contract.

Attention was also drawn to the particular issue of state authorised conditions, which are particularly prominent in state-controlled enterprises, including those offering a public service. To what extent were such clauses subject to judicial scrutiny and control? It was generally agreed that this was a matter that fell to be answered in principle by reference to the proper law of the contract. Most countries did not preclude judicial review of such clauses so that the problem would not arise frequently. Where such review was preclude by legislation enacted in the country of the law that was applicable then in principle that law ought to be respected by a foreign court seized of the matter, although some doubt was expressed as to whether all foreign courts would feel constrained to hold themselves precluded from review, particularly where such restraint was not a feature of the *lex fori.* Apart from this latter qualification, it was also agreed that the proper law should govern such matters as requirements as to deposit or registration of general conditions with the court or other such instance at the place of business or establishment of the author of the conditions. Where such requirement is not a feature of the governing law but of another law, e.g., the seller's, then it ought not to be regarded as operative in the relations between the parties, subject to resort being had to Article 7 of the Contractual Obligations Convention.

The Chairman expressed his thanks to the reporters and closed the session.

SOLE DISTRIBUTOR

THE SOLE DISTRIBUTOR IN THE COMMON LAW

by J.L. Yelland

1. INTRODUCTION

1.1. Purposes of Sole Distributorship Contracts

On the assumption that at least a large measure of freedom surrounds the negotiation of a sole distributorship contract, the parties' motives for making it may be various. The prospective advantages may be magnified or eroded by the particular terms which are finally agreed, but one may guess that most such contracts are influenced by at least some of the following considerations.[1]

The distributor desires a steady and assured supply of goods, and at prices which, if unlikely nowadays to be static, at least relieve him of much of the otherwise constant need to assess (or speculate upon) market price trends. A small distributor acting for a large manufacturer may be able to specialise in particular product lines in a way which would be impossible if all supplies had to be obtained on a completely open market. The distributor gains the major advantage of a monopoly in sales of the goods within the distributorship territory. This not only helps to stabilize his supplies and prices, but may often enable him to develop his own business in circumstances which the buffeting of competition from larger rivals might otherwise prevent. He will hope to gain expertise and know-how valuable even when the distributorship may have gone. He may sometimes hope for discounts on the manufacturer's prices, and even, in some cases, for direct financial assistance in expansion.

The advantages to the manufacturer are in large measure complementary. He is to be given a more or less assured market at assured prices. Whether or not he has to provide early technical or financial aid, he will expect the market to be developed for him by the distributor without what might well be a very large initial commitment of manpower and resources involved in procuring that market by his own efforts. He may also be able to guarantee an after-sales service for his products which, again, might not have been possible if he stood alone.

Not all these advantages can be entirely mutual, and some will be gained or lost in negotiations for the contract. A weak manufacturer, for example, may have to pay heavily for a distributor's energies in the form of large discounts or commissions.

More cynical motives may also be present. The first (and obvious) is the stifling of competition and the achievement of a monopoly, whether in new or established products. The law may have something to say about this. The second, about which the law can do little, is sheer inertia. A manufacturer may be too cautious, or too feeble, to develop new markets for himself. Exclusive dealing agreements might provide a comfortable cushion and further discourage any competitive drive in the manufacturer.

1. See, Stockhausen, (1948) 23 NYULR 412; Neale and Goyder, *The Antitrust Laws of the USA*, 3rd ed., at pp. 148-149, 151-152, 286-287.

It will be noticed that the bulk of English material concerns import/export agreements, usually with a foreign manufacturer selling into the United Kingdom via an English agent. Where an inter-state agreement is involved, other considerations may influence the manufacturer. He may be faced with a market of which he knows little, and which he is prepared to enter only with the benefit of local knowledge and assistance. Even when he knows the market, however, and may be considering the creation of a local branch or subsidiary, the financial and fiscal implications may deter him.

1.2. Range and scope of agreements

The common law moved remarkably smoothly from a set of procedural and remedial rules to a generalised law of contract. There is almost no trace in recent English legal history of a stage at which there existed a "Law of contracts". Even an undoubtedly specialised agreement like the sale of goods, which has many particular rules of its own, is the product as much of the general merchant law and the law of property as of any special law of contract. The generalisation of the law is reflected in the traditional view of the English judiciary that their task is to enforce agreements and not to make them or remould them for the parties. One of the clear results is that relationships commonly collected under the broad heads of "commercial agency" or "sole distributorship" contracts are entirely matters of contract law. Unlike some systems, English law knows no "commercial representative", and has no special rules to govern such agreements. They are a matter of contract, not of status.[2]

Because of the concentration on agreement rather than on status, the label which parties may choose to attach to their contract will be just that – a label, being no more than a preliminary indication of what may be expected to be the contents of the contract, and, perhaps, a guide to the interpretation of those terms whose meaning may be left in doubt. So, indeed, we find the same words (in particular, "agency") being used by parties to describe legally quite distinct contracts, and different words being used to describe identical agreements. Only occasionally do the judges protest at the abuse of the language, since it is a matter of little importance.

2. Significantly, there is only one major English textbook dealing specifically with distributorship contracts as part of trade law: see Schmitthoff, *The Export Trade,* 7th ed., (1980), Ch. 14, 15; see also Heydon, *Restraint of Trade,* Ch. 9. The practical aspects of such contracts are, however, not ignored. Standard forms of sole agency and distributorship agreements can be found in the Encyclopaedia of Forms and Precedents, 4th ed., Vol. I. Some trade associations publish booklets or draft agreements, e.g., British Agents' Register publishes a master agreement for selling agents and at a different level, the International Chamber of Commerce publishes a guide to transnational contracts. The contracts which caused litigation in the cases discussed below were, in contrast, *ad hoc* and in some instances rather crude. British lawyers have shown an interest in the implications of agency and distribution contracts under foreign laws; see, e.g., Thompson, ed., *Commercial Agency and Distribution Agreements in Europe* (British Institute of International and Comparative Law, 1964).

The subject of the paper is "sole" agency or distributorship contracts. In certain older cases the word "sole" is used to describe agents having the exclusive right to deal in the manufacturer's goods, but having at the same time power to deal in competing goods.[3] More recent cases show the expression "sole" agent, etc., being used to describe the classic contract where there is a double bar on competition: as far as the agreed territory extends, the manufacturer must sell only to the "agent", and the latter must not deal in competing goods.[4] It is in this narrower sense that "sole" agreements will be discussed here.

The next question will be the precise nature of the agreement. Again, the parties' description of the contract may be at variance with correct legal analysis. In *W.T. Lamb & Sons* v. *Gosling Birch Co. Ltd.*[5], for example, the Court of Appeal noted with an air of weary resignation that the "sole selling agent" in that case was in fact a purchaser with exclusive rights of resale. Although there are many possible variations, there seem to be four principal arrangements for exclusive dealing contracts:

(i) the appointment of an "agent" whose authority is limited to the transmission of orders from potential customers to the manufacturer.[6];

(ii) the appointment of an agent with full power (or at least, a considerable measure of power) to make binding contracts between the manufacturer and customers [7];

(iii) "hybrid" contracts, involving the appointment of an "agent" to sell goods on the manufacturer's behalf, the "agent" being treated as agent (and not buyer of goods) as between himself and the manufacturer, but selling as principal as far as third parties are concerned [8];

(iv) the appointment of an "agent" who buys goods from the manufacturer for resale.[9]

The first three are, of course, the "agency" contracts, although only (ii) unequivocally exhibits that aspect of authority to act and to bind a principal which is normally regarded as the hallmark of agency. (iv) is the distributorship agreement. The commercial purposes of the agreements are very similar, but the legal distinction between the agent, introducing or binding the manufacturer and customer to a single sale, and the distributor, acting usually as an independent merchant buying

3. Saccharin Corpn. Ltd. *v.* Chemische Fabrik von Heyden [1911] 2 K.B. 516; Okura & Co. Ltd. *v.* Forsbacka Jernverks Actiebolag [1914] 1 KB 715; W.T. Lamb & Sons *v.* Goring Brick Co. Ltd. [1932] 1 KB 710.

4. See, e.g., Martin-Baker Aircraft Co. Ltd. *v.* C.F.L.E. Ltd. [1944] 2 QB 556 (agency); Evans Marshall & Co., Ltd. *v.* Bertola SA [1973] 1 WLR 349 (distributorship described as agency).

5. [1932] 1 KB 710.

6. See, *Okura, supra;* n. 3. Here the agent was allowed to compete.

7. See, *Saccharin Corpn., supra* n. 3. Again the agent was allowed to compete.

8. Such contracts are not unknown to English law (see, *Bowstead on Agency,* p. 6 and cases cited) but are commonly made with buying rather than selling agents. See also, *Romalpa, infra,* section 2.1.3.

9. The possibility of sale or return contracts is considered in section 2.1. *infra.*

and then reselling, is a clear one.[10] Although, as observed, these agreements occupy no special legal position of their own, it may nevertheless be of some help to see how the English courts have regarded them before turning to particular aspects of the relationships.

In the case of agencies the nearest analogous contract, at first sight, is the contract of employment. This analogy will be most impressive where the agent is an individual; but it can of course be pressed whenever the manufacturer directs operations, sends out publicity material and supervises the agent's promotions, vets sales, controls credit lines, etc. In *Martin Baker Aircraft Company Ltd.* v. *Canadian Flight Equipment Ltd.* [11] McNair, J. was prepared to accept the comparison. But it is submitted that this can be done only in exceptional cases, of which *Martin-Baker* was clearly one. The plaintiffs had been anxious to get their product off the ground in North America. The defendant company was therefore created to manufacture the goods under licence. The second defendant, Murison, was a director of the defendant company. Having been an employee of the plaintiffs for many years, he had been sent to Canada specifically to market the goods. It was because performance of the licence agreement was not proving satisfactory to the plaintiffs that Murison was personally appointed as the plaintiff's sole agent for North America. He was also, it seems, obliged to pay the commission which he might earn into the defendant company. It is not difficult to see why McNair, J. was prepared to treat the agreement in this case almost as one of employment. But if a manufacturer approaches an independent agent (whether already dealing in goods of the same sort or not) there will be none of those elements of personal obligation which Murison already owed to the plaintiffs and which were emphasised in his agency contract.

McNair, J. in *Martin Baker* also stressed that the contract was one involving mutual trust and confidence. So, of course, are many contracts other than employment agreements. Further, there is a distinction between different types of confidence and trust; some trust is purely commercial in nature. Thus distributorship agreements (class (iv)) necessarily involve inter-dependence and reliance; but when an attempt was made in *Decro-Wall International S.A.* v. *Practitioners in Marketing Ltd.* to argue from this to an analogy with employment contracts, it was speedily and unanimously rejected by the Court of Appeal.[12] Here there had been slight delays by the distributor in paying for goods supplied to him. These caused a loss of some £ 20 in all, which the manufacturer could have debited to the distributor's account. Instead, he sought to treat it as a repudiatory breach of contract, entitling him to treat the agreement as discharged. The court held that the breach did not have this effect; but "the case would have been quite different if the defendant's breach had been such as reasonably to shatter the plaintiffs' confidence in the defendants' ability to pay for the goods".[13] This is the language of commercial

10. Except in case (iii). The legal independence of the distributor may be a factor influencing the choice of the type of agreement.
11. [1944] 2 QB 556.
12. [1971] 1 WLR 361, at pp. 369, 376 and 381.
13. Ibid., at p. 369 (Salmon, L.J.).

dealing, not of employment. It is thought that the same attitude could be taken to an agency; it is usually no more than a well-defined contract for the mutual benefit of two independent businessmen. So far as the agent has no other business but the sale of the manufacturer's goods, there will be some resemblance to employment. But generally speaking, no great reliance can be placed on the law of master and servant.

Nor, it appears, does the considerable degree of co-operation involved both in agency and in distributorship contracts enable us to treat them as "joint-ventures"[14], still less as partnerships. Although agency may be one of the essential features of partnership, the reverse is not true.

A further, if remote, analogy may be made with licensing agreements authorising a producer to have the use, and often the sole use, of a famous name on his goods.[15] The resemblance is slight, since the "sponsor" supplies his name and little else in many cases. Where, however, he contributes (for example in design or quality control) a similar though relatively slight element of mutual dependence can be seen. Such a comparison, however, serves principally to emphasise that the sole agency or distributorship is merely another "commercial relationship of a commonplace character".[16]

Distributorships are perhaps more easy than agency to regard as commercial dealings between parties at arms' length. We have already seen that attempts to invoke comparisons with master and servant law or elements of "joint-venture" have been rejected in such cases. Indeed, the fact that there is a sale of goods to an independent merchant for resale by him might lead one to suppose that the distributorship contract was merely a master agreement for the sale of goods between manufacturer and distributor. This is not so, however. The contract involves long-standing obligations on both sides of co-operation and promotion of sales which give it a far wider ambit than a simple sale.[17] That the contract is also distinct in law from the sales made in pursuance of it is adequately demonstrated by *Cebora S.N.C.* v. *S.I.P. (Industrial Products) Ltd.* [18] Here there had been a breakdown in the relations between manufacturer and distributor. The latter dishonoured bills of exchange drawn on them in payment for goods supplied. As a defence to an action on the bills, they sought to rely upon an alleged repudiation of the main agreement. The Court of Appeal rejected the defence. Although the sales took place "under the general umbrella" of the main agreement, the distribution agreement was a separate contract, breach of which would generate a counterclaim, but not a defence on the bills.

14. Evans Marshall *v.* Bertola, *supra* n. 4.

15. E.g., in Re Berkertex Sportcraft Ltd.'s Agreement (1947) 177 LT 420: licence to manufacture dresses for export under Norman Hartnell's name, he promising not to sponsor competitors.

16. Schuler A.G. *v.* Wickman Machine Tool Sales Ltd. [1974] AC 235 at p. 270 *per* Lord Wilberforce.

17. See, *Decro-Wall, supra* n. 12 at p. 373 *per* Sachs, L.J.

18. [1976] 1 Lloyds R. 271. Other defences on the bills also failed.

2. ASPECTS OF THE PARTIES' DEALINGS

2.1. The sale element

2.1.1. Distributorship contracts

These involve two sets of sale agreements, between manufacturer and distributor, and between distributor and customer, and both will be governed by the Sale of Goods Act 1979, with appropriate modifications introduced by the parties. The fact that the distributor's profit may be described as "commission" will not alter his status as a purchaser of the goods from the manufacturer; frequently the manufacturer is prudent enough to make it clear in the principal agreement that the distributor is in no way to hold himself out as an agent.

Looking first at the sales by the manufacturer to the distributor, if no specific provision is made for the passing of property and risk in the goods, this will be governed by ss. 16-20 of the 1979 Act. The overriding provision, which the parties cannot exclude, is that property cannot pass to the distributor until the goods are ascertained.[19] Nor may the distributor argue that an order placed under the main agreement generates in him an equitable interest in the goods; the rule in sales contracts is that if property has not passed, no lesser interest may be claimed.[20] On the insolvency of a manufacturer who has received payment without delivering or appropriating goods to the distributor's order, therefore, the latter is limited to a proof in the insolvency, subject to any rights he may have to assert a set-off based on the parties' mutual dealings.[21] Similarly, risk in the goods prima facie will not pass until property has passed; and even though there is nothing in law to prevent risk in unascertained goods passing, the practical difficulties involved will be so great as to preclude such a finding in the absence of a very clear intention to this effect.[22]

Subject to this, it is the parties' actual or presumed intention which is to govern the passing of property.[23] The commonest express provision, naturally enough, is that property should pass on payment. If the contract involves shipment of goods, the parties will often have introduced f.o.b. terms of payment. This may imply that property is to pass on shipment; but the manufacturer would be wise to require prepayment as a further condition.

Where no intention can be elicited from the contract, s.18 r.5(1) provides that property is to pass when goods of the contract description are unconditionally appropriated to the contract, usually by the seller with the buyer's assent. The assent

19. Section 16. Property will in most cases not pass *merely* because of ascertainment.

20. Re Wait [1927] 1 Ch. 606 is usually taken to decide this.

21. Bankruptcy Act 1914, s. 31. The right to set-off cannot be excluded by agreement: see, e.g., Rolls Razor Ltd. *v.* Cox [1961] 1 QB 552.

22. Sale of Goods Act 1979, s. 20. The decision placing risk on the buyer in Sterns Ltd. *v.* Vickers Ltd. [1923] 1 KB 78 was in every way exceptional, since the seller had lost all control over the goods in storage.

23. Ibid., ss. 17 and 18. See also Re Bond Worth, *infra* section 2.1.3.

(which may precede appropriation) may be easy to imply in a case where the distributor is placing regular orders under the main agreement; if the manufacturer actually has a stock of goods available for collection, the roles may be reversed, with the distributor himself appropriating goods to the contract. The distinctive feature of these rules is that the transfer of property is, in theory, divorced from the act of delivery, a doctrinal result which has often attracted critical comment. Where the manufacturer delivers goods to an independent carrier for transmission to the distributor, however, this is prima facie both a delivery (s.32) and an unconditional appropriation (s.18 r.5(2)) which brings delivery and the passing of property close together.

An entirely different approach may sometimes be adopted, with goods consigned to the distributor on a sale or return basis. Although useful in respect of small goods and traders, this would be a clumsy approach to a large commercial dealing. Where sale or return terms are used [24], property (and risk) prima facie pass on acceptance by the distributor, on the expiry of a reasonable time, or when the distributor "adopts" the transaction, which he would most clearly do by reselling the goods, though not necessarily by forwarding them to a customer on sale or return terms.

Returning to more orthodox sales, the quality of the seller's performance will be measured by the usual provisions of the Sale of Goods Act. Time of delivery is prima facie of the essence [25]; the manufacturer, apart from passing a good title, must supply goods of the correct description, of merchantable quality and reasonable fitness for purpose and corresponding with any sample which has been given contractual force [26]; and of course, any express terms relating to the goods (e.g., "guaranteed dispatched in good order") must be observed. The manufacturer may attempt to exclude, limit, or vary his obligations. As to the statutory terms, he may not exclude his duty to pass a good title. This is unlikely to affect a manufacturer's sales, since even where his own suppliers have reserved title to raw materials supplied to him, he will normally be able to pass a good title to the finished goods to the distributor [27], and a security by way of fixed charge on such materials is unlikely to be encountered. The other implied terms may be excluded, by the principal agreement, or by the terms of sale, to the extent to which the exclusion passes the "requirement of reasonableness" under the Unfair Contract Terms Act 1977.[28] Provisions excluding liability for delay or breach of express terms would also be subject to this statutory test, provided that the distributor can be held to be "dealing" on the manufacturer's written standard terms of business.[29] Where the terms of the

24. Such an arrangement may amount to a mercantile agency, in which case it will not be treated as sale or return, even if that description is used by the parties.

25. Time of payment is not. See, e.g., *Decro-Wall, supra* n. 12. As to time of delivery, see section 10 of the Sale of Goods Act and Hartley *v.* Hymans [1920] 3 KB 475, and, as to time stipulations in general, Bunge Corpn. *v.* Tradax SA [1981] 2 All ER 513.

26. Sale of Goods Act 1979, ss. 12-15.

27. Borden UK Ltd. *v.* Scottish Timber Products Ltd., *infra* n. 56.

28. Sections 6 and 11 and Schedule 2.

29. Section 3.

agreement are freely negotiated by the parties, there may be considerable scope for argument – and therefore compromise – of the question of "dealing" on "standard" terms; for example, if the parties agree specially tailored terms and conditions which are inserted into a standard form of agreement proferred by the manufacturer. It must always be remembered, too, that the first step in dealing with such terms must always logically be to construe them, as part of the contract as a whole, to determine whether they do indeed purport wholly or partly to protect the manufacturer against liability for an alleged breach.[30]

Where liability exists, it would, if litigated, generally sound in damages. In the case of a failure to deliver, no order will be given, compelling specific performance of a contract for the sale of ordinary commercial goods.[31] To this general rule, three cautions may be entered. First, an injunction equivalent to an order to deliver petrol (which did not even constitute ascertained goods) has been granted in one case on the basis that the alternative was that the buyer would be forced out of business.[32] Secondly a failure to deliver may be accompanied by, and will probably constitute, a breach of the main agreement, as well as of the sale contract. Where this is accompanied by a threat to appoint a new distributor, the court may grant an injunction to restrain that breach.[33] Unless relations have broken down completely, and the manufacturer is prepared to forego selling in the territory pending a lawful termination of the contract, such an order will, to put it at its lowest, encourage him to perform his sales agreement. Thirdly, a buyer who has paid for particular goods may have an action in the tort of conversion against the manufacturer; though this is unlikely substantially to add to his chance of obtaining their delivery, he may be able to claim any extra profit which the manufacturer makes on a resale in an action for money had and received.

Finally, it should not be overlooked that the distributor may be able to reject tenders or supplies of defective goods on the grounds of failure to comply with the terms implied under the Sale of Goods Act 1979 or with express terms of the contract. Where the power to reject is exercised, the distributor may also be able to claim damages for any resulting loss from what is now a non-delivery. In practical terms, the distributor will usually accept substitute goods and try to negotiate compensation for any financial loss suffered.[34] It does not follow from breach of terms as to quality that the distributor is entitled to regard the distributorship itself as broken in such a way as to justify his treating it as discharged. This would

30. See, Photo Productions Ltd. *v.* Securicor Transport Ltd. [1980] AC 827.

31. Re Wait [1927] 1 Ch. 606.

32. Sky Petroleum *v.* V.I.P. Petroleum Ltd. [1974] 1 WLR 576 (no other supplies because of fuel crisis).

33. Evans Marshall & Co., Ltd. *v.* Bertola SA [1973] 1 WLR 349.

34. He may in at least some circumstances be forced in law to accept substitute goods if the manufacturer is able to deliver within the period fixed by the order: see, e.g., Borrowman *v.* Free (1879) 4 QBD 500; E.E. & Brian Smith *v.* Wheatsheaf Mills [1939] 2 KB 302. This conflicts in spirit, if not in the letter, with the commonly held view that rejection of goods always puts an end to the sale contract, a view which may be argued to be implicit in s. 11 of the Sale of Goods Act 1979; but there is respectable support for the alternative view outlined above: see, Devlin (1966) CLJ 192 at p. 194.

be the case if, and only if, the seriousness of the breach or its actual or likely repetition show clearly that the manufacturer cannot, or will not, perform.

The rules governing the resale contracts made by the distributor will follow the same general lines. If the customer is a consumer within the meaning of the Unfair Contract Terms Act, it will be impossible for the distributor to exclude his own liability for breaches of the implied terms in the sale agreement.[35] In other cases, it will often be desired to achieve symmetry, so that where the manufacturer is liable or exempt, so is the distributor. There may be various reasons why such symmetry cannot be complete. In the first place it is difficult to envisage a court upholding a distributor's exclusion of liability under the Unfair Contract Terms Act *merely* on the grounds that he cannot pass it on to his own seller (other reasons may be relevant, however). On the other hand, a distributor's exclusion of liability for e.g., delays caused by the fault of the manufacturer may perhaps be adjudged more reasonable than an attempt by the manufacturer to exclude his own liability for not having the goods ready on time.

The distributorship contract may oblige the distributor to sell only on the terms laid down therein. Certain provisions, such as attempts to impose a price structure, involve special considerations which are dealt with separately; but what of a provision simply that the distributor, in reselling, will contract on the same terms as those on which he purchases? There may be good commercial reasons for such a provision, but they do not bind third parties who are not privy to the distributorship contract. The distributor who contracts on other terms is of course in breach of contract with the manufacturer. It may also be that a third party who, with actual knowledge of the terms, induces the distributor to sell in breach is liable in tort for inducing a breach of contract.[36]

If a manufacturer supplies his distributor with defective goods which are then resold, loss, damage or injury may be caused to the ultimate buyer. Frequently the liability for this loss may be passed on in the form of consecutive (and consolidated) actions in contract, with customer suing retailer, retailer suing wholesaler or distributor, and the latter seeking redress from the manufacturer. In the course of these actions, the liability may change in nature. For instance, a defective product may cause the consumer physical injury, for which it may be assumed the retailer is likely to be liable under s.14 of the Sale of Goods Act. On the further assumption that the supply of the defective goods to the retailer was itself a breach of contract, the retailer's liability may then be passed on, but the loss claimed is now a financial loss, i.e., the liability to compensate the customer. Of course, liability

35. Unfair Contract Terms Act 1977, s. 6. Exclusion of liability in other respects is also governed by this Act; in particular, s. 3. will often control the exclusion of liability for breaches of contract. Section 2 governs exclusion of liability in negligence. The manufacturer or distributor will expect to be sued in negligence only by parties with whom there is no privity of contract. Liability for negligence causing death or injury cannot be excluded. In other cases, liability can be excluded if and only if the exclusion is shown to be reasonable. For a brief consideration of tortious liability for defective supplies, see *infra,* section 2.1.1.

36. Lumley *v.* Gye (1852) 2 E & B 216; see also, Swiss Bank Corpn. *v.* Lloyds Bank Ltd. [1979], reversed on other grounds [1980] 2 All ER 419.

may stop before the manufacturer is reached, e.g., because a party in the chain of sales has successfully excluded or modified his duties or liabilities or because a party is insolvent and uninsured and therefore not worth suing. In addition there may be some cases in which loss cannot be passed on because it is too remote a consequence of the breach, or is not caused by it. In *Lambert* v. *Lewis* [37] the situation arose that the ultimate buyer of a defective product was himself at fault in his use of it. A manufacturer had marketed a towing attachment for motor vehicles which was dangerous in operation because of a design fault. Thus each party who in the course of his business sold the attachment was prima facie in breach of the obligations implied by s.14 of the Sale of Goods Act.[38] But the last buyer, the consumer (in a non-technical sense), failed to detect or to deal with the attachment's dangerous condition after some months of use. For this failure he was held liable in negligence for the death of a third party in an accident. He sought to pass this liability to the retailer in an action on the sale, and failed. It was held that his tortious liability arose from his negligent use of the defective attachment, and that at the time of the sale it could not reasonably have been contemplated that he would be likely to act with this degree of carelessness. Accordingly his loss was too remote a consequence of the retailer's breach of contract to be recoverable.[39] Short of an express warranty that goods may be used in a defective condition, the seller escapes liability in such circumstances. So will those who supplied him with the goods, as far as actions in contract are concerned. Somewhat similarly, if a buyer resells goods which he knows or should realize to be defective, his seller will not be liable to reimburse the buyer's liability to customers or third parties.[40] Where this sort of "risk taking" occurs, the precise pattern of liability will depend on the point of occurrence – i.e., whether it is distributor, retailer, last buyer who is at fault.

The manufacturer marketing defective goods may well also be liable to those injured by them in an action for negligence, cutting out the intermediate parties. Thus in *Lambert* v. *Lewis* [41] the trial judge found the manufacturer liable in negligence as to 75% for the third party injuries (the customer being liable as to the remainder). Tortious liability will normally arise only where non-contracting third parties are seeking redress, since a buyer will normally prefer proof of breach of contract to the rather more difficult task of proving negligence. But even a party in the chain of distribution may sometimes choose or be forced to sue in negligence, perhaps to by-pass an insolvent supplier. In *Lambert* v. *Lewis* the retailer

37. [1981] 1 All ER 1185.

38. Notably that the goods should be reasonably fit for their purpose.

39. Alternatively, the loss can be said to be caused by the buyer's negligence and not by the breach of contract. It should be noted that nobody argued for any apportionment of loss, for example by finding of contributory negligence.

40. British Oil and Cake Co. Ltd. *v.* Burstall & Co. (1923) 29 TLR 406; G.C. Dobell & Co. Ltd. *v.* Barber and Garrett [1931] 1 KB 219. Where the buyer is not negligent and relies on his seller's undertakings, express or implied, he should be able to recover from his seller the amount of his own liability to his customer: see, *Benjamin's Sale of Goods,* para. 1315.

41. [1979] RTR 61.

took action directly against the manufacturer because he had lost his records and could not identify the distributor who had sold the attachment to him. In the Court of Appeal [42] his claim was refused on the ground that his loss (his liability to compensate his customer for his liability to the third party) was purely economic and therefore not recoverable in negligence, or at least in this type of action for negligence. On this basis the chance loss of a party produced by the loss of the records would produce a completely different spread of loss between manufacturere, distributor and retailer from the "normal" contractual actions. In the House of Lords this question did not call for decision since, for the reasons described above, the retailer was held not liable to indemnify his customer at all, so that there was no loss. Whether the Court of Appeal's decision is correct is uncertain; Lord Diplock, delivering the opinion of the whole House, left open the question of recovery of economic loss in these circumstances in a way that seems to leave the issue very arguable, at least at the highest level.[43]

2.1.2. Agency contracts

Here the position is usually simpler. Whether the agent is merely acting as a go-between or has authority to bind the manufacturer, there will be a single contract of sale between manufacturer and customer, to which the rules and considerations already mentioned apply. The agent himself is usually not liable under the sale contract. Insofar as the agent exceeds his authority in contracting, special problems arise which are considered in the next section.

The most difficult point for an overseas manufacturer will be to guarantee payment by the customer. Although the imposition of del credere terms would be the obvious answer, and would require no special formalities to create, most commercial agents would be reluctant to undertake such liability, even for extra commission. Either payment by bank credits, or the use of credit insurance, would be the most practical way to guarantee performance.

Similar problems seem to be generated by the "hybrid" contract in which the relationship between manufacturer and distributor is that of principal and agent, but the distributor is obliged to sell as principal to customers. There might appear to be doctrinal difficulties in such an arrangement [44] but it has the sanction both of the leading English textbook on agency and of the courts.[45] Whatever the commercial attractions of such an arrangement, the principal's redress against customers is more remote; indeed, it will usually be non-existent.

2.1.3. Insolvency of the distributor

The insolvency of the distributor, owing sums of money to the manufacturer

42. [1980] 2 WLR 299.
43. [1981] 1 All ER 1185, 1192.
44. In particular with regard to s. 12 of the Sale of Goods Act 1979.
45. See, *Bowstead on Agency*, pp. 6-7 and cased cited; and see, *Romalpa, infra*, section 2.1.3.

and with goods and proceeds in his hands which may be swallowed in that insolvency is a major headache for all manufacturers, but particularly for those without direct representation in the distributorship territory. A possible solution may be to take a floating charge over the distributor's assets. Such a security, however, cannot be taken from an individual trader [46], is vulnerable to certain other creditors, and steps will normally have to be taken to crystallize it.[47] A fixed charge on the goods and proceeds would avoid these problems, but would entail either the paralysis of the distributor's business or a clause entitling the distributor to deal with the goods, and probably their proceeds, free of the charge. The grant of such freedom might itself lead a court to decide that the security is in law a floating charge.[48] Such a fixed charge over fluctuating assets could not be taken from an individual trader.[49] Either form of security may be unobtainable or at least unsatisfactory if there is already a first charge to the distributor's bank.

To avoid these problems, and also the publicity attendant upon the registration of a company charge [50], many English suppliers have adopted the continental form of security through reservation of title to the goods as security for payment of all sums owed to the supplier. The aim is to remove the goods, and the proceeds of sale of the goods, from other creditors.

It will be assumed that the distributor is a company. If he is an individual, the reservation of title is likely to face an immediate challenge under the "reputed ownership" provisions of the Bankruptcy Act 1914, s.38 though it may be possible to draft a clause avoiding this risk.[51] The first reported case in which a reservation of title was tested was *Aluminium Industrie Vaassen B.V.* v. *Romalpa Aluminium Ltd.* [52] Here the plaintiffs supplied aluminium to the defendants. Under their contract, title to the goods was not to pass [53] until all debts owed by the defendants to the plaintiffs had been paid. A receiver was appointed over the defendant's property by debenture-holders, and the plaintiffs claimed:

(i) goods supplied by them and still in the defendant's possession; and

(ii) the proceeds of sales of goods supplied by the plaintiffs and resold by the defendants.

46. The Bills of Sale Acts 1878 and 1882 effectively prevent an individual from charging future goods. Although charges on imported goods escape from these Acts under the 1890 and 1891 Acts, these Acts apply only to identified consignments, and not to charges embracing all future consignments: NV Slavenburg's Bank *v.* I.N.R. Ltd. [1980] 1 All ER 955, at 977; and see, *Halsbury's Laws of England,* 4th ed., Vol. 4, para 636.

47. This is not entirely free from doubt; see, Farrar (1976) 40 Conv. 397: *Gore-Browne on Companies,* 43rd ed. 18-5.

48. Siebe Gorman & Co. Ltd. *v.* Barclays Bank Ltd. [1979] 2 Lloyds R. 142.

49. See, *supra* n. 46.

50. Where property charged is in England, the charge must be registered under the Companies Act 1948 even if the company is incorporated outside England: s. 106; and see, NV Slavenburg's Bank *v.* Intercontinental Natural Resources Ltd. [1980] 1 All ER 955 which applied s.106 even though the company had no property in England when the charge was created. This decision is giving rise to many difficulties.

51. See, Smart *v.* Holt [1929] 2 KB 303, a decision on the somewhat remote contract of hire purchase.

52. [1976] 1 WLR 676.

53. This may prevent VAT relief on bad debts: Finance Act 1978, s. 12(2)(c).

The first claim succeeded on the basis of the reservation of title. The Court of Appeal also allowed the second claim. The agreement contemplated, it was held, that the supplier's rights should extend to the proceeds of resale, and created a relationship between the parties greater than that merely of vendor and purchaser. It was a bailment generating an equitable right in the supplier to the proceeds of goods. Subject to the identification of the proceeds (and to claims of third parties who acquired legal title of the proceeds without notice of the supplier's equitable right) the claim could be maintained against the purchaser and the receiver and, it also follows, against third parties.

As far as the distributor's customers are concerned, the result is not very startling. It is unlikely in the extreme that the reservation of title would deny ownership of the the goods to a customer who buys goods from the distributor bona fide and in the ordinary course of business.[54] From the point of view of others dealing with the distributor, however, the decision was more far-reaching. The distributor's balance sheets (which even if in full compliance with the Companies Act 1948-1981 are unlikely to be completely up to date) may or may not reveal that stock carried by the distributor in fact belongs to the manufacturer. Those balance sheets would certainly be unlikely to reveal the claim to proceeds (in the *Romalpa* case the proceeds consisted of money in a special bank account). But all these assets would be removed from the general creditors in an insolvency and also, subject to any question of priorities or bona fide acquisition without notice [55], from any other party relying on a security over the distributor's assets. The manufacturer could thus achieve all the advantages of a fixed charge on assets with none of the disadvantages; in particular, the publicity attendant upon registration of a charge under the Companies Act 1948.

The full impact of the *Romalpa* case has been challenged, if not necessarily overthrown by the subsequent decision in *Borden (U.K.) Ltd.* v. *Scottish Timber Products Ltd.* [56] Borden supplied the defendants with resin for chipboard manufacture. Property in the resin was to pass only when that resin and all other goods supplied by Borden had been paid for. There are certain very clear differences between this case and *Romalpa*. The contract did not, expressly or by clear implication, contemplate a claim to proceeds. There was no obligation on the defendants to keep the goods supplied separate from other stock (as there was, albeit in a rather tenuous form, in Romalpa). The defendants' ability to store resin was very limited, and it was unlikely that resin would be stored, unused, for more than two days. Consequently, it would be quite normal for the goods to be used before being paid for. Finally, Borden's claim, on the defendants' insolvency, was not for the proceeds of resale, but to an interest in chipboard manufactured using their

54. The customer would acquire title under s.21 or 25(1) of the Sale of Goods Act 1979.

55. Possibly a factor purchasing the distributor's receivables. Here the priority position is not free from doubt. See in particular, Goode (1976) 92 LQR 528, at pp. 554-559; Donaldson (1977) 93 LQR 324; Goode (1977) 93 LQR 487; McLauchlan (1980) 96 LQR 90.

56. [1981] Ch. 25 (a very differently constituted court from that which decided *Romalpa*).

resin. Once the resin had been used, it was impossible either to recover it or, it seems, to calculate how much of the chipboard by weight or by value represented Borden's resin.

The Court of Appeal rejected the claim. The case is distinguishable from *Romalpa* in view of the different type of claim to "proceeds", and in view of the circumstances referred to in the previous paragraph. The Court was, however, openly hostile to title reservations as concealed security devices.[57] Its reasoning, moreover, tends to erode the most obvious basis of the *Romalpa* case.

First, the Court distinguished the case where goods are resold, and where the supplier has a good chance of showing which assets of the insolvent purchaser (whether goods, cash, book debts, etc.) represent the goods supplied, from the case of goods used for manufacture. Once these lost their identity, the supplier loses both his legal title by reservation and any claim to the end product or its proceeds. This raises no obstacle to a manufacturer seeking to claim against a distributor.

The Court went on, however, to deny the supplier a remedy at all, and not merely to deny him a remedy once identification had become impossible. This was done by holding that the relationship between the parties was little more than that of vendor-purchaser. In *Romalpa,* the defendants in fact conceded in argument that the purchaser was a bailee of the goods, and the relationship of bailor (manufacturer/supplier) and bailee (distributor/purchaser) was held to generate the claim to proceeds of sale. In *Borden* no such concession was made, and Borden failed to establish a sufficient "trust bailment" to generate any claim to proceeds. The Court was of the opinion that no such relationship could be implied unless the parties contemplated the return of the goods to the bailor. This effectively excludes bailment as the basis of a remedy for the manufacturer.[58]

Thirdly, the two members of the court who dealt with the point considered that if Borden had established a right to proceeds, they would have done so by virtue of the agreement, and not by any intrinsic quality of their relationship with the defendants. The agreement would therefore have been registrable as a charge under the Companies Act 1948, and, if unregistered, would have been void against the purchaser's liquidator and creditor. Whilst it seems that the claims flowing from a genuine "trust-bailment" would not require registration in this way, it is clear that the onus on the supplier seeking to establish such a relationship will be heavy. Whether a duty to keep stock separately would be enough is very doubtful.

Unfortunately, there was no further appeal from the Court of Appeal's decision in *Borden,* and until the House of Lords has the chance to dispose of these questions authoritatively, the efficacy of title reservations by a manufacturer against a distributor is clouded with doubts.

Ironically, an alternative basis of the decision in *Romalpa* is that the relationship of the parties is that of principal and agent. Since a fully drafted distributorship contract excludes such a relationship, the manufacturer is unlikely to be able to rely

57. See especially, Templeman, L.J., ibid., at p. 42.

58. The mere fact that the distributor may in certain circumstances have to return the goods would not be sufficient.

on this part of the decision, which is not affected by *Borden.* He will, however, apparently be able to do so in the case of sole agency contracts, even where the contract is a "hybrid" in which the manufacturer and distributor are (inter se) principal and agent, but the agent himself is to sell to his customers as a principal vendor. (This in fact is expressly approved in the *Romalpa* case). Here no question of registration as a charge of the reservation of title or the claim to proceeds arises, since the "security" is inherent in the parties' relationship and not imposed upon it by a special term of the agreement.

For the sake of completeness, mention should also be made of the decision of Slade, J. in *re Bond Worth* [59] which preceded *Borden.* Again the contract was for the supply of goods mainly for manufacture, not for resale. The significance of the case is reduced by the rather obscure and unusual terms of the security clause. This provided that:

(1) "equitable and beneficial ownership" was reserved till payment;

(2) if the goods were resold, this interest should attach to the proceeds of resale; and

(3) if the goods were incorporated into a new product, the interest should attach to that.

It was held that legal title to the goods passed to the buyer on delivery. The suppliers argued that the agreement reserved to them the equitable rights outlined above. Slade, J. held, however, that, since the buyers were given a right absolutely and freely to deal with the goods, the real nature of the transaction was that the buyers acquired full ownership and then granted a charge over the goods (which he took to be a floating charge).[60] This, being unregistered, was void against the liquidator and creditors. The judgment assumes that the owner of property cannot simultaneously pass legal title and reserve an equitable title to himself, a question which has troubled the courts in a different context.[61] Since a reservation of title in this form is unlikely to be attempted in a distributorship agreement, however, the problem is unlikely to cause further difficulties.

2.2. General agency aspects of exclusive dealing contract

Whilst the distributor is essentially an independent merchant, the sole agent's activities fall within the general law of agency. The agent's authority to deal with third parties will normally be analysed in terms of the first two of the following three categories.

2.2.1. Actual authority

This, naturally, will be found in the express terms of the agency agreement (coupled

59. [1980] Ch. 228.

60. In *Borden*, opinion was divided as to whether the charge would be fixed or floating. A charge taken closely in time to the receivership might encounter difficulties under the Companies Act 1948, ss. 320-322.

61. See, Vandervell *v.* I.R.C. [1967] 2 AC 291 (tax liability).

if relevant and where permissible, with any additional terms agreed elsewhere by the parties) and in any terms implied into the agreement in order to give it business efficacy. Actual authority includes, to the extent that the contract does not restrict it, the power to do what is ordinarily incidental to the effective fulfilment of the express authority.[62] Although a sole agent may therefore have implied authority to do whatever is incidental to or within the ordinary scope of such a promotion of sales enterprise, there will be matters which are not free from doubt; for example, whether he has authority to receive payment, to give warranties concerning the goods, or to compromise claims against the manufacturer. These are the sorts of matters which should, if possible, be dealt with expressly.

2.2.2. Apparent authority

Where the manufacturer holds the agent out as having a particular authority, or knowingly permits him to hold himself out, the manufacturer will be estopped from denying the apparent (or "ostensible") authority of the agent, if sued by a third party who acted in reliance on the represented authority. This may be of particular significance where there are restrictions on authority unknown to the third party. Naturally, a third party who has notice that the agent is exceeding his authority cannot rely on apparent authority. On the other hand, the manufacturer will be bound by acts done within the scope of authority, notwithstanding that the agent is acting in furtherance of his own interests or even in fraud of the manufacturer.[63]

2.2.3. Usual authority

It may be that the manufacturer is simply liable on any contract made by the agent within such powers as are usually possessed by a person in his position.[64] This is a highly controversial question, however, and it is usually assumed that only the first two categories of authority have to be considered, and that "usual" authority is restricted to cases where there is implied authority or a holding out by an appointment to a particular position.[65]

Probably the three commonest limitations contained in sole agency agreements are these:

(a) that the agent is to sell only as principal and is not to incur liability on the part of the manufacturer (the "hybrid" agency);

(b) that the agent is not to sell the goods at all but is to transmit customers' orders for approval, or is to sell only subject to the manufacturer's approval;

62. See, e.g., The Huntsman [1894] P. 214. The agent may also have authority to act according to the usage of the place or business in which he is "employed"; but the usage must be "reasonable", e.g., not a usage allowing him to accept payment in the form of a set-off: Pearson *v.* Scott (1878) 9 Ch. D. 198.

63. Oppenheimer *v.* Attenborough & Sons [1908] 1 KB 221.

64. Watteau *v.* Fenwick [1893] 1 QB 346 (undisclosed principal).

65. Freeman & Lockyer *v.* Buckhurst Park Properties (Mangal) Ltd. [1964] 2 QB 480 (company directors).

(c) that the agent is to sell only on the terms and conditions approved in the agency contract, and is to allow no variations to be negotiated and to give no warranties, etc.

These limitations, built into and defining the scope of the agent's powers, will bind third parties unless the agent is somehow given apparent authority to do one of the prohibited acts. The first point to be made is that merely to deliver goods to another does not clothe him with any authority, actual or apparent, to sell them.[66] Although the agent will not usually have possession of the contract goods at all, where he does so this rule is doubly important in case (b), in that it not only prevents the creation of a contract between the manufacturer and customer, but also prevents the latter from claiming title to the goods under s.21 of the Sale of Goods Act (although be may sometimes have a claim under s.2 of the Factors Act 1889). Secondly, since proof is required of the manufacturer's representation that the agent had a wider authority, or at the least such an acquiescence in the representation as to constitute permission or encouragement to the agent to make such representations, a manufacturer who clothes the agent with such apparent authority will usually have only himself to blame. Thirdly, and more difficult, it is sometimes suggested that there is a distinction between restriction (c) and the others. For (it is argued) restriction (c) does not prevent an agent who is entitled to sell from selling on the principal's behalf, but merely provides that certain transactions are unauthorised if they contain terms and conditions not agreed upon in the agency contract. So, partly by analogy with the much-debated decision in *Watteau* v. *Fenwick* [67], partly by analogy with the doctrine of vicarious liability in tort[68], and partly in reliance on certain old-cases dealing with mortgages of real property, it is argued that the agent who acts "*within the course of his employment* as an agent binds the principal even though he exceeds his actual authority." [69] On the other hand, such a result is impossible to reconcile with general propositions that an agent must act within the scope of his actual or apparent authority in order to bind the principal. The better view is probably that the old mortgage cases are anomalous [70] and that the agent cannot normally bind his principal unless acting within one of the recognised forms of authority.

The agent himself may incur liability to the customer in a number of ways. He may undertake personal liability either alone or jointly and severally with his principal, as surety for his principal, as an alternative to his principal, or on a contract collateral to the agreement between the principal and the customer.[71] Most sole agency contracts will compel the agent to disclose to the customer that he is acting as such. If he fails to do so, the manufacturer can still sue and be sued on the con-

66. Central Newbury Car Auctions Ltd. *v.* Unity Finance Ltd. [1957] 1 QB 371.

67. [1893] 1 QB 346.

68. Employer liable even for forbidden acts of employee if done in the course of employment.

69. Atiyah, *Sale of Goods*, 5th ed., p. 192 (emphasis added): Treitel, *Law of Contract*, 5th ed., pp. 541-542.

70. *Bowstead on Agency*, pp. 295-297: *Chitty on Contracts*, 24th. ed., Vol. 2, para. 2061.

71. *Bowstead on Agency*, pp. 353-354. A *del credere* agent is normally liable to the seller not the buyer.

tract (provided that it was otherwise in accordance with the agent's authority; an undisclosed principal may not ratify a completely unauthorised contract [72]); but the agent will be personally liable on the contract. Finally, special considerations sometimes apply where the agent is acting for a foreign principal, which is not unlikely to be the case in a sole agency contract. Older cases seemed to establish a presumption, rebuttable only by clear evidence of authority, that such an agent contracted personally and to the exclusion of liability in the "foreign principal". There may or may not have been a justification for this rule in the supposed reluctance of parties, who regarded themselves as entering into a domestic transaction, to become involved with foreign law and foreign jurisdiction questions. Normally, however, the terms of the sole agency would be sufficiently clear evidence of authority to displace any such presumption, at least if the agent made it clear that he was acting as such.[73] More recently, it has been said that the existence of a foreign principal may have some, perhaps minimal, weight in determining whether the customer contracts with the principal, and rather more weight in determining whether the intention of the agent and customer is that the agent should be liable as well as the principal.[74]

Apart from his possible liability directly under the contract negotiated, the agent may incur liability to the customer in other ways. The chief of these is through the warranty of authority. Every agent who by words or conduct represents his authority to act on the principal's behalf is treated as warranting his authority to do so, whether he acts in good faith or not; and by purporting to act as agent he represents his authority to do so. Thus a person acting as broker for seller and buyer impliedly warrants that he has been authorised by each.[75] Although the matter is not free from doubt, the liability appears to be contractual so that it does not matter whether the agent acts negligently or not.[76] It is unclear whether there is a breach of warranty where the agent renders the principal liable through *apparent* authority, since this is not a real authority. It may be that the point is academic, since normally the breach of warranty, if there is one, will cause no loss.[77] Finally, there may be circumstances in which an agent incurs liability in tort for fraudulent misstatements, either of his authority or concerning the proposed transaction; he may also, by assuming a position of adviser to a customer, come under a duty of care not to give advice and information negligently.[78]

72. Keighley, Maxsted & Co. *v.* Durant [1901] AC 240; see, Schmitthoff (1970) Vol. 1 *Hague Recueil des Cours* 148.

73. Miller, Gibb & Co. *v.* Smith and Tyrer Ltd. [1917] 2 KB 141.

74. Teheran-Europe Co. Ltd. *v.* S.T. Belton (Tractors) Ltd. [1968] 2 QB 545, at p. 558 *per* Diplock, L.J.

75. Hughes *v.* Graeme (1864) LJQB 335.

76. Yonge *v.* Toynbee [1910] 1 KB 215.

77. Even if the manufacturer is insolvent, this potential source of loss to the customer would not flow from the breach of warranty.

78. Esso Petroleum Ltd. *v.* Mardon [1976] 2 QB 801.

Where the "contract" between the customer and the manufacturer is void for the agent's lack of authority, the customer will be able to recover sums paid to the agent. If the agent has (acting innocently throughout) paid them to the manufacturer, the agent may no longer be liable to make restitution. If the manufacturer keeps the money, this is, at the least, evidence of ratification validating the contract. If there is no ratification, then in principle the customer should be able to recover the money in an action for money had and received on a total failure of consideration.[79]

Where the agent exceeds his authority, he is in breach of his contract with the manufacturer and liable for any loss resulting. The agent is also a fiduciary for the manufacturer, a relationship which is less than that of a trustee to his cestui que trust, but which nevertheless has considerable implications. The agent must disclose any conflict of interest, and in contracting with his principal must make full disclosure of all material circumstances, is liable to account to the principal for secret payments or bribes received or for benefits obtained by taking advantage of his position to make secret profits, and must account strictly to his principal. So, for instance, if the agent in breach of the agency contract carries on a business competing with, rather than developing, the manufacturer's, the profits received may belong, in equity, to the manufacturer.[80] If the agent (without authority) makes a contract which the manufacturer adopts, the agent must account in the normal way to the manufacturer for money received from the customer.

2.3. Controls on restrictive trading agreements

2.3.1. Restraint of trade at Common Law

A comprehensive sole distributorship contract will contain provisions on the following lines:

(1) A general recital clause appointing the agent or distributor as exclusive distributor for all or some of the manufacturer's products within a defined distributorship territory.

(2) An undertaking by the distributor not to be concerned in the promotion or sale of competing goods during the currency of the agreement (except, perhaps, with the consent of the manufacturer and/or to safeguard existing and valued customers, if the manufacturer cannot meet an order).

(3) An undertaking by the distributor not to take orders from, or sell to, buyers outside the territory (including buyers who he may believe are likely to resell the goods outside the territory).

(4) An undertaking by the manufacturer not to sell goods to which the contract relates within the territory, or outside the territory if there may be a resale or use within the territory.[81]

79. Goff & Jones, *Law of Restitution*, 2nd ed., p. 302.
80. Phipps *v.* Boardman [1967] 2 AC 46.
81. There may be a limited power to sell within the territory, with a right to commission

(5) An undertaking by the distributor not to deal in competing goods for a fixed period after the termination of the agreement without the manufacturer's consent.

Clause 5 is clearly subject to the restraint of trade doctrine and if it infringes it, pro tanto ineffective. Consequently, if a manufacturer sought to enforce it, he would have to justify it as being (a) reasonable between the parties and (b) not contrary to the public interest. In applying the first test, the court will compare the geographical area of restraint with the area of the territory, the length of the restraint, the activities and goods covered and degree to which the agent is to benefit from the agreement and, therefore, to receive a quid pro quo for the restraint.[82] Of these factors, the length of the restraint may often prove decisive if, as is usually the case, the restraint is tied to the territory. It is often said that in determining whether the agreement is reasonable between the parties, it is necessary that the party seeking to enforce the restrictive term must be protecting a legitimate interest; in particular, that it is not enough that he is merely seeking to avoid competition.[83] The word "interest" does not connote any independently enforceable legal right; for example, the interest of an employer or a purchaser of a business in taking a reasonable non-competition covenant from his employee or vendor is sufficient. The "interest" really lies in protection of established or likely business from a party who has gained knowledge of customers or other specialised information of which he can take unfair advantage. So by analogy with employment cases, the manufacturer may protect the territory established during the distributorship against the distributor's subsequent use of specific knowledge of, or influence over, customers gained during the course of the contract. Although the manufacturer cannot (on a traditional analysis) simply prevent the distributor from using the general skill or expertise gained during the distributorship [84], it is possible that the English Courts may come to recognise "know-how" as an interest meriting protection.[85] A search for a clear and universal criterion of "interest" seems, in reality, to be futile. Just as the question of what is "reasonable" between the parties must depend on the facts of each case (e.g., the extent of the territory, the degree to which the manufacturer is to "teach" the distributor about the products, the degree to which he was to set up the distributor's business, and the value to be received by the distributor in return for the restraint) so the "interest" of the manufacturer is likely to be inextricably bound up with the details of the agreement. It is clear, however, that the validity of the restraint is to be judged as at the time of making the contracts.[86]

---

in the distributor. In some states, government buying agencies will deal only directly with the manufacturer.

82. Esso Petroleum Ltd. *v.* Harper's Garage (Stourport) Ltd. [1968] AC 269. To this extent the adequacy of consideration will be considered.

83. McEllistrim's Case [1919] AC 548.

84. Herbert Morris Ltd. *v.* Saxelby [1916] 1 AC 688.

85. Commercial Plastics Ltd. *v.* Vincent [1965] 1 QB 623 at p. 642 *per* Pearson, L.J.

86. *Pace* Lord Denning M.R. in *Lostock, infra* n. 102.

Rather more difficult questions are raised by clauses such as 2, 3 and 4 above. First, it is not clear whether, or to what extent, the doctrine of restraint of trade applies. There are several cases in which agreements to some extent resembling distributorships have been enforced. In *Donnel* v. *Barnett* [87] an agreement to sell certain goods (the by-product of a fish curing process) only to a particular purchaser (there being no obligation actually to sell them at all) was enforced. Conversely, in *Metropolitan Electric Co.* v. *Grinden* [88] an agreement to take supplies only from a particular supplier in a period of five years was enforced. Further, it is not difficult to find cases where the courts have enforced what are clearly sole agency or distributorship contracts. Thus in *Decro-Wall S.A.* v. *Practitioners in Marketing Ltd.* [89] the Court of Appeal gave judgment on unpaid bills of exchange drawn by a French manufacturer on his English distributor. This is a somewhat unusual case, in that the contract seems to have been completely oral, although it is clear that the relevant undertakings not to compete had been given; but no time limit at all for the duration of the agency had been agreed.[90] Again, a sole agency was enforced in *Martin-Baker Aircraft Co. Ltd.* v. *CFE Ltd.*[91] the only substantial issue raised being the length of notice required to terminate the contract.

In none of these cases, however, was a challenge made on the grounds that the agreement was an unenforceable restraint of trade. In *Evans Marshall & Co. Ltd.* v. *Bertola S.A.*[92] the defence was taken in proceedings for an interlocutory injunction. The agreement was a sole agency and distribution contract, with a Spanish sherry maker agreeing to sell only in the United Kingdom through the English agents, who in turn agreed not to deal with competing goods. At first instance, Kerr, J. thought that the defence was not a serious threat to the agent's prospects of eventual success in the action. In the Court of Appeal, only Sachs, L.J. referred to the point, agreeing with Kerr, J. and adding that no case had been cited where the doctrine of restraint of trade had been applied to such an agreement. This, although suggestive, does not clearly answer the question whether the position is that the doctrine applies the body of sole agency agreements, but is unlikely to strike them down, or that the doctrine is simply inapplicable to such agreements.

This question was raised, obliquely, in *Esso Petroleum Co. Ltd.* v. *Harper's Garage (Stourport) Ltd.*[93] This concerned an oil company's "solus" agreement with a garage. It is no longer necessary to consider such agreements in detail, since they have been overtaken by events. The agreements are different from sole distributorships in that (a) there is no "monopoly territory" for the distributor and (b) the agreement, though a personal covenant, is to buy the supplier's petrol for a particular site, and not a general non-competition contract. The House of Lords struck

87. (1883) 22 Ch. D. 835.
88. [1901] 2 Ch. 799. See also, British Oxygen Co. Ltd. *v.* Liquid Air Ltd. [1925] 1 Ch.. 383.
89. [1971] 1 WLR 361.
90. A reasonable period of notice was necessary to determine the contract.
91. [1955] 2 QB 556. See also, W.T. Lamb & Sons *v.* Goring Brick Co., Ltd., *supra* n. 3.
92. [1973] 1 WLR 349.
93. [1968] AC 269.

down a 21 year agreement but upheld a five year tie. It might be thought that a sole distributorship contract, involving a double loss of the parties' freedom to compete, would be an even stronger case for the doctrine to apply. During the course of wide-ranging speeches, a number of obiter dicta shed some light on the present issue, the application of the doctrine. The clearest statement is perhaps that of Lord Pearce:

"The doctrine does not apply to ordinary commercial contracts for the regulation and promotion of trade during the existence of the contract, provided that any prevention of work outside the contract, viewed as a whole, is directed towards the absorption of the parties' services and not their sterilisation. Sole agencies are a normal and necessary incident of commerce and those who desire the benefit of a sole agency must deny themselves the opportunities of other agencies . . . if during the contract one of the parties is too unilaterally fettered so that the contract loses its character of a contract for the regulation and promotion of trade and acquires the predominant character of a contract in restraint of trade [it would be unenforceable]"[94]

The other speeches, though not free from ambiguity, are to similar effect. The best view appears, therefore, to be that the doctrine of restraint of trade does apply but in very remote fashion; since these contracts are "matters of every-day occurrence" which generally can be seen as "encouraging or strengthening trade, rather than as limiting trade" [95], they will usually be upheld.[96] It may, indeed, be that an intermediate position has been reached in relation to such agreements, in which the onus is on the party seeking to evade the contract to show that there is an unreasonable restraint of trade, rather than on the other to show that the restraint is reasonable. The fact that an agency agreement is freely negotiated; that its aim is to generate a new and stable market, perhaps with relatively stable prices, for the distributor's goods; that each party receives a solid recompense for the surrender of his freedom to compete; that each side may have an investment of capital, effort and know-how; that it is not of excessive duration[97]; that the Courts recognise the difficulty inherent in putting themselves in the parties' position and judging the commercial factors influencing the terms agreed; and the overall dangers of an unjust benefit accruing to a party who is allowed too readily to evade his obligation – all suggest the bulk of agency contracts will survive any attack.

They must, however, not be contrary to the *public* interest.[98] The reasoning already referred to implies that an attack on this basis would have to demonstrate a

94. Ibid., at p. 328.

95. Ibid., at p. 336.

96. See, Graupner (1969) 18 ICLQ 879, at p. 881. There is a suggestion in some cases that the loss of existing freedom is viewed more seriously than a restraint placed upon a new trader. If accepted, this view might be significant in distributorship contracts. Certainly, the court would look to see that the distributor is properly compensated by the terms of the agreement for his loss of competitive freedom.

97. The agreement in *Evans Marshall, supra* n. 92 was for 20 years; in *Cebora, supra* n. 18, the restraint appeared to extend outside the distributorship territory, though nothing was made of this.

98. This was Lord Hodson's *ratio decidendi* in *Esso.* Government policy, such as discouraging imports is not the same thing as public interest.

very prejudicial monopoly effect before it was likely to succeed. Indeed, the court may once again, begin with a presumption in favour of the sole agency agreement, particularly where the manufacturer would be unable or unwilling to enter a new market on other terms. In *Servais Bouchard* v. *The Prince's-Hall Restaurant* [99] a contract giving French wine merchants the exclusive right to supply burgundy for sale at the defendant's restaurant was upheld. Collins, M.R., considered that such contracts were "for the benefit of the community".

If a contract is held to contain an invalid restraint of trade, it becomes unenforceable to that extent. This would not prevent actions to enforce transactions with third parties made in pursuance of it (e.g., actions on contracts of sale), but might very well affect the enforceability of separate arrangements between the parties, e.g., for payment by the distributor by bill of exchange.[100] As to the main agreement, it is theoretically possible to sever the illegal part of a restrictive contract from the rest, which may remain enforceable; but since this would entirely alter the nature of the agreement, it is thought that severance of the exclusive rights from the rest of the agreement would not be possible [101] (in contrast to the position where a post-contract restraint is struck down or a minimum price clause becomes void by statute: see below). There is some authority that a party who is pressurised into performing an unlawful agreement against his will may claim compensation, but this is far from established doctrine.[102]

Finally, we must consider the position of third parties, such as other hopeful distributors. There are cases where third parties whose livelihood has been threatened have been allowed declarations that collective agreements, schemes or rules and arrangements excluding them were invalid.[103] It seems unlikely, however, that trade rivals, or members of the public, could successfully attack a distributorship agreement which both parties were observing.

2.3.2. Resale price maintenance

Both distributorship and agency contracts will often provide that the goods are not to be offered for sale except at the price for the time being fixed by the manufacturer. As far as the common law is concerned, such clauses were valid and enforceable but did not bind third parties who were not privy to the contract [104] except where the person selling to the third party was doing so under a licence to deal with patented articles, in which case a third party with knowledge of the con-

99. (1904) 20 TLR 574.

100. This would probably not affect the position of a holder in due course of the Bill.

101. Cf. Attwood *v.* Lamont [1920] 3 KB 571.

102. Shell U.K. Ltd. *v.* Lostock Garages [1976] 1 WLR 1187. A restitutionary remedy seems more appropriate than damages, although the facts do not quite fit into existing categories of economic duress, on which see, Goff & Jones, op.cit., pp. 176-186. It may be that in some cases only an award of damages will fully compensate the distributor.

103. See, Eastham *v.* Newcastle Utd. F.C. Ltd. [1964] Ch. 413 (football retain and transfer system): Nagle *v.* Fielden [1966] 2 QB 633 (membership of Jockey Club): Greig *v.* Insole [1978] 1 WLR 302 (rules of Test and County Cricket Board).

104. Dunlop *v.* Selfridge [1915] AC 847.

ditions attached to the licence was bound by those conditions.[105] Nor were such clauses per se illegal restraints of trade.[106]

By statute, however, terms or conditions in sales or other contracts (such as a distributorship) by a supplier (including a manufacturer) and dealers providing for a minimum resale price are void.[107] In addition the imposition of a minimum price resale condition on the sale to a dealer of patented articles is now prohibited.[108] The rest of the contract of sale remains valid and enforceable. There are certain exceptions:

(i) The Act applies only to minimum price maintenance. A provision for a maximum resale price is perfectly valid.

(ii) The Act does not prevent a seller from notifying or publishing recommended retail prices.[109]

(iii) Application may be made to the Restrictive Practices Court for an order exempting goods from these provisions.[110] To obtain an exemption, it must be shown that the goods fall within one of five "gateways", each of which involves a detriment or danger to the public:

(a) a reduction in quality or varieties available;

(b) a reduction in the number of retailers;

(c) a general, long term, increase in prices;

(d) a danger to health from the conditions of sale; or

(e) a substantial reduction in "necessary services" [111] provided in connection with or after the sale of the goods.

It must also, in each case, be shown that such a detriment outweighs the detriment caused to the public by resale price maintenance. The onus of proof on applicants has proved to be a heavy one.

In order to prevent evasion, the Act makes it unlawful for a supplier to withhold supplies by refusing orders, by supplying on significantly less favourable terms, or by treating the dealer significantly less favourably "in the execution of the contract", if the reason for withholding is that the dealer has resold the supplier's goods at below a recommended or agreed price, or sold to another person who has done so (or that he is likely to do so in future).[112] But a supplier may rely on any other legitimate grounds for withholding supplies, even though part of his reason

105. Dunlop *v.* Longlife Battery Ltd. [1958] 1 WLR 1033; subject now to the Patents Act 1977, s.44, which, however, does not prevent the licensor from imposing price conditions.

106. Palmolive Co. Ltd. *v.* Freedman [1928] Ch. 264; otherwise, perhaps, if the market has been cornered in an essential commodity (ibid) or the agreement may drive the buyer out of business: Evans *v.* Heathcote [1918] 1 KB 418.

107. Resale Prices Act 1976, s.9 (consolidating earlier legislation).

108. Ibid., s.10. To this extent the protection of patent law is lost.

109. Recommended prices are usually free from the intricacies of the Price Marking (Bargain Offers) Order 1979, as amended: S.I. 1979 Nos. 365 & 633.

110. Resale Prices Act 1976, ss. 14-19 (applications by suppliers, trade associations or Director General of Fair Trading).

111. I.e., necessary to prevent injury or otherwise for the protection of consumers or users.

112. Resale Prices Act 1976, ss. 11-12.

for doing so are unlawful, if those grounds alone would have led him to the same course of action.[113] Further, the Act allows wihtholding of goods which the dealer has, within the previous 12 months, been using as loss leaders.[114]

There are no criminal sanctions for contravention of these provisions of the Act. But a person affected by such a contravention may bring an action for an injunction or damages for breach of statutory duty; and the Crown may seek an injunction of its own motion.[115] Where, on the contrary, the resale price restriction is not contrary to the Act, s.26 actually helps the supplier to enforce it. This section provides that a term [116] as to resale price maintenance may be enforced even against a person not privy to the contract, if he had notice of it (to this extent reversing *Dunlop* v. *Selfridge)*.[117] Notice here means that the third party knew of the existence of the condition, and could easily discover details of it, even though he has not been given all the details.[118]

Finally, the territorial scope of the provisions should be noted. They apply to all attempts at resale price maintenance on the resale of goods in the United Kingdom.[119] Consequently, they apply whether or not the parties (or either of them) are English, and as far as the distribution agreement is to be executed in the United Kingdom, they apply whatever may be the governing law of that contract, or of any sales made in pursuance of it.

2.3.3. Collective price maintenance

The Resale Prices Act 1976 also controls collective agreements or arrangements by suppliers and dealers for the fixing of prices (whether maximum or minimum prices are involved). Briefly, it is unlawful to make or carry out such arrangements:

(a) to withhold goods from dealers not observing a price structure;

(b) to supply goods to such dealers only on less favourable terms;

(c) to supply goods only to dealers who observe the terms of the arrangement;

(d) to recover penalties or conduct domestic proceedings (e.g., within a trade association) against such dealers;

(e) to boycott or discriminate against suppliers who are not observing the terms of such an arrangement or to take action of the sort described in (a) above against them; or

(f) to recommend to other suppliers or dealers that they should take such action.
The prohibition extends to trade associations.[120]

113. Ibid., s.11(2). E.g., trader encouraging sales of rival goods.
114. Ibid., s.13, i.e., to drum up trade rather than make a profit on the goods. Seasonal or clearance sales are not loss leaders.
115. Ibid., s. 25.
116. The Act refers to a "condition" but probably means any term of the contract.
117. [1915] AC 847.
118. Goodyear Tyre Co. Ltd. *v.* Lancs Batteries (1958) LR 1 RP 22.
119. Resale Prices Act 1976, s.9.
120. Ibid., ss.1-3.

The scope of these provisions is of interest to a manufacturer exporting goods to the United Kingdom under a distributorship agreement. In the first place, the prohibitions do not cover either the distributorship itself, or sales made in pursuance of it, provided that there are only two parties to the transaction.[121] These parties would, as seen, normally be unable lawfully to fix minimum resale prices to the extent to which goods are destined for resale within the United Kingdom. Secondly, the prohibitions cover suppliers or dealers carrying on business in the United Kingdom and trade associations whose membership includes those carrying on such a business. For the purposes of the prohibitions on collective price fixing, it is interesting to note that s.8(3) of the Act specifically provides that a person is not deemed to carry a business in the United Kingdom only because he is "represented" [122] "for the purposes of that business by an agent within the United Kingdom".

As in the case of individually agreed minimum price maintenance, there is no criminal sanction for entering into an unlawful collective arrangement; but either the Crown, or a person "affected" by the arrangement, may seek redress in the Restrictive Practices Court.[123]

2.3.4. Restrictive Trade Practices

Although it is not of direct relevance to the distributorship agreement, a brief account of the Restrictive Trade Practices Act 1976 [124] may help to place such agreements in the proper context. Under this Act, certain "restrictive agreements" or arrangements relating to the supply of goods must be registered with the Director General of Fair Trading. He must take proceedings before the Restrictive Trade Practices Court which may prohibit the enforcement of the agreement.[125] The thrust of the Act is directed at agreements between suppliers of goods (and services) aimed at fixing the prices at which they will supply their products or otherwise restricting competition.[126] Such agreements may be direct, or in the form of "information agreements" under which suppliers are obliged to give each other details of prices, dealers to whom goods are sold, etc. Once such an agreement is before the Court, it is deemed to be contrary to the public interest (and therefore to be prohibited) unless the parties can prove that it escapes through one of eight statutory "gateways" of benefit to the public *and* that this benefit is not outbalanced by detriment caused to the public or dealers in the goods.[127]

121. Ibid., s.4.

122. There may be doubt whether an agency is more than "representation".

123. Resale Prices Act 1976, ss. 25, 27.

124. Another consolidating Act.

125. Orders may be made only against those carrying on business in the United Kingdom, and by s. 43(4) a person does not do this merely by being "represented" by an agent. An unregistered agreement is void and third parties may sue for loss suffered. The office of Director General of Fair Trading was established by the Fair Trading Act 1973, ss. 1 and 2.

126. E.g., by manufacturers establishing territories in which they will not compete with each other.

127. Sections 6, 7 and 10.

Although a foreign manufacturer with English distributors must keep a weather eye on this Act, there is a number of reasons why an exclusive distributorship agreement for an English territory will, by itself, not attract the Act. In the first place, the controls (as in the case of collective price fixing) are at a "horizontal" level and do not affect agreements for the supply of goods under which a manufacturer agrees to market his goods only through the distributor and the distributor agrees not to purchase goods of that description from other suppliers, or to resell them only within the distributorship territory. Secondly, even if one of the parties is a party to a collective restrictive agreement, the Act applies only to agreements made between two or more persons carrying on business in the United Kingdom so that the Act will not be attracted to agreements between foreign manufacturers only. It is possible, however, that agreements might be referred by the Director General of Fair Trading to the Monopolies Commission.[128]

2.3.5. Competition Act 1980

Further controls are imposed by the Competition Act 1980, which is designed to provide a simple and quick means of investigation. The Act regulates "anti-competitive practices". Such a practice is defined by s.3 of the Act as a course of conduct by a person in the course of business which has, or is intended or likely to have, the effect of restricting or preventing competition in the production, supply or acquisition of goods or services in any part of the United Kingdom. Although a course of conduct may have this effect when taken together with conduct of associates, one of the most striking features of the definition is that the practices of a single firm are now caught, whether or not the practices are concerted with other firms.[129] Previously this was not the case, in the absence of a monopoly, unless there was a "consumer trade practice" adversely affecting supplies of goods or services to non-business customers.[130] Equally notable is the emphasis on the effects rather than the form of the practice. In this respect the new Act resembles E.E.C. rather than the earlier United Kingdom rules. The width of definition of "anti-competitive practices" has been the subject of comment since it was first debated [131], and is clearly apt to catch distributorships. Even if such agreements may be investigated, however, inhibitions on smaller or newer markets are removed by the exclusion from the Act of enterprises with an annual turnover in the United Kingdom of less than £.5.000.000.[132]

128. Fair Trading Act 1973, s. 44 et seq.

129. One of the first issues to be raised under the Act has been the refusal of a bicycle manufacturer to supply his product to discount shops and ware houses. The refusal is justified by the manufacturer on the basis that such outlets provide no after-sales services and not only distort the selling market but may damage the manufacturer's name. Regardless of the merits of this argument, the refusal is clearly within the scope of section 3 of the Act.

130. Fair Trading Act 1973, ss. 13-17.

131. See, e.g., H.C. Deb., Vol 971, column 152. See also, Korah, (1980) JBL 255; Merkin and Williams (1980) 43 MLR 529.

132. Anti-Competitive Practices (Exclusion) Order 1980, SI 1980 No. 979.

The Director General of Fair Trading may investigate any firm or firms which he believes to be pursuing an anti-competitive practice.[133] The Director's task is to determine the existence of the practice, not to consider the public interest – although it is hard to see how he can ignore it given the limited number of investigations which resources will allow.[134] If he considers it appropriate he will, in the absence of an undertaking by the firm, refer the matter to the Monopolies and Mergers Commission. The Commission must then decide whether the practice indeed falls within s.3 and whether it is contrary to the public interest. On a finding against the firm, the Secretary of State is empowered to prohibit the practice. Given the probability that the Director will refer only a few, selected cases to the Commission, it may well be that the very fact of finding an anti-competitive practice to exist will place a considerable onus on the firm to justify it.

2.3.6. Antitrust law: an outline of the American position

It may be helpful to compare the *ad hoc* English controls with the theoretically more systematic controls in force in the United States. What is revealed, however, is a difference mainly in the thoroughness of the approach. Although this leads to results which would not obtain in England, few of the rules are so different as to be unrecognizable; but the amount and concentration of analysis is in stark contrast to the English position.

American antitrust law is found in a few, short sections of Federal legislation [135] and a mass of interpreting caselaw. The two main provisions which have affected the various forms of distributorship [136] are–

(i) Section 1 of the Sherman Act 1890, providing:

"Every contract, combination in the form of trust or otherwise, or conspiracy, in restraint of trade or commerce among the several States or with foreign nations, is hereby declared to be illegal."

(ii) Section 3 of the Clayton Act 1914, providing:

133. Once investigation has commenced, he may only terminate it by publishing his report, unless the Secretary of State consents.

134. See, Korah, loc.cit., at p. 256.

135. The Acts do not affect purely intra-State business, but inter-State effects are readily found. Some States, such as Texas, have enacted and enforced antitrust legislation of their own. For accounts of antitrust laws see: Neale and Goyder, *The Antitrust Laws of the USA*, 3rd ed. (1980, Cambridge); Sullivan, *Handbook of the Law of Antitrust*, (1977, West Publishing Co.).

136. Here, as in English law, terminology used by judges and commentators cannot be taken at face value. For examples of the range of usages, see, Pitofsky (1978) 78 Col. LR at pp. 1-5; Posner (181) 48 U. Chicago LR at pp. 6-7. Whilst the English cases tend to concern intermediate distributors, many of the US cases involve retailers described as "distributors". Intermediates are also described in this way: see *Pearsall Butter, infra* n. 142. The difference in analysis of damage to competition amongst "first-line" and "second-line" parties seems to be of degree, not of kind.

"It shall be unlawful for any person engaged in commerce, in the course of such commerce, to lease or make a sale or contract for sale of goods, wares, merchandise, machinery, supplies or other commodities . . . for use, consumption or resale . . . or fix a price charged therefor, or discount therefrom, or rebate upon such price, on the condition, agreement or understanding that the lessee or purchaser thereof shall not use or deal in the goods, wares, merchandise, machinery, supplies, or other commodity of a competitor or competitors of the lessor or seller where the effect of such a lease, sale or contract for sale or such condition, agreement or understanding may be substantially to lessen competition or tend to create a monopoly in any line of commerce."

It is the second provision which more directly affects exclusive distributorships but the most recent, and more interesting, caselaw has arisen under the Sherman Act. Enforcement of the Acts lies in the hands of the United States Department of Justice and the Federal Trade Commission.[137] Although the Sherman Act creates criminal offences much of the caselaw has arisen on applications by the Federal agencies for injunctions against violations. In addition, a private subject suffering loss through a violation of the Acts is permitted to recover "threefold the damages by him sustained".[138]

2.3.6.1. *The Clayton Act*

This Act does not affect the grant of an exclusive distributorship territory nor a restriction of customers to whom the distributor may resell. Neither does it prevent a manufacturer agreeing to supply goods only to a particular distributor. It does apply, however, to one of the characteristic terms of exclusive contracts, i.e., the distributor's agreement only to handle the manufacturer's goods and not to deal in competing products. Although the Act speaks in terms of "sales", it is clear that a sale disguised as an agency is caught by the Act [139] though not, apparently, bona fide agency agreements.

The most important question is the effect of an agreement upon competition. The words "may . . . substantially lessen competition" are "intended to prevent such agreements as would, under the circumstances disclosed, probably lessen competition, or create an actual tendency to monopoly".[140] At one extreme, a manu-

137. Created by the Federal Trade Commission Act 1914, which incidentally also declared illegal "unfair methods of competition in commerce". The Commission may declare practices to be unfair if against the policy of the Sherman and Clayton Acts whether or not there is an actual violation. Thus an "incipient attempt" to reduce competition may fall within the Act without proof of actual damage to competition already manifested: F.T.C. *v.* Brown Shoe Company (1966) 384 US 316.

138. Accordingly the termination of a distributorship often produces an antitrust suit against the manufacturer, usually unsuccessful. See, Buxbaum, (1966) Mich. L.R. 671; Barber (1955) 103 U.Pa.L.R. 847. Such a distributor, in the absence of a conspiracy (which would itself attract the antitrust laws), will have no other redress unless the termination is in breach of contract: Horton (1970) 3 Creighton LR 88; Bohling (1975) Tex. LR 1180-82.

139. Standard Fashion Co. *v.* Magrane-Houston Co. (1922) 258 US 346.

140. Ibid., *per* Justice Day.

facturer with 40% control of the relevant market falls within the Act [141]; but a manufacturer with only a 1% share who appointed an exclusive distributor selling only the manufacturer's margarine was held to have acted lawfully.[142] The courts are readiest to intervene in the case of tying contracts, under which the manufacturer agrees to supply product A (the tying product) only on condition that the distributor agrees to obtain supplies of product B (the tied product) from him.[143] It has indeed been said that such contracts "serve hardly any purpose beyond the suppression of competition" [144], and that once it is shown that the manufacturer has a monopolistic position in the tying product or that a substantial volume of trade in the tied product is restrained, the requisite potential lessening of competition is to be inferred.[145] In other words, as long as the volume of trade affected is not insubstantial, a rigorous forensic inquiry into the market is unnecessary. A tie may, however, be justified if the tying and tied products are so closely linked that the manufacturer's goodwill may be damaged by the use or resale of the one without the other.[146]

A more generous but still cautious attitude is taken to the requirement contract, under which the distributor agrees to obtain his whole requirement of a particular product from the manufacturer. Such contracts are said to assure steady supplies at stable prices and to avoid the risks and expenses of storage, as well as reducing the manufacturer's selling expenses [147], and therefore to be of indirect advantage to the public as well as to the parties. The criterion is whether competition has been "foreclosed in a substantial share in the line of commerce affected".[148] Thus a manufacturer with a dominant position [149] or with a wide range of outlets having overall substantial sales and all subject to the same restrictions [150] may well infringe Clayton unless there are very strong arguments of public interest in his favour.[151] If the proportion of the market affected is substantial, it appears to be no defence either that distributors not wishing to enter the manufacturer's exclusive contract can easily find other sources of supply or that the manufacturer has trained the distributors at his own expense.[152] It has been suggested that ex-

141. Standard Fashion Case, n. 139, *supra.*

142. Pearsall Butter Co. *v.* F.T.C. (1923) 292 F. 720 (7th Circuit Court of Appeals).

143. Particular hostility is shown to "full-line forcing", where the manufacturer makes the distributor carry his full range of products.

144. International Salt Co. *v.* US (1947) 332 US 392, *per* Justice Frankfurter.

145. Times-Picayune Publishing Co. *v.* US (1953) 345 US 594, *per* Justice Clark. Contrast the more generous approach in F.T.C. *v.* Gratz (1920) 253 US 421. If both conditions are met, the Sherman Act will also be violated.

146. U.S. *v.* Jerrold Electronics (1960) 187 F. Supp. 545; (1961) 365 U.S. 567 (TV equipment apt to fail unless used with other equipment of same manufacturer).

147. Particularly important for new entrants in the market.

148. Standard Oil of California *v.* U.S. (1949) 337 U.S. 293. This case tended to ignore the actual market performance, which might be considered under the Sherman Act.

149. See, *supra* n. 139.

150. As in *Standard Oil, supra* n. 148.

151. As in *Tampa Electric* (1961) 365 U.S. 320, a public utility case, in which the relevant market foreclosure was in any event smaller.

152. Mytinger and Casselbury Inc. *v.* F.T.C. (1962) 301 F: 2d 534 (District of Columbia Court of Appeals).

clusive arrangements may be permissible under Clayton for new entrants to the market who would not reasonably be expected to enter that market without the assurance of bound distributors.[153]

Summarizing briefly, it may be said that exclusive distributorships, but not pure agencies, are subject to Clayton whilst they tie the distributor to the product; that the test generally speaking is a rough and ready measurement of the volume of competition foreclosed; and that despite judicial awareness of the competing business and economic arguments in favour of such ties, it is only exceptionally that the courts are prepared to embark upon a more sophisticated inquiry.[154]

2.3.6.2. *The Sherman Act*

Clayton is limited in scope; for example, it does not catch territorially exclusive agreements in themselves. Distributorships are often, therefore, tested under the much wider Sherman Act. Although a similar question could perhaps be raised under Clayton, it is under Sherman that the issue is more frequently: "is an agreement illegal *per se* or subject to the rule of reason? " Sherman outlaws certain restraints of trade. Although clearly modelled, to this extent, on the common law notions of "unreasonable restraint of trade", those notions themselves are not sufficiently precise to be read as more than a statement of intention by Congress when the Act was passed. What has happened is that certain agreements, on an examination of their anti-competitive features as well as of the economic, business or social factors which might justify them, have been found by the Federal courts to be "so pernicious and lacking in redeeming value" [155] that they are now treated as automatic, *per se* violations of the Act. They are condemned as soon as they are shown to have been made. This is said to have the merit of avoiding expensive and prolonged litigation which could, in any case, have only one result. The two clearest examples [156] are horizontal divisions of markets [157] and vertical price fixing or price maintenance [158] (even otherwise acceptable practices may be struck down if tainted with such purposes).

153. Bok, *Supreme Court Review* (1961) p. 267. But even here, once the product is established, the agreements would begin to violate Section 3. It is also possible that the arrangements could be declared "unfair trade practices" by the F.T.C. under s.5, Federal Trade Commission Act: see, Neale and Goyder, *The Antitrust Laws of the U.S.A.*, 3rd ed., p. 273.

154. E.g., whether the manufacturer's position would actually have deteriorated if he had not imposed the restraints upon his distributors. The perceptible tendency of the cases is (willingly or not) to encourage integration by ownership, since integration by contract is obstructed. Of course, this in turn can lead to challenges under the monopoly-trust rules.

155. Northern Pacific Railway *v.* U.S. (1958) 356 US 1 at p. 5.

156. There may be others in the area of exclusive distributorship, but it is unclear what they are: see, *Sylvania, infra* n. 160.

157. Timken Roller Bearing Co. *v.* U.S. (1951) 341 U.S. 593 and see, *Cernuto, infra* n. 178.

158. Dr. Miles Medical Co. *v.* John D. Park & Sons (1911) 220 U.S. 373, 408. This *per se* rule was approved in Continental TV Inc. *v.* GTE Sylvania Inc. but is not without its critics: see, Posner, loc.cit., at pp. 9-10. There is clearly no prospect of the rule's reversal whilst judges regard the price mechanism as the single most important hallmark of competitiveness – "the central nervous system of the country": U.S. *v.* Socony-Vacuum Oil Co.

In most cases, on the other hand, the Sherman Act applies only if the agreement fails under the "rule of reason".[159] The court has to evaluate the impact of the practice upon competition. Two points emerge. First it is assumed that exclusive distributorships reduce "intrabrand" competition amongst the manufacturer's distributors, which is agreed to be a bad thing. To be weighed against this, however, is the assumption that such agreements in fact promote "interbrand" competition with rival products, a "redeeming virtue" which often allows them to be upheld.[160] Secondly, there arises the question of the precise content of the "rule of reason". One view is that it simply has no content.[161] It is true that courts tend to fall back on the very generalised formulation of the rule by Justice Brandeis in the leading case, *Chicago Board of Trade* v. *U.S.* [162]:

"The true test of legality is whether the restraint imposed is such as merely regulates and perhaps thereby promotes competition or whether it is such as may suppress or even destroy competition. To determine that question the court must ordinarily consider the facts peculiar to the business to which the restraint is applied; its condition before and after the restraint was imposed; the nature of the restraint and its effect, actual or probable. The history of the restraint, the evil believed to exist, the reason for adopting the particular remedy, the purpose or end sought to be attained, are all relevant facts. This is not because a good intention will save an otherwise objectionable regulation or the reverse; but because knowledge of intent may help the court to interpret facts and to predict consequences".

It is said that this invites an "unlimited, free-wheeling inquiry" which neither the judges nor jurors are equipped to undertake.[163] Whether this is true or not, some courts have tried to reduce the temptation offered by treble-damage suits by requiring the plaintiff to show that the defendant had a substantial power in the relevant market before the rule of reason even applied [164], but this is far from established law.[165]

(1940) 310 U.S. 150 at p. 226, cited with relish in National Society of Professional Engineers *v.* U.S. (1978) 435 U.S. 679 at p. 692.

159. Standard Oil Co. *v.* U.S. (1911) 221 U.S. 1.

160. Continental TV Inc. *v.* GTE Sylvania Inc. (1977) 433 U.S. 36. It is precisely because of these redeeming features that the Supreme Court in this case refused to apply a *per se* rule to distributorships, overruling the much criticized decision in U.S. *v.* Arnold Schwinn & Co. (1967) 388 U.S. 365.

161. See, e.g., Posner, loc.cit., at p. 14 et seq. (the "Vacuity of the Rule of Reason"). Attempts to restate the rule in other contexts have also been mauled: see (1980) Col.LR 14, criticizing National Society of Professional Engineers *v.* U.S. (1978) 435 U.S. 679.

162. (1918) 246 U.S. 231 at p. 238: Louis, (1977) 76 Mich. L.R. 265 at p. 271 ("totally unilluminating"). Cf. Esso Petroleum *v.* Harper [1968] A.C. 269 at p. 328, *supra* n. 94.

163. Posner, loc.cit., at pp. 14-15.

164. See, e.g., Gough *v.* Rossmoor Corpn. (1978) 585 F. 2d 381 at p. 390: Oreck Corp. *v.* Whirlpool Corp. (1978) 579 F. 2d. 126, (1979) 439 U.S. 446: Donald B. Rice Tire Co. *v.* Michelin Tire Corp. 483 F. Supp. 750.

165. Contrast with the examples in n. 164, Eiberger *v.* Sony Corpn. of America (1980) 622 F. 2d. 1068; Harold Freidman Inc. *v.* Thorofare Markets Inc. (1978) 587 F. 2d. 127 ("no single aspect is dispositive"). It is interesting that the F.T.C. resisted the substantial market approach: *Coca-Cola Co.* (1978) CCH Trade Reg. Rep. 21,509. Congress then passed the Soft Drink Interbrand Competition Act 1980, allowing exclusive territories for bottlers as long as there existed "substantial and effective interbrand competition".

It is fairly clear that the agreements most commonly described as "exclusive distributorships" in the United States are those in which the manufacturer agrees to appoint one distributor only in a given area. These agreements are subject to the rule of reason (unless there is a price-fixing element) and seem usually to be upheld.[166] Difficulties under Sherman are encountered only when the distributor is tightly circumscribed in the range of selling permitted, e.g. –

(a) an "airtight" territory, the dealer being forbidden to trade in the manufacturer's goods outside his allocated territory;

(b) restricted customer allocation, the dealer being forbidden to sell (for example) except to franchised retailers.

There may be sanctions for breach of such undertakings, (notably, termination of the distributorship); or the distributor may be subject to a "profit pass-over", requiring him to pay part of his profit to another distributor on whose territory he has trespassed. Where the dealer is subject to such restrictions, it has been suggested [167] that the rule of reason is to take into account at least some of the following factors–

(1) the need to attract a substantial number of distributors. This was mentioned in the leading case, *Sylvania* [168], justifying vertical ties on the grounds that distributors (actually retailers in this case, as in many others) would, in return for the restriction, invest capital and labour to develop the market. Where the restrictions apply to protect other distributors in the manufacturer's sales system, the ties may also be justified as compensating distributors who are required to provide substantial services both in promotion and sales and in after sales services. In return they are protected from intra-brand competition, but (in theory) encouraged to promote inter-brand competition. There is clearly a question whether these purposes and their assumed improvement in sales efficiency could not be achieved in other ways (such as quotas). The assumption is that the extra profit available to each distributor by the restriction on intra-brand competition will be rechanneled into enhanced sales against competitors. Whether this is likely, except in the case of new entrants, is obviously debatable. Where the justification operates, it also attempts to deal with the problem, actual or imagined, of the "free rider", i.e., the rival distributor relying on volume sales at low margins and rapid turnover, who exploits the market created by the less "efficient" but more hard working distributor who creates the market and provides a full range of services as well as merely selling the product. The anti-free rider effect apparently has judicial approval [169], but may be very hard to distinguish from a form of resale price maintenance, which is illegal *per se.*

166. See, Packard Motor Car Co. *v.* Webster Motor Ca. Co. (1957) 243 F. 2d. 418, 355 U.S. 822; Joseph E. Seagram & Sons *v.* Hawaiian Oke and Liquors Ltd. (1969) 416 F. 2d. 71, (1970) 396 U.S. 1062; Ark Dental Supply Co. *v.* Cavitron Corp. (1972) 461 F. 2d. 1093.

167. Pitofsky, loc.cit., at pp. 18-27.

168. Continental TV Inc. *v.* GTE Sylvania Inc. (1977) 433 U.S. 36.

169. Ibid., 55.

(2) Health, safety and product liability considerations.[170] Even before the *Sylvania* case, at a time when it was possible that *per se* rules applied to many vertical ties, a manufacturer was allowed to direct his wholesalers to sell certain very sensitive products only to outlets capable of selling them and using them properly.[171] There is of course a competitive aspect to these considerations, since it is arguable that safe, high quality goods will provide more effective inter-brand competition. Whether this in itself would justify raising, and protecting, distributor's margins either to attract them to the product or to counter free-riders and other rivals, is doubtful.

(3) The protection of valid exclusive distributorships (in the sense outlined at the start of this paragraph). This apparently justifies "location" clauses, under which a distributor (or, more often, a retailer) agrees to sell only from particular premises.[172]

(4) Other suggestions include the avoidance of duplication in the provision of services and economy of scale in the numbers and efficiency of distributors. These arguments are primarily of importance in the case of retailers, and again it is arguable whether the same ends could not be achieved by the use of quotas under "primary responsibility" clauses.[173]

2.3.6.3. *'Horizontal' vertical agreements under Sherman*

A simple refusal to deal with a distributor is perfectly lawful, even if the underlying reason is his refusal to abide by prescribed or understood resale prices.[174] But once a distributor has become part of the manufacturer's distribution system, which imposes restrictions on all distributors, it becomes much harder to drop him, since he is allowed to call the whole distribution system into question.[175] The "Colgate doctrine" allowing refusal to deal is therefore of limited utility.

An interesting development is the apparent readiness of some courts to see a horizontal (and therefore illegal) element in an apparently vertical agreement or refusal to deal.[176] Two cases stand out, if only for the difficulty in reconciling the decisions. In the first, *Oreck Corp.* v. *Whirlpool Corp.*[177] the defendant manufactured, *inter alia*, vacuum cleaners. Most of their business was done through Sears, selling the cleaners as "Kenmores" (sale of which accounted for more than 90% of Whirlpool's vacuum cleaner sales). Whirlpool appointed Oreck as exclusive distributors of "Whirlpool" vacuum cleaners. At the end of the agreement, Whirlpool refused to renew, and in fact terminated, Oreck's distributorship. The court

170. Ibid., n. 23.

171. Tripoli Co. *v.* Wella Corpn. (1970) 400 U.S. 831.

172. *Sylvania*, 9th Circuit decision, (1976) 537 F. 2d. 980 at p. 997.

173. Pitofsky, loc.cit., at p. 22.

174. U.S. *v.* Colgate & Co. (1919) 250 U.S. 300. But a refusal to deal may be part of a general scheme to control prices, and would then run into difficulties: see F.T.C. *v.* Beech Nut Packing Co. (1922) 257 U.S. 441; U.S. *v.* Parke, Davis & Co. (1960) 362 U.S. 29.

175. It may be significant that most of the cases upholding exclusive distributorships involve the replacement of the terminated distributor, not merely his disappearance.

176. See especially, (1980) U.Pa.L.R. 622.

177. (1978) 579 F. 2d. 126; 439 U.S. 946: 92 Harv. L.R. 1160.

held that this was a vertical restraint and subject to the rule of reason. In the second case, *Cernuto Inc.* v. *United Cabinet Corp.*[178], Cernuto was given a two year contract for the supply of kitchen cabinets. This was not in fact an exclusive distributorship. After a short time, United Cabinet terminated the agreement. Cernuto claimed that this was done because of complaints by another distributor that Cernuto was competing as a "low price volume dealer" – a free rider. Cernuto could not prove any actual anti-competitive effects of the termination, but the Court held that this might be a *per se* violation if it were shown [179] that United Cabinet and the other distributor had conspired to prevent price competition by Cernuto. Following *Cernuto*, "vertical" restraints tainted with "horizontal" agreement are, or may be, removed from the rule of reason laid down for purely vertical restraints (other than price-fixing) in *Sylvania*. The distinction between *Colgate* and *Sylvania*, on the one hand, and *Cernuto*, on the other, seems to be that restraints imposed as a result of pressures by third parties, such as rival distributors, will not be treated as being imposed unilaterally by the manufacturer.

Whether *Oreck* and *Cernuto* can be reconciled at all is debatable. Oreck had specifically argued that Whirlpool's refusal came at the "behest and insistence" of Sears and the court in *Cernuto* was "not convinced" [180] that it would have decided *Oreck* in the same way. It is clear that *Cernuto* does not require a cartel or general conspiracy amongst dealers. Pressure from a single powerful distributor would be sufficient. It has been argued, approving *Cernuto* [181], that the intra-brand restraints permitted by exclusive distributorships are usually effectively balanced by pro-competitive inter-brand effects [182]; that replacing one distributor by another does not generally affect intra-brand competition anyway [183]; and that because distributors are competing for the manufacturer's contract, the possibility of their coercing the manufacturer is remote, so that generally a vertical analysis is appropriate. The position is different, however, where the terminated distributor is a competitor of another (possibly exclusive) distributor. A distributor is then removed, intra-brand competition reduced, and, if the pressure comes from another distributor, horizontal analysis is appropriate.[184]

2.4. Duration and termination of the agreement

It was explained earlier that neither sole agents nor distributors enjoy any special status under English law. Consequently, all matters relating to the duration

178. (1979) 595 F. 2d. 164.

179. The question arose on the defendant's motion for summary judgment. The case could have been decided on the price maintenance point alone, and it is a mark of the court's determination that it insisted on opening the "horizontal" aspects of a vertifical termination.

180. 595 F. 2d., 169.

181. (1980) 128 U.Pa.L.R., 643.

182. But Posner argues that this balance is untenable: (1981) 48 U. Chichago L.R. 1.

183. See, *supra* n. 175.

184. Quite what happens if the other distributor's justification is that the removal of his rival would promote inter-brand competition is unclear. If he could prove this the fact would remain that he was conspiring with the manufacturer, and probably, under *Cernuto*, this would be enough to attract *per se* illegality.

of the contract, the manner and length of notice by which it may lawfully be terminated and the compensation (if any) payable on termination are for the parties to agree.

2.4.1. Duration

There is nothing to prevent the parties fixing any period which they may choose; they may even provide for a perpetual agreement.[185] The period chosen depends, at least in part, on the parties' commercial judgment of the time required to build up a sales network, the extent to which each should benefit from the initial spadework and expenditure of money and effort. No doubt the bargaining power of the parties will not be entirely irrelevant. Where no period is fixed, the question becomes effectively one of the length of notice required to terminate the contract.

2.4.2. Notice

The contract may make specific provision both for the projected duration of the contract, and for the power of either or both of the parties prematurely to terminate it, for example, a four and a half year contract terminable (in certain events) by 12 months' notice.[186] Where there is no express provision dealing with notice, the court will have to decide (a) whether the agreement, if for a fixed period, is determinable at all and (b) in any case the length of notice if determination is permitted.

It seems that the court will readily imply a power to terminate. The agreements after all, are of a sort which requires co-operation and mutual confidence, and even in the absence of a breach it would be unreasonable to hold the parties to the contract for an indefinite period. The longer the duration of the contract, the more readily such a power will be implied, since again, it will often be unreasonable to hold parties to a contract when the commercial circumstances may change dramatically during the course of time (even though that would not permit a plea that

185. Subject to the restraint of trade rules. Some agreements have been very long term: see, *supra* n. 97.

186. Schuler A.G. *v.* Wickman Machine Tool Sales Ltd. [1974] A.C. 235. Whether and when the distributor is able to claim payment under the contract depends upon the contract. How far he in turn is liable to place orders and pay for a particular quantity of goods is again a matter of construction. The question is whether he has merely agreed to use his best endeavours to drum up trade or has committed himself to place a minimum order in a particular period: James Shaffer Ltd. *v.* Findlay Durham & Brodie [1953] 1 WLR 106. Similarly an agent's entitlement to remuneration for introducing a willing buyer depends on the contract: *Bowstead on Agency,* at p. 168; although generally this will be decided in his favour (see Alpha Trading Ltd. *v.* Dunnshaw-Patten Ltd. [1981] Q.B. 290 – a "one-off" agency), this is only a safe *assumption* where the agent has power to bind. Because of the difficulties that have arisen (see, e.g., *Alpha Trading* itself) it is very important to draft the contract to deal with remuneration properly. Particular problems may arise if the contract deals with remuneration for certain types of service and the agent claims in different circumstances.

the contract was discharged by frustration). Certainly, where no duration is fixed, the court will imply (and indeed, impose) a power to terminate.[187]

The more significant question is the length of the notice required where there is no express provision in the contract. Here, it seems, it will not matter whether the contract is one of agency or of distributorship, nor whether the agent is a "quasi-employee" or an independant merchant. The length of notice must be "reasonable", judged at the time when notice is given. What is "reasonable" depends upon the facts of the case. Where the distributor has had to make considerable efforts to get the sales process moving, this is likely to mean a period of at least one year, particularly if there is no provision in the contract for compensation for early termination. In *Decro-Wall S.A.* v. *Practitioners in Marketing Ltd.*[188] a French manufacturer of decorative wall tiles appointed the defendants as "sole consessionaires" in the United Kingdom. To promote the product the defendants had undertaken a nationwide advertising campaign, expending some £ 30,000, had increased their accommodation for stock, and were planning to double their sales staff. Although the defendants were an established marketing company, their sales of other (non-competing) products had dropped to some 17 per cent only of their main business within three years of the main agreement. Judged also in absolute terms, there was no doubt that the defendants' marketing drive had been very succesful; in four years, the turnover of the plaintiffs' goods in the U.K. had risen from none to a projected million boxes per annum. In these circumstances, the Court of Appeal unanimously held that the contract could not be terminated by notice of less than 12 months.

If the manufacturer gives a wrongful notice of termination, that is ineffective.[189] The notice may fail for a number of reasons, in particular, by giving less than a reasonable time or by relying on a ground which, under the terms of the contract, does not justify termination. In the former case, it is not clear whether the notice will eventually have effect, after a reasonable period of time or whether, as seems to be the better view in the interests of the agent or distributor, a fresh notice has to be served.[190] In the second case, there is simply no power to terminate, and an attempt to do so will often constitute a repudiation of the contract.[191] Where the manufacturer has contractual power to terminate with or without cause, however, the only issue will be the requisite period of notice.

187. Decro-Wall S.A. *v.* Practitioners in Marketing Ltd. [1971] 1 WLR 361. Summary termination of agency contracts has been allowed only where the parties were not actually obliged to perform at all.

188. [1971] WLR 361.

189. Ibid.

190. In *Decro-Wall* a fresh notice was served before the hearing in the Court of Appeal, but neither its efficacy, nor that of the earlier notice once a reasonable time elapsed, was tested.

191. See, *Cebora, supra* n. 18. But it seems that there must be evidence that the manufacturer intended to stop performance whether or not he was justified before an unsuccessful attempt to terminate amounts to a repudiation: Woodar Investment Ltd. *v.* Wimpey Construction Ltd., [1980] 1WLR 277.

2.4.3. Compensation

Unless the contract makes provision for compensating wasted expenditure or for the loss of future profit or commission, the distributor or agent has no claims upon the manufacturer who terminates the contract. Only if a purported termination is wrongful will a claim to monetary compensation, in the form of damages, arise.[192]

It is obvious that the absence of a special legal regime for the protection of the distributor may mean that the contract operates very harshly against him. It is for this reason that the courts are wary of claims to terminate, particularly those which appear to be attempts to take advantage of the spadework done by the distributor; the same attitude may explain decisions where the English Courts have very readily allowed service of writs or issued injunctions against manufacturers in circumstances which might, at first sight, appear inappropriate.[193]

2.5. Terms of the agreement

The most central terms of the distributorship contract relate to sales of goods, the exclusive rights of the parties, and the extent to which an agent or distributor may legally bind the manufacturer. The agreement will often be very complex and may contain some or all of the following undertakings:

(a) by the distributor to promote the goods throughout the territory, by visits, correspondence, circulars, mail-shots, advertising, etc. and to deal promptly with orders;

(b) by the distributor to pass on useful information to the manufacturer, to keep accounts and make returns;

(c) by the distributor to draw to the manufacturer's attention any wrongful use of trade marks, etc.;

(d) by the distributor not to tamper with the goods in their markings;

(e) by the distributor to maintain stocks, spares, after-sales services, etc.;

(f) by the distributor only to employ particular salesmen;

(g) by the distributor not to assign the distributorship [194];

(h) by the manufacturer to supply instructions and samples, and to assist with advertising and promotion, and to send representatives;

(i) by the manufacturer to protect the distributor's exclusive rights;

(j) by the manufacturer to allow discounts or extra commission in specified circumstances.

This list cannot, by its very nature be exhaustive. There will often be terms permitting variations of prices or delivery terms or, of course, changes in the product.

192. Schuler AG *v.* Wickman Machine Tool Sales Ltd. [1974] AC 235.

193. See, Evans Marshall *v.* Bertola, *supra* n. 4.

194. He may be able to employ sub-agents. Further, this provision would not prevent factoring of receivables.

The first observation must be that some of the parties' undertakings are obligations of strict liability; the liability of the manufacturer to deliver goods contracted for on time, of the correct type and quality, to supply samples, discounts, etc., and of the distributor not to tamper with the goods, are obvious candidates, subject to what the contract may lawfully provide. So, indeed, are the exclusive dealing obligations of the parties. There are certain terms which can usually only be broken deliberately, e.g., the prohibition on assignment of the contract. Other terms, however, constitute only an undertaking that the parties will use their best endeavours – for example, the manufacturer's obligations to have goods available to meet orders, and to protect the exclusive rights of the distributor, and the latter's duties to promote the product, cannot normally be construed as absolute obligations.[195] The significance of the distinction will be apparent where the manufacturer tries to revoke the contract on the basis of the distributor's allegedly unsatisfactory performance in developing the market.

Generally, however, the more important question will be not whether a breach has occurred, but whether the breach entitles the other party to treat the contract as discharged, releasing him from further performance. Here, the "general contract law" nature of the agreement is most apparent. Terms can be divided into three sorts –

(i) "conditions", i.e., terms the breach of which (however trivial in itself) entitles the other party to treat the contract as discharged;

(ii) "warranties", the breach of which sounds in damages only[196]; and

(iii) intermediate, innominate terms, generating only a right to damages under the breach unless sufficiently serious as "to go to the root of the contract" or to "destroy the basis of the contract" or to be characterised as "fundamental".

Certain terms have been established by statute [197] or by common law [198] invariably to be conditions or warranties. Modern cases have shown a strong, though not exclusive, bias in favour of the third category.[199] Where the court is not legally bound to place a term within a particular category, the characterisation of that term becomes a matter for construction of the contract. The basic question is the degree of importance which reasonable commercially-minded parties would attach to a term and to the effects of possible breaches of the term, if, as is assumed, they considered the matter at the time when they made the contract. The wording of the contract is obviously some indication of this, but, since the test is at least partly an objective one, the words used cannot be more than an indication of

195. See, Schuler AG *v.* Wickman, *supra* n. 186. But an obligation to order a minimum quota would be absolute, and an obligation to pass on a minimum number of orders may well be: see, *Shafter, supra* n. 186. As discussed below (section 2.5.) it does not follow that breach of an absolute obligation necessarily entitles the other party to end the contract.

196. A substantial or repeated breach of warranty might conceivably amount to evidence that the party was unwilling or unable to perform at all.

197. E.g., Sale of Goods Act 1979, ss. 12-15.

198. E.g., The Mihalis Angelos [1971] 1 Q.B. 165 ("expected ready" in charterparty a condition).

199. Hong Kong Fir Shipping Ltd. *v.* Kawasaki [1962] 2 Q.B. 26; *Schuler supra* n. 186; The Hansa Nord [1976] Q.B. 44.

what the parties, acting "reasonably", intended. The tension between the subjective and objective approach, and the vagueness which the latter introduces, has led to judicial doubts about the wisdom of ignoring the words of the contract.[200] It is however, too late to alter the course which the Courts have taken, although it is clear that many terms remain to be treated as conditions.[201] The leading case as far as distributorship is concerned is *Schuler A.G.* v. *Wickman Machine Tool Sales Ltd.*[202] A German manufacturer appointed Sales for four and a half year as sole agents for certain panel presses and as distributors for other products. The agreement provided, inter alia, that "It shall be [a] condition for this agreement that . . . Sales shall send its representatives to visit [certain major motor-car firms] at least once every week". This was the only term of the agreement described as a "condition". Schuler later alleged that failure to comply with this term amounted to a breach of condition entitling them to treat the agreement as discharged. A majority of the House of Lords held that the term was not a "condition" in this sense. Some 1400 visits would be required during the contract, and the House was not prepared to hold that a failure in respect of even a single visit would have the effect contended for. This was a result which was considered too unreasonable to have been intended.

This is not to say that the use of words like "conditions" is to be ignored, and a majority of the House would at least have given it its prima facie effect but for what was considered the absurd results which this would have produced. If, therefore, parties wish to impose what a court might consider a very harsh burden upon one of them, it will be necessary to make it clear that this really is their intention. In most of the other cases discussed here, however, the question of characterising the term has not arisen. More often the issue has been whether an undoubted intention by the manufacturer to put an end to the contract has been lawfully manifested or not. In *Evans Marshall* v. *Bertola,* the issue was whether the agent had broken the contract at all. In the *Decro-Wall* case the manufacturer attempted to rely upon a breach of a term (prompt payment) which is normally regarded as only a warranty.

Where the breach relied upon is not a breach of condition in the strict sense, the ability to terminate the contract will turn upon the seriousness of the effect of the breach. If it destroys the basis of commercial confidence, or manifests an unwillingness to perform in accordance with the contract (or at all), then it will justify the other party in refusing further performance. It cannot be doubted that this produces a vagueness which is in contrast to the relative clarity of the rules governing conditions and warranties, and it has been criticised accordingly.[203]

200. Lord Wilberforce (dissenting) in *Schuler, supra* n. 186.

201. Bunge Corpn. *v.* Tradax S.A. [1981] 1 WLR 711. In particular, stipulations as to time of performance (though not of payment) will usually be found to be conditions in commercial contracts. Attempts to argue that "conditions" as such were no longer part of English law have been firmly resisted by the House of Lords in *Bunge.*

202. [1974] AC 245.

203. Weir (1976) CLJ 33.

The party suffering a major breach or a breach of condition need not treat the contract as discharged. The remedy is elective. Where, however, the manufacturer repudiates, then although the distributor theoretically has a choice, he may be driven to accept the breach as destroying the contract. This will be in part because the manufacturer may be able lawfully to terminate within a reasonable period of time in any case. Just as importantly, however, it is said that the distributor's right to damages will be adversely affected if he fails to take steps to mitigate his loss, for example, by finding an alternative source of business.[204] Whether this view is reconcilable with the rule that an unaccepted repudiation in itself has no effect [205] is doubtful. Certainly, it is open to the distributor who can perform without the assistance of the manufacturer to press on and do so, at least where the damage to his business by a summary end to the contract would be great. To the extent that he may earn commission by introducing orders which the manufacturer accepts, he is entitled to that commission as a contract payment, and not merely to damages.[206] On the other hand, cases in which the distributor can unilaterally perform will be limited by the very nature of the agreement. In most cases, therefore, the distributor will have to accept the breach as putting an end to the contract, subject to what is said in the next section.

2.6. Breach and remedies

As already indicated, the normal redress for the innocent contracting party is damages. Distributorship agreements may raise considerable difficulties in assessment of loss suffered either by manufacturer or distributor. Factors such as the unpredictability of markets and marketing efforts, the availability and cost of alternative suppliers or distributors on breach, coupled with the long term nature of many of the contracts, will necessarily make the assessment of a final loss speculative. This, in itself, is no obstacle to an award of damages.[207]

A general survey of contractual remedies would be out of place here. It will be necessary, however, briefly to examine the remedies other than monetary redress which may be available. The English cases have invariably concerned attempts to enforce agreements on behalf of the distributor rather than the manufacturer. Provided that the latter is prepared to give suitable undertakings, a simple declaration that the agreement is still subsisting will often be sufficient. In *Decro-Wall*, where the distributor refused to accept a termination or a repudiation by the manufacturer, a declaration was granted that the agreement continued in force

204. *Decro-Wall, supra* n. 187, at pp. 369-170. Sachs, L.J. at p. 375 is more guarded. In later proceedings in *Evans Marshall* the Court of Appeal gave damages for the period between repudiation and its acceptance without apparent regard for any supposed duty to mitigate *at that stage,* and this was not challenged in the House of Lords: [1975] 2 Lloyds R. 373, [1976] 2 Lloyds R. 17.

205. Heyman *v.* Darwins Ltd. [1942] AC 356.

206. White and Carter (Councils) Ltd. *v.* McGregor [1962] AC 413.

207. Chaplin *v.* Hicks [1911] 2 KB 786 (exclusion from beauty contest): and see *Evans Marshall, supra* n. 204.

and could be determined only by giving the required 12 months' notice. The manufacturer had undertaken (a) to continue supplying products during the period of the notice and (b) not to appoint any other distributor or themselves to sell within the territory during that period.

Undertaking (a), however, was tantamount to a positive injunction to perform the contract. This undertaking was discharged in the Court of Appeal. To put it crudely, although undertaking (b) might, commercially, compel the manufacturer to act in accordance with undertaking (a), the latter undertaking had not been sought, in the form of an injunction or otherwise, and could not have been granted. The reason is simple. The courts will grant injunctions to enforce only certain types of contractual promise. Nothing that amounts directly or indirectly to a positive promise of performance will be the subject of an injunction; but breach of an express or clearly implied negative stipulation may be prevented. So in *Decro-Wall* it was permissible to encourage, but not to enforce, the manufacturer's duties to supply goods; it would not be permissible to order him to supply goods.

To this extent, it does not matter whether the remedy granted is a declaration (having no coercive effect) or an injunction. It might be thought that a simple declaration would be available in at least one case where an injunction would not be, i.e., where the contractual performance is to run for a considerable time in the future. Even here, however, the Court of Appeal has been prepared to contemplate an injunction for up to 14 years, though it was expected to be rather less [208], and the decision was a preliminary issue. Normally, the grant of an injunction will be a preliminary to an orderly winding-up of the arrangements between the parties. It appears not to have been considered whether the power of the manufacturer lawfully to terminate the contract within the life span of the injunction ought to discourage the grant of this remedy.

An injunction is an equitable remedy and originally was granted to a plaintiff whom damages could not compensate. It is not difficult to see why an injunction may be granted, on this basis, to restrain a manufacturer from wrongfully ending his contract:

"If [Decro-Wall] were released from [their undertakings] they and the concessionaires they appointed in breach of their contract with the defendants would be free to take advantage of the breach and enjoy the fruits of the time, effort and money which the defendants have expended during the last three years in creating and building up a thriving market for [Decro-Wall's] goods in the United Kingdom. Damages in such a case are very difficult to prove and I do not believe that they would by themselves be an adequate remedy".[209]

It is possible that one consideration, not mentioned in this passage, is the ability of the manufacturer to pay the damages necessary to recompense the defendant, which will often be very large indeed. It is also possible that the modern test

208. Evans Marshall *v.* Bertola SA [1973] 1 WLR 349.
209. *Decro-Wall, supra* n. 187 at pp. 371-2 *per* Salmon, L.J.

is not simply whether damages constitute an adequate remedy but whether it is just that the plaintiffs should be *confined* to damages.[210] This enables the court in some cases adequately to prevent an unjust enrichment of the manufacturer, as well as an uncompensated impoverishment of the distributor.

3. DISTRIBUTORSHIP AGREEMENTS IN ENGLISH CONFLICT OF LAWS

Distributorships may be complex agreements, and involve contract law, agency, sale, personal property law and sometimes security law. There is ample scope for conflicts to arise where there is an inter-state distributorship, since different systems may hold the contracts very differently, particularly with regard to the protection of the distributor and the public policy aspects of exclusive dealings. What follows is necessarily a very cursory account of the approach which English courts will adopt to these problems. Apart from a few special points, most of what is said will have to be in the form of an outline only.

3.1. The law governing the distributorship

The agreement will be governed by its "proper law", i.e., that system of law which the parties have expressly or impliedly selected to govern it, or with which it has the "closest and most real connections".[211]

3.1.1. Express choice of law

There is almost unfettered power in the parties to choose any system of law to govern the contract, although the choice may sometimes be partly nullified by statute or rules of public policy. Subject to this, the only substantial limit upon the parties' freedom lies in a requirement that the choice must be "bona fide and legal".[212] This requirement is not infringed merely because the court cannot see why a particular law, apparently unconnected with the contract, has been selected. But, although there is no general doctrine of "law evasion", it may be that a choice which is tricky (e.g., designed solely to evade otherwise relevant antitrust or public policy rules) may be ignored.[213]

It is, unfortunately, unclear what weight is to be given to a choice of law by the parties which fails, through, for example, ambiguity.[214] If the parties selected "United Kingdom law" to govern a distributorship between a domestic distributor and a foreign manufacturer, it is not certain how far, once this choice fails

210. *Evans Marshall, supra* n. 208.
211. Dicey & Morris. *Conflict of Laws,* 10th ed., (1980) Rule 145.
212. Vita Food Products Ltd. *v.* Unus Shipping Co. [1939] AC 277 at p. 290.
213. Dicey & Morris, op.cit., pp. 755-756.
214. See, Cie. Tunisienne de Navigation SA *v.* Cie d'Armement Maritime SA [1971] AC 572.

for uncertainty, it may nevertheless be taken to exclude the law of the manufacturer's state.

3.1.2. Implied choice of law

Even where the contract makes no express choice, it may contain provisions which imply a choice. The commonest such provisions are choice of jurisdiction or arbitration clauses. So, in *Evans Marshall Ltd.* v. *Bertola S.A.*[215] a distributorship for Spanish wines in the United Kingdom had two references of disputes to Spanish arbitration. Although the issue was not directly concerned with the governing law, it was taken without argument that the law was Spanish.

But where the other "connecting factors" with different systems of law are not as evenly balanced as in *Evans Marshall,* the inference that the arbitral law has been chosen may be displaced.[216] This will be particularly so where the arbitration clause is the only connection between the contract and the arbitral state.

It may also be possible to find a choice by a negative implication. If, for instance, the manufacturer insists that sales in pursuance of the contract are not to be governed by the law of the distributorship territory, this may be some indication that the distributorship itself is not to be governed by that law.

Finally it should not be overlooked that jurisdiction and arbitration clauses may be merely matters of convenience, not indicating a choice of law at all.

3.1.3. Proper law in the absence of any choice

In this case the court must try to discover the system of law which has the closest connection with the contract. Relevant factors [217] may include the parties' place of business, the place of performance, the currency of payment, the use of terms or legal forms appropriate to a particular system and, where it is not entirely fortuitous, the place where the contract was made. Unfortunately, the first two factors, which are the most obviously powerful, will be of little help in the case of an inter-state distributorship.

The only case, apparently, in which a distributorship or agency has raised this problem is *Maroux* v. *Pereira.*[218] Maroux, a Frenchman resident in England wrote from England to the company in Portugal seeking the sole agency in England for their wines, and asking for samples, catalogues, etc. The defendants arranged a meeting in London, after which Maroux sent to the defendants a "certificate of agency" (in English). This was signed and duly returned. By now the agreed territory had been enlarged to embrace not only England, but also Scotland, Ireland and the Channel Islands. The judge held that the proper law of the contract was Portuguese:

215. See, *supra* n. 208.

216. *Cie Tunisienne, supra* n. 214; Atlantic Underwriting Agencies Ltd. *v.* Cia. di Assicurazione di Milano S.P.A. [1979] 2 Lloyds R. 240.

217. None of the factors raises any assumption: The Assunzione [1954] p. 150.

218. [1972] 1 WLR 962.

(i) It was not argued that the *lex loci contractus* was other than Portuguese. In the circumstances, however, this factor had no great independent weight, since the contract had been negotiated through the post. Under English law, therefore, the place of contracting was the place where the offer was effectively turned into a contract by acceptance, i.e., where the acceptance was posted. But this was largely fortuitous. Pereira might easily have varied the terms of Maroux's offer, making a counter offer which Maroux might have accepted in England.

(ii) However, although the English postal rules reduced the importance of the *lex loci contractus,* that law had some significance when coupled with the fact that Maroux had "sought out" Pereira in Portugal. In these circumstances, Megarry, J. was prepared to give some "real weight" to the claims of the manufacturer's law.[219]

(iii) It was difficult to say what was the *lex loci solutionis.* There was no single system of law under which the agent was to act, since the proposal for an agency in England had now extended to three other jurisdictions. Furthermore, the court did not accept the proposition that a distributorship involves a "localization" of the contract in the territory granted to the distributor, stressing Pereira's obligations to dispatch samples, literature and goods from Portugal. This rightly suggests a cautious approach to attempts to "localize" distributorship agreements in the agent's territory.

(iv) Whilst the "certificate of agency" was in English, and payments for the goods and of agent's commission was to be in sterling, the prices quoted for the goods were f.o.b. Lisbon.

Megarry, J. treated the case as a borderline one. It may be that the decisive factor, all other things being equal, was the impossibility of connecting the contract with any single system of law within the United Kingdom. It is true that in *Maspons Y Hermano* v. *Hildred, Goyeneche & Co.*[220] a simple agency contract between a Spanish merchant and a company was held, without any explicit reason, to be governed by English law. *Maroux* v. *Pereira* illustrates, however, that the court's inclination to apply the *lex fori,* where that is also the law of the distributorship territory, may be displaced.

3.1.4. Tortious liability

The possibility that the manufacturer of a defective product might find himself liable in tort to injured third parties has already been considered briefly (see 2.1). If the manufacturer is foreign and operates in England via a distributor, it has been held that process may be served on him out of the English jurisdiction. This is on the basis that his wrongdoing is committed by putting defective goods on the English market. He therefore commits an "English" tort.[221] As far as injury

219. See also, Arnott *v.* Redfern (1825) 2 Car. & P. 88.
220. (1882) 9 QBD 530, affirmed (1883) 8 App.Cas. 874 (unidentified principal).
221. Castree *v.* E.R. Squibb & Sons Ltd. [1980] 1 WLR 589.

or damage caused abroad is concerned, this will be actionable in tort in England only where the act causing it would be actionable if done in England and also by the law of the place where the act occurred.[222] It should be noted that there is no doctrine of the "proper law of the tort" in the English conflict of laws.

3.2. The law governing the sales

Finding a proper law for these contracts involves the same considerations as finding the proper law of the distributorship contract, although in some cases (e.g., the sale by a manufacturer to the distributor) it may be possible to identify the governing law with the law which is held to govern the principal agreement. There may also be contracts which raise no substantial conflict at all (e.g., the resales by distributor within the distributing territory) unless a foreign law is sought to be applied to the contract by one of the parties (e.g., where the distributor wishes to apply the foreign law of the distributorship to his resales).

Where a conflicts problem arises, it will have to be solved, in the absence of an express or clearly implied choice of law, by reference to the same connecting factors as would be applied to the principal agreement. There may be significant differences in the manner in which the factors can be applied between the distributorships and sales (for instance, as to the places of performance and the places of business of the parties) and between distributorships and agencies (the sale by the manufacturer to the customer may well be a "foreign-element" transaction when the distributor's resale to his customer is not). Agency sales may also raise difficulties of the agent's authority in the conflict of laws which do not appear in distributorships (these are considered in section 6 below).

There has been some tendency in English law to adopt the *lex loci contractus* of an agent's sale as the proper law which then governs the resulting contract between principal and customer. This should now be regarded as no more than one possible solution to the search for a proper law. Where no hard-and-fast method of negotiations has been laid down in the agency contract itself, it may also be objected that the *locus contractus* between manufacturer and customer will often be purely a matter of chance.

The "hybrid" agency (see section 1.2. above) falls between distributorships and "pure" agencies. Whilst, between manufacturer and agent the proper law of the agency will govern, it is thought that the sales to customers, in which the agent must act as principal, should be treated in the same way as resales by a distributor.

4. THE IMPACT OF STATUTE UPON THE SALES AGREEMENTS

A sale with an English connection may attract the provisions of the Unfair Contract Terms Act 1977, which severely limits the ability of a party to exclude

222. Dicey & Morris, op.cit., Rule 172.

contractual liability and liability in negligence. Where the Act applies, it will govern attempts to exclude liability in the sale itself, or (where the rules of privity permit such an exclusion) in a separate contract [223], such as the distributorship.

4.1. **Foreign manufacturer: distributor in England: English customers**

4.1.1. Contracts between manufacturer and distributor

Assuming in the first place that English law does govern the sales, the Act will not apply if the sales are "international supply contracts" within s.26. These are defined as (inter alia) sales by parties whose places of business are in the territories of different states if one of the following conditions is met:–

(i) the goods will be taken from one state to another; or

(ii) offer and acceptance take place in different states; or

(iii) the goods are to be delivered to a state other than the state in which offer and acceptance took place.[224]

If the manufacturer does not himself carry on business in the United Kingdom, it is clear that agreements of the sort presently under consideration will fall within the definition. Possibly, if the manufacturer has already shipped goods to England for storage before any order has been placed, the sale would not be able to meet condition (i), and if the orders were placed with an authorised representative of the manufacturer in England, it would not meet (ii) or (iii) either. If, in these circumstances, the manufacturer has given part only of the United Kingdom to the distributor, and himself sells the products in the rest, he would be carrying on business in the United Kingdom. This would conclude the question; the sales could not then be "international supply contract" at all.[225]

4.1.2. Contracts between distributor and customer

Section 26 cannot here apply since the contract will be made between parties carrying on business in the same State or, if the buyer is a consumer, because his "habitual residence" is in the same State as the distributor's business. One would expect this, a purely "domestic" sale, to be governed by English law. Connecting factors with other systems of law are weak. If the contract then proceeds expressly (or by a clear reference to a foreign judicial or arbitral law) to select a law other than English, what consequences flow? It may be that the choice of law can be ignored or overridden as not "bona fide and legal" or that the arbitration clause can be outweighed by the opposing connecting factors. Regardless of this, s.27(2)

223. Section 10.

224. Cf. Uniform Laws on International Sales Act 1967, s. 1(3). It is assumed that the parties are not choosing to apply this Act.

225. If English law does not apply, it may be necessary to consider s. 27, dealt with below.

of the Act may apply. Under this provision the Act itself is to apply, despite any contract term which applies or purports to apply a foreign law, if either or both of two conditions are met:–

(i) that the buyer can show that the term was "imposed wholly or mainly for the purpose of enabling the party imposing it to evade the operation of this Act"; or

(ii) if the buyer is a consumer habitually resident [226] in England at the time of the contract and that "the essential steps necessary for the making of the contract were taken there . . ."

As to (i), the general meaning is clear. A preponderant intention, in choosing the foreign law, of avoiding the provisions of the Act, will be self-defeating. There are detailed difficulties in interpreting (i) [227], in particular the precise meaning of the word "impose". This suggests a lack of freedom as far as the buyer is concerned; he must take the choice of law or not take the goods. To this extent, the Act contains a form of "abuse of rights" doctrine; and it may be that the English court would hold that a freely chosen foreign law is not subject to s.27(2) at all. Again, (ii) is clear enough in general, though there are difficulties in its precise interpretation.

Section 27(2) is an English conflicts rule.[228] As such, a foreign court would not be concerned with it. If the foreign court decides English law is the proper law, the whole Act applies. If it decides otherwise, s.27(2) will not change anything. In contrast, s.26 is a domestic English rule, applicable once English law is chosen or applied, and a foreign court would, no doubt, apply that section.

4.2. Foreign manufacturer: sole agent in England: English customers

In this case, we will probably have to consider one contract only, by which the manufacturer, through the agent, sells goods to the English customer. If the contract is governed by English law, any attempts to exclude liabilities within the 1977 Act will be caught, unless the sale qualifies as an "international supply contract" within s.26. This might seem an odd result in relation to a semi-domestic contract. In fact, the Law Commission in recommending the equivalent of s.26 to the legislature had a view to export transactions between large businesses.[229] As enacted, s.26 clearly applies to imports, and to transactions where the buyer may or may not be able to deal at arm's length with the seller.

Before s.26 can apply, however, the parties must have places of business in the territories of different states, which appears to exclude the case where the manufacturer has a place of business in England (as well as a principal business abroad).[230] If the manufacturer has premises in England from which he regularly

226. For "consumer" see s.12. "Habitual residence" is not defined.
227. See, F.A. Mann (1978) ICLQ 661.
228. Ibid.
229. *First Report on Exemption Clauses,* Law.Com.No. 24, para. 120.
230. Cf. Graveson, Cohn and Graveson, *ULIS*, pp. 48-49.

trades, therefore, s.26 would not apply. It is less clear whether the sole agent's place of business could be treated as the manufacturer's place of business for these purposes. The question seems to have arisen mainly in relation to service of writs issued by the English courts and to tax liability, neither of which is necessarily a guide to the interpretation of the 1977 Act. The distinction to be drawn is imperfectly expressed as the difference between "doing business here by a person" or merely "through a person". Thus in *Saccharin Corp. Ltd.* v. *Chemische Fabrik von Heyden A.G.*[231] a German manufacturer employed an agent in the United Kingdom, who carried on business at premises in London. The following facts are noteworthy:—

(i) the agent had power to enter into contracts of sale binding the manufacturer;

(ii) he had stocks of the manufacturer's goods available in London (some at his own premises) to fulfil their contract;

(iii) the manufacturer's name and address in the United Kingdom was, in all transactions, stated to be that of the agent.

In these circumstances, the Court of Appeal held that the manufacturer was carrying on business at the agent's address in London. The question is one of fact.[232] The fact that the agent is a sole agent in the sense that he must submit *all* orders for the relevant types of goods to the manufacturer might strengthen the argument that the manufacturer is carrying on business "by" the agent, i.e., has a place of business in England.[233] But, in so far as any single issue is decisive, this issue seems to be the extent of the agent's authority to bind the manufacturer to sales without submitting orders for his prior approval or subsequent ratification. In *Okura & Co. Ltd.* v. *Forsbacka Aktiebolag*[234] the "sole agents" (who were very far from "sole agents" in the sense used here) had to place orders with the Swedish manufacturer and had no general authority to accept offers. It was held that the manufacturer was not 'here' by an "alter ego who does business for them here, or who is competent to bind them in any way".[235] It is also clear from the cases that the mere fact that payment for the goods is made *via* the agent does not affect the matter.[236]

This assumes that English law governs the sales. It might well be that, even in the absence of an express choice of law, the proper law of the contract would not be English. The 1977 Act would not apply. In a case like the *Saccharin Corp.*, however, the contract has a strong connection with England and might well be held to be governed by English law. If in such a case the contract contains a choice of foreign law (expressly, or because an arbitration or jurisdiction clause

231. [1911] 2 KB 516.
232. Ibid.
233. Okura *v.* Forbacka [1914] 1 KB 715 at p. 720 *per* Buckley, L.J.; see also, Vogel *v.* Kohnstamm [1971] 3 WLR 537 (agency); Grainger *v.* Gough [1896] AC 235 (tax liability).
234. Ibid.
235. Ibid. at p. 721 *per* Buckley, L.J.
236. Ibid.; Grainger *v.* Gough, *supra* n. 233.

clearly point to a foreign law) an English court might well be faced with a challenge to that choice, as far as exclusions of liability are concerned, under s.27(2) of the 1977 Act. Though the challenge would, in a strict analysis, be weaker than in the case of the distributor-customer contract considered above, broadly the same consideration would apply. If confirmation of the order is necessary before a binding contract between customer and manufacturer is made, however, the customer's attempt to invoke s.27(2) faces an added difficulty. If he cannot show that the choice of law was "imposed" with an "evasive" intent, he must rely on his status as a consumer (if such he is). If he does so, he must also show that "the essential steps necessary for the making of the contract were taken" in England: s.27(2)(b). Whether or not the agent's transmission of the order to the foreign manufacturer has to be regarded as a step taken "by others on his behalf" it is not at all clear that an offer made in England and accepted abroad would satisfy the requirement of the section.

4.3. **English manufacturer: distributor abroad: foreign customers**

4.3.1. Contract between manufacturer and distributor

This is precisely the sort of contract to which, it was anticipated, the 1977 Act should not apply, even if the proper law were English.[237] Section 26 will almost inevitably make the sale an international supply contract, so that the English manufacturer is (as far as that Act is concerned) free to limit his liability as he pleases.[238]

Again, if the law of the contract is a foreign law, there seems little possibility of s.27(2) (above) being applied by an English court, since the choice of the foreign law is unlikely to be characterised as "evasive" in the circumstances.

4.3.2. Contract between distributor and customer

One would expect this to be governed by the law of the distributorship territory. If, however, English law is chosen, s.27(1) may apply. This provides that most of the restrictions on exclusion of liability are not to apply:–

"where the proper law of a contract is the law of any part of the United Kingdom only by choice of the parties (and apart from that choice would be the law of some country outside the United Kngdom)."

This section has not escaped criticism [239] but its intention (though not perhaps its application) seems in the present case to be clear. If the court concludes that the closest connection is with a foreign law, it must still uphold the choice of English law (provided it is "bona fide and legal", etc.). But "English law" does

237. See, *supra* n. 229.
238. Unless the manufacturer has a place of business within the United Kingdom.
239. See, F.A. Mann, loc.cit.: "almost perverse in character".

does not include the restrictive provisions of the 1977 Act.[240] There may be difficulties in deciding whether English law governs "only by choice of the parties", in particular in determining whether and to what extent a choice by arbitration or jurisdiction clause (a) amounts for these purposes to a choice of English law and (b) is to be disregarded entirely in deciding if the contract is more closely connected with a foreign law (if the answer to (a) is affirmative, the answer to (b) is presumably the same). Many problems will not materialise if the courts take the view that an arbitration clause choosing English law can be overridden by stronger connections with a foreign law; in this case the proper law will be that foreign law and s.27(1) will not fall to be considered.

4.4. English manufacturer: sole agent abroad: foreign customers

Assuming again that only one contract falls for consideration here, the first step is to determine the proper law. Neither a choice of English law nor a choice of the foreign law would be capricious. If no choice is made, clearly both laws would have a claim for consideration.

If the English law applies, there is, once again, a strong possibility that s.26 will make the contract an international supply contract, so that the rest of the 1977 Act will not apply. If, for some reason, it does not, one would have to consider the possible impact of s.27(1), but it seems improbable that an English court would decide that English law is the proper law "only by choice of parties" in these circumstances.

If the foreign law applies, the only possible application of the Act lies in s.27(2), and it is unlikely that the customer will be able to show that the choice of the foreign law was "wholly or mainly for the purpose of" evading the Act.[241]

4.5. Foreign manufacturer: foreign distributor: foreign customers

For present purposes, it will not matter a great deal whether the manufacturer is in a different state from the other parties or not, since the brief discussion will deal both with "domestic" and "international" agencies. It is clear that in the absence of a choice by the parties, English law will not apply, whether we are talking of a distributorship or an agency. If, however, English law is chosen or implied by an arbitration clause, and the choice is upheld, s.27(1) of the 1977 Act must apply here: the restrictive provisions of the Unfair Contract Terms Act are therefore excluded. This is in line with the policy behind the section, which is to ensure that foreign parties are not deterred from coming to the United Kingdom for arbitration of their dispute by the possibility that the 1977 Act might invalidate contractual terms which were perfectly acceptable to them.[242]

240. Except for s. 8 (exclusion of liability for misrepresentation).

241. Even if the buyer is a "consumer", he will not be habitually resident in the United Kingdom.

242. Law Com. No. 24, *supra* n. 229, paras. 232-233.

It may be that, as far as the 1977 Act is concerned, a "choice" of English law may be made otherwise than expressly or by implication from an arbitration clause, e.g., by the entire contract being in an English form, with prices, etc. in sterling. To decide otherwise would be to hold s.27(1) inapplicable, and the rest of the Act to apply; even if the contract were then extricated from the Act via s.26, this would be an odd result.

5. THE DISPOSITIVE EFFECTS OF THE CONTRACT

Whilst the contract is governed by its proper law, its effect on the ownership of the goods will, generally speaking, be dictated by the *lex situs* of the goods when the transfer is made [243], although a transfer effective by the proper law of the contract will probably be recognised in England if made whilst the goods are in transit.[244]

It follows that the proprietary effects of the initial sale by manufacturer to distributor will probably be governed by the law of the manufacturer's place of business, the resales by the distributor more often by the law of the distributorship territory (in the case of agencies, much will depend upon where stocks of goods to meet the orders are kept). The distributor's title under the manufacturer's law would then be recognised in England even though it might not be effective by the distributor's own law. When the distributor resells, English law will judge the dispositive effect of that sale by the new *lex situs*, applied to a title already established under the old *lex situs*, and without resort to any provisions of that law giving effect to sales by non-owners.

The efficacy of securities over the goods, in particular of reservations of title by the manufacturer, will be dealt with in the same way, since all the securities will involve the retention or transfer of interests in movable property.[245] Thus a reservation of title valid by the *lex situs* should be effective even when the goods are transferred to a territory whose law would have avoided it (e.g., for non-registration).

243. Dicey & Morris, op.cit.

243. Dicey & Morris, op.cit., Rule 79. In Winkworth *v.* Christie, Manson and Woods Ltd. [1980] Ch. 496, Slade, J. held that the rule applies not only as between the parties to the disposition, but also so as to bind third parties who did not assent to it but claim title recognized by the law of another jurisdiction and prior in time to the disposition. The goods in question had been stolen in England, sold in Italy, and then returned by the Italian buyer for auction in England. The original owner's title was held to be defeated by the sale in Italy, on the assumption that this would be the result under Italian domestic law. An argument that as the goods had never left England with the owner's consent and were now back in England, the "real" situs was English, was rejected. For a general discussion of prior titles in the conflict of laws see, Davis (1964) ICLQ 53 (listing the copious literature on the subject).

244. Dicey & Morris, op.cit., pp. 560-561. What happens if the transfer is invalid by the proper law is less clear.

245. Ibid., at p. 563 et seq.

The purpose of title reservation is to defeat third party claims as much as the distributor's. If the distributor is insolvent, the actual administration and distribution of the property is, with some exceptions, regarded as a matter for the *lex fori*.[246] This applies once the distributor's property is determined. But third party claims to own the goods will have to be decided according to the relevant *lex situs*, and an initially valid reservation may later be defeated by a transfer sufficient under the new *lex situs* to transfer ownership to a buyer (e.g., by recognition of transfer by non-owning mercantile agents).

If the initial reservation of title is void by the manufacturer's law, the effect of the transaction between manufacturer and distributor may be to vest property in the latter (unless the effect of the invalidity by that *lex situs* is merely to avoid the manufacturer's claim against other creditors). The efficacy of the distributor's resale may then be judged by the ordinary rules of the new *lex situs*.

A successful reservation of title may carry with it a claim to the proceeds of resale of the goods. If the claim is proprietary (as in the case of an English equity) the title to the proceeds should be governed by the *lex situs* of the proceeds when they were dealt with (rather than, it is thought, the *lex situs* of the goods when resold, if that is different). If the claim is personal (e.g., a bare duty to account) then its efficacy should probably be judged by the proper law of the distributorship (or other agreement) upon which the claim is based. If, however, in any case the proceeds are intangible property, such as a book debt, claims to proceeds and questions of priority against rival claimants would, it seems, be governed by the proper law of the contract creating the debt.[247]

6. THE AGENT'S AUTHORITY

The rights and duties of manufacturer and sole agent inter se will be governed by the proper law of the agency. It is also usually stated that the substantive effects of the contract which the agent procures for his principal is governed by the proper law of the contract, and also that the extent of the agent's actual or apparent authority is to be judged by that law [248] (even though the connection between apparent authority and estoppel might at first sight lead one to regard it as a procedural matter for the *lex fori*, this would be an odd result).

There is, however, a long-standing confusion in the English cases, since it has also been held [249] that the agent may be able to affect the relationship between principal and third party if he had power to do so under the proper law of the agency, and although he had no such power under the proper law of the contract between principal and third party.

246. Ibid., Rules 127 and 209.
247. Ibid., Rule 83. The authorities are not very clear.
248. Ibid., at pp. 909-910.
249. Ruby S.S. Corpn. Ltd. *v.* Commercial Union Assurance Co. Ltd. (1933) L.T. 38.

Whether the agent has himself undertaken liability by his acts (i.e., liability under or collateral to the agreement between the manufacturer and customer) should depend upon the proper law of the contract which he negotiates for the manufacturer.[250]

7. RESTRAINT OF TRADE AND ILLEGALITY OF CONTRACTS

The validity of the distributorship must be determined by its proper law. English courts will not enforce an agreement invalid by that law even though it may be valid by English law and by the *lex loci contractus.*[251] The theoretical dangers of evasive choices of law do not yet appear to have materialised in practice. There are, moreover, substantial inroads on the primacy of the proper law.

7.1. Where the contract is contrary to English public policy

If a contract infringes a basic policy rule of English law, then an English court will refuse to enforce it. So, a contract valid by its proper law, will not be enforced in England if it constitutes an unreasonable restraint of trade, at least where enforcement would produce in England some of the effects which it is the purpose of the restraint rules to avoid.[252] Oddly enough, the same does not appear to be true of English statutory rules; here the effect of the Act on the contract is a matter, in the absence of express provision, of statutory interpretation.

7.2. Where performance of the contract would be illegal by the lex loci solutionis

A contract valid by its foreign proper law will not be enforced by an English court if its performance in England would breach English law (a rule basically similar to (i) but not dependent upon any initially invalidating element of public policy); and an English court will not enforce a contract governed by English law if its performance would violate the foreign *lex loci solutionis.*[253] The extent to which the court would also refuse to enforce a contract valid by its foreign proper law but whose performance is illegal by the (different) foreign *lex loci solutionis* is uncertain.[254] The place of performance of a distributorship may very well be twofold, the place where the manufacturer performs, and the place where the agent performs, and it is not difficult to envisage the complexities which this may produce.

250. Dicey & Morris, op.cit. at p. 916.
251. Kahler *v.* Midland Bank Ltd. [1950] AC 24.
252. Rousillon *v.* Rousillon (1880) 14 CH. D. 351.
253. Ralli Bros. *v.* Cia Naviera [1920] 1 KB 614.
254. "Doubtful and highly controversial": Dicey & Morris, op.cit. at p. 795.

THE SOLE DISTRIBUTOR IN COMPARATIVE AND PRIVATE INTERNATIONAL LAW

by J.A. Wade

1. INTRODUCTION

The subject-matter of this paper begets a multitude of closely interrelated issues. It is not possible within a reasonable compass to consider the totality of issues arising: delimitation is essential. One is here concerned with international transactions for the market distribution by way of sale of movable tangibles where the distributor fulfills the economic role of middleman between the producer or supplier [1] of goods and the next purchaser. Each of the legal systems within Europe recognizes such middlemen. The nature of such figures and the incidents attaching to and flowing from their functioning reflect the legal regulation of norms recognised as requiring protection, certainly within the territorial jurisdiction. When such local law figures are involved in international commerce, differences in their natures and functioning lead to practical as well as theoretical problems when the consequences of the relationship call for regulation.

There are two principal methods open to the supplier wishing to ensure accessibility [2] of his goods in a foreign market. He can distribute directly by establishing his own sales and distribution network there or he can operate indirectly by means of, first, concluding agreements with intermediaries already established in the market, i.e., by concluding either agency or distributorship contracts, or, secondly, by way of licensing agreements, which last might be termed passive distribution.[3]

Both agency and distributorship agreements have grown in commercial importance in recent years. This fact was influential in the decision to give priority to a convention on agency in the future work of the Hague Conference on Private International Law, which led to the Convention on the Law Applicable to Agency of 1978.[4] The establishment of the European Economic Community has also led to the increased use of commission agents and distributors by producers and suppliers not established within the Community. It may be noted that during the Thirteenth session of the Hague Conference, the Netherlands proposed that the Draft Agency Convention be extended to apply also, "to the relationship between the parties to a contract under the terms of which one party grants to the other the exclusive right to sell a product or a service (sole distributor)" [5], on the ground that such relationships were similar to agency relationships for all practical purposes. The proposal was supported by Switzerland but failed to secure adop-

1. More usually the latter: van Rooij, (1980) 27 NILR 371 at p. 374, commentary to Hof Amsterdam, 8 June 1977, NJ 1978, 191.

2. On methods of market penetration generally see, Schmitthoff, *Export Trade,* 7th ed., (1980) p. 153 et seq., and van Gerven and Lukoff, eds., *Commercial Agency and Distribution Agreements* (1970) passim.

3. On this see, e.g., Jones, "Fundamentals of International Licensing Agreements and their Application in the European Community", CMLRev (1973) p. 3 et seq. On the approach of the Community to the use of industrial property see, Cohen Jehoram, "The Delicate Balance between Industrial Property and European Law: the Law as it stands", *Legal Issues of European Integration* (1972) No. 2, p. 71 et seq.

4. See, Pelichet, "Report on the Law Applicable to Agency", *Actes et Documents* (1976) Vol. IV, p. 10.

5. See, *Actes et Documents,* (1976) Vol. IV, Document du Travail No. 29.

tion principally on the reasoning that despite the coincidence of economic function, the legal bases were sufficiently distinct to justify individual treatment.[6]

The subject under discussion is a forcing ground for the interplay of economic forces and legal regulation. A dominant motivation for the various contractual arrangements devisable, turning as they do on the central notion of exclusivity, is essentially the same: the economic need to compete, whether that manifests itself as a desire to achieve extensive monopoly or as protection for a limited and vulnerable market in goods and services. The scale of possibilities represents the trader's inventiveness in harnessing the power of competition [7], and in utilizing the scope and limitations of the private law options available. Although the rule of survival, arguably the most fundamental rule, may motivate the trader towards continuing expansion and elimination of competition, thus leading to a concentration of control over scarce goods, in particular money, this course is increasingly being strewn with obstacles as efforts are continued to regulate the distorting effects of competition either directly through the mechnism of anti-trust and restrictive parctices legislation or indirectly by protecting or alleviating the position of the economically weaker party. Within the European community these processes occur at both national and Community levels [8], and can lead to condemnation in the same area of control at both levels.[9] The motivation for such in-

6. Ibid., pp. 164, 260-61, 273-74, 418.

7. On the driving power of competition within an integrated Common Market see, van Gerven, "Het concurrentiebeleid van de gemeenschap en de economische crisis", *Nieuw Europa* (1978) No. 3, p. 1 at p. 4. On the economic motivations for concerted practices see, de Jong, "The Economics of Concerted Practices (Collusion)", in *European Competition Policy,* edited by Europa Institute, Leiden (1973) p. 92 et seq. See also, Downes, "Exclusive Dealing Agreements: A Change for the Worse? ", *European Law Review* (1979) Vol. 4, p. 166 et seq.

8. Art. 85(1), EEC Treaty, which seeks to prevent practices, "which may affect trade between Member States and which have as their object or effect the prevention, restriction or distortion of competition within the common market . . .": Ets. Consten S.A. and Grundig – Verkaufs GmbH *v.* EEC Commission (56/64, 58/64) [1966] CMLR 418. See further, *infra*, section 5. For a similar provision see, (UK) Competition Act 1979, s. 2. For price maintenance clauses see, *UK:* Resale Prices Act 1976, s. 9. The Act only applies to resale within the United Kingdom. Sole agency and exclusive distributorship agreements are exempted from the scope of the UK Restrictive Trade Practices Act 1976, where the agreement is concluded between not more than two parties: Schedule 3, para 2; *France:* Decree of 30 June 1945, Art. 37(4), Decree No. 45-1483 as amended; see Focsaneanu, "Les prix imposés dans la Communauté Economique Européene, droits nationaux et droit communautaire", Rev. trim. de droit europ. (1976) p. 12 at p. 185 et seq.; *Germany:* Law against Restraints of Competition (*Gesetz gegen Wettbewerbsbeschränkungen*) of 27 July 1957, paras. 15 et seq.: see Focsaneanu, ibid., at p. 199 et seq.; Joliet, "Prix imposés et droit européen de la concurrence", *Cahiers de Droit Européen* (1971) p. 16 at p. 42 et seq.; *The Netherlands:* Law on Economic Competition (*Wet economische mededinging*) of 28 June 1956, Stb. 1958, No. 413 appears to have been invoked only exceptionally. Recent cases show that vertical price-fixing achieved by means of national distributorship agreements can be protected by litigation: Rb. Amsterdam, 16 September 1975, NJ 1976, 93; except where the supplier fails to prove actual loss occasioned by the retailer: Rb. Utrecht, 22 September 1975, NJ 1976, 94 and 95; *EC Art. 85,* complemented by Council Reg. 17 of 6 February 1962, OJ 1962/13, and various Commission regulations: see, *Guide to EEC-Legislation* (1979) ed. Kellermann, Esselaar, Tromm, Grondman.

9. See, Wilhelm *v.* Bundeskartellambt [1969] CMLR 100. According to an earlier decision of the French *Cour de Cassation, Chambre Criminelle,* Decision of 22 October 1964 [1965]

tervention is that competition is thereby ensured, at least at the supra-national level. Other motivations certainly play a role at the national level when it is accepted that restrictions on play are necessary in the interests of the game [10], motivations which in turn are now appearing at Community level.[11] As one commentator has expressed it, the absoluteness of the goal rules is now substantially qualified by the operation of the game rules.[12] As another has recently and incisively pointed out:

"[It is] an important economic phenomenon too often ignored by courts and governments: that individuals and firms are not automatons and will adapt their behaviour to any potentially disadvantageous legal change."[13]

Not surprisingly, the vocabulary encountered in the field is not only extensive, its use is sometimes idiosyncratic and frequently lacking in precision.[14] Confusion

---

CMLR 36 (*Nicholas No. 2*) a decision of the Commission exempting under Art. 85(3) an agreement from invalidity under Art. 85(1) would not exempt the agreement from conformity with national restrictive practices legislation of the same type as Art. 85(1). The United Kingdom Restrictive Trade Practices Act 1976 applies also to agreements authorised by directly applicable Community provisions; s. 5(1).

10. For a play on the French and Italian texts of Art. 85: "*jeu de la concurrence*", "*gioco della concurrenza*", Drion, "Restraint of Buyer's Freedom under Article 85", CMLRev (1963-64) p. 148 et seq. In the United Kingdom the House of Lords, in the context of solus agreements, stated that, "restrictions may in some contexts be imposed, and upheld, where they have become part of the accepted pattern or structure of trade, rather than as limiting trade": Esso Petroleum Co. Ltd. *v.* Harper's Garage (Stourport) Ltd. [1968] AC 269 at p. 336, *per* Lord Wilberforce.

11. Draft EEC Council Directive to coordinate the laws of the Member States relating to self-employed commercial agents, OJ 18 January 1977, C 13/2, amended, OJ 2 March 1979, C 56/5, see, *infra*, text to n. 97 et seq.

12. For an account of the interplay between economist and lawyer, respectively employing goal rules and game rules, see, Brinkmann, "Steeplechase voor juristen en economen", AAe (1966) p. 36 et seq.

13. Bishop [1981] 44 MLR 282 at p. 291.

14. "In certain trades the word 'agent' is often used without any reference to the law of principal and agent", W.T. Lamb & Sons *v.* Goring Brick Co. [1932] 1 KB 710 at p. 717 *per* Scrutton LJ. The European Court of Justice in Consten and Grundig *v.* EEC Commission [1966] CMLR 418 at p. 470 confused the economic and legal connotation of agency and distribution: "It is pointless to compare . . . the situation under Art. 85 of a producer bound by a sole agency agreement to a distributor of his products . . ." The Court soon clarified its meaning: "It is vain to compare the position of the producer bound by an exclusive dealing agreement to the distributor of his products . . . " in Italy *v.* EEC Council and Commission, Case 32/65 [1969] CMLR 39 at p. 63. The distributor (*concessionaire*) is frequently termed agent (*agent* or *représentant*), see Theux, *Le droit de la représentation commerciale*, Vol. I, p. 302 n. 154. For a typical example see, Evans Marshall & Co. *v.* Bertola SA [1973] 1 WLR 349, where the parties had concluded a sole agency contract referring to "sole agents and representatives", which was in fact an exclusive distribution agreement: see, Wade, "Actions in personam – assumed jurisdiction of the English Court", [1974] 21 NILR 1 at p. 17 n. 90. Suetens, "Exclusiviteitsovereenkomsten, exportverboden en het EEG-Kartelrecht", RW (1962-63) no. 2214, not only distinguishes between pure exclusive contracts and those containing additional clauses but divides the former into three classes. The analysis derived from a criticism of the European Commission's use of terminology as economically unfortunate in its Announcement of 24 December 1962, OJ 1962, 2921, the so-called Christmas Message. The usefulness of this analysis has itself been questioned, see, van Damme, "La Mise en Oeuvre des Articles 85 et 86 du Traité de Rome", *Cahier de droit européen* (1967) p. 49 at p. 64.

is almost unavoidable. At the private law level economic objectives are brought within a range of legal concepts which from one legal system to another are either basically or otherwise significantly different. In addition, European Community competition law is concerned predominantly with international effects and consequently its provisions cut across diverse categories of agreement.[15]

The thrust of the following discussion is towards the contractual relationship between a producer-supplier established in one country, who wishes to create or expand an economic relationship with purchasers-users in another country, and another person, established in either country, who carries on an activity that is suitable for effecting such economic relationship, the contractual relationship serving to confer upon that other person the economic function of distributor. It is intended, without more ado, to limit this function to that of distributing goods produced or supplied, and to concentrate attention almost exclusively on the contractual aspects of the relationship, to the exclusion of proprietary aspects.

This approach encompasses both the relationship with the distributor and his with the third party. In the case of an exclusive distributorship agreement the relationship between producer-supplier and third party is contractually non-existent.[16] The economic relationship breaks down into one contract of sale between distributor and third party, and another, within the framework of the contract of exclusive distributorship, between producer-supplier and distributor. When the distributor is invested with the legal character of agent, the matter is conceptually more complex for although one is still dealing with contract of sale, it may, depending on the type of agent, be a direct sale not involving the agent, or a sale to or from the agent with a further transfer of property from the agent or even raise the question whether a sale has been effected, depending on the existence or extent of the agent's authority. In consequence, the issue of the governing law is equally complex. The discussion of these matters will fall within two broad divisions; parties to the agreement (Part 2) and the laws governing the relationship (Parts 3, 4 and 5).

2. PARTIES TO A DISTRIBUTION AGREEMENT

In this section an attempt will be made to indicate that the legal nature which may be ascribed to the distribution agreement concluded between businessmen may depend at least in part on the legal nature accorded to one or both of the parties or to their acts.

15. See, e.g., Commission Regulation 67/67, OJ 1967, No. 57/849, *infra*, section 5, which grants a block exemption to certain exclusive dealing agreements from the prohibition of Art. 85(1) EEC Treaty, listing in consecutive order what in essence constitute unilateral distributorship contracts, requirements contracts and bilateral distributorship contracts: for the distinction see, *infra*, section 2.2.1.

16. In the case of consumer sales there may be a defective goods 'guarantee', At the Community level, Moulinex (France) and Bauknecht (Germany) have recently joined the Euro guarantee system initiated by the EC Commission, which began with Zanussi (Italy) in 1978.

2.1. The supplier-principal

It has already been seen that the supplier is the party who concludes a contract with another with a view to ensuring the distribution abroad of goods. However, it may often be the case that the supplier (principal) in one relationship will stand as 'agent' in relation to his own principal in another commercially linked transaction. The clearest example is that of indirect agency [17] (commission agent or merchant) [18], where the agent is himself a principal in the transaction with the third party but an agent in relation to his supplier from whom he received the instruction to act in his own name. Again, the supplier of goods, having concluded a "sole agency" agreement as principal with another may in turn be party to a contract in which he is described as "sole agent" with a manufacturer of those goods. "There is no magic in the word 'agency'. It is often used in commercial matters where the real relationship is that of vendor and purchaser." [19] The 'sole agency' agreement between the supplier and the manufacturer, as well as that between the supplier and his 'sole agent', may be either an agency or a distributorship agreement or a mixed contract embodying features of both. The solutions accorded to various matters may turn on these distinctions. In short, each relationship must be examined on its facts.[20]

A pertinent illustration is afforded by the export or confirming house [21], which enters into two legal relationships, one with an importer-purchaser abroad, the other with the exporter-seller in the home market. In relation to the importer it stands as agent, to the exporter either as buyer (principal), or as agent for the importer. In practice, the more typical arrangement is that it stands as agent for the importer but by personally confirming performance of the order as principal (buyer) in relation to the exporter.[22] It is clearly established that there is no contradiction in combining these two figures in one person.[23]

2.1.1. The option of direct distribution

Distribution may also be achieved by the supplier establishing himself in the foreign market and conducting his own distribution by means of employees operating from a branch office (also termed an agency) or subsidiary company created under the laws of that foreign country. The overseas subsidiary [24] is a use-

17. See further, *infra,* section 2.3.2.
18. Hill, "The Commission Merchant at Common Law", (1968) 31 MLR 623.
19. Ex p. White, re Neville (1871) 6 Ch. App. 397 at p. 399.
20. See generally, *Bowstead on Agency,* 14th ed. (1976) by Reynolds and Davenport, p. 6 et seq.
21. See, Schmitthoff, *Export Trade,* p. 173 et seq.
22. Sobell Industries Ltd. *v.* Cory Bros & Co. Ltd. [1955] 2 Lloyd's Rep. 82.
23. R. & J. Bow, Ltd. *v.* Hill (1930) 37 Ll.l.R. 46.
24. Adopting this method of penetration makes the supplier a multinational, which has been defined as, "a combination of companies of different nationality, connected by means of shareholdings, managerial control or contract and constituting an economic unit", in Schmitthoff, *Export Trade,* p. 194.

ful tool for medium and large suppliers and offers considerable flexibility. It can serve the purposes of two or more suppliers in the home state who combine forces in a consortium or joint venture; similarly where two or more foreign suppliers associate in the establishment of a subsidiary in the host state. Such subsidiaries frequently take on the specific role of acting as branch office, agent or exclusive distributor for the parent company. The last two roles fulfill the functions that would otherwise be performed by persons already established in the foreign market were the supplier to opt for indirect distribution.[25]

It is clear that, viewed economically, the function performed is of greater significance than the legal mechanism chosen to effect that function. On the other hand, legal mechanisms adopted to disguise economic function do not allow the trader to escape the regulatory restriction of the law of competition. Thus, the EC Court of Justice lifted the veil of corporation and assumed jurisdiction over a parent company incorporated in a non-Member State and having a subsidiary in a Member State where that subsidiary did "not determine its behaviour on the market in an autonomous manner but essentially [carried] out the instructions of the parent company." [26]

Conversely, the legal mechanism adopted to perform the desired economic function brings with it a range of legal consequences attaching to categories of legal persons as these are regulated under the laws of either or both the home and the host state. To give but a small example.[27] A branch office abroad is normally staffed by two types of employee, namely, those sent to the foreign country by the supplier and those recruited locally. The employment contracts of the former must satisfy the employment law of the home country as well as the place of employment; those of the latter only the foreign law. In the case that the contracts of the locally recruited personnel provide that the law of the supplier's country shall govern, nevertheless the mandatory provisions of the local foreign law apply.[28]

Although the option of direct distribution offers significant advantages, particularly those of maximum measures of control over personnel and methods of promotion of sales and distribution together with maximum profit potential by reason of the degree of vertical integration, nevertheless it is not an obvious choice. Direct distribution calls for decided risks in the outlay of considerable expense, the tying up of capital, perhaps for an extensive and unprofitable period, the recruitment and training of local personnel by experienced managerial staff sent out from the home state, all this in the expectation that the market exploitability has not been over-estimated or does not subsequently contract. On the

25. See, *infra,* sections 2.2., 2.3. The influence of direct and indirect methods leading to identical problems can be seen in the recent Commission Decision in *Pioneer, infra,* n. 310 and related text.

26. ICI Ltd. and others *v.* EC Commission (48/69) [1972] CMLR 557 at p. 629. For a trenchant criticism of this "Dyestuffs case" see, Mann (1973) 22 ICLQ 35. Cf. *infra,*.n. 280.

27. Taken from Schmitthoff, *Export Trade,* pp. 183-4.

28. Sayers *v.* International Drilling Co. NV [1971] 1 WLR 1176. Here the local Dutch law appears to have been misapplied, see, Wade (1976) 23 NILR 205 at n. 5.

other hand, the commitment necessary to generate sufficient goodwill effectively and lastingly to penetrate a new market may be too great to be entrusted to a stranger.

Ultimately, the choice is an economic one. Where the risks are too great or the problems unnecessarily too complicated to overcome, or simply where it is more prudent to test the market with a view to subsequent direct involvement, it may be thought wiser to use the expertise and know-how of persons already established in the foreign market.

2.2. The exclusive distributor

This figure [29] is identifiable only by reference to the nature of the agreement concluded with the supplier. Apart therefrom, one thing is clear: the distributor is in business for himself; he is an independent trader, not an employee. However, the same is equally true of the agent acting economically as distributor.

2.2.1. Exclusive distributorship: definition and legal nature

The 'legal' concept of exclusive distributorship is somewhat easier to define and thus to identify in general terms than that of sole agency.

An exclusive distributorship agreement is one where the supplier agrees to the sale of defined goods only to an independent trader for resale within a particular area or to particular customers. The agreement is, naturally, seldom so limited and is usually clothed with extensive mutual obligations.[30] An essential element of the agreement is that the distributor shall buy and resell the goods in his own name and for his own account. It envisages thus a double sale. The supplier does not stand in any contractual relationship with the next purchaser.[31] He trades only with his distributor [32], and their mutual rights and duties are founded in principle

29. *Concessionnaire; concessiehouder* or *distributor; Vertragshändler; concessionario.* On the distrinction between *distributor* and *handelsagent,* HR 20 January 1956, NJ 1956, 335, *Turkstra-Staal, infra,* text to n. 55. See also, *Consten-Grundig,* and Italy *v.* EEC, *infra,* n. 294.

30. See generally, Graupner, "Sole Distributorship Agreements – A Comparative View" (1969) 18 ICLQ 879 et seq., also "Alleinvertriebsverträge im englischen Recht und rechtsvergleichende Probleme", 16 AWD (1970) 49-55; Carbonneau, "Exclusive Distributorship Agreements in French Law" (1979) 28 ICLQ 91 et seq.; van Gerven and Lukoff, eds., op. cit., passim; Schmitthoff, *Export Trade,* Chap. 14; Gijlstra and Murphy, "Distribution Systems and EEC Competition Law: The Law as it stands", Legal Issues of European Integration (1976) p. 81 at p. 92 et seq.; van Damme, loc.cit., p. 63 et seq. Theux, op.cit., Vol. I, p. 301 et seq.

31. Naturally, a tortious relationship may exist: see, Duintjer Tebbens, *International Product Liability* (1979); Castree *v.* E.R. Squibb & Sons Ltd. (1980) 1 WLR 1248 (CA).

32. This fact may offer an advantage over the sole agency agreement. The supplier is thus not concerned with the credit worthiness of innumerable unknown purchasers, merely that of one purchaser, the distributor: see, Schmitthoff, *Export Trade,* p. 154. The same advantage is obtained where the sole agent agrees to act as *del credere* agent (*commissionnaire – du croire*): HGB Art. 394, Italian CC Art. 1736, French Decree of 23 December 1958, Art. 1(4).

on the contract between them and subject to the governing laws of contract and sale of movable tangibles.[33]

An exclusive distributorship agreement is thus identifiable by reference to three factors. The agreement is not a sale of specific goods, nor is it a contract to conclude future contracts. It is a contract under which its restrictive provisions are at once effective and enforceable without reference to the eventual conclusion of the separate contracts of sale envisaged by it.[34] It may be likened to the *Rahmenvertrag* of German law and *contrat-cadre* of French law.[35] Secondly, it stipulates for the sale of goods by one independent trader, the supplier, to another, the distributor, who buys in his own name and for his own account and who, upon resale, sells in his own name and for his own account.[36] Where the distributor buys or sells in his own name but for the account of the supplier he does so as agent (*commissionnaire*) and not as distributor.

The final factor is the obligation on the part of the supplier to sell defined goods to the distributor on the condition that if those goods be resold, they be sold within a particular area or to particular customers. This latter qualification of exclusivity in respect of area or customers is an almost invariable one, with the result that it is regarded as being the most characteristic element of exclusive distributorship agreements.[37]

The reciprocal obligation on the part of the distributor would appear to be the specific one of promoting the resale of the goods within the area or to the customers reserved.[38] This is in line with the economic motivations underpinning such agreements. Further, such an analysis avoids confusion between apparently similar agreements, in particular between bilateral distribution agreements and requirements contracts.

2.2.1.1. Unilateral and bilateral agreements

The definition of exclusive distributorship which has already been given identifies what may be termed a unilateral exclusive distributorship agreement.

Where the agreement is extended so that the distributor accepts the obligation of buying defined goods for resale within a particular area or to particular cus-

33. See, however, the discussion on distributorship as a contract *sui generis, infra,* section 3.2.

34. See, Schmitthoff, *Export Trade,* p. 154. See, Rose and Franck Co. *v.* J.R. Compton Bros. Ltd. [1925] AC 445, in which the agreement was held to be unenforceable without this vitiating the individual contracts.

35. See, Graupner, loc.cit., p. 884.

36. Ibid., pp. 884-5; see also, Theux, op.cit., Vol. I, p. 302.

37. See, Theux, ibid., p. 312.

38. See, Graupner, loc.cit., p. 885. This is expressly stipulated in Italian CC Art. 1568(2). It has recently been held in England that where the distributor is expressly required by the agreement to make "every endeavour" to sell the supplier's product, failure to do so, as by selling competing products, constitutes a serious breach of contract justifying termination by the supplier; Re Arbitration between Deb Chemical Proprietaries Ltd., and Dreumex Chemie BV, 2 November 1979, *European Law Letter,* February 1980, p. 4.

tomers only from the supplier, it may be termed a bilateral exclusive distributorship agreement and this is the normal type of basic arrangement.[39]

2.2.1.2. Requirements contract

A requirements contract [40] resembles an exclusive distributorship agreement but is in fact totally distinct, both economically and legally. Under such a contract an independent trader agrees to purchase all the goods he needs for resale only from the supplier. He is under no obligation to the supplier to promote the resale of the supplier's product, either generally or in relation to a reserved area or customers. The supplier, consequently, is under no reciprocal obligation as to exclusivity. The economic motivations underpinning such arrangements are guaranteed stocks and supplies on the part of the trader and some guarantee of sales and movement of stock on the part of the supplier. It is a simple, albeit reinforced, link in the distribution chain.

Such contracts are to be found predominantly in the petrol resale and brewery trades. Most are purely national arrangements concluded between supplier and dealer established within a single Member State of the European Community and concern the resale of the supplier's product within that State. Consequently, they benefit by the block exemption granted by the European Commission [41] even though the existence of an extensive network of such intra-state agreements may in fact have a distorting effect upon inter-state trade by effectively closing the market in that State to penetration from outside.[42]

2.3. **The sole agent**

This figure is not readily amenable of definition in comparative law though often not too difficult to identify in the trading practice between the parties. The difficulty lies in the substantial differences existing between the notion of agency as understood in the Common Law and the institution of *représentation* or *Vertretung* as variously elaborated in or developed from the Civil and Commercial Codes.[43]

39. See, Theux, op.cit., Vol. I, p. 308; also, Champaud, "The Group Exemptions of EEC Regulation 67/67" (1967-68) CMLRev 23 at p. 27.

40. *L'exclusivité de fourniture, alleenkoopovereenkomst.* Such contracts are variously termed solus agreements, sole purchasing contracts, etc.

41. Reg. 67/67, Art. 1(2), OJ 1967, 849.

42. This danger was recognised by the European Court in Brasserie de Haecht *v.* Wilkin (No. 1) [1968] CMLR 26 in reply to a request for a preliminary ruling by the Liège Commercial Court. Since then the Court appears to have ignored the danger: S.A. Fonderies Roubaix – Wattrelos *v.* Fonderies Roux [1976] 1 CMLR 538; De Norre *v.* NV Brouwerij Concordia [1977] 1 CMLR 378. The Commission has since proposed to delete Art. 1(2): *Seventh Report on Competition Policy* OJ 1978 C 31/2; critically discussed by Downes, loc.cit., pp. 174-178. Reg. 67/67 expires on 31 December 1982.

43. See generally, Asser-van der Grinten, *Vertegenwoordiging en rechtspersoon* (1973); Asser-Kamphuizen, *Bijzondere Overeenkomsten,* Vol. 3 (1977); *Bowstead on Agency,* op.cit.; Fridman, *Law of Agency,* 4th. ed. (1976); Pelichet, loc.cit.; Regaux, Int. Ency. Comp. Law,

2.3.1. Definition

For present purposes the following is advanced: a sole agency agreement is one where the supplier of goods, the principal, authorizes another, being an independent trader, the agent, to procure or conclude contracts, whether or not in his own name, for the account of the principal, for the sale of those goods to third parties within a particular area or to particular persons, and that person agrees to do so.

2.3.2. Nature

The first observation relates to semantics. There exists little harmonisation of terms in this field. Nevertheless, for present purposes it is useful to restrict the multifarious terminology to a select number of expressions. By "principal" one understands, as already discussed, the producer-supplier of the goods to be distributed. "Agent" is a far more complex figure and must be taken to mean *"intermédiaire"* in the broad sense of encompassing *"représentant"* and *"commissionnaire"*, except where otherwise specifically indicated. The generic term "agency" creates particular problems for it corresponds to, but does not equate with, *représentation* or *Vertretung*. Similar difficulties attach to the use of expressions such as mandate, authorization, power of representation, direct and indirect agents. Where possible the terms used will also indicate the scope of meaning that should be ascribed to them.

Secondly, as this report is directed towards commercial transactions, attention will be paid only to the agency relationship arising by virtue of an agreement [44] (*représentation conventionnelle* [45] or *représentation volontaire, gewillkürte Vertretung* [46], *lastgeving* [47]), ignoring all agency relationships arising from judicial order (*représentation judiciaire* [48]) or operation of law (*représentation légale, gesetzliche Vertretung* [49]).

The agency contract between principal and agent gives rise to what is now generally characterised as the internal relationship, that, termed the main contract (*opération* or *relation principale, Hauptgeschäft*), between principal and/or agent and third party, as the external relationship. The definition of sole agency already given encompasses both this tripartite feature as well as the doctrinal differences existing between the Common Law understanding of agency and

---

Vol. 3, Chap. 29 (1970); Schmitthoff, "Agency in International Law", *Recueil des Cours de l'Académie de droit international* (1970) Vol. 1 (hereafter, *Recueil*); Theux, op.cit., Vol. 1 (1975), Vol. 2 (1977); Treitel, *Law of Contract*, 5th ed. (1979) Chap. 17.

44. This is the normal basis for the relationship between principal and agent: see, Garnac Grain Co. Inc. *v.* Faure & Fairclough Ltd. [1968] AC 1130.

45. Pelichet, loc.cit., p. 11.

46. Rigaux, loc.cit., p. 3.

47. Art. 1829 BW: see, Asser-van der Grinten, op.cit., p. 16; Art. 7.7.2.1. NBW: see, Asser-Kamphuizen, op.cit., p. 74 et seq.

48. Pelichet, loc.cit., p. 11.

49. Ibid.; Rigaux, loc.cit., p. 3.

représentation - Vertretung. In this context it is necessary to distinguish broadly between two groups of commercial agent. The first comprises those who may be described as having a mandate and a power of representation and who may negotiate and conclude contracts with a third party for the account of and on behalf of the principal and in his name. Within this group one finds the French *l'agent commercial* [50], the Italian *agente* [51], the Dutch *handelsagent* [52] and the German *Handelsvertreter.*[53] The second considerably looser group encompasses those having what one may term a mandate without power of representation who may conclude contracts with a third party for the account of and on behalf of the principal, not in his name but in their own.[54] Here one finds the French *commissionnaire,* the Italian *commissionario*, the Dutch *commissionair,* and the German *Kommissionär.*[55]

The legal distinction between the two groups was firmly stated by the Dutch *Hoge Raad* [56] in an appeal *in cassatie* directed to the jurisdictional competence of the *Kantonrechter* to hear a claim brought by a plaintiff petitioning as *handelsagent.* The *Hoge Raad* held that where it appeared from the pleadings that the plaintiff might not be a *handelsagent* by virtue of the fact that he allegedly bought and sold in his own name, the *Kantonrechter* was obliged to determine his own competence, which depended *in casu* on the status of the plaintiff, which was conditional on his not doing more than acting in the name and for the account of the principal. It may be noted that this judgment is also used as authority for the distinction between *handelsagent* and distributor.

An immediate qualification pertains to the vast body of commercial representatives who also fulfill a role as *intermédiaires* (*tussenpersonen*). Such person may be left out of consideration here to the extent that he is a *représentant salarié*

50. The French Decree of 23 December 1958 regulates the position of the commercial agent as being a *mandataire* who ordinarily in an independent professional capacity carries on the activity of negotiating or concluding contracts of, *inter alia,* sale for and on behalf of the principal.

51. Italian CC Art. 1742 specifies that an *agente* is one who on a continuing basis undertakes for remuneration to procure contracts for the account of the principal within a given territory. The agent may be granted a power of representation also authorising him to conclude contracts in the principal's name: Art. 1752.

52. WvK Art. 75a. See further, Doorhout-Mees, *Kort begrip van het Nederlands handels- en faillissementsrecht* (1971) 5th ed., paras. 2.47-48.

53. HGB Art. 84 emphasises the agent's independence as a *Selbständiger Gewerbetreibender* acting for the account of another *Unternehmer.*

54. Mention should be made of the class of independent commercial auxiliaries who may be termed brokers (*Courtier* Art. 64 Belgian CC, Art. 74 French CC, *Makelaar* Art. 62 WvK, *Handelsmäkler*Art. 99 HGB, *Mediatore* Art. 1754 Italian CC). See further, Theux, op. cit., Vol. I, pp. 265-77.

55. See, Italian CC Art. 1731 specifying the mandate of the *commissionario* to buy and sell in his own name but for the account of the principal (*committente*); HGB para. 383 which defines a *Kommissionär* as one who buys or sells goods in his own name for another; French C.Comm. Art. 94 defines a *commissionnaire* as a person who acts for a principal but in his own name; similarly the *commissionair* under Dutch law who acts in his own name for the *committent:* WvK Art. 76. Cf. Mercantile agent, s.1(1) Factors Act 1889, *infra,* n. 66 and related text.

56. HR 20 January 1956, NJ 1956, 335, *Turkstra-Staal.*

who undertakes a representative task within the cadre of an employment contract (*contrat d'emploi, arbeidsovereenkomst, Anstellungsvertrag* or *Arbeitsvertrag*) [57], not by virtue of an agency contract (*contrat d'agence, agentuurovereenkomst, Agenturvertrag*) [58] in the sense of a contract for particular services (*overeenkomst tot het verrichten van enkele diensten*) to be performed by an independent trader (*ondernemer, Unternehmer*). It need hardly be remarked that it is not always a clearly recognisable distinction.[59]

There are clear doctrinal differences between agency and *représentation - Vertretung.* It has been said that the fundamental difference is to be found in the civil law concept of separation and in the Common Law concept of identity.[60] According to the former, *représentation - Vertretung* is characterised by the strict separation of the agency relationship agreement concluded between principal and agent, being the mandate authorizing the agent to act [61], from the power of representation, being the power to act on the principal's behalf and for his account.[62] By contrast, Common Law agency is founded on the maxim *qui facit per alium facit per se* : in short, identity of parties. In Pelichet's illuminating phrase, "the agent is to some extent the *alter ego* of the principal from whom he has received full authority and . . . acts within the limit of this full authority." [63]

The difference of approach leads not surprisingly to very different results. The most striking is that the civil law concept of separation tends to the protection of the third party who contracts with the agent, whereas the concept of identification tends to the protection of the principal.[64] The tendency towards protection of the third party results from an emphasis on the external relationship and the power of the agent to bind the principal, whereby *représentation - Vertretung* is viewed as an abstraction independent of the internal relationship imposing limits on the authority of the agent.[65] The Common Law views representation not as an abstraction but as the result, indeed the purpose of the mandate, so that, as a general rule, the acts of the agent who lacks sufficient authority do not bind the principal.

Commercial practice, as indorsed by legislation and caselaw, has built upon these doctrinal foundations.

Even before the Factors Act 1889, the Common Law had recognised a factor as an agent entrusted with possession of the principal's property for purposes of sale, sometimes in his own name and without disclosing his principal.[66] The Factors Act 1889 created the term mercantile agent "having in the customary course of his business as such agent authority to sell goods or to consign goods

57. Art. 75q WvK; HGB Art. 60.
58. Artt. 75a and 75c WvK; HGB Art. 84.
59. See, Rb. Roermond, 27 February 1975, WPNR 1977, 281, *infra,* text to n. 212.
60. Pelichet, loc.cit., pp. 13, 15.
61. *Lastgeving zonder volmacht:* Artt. 76 and 86 WvK.
62. *Volmacht:* Art. 3.3.1. NBW.
63. Pelichet, loc.cit., p. 15.
64. Schmitthoff, *Recueil*, pp. 132-33.
65. Rigaux, loc.cit., p. 2.
66. For older authorities see, Fridman, op.cit., p. 28.

for the purpose of sale, or to buy goods, or to raise money on the security of goods" [67], which term also encompasses brokers, who are not, however, given possession of goods or documents of title, nor are they permitted to sell in their own name, and *del credere* agents.[68]

A further development is that where a Common Law agent concludes a contract with a third party without authority but on behalf and for the account of his principal, the principal may, subject to conditions, ratify the agent's contract, thereby creating both an internal relationship with the agent and an external relationship with the third party. It is important to note that where ratification is valid and effective, the principal confers authority [69] on the agent retrospective to the moment of the act of the agent. Equally, the privilege of ratification is available only to a named or disclosed principal, never to an undisclosed principal.[70] In such a case there is, in civil law terms, no representation, although there is agency (authority). This is in direct contrast to the civil law position, where contracts may be concluded by a *commissionnaire* in his own name but for the benefit of an 'undisclosed principal' who can later 'ratify' the contract even though when the contract was concluded by the agent, he had no specific authority to so act [71] and the third party had no knowledge of the principal. The civil law recognises the *ius quaesitum tertio.*[72] English law has been pushed in the opposite direction by its insistence that consideration must move from the promisee [73], with the consequence that simple contracts for the benefit of a stranger cannot be enforced.

The most important limitations to the Common Law rule that an agent acting without authority does not bind the principal are contained in the notions of apparent or usual authority, which may for general purposes be subsumed under the term agency by estoppel.[74] These limitations are of significance in the present context in that they encompass cases where it appears that, in civil law terms, the agent is recognised as having the power to bind his principal on the basis of representation, not on the basis of authority within the terms of the mandate.[75]

An agent's usual authority may be a semantic distinction without a difference when one is concerned with an agent who carries on a trade, profession or business as an agent (what may be termed a permanent agent) [76] and as such is regarded as having an implied authority to perform such acts as are usual in that trade,

67. s. 1(1).
68. See further, Fridman, op.cit., pp. 28-31; Schmitthoff, *Export Trade,* pp. 170-71; Treitel, op.cit., pp. 546-50.
69. Re Mawcon, Ltd. [1969] 1 WLR 78.
70. Keighley, Maxted & Co. *v.* Durant [1901] AC 240.
71. Asser-van der Grinten, op.cit., p. 52; Italian CC Art. 1711, para. 1.
72. French CC Art. 1121; Italian CC Art. 1141; BGB Artt. 328-335; NBW Art. 6.5.3.5.
73. Dunlop Pneumatic Tyre Co. *v.* Selfridge [1915] AC 847; Scruttons *v.* Midland Silicones [1962] AC 446. See now, The Eurymedon [1975] AC 154, which appears not to have been followed in the Commonwealth: Clarke [1980] 29 ICLQ 132. Cf. Rb. Rotterdam 9 January 1978, S & S 1978, 56.
74. Pelichet, loc.cit., pp. 16-17; Fridman, op.cit., pp. 70-71.
75. Schmitthoff, *Recueil,* p. 133.
76. E.g., factors and brokers, see, *supra,* text to notes 66, 67.

profession or business, on the reasoning that the agent by logical inference must have been authorised to perform acts necessary for the execution of his express authority.[77] However, where the principal expressly places restrictions on the agent's usual authority, such restrictions will not affect a third party unaware of them. A good illustration, albeit much criticized, of the scope of this rule, is *Watteau* v. *Fenwick* [78], where the third party successfully sued the principal (whose existence was unknown to the third party at the time of his dealings with the agent), for debts incurred by the agent where the latter had been expressly forbidden to enter into such transactions, of which restriction the third party was ignorant. This must be distinguished from the principle of apparent authority where both the agency relationship and the identity of the principal must be apparent to the third party, but the agent acts outside his authority. However, the third party will not be able to rely on apparent authority if he had actual or constructive notice of the excess of authority, or even when the facts should have aroused his suspicion.[79] This may be contrasted with the position under German law where a third party dealing with a permanent agent is not affected by an excess of authority even where he knows that the agent has exceeded the authority.[80]

The distinction drawn between a named, unnamed (existence disclosed) and an undisclosed principal is a peculiarity of the Common Law. Cases of a disclosed principal can be comfortably equated with the civil law notion of direct representation. The situation of the undisclosed principal differs fundamentally, by virtue of the doctrinal divergence already indicated, from that of civil law indirect representation.[81]

When the agent, whether Civil or Common Law, acts on behalf and for the account of his principal (direct representation) [82], the contract concluded is one between third party and principal [83] with the result, for example, that goods 'bought' by the agent pass directly into the ownership of the principal.[84] By contrast, the indirect representative concludes contracts with third parties in his own name.[85] The contractual relationship of the third party is not with the principal, whether disclosed or not, but with the agent (*commissionnaire*) [86], with the result that ownership in goods bought for the principal by the agent normally vests in the agent and requires, in most cases, to be separately transferred by the

77. Italian CC Art. 1708.
78. [1893] 1 QB 346.
79. Overbrooke Estates Ltd. *v*. Glencombe Properties Ltd. [1974] 1 WLR 1335.
80. HGB Art. 50; Schmitthoff, *Recueil*, pp. 132-33.
81. Asser-van der Grinten, op.cit., p. 65: "The coupling of *lastgeving* and *volmacht* is not accepted in the law at present".
82. See, Asser-Kamphuizen, op.cit., p. 76: *onmiddellijke vertegenwoordiging met volmacht.*
83. Art. 1843 BW; Art. 7.7.2.1. NBW: *lastgeving met volmacht.*
84. Asser-van der Grinten, op.cit., p. 41.
85. Art. 7.7.2.1. NBW; Asser-Kamphuizen, op.cit., p. 74: *middellijke vertegenwoordiging.*
86. Asser-van der Grinten, op.cit., pp. 62-63; Art. 1376 BW: "Contracts are binding only as between the contracting parties"; Art. 78 WvK: "The principal incures no liability or contractual responsibility to the third party with whom the *commissionair* has dealt". See, also, Italian CC Art. 1705.

agent to the principal.[87] As already indicated, where a Common Law agent acts for an undisclosed principal and concludes a contract with the third party in his own name he also creates no contractual relationship between third party and principal, but he does create a situation wherein each party can bring proceedings directly against the other [88], the third party also having a right of election to proceed against the agent.[89] If he does so the principal's liability is thereupon discharged. The election is irrevocable. If he pursues the wrong party he cannot remedy his mistake by pursuing the other.[90] It is important to note, however, that the undisclosed principal's so-called right of intervention, which is perhaps best regarded as *sui generis* [91], is dependent upon the agent having the authority to act at the time of the contract with the third party. If he had then the principal may take the benefit of the contract without more. The agent who agrees to acquire property on behalf of the principal but in his own name becomes a trustee of the property for his principal.[92]

Intervention by the principal consequent upon exercise of authority by the agent is distinguishable from the principal's right of ratification where the agent acted without authority but on behalf of the principal; in short, for a named or disclosed principal. In other words, ratification is possible where there is representation, but only retroactive authority, whereas intervention is dependent on authority, not on representation. This would seem to bring the case of the undisclosed principal very close to indirect representation. The differences remain, however, fundamental. The 'undisclosed' principal is not a party to the contract concluded by the *commissionnaire.* The undisclosed principal under the Common Law is also not a party to the contract, whether he intervenes or not, although the third party can elect to proceed directly against him. The *commissionnaire* must normally transfer the ownership acquired from the third party to the 'undisclosed' principal, who can, furthermore, directly take the benefit of a contract made by the *commissionnaire* even though the agent exceeded his authority if the object of the transaction was to benefit the principal.[93] If the Common Law undisclosed principal wishes to take the benefit of a contract concluded by an agent in his own name but without authority he must do so by assignment from the 'agent', for he cannot intervene and the agent is not a trustee of the property.

87. Asser-van der Grinten, op.cit., pp. 70-76. Cf. Italian CC Art. 1706, para 1: principal can claim goods bought by his *mandatorio* but without prejudice to third parties in good faith.

88. Cf. Art. 240 WvK giving the principal the exceptional right to sue the third party directly for the price of goods sold by the *commissionair* prior to the latter's bankruptcy.

89. Pople *v.* Evans [1969] 2 Ch. 255, *infra,* n. 92.

90. Schmitthoff, *Recueil,* p. 142.

91. Ibid., pp. 141-43. It now appears that a foreign principal has the same right of intervention: Teheran-Europe Co. Ltd. *v.* S.T. Belton (Tractors) Ltd. [1968] 2 QB 545; Schmitthoff, *Export Trade,* p. 164; Rigaux, loc.cit., p. 16.

92. Rochefoucauld *v.* Boustead [1897] 1 Ch. 196: even a *bona fide* purchaser for value from the agent will not be protected. However, an agent who brings an action on behalf of his undisclosed principal is not regarded as a trustee for purposes of estoppel *per rem judicatum* where the agent's action is discontinued and the principal later commences new proceedings: Pople *v.* Evans [1969] 2 Ch. 255.

93. BGB Artt. 328-335.

This last situation has affinities with the situation where the agent acts in exercise of his commission from the principal to procure goods for the latter, but he does so by way of purchase from the third party and then resells to the principal. In such a case he may avail himself of all the normal remedies open to a seller.

The commission agent, what one may call the Common Law indirect agent, although buying from the third party as principal and selling to his own principal as agent, would look to renumeration by commission rather than by profit on resale and, consequently, his duties would not be those of a seller but that of an agent to exercise reasonable diligence in carrying out his principal's instructions.[94] He would nevertheless have the rights of an unpaid seller as against his principal, namely those of lien, stoppage *in transitu* and resale of the goods.[95] However, being an agent, it is an open question whether he could reserve property in the goods as against the principal.[96] This aspect raises questions relating to proprietary rights and the role of the *lex situs*, or alternatively the proper law of the transfer where the goods are in transit, and must be here left aside.

3. LAW APPLICABLE TO A DISTRIBUTION AGREEMENT

The law applicable to the agreement depends in varying degrees on whether the relationship between the parties to the agreement is characterised, or simply regarded, as one of agency, distributorship or, which is almost invariably the case with distribution agreements, sale.

The contract of sale, considered from the point of view of its contractual effects, is not regarded as fundamentally different from other commercial contracts and as such is normally governed by the "proper law". However, sale is both a contractual and a proprietary transaction in that it operates both as a contract and as a conveyance, i.e., as a mode of transferring property. There is also a third function. At the level of commerce, as distinct from individual transactions between private persons, sale serves as a mechanism to ensure or assist in the continuation, both spatially and temporally, of production.

In the case of distribution agreements, the mutual rights and duties falling to be governed by the proper law will differ *ex çontractus* and *ex lege* depending not just on the specific contractual stipulations reflecting the economic goal of the particular arrangement but also on the legal character of the distributor, as previously discussed. In addition, account needs to be taken of the possible applicability of legal provisions intended to benefit the distributor or the third party, or to protect market interests.

94. Ireland *v.* Livingston (1872) LR 5 HL 395. Cf. Italian CC Art. 1710, para. 1: "The *mandatorio* must perform the mandate with the diligence of a good *pater familias*".

95. Sale of Goods Act 1979, ss. 38, 39. Cf. Italian CC Artt. 1721, 2761, para 1, permitting charges on monies and property held by the *mandatario.*

96. See, *Benjamin's Sale of Goods* (1974) ss. 1416-1419.

It may here be mentioned that the EC Commission has proposed an EEC Council Directive to coordinate the laws of the Member States relating to self-employed commercial agents.[97] Criticism from the Economic and Social Council and from the European Parliament led to submission of an amended version.[98] The Directive is intended to correct the inequality in conditions of competition resulting from differences in the national laws relating to commercial agents, which constitutes a barrier to the freedoms of establishment and provision of services. The subject of the Directive is the "self-employed intermediary who has continuing authority . . . to negotiate and/or to conclude an unlimited number of commercial transactions in the name and for account of another person." [99] The harmonized rules are in general to be regarded as mandatory in the sense of establishing minimum standards.[100] The Draft Directive received extensive criticism from the Law Commission for England and Wales [101], which the amended version of 1979 did not fully meet. The Directive is not yet in force.

The law which is now widely regarded as normally governing the rights and duties of the parties to a contract is what the Common Law would term the proper law and what otherwise might be termed the law of closest connection.[102] The proper law has been defined as, "the system of law by which the parties intended the contract to be governed, or, where their intention is neither expressed nor to be inferred from the circumstances, the system of law with which the transaction has its closest and most real connection." [103] The answers arrived at in determining the proper law vary as between different countries.[104] Whatever the proper law may be in a particular situation, it will normally govern such matters as the capacity of the parties to contract; the formalities required, if any; the essential validity of the contract, including mistake, misrepresentation, effect and implication of terms of the contract; legality; and discharge by performance, breach, subsequent agreement or frustration. Questions relating to time, mode, and manner of performance are in some countries governed not by the proper law of the contract but by the law of the place of performance.[105]

97. Proposal of 17 December 1976, OJ 18 January 1977, C 13/2.

98. Proposal of 29 January 1979, OJ 2 March 1979, C 56/5.

99. Art. 2.

100. Art. 35, para 1.

101. *Report on the Proposed EEC Directive on the Law Relating to Commercial Agents,* Law Com. No. 84, 12 October 1977, Cmnd. 6948; see further, Lando (1980) 44 RabelsZ 1 et seq.

102. Dicey and Morris, *Conflict of Laws,* 10th ed. (1980) Vol. 2, p. 747; Batiffol and Lagarde, *Droit international privé*, Vol. 2 (1976) p. 259; Lemaire, *Internationaal Privaatrecht* (1968) (hereafter, *IPR*); Drobnig, *American-German Private International Law* (1972) p. 225; Lando, *International Encyclopedia of Comparative Law,* Vol. 3, Chap. 24 (1974-76), s. 215, p. 116 (hereafter, *Contracts*).

103. Dicey and Morris, op.cit., p. 747. See also, Cheshire and North, *Private International Law*, 10th ed. (1979) p. 195 et seq.; *Benjamin's Sale of Goods,* op.cit., s. 2294 et seq.

104. See generally, Lando, *Contracts*, s. 215 et seq.

105. Dicey and Morris, op.cit., p. 813 et seq.

Further, a number of countries have enacted legislation providing a varying measure of protection to agents. Where the 'proper law' is the law of such country those protective provisions [106] will normally [107] apply where that law is also the *lex fori*, and will have a claim to be applied in other cases.[108]

The parties are in principle free to select the proper law of the contract and may do so expressly, impliedly or, in some countries, tacitly. The distinction between implied or tacit choice and objective determination of the proper law or closest connection, is frequently blurred, not least due to the fact that there is overlap of the elements to be taken into consideration in each inquiry. The issue of express choice of law is considered further in Part 4. Here attention will be directed to the applicable law in the absence of an effective choice of law and the three alternatives of sale, distributorship and agency will be considered in turn.

3.1. Distribution agreement as a sale contract

Although some authors argue that distributorship contracts should be regarded as contracts *sui generis* and as such subject to their own conflict rules [109], the general approach is to view them as sale contracts governed by the law applicable to contracts generally and sale of tangible movables in particular.

A number of connecting factors have come to the fore as determining the proper law, operating in this respect as fixed rules or as presumptive indications in the objective determination of a more flexible concept of the proper law.

In those countries that have ratified the Hague Sales Convention of 1955 [110] the fixed rule for sales is that the law of the country of the seller's place of business governs. The Convention provides [111] that a sale is governed by the substantive law of the country where the seller was habitually resident at the time of receiving the order. Where a branch office of the seller receives the order, the law of the country where the branch is located governs. Alternatively, where the seller or his agent receives the order in a country where the buyer is habitually resident or has a branch office, the substantive law of that country governs.[112] The adoption of such rigid conflict of laws rules has superseded a variety of

106. Belgium: Laws of 27 July 1961 and 13 April 1971, see, further, *infra*, text to n. 181 et seq.; France: Decree no. 58-1345, 23 December 1958, supplemented by Decree no. 68-765, 22 August 1968; Germany: HGB Artt. 84-92e; Italy: CC Artt. 1731-1952; The Netherlands: WvK Artt. 74-74s.

107. Cf. BGH 30 January 1961, *infra*, n. 272.

108. Cf. Trib. comm. Brussels, 6 May 1969, *infra*, n. 274.

109. See, *infra*, section 3.2.

110. Belgium, Denmark, Finland, France, Italy, Norway (in force 1 September 1964); Sweden (in force 6 September 1964); Switzerland (in force 27 October 1972); Niger has adhered (10 December 1971); Luxemburg, The Netherlands, Spain have signed: see (1981) 28 NILR 224-225; Sumampouw, *Les Nouvelles Conventions de la Haye*, (1980) Vol. 2, p. 189.

111. Art. 3, para. 1. See, Cour d'appèl de Lyon, 28 February 1979, Clunet 1980, 104; see, further, Sumampouw, op.cit., p. 27.

112. Art. 3, para. 2. Para. 3 provides for sale by public auction or at a commodity ex-

earlier approaches to determining objectively the governing law. Italy [113] and Belgium [114] had remained faithful to the law of the place of contracting. France had come to regard this as one element to be given weight to in assessing the circumstances of the contract in determining where it was localized [115], in contrast to seeking to ascertain the presumed intention of the parties.[116] The Belgian courts appeared to assume that the *lex loci contractus* represented the presumed intention of the parties.[117] Switzerland had adopted an objective closest connection approach [118] but then began considerably to develop the theory of the characteristic performance.[119]

In The Netherlands, the influence of the Hague Sales Convention of 1955 has led to a number of decisions in favour of the law of the seller's place of business [120], even though The Netherlands has not ratified the Convention, on the reasoning that, "even though [the Convention] is as such not yet in force . . . nevertheless, it is proper that [the rule in Art. 3, paragraph 1] be applied *in casu* as a norm of private international law." [121] This approach has met with the pertinent observation that the court ought to give consideration to the question why The Netherlands has not ratified the Convention [122], but instances are still not uncommon.[123]

---

change: law of country of location governs. Cf. Cammell *v.* Sewell (1860) 5 H. & N. 728: Prussian ship carrying cargo from England to Russia wrecked off Norway; without owner's authority captain sold cargo at public auction; good title according to *lex situs;* Winkworth *v.* Christie Manson & Woods Ltd. [1980] 2 WLR 937: goods stolen in England, sold in Italy by contract governed by Italian law, resold by auction in England, ownership to be governed by Italian law as *lex situs.*

113. CC Art. 25, prelim. provs., with exceptions contained in Code of Navigation 1942, artt. 9, 10.

114. See, Trib. comm. Brussels, 28 November 1969, Clunet 1971, 885; Trib. comm., Brussels, 9 June 1972, JCB 1974, IV, p. 99, AK 10091.

115. See, Cass. civ. 15 February 1972, Rev. crit. 1973, 77; Cour de Paris, 23 April 1971, Rev. crit. 1973, 58.

116. Lando, *Contracts*, s. 117.

117. Ibid., s. 119.

118. BG 12 February 1952, BGE 78 II 74, *Chevalley-Genimportex.*

119. BG 13 August 1953: "Beim Fehlen einer Parteivereinbarung ist das Recht desjenigen Landes anwendbar, mit dem das Rechtsverhältnis den engsten räumlichen Zusammenhang aufweist; dieser besteht in der Regel mit dem Recht des Landes derjenigen Partei, welche die charakterische Leistung des in Frage stehenden Vertragsverhältnisses zu erbringen hat": cited Lemaire, *IPR*, p. 272. Swiss Draft Federal Law on private international law, Art. 121, para 1: "Lorsque la prestation caractéristique détermine le rapport le plus étroit, comme par exemple dans les contrats visés au second alinéa, le contrat est soumis à loi de l'établissement commercial ou, à défaut d'un tel établissement, à la loi de la résidence habituelle du débiteur de cette prestation". Para. 2, *inter alia,* saves the application of the Hague Sales Convention 1955.

120. Rb. Leeuwarden, 4 June 1964, NJ 1966, 12, AK 2107; 30 November 1968, 44 (1971) NTIR 342, commentary Verheul; Rb. Den Haag, 31 March 1977, AK 10728.

121. Rb. Arnhem, 14 November 1968, approved Hof Arnhem, 2 June 1970, AK 6047.

122. Lemaire, *Rechtspraak overzicht ipr 1970-72,* ed. Voskuil and Verheul (1975) p. 118 (hereafter, *Overzicht*).

123. See, Rb. Breda, 5 November 1974, WPNR 1977, 278 and 294; Rb. Arnhem, 15 February 1979, NJ 1979, 579,(reservation of title); 21 June 1979, AK 11904, (express choice of German law contained in seller's conditions of sale). See, also, Sumampouw, op. cit. (1976) Vol. 1, for other instances.

Developing from a closest connection approach in contrast to the parties' presumed intention [124], the Dutch courts have in recent years moved also to adoption of the law of the place of business of the party whose performance is regarded as characteristic of the contract.[125]

The closest connection approach had rightly been criticized as producing arbitrary results which fostered legal uncertainty.[126] In some instances, the approach tended towards the error of counting contacts.[127] The conscious use of the characteristic performance approach by the Dutch courts has been seen as a correction to the defects of the rule of closest connection [128], although it had 'unconciously' been employed in earlier caselaw.[129] In the words of one commentator, the substance of this secondary conflict of laws rule is that,

"the contract, in regard to its valid formation and its effects, is governed by the law of the country with which it is most closely connected. In order to determine this, the connections of the contract as well as the circumstances under which it arose, are to be considered in relation particularly to the characteristic performance. By means of legal comparison, particularly as regards contracts having a clear international character, for example, contracts for maritime transport, a uniform international solution ought to be sought."[130]

Further:

"The final determination of the characteristic performance ought, in my view, equally to be arrived at in the light of an examination of the socio-economic function of the contract, whereby the relationship of the parties prior to conclusion of the contract can be of interest."[131]

Surveying the recent caselaw reveals that the characteristic performance approach, although perhaps not quite in the terms above, has been readily embraced in The Netherlands for a range of legal transactions [132], although it has not displaced the closest connection approach.[133] The difficulty of establishing a performance on one side that can be regarded as more characteristic of the transaction than a counter-performance on the other has also not escaped attention.[134]

124. Criticized, Deelen, *Rechtskeuze in het Nederlands internationaal privaatrecht* (1965) pp. 281-82. See, Hof Den Haag, 15 March 1910, W. 8984; Hof Amsterdam, 13 February 1957, NJ 1958, 230. See, also, Lemaire, *IPR*, p. 270.

125. HR 17 April 1964, NJ 1965, 22; Hof Arnhem, 9 January 1974, NJ 1974, 276.

126. Lemaire, *Overzicht*, p. 111.

127. Hof Amsterdam, 12 March 1971, NJ 1972, 64; Pres. Rb. Arnhem, 6 April 1972, AK 7255.

128. Lemaire, *Overzicht*, p. 113.

129. Lemaire, *IPR*, p. 272: HR 2 April 1942, NJ 1942, 468, *Jurgens-van Heesch;* Rb. Amsterdam, 25 March 1964, NJ 1964, 437.

130. Lemaire, *IPR*, p. 273.

131. Ibid., *Overzicht*, p. 113.

132. HR 21 October 1972, NJ 1973, 121, *Neska-De Beijer;* HR 6 April 1973, NJ 1973, 371, *Topsøe-Del Prado;* HR 8 June 1973, NJ 1973, 400, *Mackaay-American Express.*

133. Hof Arnhem, 4 November 1975, AK 9774; Rb. Breda, 12 December 1978, AK 11722.

134. Kisch, "Een Onduidelijke Bepaling", (1970) 17 NTIR 275, at pp. 278-279. Characteristic performance as the localizing test has been adopted in Art. 4 EC Contractual Obligations Convention 1980. For searching criticism see, Lando, von Hoffmann, Siehr, ed., *European PIL of Obligations* (1975) passim; Collins (1976) 25 ICLQ 35, at pp. 46-49.

The rule has been stated judicially as follows:

"According to Dutch private international law, an international contract is governed by the law of the country where the contracting party, who under the contract must accomplish the most characteristic performance, is resident or has the centre of his activities . . . in the case of a contract of purchase and sale the seller . . . accomplishes the most characteristic performance." [135]

The rule has not, however, become an empty formalism. Thus, where an American seller of certain chemicals was not the manufacturer but had to buy from a third party in order to sell to a Dutch purchaser, the court held that the establishment of the seller in New York was of insufficient significance in deciding whether the duty to deliver was more characteristic than the duty to pay, and in consequence the court made use of the closest connection approach, placing most weight on the facts that the duty to deliver was c.i.f. Rotterdam and that the payment could be made in the Netherlands.[136] In a number of cases the reference to characteristic performance is buttressed by reference to other facts in a way that resembles the search for the law of closest connection.[137] In other cases the rule is simply stated to be that the law of the seller's establishment governs, without further reference to that being the most characteristic performance.[138]

Germany, which likewise has not ratified the Hague Sales Convention of 1955, does not make use of the seller's place of business as a fixed rule [139], but rather as an indicator of the presumed intention of the parties [140], which is determined by an objective appraisal of the facts and interests involved.[141] The law of the place of performance is often held to be the governing law [142], and for certain purposes this might be the place of payment of the price.[143]

Under English law a contract for the sale of goods is governed by the proper law of the contract [144], and the proper law is determined in accordance with the

135. Rb. Alkmaar, 19 June 1980, AK 11994: Danish seller sold and delivered goods to Dutch buyer, Danish law governed; Rb. Amsterdam, 28 March 1979, AK 11670; Rb. Rotterdam, 9 January 1981, AK 12419, *Handelsmaatschappij Klarholz, Import-Export BV - Riethmann & Brunet.*

136. Hof Amsterdam, 8 June 1977, AK 10921.

137. Rb. Amsterdam, 11 April 1979, AK 11671: although a clear implied choice of Dutch law, court also concluded that The Netherlands was the country where characteristic performance to be effected as being place of residence of seller plus payment of price stipulated in guilders at Amsterdam.

138. Rb. Amsterdam, 12 November 1975, AK 9743.

139. BGH 22 September 1971, IPRspr. 1971, no. 133. See, generally, Drobnig, op.cit., pp. 232-34, 240-42.

140. BGH 19 September 1973, IPRspr. 1973, no. 11.

141. BGH 10 January 1958, IPRspr. 1958/59, no. 37.

142. BGH 14 February 1958, IPRspr. 1958/59, no. 39: Italian purchaser, German seller, Italian law governed; BGH 15 March 1962, IPRspr. 1962/63, no. 41: commercial agency, law of agent's place of business governed; BGH 22 September 1971, IPRspr. 1971, no. 133: French distributor, German seller, French law governed.

143. LG Hamburg, 10 June 1974, IPR spr. 1974, no. 154: German seller, French buyer, French law as law of place of payment to govern: meaning of place of performance a matter for German law to decide; renvoi from French law, whereby law of seller's habitual residence governs, accepted. See, also, Sumampouw, op.cit., Vol. 2, pp. 26-27.

144. See, Dicey and Morris, op.cit., p. 747 et seq.

principles which have been developed in English conflict of laws.[145] In the absence of an express choice of law the court will seek to determine an implied choice of law. Exclusive jurisdiction clauses and arbitration clauses may provide strong indications of the parties' intention.[146] Where such intention is not discoverable the court must select the system of law [147] with which the transaction has its closest and most real connection. This involves an examination of the contract terms and all relevant circumstances connected with the making of the contract.[148] To this end, decisions have been reached which could serve as examples for most of the approaches seen to exist in the other European countries.

Where both parties have a place of business or are habitually resident in, or where one party is represented by an agent in, the same country, the law of that country is likely to be held to be the proper law.[149] Where each party has a place of business in a separate country and the contract was negotiated and concluded in one of the countries, the law of that country may likewise be held to be the proper law.[150] The *lex loci contractus* has been regarded as being *prima facie* the proper law [151], but it is unlikely now to be resorted to unless there exist supporting connections, such as the place of business of one of the parties or as being also the *lex loci solutionis.*

The law of the country of performance is to be regarded as a significant pointer to the proper law where it is reinforced by other factors, but not otherwise, with the probable exception of f.o.b. contracts not being a multiport contract. Performance normally relates to discharge of all or most of the principal obligations imposed by the contract in one country.[152] As amongst the various acts to be performed, that of delivery, whereby the seller or his agent places the goods at the disposition of the buyer or buyer's agent, or of a carrier for transport to the buyer, is generally to be regarded as the most principal act of performance. Provided that the contract stipulates for delivery by the seller, this obligation might well be termed the characteristic obligation and to the extent that it is reinforced by other factors it will often be enough to "localize" the proper law. This will be negatived where the seller has the contractual right to choose the country of delivery on the reasoning that he would thereby be unilaterally specifying the proper law of the contract. The weight of the other factors may, in turn, be sufficient to balance this.

145. James Miller & Partners, Ltd. *v.* Whitworth Street Estates (Manchester) Ltd. [1970] AC 583; Compagnie d'Armement Maritime SA *v.* Compagnie Tunisienne de Navigation SA [1971] AC 572.

146. NV Kwik Hoo Tong Handel Maatschappij *v.* James Findlay & Co. [1927] AC 604; see further, *infra*, n. 200.

147. Sayers *v.* International Drilling Co. NV [1971] 1 WLR 1176; Coast Lines Ltd. *v.* Hudig & Veder Chartering NV [1972] 2 QB 34.

148. Jacobs *v.* Crédit Lyonnais (1884) 12 QBD 589.

149. Ibid.; A.V. Pound & Co. Ltd. *v.* M.W. Hardy & Co. Inc. [1956] AC 588.

150. H. Glynn (Covent Garden) Ltd. *v.* Wittleder [1959] 2 Lloyd's Rep. 409.

151. Kahler *v.* Midland Bank Ltd. [1950] AC 24.

152. Benaim & Co. *v.* Debono [1924] AC 514; NV Handel Maatschappij J. Smits *v.* English Importers (London) Ltd. [1955] 2 Lloyd's Rep. 317.

In the case of f.o.b. contracts imposing an obligation on the seller to consign goods to the buyer from a specified place, shipment at a stipulated port can often be considered to be the most important act of performance and has been held to be decisive.[153] Often, the *lex loci solutionis* will also coincide with the seller's place of business and/or the place of payment. The same will hold true for many c.i.f. contracts.

The various factors to be taken into account, other than those already mentioned, include the form, language and terminology of the contract, the currency involved, the nationality and residence of the parties, any previous dealings between them as well as their dealings in regard to the particular contract under consideration, together with considerations of business efficacy and commercial convenience.[154] Not just the length of the list but also its openness has caused concern among commentators: all is grist to the mill.

Despite the variation in particular approaches existing amongst the European countries, one may suggest that, at the risk of a too great over-simplification, as a general indicator of the present state of European conflict of laws, the law of the place of the seller governs the international contract of sale of goods, whether this be by way of (characteristic) performance, e.g., delivery within the seller's country, or by virtue of conclusion of the contract within the seller's country or within the buyer's country in which the seller is also there established.

It is also worthy of note that three of Europe's most active international trading countries, Germany, The Netherlands and England, have persisted in their adherence to the use of open-textured conflict of laws rules in contrast to the adoption of fixed rules.[155]

3.2. Distribution agreement as a distributorship contract *sui generis*

Although being a contract envisaging sales of goods, such contracts include clauses relating to the distribution of the goods sold, publicity, advancement of "brand name", etc., and non-competion by way of establishing exclusive trading zones. The relationship envisages, *inter alia,* the creation of a 'clientele'. Further, the 'distributor' may be an agent.

There is a strong body of opinion [156] that exclusive distributorship agreements are contracts *sui generis* and it must be conceded that to treat such contracts as not different to sale contracts may be at best conceptually inelegant and at

153. Benaim & Co. *v.* Debono [1924] AC 514: seller with place of business in Gibraltar sold anchovies f.o.b. Gibraltar to a buyer in Malta, payment against documents through a bank in Gibraltar; law of Gibraltar governed as *lex loci solutionis* of f.o.b. contract. Cf. Lando, *Contracts,* s. 239, n. 1029, who construes this case as a further example of application to commercial contracts of the *lex fori* by the English courts, the case being heard by the Privy Council.

154. See, *Benjamin's Sale of Goods,* op.cit., ss. 2300-2305.

155. For criticism of this fact, see, Lando, *Contracts,* s. 116 (England) and s. 238 (Germany).

156. See the authors cited by Theux, op.cit., Vol. I, p. 310, n. 185, n. 187, and p. 320, n. 240. See, also, Lando, *Contracts,* ss. 254-57.

worst abusive of the proper determination of rights not directly pertinent to the sale aspects.

This can be interpreted restrictively or extensively. The restrictive view allows for judicial construction of the contract to the extent necessary to give it what may be termed business efficacy. The alternative is to identify in the relationship those elements that have an affinity with contracts of agency and mandate, which leads to the conclusion that the incidents of such agreements should not be regulated principally by reference to the law of contract but equally by reference to the mutual rights and obligations pertaining to *représentation*, and even employment.

This broad view manifests itself in a general approach and a particular approach. The former encompasses the device of reading into the contract far wider rights and duties than those treated by the parties, either expressly or capable of being found by construction of the language adopted. Thus, regarding the distributorship agreement as being in essence also a contract to perform particular services [157] would allow the court to incorporate into the relationship a number of analogous obligations, such as the duty of loyalty owed by an agent under which may be subsumed the duty on the distributor to provide the supplier with full and necessary information and to refrain from divulging trade secrets.

The particular approach is directed to developing the protection which the distributor can claim in the event that he suffers real economic damage not constituting legally recognised damage upon unilateral termination by the supplier. Having regard to the degree of economic dependence between the supplier and his exclusive distributor, which is often considerable, and to the very real prejudice occasioned by the termination of the relationship by the supplier, it is understandable that attempts should be made to import notions of *mandat d'intérêt commun* in order to allow the distributor a claim to compensation analogous to that available to agents upon unilateral termination by the principal.[158] The view that both sole agency and exclusive distributorship agreements share the common objective of developing a *clientèle* and an element of continuity, is attractive but not entirely convincing.[159] On the other hand, there is much substance in the claim that, where the manufacturer-supplier effectively controls the distributor's business organization and dictates his commercial policy (and may legally do so under the terms of the contract – often a contract of adhesion), the distributor functions more as an employee than as an independent trader.[160] If the manufacturer terminates or does not renew the contract the distributor may be left in a very weak economic position.[161] It is argued that to leave him to seek judicial redress on the ground of breach of contract by abusive termina-

157. E.g., as falling under BGB para. 675.

158. E.g., in France under the terms of the Decree of 23 December 1958 or otherwise by judicial recognition of a *mandat intérêt commun.* The right of the principal to revoke at will is contained in French CC Art. 2003: see also, BGB paras. 649 and 671.

159. Compare, Theux, op.cit., Vol. I, pp. 306, 311, 312.

160. See, Carbonneau, loc.cit., p. 93.

161. There is no recognized right to have the contract extended beyond what is provided

tion is tantamount to leaving him without redress.[162] Accordingly, it is contended that the courts should recognise the concept of 'employed merchant' and allow (analogous) claims deriving from employment protection and social legislation.[163]

However, the rule remains that the distributor is not *per se* entitled to an *indemnité de cessation* [164], and is not to be regarded as an employed merchant. Nevertheless, he has not been abandoned entirely to his own devices. Although the Italian [165] and French [166] courts have refused to interprete extensively in favour of the distributor, the West German *Bundesgerichtshof* [167] has extended the provisions of the Commercial Code relating to the agent's compensation for serious breach and *indemnité de clientèle* [168] to the distributor, but only where the distributor fulfills in fact the function of a commercial agent and has been effectively assimilated into the supplier's sales organization. The Swiss Code of Obligations, Article 418b, paragraph 2 [169] provides that, "the legal relationship between the parties to a commercial agency agreement is governed by Swiss law if the area covered by the agent's activity is situated in Switzerland" [170], and the Swiss *Bundesgericht* has held that in cases where the distributorship relationship has existed for some years, and has resulted in a considerable sale of the producer-supplier's goods consequent upon the distributor's devotion to promotion, the legal position of the distributor, for the purposes of ascertaining the proper law, may be compared to that of the commercial agent.[171] In The Netherlands it has been held that the law governing a sole importer contract is that which by analogy applies to a contract of agency.[172] This would appear, however, to be an isolated instance, the normal approach being to regard the sole importer as a co-seller.[173] In other cases, the various approaches available to the Dutch court in ascertaining the governing law are employed, and indicate something of a homeward trend.[174]

---

for in the contract: French CC Art.1134 and cf. Martin-Baker Aircraft Co. Ltd. *v.* Canadian Flight Equipment Ltd. [1955] 2 QB 556.

162. See, Carbonneau, loc.cit., p. 94.

163. Ibid., p. 113.

164. Theux, op.cit., Vol. I, p. 306.

165. See the authorities cited, ibid., p. 312, n. 194.

166. Ibid., p. 318, n. 230.

167. BGH, 11 December 1958, NJW 1959, p. 144.

168. HGB 89b.

169. Federal Law of 4 February 1949, inserting in the Code of Obligations a rule deriving from caselaw: BG 18 September 1934, BGE 60 II 322, see, Rigaux, loc.cit., n. 24.

170. Translation taken from Lando, *Contracts*, s. 254. Cf. Rigaux, loc.cit., s. 7: "When the agent's centre of activity lies in Switzerland the legal relations between principal and agent are governed by Swiss law".

171. BG 3 August 1962, BGE 88 II 474, *Fadyco Handels AG-Seybert & Rahier,* cited Lando, *Contracts,* s. 254.

172. Rb. Groningen, 23 January 1970, AK 5844.

173. Rb. Amsterdam, 29 January 1975, AK 9093: Dutch agent of an Italian firm also given sole importer function; Dutch law also governed this aspect.

174. Hof Den Bosch, 10 April 1972, AK 8012, *Matram-Konrad Hornschuh AG:* Dutch firm granted exclusive selling rights in the exclusive selling zone of the Netherlands by German firm; law where exclusive seller had his place of business, the Netherlands, governed; Rb. Breda, 12 December 1978, AK 11722: exclusive selling zone, "most characteristic of this contract being its exclusive territory", covered Benelux and Germany; place of business

This is further than the English courts have been prepared to go, although comparison may be drawn with one decision where a contract of sole agency was regarded as not significantly different from an employment contract in the situation where the agent was effectively part of the principal's organization.[175] Extension of this approach to the distributor has more recently been denied in a case which held that the supplier could not escape from the agreement by pleading that minor failures to perform constituted a breach amounting to repudiation of the contract by the distributor, with the result that the contract was held to be still subsisting, and that where the agreement was of indefinite duration it could only be terminated by reasonable notice.[176] The judicial incorporation of such a term into the parties' contract allows the court to employ the precept that contracts are to be performed in good faith [177] and in this way to effect a measure of relief. Similarly, and for the first time in regard to international commercial agency, the Court of Appeal has recently held [178], that where a commercial agent had introduced the (Dutch) buyer willing and able to perform to the (English) seller and a contract of sale was concluded between those parties, the principal (seller) remained liable to pay the full amount of the agent's agreed commission even though the principal was later unwilling or unable to perform his contractual obligations to the buyer. The court implied a term into the contract that the principal would "not fail to perform [the] contract with the buyer so as to deprive the agent of the remuneration due to him under the agency contract".[179] "[The] whole relationship of principal and agent depends upon the principal accepting his obligations to the agent once the agent has done his work and the principal has accepted the benefit of it." [180] However, this must be read in the light of an earlier decision by the House of Lords that the principal incurs no liability to the agent where the principal disposes of his property to the third party during the con-

in The Netherlands, therefore basis of sales activities, led to closest connection with Dutch law; cf. Rb. Rotterdam, 16 November 1971, AK 7031, affirmed, Hof Den Haag, 29 June 1973, AK 8015, *C.A.L. - Ligtermoet & Cyanamid:* Dutch supplier granted distributor in Lebanon exclusive selling rights there; written offer sent from, written acceptance received in The Netherlands, where contract orally amended and written confirmation despatched; relationship "must be seen as having most connection with Dutch legal sphere."

175. Martin-Baker Aircraft Co. Ltd. *v.* Canadian Flight Equipment Ltd. [1955] 2 QB 556.

176. Decro-Wall SA *v.* Marketing Ltd., [1971] 1 WLR 361.

177. This is an active principle in Dutch law, expressed in Artt. 1374(3) BW and 1375 BW. Its application has led to prevention of reliance on an unconscienable exemption clause contained in an adhesion contract: HR 19 May 1967, NJ 1967, 261. The corresponding provision in the French CC 1134(3) appears to allow repudiation rather than to prevent it.

178. Alpha Trading Ltd. *v.* Dunnshaw-Patton Ltd. [1981] 2 WLR 169 (CA).

179. Ibid., at p. 180, *per* Brandon LJ.

180. Ibid., at p. 183, *per* Lawton LJ. this decision is capable of a narrower *ratio:* on the facts set out in the parties' pleadings, agent's commission was calculated on the basis of the sale price and due upon performance; therefore, implied term could be that principal would not cause agent to be deprived of commission by committing breach of contract releasing buyer from obligation to pay purchase price, being the sole agreed source of agent's commission; see, Templeman LJ at p. 183.

tinuance of the contract brought about by the agent, thus bringing the contract to an end, even though the agent's commission has been calculated on the basis of the contract persisting for its agreed period. The agent's claim that he had a vested interest in the continued performance of the contract, and that termination by the deliberate act of the principal deprived him of commission which he would otherwise have received, was denied.[181]

Only in Belgium is there specific legislation directed to exclusive distributorship agreements, and even this is confined to the unilateral termination of such contracts of indefinite duration [182] and intended to provide such distributors with a certain measure of protection. This has been extended to certain non-exclusive distributors under agreements for a specified duration.[183]

The scope of the legislation is restricted. It applies only to agreements relating to sale of goods within a reserved territory by an independent trader. It appears that the courts have excluded the case of the distributor whose exclusive right is restricted to a reserved class of customers.[184] The innovatory character of the legislation is to be found most clearly in Article 3 of the 1971 Law, which provides that where a distributorship agreement is terminated by the supplier for reasons other than serious default of the distributor or where the distributor terminates the agreement for serious default of the supplier, the distributor may claim *"une indemnité complémentaire équitable."* The assessment of this compensation takes into account the increased benefit accruing to the supplier in terms of *clientèle* developed by the distributor, the cost to the distributor in exploiting the distributorship and the cost to him, such as severance pay to personnel, resulting from the loss of concession. This extends the provisions of the 1961 Law which is in terms of unilateral termination for serious default of either party or by either giving reasonable notice or a fair compensation at the choice of the party terminating.[185]

Paradoxically, Belgian law appears to be an exception to the rule in France and Germany in that it does not grant an *indemnité de clientèle* to commercial agents [186] but now grants as much, if not more, to distributors. These other laws do not, in the main, protect their distributors, only their commercial agents.

Of particular interest here is that the Law of 1961 contains a conflict of laws rule whereby Belgian law is the governing law, to the exclusion of any foreign choice of law, when the court has jurisdiction on the basis of the Law [187] , which

181. L. French & Co. Ltd. *v*. Leeston Shipping Co. Ltd. [1922] 1 AC 451: shipbrokers effected upon request ship charter for 18 months; charterparty terminated after 4 months when shipowner sold vessel to charterers; shipbrokers claimed 14 months' commission.

182. Law of 27 July 1961. See, Theux, op.cit., Vol. I, p. 320 et seq.; Gutt, "Commercial Agency and Distribution Agreements and Related Problems of Licensing in Belgium and Luxemburg", in van Gerven and Lukoff, eds., op.cit., p. 7 et seq.

183. Law of 13 April 1971. See, Theux, ibid.

184. See, Gutt, loc.cit., p. 9, n. 2 and the authorities cited there.

185. Cass. civ., 16 September 1965, JT 1966, 77.

186. Belgian CC Artt. 1984-2010 is silent on this point.

187. Art. 4, para. 2.

provides that a distributor who is a party to a contract producing its effects wholly or in part in Belgium may bring proceedings before the court on the ground of unilateral termination.[188] This conflict of laws rule is not applicable where the Belgian court has jurisdiction by virtue of its ordinary rules of jurisdiction [189], in which case general Belgian conflict of laws rules will apply. Being a unilateral and not a bilateral rule, it will have 'extraterritorial' effect to the extent that a foreign court gives consideration to the impact of the law of the place of performance upon the otherwise proper law governing the distributorship contract.

Finally, it has been pointed out that if the distributorship contract were to be regarded as a contract *sui generis*, and not as a contract of sale, the Hague Sales Convention of 1955 would not *per se* apply.[190]

3.3. Distribution agreement as an agency contract

When one turns to transactions effected by an agent, the issue of the applicable law usually turns upon the distinction between the internal and the external relationship, together with the issue, truly peculiar to agency, of the effects of the agent's authority.

The EC Contractual Obligations Convention of 1980 will apply to the internal relationship but only to the external relationship to the extent that it relates to the relationship agent-third party. The external relationship principal-third party is excluded [191], on the reasoning that such instances relate to the effect of the agent's authority, which is not germane to party autonomy.[192] On the other hand, the Hague Agency Convention of 1978 does encompass the effects of the agent's exercise or purported exercise of his authority as an issue in the relationship of principal-third party, but it does not apply to the transaction made by the agent.[193]

With the exception of France, which adopts a unitary approach whereby in principle all issues are subjected to the law of the place of the most characteristic obligation [194], most other countries accept this distinction, which can lead to the application of different laws to the one tripartite relationship.

In broad outline it is possible to say that the internal relationship, i.e., between principal and agent, is governed by the 'proper' law of that agency contract,

188. Art. 4, para. 1. As between Parties to the EC Convention on Jurisdiction and Recognition and Enforcement of Judgments in Civil and Commercial Matters of 1968, the rules of jurisdiction contained in Title 2 of the Convention are applicable.

189. See, Judicial Code, Art. 624, para. 2: proceedings may be brought by the claimant before the court of the place where the obligations in dispute, or any of them, are created or where they are, have been or ought to have been performed.

190. Lando, *Contracts*, s. 255.

191. Art. 1, para. 2(f).

192. See, Giuliano and Lagarde, *Report on the Convention on the law applicable to contractual obligations*, 1980 C 282, 31 October 1980, p. 13.

193. Art. 11.

194. See, Pelichet, loc.cit., pp. 20-23; Battiffol and Lagarde, op.cit., Vol. 2 no. 603; Cour de Paris, 21 May 1957, Rev. cit. 1958, 128; 4 December 1970, Rev. Crit. 1971, 703; Cour d'appèl de Lyon, 21 March 1973, Clunet 1974, 345, AK 10062.

whereas the external relationship, i.e., between principal and/or agent (which may depend on the further distinction between direct and indirect representation) and the third party is governed by the 'proper' law of the main contract concluded with the third party. As between the different countries, however, the application of the broad rule can differ significantly.

3.3.1. Internal relationship

Under English law, in accordance with the normal conflict of laws rule for contracts, the internal relationship is governed by the proper law of the agency contract.[195] Thus, in *Mauroux* v. *Pereira* [196], application by an English agent for leave to serve notice of a writ out of the jurisdiction [197] upon a Portuguese principal was refused on the ground that Portuguese law was the proper law of the contract.

In general, the proper law will be the law of the country where the principal is established and where the agency relationship is constituted.[198] When the parties are established in different countries, or even in the same country, the implied intention may be that the law of another country than that of the principal's establishment is to apply. The same is true in regard to determining the closest connection. In another recent case [199], also on an application for leave to serve notice of a writ out of the jurisdiction for alleged breach of a contract concluded in Italy between a principal established there and an underwriting agent established in the British Virgin Islands, the agreement providing for ICC arbitration in Geneva, leave was refused on the grounds, *inter alia*, that the contract was governed either by Italian law as being the law of the place where the principal was resident and where the contract was concluded or by Swiss law as being an implied choice of law.[200]

The true position is not, however, quite so certain. It has been held that the extent of the agent's authority, in addition to being governed by the proper law

195. Dicey and Morris, op.cit., p. 910; Cheshire and North, op.cit., p. 237.

196. Mauroux *v.* Sociedade Comercial Abel Pereira Da Fonseca S.A.R.L. [1972] 1 WLR 962.

197. Under Rules of The Supreme Court, Order 11 rule 1(f): discussed generally, Wade (1974) 21 NTIR 1.

198. Albeko Schuhmaschinen AG *v.* Kamborian Shoe Machine Co. Ltd. (1961) 111 LJ 519.

199. Atlantic Underwriting Agencies and David Gale (Underwriting) *v.* Compagnia di Assicurazione di Milano S.p.A. [1979] 2 Lloyd's Rep. 240.

200. Arbitration clauses and to a less extent jurisdiction clauses provide strong indications of an implied choice; Tzortzis *v.* Monark Line A/B [1968] 1 WLR 406 (CA): arbitration in London clause only connection with England of contract made and to be performed in Sweden for sale of a ship by Swedish sellers to Greek buyers, English law governed; cf. Compagnie Tunisienne de Navigation SA *v.* Compagnie d'Armement Maritime SA [1971] AC 572: similar clause only connection with England of contract for sea carriage of oil from Tunisia to France made between Tunisian company and French shipowners, French law governed: "An arbitration clause must be treated as an indication . . . Always it will be a strong indication", at p. 600 *per* Lord Wilberforce. Dutch law refuses to construe a tacit choice of law from such clauses: Hof Amsterdam, 7 February 1963, NJ 1963, 197.

of the agency contract with the principal, may be enlarged by powers deriving from the law governing the main contract with the third party.[201] Furthermore, the question of the agent's apparent authority may be governed by the law under which the agent acted.[202] Although the law governing the agency contract may lead to the conclusion that the agent had no implied authority from the principal so to act, the law of the place where the agent acted may conclude that the agent had apparent authority to act.[203]

German and Swiss law adopt the rule that the internal relationship is generally governed by the law of the place of performance of the agent's duties as being the law of closest connection, which in the case of commission and mercantile agents is generally that of the agent's business residence.[204]

Dutch law now [205] adopts the rule that the internal relationship is governed by the law of the country where the agent is established.[206] This rule is subject to the proviso that there exist no factors that would lead to the conclusion that another law ought to govern.[207] This connecting factor of establishment of the agent has increasingly been coupled with or replaced by reference to the law of the place where the agent acts or performs his contractual obligations [208], that being the place of the characteristic performance.[209] This appears to be motivated not so much by doctrinal considerations related to characteristic performance but by a need to localize the agent's activities in order to ensure the application of local protective legislative measures.[210] Where the agent is Dutch, it appears that the Dutch court will require much convincing that Dutch law should not apply. Thus, as between a Dutch agent and a German

201. Ruby SS Corporation Ltd. *v.* Commercial Union Assurance Co. [1938] All ER Rep 711: law of agency contract (New York) governed agent's power to cancel insurance contract with third party, governed by English law, which conferred no such power on agent. Criticised, Dicey and Morris, op.cit., pp. 913-14, condemned, Cheshire and North, op.cit., p. 238 n. 3. Cf. Rb. Dordrecht, 22 June 1976, AK 10194, *infra*, n. 206 and text to n. 223.

202. Dicey and Morris, op.cit., p. 874, Cheshire and North, op.cit., p. 234.

203. Rigaux, loc.cit., s. 17.

204. OLG Hamburg, 20 June 1909, cited Rigaux, loc.cit., s. 5 n. 19; BGH 5 February 1958, IPRspr. 1958/59 no. 38; for commission and mercantile agents see, BGH 23 November 1964, and BGH 15 March 1962, IPRspr. 1962/63 no. 41, both cited, Drobnig, op.cit., p. 235, n. 67, 70. BG 15 May 1962, BGE 88 II 191; 5 October 1965, AK 3319. Cf. Swiss Draft Federal Law on p.i.l., Art. 127, para. 1: "Dans la représentation contractuelle les rapports entre représenté et représentant sont régis par la loi applicable à leur contrat."

205. Compare Ktg. Amsterdam, 25 January 1963, NJ 1965, 223: "There are reasonable arguments to proceed from the principle that agency contracts are governed by the law of the principal for it cannot be demanded of him, when he has appointed agents in different countries, that they be apprised of the various laws applicable to the respective contracts."

206. Rb. Amsterdam, 29 January 1975, AK 9093; Rb. Dordrecht, 22 June 1976, AK 10194: "One may certainly, when someone in The Netherlands is authorised as agent for a foreign firm to conclude contracts, accept in general that such agent is also authorised to receive payment". See further, *infra,* text to n. 223.

207. HR 6 April 1973, NJ 1973, 371, *Topsøe-Del Prado;* Rb. Roermond, 27 February 1975, WPNR 1977, 281; Rb. Arnhem, 6 February 1975, AK 9463.

208. Ktg. Den Haag, 7 August 1964, AK 6758; President Rb. Roermond, 13 October 1969, AK 7851.

209. Lemaire, *Overzicht,* p. 116.

210. Ktg. Den Haag, 7 August 1964, AK 6758.

principal, it was held that, as the territory of the agent was predominantly in The Netherlands, with which there were several other connecting factors, the regulations in force in Germany concerning agency contracts were not of application: "the legislative regulation of agency contracts places the centre of gravity in the protection of the agent, whereby the law of the country where the agent is active must prevail." [211] However, where a Dutch agent of a Dutch company (the court holding that there was no employment contract) was required to perform his sales activities predominantly in Belgium, to such an extent that he had to have an office and living quarters there, it was held that, considering his Dutch nationality, the maintenance of another home in The Netherlands, the conclusion of the contract there, the settling of accounts between agent and principal always having been in Dutch guilders and the agent's participation in The Netherlands in the liquidation of the Dutch principal, the agency relationship was the most closely connected with The Netherlands, and that law governed.[212] In the case of non-permanent or *ad hoc* agents commissioned to perform a specific task, the law of the country where the principal is established will have a claim to be applied.[213]

The cases exhibit such flexibility that, as one commentator has observed [214],

"the court in a given case will, without much difficulty, be able to apply the legal system containing a public law regulation that will operate upon the legal relationship, and whose claim to be applied is justified in the light of the specific connecting factors."[215]

3.3.2. External relationship

3.3.2.1. *Principal-third party*

The issue of the principal-agent relationship is seldom litigated as between principal and third party, although it has been extensively discussed in legal literature.[216] The question of the law governing the agent's authority is distinct from the question of the law governing the transaction concluded by the agent with the third party. Thus the Hague Agency Convention of 1978 deals with the former question, whereas the EC Contractual Obligations Convention of 1980 deals with the latter.

The widely accepted rule is that the effects of the agency relationship upon

211. President Rb. Roermond, 13 October 1969, AK 7851.

212. Rb. Roermond, 27 February 1975, WPNR 1977, 281.

213. Rb. Den Bosch, 15 October 1971, NJ 1973, 118: economic and legal adviser agreed with Dutch company to seek a buyer in the US and elsewhere for company's shares, Dutch law governed.

214. In regard also to employment contracts, see, HR 8 June 1973, NJ 1973, 400, *Mackaay-American Express 2.*

215. Van Rooij, *De positie van publiekrechtelijke regels op het terrein van het internationaal privaatrecht* (1976) p. 250.

216. For extensive citation of authorities see, Rigaux, loc.cit., ss. 8-29; Pelichet, loc.cit., p. 25, n. 61.

third parties with whom the agent transacts, in other words, the question whether the act of the agent binds the principal, are to be governed by the 'proper' law of the transaction, the main contract, concluded with the third party. In practice this will usually amount to application of the law of the place where the agent has acted.

Both the *Bundesgerichtshof* and the *Bundesgericht* have expressly affirmed that the external relationship is autonomous and thus subject to its own conflict of laws rule.[217] In principle this is the law of the place where the agent's power is to operate (*Wirkungsland* [218] or *Wirkungsort* [219]). Swiss law, however, has introduced the distinction that the question whether the principal in fact authorized the agent to act is to be resolved by reference to the law of the principal's domicile [220], a distinction which German law appears to ignore.[221]

Dutch law adopts the same approach:

> "The agent's authority to bind the principal is governed by the internal law of the country where the agent acts."[222]

Thus, where a third party bought goods in The Netherlands from an agent appointed by an Italian principal as its Dutch agent and paid the agent, who was not authorised to receive payment and who failed to remit the price to his principal, the latter's claim that the third party should have paid the price directly and not to the agent was rejected on the ground that under Dutch law an agent authorised to conclude contracts must in principle be taken to be authorised to accept payment under those contracts.[223]

English law conforms to the rule that the proper law of the main contract concluded by the agent with the third party governs the principal-third party relationship.[224] In the case of 'direct representation' it could scarcely be otherwise, for as was pointed out in *Pattison* v. *Mills* [225], where an English principal commissioned a Scottish agent to conclude a contract in Scotland with a third party: "If I, residing in England, send down my agent to Scotland, and he makes

217. BGH February 1958, IPRspr. 1958/59 no. 38: "According to German Private International Law agency is an independent legal transaction and is therefore subject to a special conflicts rule"; BG 15 May 1962, BGE 88 II 191: "The relations which have thus been created (between principal and third party) are subject to their own choice of law rule in Private International Law"; translations taken from Rigaux, loc.cit., s. 11 n. 40.

218. BGH 13 July 1954, NJW 1954, 1561.

219. Trib. supérieur de Zurich, 14 June 1973, RSJ 1975, 354, AK 9862. Cf. Swiss Draft Federal Law on p.i.l., Art. 127, para 2.

220. BG 26 June 1962, BGE 88 II 195.

221. BGH 5 February 1958, IPRspr. 1958/59, no. 38. See, also, BGH 9 December 1964, 23 October 1963, cited Drobnig, op.cit., p. 248, n. 161.

222. Rb. Amsterdam, 18 June 1975, S & S 1976, 51, AK 9744, (1980) 27 NILR, p. 391; also, 27 January 1976, AK 10458; 19 April 1977, AK 10723.

223. Rb. Dordrecht, 22 June 1976, AK 10194. See also, Rb. Rotterdam, 13 February 1976, AK 10241, (1980) 23 NILR, p. 391: "The question whether the agent has authority to commit his employer is governed by German law, since the place of business of the principal is located in Germany, whilst the agent was also to carry out his duties in that country."

224. Dicey and Morris, op.cit., p. 911; Cheshire and North, op.cit., p. 237.

225. (1828), 1 Dow & Cl. 342, at p. 363.

contracts for me there, it is the same as if I myself went there and made them." Similarly, where a Brazilian principal executed in Brazil a power of attorney in Portuguese authorising an English agent to buy and sell shares in London, and it was questioned whether the agent had validly sold some of the principal's shares to third parties, it was held that the issue was governed by English, not Brazilian law.[226]

Where the principal is undisclosed, the matter remains open to some doubt, although it is submitted that the rule should also encompass undisclosed principals.[227] As a preliminary, it should be noticed that confusion continues to persist in distinguishing between the unnamed and the undisclosed principal. A clear example is provided by *Teheran-Europe Co. Ltd.* v. *S.T. Belton (Tractors) Ltd.* [228], where it was stated that, "Their identity was not disclosed. Their existence as principals was not disclosed." [229] Yet it was clear from the correspondence between the agent and third party that the latter knew or must have known that the agent was acting for a principal, though not necessarily a foreign principal.

The leading case of *Maspons Y. Hermano* v. *Mildred, Goyeneche & Co.* [230] is sometimes advanced as authority for the proposition that the law of the main contract governs the liability of the undisclosed principal.[231] It is clear from the facts, however, that the principal in that case was unnamed and that the fact of the agency was disclosed to the third party. To this extent it is unsafe to rely on *Maspons* v. *Mildred* as authority for the wider rule; certainly, it is unnecessary to distinguish it when advancing the reasoning that English law is one with German and Swiss law in subjecting the external relationship to the *lex loci actus* of the agent.[232]

Nevertheless, there does not appear to be any compelling reason why the law governing the case of the undisclosed principal should be different to that of the disclosed principal situation, and the trend of the judicial decisions suggests strongly that also here the law governing the main contract with the third party applies to the relationship of undisclosed principal-third party. The latter has a right of election against either the agent or the principal, and the same conflict of laws rule ought to govern both cases. Similarly, if the undisclosed principal exercises the right of intervention he ought not to be able to surprise the third party by bringing with him a governing law of which the third party was ignorant.

Nor is this a matter of purely theoretical interest. In a multitude of transactions carried out by commercial agents known in their particular trade, it will often not be specified, or indeed even clear, whether they are acting as agent or not in the particular transaction. When disputes arise, the third party will

226. Chatenay *v.* Brazilian Submarine Telegraph Co. Ltd. [1891] 1 QB 79.
227. Dicey and Morris, op.cit., p. 912.
228. [1968] 3 WLR 205 (CA).
229. Ibid. at p. 209, *per* Lord Denning MR.
230. (1882) 9 QBD 530, upheld on appeal, (1883) 8 App. Cas. 874.
231. Cheshire and North, op.cit., p. 238; Rigaux, loc.cit., s. 13.
232. Cf. Rigaux, ibid., s. 29.

naturally expect the agent to be liable on the basis of the law governing the transaction between them. When the figure of the undisclosed principal is revealed and the sometimes difficult issue of election arises, it would hardly do justice to legitimate commercial expectations to allow the principal to escape liability by pleading a law other than that governing the main contract.

It may be noted that the Hague Agency Convention of 1978 makes no distinction based on the undisclosed principal.[233]

3.3.2.2. *Agent-third party*

The position here seems relatively straightforward. Where the agent has acted fully within his authority, his principal will be bound by the transaction effected. The agent is normally neither liable to the thrid party, unless he has undertaken personal liability jointly with the principal [234] or acted in his own name [235], nor does he acquire rights under the transaction. Where the agent has acted in excess of his authority, so that the principal is not bound, his conduct normally creates personal liability to the third party, which in differing countries will be of a contractual or (quasi-)delictual nature. The agent's liability may not necessarily be co-extensive with that of the putative principal.[236]

The law under which the agent acts or purports to act governs.[237] Consequently, in a number of cases, this law will be that which would have governed the main contract if it had been found that the principal was bound.

4. EXPRESS CHOICE OF THE APPLICABLE LAW

Although this matter is of general practical importance, the difficult issues which arise under the notion of party autonomy are not specific to distribution agreements and do not call for detailed elaboration. The following discussion will in consequence be concise.

The principle of party autonomy in contract is, and has been for a long time [238], almost universally accepted [239], and for very good reasons, not least of which is commercial certainty.[240]

233. Art. 1.

234. Art. 1843 BW.

235. Asser-van der Grinten, op.cit., p. 9.

236. BGB Art. 179.

237. Dicey and Morris, op.cit., p. 916; Kahler *v.* Midland Bank Ltd. [1949] 2 All ER 621; Swiss Draft Federal Law on p.i.l., Art. 127, para. 3: "Les effets de la représentation sans pouvoir entre le représentant et le tiers sont régis par la loi du lieu d'établissement commercial du représentant et, à défaut d'un tel établissement ou si l'existence n'en est pas reconnaissable pour le tiers contractant, par la loi du lieu où le représentant a eu son activité principale dan le cas d'espèce."

238. See, Hamlyn *v.* Talisker Distillery [1894] AC 202; Cass. civ. 5 December 1910, S. 1911. 1.129; BGH 30 September 1952, Clunet 1958, 224; HR 13 May 1966, NJ 1967, 3.

239. See generally, Int. Ency. Comp. Law, Vol. 1, National Reports. See, also, Perovic, "Les Principes et les Règles générales de la nouvelle loi Yougoslave sur les obligations en matière de contrats", (1979) *Revue int. de droit comparé*, p. 749.

240. Rabel, *Conflict of Laws*, Vol. 2, ed. Drobnig, p. 362.

Choice is often given a very flexible meaning. "The choice must be expressed or demonstrated with reasonable certainty by the terms of the contract or the circumstances of the case." [241] The distinction between choice as here intended [242] amd closest connection is that the latter objective determination by the court is ousted by an effective agreement between the parties, either expressed or implied, that a particular law should govern. The fact of agreement is central.[243] The scope of determination of the implied agreement is not always the same and differing results can be reached by different national courts simply on this ground. Thus, the terms of Article 3 of the EC Contractual Obligations Convention of 1980, which correspond to the approach adopted by the English court [244], are wider than the present approach of the Dutch courts, where the enquiry is restricted to the terms of the contract [245], i.e., to express or implied choice, but not tacit choice, which is also the case in those countries that are Parties to the the Hague Sales Convention of 1955.[246]

There are certain restrictions imposed on the parties' freedom to choose the applicable law, the content of which differs from one country to another. In general it may be said that the choice will be conclusive provided it is "bona fide and legal" [247], forms part of a contract regulating an international transaction and is not amended by mandatory provisions.

'International' would at first sight appear to cause no great problems. Certainly, where there is bordercrossing of goods or payment, particularly where the parties are established in different states, there will be general agreement that the transaction is of an international character. It is, however, striking that recent conventions show no uniformity of approach to this issue and that some have been drafted on the basis either that is has proved to be impossible to define the term [248] or that no more can be done than to delimit it negatively.[249] In the result, the determination is a matter for the *lex fori.*[250] In the event of a so-called 'unconnected' choice of law, the approach adopted by the forum may have

241. EC Convention of the Law Applicable to Contractual Obligations, 1980, Art. 3, para. 1.

242. Cf. Art. 4, para. 1 on closest connection in the absence of a choice in such terms.

243. Whitworth Street Estates (Manchester) Ltd. *v.* James Miller and Partners Ltd. [1970] AC 583; Hof Amsterdam, 1 April 1970, NJ 1971, 115. On the different approach to arbitration clauses see, *supra*, n. 200.

244. See, Dicey and Morris, op.cit., p. 753 et seq. (express), p. 761 et seq. (implied/tacit), p. 769 et seq. (closest connection).

245. Hof Amsterdam, *supra*, n. 243; Lemaire, *IPR*, p. 254, *Overzicht*, p. 107.

246. Art. 2, para. 2.

247. Vita Food Products Inc. *v.* Unus Shipping Co. Ltd. [1939] AC 277 at p. 290.

248. Hague Convention on the Law Applicable to Agency 1978, Art. 1, para. 1: see, Pelichet, loc.cit., p. 30; Karsten, Report on the Convention, *Actes et Documents* (1976) Vol. 4, p. 407. On the impossibility of defining 'international' see, Siesby in, *European PIL of Obligations* (1975) ed. Lando, von Hoffman, Siehr, p. 206 at p. 213.

249. Hague Sales Convention, 1955, Art. 1, paras. 1 and 4.

250. See, UN Convention on Contracts for the International Sale of Goods, 1980, Art. 1, paras. 1 and 2; EC Convention on the Law Applicable to Contractual Obligations, 1980, Art. 1, para. 1.

the result of negativing the choice [251], though this result is seldom arrived at.[252] Where the only 'foreign' element present is a choice of law clause, the determination of 'international' may simply be another way of raising the issue whether the choice was *bona fide.*[253] However, a finding that the choice of law was intended to evade otherwise applicable domestic law and thus *mala fide* would not appear to deny the quality of international to all contracts with an unconnected choice of law clause, merely to deny the operativeness of the choice *in casu.*

At this juncture it is important to distinguish three separate issues, which, being closely connected, are often intermingled, even confused. The duty of the court to determine the actual existence of an alleged choice of law reflecting the agreement of the parties is not the same as determining the extent of the freedom of the parties effectively to submit their relationship to a governing law, i.e., the issue of the unconnected law, which in turn is not the same as the material scope of the chosen law, i.e., the issue of restriction by operation of mandatory rules. However, the existence of other closely related matters renders it at best difficult to reduce the problematic to clear logical exposition. For example, by agreeing not to plead foreign law, parties can always make English law applicable to a contract totally unconnected with England.[254] Conversely, in those countries where it is for the court to determine *ex officio* the applicable law the parties are given sometimes considerable freedom to make mutual submissions to the court prior to or even during the proceedings [255] that the parties have agreed

251. Under French law, the contract must be localized by virtue of its factual circumstances and the localizing elements "are in general the same ones that disclose the parties' intention" as to the chosen law: Delaporte, Rev. crit. (1978) at p. 693. See, further, Batiffol and Lagarde, op.cit., Vol. 2 (1976), pp. 229-41: where the chosen law is held to govern it does so by virtue of the localization of the contract in its economic sphere; thus, where all the elements are otherwise localized in Italy, Italian law governs: Ire Cham. civ., 29 April 1970, Rev. crit. 1971, 270. Cf. Cass.civ. 27 January 1931, S. 1933.1. 41.: contract for sale of corn between two French merchants established in France, payment in France, choice of English standard form contract, shipment c.i.f. of Canadian wheat from American port; international contract.

252. The localization theory has had an influence in Dutch literature and in the lower courts: see, generally, Lemaire, *IPR*, p. 258 et seq.; see, also, original Art. 13 Benelux Uniform Law on PIL. HR 13 May 1966, NJ 1967, 3, *Alnati,* settled the question for all practical purposes. It remains theoretically open in English law: see, Dicey and Morris, op. cit., Vol. 2, p. 756. It should not be forgotten that the reason for the choice may not appear from the contract but yet be a commercially reasonable object: Getreide-Import-Gesellschaft m.b.H. *v.* Contimar S.A. [1953] 1 WLR 793, mutually acceptable 'neutral' law. There appears to be no instance under English or German law (see, Drobnig, op.cit., p. 228) where a choice of law has not been recognised for lack of connection.

253. See the line of reasoning of Batiffol, Rev. crit. (1980) 579, commentary to Cour de Cass. (Ire Ch.civ.), 25 March 1980.

254. This appears to have been the position in Suisse Atlantique Société d'Armement Maritime SA *v.* NV Rotterdamsche Kolen Centrale [1967] 1 AC 361.

255. Rb. Rotterdam, 28 March 1961, S & S 1961, 38; 2 April 1963, S & S 1963, 52; Hof Amsterdam, 31 March 1926, W 11513; BGH 17 December 1957, IPRspr. 1956/57 no. 23d; 7 March 1962, NJW, 1005. Swiss Draft Federal Law on private international law, Art. 118, para. 2.

that a particular law should be applicable to the matter in dispute (*procespartijkeuze* or *rechtskeuze achteraf* [256]; *Rechtswahl im Prozess* [257]).

The matter remains, therefore, one of some difficulty, for it touches upon two further issues, the first being the moment of agreement as to the governing law, the second being the power or not to agree to a change of governing law, which issues are further complicated by the question whether the contract may be split and the separate parts submitted to different laws.[258]

The EC Contractual Obligations Convention of 1980 allows for severance and for choice of law applicable to "a part only of the contract" [259], which choice(s) may be made "at any time" [260], but with the saving that any variation, including substitution of the objectively determined law of closest connection by an express choice, shall not, *inter alia*, "adversely affect the rights of third parties." [261] This accords with German.[262], French [263], Swiss [264] and Dutch [265] law, and in as far as splitting the contract is concerned theoretically with English law.[266] It does not accord with English law unless the subsequent choice amounts to an agreement to discharge the contract and to enter into a new transaction governed by the new choice of law.[267]

The EC Contractual Obligations Convention of 1980 clearly adopts the position that connection is unnecessary [268], subject to the reservation that an un-

256. Kollewijn, "De Rechtskeuze achteraf", (1964) NTIR 225 et seq.; Lemaire, *IPR*, pp. 265-67.

257. Schulze, *Die Kodification des Vertragsstatuts im internationalen Privatrecht* (1980) pp. 35, 56 et seq.; Drobnig, op.cit., pp. 229-30. It is not yet settled whether the procedural choice is autonomous and conclusive or whether it should be supported by closest connection elements to be identified by the court. Cf. Rb. Amsterdam, 5 May 1971, S & S 76 (acceptance without more) and Rb. Almelo 21 January 1970, AK 5843 (other factors); similarly, BGH 23 November 1964, and others cited, Drobnig, op.cit., p. 230 n. 28 (acceptance without more) and 17 December 1957, IPRspr. 1956/57 no. 23d (other factors). Cf. Vita Food Products Inc. *v.* Unus Shipping Co. [1939] AC 277, Privy Council, *obiter*, that proper law was English even though counsel for both parties pleaded Newfoundland law applicable. See also, Tomaszewski, (1972) Rev. crit. p. 568 et seq.

258. Soek, "De partiële conflictenrechtelijke Rechtskeuze", *Tien Jaren T.M.C. Asser Instituut* (1975) p. 33 et seq. The *Hoge Raad* has not yet given an unambivalent answer: HR 13 June 1924, NJ 1924 859, *Nicolaas;* HR 19 February 1971, NJ 1971 299, *Katsedijk;* HR 31 May 1974, S & S 1974, 68. English law allows for splitting but the court has expressed extreme reluctance: Kahler *v.* Midland Bank [1950] AC 24.

259. Art. 3, para. 1.

260. Art. 3, para. 2.

261. Ibid. Swiss Draft Federal Law on p.i.l., Art. 119.

262. Drobnig, op.cit., p. 228.

263. Batiffol and Lagarde, op.cit., Vol. 2, p. 243; Cass.civ. 18 November 1959, Rev. crit. (1960) 83.

264. Schulze, op.cit., pp. 56-57.

265. Lemaire, *IPR*, pp. 265-67.

266. Kahler *v.* Midland Bank [1950] AC 24.

267. Whitworth Street Estates (Manchester) Ltd. *v.* James Miller and Partners Ltd. [1970] AC 583; Armar Shipping Co. Ltd. *v.* Caisse Algerienne d'Assurance et de Reassurance [1981] 1 WLR 207 (CA): " . . . unanswerable legal logic, that there must be a proper law of any contract - a governing law - at the time of the making of that contract", *per* Megaw LJ at p. 215. Italy: Cour.cass. 28 June 1966, cited Tomaszewski, loc.cit., p. 579.

268. Cf. EC Jurisdiction and Judgments Convention, 1968, Art. 17 which allows the parties to choose a foreign court even though the transaction does not contain a foreign element.

connected choice shall not oust the application of the mandatory rules of the putative proper law. However, the limitation is itself severly restricted. The Convention provides that the choice of foreign law shall not prevail over the mandatory rules of the law of the "one country" with which "all the other elements relevant to the situation" are connected.[269] This formulation is narrower than the approach adopted in certain Member States, although it may be read together with the discretion allowing for application of the mandatory rules of another law having a close connection [270], and with the saving for application of the law of the forum.[271] Against this must be set the fact that the *Bundesgerichtshof* has held [272] that parties are free to choose a foreign law which does not contain protective measures conforming to those laid down in Article 89b Commercial Code, even in the event of a German agent active in West Germany.[273] An analogous result has also been reached under Belgian law [274] where a Belgian national contracted as *représentant de commerce* with a German company. The contract was expressed to be governed by German law but to the exclusion of the protective Articles 87, 89b and 92a of the German Commercial Code. At issue was whether the clause renouncing a later claim for compensation for termination of the contract [275], valid under German law where the representative is not established within the Federal Republic [276], could be upheld under Belgian law as the *lex fori* [277] in an action brought by an inheriting dependant. The court held that, as the German law did not discriminate on gounds of nationality but rather laid down an objective criterion applicable to all persons, and as the Belgian law was not a matter of *ordre public,* although certainly "*une disposition impérative protégeant des intérêts privés*", the submission of the contract to German law would not be impugned.[278]

Dutch law, although stressing that Dutch mandatory provisions and interests of a public law nature may not be avoided [279], certainly allows for the possibility that the court should take into account a foreign State's interests in preference to the law chosen by the parties [280], even, possibly, where the law of that foreign

269. Art. 3, para. 3.

270. Art. 7, para. 1.

271. Art. 7, para. 2. Art. 16 saves the public policy of the forum.

272. BGH 30 January 1961, IPRspr. 1960/61, no. 39: choice of Dutch (principal's) law prevailed over German agent's claim for *Ausgleichanspruch.*

273. The EC Draft Directive on Commercial Agents, *supra*, text to n. 97-101, allows derogation from mandatory protective laws only for activities outside the EEC: Art. 35 (2).

274. Trib. de Comm. Brussels, 6 May 1969, AK 7337.

275. Art. 89b provides that a representative may claim reasonable compensation for termination from the employer.

276. Art. 92c.

277. Art. 23, Law of 30 July 1963 on commercial representatives prohibits derogation from the Law to the detriment of the representative. See, generally on this Law, Houtekier, *Rechtskundig Weekblad* (1968-69) p. 337 et seq.

278. The court also concluded that the claimant as dependant did not have a right of action under the law. Whichever law was applicable, the result *in casu* would have been the same.

279. HR 12 December 1947, NJ 1948, 608, *Solbandera.*

280. HR 13 May 1966, NJ 1967, 3, *Alnati.* Cf. the German position particularly *vis-a-vis* the long-arm nature of American anti-trust legislation, e.g., Regulation of 14 De-

State would not be the putative proper law.[281] Certainly it has been held that parties may not avoid the mandatory provisions of the putative proper law where such provisions form part of a uniform law pursuant to an international convention.[282] The practice of the Dutch courts in what Dutch commentators term 'bilateralising' the concept of State interests in furtherance of the aims of international commerce may be seen to offer a useful working model by which the inherent uncertainties contained in the formulation of Article 7 EC Contractual Obligations Convention of 1980 and Article 16 Hague Sales Convention of 1978 may be rendered managable.[283]

5. EFFECT OF EEC COMPETITION LAW

The exclusivity of distribution agreements if often referred to as the most characteristic element of sole agency and exclusive distributorship contracts. There is a danger that this element becomes over-emphasised and over-valued, both legally and economically. Put at its most simple, every agreement between traders whereby one is supplied with goods by the other incorporates an aspect of exclusiveness of supply with a corresponding effect on availability to meet demand: in other words, an effect on competition.[284] The importance of this element should not be sought in the notion itself but in the degree of its role in the relations between the contracting parties, that is, in the consequences both internally as between themselves and externally in relation to third parties.

The consequences attaching to the exclusiveness of the trading relationship derive from the agreement, from national legal provisions pertaining to the class of relationship [285] and from European Community law governing competition. The starting-point must be the contract between the parties but in view of the overriding force of European Community law it is always necessary to evaluate the effect of the contractual provisions in the light of these rules on competition. Here it should be noted that the rules relating to both restrictive practices (Art. 85 EEC) and abuse of dominant position (Art. 86 EEC) are aimed at imposing restrictions on effect. The intentions of the parties are here not determinative. What is of importance is the substantive effect on competitive structures and on

cember 1966: Drobnig, op.cit., pp. 311-314. For an analogous response to the extraterritorial reach of US domestic law, see (UK) Shipping and Commercial Documents Act 1964, repealed but more extensively replaced by Protection of Trading Interests Act 1980.

281. Deelen, (1968) 15 NTIR at p. 94.

282. Rb. Rotterdam, 28 November 1967, NJ 1969, 55.

283. See also, for criticism of and a suggested alternative to Art. 7, Drobnig, in *European PIL of Obligations* (1975) ed. Lando, von Hoffmann, Siehr, pp. 82-86. Also, Collins, loc.cit., pp. 49-51.

284. See, Champaud, "La Concession commerciale", Rev. trim. de droit comm., (1963) p. 451 et seq.

285. See generally, Theux, op.cit., Vol. II, p. 263 et seq.

the degree of competition within those structures.[286] Whether such effect is determinable remains open to discussion.[287]

The principal regulation is Article 85 EEC Treaty. Paragraph 1 declares incompatible with the objectives of the Common Market and prohibits

> "all agreements between enterprises, all decisions of associations of enterprises and all concerted practices, which are liable to affect trade between Member States and whose purpose or effect is to prevent, restrict or distort competition within the Common Market."[288]

Agreements or provisions falling within the ambit of Article 85 "shall be automatically void." [289] The European Court has held that the invalidity affects only those elements of the agreement offending Article 85(1), unless they cannot be severed, in which case the entire agreement is rendered void.[290] Where an agreement falls within the terms of Article 85(1) but, *inter alia* "contributes to improving the production or distribution of goods . . . and which does not: (a) impose . . . restrictions which are not indispensable to the attainment of these objectives; (b) afford . . . the possibility of eliminating competition . . ." [291], the Commission may on the application of a party grant a declaration of inapplicability.[292]

The EEC law on competition is concerned with vertical as well as horizontal agreements [293], but it is not concerned with the (sole) agent, whether or not he concludes contracts in his own name, provided the relationship is a genuine one of agency, whereby he acts on behalf of his principal, and accepts no financial risk for the transactions concluded other than that assumed by the *del credere* agent.[294] The decisive criterion, however, is the economic function exercised, and

286. See, Van der Esch, "EEC Competition Rules: basic principles and policy aims", *Legal Issues of European Integration* (1980) No. 2 p. 75 at p. 76.

287. For a trenchant criticism along these lines of recent price discrimination cases, in particular Case 27/76, United Brands *v.* EC Commission [1978] CMLR 429, see, Bishop [1981] 44 MLR 282.

288. This clause has been judicially interpreted to mean 'to a noticeable extent': Case 5/69 Volk *v.* Vervaecke [1969] CMLR 273; Case 22/71 *Béguelin* [1972] CMLR 81.

289. Art. 85(2), EEC.

290. Case 56/65, La Technique Minière *v.* Maschinenbau GmbH (the LTM Case) [1966] CMLR 357; The European Court also held that the relevant national law governs which elements are capable of severance: cf. BGH 27 February 1969, [1969] CMLR 123, *Yoga Fruit Juice Case;* Attwood *v.* Lamont [1920] 3 KB 571, holding that, e.g., restraint of trade clauses cannot be severed if that would entirely alter the scope and intention of the agreement.

291. Art. 85(3), EEC.

292. Where the parties seek clarification that their agreement falls outside Art. 85(1) they should request a negative clearance under Reg. 17/62: see, e.g., Mertens and Straet-Bendix Decision 64/344 of 1 June 1964, OJ 1426/64 of 10 June 1964.

293. Case 56/64, 58/64, Consten and Grundig *v.* EEC Commission [1966] CMLR 418.

294. See, Announcement of 24 December 1962: Exclusive Agency Contracts made with Commercial Agents, OJ 1962/2921 - the so-called Christmas Message. On the nature of agents and distributors for the purposes of Art. 85 see, Consten-Grundig, ibid., at p. 470 and Italy *v.* EEC Council and Commission [1969] CMLR 39 at 63; more generally, van Damme, loc. cit., p. 60 et seq.

not the designation accorded. Thus, where the "agent" maintains or is contractually required to maintain significant stocks in his own name, is required to organize, maintain or guarantee substantial services to the customer at his own expense, or is free to determine or does so determine the price or other terms of the contracts to be concluded, he will constitute an independent trader exercising a degree of economic independence, and thus risk-bearing, that takes him outside the scope of the exception för agents and the agreement will be subject to the law on competition.

The primary category of rights and duties contained in the parties' contract is the supplier's obligation to sell to the distributor, and, where the distributorship is exclusive, only to that distributor, goods for resale within a specified area, the contract area. Limited in such terms the agreement will benefit from the block exemption for certain exclusive dealing agreements granted by the Commission under Regulation 67/67 [295], provided that not more than two parties are concerned in the arrangement. To this primary category, one usually finds a complementary obligation accepted by the distributor to purchase the goods only from the supplier, as a result of which he is prevented from obtaining such goods from other sources. Regulation 67/67 also grants block exemption to such reciprocal arrangements.[296]

The importance of the primary obligation towards the distributor is that, regarded logically, it requires the complementary obligation to refuse to sell to other distributors in the contract area and not to sell to customers from that area approaching the supplier directly. This is of importance at both national and EEC level, in that it may constitute an unlawful restrictive practice. Thus, in France [297] considerable attention has been focused on the question whether the prohibition of *réfus de vente* contained in Article 37 of the Ordinance of 30 June 1945 is justifiable on the ground that the party refusing to sell is bound by the terms of an exclusive distributorship agreement. In the leading case of *Nicholas, Société Brandt Frères* [298], the *Cour de Cassation* ruled that it is justifiable provided the agreement is not a disguise for fixing prices and, further, that the arrangement can be shown as tending to an improvement of services to the benefit of customers. It does not have extra-territorial effect and a refusal to sell by a foreign supplier to persons within the French contract territory is considered as taking place abroad so that Article 37 is not relevant.[299]

295. Art. 1(1)(a).

296. Art. 1(1)(c). See, *supra*, s. 2.2.1. However, disguised closed agreements will fail by virtue of Art. 85(1) and (3): see, Belgian Tile Recommendation 1964 (mutual exclusive dealing), German Ceramic Tiles Decision, OJ L 10/15, 1971, (system of aggregated rebates), or Art. 86: see, Hoffman-La Roche *v.* EC Commission, Case 85/76 [1979] CMLR 211.

297. See, Carbonneau, loc.cit., p. 98 et seq. Cf. Tribunal de Commerce, Brussels, 2 December 1963, *Bara - Philips*, upholding the manufacturer's right of refusal to sell in conformity with his contract: [1964] CMLR 379.

298. Ibid., pp. 104-108.

299. See, Jacquemaire, "Commercial Agency and Distribution Agreements and Related Problems of Licensing in France", in van Gerven and Lukoff, eds., op.cit., passim.

Such a refusal to sell is in principle valid under EEC law, in accordance with the concept of strict exclusivity.[300] However, where the exclusivity is absolute [301], as where the supplier's obligations under the contract include a clause obliging him to prevent other distributors from selling in the contract area, by agreeing to impose export prohibitions on all other distributors or by exploiting industrial property rights [302], then the degree of exclusivity is excessive and will be condemned.[303] In short, exclusivity clauses that confer absolute territorial protection are regarded as being too exclusive, even though such a clause is the logical concommitant to the supplier's essential obligation. Most recently, in *Distillers Company Ltd.* v. *EC Commission* [304], the EC Court of Justice upheld [305] the decision of the EC Commission condemning an export prohibition, and a double pricing system, intended to prevent whisky sold at lower prices in the United Kingdom from being exported to the continent where higher prices prevailed. The balance which has been found between contractual freedom to restrict competition and legal intervention to ensure freer competition is the mechanism of allowing for parallel imports. This entails that distributors bound to the same supplier must not be prevented by the imposition of export prohibitions from selling to customers within the contract area of other distributors, nor, which amounts to the same thing, must the distributor be contractually bound to sell only within his contract area. Provided the agreement allows for the possibility of parallel imports, thus conferring only relative protection within the contract area, which thus becomes an area of primary responsibility [306], the degree of exclusivity may contractually be very great.[307]

300. On which, see Champaud, loc.cit., at p. 34.

301. The concept of absolute territorial protection reached its zenith in The Netherlands with *Kolynos* in 1937 when the *Hoge Raad,* HR 11 November 1937, NJ 1937, 1096, ruled that reselling below fixed prices goods obtained from a trader without the imposition of the minimum price obligations to which that trader was subject by agreement with the manufacturer could constitute tortious conduct by the buyer as against the manufacturer where the buyer was (or should have been) aware that by selling to him the trader was in breach of his contract with the manufacturer. Attempts to extend this protection by actions based on industrial property rights against a parallel importer failed: HR 14 December 1956, NJ 1962, 242, as did later attempts to prevent parallel imports by tortious actions to prevent harm to the supplier: HR 13 January 1961, NJ 1962, 245; HR 12 January 1962, NJ 1962, 246. Cartels are generally viewed with rather more leniency when the market is endangered by deflation leading to lack of demand, certainly where they have a stabilizing and strengthening effect on falling prices.

302. As by reliance upon an assignment of a trademark from the supplier to his distributor whereby the latter is thus enabled to bring proceedings under national law for trademark infringement against competitors bringing such products onto the market in the area reserved to the distributor: Consten and Grundig *v.* Commission [1966] CMLR 418; Sirena *v.* Eda, Case 40/70 [1971] CMLR 260.

303. Consten and Grundig *v.* Commission [1966] CMLR 418; Béguelin Import *v.* SAGL Import-Export SA [1972] CMLR 81.

304. Case 30/78, 10 July 1980 [1980] CMLR 121.

305. The actual decision turned on the failure to notify in accordance with Reg. 17.

306. Quite extensively restrictive agreements have been permitted in markets where technical expertise is essential: *Kodak*, OJ L 147/24, 1970; *Omega* OJ L 242/22, 1970; but on condition that the import-export prohibitions were deleted.

307. The closed agreement is thus rendered an open agreement. See, Gijlstra and Murphy, loc.cit., pp. 93 and 98.

In practice, however, the actual extent of the protection conferred by the parties' agreement will depend as much (if not more) on market forces as on contractual terms. Where prices are relatively stable and equal in all parts of the market, there will be little incentive for competitors to become involved in importing products into the local market from outside. Viewed economically, it is sensible to obtain the products from the local distributor. Where price differentials exist, however, then it may become economically attractive to buy in a different part of the market and import the products into the local distributor's reserved area.[308] This phenomenon is well-illustrated by a recent EC Commission condemnation of concerted practices in the field of hi-fi equipment. The subsidiaries, incorporated in various European States, of a Japanese parent company, together with their national distributors, entered into a gentleman's agreement designed to prevent a French competitor of the French distributor from obtaining supplies from, e.g., the UK and Germany and selling them in France where prices were significantly higher following the expiry of a Commission decision [309] which had led to national protective measures. The distributorship agreements involved did not contain objectionable clauses but the agreement and subsequent action to resist changed market conditions were judged objectionable as being in contravention of Article 85(1) EEC Treaty.[310]

Here it may be emphasized that whereas price differentials are permitted, price discrimination is unlawful. In the case of the former any other approach would be manifestly untenable. Such factors as different climatic conditions, infrastructure development and socio-cultural patterns combine to produce regional price divergence. The extent to which such variables may legitimately be taken into account has recently been the subject of scrutiny by the EC Court of Justice.[311] What is clear is that price discrimination is unlawful. What will not always be clear is when one has departed from lawful price divergence and transgressed into unlawful price discrimination. One touchstone offered by the Court is that the operation of a price divergence mechanism is lawful when resorted to by a trader who bears the risk of the market. To the extent that this is a workable proposition it will be one more factor to be weighed by suppliers considering whether to embark upon direct as opposed to indirect distribution.

In the result, one is faced with a range of agreements by which the parties seek to protect and advance their own economic interests by means of a range of exclusivity clauses, which device is certainly recognised as lawful in every European legal system. Yet agreements run the risk of being invalidated. The answer to this seeming paradox is to be found in the initial premise that competition is

308. See, Centrafarm BV *v.* Sterling Drug Inc., [1974] 2 CMLR 480; A. Bulloch & Co. *v.* Distillers Co. Ltd. [1978] 1 CMLR 400.

309. OJ L 121/71.

310. Commission Decision 80/256 of 14 December 1979, OJ L 60/21 of 5 March 1980, [1980] CMLR 457.

311. Case 27/76, United Brands *v.* EC Commission [1978] CMLR 429; Case 85/75, Hoffmann-La Roche *v.* EC Commission [1979] CMLR 211.

to be encouraged as being beneficial to the entire community, including consumers, which is qualified by the second premise, provided only that it is not diversive. On the other hand, it is also integrative. It is the trading advantage offered by the former that is the inducement to the trader to accept the economic risk attaching to the latter. In short, no exclusivity, no concession and thus no integration. Put another way, the process of integration is only possible if the trader is allowed to trade with a degree of exclusivity. It appears that it is the balance in favour of the integrative process between supplier and distributor that draws the line between acceptable (integrative) and excessive (diversive) exclusivity.[312] The former is encouraged and therefore positively regulated, albeit in differing ways and to different extents. The latter is negatively regulated and liable to be condemned. Achieving the correct balance is not just a matter of careful drafting but one of realistic assessment of the extent to which individually desired economic goals will be permitted.

312. See generally, Champaud, loc.cit.

ANNEX 1

EEC TREATY RULES ON COMPETITION APPLYING TO UNDERTAKINGS (ARTT. 85 - 86)

Article 85

1. The following shall be prohibited as incompatible with the common market: all agreements between undertakings, decisions by associations of undertakings and concerted practices which may affect trade between Member States and which have as their object or effect the prevention, restriction or distortion of competition within the common market, and in particular those which:

(*a*) directly or indirectly fix purchase or selling prices or any other trading conditions;
(*b*) limit or control production, markets, technical development, or investment;
(*c*) share markets or sources of supply;
(*d*) apply dissimilar conditions to equivalent transactions with other trading parties, thereby placing them at a competitive disadvantage;
(*e*) make the conclusion of contracts subject to acceptance by the other parties of supplementary obligations which, by their nature or according to commercial usage, have no connection with the subject of such contracts.

2. Any agreements or decisions prohibited pursuant to this Article shall be automatically void.

3. The provisions of paragraph 1 may, however, be declared inapplicable in the case of:

- any agreement or category of agreements between undertakings;
- any decision or category of decisions by associations of undertakings;
- any concerted practice or category of concerted practices;

which contributes to improving the production or distribution of goods or to promoting technical or economic progress, while allowing consumers a fair share of the resulting benefit, and which does not:

(*a*) impose on the undertakings concerned restrictions which are not indispensable to the attainment of these objectives;
(*b*) afford such undertakings the possibility of eliminating competition in respect of a substantial part of the products in question.

Article 86

Any abuse by one or more undertakings of a dominant position within the common market or in a substantial part of it shall be prohibited as incompatible with the common market in so far as it may affect trade between Member States. Such abuse may, in particular, consist in:

(*a*) directly or indirectly imposing unfair purchase or selling prices or other unfair trading conditions;
(*b*) limiting production, markets or technical development to the prejudice of consumers;

(*c*) applying dissimilar conditions to equivalent transactions with other trading parties, thereby placing them at a competitive disadvantage;

(*d*) making the conclusion of contracts subject to acceptance by the other parties of supplementary obligations which, by their nature or according to commercial usage, have no connection with the subject of such contracts.

ANNEX 2

EEC REGULATIONS IMPLEMENTING RULES ON COMPETITION (REGS. 17/62, 67/67)

REGULATION No 17

First Regulation implementing Articles 85 and 86 of the Treaty

THE COUNCIL OF THE EUROPEAN ECONOMIC COMMUNITY,

Having regard to the Treaty establishing the European Economic Community, and in particular Article 87 thereof;

Having regard to the proposal from the Commission;

Having regard to the Opinion of the Economic and Social Committee;

Having regard to the Opinion of the European Parliament;

Whereas, in order to establish a system ensuring that competition shall not be distorted in the common market, it is necessary to provide for balanced application of Articles 85 and 86 in a uniform manner in the Member States;

Whereas in establishing the rules for applying Article 85 (3) account must be taken of the need to ensure effective supervision and to simplify administration to the greatest possible extent;

Whereas it is accordingly necessary to make it obligatory, as a general principle, for undertakings which seek application of Article 85 (3) to notify to the Commission their agreements, decisions and concerted practices;

Whereas, on the one hand, such agreements, decisions and concerted practices are probably very numerous and cannot therefore all be examined at the same time and, on the other hand, some of them have special features which may make them less prejudicial to the development of the common market;

Whereas there is consequently a need to make more flexible arrangements for the time being in respect of certain categories of agreement, decision and concerted practice without prejudging their validity under Article 85;

Whereas it may be in the interest of undertakings to know whether any agreements, decisions or practices to which they are party, or propose to become party, may lead to action on the part of the Commission pursuant to Article 85 (1) or Article 86;

Whereas, in order to secure uniform application of Articles 85 and 86 in the common market, rules must be made under which the Commission, acting in close and constant liaison with the competent authorities of the Member States, may take the requisite measures for applying those Articles;

Whereas for this purpose the Commission must have the co-operation of the competent authorities of the Member States and be empowered, throughout the common market, to require such information to be supplied and to undertake such investigations as are necessary to bring to light any agreement, decision or concerted practice prohibited by Article 85 (1) or any abuse of a dominant position prohibited by Article 86:

Whereas, in order to carry out its duty of ensuring that the provisions of the Treaty are applied, the Commission must be empowered to address to undertakings or associations of undertakings recommendations and decisions for the purpose of bringing to an end infringements of Articles 85 and 86;

Whereas compliance with Articles 85 and 86 and the fulfilment of obligations imposed on undertakings and associations of undertakings under this Regulation must be enforceable by means of fines and periodic penalty payments;

Whereas undertakings concerned must be accorded the right to be heard by the Commission, third parties whose interests may be affected by a decision must be given the opportunity of submitting their comments beforehand, and it must be ensured that wide publicity is given to decisions taken;

Whereas all decisions taken by the Commission under this Regulation are subject to review by the Court of Justice under the conditions specified in the Treaty; whereas it is moreover desirable to confer upon the Court of Justice, pursuant to Article 172, unlimited jurisdiction in respect of decisions under which the Commission imposes fines or periodic penalty payments;

Whereas this Regulation may enter into force without prejudice to any other provisions that may hereafter be adopted pursuant to Article 87;

HAS ADOPTED THIS REGULATION:

Article 1

Basic provision

Without prejudice to Articles 6, 7 and 23 of this Regulation, agreements, decisions and concerted practices of the kind described in Article 85 (1) of the Treaty and the abuse of a dominant position in the market, within the meaning of Article 86 of the Treaty, shall be prohibited, no prior decision to that effect being required.

Article 2

Negative clearance

Upon application by the undertakings or associations of undertakings concerned, the Commission may certify that, on the basis of the facts in its possession, there are no grounds under Article 85 (1) or Article 86 of the Treaty for action on its part in respect of an agreement, decision or practice.

Article 3

Termination of infringements

1. Where the Commission, upon application or upon its own initiative, finds that there is infringement of Article 85 or Article 86 of the Treaty, it may by decision require the undertakings or associations of undertakings concerned to bring such infringement to an end.

2. Those entitled to make application are:

(a) Member States;

(b) natural or legal persons who claim a legitimate interest.

3. Without prejudice to the other provisions of this Regulation, the Commission may, before taking a decision under paragraph 1, address to the undertakings or associations of undertakings concerned recommendations for termination of the infringement.

Article 4

Notification of new agreements, decisions and practices

1. Agreements, decisions and concerted practices of the kind described in Article 85 (1) of the Treaty which come into existence after the entry into force of this Regulation and in respect of which the parties seek application of Article 85 (3) must be notified to the Commission. Until they have been notified, no decision in application of Article 85 (3) may be taken.

2. Paragraph 1 shall not apply to agreements, decisions or concerted practices where:

(1) the only parties thereto are undertakings from one Member State and the agreements, decisions or practices do not relate either to imports or to exports between Member States;

(2) not more than two undertakings are party thereto, and the agreements only:

  (a) restrict the freedom of one party to the contract in determining the prices or conditions of business upon which the goods which he has obtained from the other party to the contract may be resold; or

  (b) impose restrictions on the exercise of the rights of the assignee or user of industrial property rights—in particular patents, utility models, designs or trade marks—or of the person entitled under a contract to the assignment, or grant, of the right to use a method of manufacture or knowledge relating to the use and to the application of industrial processes;

(3) they have as their sole object:

  (a) the development or uniform application of standards or types; or

  (b) joint research for improvement of techniques, provided the results are accessible to all parties thereto and may be used by each of them.

These agreements, decisions and practices may be notified to the Commission.

Article 5

Notification of existing agreements, decisions and practices

1. Agreements, decisions and concerted practices of the kind described in Article 85 (1) of the Treaty which are in existence at the date of entry into force of this Regulation and in respect of which the parties

seek application of Article 85 (3) shall be notified to the Commission before 1 August 1962.

2. Paragraph 1 shall not apply to agreements, decisions or concerted practices falling within Article 4 (2); these may be notified to the Commission.

Article 6

Decisions pursuant to Article 85 (3)

1. Whenever the Commission takes a decision pursuant to Article 85 (3) of the Treaty, it shall specify therein the date from which the decision shall take effect. Such date shall not be earlier than the date of notification.

2. The second sentence of paragraph 1 shall not apply to agreements, decisions or concerted practices falling within Article 4 (2) and Article 5 (2), nor to those falling within Article 5 (1) which have been notified within the time limit specified in Article 5 (1).

Article 7

Special provisions for existing agreements, decisions and practices

1. Where agreements, decisions and concerted practices in existence at the date of entry into force of this Regulation and notified before 1 August 1962 do not satisfy the requirements of Article 85 (3) of the Treaty and the undertakings or associations of undertakings concerned cease to give effect to them or modify them in such manner that they no longer fall within the prohibition contained in Article 85 (1) or that they satisfy the requirements of Article 85 (3), the prohibition contained in Article 85 (1) shall apply only for a period fixed by the Commission. A decision by the Commission pursuant to the foregoing sentence shall not apply as against undertakings and associations of undertakings which did not expressly consent to the notification.

2. Paragraph 1 shall apply to agreements, decisions and concerted practices falling within Article 4 (2) which are in existence at the date of entry into force of this Regulation if they are notified before 1 January 1964.

Article 8

Duration and revocation of decisions under Article 85 (3)

1. A decision in application of Article 85 (3) of the Treaty shall be issued for a specified period and conditions and obligations may be attached thereto.

2. A decision may on application be renewed if the requirements of Article 85 (3) of the Treaty continue to be satisfied.

3. The Commission may revoke or amend its decision or prohibit specified acts by the parties:

(a) where there has been a change in any of the facts which were basic to the making of the decision;

(b) where the parties commit a breach of any obligation attached to the decision;

(c) where the decision is based on incorrect information or was induced by deceit;

(d) where the parties abuse the exemption from the provisions of Article 85 (1) of the Treaty granted to them by the decision.

In cases to which subparagraphs (b), (c) or (d) apply, the decision may be revoked with retroactive effect.

Article 9

Powers

1. Subject to review of its decision by the Court of Justice, the Commission shall have sole power to declare Article 85 (1) inapplicable pursuant to Article 85 (3) of the Treaty.

2. The Commission shall have power to apply Article 85 (1) and Article 86 of the Treaty; this power may be exercised notwithstanding that the time limits specified in Article 5 (1) and in Article 7 (2) relating to notification have not expired.

3. As long as the Commission has not initiated any procedure under Articles 2, 3 or 6, the authorities of the Member States shall remain competent to apply Article 85 (1) and Article 86 in accordance with Article 88 of the Treaty; they shall remain competent in this respect notwithstanding that the time limits specified in Article 5 (1) and in Article 7 (2) relating to notification have not expired.

Article 10

Liaison with the authorities of the Member States

1. The Commission shall forthwith transmit to the competent authorities of the Member States a copy of the applications and notifications together with copies of the most important documents lodged with the Commission for the purpose of establishing the existence of infringements of Articles 85 or 86 of the Treaty or of obtaining negative clearance or a decision in application of Article 85 (3).

2. The Commission shall carry out the procedure set out in paragraph 1 in close and constant liaison with the competent authorities of the Member States; such authorities shall have the right to express their views upon that procedure.

3. An Advisory Committee on Restrictive Practices and Monopolies shall be consulted prior to the taking of any decision following upon a procedure under paragraph 1, and of any decision concerning the renewal, amendment or revocation of a decision pursuant to Article 85 (3) of the Treaty.

4. The Advisory Committee shall be composed of officials competent in the matter of restrictive practices and monopolies. Each Member State shall appoint an official to represent it who, if prevented from attending, may be replaced by another official.

5. The consultation shall take place at a joint meeting convened by the Commission; such meeting shall be held not earlier than fourteen days after dispatch of the notice convening it. The notice shall, in respect of each case to be examined, be accompanied by a summary of the case together with an indication of the most important documents, and a preliminary draft decision.

6. The Advisory Committee may deliver an opinion notwithstanding that some of its members or their alternates are not present. A report of the outcome of the consultative proceedings shall be annexed to the draft decision. It shall not be made public.

Article 11

Requests for information

1. In carrying out the duties assigned to it by Article 89 and by provisions adopted under Article 87 of the Treaty, the Commission may obtain all necessary information from the Governments and competent authorities of the Member States and from undertakings and associations of undertakings.

2. When sending a request for information to an undertaking or association of undertakings, the Commission shall at the same time forward a copy of the request to the competent authority of the Member State in whose territory the seat of the undertaking or association of undertakings is situated.

3. In its request the Commission shall state the legal basis and the purpose of the request and also the penalties provided for in Article 15 (1) (b) for supplying incorrect information.

4. The owners of the undertakings or their representatives and, in the case of legal persons, companies or firms, or of associations having no legal personality, the persons authorised to represent them by law or by their constitution shall supply the information requested.

5. Where an undertaking or association of undertakings does not supply the information requested within the time limit fixed by the Commission, or supplies incomplete information, the Commission shall by decision require the information to be supplied. The decision shall specify what information is required, fix an appropriate time limit within which it is to be supplied and indicate the penalties provided for in Article 15 (1) (b) and Article 16 (1) (c) and the right to have the decision reviewed by the Court of Justice.

6. The Commission shall at the same time forward a copy of its decision to the competent authority of the Member State in whose territory the seat of the undertaking or association of undertakings is situated.

Article 12

Inquiry into sectors of the economy

1. If in any sector of the economy the trend of trade between Member States, price movements, inflexibility of prices or other circumstances suggest that in the economic sector concerned competition is being restricted or distorted within the common market, the Commission may decide to conduct a general inquiry into that economic sector and in the course thereof may request undertakings in the sector concerned to supply the information necessary for giving effect to the principles formulated in Articles 85 and 86 of the Treaty and for carrying out the duties entrusted to the Commission.

2. The Commission may in particular request every undertaking or association of undertakings in the economic sector concerned to communicate to it all agreements, decisions and concerted practices which are exempt from notification by virtue of Article 4 (2) and Article 5 (2).

3. When making inquiries pursuant to paragraph 2, the Commission shall also request undertakings or groups of undertakings whose size suggests that they occupy a dominant position within the common market or a substantial part thereof to supply to the Commission such particulars of the structure of the undertakings and of their behaviour as are requisite to an appraisal of their position in the light of Article 86 of the Treaty.

4. Article 10 (3) to (6) and Articles 11, 13 and 14 shall apply correspondingly.

Article 13

Investigations by the authorities of the Member States

1. At the request of the Commission, the competent authorities of the Member States shall undertake the investigations which the Commission considers to be necessary under Article 14 (1), or which it has ordered by decision pursuant to Article 14 (3). The officials of the competent authorities of the Member States responsible for conducting these investigations shall exercise their powers upon production of an authorisation in writing issued by the competent authority of the Member State in whose territory the investigation is to be made. Such authorisation shall specify the subject matter and purpose of the investigation.

2. If so requested by the Commission or by the competent authority of the Member State in whose territory the investigation is to be made, the officials of the Commission may assist the officials of such authorities in carrying out their duties.

Article 14

Investigating powers of the Commission

1. In carrying out the duties assigned to it by Article 89 and by provisions adopted under Article 87 of the Treaty, the Commission may undertake all necessary investigations into undertakings and associations of undertakings. To this end the officials authorised by the Commission are empowered:

(a) to examine the books and other business records;

(b) to take copies of or extracts from the books and business records;

(c) to ask for oral explanations on the spot;

(d) to enter any premises; land and means of transport of undertakings.

2. The officials of the Commission authorised for the purpose of these investigations shall exercise their powers upon production of an authorisation in writing specifying the subject matter and purpose of the investigation and the penalties provided for in Article 15 (1) (c) in cases where production of the required books or other business records is incomplete. In good time before the investigation, the Commission shall inform the competent authority of the Member State in whose territory the same is to be made of the investigation and of the identity of the authorised officials.

3. Undertakings and associations of undertakings shall submit to investigations ordered by decision of the Commission. The decision shall specify the subject matter and purpose of the investigation, appoint the date on which it is to begin and indicate the penalties provided for in Article 15 (1) (c) and Article 16 (1) (d) and the right to have the decision reviewed by the Court of Justice.

4. The Commission shall take decisions referred to in paragraph 3 after consultation with the competent authority of the Member State in whose territory the investigation is to be made.

5. Officials of the competent authority of the Member State in whose territory the investigation is to be made may, at the request of such authority or of the Commission, assist the officials of the Commission in carrying out their duties.

6. Where an undertaking opposes an investigation ordered pursuant to this Article, the Member State concerned shall afford the necessary assistance to the officials authorised by the Commission to enable them to make their investigation. Member States shall, after consultation with the Commission, take the necessary measures to this end before 1 October 1962.

Article 15

Fines

1. The Commission may by decision impose on undertakings or associations of undertakings fines of from 100 to 5000 units of account where, intentionally or negligently:

(a) they supply incorrect or misleading information in an application pursuant to Article 2 or in a notification pursuant to Articles 4 or 5; or

(b) they supply incorrect information in response to a request made pursuant to Article 11 (3) or (5) or to Article 12, or do not supply information within the time limit fixed by a decision taken under Article 11 (5); or

(c) they produce the required books or other business records in incomplete form during investigations under Article 13 or 14, or refuse to submit to an investigation ordered by decision issued in implementation of Article 14 (3).

2. The Commission may by decision impose on undertakings or associations of undertakings fines of from 1000 to 1 000 000 units of account, or a sum in excess thereof but not exceeding 10% of the turnover in the preceding business year of each of the

undertakings participating in the infringement where, either intentionally or negligently:

(a) they infringe Article 85 (1) or Article 86 of the Treaty; or

(b) they commit a breach of any obligation imposed pursuant to Article 8 (1).

In fixing the amount of the fine, regard shall be had both to the gravity and to the duration of the infringement.

3. Article 10 (3) to (6) shall apply.

4. Decisions taken pursuant to paragraphs 1 and 2 shall not be of a criminal law nature.

5. The fines provided for in paragraph 2 (a) shall not be imposed in respect of acts taking place:

(a) after notification to the Commission and before its decision in application of Article 85 (3) of the Treaty, provided they fall within the limits of the activity described in the notification;

(b) before notification and in the course of agreements, decisions or concerted practices in existence at the date of entry into force of this Regulation, provided that notification was effected within the time limits specified in Article 5 (1) and Article 7 (2).

6. Paragraph 5 shall not have effect where the Commission has informed the undertakings concerned that after preliminary examination it is of opinion that Article 85 (1) of the Treaty applies and that application of Article 85 (3) is not justified.

Article 16

Periodic penalty payments

1. The Commission may by decision impose on undertakings or associations of undertakings periodic penalty payments of from 50 to 1000 units of account per day, calculated from the date appointed by the decision, in order to compel them:

(a) to put an end to an infringement of Article 85 or 86 of the Treaty, in accordance with a decision taken pursuant to Article 3 of this Regulation;

(b) to refrain from any act prohibited under Article 8 (3);

(c) to supply complete and correct information which it has requested by decision taken pursuant to Article 11 (5);

(d) to submit to an investigation which it has ordered by decision taken pursuant to Article 14 (3).

2. Where the undertakings or associations of undertakings have satisfied the obligation which it was the purpose of the periodic penalty payment to enforce, the Commission may fix the total amount of the periodic penalty payment at a lower figure than that which would arise under the original decision.

3. Article 10 (3) to (6) shall apply.

Article 17

Review by the Court of Justice

The Court of Justice shall have unlimited jurisdiction within the meaning of Article 172 of the Treaty to review decisions whereby the Commission has fixed a fine or periodic penalty payment; it may cancel, reduce or increase the fine or periodic penalty payment imposed.

Article 18

Unit of account

For the purposes of applying Articles 15 to 17 the unit of account shall be that adopted in drawing up the budget of the Community in accordance with Articles 207 and 209 of the Treaty.

Article 19

Hearing of the parties and of third persons

1. Before taking decisions as provided for in Articles 2, 3, 6, 7, 8, 15 and 16, the Commission shall give the undertakings or associations of undertakings concerned the opportunity of being heard on the matters to which the Commission has taken objection.

2. If the Commission or the competent authorities of the Member States consider it necessary, they may also hear other natural or legal persons. Applications to be heard on the part of such persons shall, where they show a sufficient interest, be granted.

3. Where the Commission intends to give negative clearance pursuant to Article 2 or take a decision in application of Article 85 (3) of the Treaty, it shall publish a summary of the relevant application or notification and invite all interested third parties to submit their observations within a time limit which it shall fix being not less than one month. Publication shall have regard to the legitimate interest of undertakings in the protection of their business secrets.

Article 20

Professional secrecy

1. Information acquired as a result of the application of Articles 11, 12, 13 and 14 shall be used only for the purpose of the relevant request or investigation.

2. Without prejudice to the provisions of Articles 19 and 21, the Commission and the competent authorities of the Member States, their officials and other servants shall not disclose information acquired by them as a result of the application of this Regulation and of the kind covered by the obligation of professional secrecy.

3. The provisions of paragraphs 1 and 2 shall not prevent publication of general information or surveys which do not contain information relating to particular undertakings or associations of undertakings.

Article 21

Publication of decisions

1. The Commission shall publish the decisions which it takes pursuant to Articles 2, 3, 6, 7 and 8.

2. The publication shall state the names of the parties and the main content of the decision; it shall have regard to the legitimate interest of undertakings in the protection of their business secrets.

Article 22

Special provisions

1. The Commission shall submit to the Council proposals for making certain categories of agreement, decision and concerted practice falling within Article 4 (2) or Article 5 (2) compulsorily notifiable under Article 4 or 5.

2. Within one year from the date of entry into force of this Regulation, the Council shall examine, on a proposal from the Commission, what special provisions might be made for exempting from the provisions of this Regulation agreements, decisions and concerted practices falling within Article 4 (2) or Article 5 (2).

Article 23

Transitional provisions applicable to decisions of authorities of the Member States

1. Agreements, decisions and concerted practices of the kind described in Article 85 (1) of the Treaty to which, before the entry into force of this Regulation, the competent authority of a Member State has declared Article 85 (1) to be inapplicable pursuant to Article 85 (3) shall not be subject to compulsory notification under Article 5. The decision of the competent authority of the Member State shall be deemed to be a decision within the meaning of Article 6; it shall cease to be valid upon expiration of the period fixed by such authority but in any event not more than three years after the entry into force of this Regulation. Article 8 (3) shall apply.

2. Applications for renewal of decisions of the kind described in paragraph 1 shall be decided upon by the Commission in accordance with Article 8 (2).

Article 24

Implementing provisions

The Commission shall have power to adopt implementing provisions concerning the form, content and other details of applications pursuant to Articles 2 and 3 and of notifications pursuant to Articles 4 and 5, and concerning hearings pursuant to Article 19 (1) and (2).

This Regulation shall be binding in its entirety and directly applicable in all Member States.

Done at Brussels, 6 February 1962.

For the Council

The President

M. COUVE DE MURVILLE

REGULATION No 67/67/EEC OF THE COMMISSION

of 22 March 1967

on the application of Article 85 (3) of the Treaty to certain categories of exclusive dealing agreements

THE COMMISSION OF THE EUROPEAN ECONOMIC COMMUNITY,

Having regard to the Treaty establishing the European Economic Community, and in particular Articles 87 and 155 thereof;

Having regard to Article 24 of Regulation No 17 of 6 February 1962[1];

Having regard to Regulation No 19/65/EEC of 2 March 1965[2] on the application of Article 85 (3) of the Treaty to certain categories of agreements and concerted practices;

Having regard to the Opinions delivered by the Advisory Committee on Restrictive Practices and Monopolies in accordance with Article 6 of Regulation No 19/65/EEC;

Whereas under Regulation No 19/65/EEC the Commission has power to apply Article 85 (3) of the Treaty by regulation to certain categories of bilateral exclusive dealing agreements and concerted practices coming within Article 85;

Whereas the experience gained up to now, on the basis of individual decisions, makes it possible to define a first category of agreements and concerted practices which can be accepted as normally satisfying the conditions laid down in Article 85 (3);

Whereas, since adoption of such a regulation would not conflict with the application of Regulation No 17, the right of undertakings to request the Commission, on an individual basis, for a declaration under Article 85 (3) of the Treaty would not be affected;

[1] OJ No 13, 21.2.1962, p. 204/62.

[2] OJ No 36, 6.3.1965, p. 533/65.

Whereas exclusive dealing agreements of the category defined in Article 1 of this Regulation may fall within the prohibition contained in Article 85 (1) of the Treaty; whereas since it is only in exceptional cases that exclusive dealing agreements concluded within a Member State affect trade between Member States, there is no need to include them in this Regulation;

Whereas it is not necessary expressly to exclude from the category as defined those agreements which do not fulfil the conditions of Article 85 (1) of the Treaty;

Whereas in the present state of trade exclusive dealing agreements relating to international trade lead in general to an improvement in distribution because the entrepreneur is able to consolidate his sales activities; whereas he is not obliged to maintain numerous business contacts with a large number of dealers, and whereas the fact of maintaining contacts with only one dealer makes it easier to overcome sales difficulties resulting from linguistic, legal, and other differences; whereas exclusive dealing agreements facilitate the promotion of the sale of a product and make it possible to carry out more intensive marketing and to ensure continuity of supplies, while at the same time rationalising distribution; whereas, moreover, the appointment of an exclusive distributor or of an exclusive purchaser who will take over, in place of the manufacturer, sales promotion, after-sales service and carrying of stocks, is often the sole means whereby small and medium-size undertakings can compete in the market; whereas it should be left to the contracting parties to decide whether and to what extent they consider it desirable to incorporate in the agreements terms designed to promote sales; whereas there can only be an improvement in distribution if dealing is not entrusted to a competitor;

Whereas as a rule such exclusive dealing agreements also help to give consumers a proper share of the resulting benefit as they gain directly from the improvement in distribution, and their economic or supply position is thereby improved as they can obtain products manufactured in other countries more quickly and more easily;

Whereas this Regulation must determine the obligations restricting competition which may be included in an exclusive dealing agreement; whereas it may be left to the contracting parties to decide which of those obligations they include in exclusive dealing agreements in order to draw the maximum advantages from exclusive dealing;

Whereas any exemption must be subject to certain conditions; whereas it is in particular advisable to ensure through the possibility of parallel imports that consumers obtain a proper share of the advantages resulting from exclusive dealing; whereas it is therefore not possible to allow industrial property rights and other rights to be exercised in an abusive manner in order to create absolute territorial protection; whereas these considerations do not prejudice the relationship between the law of competition and industrial property rights, since the sole object here is to determine the conditions for exemption of certain categories of agreements under this Regulation;

Whereas competition at the distribution stage is ensured by the possibility of parallel imports, whereas, therefore, the exclusive dealing agreements covered by this Regulation will not normally afford any possibility of preventing competition in respect of a substantial part of the products in question;

Whereas it is desirable to allow contracting parties a limited period of time within which they may, in accordance with Article 4 of Regulation No 19/65/EEC, modify their agreements and practices so as to satisfy the conditions laid down in this Regulation, without it being possible, under Article 4 (3) of Regulation No 19/65/EEC, to rely thereon in actions which are pending at the time of entry into force of this Regulation, or as grounds for claims for damages against third parties;

Whereas agreements and concerted practices which satisfy the conditions set out in this Regulation need no longer be notified; whereas Article 4 (2) (a) of Regulation No 27,[1] as amended by Regulation No 153,[2] can be repealed, since agreements which it was possible to notify on Form B 1 would normally come within the scope of the exemption;

Whereas agreements notified on Form B 1 and not amended so as to satisfy the conditions of this Regulation should be made subject to the normal notification procedure, in order that they may be examined individually;

HAS ADOPTED THIS REGULATION:

Article 1

1. Pursuant to Article 85 (3) of the Treaty and subject to the provisions of this Regulation it is hereby declared that until 31 December 1972 Article 85 (1) of the Treaty shall not apply to agreements to which only two undertakings are party and whereby:

(a) one party agrees with the other to supply only to that other certain goods for resale within a defined area of the common market; or

(b) one party agrees with the other to purchase only from that other certain goods for resale; or

(c) the two undertakings have entered into obligations, as in (a) and (b) above, with each other in respect of exclusive supply and purchase for resale.

2. Paragraph 1 shall not apply to agreements to which undertakings from one Member State only are party and which concern the resale of goods within that Member State.

Article 2

1. Apart from an obligation falling within Article 1, no restriction on competition shall be imposed on the exlusive dealer other than:

(a) the obligation not to manufacture or distribute, during the duration of the contract or until one year after its expiration, goods which compete with the goods to which the contract relates;

(b) the obligation to refrain, outside the territory covered by the contract, from seeking customers for the goods to which the contract relates, from establishing any branch, or from maintaining any distribution depot.

2. Article 1 (1) shall apply notwithstanding that the exclusive dealer undertakes all or any of the following obligations:

(a) to purchase complete ranges of goods or minimum quantities;

(b) to sell the goods to which the contract relates under trade marks or packed and presented as specified by the manufacturer;

[1] OJ No 35, 10.5.1962, p. 1118/62.

[2] OJ No 139, 24.12.1962, p. 2918/62.

(c) To take measures for promotion of sales, in particular:

— to advertise;

— to maintain a sales network or stock of goods;

— to provide after-sale and guarantee services;

— to employ staff having specialised or technical training.

Article 3

Article 1 (1) of this Regulation shall not apply where:

(a) manufacturers of competing goods entrust each other with exclusive dealing in those goods;

(b) the contracting parties make it difficult for intermediaries or consumers to obtain the goods to which the contract relates from other dealers within the common market, in particular where the contracting parties:

(1) exercise industrial property rights to prevent dealers or consumers from obtaining from other parts of the common market or from selling in the territory covered by the contract goods to which the contract relates which are properly marked or otherwise properly placed on the market;

(2) exercise other rights or take other measures to prevent dealers or consumers from obtaining from elsewhere goods to which the contract relates or from selling them in the territory covered by the contract.

Article 4

1. As regards agreements which were in existence on 13 March 1962 and were notified before 1 February 1963, the declaration contained in Article 1 (1) of inapplicability of Article 85 (1) of the Treaty shall have retroactive effect from the time when the conditions of application of this Regulation were fulfilled.

2. As regards all other agreements notified before the entry into force of this Regulation, the declaration contained in Article 1 (1) of inapplicability of Article 85 (1) of the Treaty shall have retroactive effect from the time when the conditions of application of this Regulation were fulfilled, but not earlier than the day of notification.

Article 5

As regards agreements which were in existence on 13 March 1962, notified before 1 February 1963 and amended before 2 August 1967 so as to fulfil the conditions of application of this Regulation, the prohibition in Article 85 (1) of the Treaty shall not apply in respect of the period prior to the amendment, where such amendment is notified to the Commission before 3 October 1967. The notification shall take effect from the time of receipt thereof by the Commission. Where the notification is sent by registered post, it shall take effect from the date on the postmark of the place of dispatch.

Article 6

The Commission shall examine whether Article 7 of Regulation No 19/65/EEC applies in individual cases, in particular when there are grounds for believing that:

(a) the goods to which the contract relates are not subject, in the territory covered by the contract, to competition from goods considered by the consumer as similar goods in view of their properties, price and intended use;

(b) it is not possible for other manufacturers to sell, in the territory covered by the contract, similar goods at the same stage of distribution as that of the exclusive dealer;

(c) the exclusive dealer has abused the exemption:

(1) by refusing, without objectively valid reasons, to supply in the territory covered by the contract categories of purchasers who cannot obtain supplies elsewhere, on suitable terms, of the goods to which the contract relates;

(2) by selling the goods to which the contract relates at excessive prices.

Article 7

1. Article 4 (2) (a) of Regulation No 27 of 3 May 1962, as amended by Regulation No 153, is hereby repealed.

2. Notification, on Form B 1, on an exclusive dealing agreement which does not fulfil the conditions contained in Articles 1 to 3 of this Regulation shall, if such agreement is not amended so as to satisfy those conditions, be effected before 3 October 1967, by submission of Form B, with annexes, in accordance with the provisions of Regulation No 27.

Article 8

Articles 1 to 7 of this Regulation shall apply by analogy to the category of concerted practices defined in Article 1 (1).

Article 9

This Regulation shall enter into force on 1 May 1967.

This Regulation shall be binding in its entirety and directly applicable in all Member States.

Done at Brussels, 16 June 1967.

For the Commission

The President

Walter HALLSTEIN

ANNEX 3

HAGUE SALES CONVENTION 1955 (TEXT AND RATIFICATIONS)

1. CONVENTION SUR LA LOI APPLICABLE AUX VENTES A CARACTÈRE INTERNATIONAL D'OBJETS MOBILIERS CORPORELS

(Conclue le 15 juin 1955)

Les Etats signataires de la présente Convention;

Désirant établir des dispositions communes concernant la loi applicable aux ventes d'objets mobiliers corporels;

Ont résolu de conclure une Convention à cet effet et sont convenus des dispositions suivantes:

Article premier

La présente Convention est applicable aux ventes à caractère international d'objets mobiliers corporels.

Elle ne s'applique pas aux ventes de titres, aux ventes de navires et de bateaux ou d'aéronefs enregistrés, aux ventes par autorité de justice ou sur saisie. Elle s'applique aux ventes sur documents.

Pour son application sont assimilés aux ventes les contrats de livraison d'objets mobiliers corporels à fabriquer ou à produire, lorsque la partie qui s'oblige à livrer doit fournir les matières premières nécessaires à la fabrication ou à la production.

La seule déclaration des parties, relative à l'application d'une loi ou à la compétence d'un juge ou d'un arbitre, ne suffit pas à donner à la vente le caractère international au sens de l'alinéa premier du présent article.

Article 2

La vente est régie par la loi interne du pays désigné par les parties contractantes.

Cette désignation doit faire l'objet d'une clause expresse, ou résulter indubitablement des dispositions du contrat.

Les conditions, relatives au consentement des parties quant à la loi déclarée applicable, sont déterminées par cette loi.

Article 3

A défaut de loi déclarée applicable par les parties, dans les conditions prévues à l'article précédent, la vente est régie par la loi interne du pays où le vendeur a sa résidence habituelle au moment où il reçoit la commande. Si la commande est reçue par un établissement du vendeur, la vente est régie par la loi interne du pays où est situé cet établissement.

Toutefois, la vente est régie par la loi interne du pays où l'acheteur a sa résidence habituelle, ou dans lequel il possède l'établissement qui a passé la commande, si c'est dans ce pays que la commande a été reçue, soit par le vendeur, soit par son représentant, agent ou commis-voyageur.

S'il s'agit d'un marché de bourse ou d'une vente aux enchères, la vente est régie par la loi interne du pays où se trouve la bourse ou dans lequel sont effectuées les enchères.

Article 4

A moins de clause expresse contraire, la loi interne du pays où doit avoir lieu l'examen des objets mobiliers corporels délivrés en vertu de la vente est applicable, en ce qui concerne la forme et les délais dans lesquels doivent avoir lieu l'examen et les notifications relatives à l'examen, ainsi que les mesures à prendre en cas de refus des objets.

Article 5

La présente Convention ne s'applique pas:

1. à la capacité des parties;
2. à la forme du contrat;
3. au transfert de propriété, étant entendu toutefois que les diverses obligations des parties, et notamment celles qui sont relatives aux risques, sont soumises à la loi applicable à la vente en vertu de la présente Convention;
4. aux effets de la vente à l'égard de toutes personnes autres que les parties.

Article 6

Dans chacun des Etats contractants, l'application de la loi déterminée par la présente Convention peut être écartée pour un motif d'ordre public.

Article 7

Les Etats contractants sont convenus d'introduire les dispositions des articles 1 - 6 de la présente Convention dans le droit national de leurs pays respectifs.

Article 8

La présente Convention est ouverte à la signature des Etats représentés à la Septième Session de la Conférence de La Haye de Droit International Privé.

Elle sera ratifiée et les instruments de ratification seront déposés auprès du Ministère des Affaires Etrangères des Pays-Bas.

Il sera dressé de tout dépôt d'instruments de ratification un procès-verbal, dont une copie, certifiée conforme, sera remise, par la voie diplomatique, à chacun des Etats signataires.

Article 9

La présente Convention entrera en vigueur le soixantième jour à partir du dépôt du cinquième instrument de ratification prévu par l'article 8, alinéa 2.

Pour chaque Etat signataire, ratifiant postérieurement la Convention, celle-ci entrera en vigueur le soixantième jour à partir de la date du dépôt de son instrument de ratification.

Article 10

La présente Convention s'applique de plein droit aux territoires métropolitains des Etats contractants.

Si un Etat contractant en désire la mise en vigueur dans tous les autres territoires, ou dans tels des autres territoires dont les relations internationales sont assurées par lui, il notifiera son intention à cet effet par un acte qui sera déposé auprès du Ministère des Affaires Etrangères des Pays-Bas. Celui-ci en enverra, par la voie diplomatique, une copie, certifiée conforme, à chacun des Etats contractants. La présente Convention entrera en vigueur pour ces territoires le soixantième jour après la date du dépôt de l'acte de notification mentionné ci-dessus.

Il est entendu que la notification, prévue par l'alinéa 2 du présent article, ne pourra avoir effet qu'après l'entrée en vigueur de la présente Convention en vertu de son article 9, alinéa premier.

Article 11

Tout Etat, non représenté à la Septième Session de la Conférence de La Haye de Droit International Privé pourra adhérer à la présente Convention. L'Etat désirant adhérer notifiera son intention par un acte qui sera déposé auprès de Ministère des Affaires Etrangères des Pays-Bas. Celui-ci en enverra, par la voie diplomatique, une copie, certifiée conforme, à chacun des Etats contractants. La Convention entrera en vigueur, pour l'Etat adhérant, le soixantième jour après la date du dépôt de l'acte d'adhésion.

Il est entendu que le dépôt de l'acte d'adhésion ne pourra avoir lieu qu'après l'entrée en vigueur de la présente Convention en vertu de l'article 9, alinéa premier.

Article 12

La présente Convention aura une durée de cinq ans à partir de la date indiquée dans l'article 9, alinéa premier, de la présente Convention. Ce terme commencera à courir dès cette date, même pour les Etats qui l'auront ratifiée ou y auront adhéré postérieurement.

La Convention sera renouvelée tacitement de cinq ans en cinq ans, sauf dénonciation.

La dénonciation devra, au moins six mois avant l'expiration du terme, être notifiée au Ministère des Affaires Etrangères des Pays-Bas, qui en donnera connaissance à tous les autres Etats contractants.

La dénonciation peut se limiter aux territoires, ou à certains des territoires indiqués dans une notification faite en vertu de l'article 10, alinéa 2.

La dénonciation ne produira son effet qu'à l'égard de l'Etat qui l'aura notifiée. La Convention restera en vigueur pour les autres Etats contractants.

En foi de quoi, les soussignés, dûment autorisés par leurs Gouvernements respectifs, ont signé la présente Convention.

Fait à La Haye, le 15 juin 1955, en un seul exemplaire, qui sera déposé dans les archives du Gouvernement des Pays-Bas et dont une copie, certifiée conforme, sera remise, par la voie diplomatique, à chacun des Etats représentés à la Septième Session de la Conférence de La Haye de Droit International Privé.

2. RATIFICATIONS *

Member States	Signature	Ratification or accession	Entry into force
BELGIUM	01.08.55	29.10.62	01.09.64
DENMARK	23.10.56	03.07.64	01.09.64
FINLAND	12.04.57	03.07.64	01.09.64
FRANCE	25.07.55	30.07.63	01.09.64
ITALY	13.04.56	17.03.58	01.09.64
LUXEMBURG	15.06.55		
NETHERLANDS	15.06.55		
NORWAY	24.10.56	03.07.64	01.09.64
SPAIN	12.04.57		
SWEDEN	23.10.56	08.07.64	06.09.64
SWITZERLAND	20.09.71	29.08.72	27.10.72
Other States			
NIGER	(accession)	11.10.71	10.12.71

* Taken from *Netherlands International Law Review* (1982) p. 279, being the situation as of 1 September 1982.

ANNEX 4

HAGUE AGENCY CONVENTION 1978 (TEXT AND RATIFICATIONS)

1. CONVENTION ON THE LAW APPLICABLE TO AGENCY

The States signatories to the present Convention,

Desiring to establish common provisions concerning the law applicable to agency,

Have resolved to conclude a Convention to this effect, and have agreed upon the following provisions –

CHAPTER 1 – SCOPE OF THE CONVENTION

Article 1

The present Convention determines the law applicable to relationships of an international character arising where a person, the agent, has the authority to act, acts or purports to act on behalf of another person, the principal, in dealing with a third party.

It shall extend to cases where the function of the agent is to receive and communicate proposals or to conduct negotiations on behalf of other persons.

The Convention shall apply whether the agent acts in his own name or in that of the principal and whether he acts regularly or occasionally.

Article 2

This Convention shall not apply to –

a) the capacity of the parties;
b) requirements as to form;
c) agency by operation of law in family law, in matrimonial property regimes, or in the law of succession;
d) agency by virtue of a decision of a judicial or quasi-judicial authority or subject to the direct control of such an authority;
e) representation in connection with proceedings of a judicial character;
f) the agency of a shipmaster acting in the exercise of his functions as such.

Article 3

For the purposes of this Convention –

a) an organ, officer or partner of a corporation, association, partnership or other entity, whether or not possessing legal personality, shall not be regarded as the agent of that entity in so far as, in the exercise of his functions as such, he acts by virtue of an authority conferred by law or by the constitutive documents of that entity;
b) a trustee shall not be regarded as an agent of the trust, of the person who has created the trust, or of the beneficiaries.

Article 4

The law specified in this Convention shall apply whether or not it is the law of a Contracting State.

CHAPTER II – RELATIONS BETWEEN PRINCIPAL AND AGENT

Article 5

The internal law chosen by the principal and the agent shall govern the agency relationship between them.

This choice must be express or must be such that it may be inferred with reasonable certainty from the terms of the agreement between the parties and the circumstances of the case.

Article 6

In so far as it has not been chosen in accordance with Article 5, the applicable law shall be the internal law of the State where, at the time of formation of the agency relationship, the agent has his business establishment or, if he has none, his habitual residence.

However, the internal law of the State where the agent is primarily to act shall apply if the principal has his business establishment or, if he has none, his habitual residence in that State.

Where the principal or the agent has more than one business establishment, this Article refers to the establishment with which the agency relationship is most closely connected.

Article 7

Where the creation of the agency relationship is not the sole purpose of the agreement, the law specified in Articles 5 and 6 shall apply only if –

a) the creation of this relationship is the principal purpose of the agreement, or

b) the agency relationship is severable.

Article 8

The law applicable under Articles 5 and 6 shall govern the formation and validity of the agency relationship, the obligations of the parties, the conditions of performance, the consequences of non-performance, and the extinction of those obligations.

This law shall apply in particular to –

a) the existence and extent of the authority of the agent, its modification or termination, and the consequences of the fact that the agent has exceeded or misused his authority;

b) the right of the agent to appoint a substitute agent, a sub-agent or an additional agent;

c) the right of the agent to enter into a contract on behalf of the principal where there is a potential conflict of interest between himself and the principal;

d) non-competition clauses and *del credere* clauses;

e) clientele allowances *(d'indemnité de clientèle);*

f) the categories of damage for which compensation may be recovered.

Article 9

Whatever law may be applicable to the agency relationship, in regard to the manner of performance the law of the place of performance shall be taken into consideration.

Article 10

This Chapter shall not apply where the agreement creating the agency relationship is a contract of employment.

CHAPTER III – RELATIONS WITH THE THIRD PARTY

Article 11

As between the principal and the third party, the existence and extent of the agent's authority and the effects of the agent's exercise or purported exercise of his authority shall be governed by the internal law of the State in which the agent has his business establishment at the time of his relevant acts.

However, the internal law of the State in which the agent has acted shall apply if –

a) the principal has his business establishment or, if he has none, his habitual residence in that State, and the agent has acted in the name of the principal; or

b) the third party has his business establishment or, if he has none, his habitual residence in that State; or

c) the agent has acted at an exchange or auction; or

d) the agent has no business establishment.

Where a party has more than one business establishment, this Article refers to the establishment with which the relevant acts of the agent are most closely connected.

Article 12

For the purposes of Article 11, first paragraph, where an agent acting under a contract of employment with his principal has no personal business establishment, he shall be deemed to have his establishment at the business establishment of the principal to which he is attached.

Article 13

For the purposes of Article 11, second paragraph, where an agent in one State has communicated with the third party in another, by message, telegram, telex, telephone, or other similar means, the agent shall be deemed to have acted in that respect at the place of his business establishment or, if he has none, of his habitual residence.

Article 14

Nothwithstanding Article 11, where a written specification by the principal or by the third party of the law applicable to questions falling within Article 11 has been expressly accepted by the other party, the law so specified shall apply to such questions.

Article 15

The law applicable under this Chapter shall also govern the relationship between the agent and the third party arising from the fact that the agent has acted in the exercise of his authority, has exceeded his authority, or has acted without authority

CHAPTER IV – GENERAL PROVISIONS

Article 16

In the application of this Convention, effect may be given to the mandatory rules of any State with which the situation has a significant connection, if and in so far as, under the law of that State, those rules must be applied whatever the law specified by its choice of law rules.

Article 17

The application of a law specified by this Convention may be refused only where such application would be manifestly incompatible with public policy *(ordre public)*.

Article 18

Any Contracting State may, at the time of signature, ratification, acceptance, approval or accession, reserve the right not to apply this Convention to –
(1) the agency of a bank or group of banks in the course of banking transactions;
(2) agency in matters of insurance;
(3) the acts of a public servant acting in the exercise of his functions as such on behalf of a private person.

No other reservation shall be permitted.

Any Contracting State may also, when notifying an extension of the Convention in accordance with Article 25, make one or more of these reservations, with its effect limited to all or some of the territories mentioned in the extension.

Any Contracting State may at any time withdraw a reservation which it has made; the reservation shall cease to have effect on the first day of the third calendar month after notification of the withdrawal.

Article 19

Where a State comprises several territorial units each of which has its own rules of law in respect of agency, each territorial unit shall be considered as a State for the purposes of identifying the law applicable under this Convention.

Article 20

A State within which different territorial units have their own rules of law in respect of agency shall not be bound to apply this Convention where a State with a unified system of law would not be bound to apply the law of another State by virtue of this Convention.

Article 21

If a Contracting State has two or more territorial units which have their own rules of law in respect of agency, it may, at the time of signature, ratification, acceptance, approval or accession, declare that this Convention shall extend to all its territorial units or to one or more of them, and may modify its declaration by submitting another declaration at any time.

These declarations shall be notified to the Ministry of Foreign Affairs of the Kingdom of the Netherlands, and shall state expressly the territorial units to which the Convention applies.

Article 22

The Convention shall not affect any other international instrument containing provisions on matters governed by this Convention to which a Contracting State is, or becomes, a Party.

CHAPTER V – FINAL CLAUSES

Article 23

The Convention is open for signature by the States which were Members of the Hague Conference on Private International Law at the time of its Thirteenth Session.

It shall be ratified, accepted or approved and the instruments of ratification, acceptance or approval shall be deposited with the Ministry of Foreign Affairs of the Kingdom of the Netherlands.

Article 24

Any other State may accede to the Convention.

The instrument of accession shall be deposited with the Ministry of Foreign Affairs of the Kingdom of the Netherlands.

Article 25

Any State may, at the time of signature, ratification, acceptance, approval or accession, declare that the Convention shall extend to all the territories for the international relations of which it is responsible, or to one or more of them. Such a declaration shall take effect at the time the Convention enters into force for that State.

Such declaration, as well as any subsequent extension, shall be notified to the Ministry of Foreign Affairs of the Kingdom of the Netherlands.

Article 26

The Convention shall enter into force on the first day of the third calendar month after the deposit of the third instrument of ratification, acceptance, approval or accession referred to in Articles 23 and 24.

Thereafter the Convention shall enter into force –

(1) for each State ratifying, accepting, approving or acceding to it subsequently, on the first day of the third calendar month after the deposit of its instrument of ratification, acceptance, approval or accession;

(2) for a territory to which the Convention has been extended in conformity with Articles 21 and 25, on the first day of the third calendar month after the notification referred to in those Articles.

Article 27

The Convention shall remain in force for five years from the date of its entry into force in accordance with the first paragraph of Article 26, even for States which subsequently have ratified, accepted, approved it or acceded to it.

If there has been no denunciation, it shall be renewed tacitly every five years.

Any denunciation shall be notified to the Ministry of Foreign Affairs of the Kingdom of the Netherlands at least six months before the expiry of the five year period. It may be limited to certain of the territories or territorial units to which the Convention applies.

The denunciation shall have effect only as regards the State which has notified it. The Convention shall remain in force for the other Contracting States.

Article 28

The Ministry of Foreign Affairs of the Kingdom of the Netherlands shall notify to the States Members of the Conference, and the States which have acceded in accordance with Article 24, the following –

(1) the signatures and ratifications, acceptances and approvals referred to in Article 23;
(2) the accessions referred to in Article 24;
(3) the date on which the Convention enters into force in accordance with Article 26;
(4) the extensions referred to in Article 25;
(5) the declarations referred to in Article 21;
(6) the reservations and the withdrawals of reservations referred to in Article 18;
(7) the denunciations referred to in Article 27.

In witness whereof the undersigned, being duly authorised thereto, have signed this Convention.

Done at The Hague, on the . . . day of . . . . 19 . ., in the English and French languages, both texts being equally authentic, in a single copy which shall be deposited in the archives of the Government of the Kingdom of the Netherlands and of which a certified copy shall be sent, through diplomatic channels, to each of the States Members of the Hague Conference on Private International Law at the date of its Thirteenth Session.

2. RATIFICATIONS *

Member States	Signature	Ratification or accession	Entry into force
FRANCE	14.03.78		
PORTUGAL	26.05.78	04.03.82	

* Taken from *Netherlands International Law Review* (1982) p. 294, being the situation as of 1 September 1982.

ANNEX 5

EC PRIVATE INTERNATIONAL LAW CONVENTION 1980

II

(Acts whose publication is not obligatory)

COUNCIL

CONVENTION
ON THE LAW APPLICABLE TO CONTRACTUAL OBLIGATIONS

opened for signature in Rome on 19 June 1980

(80/934/EEC)

PREAMBLE

THE HIGH CONTRACTING PARTIES to the Treaty establishing the European Economic Community,

ANXIOUS to continue in the field of private international law the work of unification of law which has already been done within the Community, in particular in the field of jurisdiction and enforcement of judgments,

WISHING to establish uniform rules concerning the law applicable to contractual obligations,

HAVE AGREED AS FOLLOWS:

TITLE I

SCOPE OF THE CONVENTION

Article 1

Scope of the Convention

1. The rules of this Convention shall apply to contractual obligations in any situation involving a choice between the laws of different countries.

2. They shall not apply to:

(a) questions involving the status or legal capacity of natural persons, without prejudice to Article 11;

(b) contractual obligations relating to:

— wills and succession,

— rights in property arising out of a matrimonial relationship,

— rights and duties arising out of a family relationship, parentage, marriage or affinity, including maintenance obligations in respect of children who are not legitimate;

(c) obligations arising under bills of exchange, cheques and promissory notes and other negotiable instruments to the extent that the obligations under such other negotiable instruments arise out of their negotiable character;

(d) arbitration agreements and agreements on the choice of court;

(e) questions governed by the law of companies and other bodies corporate or unincorporate such as the creation, by registration or otherwise, legal capacity, internal organization or winding up of companies and other bodies corporate or unincorporate and the personal liability of officers and members as such for the obligations of the company or body;

(f) the question whether an agent is able to bind a principal, or an organ to bind a company or body corporate or unincorporate, to a third party;

(g) the constitution of trusts and the relationship between settlors, trustees and beneficiaries;

(h) evidence and procedure, without prejudice to Article 14.

3. The rules of this Convention do not apply to contracts of insurance which cover risks situated in the territories of the Member States of the European Economic Community. In order to determine whether a risk is situated in these territories the court shall apply its internal law.

4. The preceding paragraph does not apply to contracts of re-insurance.

Article 2

Application of law of non-contracting States

Any law specified by this Convention shall be applied whether or not it is the law of a Contracting State.

TITLE II

UNIFORM RULES

Article 3

Freedom of choice

1. A contract shall be governed by the law chosen by the parties. The choice must be expressed or demonstrated with reasonable certainty by the terms of the contract or the circumstances of the case. By their choice the parties can select the law applicable to the whole or a part only of the contract.

2. The parties may at any time agree to subject the contract to a law other than that which previously governed it, whether as a result of an earlier choice under this Article or of other provisions of this Convention. Any variation by the parties of the law to be applied made after the conclusion of the contract shall not prejudice its formal validity under Article 9 or adversely affect the rights of third parties.

3. The fact that the parties have chosen a foreign law, whether or not accompanied by the choice of a foreign tribunal, shall not, where all the other elements relevant to the situation at the time of the choice are connected with one country only, prejudice the application of rules of the law of that country which cannot be derogated from by contract, hereinafter called 'mandatory rules'.

4. The existence and validity of the consent of the parties as to the choice of the applicable law shall be determined in accordance with the provisions of Articles 8, 9 and 11.

Article 4

Applicable law in the absence of choice

1. To the extent that the law applicable to the contract has not been chosen in accordance with Article 3, the contract shall be governed by the law of the country with which it is most closely connected. Nevertheless, a severable part of the contract which has a closer connection with another country may by way of exception be governed by the law of that other country.

2. Subject to the provisions of paragraph 5 of this Article, it shall be presumed that the contract is most closely connected with the country where the party who is to effect the performance which is characteristic of the contract has, at the time of conclusion of the contract, his habitual residence, or, in the case of a body corporate or unincorporate, its central administration. However, if the contract is entered into in the course of that party's trade or profession, that country shall be the country in which the principal place of business is situated or, where under the terms of the contract the performance is to be effected through a place of business other than the principal place of business, the country in which that other place of business is situated

3. Notwithstanding the provisions of paragraph 2 of this Article, to the extent that the subject matter of the contract is a right in immovable property or a right to use immovable property it shall be presumed that the contract is most closely connected with the country where the immovable property is situated.

4. A contract for the carriage of goods shall not be subject to the presumption in paragraph 2. In such a

contract if the country in which, at the time the contract is concluded, the carrier has his principal place of business is also the country in which the place of loading or the place of discharge or the principal place of business of the consignor is situated, it shall be presumed that the contract is most closely connected with that country. In applying this paragraph single voyage charter-parties and other contracts the main purpose of which is the carriage of goods shall be treated as contracts for the carriage of goods.

5. Paragraph 2 shall not apply if the characteristic performance cannot be determined, and the presumptions in paragraphs 2, 3 and 4 shall be disregarded if it appears from the circumstances as a whole that the contract is more closely connected with another country.

Article 5

Certain consumer contracts

1. This Article applies to a contract the object of which is the supply of goods or services to a person ('the consumer') for a purpose which can be regarded as being outside his trade or profession, or a contract for the provision of credit for that object.

2. Notwithstanding the provisions of Article 3, a choice of law made by the parties shall not have the result of depriving the consumer of the protection afforded to him by the mandatory rules of the law of the country in which he has his habitual residence:

— if in that country the conclusion of the contract was preceded by a specific invitation addressed to him or by advertising, and he had taken in that country all the steps necessary on his part for the conclusion of the contract, or

— if the other party or his agent received the consumer's order in that country, or

— if the contract is for the sale of goods and the consumer travelled from that country to another country and there gave his order, provided that the consumer's journey was arranged by the seller for the purpose of inducing the consumer to buy.

3. Notwithstanding the provisions of Article 4, a contract to which this Article applies shall, in the absence of choice in accordance with Article 3, be governed by the law of the country in which the consumer has his habitual residence if it is entered into in the circumstances described in paragraph 2 of this Article.

4. This Article shall not apply to:

(a) a contract of carriage;

(b) a contract for the supply of services where the services are to be supplied to the consumer exclusively in a country other than that in which he has his habitual residence.

5. Notwithstanding the provisions of paragraph 4, this Article shall apply to a contract which, for an inclusive price, provides for a combination of travel and accommodation.

Article 6

Individual employment contracts

1. Notwithstanding the provisions of Article 3, in a contract of employment a choice of law made by the parties shall not have the result of depriving the employee of the protection afforded to him by the mandatory rules of the law which would be applicable under paragraph 2 in the absence of choice.

2. Notwithstanding the provisions of Article 4, a contract of employment shall, in the absence of choice in accordance with Article 3, be governed:

(a) by the law of the country in which the employee habitually carries out his work in performance of the contract, even if he is temporarily employed in another country; or

(b) if the employee does not habitually carry out his work in any one country, by the law of the country in which the place of business through which he was engaged is situated;

unless it appears from the circumstances as a whole that the contract is more closely connected with another country, in which case the contract shall be governed by the law of that country.

Article 7

Mandatory rules

1. When applying under this Convention the law of a country, effect may be given to the mandatory rules of the law of another country with which the situation has a close connection, if and in so far as, under the law of the latter country, those rules must be applied whatever the law applicable to the contract. In considering whether to give effect to these mandatory rules, regard shall be had to their nature and purpose and to the consequences of their application or non-application.

2. Nothing in this Convention shall restrict the application of the rules of the law of the forum in a

situation where they are mandatory irrespective of the law otherwise applicable to the contract.

Article 8

Material validity

1. The existence and validity of a contract, or of any term of a contract, shall be determined by the law which would govern it under this Convention if the contract or term were valid.

2. Nevertheless a party may rely upon the law of the country in which he has his habitual residence to establish that he did not consent if it appears from the circumstances that it would not be reasonable to determine the effect of his conduct in accordance with the law specified in the preceding paragraph.

Article 9

Formal validity

1. A contract concluded between persons who are in the same country is formally valid if it satisfies the formal requirements of the law which governs it under this Convention or of the law of the country where it is concluded.

2. A contract concluded between persons who are in different countries is formally valid if it satisfies the formal requirements of the law which governs it under this Convention or of the law of one of those countries.

3. Where a contract is concluded by an agent, the country in which the agent acts is the relevant country for the purposes of paragraphs 1 and 2.

4. An act intended to have legal effect relating to an existing or contemplated contract is formally valid if it satisfies the formal requirements of the law which under this Convention governs or would govern the contract or of the law of the country where the act was done.

5. The provisions of the preceding paragraphs shall not apply to a contract to which Article 5 applies, concluded in the circumstances described in paragraph 2 of Article 5. The formal validity of such a contract is governed by the law of the country in which the consumer has his habitual residence.

6. Notwithstanding paragraphs 1 to 4 of this Article, a contract the subject matter of which is a right in immovable property or a right to use immovable property shall be subject to the mandatory requirements of form of the law of the country where the property is situated if by that law those requirements are imposed irrespective of the country where the contract is concluded and irrespective of the law governing the contract.

Article 10

Scope of the applicable law

1. The law applicable to a contract by virtue of Articles 3 to 6 and 12 of this Convention shall govern in particular:

(a) interpretation;

(b) performance;

(c) within the limits of the powers conferred on the court by its procedural law, the consequences of breach, including the assessment of damages in so far as it is governed by rules of law;

(d) the various ways of extinguishing obligations, and prescription and limitation of actions;

(e) the consequences of nullity of the contract.

2. In relation to the manner of performance and the steps to be taken in the event of defective performance regard shall be had to the law of the country in which performance takes place.

Article 11

Incapacity

In a contract concluded between persons who are in the same country, a natural person who would have capacity under the law of that country may invoke his incapacity resulting from another law only if the other party to the contract was aware of this incapacity at the time of the conclusion of the contract or was not aware thereof as a result of negligence.

Article 12

Voluntary assignment

1. The mutual obligations of assignor and assignee under a voluntary assignment of a right against another

person ('the debtor') shall be governed by the law which under this Convention applies to the contract between the assignor and assignee.

2. The law governing the right to which the assignment relates shall determine its assignability, the relationship betweeen the assignee and the debtor, the conditions under which the assignment can be invoked against the debtor and any question whether the debtor's obligations have been discharged.

Article 13

Subrogation

1. Where a person ('the creditor') has a contractual claim upon another ('the debtor'), and a third person has a duty to satisfy the creditor, or has in fact satisfied the creditor in discharge of that duty, the law which governs the third person's duty to satisfy the creditor shall determine whether the third person is entitled to exercise against the debtor the rights which the creditor had against the debtor under the law governing their relationship and, if so, whether he may do so in full or only to a limited extent.

2. The same rule applies where several persons are subject to the same contractual claim and one of them has satisfied the creditor.

Article 14

Burden of proof, etc.

1. The law governing the contract under this Convention applies to the extent that it contains, in the law of contract, rules which raise presumptions of law or determine the burden of proof.

2. A contract or an act intended to have legal effect may be proved by any mode of proof recognized by the law of the forum or by any of the laws referred to in Article 9 under which that contract or act is formally valid, provided that such mode of proof can be administered by the forum.

Article 15

Exclusion of renvoi

The application of the law of any country specified by this Convention means the application of the rules of law in force in that country other than its rules of private international law.

Article 16

'Ordre public'

The application of a rule of the law of any country specified by this Convention may be refused only if such application is manifestly incompatible with the public policy ('ordre public') of the forum.

Article 17

No retrospective effect

This Convention shall apply in a Contracting State to contracts made after the date on which this Convention has entered into force with respect to that State.

Article 18

Uniform interpretation

In the interpretation and application of the preceding uniform rules, regard shall be had to their international character and to the desirability of achieving uniformity in their interpretation and application.

Article 19

States with more than one legal system

1. Where a State comprises several territorial units each of which has its own rules of law in respect of contractual obligations, each territorial unit shall be considered as a country for the purposes of identifying the law applicable under this Convention.

2. A State within which different territorial units have their own rules of law in respect of contractual obligations shall not be bound to apply this Convention to conflicts solely between the laws of such units.

Article 20

Precedence of Community law

This Convention shall not affect the application of provisions which, in relation to particular matters, lay down choice of law rules relating to contractual obligations and which are or will be contained in acts of the institutions of the European Communities or in national laws harmonized in implementation of such acts.

Article 21

Relationship with other conventions

This Convention shall not prejudice the application of international conventions to which a Contracting State is, or becomes, a party.

Article 22

Reservations

1. Any Contracting State may, at the time of signature, ratification, acceptance or approval, reserve the right not to apply:

(a) the provisions of Article 7 (1);

(b) the provisions of Article 10 (1) (e).

2. Any Contracting State may also, when notifying an extension of the Convention in accordance with Article 27 (2), make one or more of these reservations, with its effect limited to all or some of the territories mentioned in the extension.

3. Any Contracting State may at any time withdraw a reservation which it has made; the reservation shall cease to have effect on the first day of the third calendar month after notification of the withdrawal.

TITLE III

FINAL PROVISIONS

Article 23

1. If, after the date on which this Convention has entered into force for a Contracting State, that State wishes to adopt any new choice of law rule in regard to any particular category of contract within the scope of this Convention, it shall communicate its intention to the other signatory States through the Secretary-Geneal of the Council of the European Communities.

2. Any signatory State may, within six months from the date of the communication made to the Secretary-General, request him to arrange consultations between signatory States in order to reach agreement.

3. If no signatory State has requested consultations within this period or if within two years following the communication made to the Secretary-General no agreement is reached in the course of consultations, the Contracting State concerned may amend its law in the manner indicated. The measures taken by that State shall be brought to the knowledge of the other signatory States through the Secretary-General of the Council of the European Communities.

Article 24

1. If, after the date on which this Convention has entered into force with respect to a Contracting State, that State wishes to become a party to a multilateral convention whose principal aim or one of whose principal aims is to lay down rules of private international law concerning any of the matters governed by this Convention, the procedure set out in Article 23 shall apply. However, the period of two years, referred to in paragraph 3 of that Article, s[illegible] reduced to one year.

2. The procedure referred to in the preceding paragraph need not be followed if a Contracting State or one of the European Communities is already a party to the multilateral convention, or if its object is to revise a convention to which the State concerned is already a party, or if it is a convention concluded within the framework of the Treaties establishing the European Communities.

Article 25

If a Contracting State considers that the unification achieved by this Convention is prejudiced by the conclusion of agreements not covered by Article 24 (1), that State may request the Secretary-General of the Council of the European Communities to arrange consultations between the signatory States of this Convention.

Article 26

Any Contracting State may request the revision of this Convention. In this event a revision conference shall be convened by the President of the Council of the European Communities.

Article 27

1. This Convention shall apply to the European territories of the Contracting States, including

Greenland, and to the entire territory of the French Republic.

2. Nothwithstanding paragraph 1:

(a) this Convention shall not apply to the Faroe Islands, unless the Kingdom of Denmark makes a declaration to the contrary;

(b) this Convention shall not apply to any European territory situated outside the United Kingdom for the international relations of which the United Kingdom is responsible, unless the United Kingdom makes a declaration to the contrary in respect of any such territory;

(c) this Convention shall apply to the Netherlands Antilles, if the Kingdom of the Netherlands makes a declaration to that effect.

3. Such declarations may be made at any time by notifying the Secretary-General of the Council of the European Communities.

4. Proceedings brought in the United Kingdom on appeal from courts in one of the territories referred to in paragraph 2 (b) shall be deemed to be proceedings taking place in those courts.

Article 28

1. This Convention shall be open from 19 June 1980 for signature by the States party to the Treaty establishing the European Economic Community.

2. This Convention shall be subject to ratification, acceptance or approval by the signatory States. The instruments of ratification, acceptance or approval shall be deposited with the Secretary-General of the Council of the European Communities.

Article 29

1. This Convention shall enter into force on the first day of the third month following the deposit of the seventh instrument of ratification, acceptance or approval.

2. This Convention shall enter into force for each signatory State ratifying, accepting or approving at a later date on the first day of the third month following the deposit of its instrument of ratification, acceptance or approval.

Article 30

1. This Convention shall remain in force for 10 years from the date of its entry into force in accordance with Article 29 (1), even for States for which it enters into force at a later date.

2. If there has been no denunciation it shall be renewed tacitly every five years.

3. A Contracting State which wishes to denounce shall, not less than six months before the expiration of the period of 10 or five years, as the case may be, give notice to the Secretary-General of the Council of the European Communities. Denunciation may be limited to any territory to which the Convention has been extended by a declaration under Article 27 (2).

4. The denunciation shall have effect only in relation to the State which has notified it. The Convention will remain in force as between all other Contracting States.

Article 31

The Secretary-General of the Council of the European Communities shall notify the States party to the Treaty establishing the European Economic Community of:

(a) the signatures;

(b) the deposit of each instrument of ratification, acceptance or approval;

(c) the date of entry into force of this Convention;

(d) communications made in pursuance of Articles 23, 24, 25, 26, 27 and 30;

(e) the reservations and withdrawals of reservations referred to in Article 22.

Article 32

The Protocol annexed to this Convention shall form an integral part thereof.

Article 33

This Convention, drawn up in a single original in the Danish, Dutch, English, French, German, Irish and Italian languages, these texts being equally authentic, shall be deposited in the archives of the Secretariat of the Council of the European Communities. The Secretary-General shall transmit a certified copy thereof to the Government of each signatory State.

SOLE DISTRIBUTOR: DISCUSSIONS

The Chair was taken by Professor Sarčević. He recommended that, having regard to the time available, the discussions be focused more on the sole distribution agreement than on the agency agreement. He then invited the reporters, Mr. Yelland and Mr. Wade, to introduce their papers.

1. INTRODUCTION

Mr. Yelland wished to confine his remarks at the present time to the central issue of what one meant by the term sole or exclusive distributorship. The characteristics identifying exclusiveness may be regarded as being the following. Where a manufacturer wishes to ensure distribution of his product he will enter into an agreement with a trader, usually a middle man rather than a retailer, whereby he agrees that within a specified territory his supply of the product onto that market will be exclusively via that trader. This undertaking may be accompanied by an undertaking not to supply other traders who would trade in that product on the territory of the sole distributor. The distributor, for his part, agrees not to deal in competing goods or products, either within the designated territory or at all. The contract of distributorship is, naturally, never so simple and will contain many other provisions ancillary to the main agreement. Although the set-up is couched in restrictive terms its purpose is not essentially restrictive for an important aspect is to encourage competition in the market with the manufacturer's rivals. When one looked to a comparison of the European and American concept of distributor, an important distinction was to be found in the nature of the distributor. In Europe the distributor is normally a wholesaler or link in the chain of supply. He is not generally a retailer, and to this extent the European distributor isolates the manufacturer from retail outlets and from consumers. The distributor acts as an independent businessman, not as an agent of the manufacturer. In the United States, on the other hand, the distributor is generally a retailer.

Mr. Wade pointed out that the wide-ranging topic under discussion touched upon several diverse yet in practice related topics, and that it had been agreed between the reporters to confine attention principally to the contractual relationships arising when a middle man is used by a manufacturer-supplier to penetrate a foreign market with his goods. Recent years had witnessed an increasing use within Europe of distributors-agents, in particular that of the continental figure of the indirect or hybrid agent. Irrespective of the national legal status of the middleman, however, attention had been focused on the relationship that is characterised by the notion of the double sale, a characteristic existing against the background of long-term mutual obligations of the first two parties, the manufacturer and his distributor. This essential characteristic is accompanied by another, namely, a degree of commercial protection. This trading exclusiveness can raise problems. In market terms an absolute exclusiveness can lead to market distortion and if it does, or threatens or is like to do so, it will increasingly attract censure for offending against national restrictive trading practices legislation, as well as against supra-national EEC regulations on competition law. In practical terms, therefore, protection can only be relative in order to achieve, not a monopoly, but a position of market strength.

When one turned to the issue of the governing law, the comparative approach demonstrated that the distributorship relationship was, generally speaking, characterised as falling under sale. Those States that are party to the Hague Sales Convention of 1955 adopt the seller's place of business as indicating the governing law. Other States adopt a range of interpretations of the concepts of proper law/closest connection objectively determined and characteristic performance, a somewhat newer concept that has been both criticised and embodied in the EC Obligations Convention 1980, Article 4. At the same time there is a move to regard the relationship as *sui generis* and independent of sale. This has led to a taking into account, more particularly in Germany and Switzerland, of national provisons aimed at protecting agents. Only in the isolated case of Belgium is there legislation (of 1961 and 1971) specifically conferring protection on distributors. The overall picture is confused, however, by the prevalent practice of applying mandatory legislative provisions invoked by the national legal status attaching to agents, even when such persons *in casu* operate not as agents *strictu senso* but as distributors.

2. LEGAL NATURE OF THE RELATIONSHIP

During the discussions a division of opinion emerged as to how the distributorship relationship should be regarded. Strong support was evinced for the view that it should be seen as a sale relationship, principally on the ground that the basic obligations of the parties, both mutually and in regard to purchasers from the distributor, were rooted in sale. The usual clauses contained in the distributorship agreement, which distinguished it from the simple contract of sale, were not such as to effect the basic nature of the contract so as to render it a different (new) category of legal relationship. This view could also be supported by reference to the economic structure of the relationship, whereby the distributor's reward was reflected in his profit on resale or, less concretely, in the potential for sale that flowed from the manufacturer's committment to supply and the market protection that was based on exclusiveness clauses.

On the other hand, it was objected that such views were too narrow and came dangerously close to the position of equating the receipt of profit on resale (distributor) with commission on sale (agent). To do so was to ignore the fundamental juridical distinction, which is still generally accepted, between the legally subordinate position of the agent to his principal and the legally unimpaired independence of the distributor *vis-à-vis* his supplier. Even though it was agreed that actual practice demonstrated that contracts were drafted in terms that allowed distributors less freedom of action than was consistent with their legal status as independent traders, and that commercial agents did act under contract in terms that made them in effect distributors, nevertheless the legal distinction ought not to be lost sight of. Rather, attention should be focused on the question whether distributorship contracts ought not to be regarded, not as extended sales contracts, but as contracts *sui generis.* Support for such an approach could be found in identyfying correctly the economic purpose of such contracts and the characteristic function or performance of the distributor. It was agreed that the economic purpose was that of penetrating a market. Such penetration would lead to, or alternatively, be evidenced by increased sales of the manufacturer's product in that market. It was argued, however, that the distributor's characteristic function was not the resale of those goods in the market but rather the promotion of the goods so as effectively to realize the sales potential of the market. On this analysis it could be argued that the distributorship relationship was not an extended sales contract but a different juridical relationship that employed the technique of sale to effect an economic objective that was more than the sale of supplied goods. In this connection reference was made to the decision of the Hague Conference not to include the distributorship relationship in its Agency Convention 1978 and also to a recent decision of the Norwegian Supreme Court, which held that, in determining the law applicable, such contracts should not be characterised as sales contracts so as to invoke the operation of the Hague Sales Convention 1955 but as contracts *sui generis.*

2.1 Protection of districutors by analogy with agents

The discussion on the legal nature of the distributorship also considered the issue of whether and to what extent distributors should be afforded some measure of protection particularly from the economic consequences attendant upon termination of the agreement by the supplier.

Attention focused on the Belgian legislation of 1961 and 1971 which allows a distributor falling within the scope of the Laws to claim damages for loss of goodwill and other damage resulting from termination. It was explained that the earlier legislation was directed at intentional termination of exclusive agreements of an unspecified duration. In order to combat the practice of successively concluding fixed-term contracts the 1971 Law extended the provisions of the 1961 Law to cover also non-exclusive agreements of a specified duration, including successively concluded exclusive agreements. It was also pointed out that, on the other hand, Belgium does not have protective legislation coverigng agents, of the type existing in France and Germany. In regard to agents the position is the same as in the UK: the remedy is the normal action for breach of contract, as it is for distributors.

On the basis that both agents and distributors may be regarded as engaged in the same activity, that of building up a clientèle which is to the benefit of the principal/supplier, there was a certain feeling that such provisions, which are mandatory in character, ought to be extended to distributors by analogy with agents. It was accepted that where an agent successfully developed a clientèle on the basis of enjoying an exclusive contract, the termination of his contract would leave him in an economically disadvantaged position, which was sought to be remedied by the right to compensation for loss of goodwill. Should not the same or an analogous right be available to distributors? On this it was argued that the correct approach would not be simply to equate distributors with agents and to extend the latter's statutory protection to the former. Given that agents were deserving of such protection and that the EEC Commission Draft Directive seeking to extend this to all the Member States was on this score to be welcomed (leaving aside criticism of the Directive on other points), it was nevertheless of importance to recognise the important legal differences between the two notions of agency (essentially a legal concept) and distributorship (primarily an economic concept). If it were to be accepted, which was not free from doubt, that distributors ought to be protected from similar economic damage, that problem ought to be solved in its own particular way. To this it was suggested that the answer might well lie in the preparation of an international Convention. It was accepted, however, that a cardinal problem in this respect would lie with establishing a sufficiently workable definition of what was meant by the term distributor. And any such definition could only be applied *in casu* by a careful examination of the contract and its underlying economic function, always being in mind that such contracts often contained clauses or terms that were inconsistent with their real nature. Nevertheless, it was generally felt that such an international instrument would in principle be welcomed by many of the larger European manufacturers and suppliers.

2.2 Exclusiveness

It was agreed that the view generally prevailed that exclusiveness was in some way a hallmark of distributorship contracts. It was suggested that this aspect of the relationship ought to be treated with some caution and that it ought not to be overvalued. Exclusiveness also found its place with agency agreements, for example. Furthermore, from an economic point of view, it was a matter of uncertainty whether exclusiveness as an element in the relationship was not more for the benefit of the supplier than for the distributor. Nevertheless, this element is of distinct importance. Such contracts would often not be concluded without it. However, its limits were increasingly being defined as a result of anti-trust and restrictive practices legislation, both at national and supra-national levels. Given that its presence in the contractual relation confers, or is intended to confer, a trading protection of mutual benefit to both parties, limits are now imposed on the degree of protection that the parties may seek to achieve for themselves. Article 85 EEC as progressively interpreted by the Commission and the Court forces the parties to allow others to deal in the same goods in the same market. The parties are entitled to seek a trading advantage over competitors so that they may trade from a position of strength, but not to the extent that that position is not vulnerable to competition. And this approach also exists under national legislation, which may go even further than the supra-national legislation, as does the UK Competition Act 1980. The agreement must be capable of withstanding challenge from both types of restriction on its operation.

3. APPLICABLE LAW

The question of the law applicable to the distributorship was seen as raising particular issues of difficulty. Little attention was given to the situation of an express choice of law otherwise than incidentally in the discussion concerning the effect of the Belgian Laws on distributors. It was explained that, although agreement on this point is not universal, the Belgian Law of 1961 may be regarded in two ways: as a unilateral rule applicable when there is another *lex contractus,* or part of the *lex contractus* when that is Belgian law. In the first case it will serve to oust a choice of non-Belgian law, given that it is operative, i.e., that the distributor trades in Belgium even if not exclusively or even predominantly there. In the second case it will operate outside its original scope so as to protect, e.g., an English distributor against a Belgian supplier. This provision is, not unexpectedly, not looked upon with favour by foreign courts. Perhaps suprisingly, the Belgian courts do not appear to take offense when these provisions of national law are not applied by foreign courts. Thus, where the court in Paris ignored the Belgian provisions and its decision came up for enforcement in Belgium, it was held there that the decision, even though it ran counter to national law conferring exclusive jurisdiction on Belgian courts and also failed to apply mandatory protective provisions, did not violate Belgian international public policy and was enforceable. This should be contrasted with the generally accepted thrust of the provisions whereby, e.g., if the distributor agrees when concluding the distributorship agreement to waive his right to claim compensation upon termination of the agreement, he may nevertheless avail himself of the Belgian protective legislation.

Where the parties do not include a valid choice of law clause in the agreement, the approach to determining the applicable law can vary substantially from one jurisdiction to another. Such differences may also exist even where different jurisdictions might appear to follow similar approaches: in short, linguistic identity may disguise juridical distinctions. For example, where the English court may find that a jurisdiction or arbitration forum clause indicates a tacit choice of law, the Dutch court will not. A tacit choice is there employed in the context of an agreement between the parties subsequent to the conclusion of the contract for the purposes of pending or active legal proceedings. By contrast, the English Court of Appeal has recently refused to entertain the notion of such type of subsequent choice of law for the purposes of legal proceedings in England, holding that it would be logically indefensible and could be permitted only where the choice of law was the subject of a new and separate contract supported by consideration.

Uncertainty as to actual content was also evidenced during the discussions in regard to employment of the characteristic performance approach, now endorsed by the Contractual Obligations Convention of 1980. Apart from a certain measure of criticism of the approach as constituting an actual improvement or useful alternative to the longer established test of closest connection, doubt was expressed also as to the feasibility in real terms of identifying the obligations of either the supplier or the distributor as the more characteristic performance. Given that the distributor's obligation is not, or at least ought not to be simply regarded as the sale of the goods, but is instead that of promoting the goods, of developing the market, of using his best endeavours to ensure increased sales, etc., it was argued that the supplier's obligations of ensuring a proper supply of the goods, of providing necessary back-up facilities and of generally not obstructing but rather of supporting and promoting the distributor's activities, made it a matter of some difficulty in deciding clearly that the former were more characteristic than the latter. On the other hand, there was a definite preference shown in favour of opting for the distributor's performance as being the more characteristic. As a test for identifying the governing law, however, its utility, it was conceded, is less obvious in those cases where the distributor must operate under the terms of the agreement in several countries. Such cases would have to be decided on their own facts, which might tend to lead the court again towards a closest connection approach. On the other hand, it was suggested, adoption by the court of a market-oriented test could, in many cases, assist in identifying the commercial centre of the distribution activities seen in the light of the contract between supplier and distributor, viewed not just "legally" but also, and even more importantly, "economically". Alternatively, one could opt instead for the "harder" rule that the law of the country of the distributor's place of business should govern.

4. TORTIOUS LIABILITY

When considering various clauses that appear in the distributorship agreement, those purporting to exclude or limit the liability of the producer/supplier will, it was agreed, be of relevance also in the litigious relations between the distributor and final purchaser/consumer. These parties are not bound by such clauses whether they proceed against the distributor in contract or in tort, or concurrently where the *lex fori* permits concurrent actions, or go directly to the manufacturer in tort. Given the difference in result that can emerge, dependent on both substantive law and conflict of laws, the choice thus presented can be of some difficulty. Where the final purchaser/consumer elects to proceed against the distributor, the latter may be met by such a clause when he attempts to join the producer/supplier in the action or when he subsequently proceeds against him in turn. In this respect a number of recent developments were noted. In an increasing number of countries legislation has strengthened the position of the consumer against, in the present context, the distributor, a development reflected by the recent Draft Hague Convention on Consumer Sales, Section 4 of the EEC Convention on Jurisdiction and Enforcement of Judgments 1978 and Article 5 EEC Contractual Obligations Convention. Secondly, some countries, e.g., Norway, Sweden and Finland, are proposing to make both the producer and distributor directly liable for defects or for damage to the ultimage purchaser/user. In a number of countries, thirdly, such exemption clauses, whether invoked by the distributor against the purchaser or by the supplier against the distributor may fall foul of unfair contract terms legislation and be struck down as invalid.

A complication that may arise here where concurrent actions in contract and tort are brought is whether there exists, and if so what is the extent and operation of, the rule that exemption clauses valid by the proper law of the contract are subject in their operation to the law governing the tort.

It was agreed, however, that such clauses as between supplier and distributor are often best regarded as in the nature of hold harmless clauses along the commercial chain, so that when one link in the chain is attacked the issue is one of bargaining as to who is to bear the risk and to effect insurance against such loss, this element to be adjusted for in respect of other elements in the commercial relationship.

The Chairman thanked both the reporters and the participants who had so actively engaged them, and concluded the session.

INTERNATIONAL ARBITRATION – NATIONAL ADJUDICATION

THE RELATIONSHIP BETWEEN INTERNATIONAL COMMERCIAL ARBITRATION AND NATIONAL ADJUDICATION

by Aleksander Goldštajn

1. INTRODUCTION

International arbitration cannot function independently of national orders. In all stages of its existence it has always been subordinated to national legal orders. In this connection it is not significant to what extent a national legal order is invoked; the fact that such a possibility exists suffices. No legal order is indifferent to proceedings before international arbitration if the latter has any real connection with such legal order whatsoever.

The relationship between international arbitration and national adjudication deserves special attention owing to the development of international commercial arbitration since the Second World War, in which period of time it has almost everywhere been accepted as the only option in the settlement of international commercial disputes. However, the most recent developments have given prominence to certain facts which impart special gravity to the present problem of the relationship between international arbitration and national adjudication.

The world market has expanded considerably since the Second World War, not only by spreading to new territories but also primarily by the growing number of entities engaging in international business transactions in newly-created States. Even in long established States changes have occurred in the structure of parties to international transactions and of such transactions themselves. From the viewpoint of international arbitration all this makes it necessary to take into consideration the varied conditions under which business transactions take place and international arbitration functions, because it is necessary to take into account the special characteristics of systems to which parties to international business transactions belong. They belong frequently to different regions of the world, and to different social, economic and legal systems, and many of them are building up new legal systems of their own. Further, international arbitration has also been accepted by States and State-controlled bodies and agencies in their business transactions.

All these indicate, in our opinion, the need to investigate the traditional roads of development of international commercial arbitration to date, and to find ways and means of making it acceptable to the international business community.

The main efforts in developing arbitration institutions came from the industrialized countries whose business firms make extensive use of arbitration in their mutual relations. As a result arbitration centres were developed particularly in the industrialized world and these centres, with their own rules, tended to become the stipulated form for arbitration. In a later stage problems of relationship in East-West trade raise also the need to reconsider the methods accepted in international commercial arbitration so far.

Third World countries do not consider the present situation as satisfactory, although most of them are favourable in principle to international arbitration. Therefore, the need to find universally acceptable solutions.

It is, therefore, not by chance that international commercial arbitration has recently attracted the attention of various international forums. The Conference on Security and Cooperation in Europe, held in Helsinki in 1975, recognized arbitration as an appropriate means of settling disputes which may arise from commercial transactions and contracts for industrial cooperation, because the prompt and equitable settlement of disputes would contribute to expanding and facilitating trade and cooperation. Because of this, the Helsinki Conference recommended that the provisions on arbitration should provide for arbitration under a mutually acceptable set of arbitration rules, and permit arbitration in a third country, taking into account existing intergovernmental and other agreements in this field.

Soon afterwards, i.e., on 15 December 1976, the United Nations General Assembly adopted a resolution expressing the view that the establishment of rules for *ad hoc* arbitration that are acceptable in countries with different legal, social and economic systems would significantly contribute to the development of harmonious international economic relations.

International commercial arbitration has been strengthened worldwide by a number of multilateral conventions and the adoption of the UNCITRAL Arbitration Rules (1976), and regionally, through the adoption of the Uniform Rules for Arbitration in the Arbitration Courts of the Chambers of Commerce of the CMEA Countries (1974).

A comparison of the relevant international texts reveals several characteristic features. First, what has been achieved on the international level only is a partial improvement, so that it is necessary to resort to other sources. However, what has been accomplished as a result of the present experience in this field and of the understanding of actual needs, and this particularly relates to the New York Convention (1958) and the Uncitral Arbitration Rules, is encouraging.

Among the sources of the law of international commercial arbitration special place is held not only by municipal legislations, but also by everything else that has been accepted in international arbitration practice and by the international business community's recognition.

Finally, it can be said that the need has been generally recognized to find universally acceptable solutions at national and international levels.

2. THE PRESENT SITUATION

International commercial arbitration is in many respects linked to national legislations, which enhances cooperation but also makes possible intervention by municipal courts. What holds true for the relationship between the autonomous law of international trade and municipal regulations, i.e., that the autonomous and municipal regulations complement each other,[1] also holds true for international commercial arbitration. In a certain sense the delicacy of the problems involved is all the greater since in the event of international arbitration, adjudication is entrusted to neutral arbitrators whose place of arbitration is frequently outside

1. Schmitthoff, "The Law of International Trade, its Growth, Formulation and Operation", in, Schmitthoff, ed., *The Sources of the Law of International Trade* (London, 1964), p. 36.

the national territories of the parties, and who conduct proceedings according to legal rules of a public and private nature. Because of this, municipal courts are called upon not only to lend assistance to parties to arbitration proceedings, but also to safeguard the broader interests of society, because parties to international arbitration proceedings come from various countries whose legal orders can have different attitudes towards questions of substantive and procedural law. Professor Schmitthoff, therefore, rightly states that the relationship between the arbitrators and the court is the core problem in the law of arbitration.[2]

Thus, the present situation is characterized, on the one hand, by the fact that there is clear evidence that effective international commercial arbitration is strongly desired by businessmen, by governments, and by arbitration organizations, but, on the other, international commercial arbitration cannot exist alone, but requires the support of the national legal systems of the countries in which it operates. Cooperation with national courts is, therefore, needed at all stages of the arbitration process. The responsibility of the judges is great, as Holtzmann says, because the wisdom with which judges decide such issues not only affects the business interests of the parties, but also often establishes conditions for international trade which have lasting influence upon the economic development of their countries.[3]

Internationalization of arbitration is a vital necessity because the parties mistrust national jurisdictions for many reasons, including political and psychological ones[4], but, on the other hand, sovereign States do exercise control over international arbitration in various ways and in various measure. Tendencies towards the internationalization of the legal rules of international commercial arbitration run counter to municipal legislations which mutually differ to such an extent that we are still rather far away from the universal standards striven for by the business community.

The organization and practice of international arbitration are based on the consent of sovereign States and on party autonomy provided for by their municipal laws. The first and foremost principle of the law of commercial arbitration is that it is founded on the parties' will [5], and since the will of the parties is paramount in arbitration, this affords them a certain amount of security, on the legal as well as the political and economic levels.

Practice has shown that parties make limited use of the possibilities which the principle of party autonomy offers them. Few arbitrators have the experience or the desire to cope with details or seek different solutions.[6] They prefer to rely on the rules of permanent arbitration bodies or on existing laws. Departure from these rules presupposes certainty not only with respect to information but also to results

2. Schmitthoff, *Commercial Law in a Changing Economic Climate* (London, 1977), p. 38.

3. Holtzmann, "Arbitration and the Courts", Report to Sixth International Arbitration Congress (Mexico City, 1978), p. 12.

4. Costet, "The Advantages of International Arbitration", Address to ICC Seminar on Arbitration (Prague, 25-27 January 1978, p. 8.

5. Schmitthoff, "Defective Arbitration Clauses", in, Schmitthoff, ed., *International Commercial Arbitration* (New York - London, 1974-1975), p. 45.

6. Costet, loc.cit., *supra* n. 4, p. 4; Goldštajn, Medunarodna trgovačka arbitraža *(International Commercial Arbitration)* Vol. III, (Zagreb 1977), p. 5; Holtzmann, loc.cit., *supra* n. 3, p. 31.

in the event of court intervention, and this is a burden parties are reluctant to bear.

We do not have at our disposal statistical data on the number of court interventions in arbitration matters in individual countries. It can be rightly presumed that this number is not large. In spite of this, the present situation cannot be considered as satisfactory because the variety of rules of arbitration law is a sufficiently strong psychologial reason to avoid States not inclined to arbitration and to accept municipal law at an appropriate price, or under economic pressure to accept the existing situation.

As a result of the present situation, the law of international arbitration consists of numerous legal sources – national and international – of a public and a private nature, so that it is possible for a concrete dispute or award to be subject to control by various municipal courts and thereby also to various legal orders. This gives rise to conflict of varied interests not only of the parties but also of national orders based on different economic, political, cultural and legal foundations, which gives international commercial arbitration a special political and psychological imprint. Efforts to overcome the present barriers will be confronted by the legal tradition and cultural and economic level of individual countries, and in particular by public policy rules, and/or municipal mandatory provisions.

Recent development gives, however, cause for optimism. What was until yesterday considered as irreplaceable, is today regarded as permissible in international commercial arbitration. An example is the change in English law where international arbitration is involved. The 1979 Arbitration Act abolished both types of special case – that stating an award and that stating a question of law arising in the course of a reference, although until then it was considered as being contrary to public policy to contract out of the case stated procedure. It also abrogated the common law jurisdiction of the High Court to set aside or remit an award on the ground of errors in fact or law on the face of the award, thus encouraging English arbitrators to adopt the practice which is normal in foreign countries of stating reasons in an award.[7]

Again, well known is the evolution of the legal orders of individual countries regarding the possibility of the State and its agencies submitting themselves to commercial arbitration [8], and of foreign awards containing no statement of reasons being recognized in continental legal systems.

Present municipal laws on arbitration were drafted to meet the needs of domestic arbitration and many of them are in need of revision.[9] Another characteristic of national laws is that their provisions relate to *ad hoc* arbitration. Fouchard

7. Marshall, "The Arbitration Act 1979", JBL (1979), p. 242; Schmitthoff, "The United Kingdom Arbitration Act 1979", *Yearbook Commercial Arbitration* V (1980), p. 231.

8. Domke, "Arbitration between Governmental Bodies and Foreign Firms", *The Arbitration Journal* (No. 3/1962), p. 129; Ibid., "Arbitration between Government-Controlled Bodies and Foreign Business Firms", Report of the Fifty-Second Conference of ILA (Helsinki, 1966), p. 804; Ibid., Report of the Fifty-Third Conference of ILA (Buenos Aires, 1968), p. 645.

9. UNCITRAL Twelfth Session, Vienna (June, 1979), Doc. A/CN. 9/169, 11 May 1979, p. 3.

draws attention to the *caractère archaique de nombre de lois nationales,* and points out that *les centres permanents d'arbitrage, leurs organisation et leurs méthodes, ne sont pas encore, en majorité, détachées complement des cadres nationaux.*[10]

Cooperation between municipal courts and international arbitrations is therefore needed at all states of the arbitration process:

i) in recognition of arbitration agreements;
ii) in conducting arbitration proceedings; and
iii) in enforcing arbitral awards.[11]

The law of arbitration is characterized by complexity and embraces several areas: arbitration agreements, i.e., conditions for the validity of such agreements; application of substantive law; rules on arbitral procedure; and provisions pertaining to the enforcement of arbitral awards.

International commercial arbitration is governed by differing rules concerning the treatment accorded to it. For it should be noted that international commercial arbitration is from the aspect of procedural rules looked upon in the home-country as domestic arbitration. On the other hand, arbitral awards made in a country other than the one where enforcement is sought, are considered as being foreign. As a result, international arbitral awards are treated differently with regard to the possibility of their enforcement.

In the home-country – according to whose rules international arbitral awards are looked upon as domestic arbitral awards – there are conditions for setting aside an award. The grounds and procedure for instituting such proceedings vary from country to country. In contrast to this, where enforcement is sought of a foreign arbitral award, there is a considerable degree of uniformity thanks to international conventions and to court practice in various countries whose courts apply the rules of international public policy. Conditions for the enforcement of an international arbitral award are not the same. There is a different situation where international conventions on enforcement refer to the application of national rules regarding the finality of awards in the home-country, from the one where awards are attacked in the home-country (i.e., in the country in which the place of arbitration is) in which they are considered as being domestic.

National rules pertaining to the setting aside or annulment of arbitral awards apply equally to domestic and international awards, since from the standpoint of the law of the home-country *(Sitzrecht)* international arbitral awards are treated as domestic. Consequently, the same international arbitral award is governed by different provisions because it is once considered as domestic and as a foreign award. Professor Sanders is therefore right in expressing doubt about the feasibility of trying to unify arbitration laws, including the grounds for setting aside or annulment of an arbitral award and the annulment of the proceeding itself.[12] National

10. Fouchard, *L'arbitrage commercial international* (Paris, 1965), no. 55, pp. 25, 29.

11. Sanders, "Appeals Procedure in Arbitration", in, Schmitthoff, op.cit., *supra* n. 5, p. 120; Holtzmann, loc.cit., *supra* n. 3, p. 13.

12. Sanders, loc.cit., *supra* n. 11, p. 119.

arbitration laws or provisions of the law of civil procedure pertaining to arbitration are closely connected with the domestic system of law and have proponderantly but not exclusively domestic needs in mind. Improvements made to date in certain national laws in favour of international commercial arbitration are limited in scope. Thus, according to the present situation, all national laws contain provisions for setting aside or annulment of arbitral awards, provisions which differ from country to country both with respect to the grounds on which these proceedings may be instituted, and with regard to the procedure. As may have become clear from what was discussed earlier: an international commercial award may be attacked owing to lack of valid arbitration agreement, irregularities in the arbitral proceedings and irregularities in the award.[13]

3. SOURCES OF THE LAW OF INTERNATIONAL COMMERCIAL ARBITRATION

It seems justifiable to speak of the sources of the law of international commercial arbitration despite the fact that this term is not known in national rules, so that international commercial arbitration is governed by general domestic rules on arbitration. Generally, international conventions only speak of arbitral awards, with the exception of the European Convention on International Commercial Arbitration (1961), which "shall apply to arbitration agreements concluded for the purpose of settling disputes arising from international trade between persons having, when concluding their agreement, their habitual place of residence or their seat in different Contracting States" (Art. I, para. 1a); the European Convention Providing a Uniform Law on Arbitration (Strasbourg, 1966), which has regard to the need to "facilitate commercial relations between the Member Countries of the Council of Europe"; and the Uniform Rules of Procedure of the CMEA Countries (1974), which applies to the settlement of disputes arising between legal persons of "various countries in the course of foreign trade and other international economic, scientific and technological relations" (para. 1).

International commercial arbitration has specific features regardless of the mandatory territorialization imposed by the laws of the countries hosting international arbitrators, and by the laws of the countries in which enforcement of arbitral awards may be sought. National courts take account of the nature of international business transactions and of international commercial arbitration, showing greater or lesser flexibility in making possible unhindered functioning of arbitration in international trade. By accepting the concept of international public policy, courts have displayed a sense of reality stemming from the need for international economic cooperation, from the interdependence of national economies and from the development of the new *lex mercatoria,* not only with respect to substantive law but also to the law of international arbitration.

13. Sanders, "Trends in the Field of International Commercial Arbitration", *Recueil des Cours,* Hague Academy of International Law (1975), II p. 275.

The law of international commercial arbitration consists of international conventions on arbitration, customs, national rules on arbitration, international arbitration practice, court practice and control of international arbitration tribunals. Nor can the important role played by doctrine in this field be neglected.

As can be seen, there are various sources of law governing international commercial arbitration. Fourchard mentions *les sources d'origine public* and *les sources d'origine privée.*[14] Among the sources of public origin he cites international conventions and national laws. By the *sources d'origine privée* he understands *les conventions arbitrales – types – documents établis soit par des associations corporatives, soit par des accords inter-corporatifs, et contenues dans les "contrat-types" ou des conditions générales,* as well as *réglements des institutions d'arbitrage.*

A comparison of the rules of international commercial arbitration bodies and Standard Contracts is indicative of the existing practice of the circles concerned. To this one should add that in the practice of international *ad hoc* arbitrations relating to international trade continuity is not so evident as it is with permanent arbitration bodies, but this practice indicates the tendency to solve various questions in this field. Awards of *ad hoc* arbitrators draw authority from their arguments and their prestige, in contrast to permanent arbitration bodies which themselves impart authority to awards made under their auspices. Herein lies not only the legal but also the sociological dimension of the problems involved.

Incompleteness is the common feature of national rules. Thus, for example, the Austrian law of civil procedure is with respect to arbitration said to be narrow and full of gaps, while the German law of civil procedure is considered to be incomplete regarding the regulation of arbitral procedure since the latter is only an accessory part *(Seitenstück)* of this law.[15] What is said about these laws can be regarded as generally true of other laws.

In view of the basic principle of the law of arbitration – party autonomy – the rules of institutional arbitration bodies, standard contracts or general conditions will be recognized by national courts provided they conform at least to public policy, if not to mandatory rules as well. Indicative in this respect are the UNCITRAL Arbitration Rules which specify that "these Rules shall govern the arbitration except that where any of these Rules is in conflict with a provision of the law applicable to the arbitration from which the parties cannot derogate, that provision shall prevail (Art. 1, para. 2)".

There will be fewer conflicts with mandatory provisions of the applicable national substantive law than in the sphere of procedural rules. Differences in the interpretation of the law of international trade are smaller than those prevailing among nations in the interpretation of procedural rules.[16] However, the application of the more restrictive standards of international public policy will make it easier to avoid difficulties where they appear to be unjustifiable.

14. Fouchard, op.cit., *supra* n. 10, pp. 41-45, 28

15. Goldštajn, op.cit., *supra* n. 4, p. 9; Fasching, *Schiedsgericht und Schiedsverfahren im österreichischen und internationalen Recht* (Vienna, 1973), p. 99; Baumbach/Schwab, *infra,* n. 36, p. 53.

As regards the sources of the law of international commercial arbitration account should also be taken of what Professor Schmitthoff considers to be a wider concept of law, notably that "we have to attribute the status of law to usage and custom generally accepted by a community, to quasi-professional bodies, gentleman's agreements and other arrangements which are regarded as binding without being enforceable in a court. Enforceability is only an incident, though not of minor importance."[17]

A test to establish whether or not something has been accepted internationally would appear to depend on determining what is normal practice when the parties are from different geographic regions and have different nationalities, that is, that which could be qualified as customary in international commercial arbitration.

It seems, however, that a distinction should be made between sources deriving from an international agency and from other associations or bodies. With some associations and bodies practice is an expression of relations between centres of economic power and their partners so that the rule take-it-or-leave-it applies here.

The greater the sense of reality shown by national courts in exercising their control, the more the interpretation of national rules will be adjustable to international needs, and thereby also to the long-term needs of every country.[18] The existence of an effective system of arbitration depends on the various systems of law that come into play due to the relevant connection of a particular case – the law of contracts, the law of the place of arbitration, and the law of the place where the arbitration award is to be enforced.

Enforcement of foreign arbitral awards is regulated by international conventions. Here public policy rules play the greatest role. In contrast to this, the setting aside of arbitral awards is regulated by the municipal provisions of the home-country, i.e., the country where the award was made. As to the nullity of the award, in all countries it is possible to have the award declared null and void by a judicial authority. Here, however, the similarity ends, as wittily noted by Professor Sanders.[19] It therefore seems to us that the basic question lies in the need to accord international commercial arbitration a special treatment.

4. PUBLIC POLICY AND INTERNATIONAL PUBLIC POLICY RULES

The Uncitral Arbitration Rules give priority to mandatory rules and do not mention public policy – a term used by conventions for the enforcement of

16. Sanders, loc.cit., *supra* n. 13, p. 224-247; Sanders, "Commentary on Uncitral Arbitration Rules", in, Sanders, ed., *Yearbook Commercial Arbitration,* Vol. II - 1977, p. 179; Coing, "Materielles Recht und Verfahrensrecht in der internationalen Schiedsgerichtsbarkeit", in, Fabricius, ed., *Law and International Trade:* Festschrift für Clive M. Schmitthoff (Frankfurt, 1973); Robert, "Administration of Evidence in International Commercial Arbitration", in, Sanders, *Yearbook Commercial Arbitration,* Vol. I - 1976, p. 226.

17. Schmitthoff, op.cit., *supra* n. 2, p. 1.

18. Schwarzenberger, *Power Politics* (London, 1964), p. 203.

19. Sanders, in, *U.I.A. International Commercial Arbitration* (Paris), Vol. I, Introduction, p. 27.

foreign arbitral awards. The question, therefore, arises as to the relationship between mandatory provisions of the applicable national law and public policy. According to Fouchard *il est devenue classique, dans la doctrine moderne de distinguer l'ordre public au sens interne, qui recouvre toutes les lois impératives, et l'ordre public au sens international, becaucoup plus restreint.*[20] However, violation of the law does not in general fall within grounds for setting aside an arbitral award. More and more a distinction can be seen between domestic public policy and international public policy as the creation of court practice and doctrine, which is confined, according to a generally accepted doctrine, to violation of a really fundamental concept of the legal order in the country concerned. The international arbitral award is, to "some extent", drawn away from the application of the pure national criterion of the domestic rules of public policy. Although the grounds for setting aside an award differ from country to country, they nevertheless have the common feature of striving to restrict grounds for annulment.

On the other hand, the Strasbourg Uniform Law on Arbitration 1966 provides that an arbitral award may be set aside if there has been disregard of any obligatory rule of the arbitral procedure (Art. 25, para. 2).

An award, not contrary to the rules of public policy in the home-country will only exceptionally be refused recognition and enforcement in a foreign country for reasons of international public policy. On the other hand, denationalization of rules of public policy in the home-country of the award is only possible on a limited scale. In the home-country domestic public policy rules still play their inevitable part.[21] Because of this, Robert speaks of the need to harmonize legal mentality.[22]

Thus, the Swiss *Bundesgericht* took the view in 1980 that,

> *der Vorbehalt der öffentlichen Ordnung im Gebied der Anerkennung und Vollstreckung ausländischer Entscheidungen enger auszulegen ist als im Gebied der direkten Gesetzanwendung.*[23]

This ruling gives expression to the distinction between domestic and international arbitration as far as public policy is concerned.[24] This certainly relates to the recognition and enforcement of foreign awards, but the problem remains unsettled of when international commercial arbitration is considered to be domestic arbitration from the viewpoint of the law of the place of arbitration. It seems that the Swiss Supreme Court restricts the scope of Swiss public policy rules when a foreign award is involved. Court practice in Switzerland has adopted a liberal view regarding the enforcement of foreign awards *dans la mesure tout au moins où des ressortissants suisses n'en seraient pas les victimes.*[25]

20. Fouchard, op.cit., *supra* n. 10, p. 526 - No. 731.
21. Sanders, loc.cit., *supra* n. 13, p. 242, 288; Robert, loc.cit., *supra* n. 16.
22. Robert, ibid.
23. BGE 84 I 39.
24. Sanders, loc.cit., *supra* n. 13, p. 227.
25. Budin, "L'execution des sentences arbitrales etrangeres en Suisse et les limits de l'ordre public", *Revue de l'Arbitrage* (2/1977), p. 118, 123-124.

In contrast to international public policy rules, international conventions refer to the public policy of a particular country. Thus the New York Convention 1958 takes into account the public policy of the country where recognition and enforcement is sought (Art. V, para. 2 (b)). The same criterion is contained in the Geneva Convention 1927 (Art. 1 (e)).

There is an interesting distinction in this respect in Swiss law in cases where Swiss public policy is not affected. The Code of Civil Procedure of the Canton of Zurich specifies in this respect the following:

> *Das Gericht braucht auf die Klage nur einzutreten, wenn eine Partei im Kanton Zürich Wohnsitz oder eine Niederlassung hat, wenn eine Partei Schweizer Bürger mit Wohnsitz im Ausland ist, oder wenn Gerichtsstandvereinbarung Bestandteil der Anleihensbedingungen einer im Kanton Zürich öffentlich zur Zeichnung aufgelegten Anliehe ist.* (Art. 11, para. 2).

The draft *Bundesgesetz über das internationale Privatrecht der Schweiz,* which contains provisions on international arbitration, provides as follows:

> *Hat keine der Parteien Wohnsitz, gewöhnlichen Aufenthalt oder Geschäftsniederlassung in der Schweiz, so können sie schriftlich vereinbaren, dass Sachurteil des Schiedsgerichts nicht an die schweizerischen Gerichte weitergezogen werden darf.* (Art. 180, para. 1).

In an explanation of the attitude that appears from the latter provision, it is said that the purpose of this provision is to ensure efficacy of arbitral awards to the greatest possible extent, and to prevent legal disputes having no real connection whatsoever with Switzerland from being brought before Swiss courts.[26]

Fouchard mentions *conceptions nationales* of public policy, which constitute a certain danger in arbitral matters,[27] while Gentinetta points out that the will of the parties may not *das Gesetz spurlos verdrängen und im rechtsleeren Raum operieren,*[28] so that, because of this, restrictions are imposed by the rules of international public policy.

As regards the setting aside of international arbitral awards, the concept of public policy differs in scope from country to country; national public policy differs with respect to the scope of application and interpretation. This is attributable not only to the traditional mechanisms of procedural law, but also to varied concepts reflecting different needs, and sometimes also to social orders. What in one country seems possible, will in another sometimes certainly be rejected, even though not every violation of the mandatory provisions provides a ground for setting aside an arbitral award. According to Professor Sanders, violation of the law does not, in general, belong to the grounds for setting aside an award, but an exception must be made for violation of rules of public policy

26. Vischer/Volken, *Begleitbericht, Schweizer Studien zum internationalen Recht,* Band 12 (Zürich, 1978), p. 180.
27. Fouchard, op.cit., *supra* n. 10, p. 345.
28. Gentinetta, *Die Lex Fori internationaler Handelsschiedsgerichte* (Bern, 1973), p. 264.

which always leads to nullity or annulment of the arbitral award. As the Swiss Supreme Court has stated:

> *angefochtener Entscheid eine Norm oder einen klaren und unumstrittenen Rechtsgrundsatz offensichtlich verletzt oder in stoszender Weise dem Gerechtsgefühl zuwiderläuft.*[29]
> *Willkür darf aber nicht mit Gesetzesverletzung verwechselt werden, da andere Lösungen ebenfalls vertretbar oder vielleicht vorzuziehen gewesen wären.*[30]

Differences of view regarding procedural questions, but also concerning substantive law, vary from country to country, and even within individual countries,[31] but this need not constitute an insurmountable obstacle to the creation of a more favourable climate for international commercial arbitration. Even within the present framework, practice in international arbitration centres has shown restraint in the application of domestic public policy rules. Thus, for example, of all arbitral awards, domestic and international, made in the last ten years in the Canton of Zurich, there have been on an average barely two cases per year where a request for setting aside the award was complied with.[32]

In the prevailing "market" situation in arbitration law the selection of the place of arbitration plays a decisive role. Judicial control of arbitral awards and suitable legislation can favour or hinder the development of international commercial arbitration.

Is a complete denationalization of international arbitration possible at all? This is a fundamental question in the present-day international economic and political constellation. Absolute denationalization would be an illusion. No country will be able to renounce its basic views, views which stem from the unequal level of economic development and different legal, political and other needs – so that a more modest approach to the finding of the common interest would seem to be more realistic. It is evident that a compromise approach should be taken and that a confrontation of views will result in an improvement in international arbitration by removing barriers which the international community finds hard to bear, and which should give way to more modern and internationally acceptable criteria.

In addition to legal possibilities for avoiding an attack on an arbitral award in the home-country and a third country in connection with its enforcement, extra-legal sanctions which often have a greater effect than legal ones, should be taken into account. Application of extra-legal sanctions is widespread in international trade when largescale business is involved, especially when an award has been made by arbitrators of a permanent arbitration body of an association. Uncontrolled primacy of the parties' will cannot be accepted as a principle, since in

29. BGE 102 Ia 3-4 E 3b.

30. BGE 99 Ia 346 E.1; 96 I 627; Jolidon, "Les motifs du recours en nullité selon la Concordat Suisse sur l'arbitrage", in Bucher/Saldin, ed., *Berner Festgebe zum Schweizerischen Juristentag 1979* (Bern, 1979) p. 325.

31. For example, in Switzerland between the Code of Civil Procedure of the Canton of Zürich and Concordat Suisse sur l'arbitrage.

32. Glattfelder, *Die internationale Schiedsgerichtsbarkeit der Züricher Handelskammer* (Zürich, 1979), p. 19.

international transactions a drastic departure from generally accepted standards is possible.

Domestic and international policy rules are encountered at the various stages of international arbitration proceedings. The question arises, therefore, whether it is possible to achieve a really international arbitration process as is the case with substantive law in the new *lex mercatoria.* We are of the opinion that national courts can contribute to it through a more liberal approach to international commercial arbitration, while municipal legislations can accomplish this by taking a modern attitude towards the needs of the international business community.

National arbitration laws are closely connected with civil procedure. In addition, the grounds for setting aside an award in a country provide a ground for refusal of enforcement in another country (party to the New York Convention).

The rules of public policy will play a varied role. They are more widely applied in setting aside an award in the home-country, while a "narrower" international public policy will be applied in the country where enforcement is sought. Therefore, there exist varied criteria for the application of the rules of public policy to the same international arbitral award: strict application of the domestic rules of public policy in the home country, i.e., of the mandatory provisions, while in a foreign country of enforcement application of international public policy rules is limited solely to really fundamental principles. In the home-country the domestic public policy rules play an inevitable part. Rules of domestic public policy will be those leading to nullity or setting aside of the award.

There is a link between international arbitration and different national arbitration laws based both on the national law of the *Sitzrecht* and the fact that international conventions refer to these laws. In this latter case there is a tendency towards a narrower interpretation [33] although there are different opinions as to the plausibility of this distinction, especially when a foreign economic relationship as an "instrument in the defence of the national economy or state finance" (Ferrante) is involved, or if the award obliges one party to make payment contrary to the currency legislation (Lew), or foreign exchange restrictions have to be taken into account (Sanders), and if matters are involved in the economic sphere which States consider as rules of *ordre public* (Fouchard). Should awards in the country of origin be set aside on the grounds other than those mentioned in the New York Convention on the Recognition and Enforcement of Foreign Arbitral Awards, these grounds will be *indirectly* introduced as grounds for refusal in the country of enforcement (Sanders). It is understandable when Professor Schmitthoff, at this stage, expressed the opinion that it is "very doubtful whether an international or transnational *ordre public* exists" having in view the modest achievement predominantly in the procedural field. Lalive recently suggested drawing distinctions between:

33. Sanders, loc.cit., *supra* n. 13, at pp. 242, 283-288; Strobach, "On Setting Aside of Arbitration Awards", in, *Hommage à F. Eisemann* (Paris), p. 79 No. 3.

– ***ordre public interne du lieu de l'arbitrage;***
– ***ordre public international du lieu de l'arbitrage;***
– ***ordre public réellement international*** [34]

having in mind the French law point of view.

5. THE POSITION OF NATIONAL COURTS IN APPOINTING ARBITRATORS

After the arbitrators have been appointed, one of the parties may challenge any of them for different reasons, such as lack of impartiality or independence, or jurisdiction. The challenge is closely connected with the appointment and therefore forms part of the appointment procedure.[35]

As regards the appointment of arbitrators, guarantees given to the parties should not be less than those accorded in proceedings before the courts. It seems that with regard to arbitration in general and international commercial arbitration in particular, additional guarantees stemming from the nature of arbitration should be recognized, because the parties select arbitrators they trust.

Two questions should be taken into consideration here: who is competent to decide on the challenge of an arbitrator, and when can such challenge be made?

There is no agreement as to whether or not the final decision on the challenge of the jurisdiction of an arbitrator should be rendered by a court. Nor may the final decision on the justifiability of such a challenge be entrusted to any third party, not even to the arbitration court.

Professor Sanders points out that a special problem arises because in many arbitration laws the decision on the challenge of an arbitrator belongs to the exclusive jurisdiction of the courts. This poses the question to what extent does such a provision influence the freedom of the parties to regulate the challenge of an arbitrator and more specifically the regulation of the challenge as usually contained in the rules of an arbitral institution to which the parties have referred. In those countries where the courts have exclusive jurisdiction,[36] the decision on

34. Ferrante, "Enforcement of Foreign Arbitral Awards in Italy", in, *Hommage a Eisemann*, ibid., p. 33, 86. Sanders, "A Twenty Years Review of the Convention on the Recognition and Enforcement of Foreign Arbitral Awards", *International Lawyer* (2/1979), p. 276; Sanders, "Procedure and Practice under the UNCITRAL Rules", AJCL (2 & 3/1979), p. 465; Lew, *Applicable Law in International Commercial Arbitration* (New York 1978), p. 565; Fouchard, op.cit., *supra* n. 10, No. 534; Schwab, *Schiedsgerichtbarkeit* (Munich 1979) p. 177; Schmitthoff, "Standard Contracts and Protection of a Weaker Party in International Trade Relations", in, *New Directions in International Trade Law* (Acts and Proceedings of the 2nd Congress on Private Law, Rome 1976, Vol. I - Dobbs Ferry, N.Y. 1977) p. 185; Lalive, J.C.C., Doc. No. 420/234, 23.11.1980.

35. Schlosser, *Recht der internationalen privaten Schiedsgerichtsbarkeit* (Tübingen, 1975), No. 517; Sanders, loc.cit., *supra* n. 13, p. 271;

36. Baumbach/Schwab, *Schiedsgerichtsbarkeit* (Munich, 1960), p. 112; For English Law: the final jurisdiction of the courts cannot be set aside - Gill, *The Law of Arbitration* (London, 1975) p. 11; Wiget, in, Sträuli/Messmer, *Kommentar zum Zürischen Zivilprozessordnung* (Zürich, 1976), p. 463, No. 9; Walder-Bohner, *Der neue Zürcher Zivilprozess* (Zürich, 1979) p. 456; Par. 244 Code of Civil Procedure of Canton Zürich and Art. 21 Swiss Intercantonal

challenge will be subject to revision by the courts, so that an intervention of the court is possible.[37] Holtzmann, too, considers that when a party is dissatisfied with the decision of the arbitration institution to which the parties have agreed that the arbitration is to be conducted in accordance with the arbitration rules specified in the contract, the challenge must usually be determined by the court at the place of arbitration.[38] Contesting the awards of all arbitration tribunals, even of institutional ones with their seat in the Canton of Zurich, falls within the jurisdiction of the court.[39] This stand has also been taken in the Draft Swiss *Bundesgesetz über das internationale Privatrecht* by providing in such cases for the jurisdiction of the court in the place where the arbitration tribunal has its seat.[40]

As regards permanent arbitration institutions, the question arises as to the jurisdiction of the courts regarding the control of the administering body. In this respect some arbitration institutions are vested under their rules with authority to perform specific administrative acts in connection with the dispute (ICC rules), while the rules of other arbitration bodies contain no such provisions (the Arbitration Court of the Zurich Chamber of Commerce). In all cases a final decision falls within the jurisdiction of the court in the place where the arbitrators, not the institution, have their seat.[41] The courts play a major role in interpreting the relationship between local law and arbitration rules.[42]

There is no available data regarding the number of court interventions in arbitration proceedings within the framework of institutional arbitration. Domke states that it may be noted that in the institutional American Arbitration Association about 20 per cent of the commercial arbitrators who had accepted appointment were subsequently replaced, either by voluntary withdrawal or disqualification by the administrative agency due to disclosure of relationship to the parties, their counsel, or prospective witnesses. This is especially the case in close-knit industries. Where the arbitrator's very close relationship to, or even identification with, one of the parties appears, the likelihood of an effort by the court to remove the arbitrator will be much greater than in the case of the latter allegation of some bias. Courts have the power to decide whether the arbitrator was subject to removal for partiality or bias even though the American Arbitration

---

Arbitration Convention (1969). The same results from the international conventions - Geneva Protocol on Arbitration Clauses 1923, para. 2, Geneva Convention for the Execution of Foreign Arbitral Awards 1927, Art. 1 c, New York Convention 1958, Art. V, para. 1 d.

37. Sanders, loc.cit., *supra* n. 13, p. 271-272.

38. Holtzmann, loc.cit., *supra* n. 3, p. 23-24.

39. Glattfelder, op.cit., *supra* n. 32, p. 15; Wiget, "Über das Verhältniss der Schiedsgerichtsordnungen ICC, UNCITRAL, ECE zum Zürcher Schiedsgerichtsrecht", in, *Schweizerische Juristen-Zeitung* (Heft 2, 1979), p. 20.

40. This is also the position of the Swiss Draft Loi fédérale sur le droit international privé, Art. 177.

41. Walder-Bohner, "Die neue Zürcher Bestimmungen über die Schiedsgerichtsbarkeit im Lichte des Konkordats", *Schweizerische Juristen-Zeitung* (Heft 16/17 - 1976). p. 249.

42. Holtzmann, loc.cit., *supra* n. 3, p. 4, 33.

Association has investigated the matter and reached a conclusion on the issue prior to an award.[43]

5.1. A Case of Violation of the Principle of Due Process

The European Contract for Coffee (E.C.C.) – General Conditions Adopted by the Committee of European Coffee Association, Lodged with the Various Arbitral Bodies in Europe (1972 edition) – specifies in Article 42:

"Any dispute incapable of solution by amicable means shall be determined by arbitration at the place stated in the contract in accordance with rules and customs admitted by the Coffee Trade Association there established."

Concerning jurisdiction, the E.C.C. reads as follows:

"Whatsoever the residence of the parties concerned, they agree that in the event of arbitration the contract shall be interpreted according to the law and the arbitration rules in force in the country where the arbitration is held." (Art. 46).

The Comments to the European Contract for Coffee (1972 edition) published by the Committee for the European Coffee Associations specify:

"As arbitrators are not lawyers and certainly not experts on international law, it was admitted that there was no other possibility than that of accepting that in case of arbitration the contract should be interpreted according to the law and jurisprudence of the country where the arbitration is held." (Artt. 46-47).

In three disputes between a Swiss defendant and plaintiffs from England and France respectively, the *Chamber Arbitrale des cafés et poivres du Havre* gave awards (*Arbitrage de principe,* Nos. AP164, 165 and 150 – all unpublished) without specifying the arbitrators who had made them, while the awards were signed by *"Le président de la Commission Arbitrale"*, whose name is typewritten above his signature.

According to the *Règlement d'arbitrage, "arbitrage de principe"* concerns *"les litiges portant sur des questions autres que la qualité et le conditionnement".* According to these rules, arbitrators decide in a tribunal as *amiable compositeurs* and *jugent en equité et sont dispensés des formalités judiciaires".* Arbitrators are appointed for one year in advance from amongst members of three merchants' syndicates, and the tribunal consists of three members. The arbitral procedure is exclusively in writing, and the award must be signed by the arbitrators.

In these three disputes the defendant contested the jurisdiction of the arbitration. The subject-matter of the disputes were legal questions, because the defendant had stated that there was reasonable ground to suspect that the relevant documents were the result of a criminal offence. Without an oral hearing, the arbitration ruled

43. Domke, *The Law and Practice of Commercial Arbitration* (Mundelein, 1968), p. 220 and 1979 Cumulative Supplement, p. 64 - 220, no. 17.

against the defendant, and the awards were signed only by the president of the tribunal.

Against these awards the defendant lodged an *opposition à ordonnance d'exequatur,* arguing, *inter alia,* that the arbitrators were not known to the parties and that they had decided the issue exclusively by written procedure, which did not provide an opportunity of ensuring a real confrontation of the parties.

Le Tribunal de grande instance du Havre rejected the defendant's complaint. In its ruling of 22 November 1979, No. 923/1978 (unpublished), it said:

Attendu que la société P. déclare en outre qu'elle était fondée à refuser la signature du compromis en raison de la nature juridique du litige, des pouvoirs d'amiables compositeurs donnés aux arbitres et du fait que ceux ci n'étaint pas connus des parties.
Attendu que par son acceptation tacite du contrat et partant de la clause compromissoire P. acceptait les conditions du Règlement du Havre et tous ses termes,
Que ces règles ne sont pas contraires à l'ordre public,
Attendu que l'acceptation du règlement d'arbitrage emportait mandat donné au Conseil d'administration de désigner trois arbitres parmi les membres du collège arbitral; que P. ne prétend pas que la désignation n'ait pas été régulièrement . . ."

The same stand was taken in other rulings of this court (No. 788/1978 of 22 November 1979) (unpublished).

Adequate information about the arbitrators and the proceedings is of particular importance in the event of an award against an absent party, and was so stated in a decision of the *Oberlandesgericht* in Cologne of 10 June 1976. Here the names of the arbitrators were not made known to the parties, except that of the president of the tribunal who signed the award. This procedure was held to violate standards of due process in that it precluded a party from effectively challenging an arbitrator.[44]

The European Contract for Coffee also provides for extra-legal measures for parties in arbitral proceedings.

"If one of the parties refuses to comply with an arbitration award held to be final and binding, the party in whose favour the award has been given may ask the Coffee Trade Association to which it is affiliated to post the name of the defaulting party and/or to bring it to notice of its members in any other way; by acceptance of these arbitration clauses the parties are deemed to have agreed to these disciplinary measures" (Art. 45).

When institutional arbitration bodies are involved, these problems provide an additional argument regarding the need for the courts to exercise control over the work of arbitration bodies, not excluding standing professional arbitration bodies which strive to ensure absolute discipline.

44. United Nations, General Assembly A/CN. 9/168, 20 April 1979.

6. SOLE ARBITRATOR OR THREE ARBITRATORS

The number of arbitrators to be entrusted with the settlement of international commercial disputes is a question of major importance in the regulation of which municipal legislations of the civil law countries differ from those prevailing in common law countries. A comparison shows that in civil law countries the prevailing rule is that disputes of a minor value are settled by a sole judge, and those of greater value by a panel of judges. In contrast to this, settlement of disputes by a sole judge is widely accepted in common law countries.[45] These differences between the civil law and common law systems also hold true for arbitration. In the United Kingdom and the US, a sole arbitrator is the norm, unless a contrary intention is expressed in the arbitration agreement,[46] while in civil law systems collegial tribunals are the rule and sole arbitrators an exception.

Different rules apply to international commercial arbitration. Apart from the reasons which had motivated municipal legislators towards one or other of the above solutions and which are associated with the traditions and judicial systems of these countries, endemic to international commercial arbitration is the fact that the parties are from different countries, often from far-away and different regions with different social, economic and political systems. For this reason, among other things, psychological and political factors play a very important role in determining the number of arbitrators, regardless of the costs incurred through proceedings conducted by a collegial tribunal instead of a sole arbitrator, since the settlement of disputes requires a good knowledge of facts and customs, and of the laws of various countries.

In international commercial arbitration disputes are, as a rule, decided by a tribunal of three members; a sole arbitrator is an exception. This holds generally true, regardless of the stand taken by the municipal legislation of the place of arbitration.

With regard to the number of arbitrators, the UNCITRAL Arbitration Rules provide that if the parties have not previously agreed on the number of arbitration (i.e., one or three), and if within 15 days of the receipt by the respondent of the notice of arbitration the parties have not agreed that there shall be only one arbitrator, three arbitrators shall be appointed (Art. 5).

The Convention on the Settlement of Investment Disputes between States and Nationals of Other States has taken the same stand, specifying that where the parties do not agree upon the number of arbitrators and the method of their appointment, the Tribunal shall consist of three arbitrators, one arbitrator appointed by each party and the third, who shall be the president of the Tribunal, appointed by agreement of the parties (Art. 37, para. 2 (b)).

45. Schlosser, op.cit., *supra* n. 35, no. 441.

46. United Kingdom Arbitration Act, Art. 6; London Court of Arbitration Rules, Art. 9, para. 1; The United States Arbitration Act, Par. 5; Commercial Arbitration Rules of the American Arbitration Association, Sec. 16.

Regionally, it is also provided that disputes are decided by three arbitrators. The Arbitration Rules of the United Nations Economic Commission for Europe 1966 contain a clause according to which, failing agreement between the parties on the appointment of a sole arbitral institution, the Appointing Authority shall invite the parties each to appoint an arbitrator, the arbitrators so appointed choosing another arbitrator as presiding arbitrator (Art. 4, para. 2).

The Uniform Rules of Procedure of the CMEA Countries provide for a tribunal of three arbitrators, unless otherwise agreed upon by the parties (Paras. 43; 14,2 e; 17,3; 19). These rules also provide, as an exception to the "customary tribunal of three", for the appointment of a single arbitrator. Here the Uniform Rules have in mind the speedy and inexpensive handling of small cases. Professor Strohbach rightly says that one cannot expect that great use will be made of the institution of a single arbitrator. The main problem probably consists in the fact that a litigation will not show, at first sight, if it is a small case, since the value in litigation alone does not decide this issue.[47]

According to municipal legislations in civil law countries there should be three arbitrators unless otherwise specified. This also holds true for the majority of arbitration institutions.[48]

Authors from both civil law and common law countries have found many reasons for disputes falling under the jurisdiction of international commercial arbitrations to be decided by three arbitrators, which is the rule in such cases, except where the parties have expressly stipulated one arbitrator. In case of doubt, as pointed out by Professor Domke, different viewpoints may be better than one arbitrator deciding the dispute; further a single arbitrator might have more difficulty in fully understanding complicated issues. Because of this, more recently it has been the AAA's practice to have three arbitrators in cases involving more than 10,000 US dollars, unless the parties have agreed otherwise in the arbitration clause.[49] Aksen supports the view whereby an international arbitration should be made up of three arbitrators. Where each party appoints one arbitrator, these two can bring to bear upon the arbitral deliberations different cultural perspectives and varied insights into national viewpoints and customs. These can be most useful in enabling the third, or presiding, arbitrator to understand and help resolve disputes growing out of widely different social, economic and legal backgrounds.[50] Pearson, too, notes that in most international commercial arbitrations the arbitration tribunal consists of at least three persons.[51]

47. Strobach, "General Introduction", in, Sanders, ed., *Yearbook Commercial Arbitration*, Vol. I - 1976, p. 11 and n. 26 on p. 17.

48. Gentinetta, op.cit., *supra* n. 28, p. 165, 171. Bucher, "Zur Unabhängigkeit des Parteibenannten Schiedsrichters", in *Recht und Wirtschaft heute, Festgabe für Kummer* (Bern) p. 599; Wiget, "Fragen der Schiedsgerichtsbarkeit in Lizenz- und Vertriebsverträgen", in, *Probleme der Schiedsgerichtsbarkeit bei Lizenz- und Vertriebsverträgen* (Zürich 1980) p. 5.

49. Domke, op.cit., *supra* n. 43, p. 199.

50. Aksen, *A Practical Guide to International Arbitration* (New York), p. 62.

51. Pearson, "The Spreading of International Commercial Arbitration", Report to III International Arbitration Congress, in, Carnacini/Minoli, ed., *Co-operation among Arbitration Organizations* (Turin, 1970) p. 310.

In his *Commentary on Uncitral Arbitration Rules,* Professor Sanders notes that the Rule in Articles 5 and 7 providing for three arbitrators corresponds to the normal practice of naming a tribunal made up of three arbitrators for the settlement of disputes arising out of international trade transactions, particularly when the parties are from different geographic regions and have different nationalities. In such a case generally, each party will appoint a national of his country as arbitrator, while Article 5 regulates what is customary in international commercial arbitration: the appointment of three arbitrators. Article 7 follows international practice in giving each party the right to appoint one arbitrator.[52]

Further arguments are given by Professor Sanders when he states that although much can be said and has been said for and against the party-arbitration-system – which need not necessarily lead to two partial arbitrators although they are party-nominated – one advantage is anyhow in international matters that the arbitrators will know the national background (law, customs and even personal circumstances) of the party who designated them.[53]

The common characteristic of clauses in current use is that they usually provide for the constitution of a tripartite tribunal, each party being entitled to appoint its own arbitrator.[54]

Fouchard cites some interesting data regarding the composition of arbitral tribunals by saying that *très généralement* an arbitral tribunal will consist of three arbitrators when institutional arbitrations are involved. According to the data of the United Nations Economic Commission for Europe, from among 127 institutions surveyed, over 100 provide for a tribunal consisting of three arbitrators. Less frequently a sole arbitrator is envisaged.[55]

Of the Arbitration Court of the Chamber of Commerce in Zurich, an institutional arbitration which decides the largest number of disputes between parties from different countries, Glattfelder says that it is normal to decide disputes by tribunals consisting of three arbitrators. Disputes of small value are decided by sole arbitrators, but only by party agreement and request. (The jurisdiction of this institutional arbitration is provided for by the *Handelsabkommen zwischen dem Ostausschuss der Deutschen Wirtschaft und China-Komitee zur Förderung des internationalen Handels (1957);* the Protocol on Commodity Exchange between the Federal Republic of Germany and the People's Republic of Romania (1959); and the Trade Agreement between the Norsk Kompensasjonsselskap A/S Oslo and the Chamber of Foreign Trade of the German Democratic Republic.[56]

Speaking of East-West arbitration, Melis notes that the question of admission of foreign arbitrators is psychologically of importance in the choice of an arbitration centre. A party considers that its interests are being taken care of and that fairness of the proceedings will be guaranteed if it has the chance of appointing

52. Sanders, loc.cit., *supra* n. 16, p. 184, 187.
53. Sanders, loc.cit., *supra* n. 13, p. 215.
54. Delaume, *Transnational Contracts, Applicable Law and Settlement of Disputes* (Dobbs Ferry, N.Y., 1978), Vol. II, Par. 14.
55. Fouchard, op.cit., *supra* n. 10, p. 165, No. 276.
56. Glattfelder, op.cit., *supra* n. 32, p. 8.

an arbitrator of its own nationality. This is especially important in arbitrations between parties from different political and economic systems.[57] Kopelmanas has arrived at the same conclusion.[58]

Thus, practice shows that in international commercial arbitration settlement of disputes by tribunals of three arbitrators is the rule, and by a sole arbitrator the exception which must be clearly indicated by the parties in the arbitration agreement. There are many reasons for this stand, and leading authors have provided many arguments showing the specific nature of disputes arising out of international commercial transactions. This in the first place relates to the application of substantive law, including customs, general conditions and the course of dealing between the parties. Furthermore, the complexity of procedural rules, in most cases the freedom of the arbitrators within the framework of the arbitration agreement and applicable legal provisions to determine their proceedings, calls for the adjustment of interests of the parties from various countries. Finally, the essence of the cases which the arbitrators have to decide demands collegial settlement, which gives much greater guarantees to the parties than a sole arbitrator can offer. To these reasons should be added the specific character of international commercial disputes. The fact that the parties are from different countries, not infrequently from different regions, even continents, and have different political and economic systems, inevitably gives significance to the political aspect of the problem involved. Nor should the generally indicated psychological aspect be neglected.

In *ad hoc* arbitrations the parties, at the conclusion of the arbitration agreement must specify the composition of the arbitral tribunal to which they want to entrust the settlement of their disputes. A dilemma can arise when the parties stipulate the jurisdiction of an institutional arbitration by simply indicating it without any additional clauses in the arbitration agreement. Various situations are possible here. For example, if the rules of the chosen arbitration institution chosen unambiguously indicate the number of arbitrators, it will be presumed that the general principle applies unless otherwise specified by the parties.

The situation is different where the parties have not clearly expressed their will in the arbitration agreement and the rules leave it to the administering body to decide whether a sole arbitrator or several arbitrators have to decide the dispute. In such a case the guiding criterion should be that "it is the spirit more than the mere wording which governs the construction of the arbitration agreement", as emphasized by Professor Domke.[59] According to American court practice, arbitration is essentially a creature of contract, a contract in which the parties themselves charter a private tribunal for the resolution of their disputes.[60] What is decisive is the intention of the parties. Here again, in the absence of a clearly expressed will of the parties in the arbitration agreement, numerous criteria stemming from the

57. Melis, "East-West Arbitration", in, *Hommage a F. Eisemann* (Publication ICC No. 321, Paris), p. 99.

58. Kopelmanas, "La rédaction des clauses d'arbitrage et le choix des arbitres", in, *Hommage a Eisemann,* ibid. p. 29.

59. Domke, op.cit., *supra* n. 43, p. 30-31.

60. Domke, ibid., cases - note 2.

fact that international disputes are involved can be taken into consideration. Various circumstances, such as the countries of origin of the parties, what their municipal rules indicate as being customary, what the practice in the trade or region involved is like, etc., as well as confidence in the work of the chosen arbitration institution, can be indicative of what the intention of the parties was at the conclusion of the arbitration agreement.

These general observations predominantly relate to cases in which an institutional arbitration is chosen, because at the conclusion of an arbitration agreement the parties usually do not go into details, but either follow the recommendation of the arbitration institution regarding the stipulation of its jurisdiction, or consider it sufficient to refer to it in some other way.

In this respect a special place is held by the Court of Arbitration of the International Chamber of Commerce.

The Rules of this court specify with respect to the choice of arbitrators as follows:

> "Where the parties have not agreed upon the number of arbitrators, the Court shall appoint a sole arbitrator, save when it appears to the Court that the dispute is such as to warrant the appointment of three arbitrators." (Art. 2, para. 5).

The 1975 ICC Rules are different from the earlier version (1955); the latter made the choice between a sole arbitrator and three arbitrators dependent on the request of one party, and the dispute appearing to the Court important enough to warrant the appointment of three arbitrators. As a result of the omission of that part of the earlier text which demanded the request of one party, it seems that not only the decision but also the initiative is left to the Court.

The ICC Rules do not lay down any criteria for deciding when a sole arbitrator or three arbitrators should be appointed. It is sufficient that it appears to the Court that the dispute "is such" as to warrant the appointment of three arbitrators, so that this depends on the Court's practice (which is not published). The value of the dispute will in all likelihood influence the Court's stand, while other elements, e.g., the complexity of the case (and other circumstances), can hardly be discerned from the request for arbitration and the answer thereto. The ICC Court of Arbitration is an administrative body because it does not itself settle disputes (Art. 2, para. 1). The view is offered that a sole arbitrator appointed by the Court has no authority to re-examine the Court's decision regarding the number of arbitrators.

In the last ten years or so three Secretaries-General of the ICC Court of Arbitration have expressed their opinions on this matter. According to one opinion, the Court is bound to appoint three arbitrators whenever a major sum is involved, even if the dispute is not of a complex nature.[61] According to the other opinion, the Court of Arbitration decides on the appointment of the arbitration tribunal, of which the parties normally will each have nominated a member.[62] According

61. Eisemann, *Welthandelsschiedsgerichtsbarkeit - heute* (Vienna 1971) p. 8.

62. Thompson, "The Procedure under the Rules of ICC", in, Schmitthoff, *International Commercial Arbitration* (London-New York 1974-1975) p. 182.

to the third opinion, it is advantageous for the parties not to determine in advance the number of arbitrators, because, for example, what sense would there be in appointing three arbitrators in a dispute involving a sum of 10,000 or 20,000 dollars? In this instance it is preferable to trust in the arbitration institution and to leave to it the determination of the number of arbitrators according to the prevailing situation.[63]

Fouchard and Buchner rank the ICC among arbitration institutions in which an arbitral tribunal consists of one arbitrator.[64]

In international commercial disputes the sum involved is not always the factor which determines the significance which the parties attach to the dispute. It is to be presumed that in international trade relations the parties will not easily decide to initiate a dispute for a small sum unless some other interest is involved, as for example, to establish some facts on the basis of which it will be possible to arrive at conclusions regarding other actions or attitudes of the parties involved or of third parties.

The problem arises as to who is competent to decide on the challenge of an arbitrator appointed by the ICC Court of Arbitration. According to the ICC Rules, the Court, as sole judge of the grounds of challenge, shall make a decision which shall be final (Art. 7). A specific feature of the ICC Court of Arbitration is seen in the fact that the place of arbitration of an arbitral tribunal may be outside the country where the Court has its seat (Art. 13). Since municipal rules and conventions provide for court jurisdiction according to the place of arbitration, the court of the country in which the arbitral tribunal has its place of arbitration will be competent.

Another question is whether the competent court may change the decision of the ICC Court of Arbitration relating to the number of arbitrators. In this respect the Swiss Supreme Court took, on 3 March 1976, the following stand:

> *Le règlement laisse à la Cour toute liberté d'appréciation. A moins que le litige ne lui paraisse particulièrement important la Cour préfère généralement désigner un arbitre unique, en partant de l'idée que, lorsque chaque partie désigne son arbitre, c'est en général le surarbitre qui prend en réalité la seul décision.*
> *Dans ces conditions, la sentence arbitrale n'aurait pu être annulée en raison de la désignation d'un arbitre unique que s'il avait été démontré, d'une façon indubitable, que dans le cas particulier, l'importance du litige était telle qu'elle appelait nécessairement la presence de trois arbitres.*
> *Il convient de relever tout d'abord que seules les décisions de la Court d'arbitrage ne sont pas motivées. Cette Court considère en effect que l'appréciation de l'importance du litige est un pouvoir discrétionnaire de la Court.*[65]

63. Derains, "Le contenu des conventions d'arbitrage", *Revue de l'arbitrage* (No. 1/1979), p. 14.

64. Fouchard, op.cit., *supra* n. 10, p. 165, footnote 14. Bucher, loc.cit., *supra* n. 48, p. 599, footnote 1.

65. BGE 102 Ia, 503-504.

It goes without saying that it is the will of the parties that should primarily be taken into consideration. In stipulating an institutional arbitration, the parties authorize it to proceed in accordance with its Rules. In such cases, too, arbitration is dependent on the voluntary agreement of the parties – the contract. Principles of the contract generally have to be observed. The same rules of construction and interpretation of contracts apply to arbitration agreements.[66]

7. CONCLUSIONS

One way to solve the problem of the present situation could be in the efforts to achieve internationally acceptable uniform rules on international commercial arbitration. We are of the opinion that it would be necessary in the first place to achieve the consensus in principle that international commercial arbitration law should be regulated by rules separate from those regulating municipal arbitration. Secondly, universally acceptable uniform rules for international commercial arbitration should be prepared. This could be done only in the framework of the United Nations using UNCITRAL Arbitration rules as a model, but in the form of non-conventional rules on arbitral procedure restricted to international commercial arbitration.[67] In this way the uniformity in this field would probably be reached in the shortest possible time. The example of UNCITRAL Arbitration Rules is encouraging and shows that it is sometimes more useful to follow such a path instead of drafting international conventions, especially when non-mandatory rules are concerned.

66. Domke, op.cit., *supra* n. 43, p. 30.
67. United Nations General Assembly A/CN. 9/190, 22 April 1980, 3.

INTERNATIONAL ARBITRATION AND NATIONAL ADJUDICATION

by H. van Houtte

1. INTRODUCTION

The relationship between international arbitration and national adjudication raises questions that are basic to the entire law on arbitration. Consequently, it is not feasible to deal fully with this relationship in an introduction of this size. However, the following three aspects of the relationship appear to be the most important ones and will be discussed in some more detail hereafter.

1. "International arbitration" is the common name for different forms of arbitration having some transnational dimension. National adjudication requires a thorough analysis of this vague concept of "international" – or rather "transnational" – arbitration, as well as the distinctions between national arbitration, anational (or quasi-international) arbitration and international arbitration in the strict sense.

2. National adjudication can monitor and enforce international arbitration. The specific powers of the national judge, in this connection, are determined by the national, anational or strictly international nature of the arbitration.

3. Finally, national adjudication can occasionally be influenced in its law-making process by transnational arbitration.

2. NATIONAL, ANATIONAL, QUASI-INTERNATIONAL AND STRICTLY INTERNATIONAL ARBITRATION

Many national legal systems, legal writers and international documents deal with international arbitration. Yet the concept of international arbitration has different meanings for each of them.

Under French law, an arbitration between private parties is "international" when its subject-matter concerns international trade.[1] Under English law, an arbitration has a specific status as an "international" arbitration when at least one party to the arbitration is not a UK citizen or when the arbitration agreement provides for arbitration outside the UK; the subject-matter of the arbitra-

1. Code de procédure civile et commerciale (CPrCCom). as amended by the Décret no. 81-500 of 12 May 1981, Dall. (1981) L 221: Art. 1492 "Est international l'arbitrage qui met en cause des intérêts du commerce international". The arbitration agreement, the arbitral procedure and the award do not need to comply with all the rules applicable to pure domestic arbitration (Art. 1495). Moreover, the "arbitrage international" has specific rules concerning enforcement and remedies (Artt. 1498-1507). Under the previous statute, the validity of the arbitration clause was not affected by the invalidity of the contract in "international arbitration". The disputes, settled through "arbitrage international" might cover public policy matters (ordre public), an area which was forbidden for common French arbitration. Finally, the State and other public entities might be parties to "international arbitrations" – which they could not be in common arbitrations. See, Fouchard, "L'autonomie de l'arbitrage international", Rev. Arb. (1965) at pp. 99-110; For recent developments, see, Level, note to French Cass. 6 June 1978, Rev. Arb. (1979) p. 233, at pp. 238-239.

tion is irrelevant for its international character.[2] For some writers an arbitration is "international" when it settles a dispute relating to an international transaction.[3] The European Convention on International Commercial Arbitration is applicable only when the parties are nationals of different countries and their dispute relates to an international transaction. Other writers give a broader definition of the concept. They consider an arbitration to be "international" when the elements of the arbitration belong to different legal systems.[4] For some authors arbitration is international when it is governed by foreign law.[5] Still, other writers consider an arbitration to be international if it is governed by an international convention on arbitration or international arbitration rules.[6] Finally, authors on international law are of the opinion that only arbitration that is governed by international law, can truly be called international arbitration.[7] Some writers recognize the difficulty of giving a definition and argue that the concept of "international arbitration" changes according to the problems which have to be solved.[8] Others omit any definition.[9]

The term "international arbitration" has too many different meanings to be useful. Yet, the different forms of "international" arbitration have something in common. Indeed, in all these arbitrations the parties, the subject-matter of the dispute, the place of arbitration, the rules applicable to the proceedings, and the substantive law applicable to the dispute, are not all linked to only one national legal system. Because of this common transnational dimension and the different concepts of international arbitration, "transnational arbitration" appears to be a more adequate term to cover all types of international arbitration. The term "international arbitration" will be used hereafter exclusively in the narrow sense of arbitration that is governed by international law.

2. Under English law and through a "non-domestic arbitration agreement" the parties may exclude in advance any right of appeal to the English courts on questions of law. In a pure domestic arbitration, parties can agree to such exclusion only after the commencement of the arbitration. See, Arbitration Act 1979 and commentary of Delaume, XVII ILM (1979) p. 1248 et seq.

3. David, "Arbitrage international ou arbitrage étranger", *Festschrift Ficker* (Frankfurt 1967) p. 121, at pp. 126-127; Foustoucos, *L'arbitrage – interne et international – en droit privé hellénique* (Paris 1976) p. 189; Fouchard, "Quand un arbitrage est-il international?" Rev. Arb. (1970) p. 59, at p. 77; Gentinetta, *Die "Lex Fori" internationaler Schiedsgerichte* (Bern 1973) at pp. 19-31; von Hoffmann, *Internationale Handelsschiedsgerichtsbarkeit* (Frankfurt 1970) at pp. 49-51.

4. E.g., Broches, "The Convention on the Settlement of Investment Disputes between States and Nationals of other States", 136 *Rec.Cours*, (1972) II, p. 331, at p. 381; Schlosser, *Das Recht der internationalen privaten Schiedsgerichtsbarkeit* (Tübingen 1975) no. 28.

5. E.g., Fouchard, loc.cit., *supra*, n. 3, at pp. 61-75; Fouchard, note to French Cass. 11 January 1972, Rev.crit. (1973) at pp. 125-126.

6. Fragistas, "Arbitrage étranger et arbitrage international en droit privé", Rev.crit. (1960) p. 1, at p. 15; Fouchard, *L'arbitrage commercial international* (Paris 1965) n. 39; Schottelius, *Die internationale Schiedsgerichtsbarkeit* (Köln 1957) p. 62.

7. Dehaussy-Goldman, "Arbitrage (en général)", *Dalloz-Droit international*, no. 2.

8. Schlosser, op.cit., no. 27.

9. E.g., the OAS Inter-American Convention on International Commercial Arbitration does not define its subject matter at all. Text: 14 ILM (1975), p. 336; Rev.Arb. (1977) p. 209.

Most transnational arbitrations have what could be called a "nationality".[10] Of course, the term "nationality" is not used here in its ordinary meaning, referring to mutual rights and duties of a State and its citizens.[11] However, in the first instance nationality does express a substantive link between a person and a country. One of its consequences is the State's basic jurisdiction over its citizens.[12] Similarly, the "nationality" of an arbitration follows from a special link between the arbitration and a specific country. Each country considers the arbitration, which has its nationality, as a "domestic" arbitration and assumes jurisdiction over it.

The determination of the "nationality" of an arbitration is not always easy. Some have proposed to use the criterion of the seat of the arbitration. This "seat" is, however, not a factual concept but a legal concept, which can be defined as the "link between the parties to the arbitration and the arbitrator on the one hand, and a judicial forum and national rules of procedure on the other hand".[13] As such, the seat is only a synonym of "nationality" of the arbitration. Others have implied that the parties to an arbitration are free to determine the nationality of their arbitration, for example, by indicating the law which is to govern the proceedings.[14] Yet, there is no doubt that parties are not free to determine the nationality of the arbitration.

Indeed, a nationality – be it of a person or of an arbitration – is not choosen by the parties, but is granted by the State. Moreover, a State may only grant or withhold its own nationality; it may not decide to grant or withhold the nationality of another State. Finally, a State is free to establish its own criteria for granting its nationality to a transnational arbitration. These criteria may differ from one State to another. For example, French law determines that an arbitration has French "nationality" if it is governed by French procedural rules.[15]

10. See also, Lew, *Applicable Law in International Commercial Arbitration* (New York 1978) at pp. 13-14.

11. See, International Court of Justice, *Reports of Judgments* (1955), *Nottebohm Case,* p. 23; "Nationality is a legal bond having as its basis a social fact of attachment, a genuine connection of existence, interests and sentiments, together with the existence of reciprocal rights and duties."

12. E.g., Greig, *International Law* (London 1976) p. 386.

13. Panchaud, "Le siège de l'arbitrage international de droit privé", Rev.Arb. (1966) p. 2, at p. 9.

14. E.g., Fragistas, loc.cit., at pp. 4-14; Klein, "Autonomie de la volonté et arbitrage", Rev.crit. (1958) p. 256, at pp. 276; Metzger, "La jurisprudence française relative aux sentences arbitrales étrangères et la doctrine de l'autonomie de la volonté en matière d'arbitrage commercial international de droit privé", *Mèlanges Maury* (Paris 1960) I, p. 273, at p. 281; Panchaud, loc.cit., at pp. 9-12; Renngli, *Die Grenzen der Parteifreiheit im internationalen privatrechtlichen Schiedsverfahren* (Bern 1955) p. 25; Schlosser, op.cit., no. 642.

15. E.g., Cour d'Appel Paris 28 April 1976, Rev. Arb. 1977, 151; Cour d'Appel Paris, 25 November 1977, Rev. Arb. (1978) p. 491 and more specifically the commentary of Alexandre, at p. 498; Cour d'Appel Paris, 21 February 1980, Dall. (1980) 568 and note Robert; See also von Hoffmann, "Zür Nationalität internationales Schiedsprüche", IPRax (1980) p. 30.

On the other hand, under English law English "nationality" is conferred on any arbitration which is held in England.[16] Some States may even grant their nationality to arbitrations on more exceptional grounds. Iran, for example, suddenly granted its "nationality" to an arbitration, which took place in Switzerland under the local law and in which the National Iranian Oil Company was the losing party.[17] Its purpose, of course, was to give the Teheran Court jurisdiction to delare the award null and void. Although the Teheran court did not explain the legal grounds for granting Iranian "nationality" to the arbitration and for interfering in it, the court implied that Iranian "nationality" was granted because the dispute concerned an oil concession in Iran.[18] However, it should be questioned most seriously whether States have the right to grant their nationality to any arbitration over a subject matter which concerns them. Such an extreme attitude would destroy the purpose of the organization of a transnational arbitration abroad, namely, to avoid the jurisdiction of the courts, which normally would have been competent over the subject matter.

The diversity of the criteria which different countries use to grant their "nationality" to an arbitration, occasionally causes an arbitration to have multiple nationalities or no nationality at all. An arbitration under French law but which is held in England, would have both French and English "nationalities". In a case of multiple nationalities, third States should recognize only that "nationality" which expresses the most substantial link between the arbitration and a judicial forum. Third states should ignore a "nationality" granted on uncommon grounds, and the jurisdiction following from it. As States grant their "nationality" according to different criteria, some arbitrations will have no nationality. For example, an arbitration which takes place in France according to English procedural rules, would be anational. It has neither English "nationality", English nationality being granted exclusively to arbitrations in England, nor French "nationality" which is available only for arbitrations organized under French law.[19] Consequently such arbitration remains "anational" as no country bestows its nationality on it.

A recent decision of the *Cour d'Appel* of Paris evidences the far-reaching consequences of the anationality of an arbitration.[20] A dispute between a Swedish shipbuilder and a Libyan shipowner was submitted to ICC arbitration.

16. Cf., Whitworth Street Estates Ltd. *v.* James Miller & Partners Ltd. [1970] AC 583; [1970] 2 WLR 728.

17. Arbitral Award 15 March 1963, Sapphire International Petroleums Ltd. *v.* National Iranian Oil Company, 35 ILR 136 et seq. The arbitrator decided that the law of the "canton de Vaud" was applicable to the arbitration "since the seat of the arbitration has been fixed at Lausanne" (at p. 169).

18. See, Court, Teheran 1 December 1963, 47 ILR 396, 397; also Matine-Daftary, in "International Commercial Arbitration", *Report of the 54th Conference ILA* (1970) p. 76.

19. See, Cour d'Appel Paris, 5 July 1955, Rev.crit. (1956), p. 79 and Rev. Arb. (1956) p. 48.

20. See, Cour d'Appel Paris, 21 February 1980, D. 1980, 568 with annotations by Robert. See also, the critical observations of von Hoffmann, loc.cit., at p. 30.

This arbitration was held in Paris under ICC rules. When the Libyan shipowner requested the Paris Court to declare the award null and void, the Court refused to intervene because it considered the arbitral procedure not governed by French law but only by the ICC rules. However, the risk that the French judge would refuse to intervene in an arbitration, taking place in France but governed by ICC rules and not by French procedural law, is actually much smaller as the French judge has now a specific jurisdiction over the "international arbitration" regardless of whether it is governed by French procedural law or not.[21]

Whereas the anational character of an arbitration results from the incidental discrepancy between the national criteria for granting "nationality", the quasi-international arbitration is intentionally and deliberately anational. The deliberate anationality of an arbitration is generally inspired by a country's unwillingness to assume jurisdiction over such arbitration. In order to avoid its involvement in the arbitration, the State simply withholds its nationality from the arbitration. This can be the case with arbitrations in which one of the parties is a private enterprise and the other is a foreign State or a public legal entity of a foreign State. The decision of the *Tribunal cantonal du canton de Vaud* illustrates such pragmatic denial of "nationality".[22]

A court can withhold nationality also from an arbitration because it is impressed by the assertion of the arbitrators that their arbitration has no link with a State but is submitted only to international law.[23] Such statements could influence the court, although judges – of course – are not bound by such allegations. But even without such a hint by the arbitrators, a court can decide to withhold nationality if it considers this arbitration – in conformity with recent legal writings – as "quasi-international" [24] or "international to a limited

21. See, *supra*, n. 1.

22. Tribunal cantonal du canton de Vaud, 12 February 1957, Rev.crit. (1958) p. 358, annotated by Aubert. The court based its denial on the consideration that the arbitration was not governed by Vaud procedure because the arbitrators had to render their award within one month while under Vaud law arbitrators have 200 days to render their award. This formalistic agreement was a false basis for the decision: Aubert, ibid., at p. 374.

23. Such assertions were for example made by the arbitrators in Aramco *v.* Saudi-Arabia, Rev.crit., (1963) pp. 304-305, and in Texaco & Calasiatic *v.* Libya, *Journal de Droit International* (1977) p. 325.

24. See, e.g., Bourquin, "Arbitration and Economic Development Agreements", *Selected readings on protection by law of private foreign investments,* (New York 1964) p. 99, at p. 111 and 113; Kipp, "Verträge zwischen staatslichen und nichtstaatlichen Partnern", 5 Ber.D.Ges.VR. (1964) pp. 161-167; Verdross, "Gibt es Verträge die weder dem innerstaatlichen Recht noch dem Völkerrecht unterliegen? ", 6 Zeitschr.f.Rvgl. (1965) p. 129, at pp. 131-132; "Die Sicherung von ausländische Privatrechten aus Abkommen zur wirtschaftlichen Entwicklung mit Schiedsklauseln", 18 ZaöRV (1957) p. 635. The theory of the "quasi-international" agreements was, however, much criticized by Batifoll, "La sentence Aramco et le droit international privé", Rev.crit., (1964) p. 647, at p. 655; Jennings, "Rules governing contracts between states and foreign nationals", in *Symposium on rights and duties of private investors abroad* (New York 1965) p. 123 et seq.; Lalive, "Contracts between a State or a State agency and a foreign company. Theory and practice: choice of law in a new arbitration case", 13 ICLQ (1964) p. 987,

extent".[25]

Finally, some transnational arbitrations are unquestionably international arbitrations, in the strict sense, namely, arbitrations governed by international law. The traditional subjects of international law (States and/or international organizations) are parties to such arbitrations.[26] These arbitrations not only have no nationality; they are truly international.

3. THE JUDICIAL MONITORING AND ENFORCEMENT OF TRANSNATIONAL ARBITRATION

At first sight transnational arbitration has no link with national adjudication. The agreement to arbitrate in principle excludes national adjudication. However, the national courts themselves have to decide whether such agreement deprives them of their jurisdiction.[27] Generally, courts will be prepared not to assume jurisdiction. In fact, the parties often choose transnational arbitration because they prefer the flexibility and secrecy of the arbitrator to the formalism and chauvinism of the court.

Arbitration appears to be independent from national adjudication. When parties submit a dispute to arbitration, they agree impliedly to honour the award. They name the arbitrator or the appointing authority. They often stipulate some details of the arbitral proceedings or refer to the procedural rules the arbitrator has to follow. To be on the safe side parties can even trust the organi-

---

at p. 997; Lalive, "Un récent arbitrage suisse entre un organisme d'état et une société étrangère", Ann. suisse dr. int. (1962) p. 273, at p. 295; Mann, "The proper law of contracts concluded by international persons", BYBIL (1959) p. 34 et seq.; Rengling, *Privatvölkerrechtliche Verträge*, (Berlin 1971) pp. 166-170; Vedel, "Le problème de l'arbitrage entre gouvernements ou personnes de droit privé", Rev.arb. (1961) p. 116, at pp. 128-130; Weil, "Problèmes relatifs aux contracts passes entre un état et un particulier", 128 *Rec.cours* (1969) III p. 101, at pp. 182-183; Wengler, "Les accords entre états et entreprises étrangères sont-ils des traités de droit international?"Rev.crit. (1972) p. 313, at p. 345; Zweigert, "Verträge zwischen staatlichen und nichtstaatlichen Partnern", 5 Ber.D.Ges.VR (1964) p. 194, at p. 199.

25. See, e.g., Böckstiegel, *Der Staat als Verträgspartner ausländischer Privatunternehmen* (Frankfurt, 1971); Fischer, *Die internationale Konzession* (Vienna 1974); Mann, "The theoretical approach towards the law governing contracts between States and private persons", *Revue belge de droit international* (1975) at pp. 562-567; Rengeling, op.cit.; Weil, ibid. However, recently, writers have doubted that an agreement to which a private person is party, could be submitted to international law. See, e.g., Verhoeven, "Droit international des contrats et droit des gens", *Revue belge de droit international* (1978-79) p. 209 et seq.

26. Dehaussy-Goldman, op.cit., no. 2.

27. See, Schlosser, op.cit., at p. 243. For example, the US courts were rather reluctant to renounce their jurisdiction. Nowadays – and through the US ratification of the UN Convention on the Enforcement of Foreign Awards (New York 1958) – they are more willing to respect an agreement to arbitrate. However, see US District Court Southern New York, 21 December 1976 (Wysmuller *v.* U.S.A.) which does not follow the general trend (*Yearbook Commercial Arbitration* III (1978) pp. 290-191 and cases cited in n. 1, p. 291).

zation of the arbitration to a specialized institution, such as the International Chamber of Commerce (ICC). If necessary, the Court of Arbitration of the ICC then appoints or replaces the arbitrator.[28] Finally, the Court even checks the form and substance of the award.[29] In brief, an arbitral institution monitors the arbitral proceedings. The national judge recognizes the monitoring role, which can be played by the institution and will refrain from monitoring such institutional arbitration. However, the jurisdiction of the arbitration institution to organize and monitor the arbitration is still based on the consent of the parties to the arbitration. For example, the ICC arbitration rules clearly reveal this consensual basis: "Where the parties have agreed to submit to arbitration by the International Chamber of Commerce, they shall be deemed thereby to have submitted *ipso facto* to the present rules" [30] and "they shall be deemed to have undertaken to carry out the resulting award without delay . . ."[31] It is true that when a party refuses to participate in an arbitration, the institution can unblock the arbitration by appointing an arbitrator. However, when the default award is not carried out, the arbitral institution will be unable to enforce it. Then only the national court, with its state-authority, can render assistance. A transnational arbitration, organized and monitored by an arbitral institution, is ultimately only truly effective if it can be enforced by a national court.

Ad hoc arbitrations, i.e., arbitrations which are not organized within the framework of an institution, have to rely even more on national adjudication. The national judge not only has occasionally to intervene to enforce the award but, moreover, he is the only authority who can monitor the arbitral proceedings. Consequently, transnational arbitration often depends on national adjudication.

The first possible role of the national judge in connection with arbitration consists in the monitoring of its proceedings. Every legal system regulates how its judges can monitor an arbitration. For example, the Belgian judge has to look at Articles 1676 to 1722 of the Code Judiciaire, whereby the Uniform Act on Arbitration, drafted by the Council of Europe, was introduced into Belgian Law. The English judge has to consult the Arbitration Acts of 1950 and 1979. For his French colleague, Articles 1442 to 1507 of the new Code de Procédure Civile et Commerciale (possibly Articles 1003 to 1028 of the old Code de Procédure Civile) and Articles 2059 to 2061 of the Civil Code are important. His German counterpart has to look at paragraphs 1025 to 1047 of the Zivilprozessordnung. However, all these national laws contain very similar principles

28. *Rules for the ICC Court of Arbitration*, Art. 2: hereafter *Rules.*

29. *Rules,* Art. 21. This supervision of the award would not affect the arbitrator's independence and freedom (Award Paris, 20 April 1972, Rev.Arb. (1973) p. 84). However, several writers criticize this control by the ICC: See, Adlerstein, "Zum Unabhängigkeit der Schiedsrichters", *Studien zum Recht der internationalen Schiedsgerichtsbarkeit* (Köln 1979) p. 9, at pp. 52-54.

30. *Rules,* Art. 8.1.

31. *Rules,* Art. 24.2.

on judicial monitoring. If a party, which had agreed to arbitration, refuses to appoint the arbitrator, the judge can appoint the arbitrator instead of the unwilling party.[32] The judge can also remove an unsuitable arbitrator or fix deadlines for an arbitral procedure which is stagnating. However, the judge will only intervene when he is convinced that the parties have a valid agreement to arbitrate.[33] The details of the rules on judicial monitoring, however, differ from one legal system to another. For example, the precise criteria to assess the validity of an agreement to arbitrate, with respect to its formal as well as to its substantial aspects, are often different from country to country. Where Belgian law forbids the insertion of an arbitration clause in a labour contract (except in a few particular cases) [34], US law permits – and even favours – such insertion. Also the requirements for a valid arbitration procedure and the court remedies for infringements vary from legal system to legal system. Consequently, it is important to know which law is applicable to arbitrations, with important transnational features, as such law decides on the fate of the arbitration.

The law on arbitration is a law on procedure. A court can only apply its own domestic law on procedure. Therefore, a judge will never monitor an arbitration according to a foreign law of arbitration.[35] The question of the applicable procedural law thus coincides with the question which judge has jurisdiction to monitor the arbitral proceedings. A judge has jurisdiction only over domestic arbitrations. Consequently, each judge has to examine whether his legal system would confer its "nationality" on the arbitration. If this is the case, i.e., when the arbitration is "domestic", the judge may monitor it.

As was indicated above, some arbitrations have a double nationality. They will be considered "domestic" and will be monitored by judges of two legal systems. On the other hand, anational arbitrations are considered by no judge as domestic arbitration. Therefore, they cannot be monitored by any national adjudication. They are doomed to float in a legal vacuum where they will be extinguished as soon as the agreement between the parties concerning the arbitration disappears.[36]

Quasi-international and truly international arbitration cannot be monitored by a national judge, as they do not have the nationality of a specific country. Some arbitrations between an investor and a foreign State, which are governed by the World Bank Convention (1965), can be monitored by an international Centre for Settlement of Investment Disputes.[37] However, in general international

32. Belgium: CJud. Art. 1684; Germany: ZPO § 1029; England: Arbitration Act 1950, s. 10; France: Cass. 5 November 1936, Gaz.Pal. 1936, 2.942; Cass. 22 January 1946, Dall. 1946.J. 239; Cass. 5 November 1962, Rev. Arb. (1963), p. 58.

33. Belgium; CJud., Artt. 1676-1678; Germany: ZPO § 1025-1027; 1033; France: CPrC, Artt. 1005-1006; CC Artt. 2059-2061; England: Arbitration Act 1950, sc. 2-3, 32.

34. Belgium: CJud, Art. 1678, 2.

35. Munzberg, *Die Schranken der Parteivereinbarungen in der privaten internationalen Schiedsgerichtsbarkeit* (Berlin 1970) p. 167.

36. See, *supra*, n. 20.

37. Broches, loc.cit., at pp. 365-370.

law no effective authority exists to monitor an arbitration. Even the Permanent Court of Arbitration, which can intervene only as long as the parties consent to its jurisdiction, is of limited efficacy.

The national judge is not restricted only to monitoring domestic arbitration. He can also enforce domestic awards if they are not carried out by the losing party but appear acceptable to the court. He will even declare the award null and void or revoke a recognition if he is convinced that the award should not bind the parties. Yet, the judge will only decide to enforce the award after a control that is even more thorough than the control he exercises as a monitoring judge.[38] Indeed, for the enforcement as well as for the monitoring, the court examines the validity of the agreement to arbitrate and verifies whether the arbitration proceedings were in conformity with the legal requirements. Moreover, an enforcing court also has to check whether the award is final and does not violate public policy ("ordre public").[39] Public policy, however, is a misty term, with a variety of meanings. Public policy, which the award, rendered in a "domestic" transnational arbitration, has to respect, would not be identified with the imperative rules of law, for example, mentioned in the French Civil Code, Article 6 ("lois qui intéressent l'ordre public"). Indeed these rules are not imperative for transnational problems, where foreign law can be applied. It would be illogical for a judge, who himself can discard such imperative rules in transnational cases, to require that the arbitrator should apply them to similar transnational problems. The arbitrator is the alternative to the judge. The "public policy" should have the same content for the domestic arbitrator as for the judge. Consequently, when a judge does not decide a case, but only has to enforce the award of his "alter-ego", the arbitrator, he should require that the latter respects the same fundamental legal and social principles of the domestic legal system as he does. In other words: the judge, who has to disregard foreign law if it is contrary to the fundamental "public policy" of the forum ("exception d'ordre public") [40], should refuse enforcement of a domestic award which ignores this public policy.[41]

Of course, not only domestic, but also foreign awards can be enforced. Such enforcement requires control, which stands midway between the comprehensive control for the enforcement of a domestic award and the more lenient control for the enforcement of a foreign judgment.

38. See, e.g., Belgium: CJud, Artt. 1704, 1711-1714; England: Arbitration Act 1950, s. 26; France: CPrCiv. Artt. 1020, 1026-1028; CPrCCom, Artt. 1484: The "public order" test for "international" domestic arbitration, put on a par with foreign arbitration (Artt. 1498 and 1502), could be less strict than the test for the purely domestic arbitration; Germany: ZPO paras. 1041-1042.

39. Ibid.

40. See, e.g., Batiffol, *Droit international privé* (Paris 1974) Vol. 1, no. 355; Cheshire, *Private international law* (London 1974) p. 148; Rigaux, *Droit international privé,* (Brussels 1978) Vol. 1, nos. 466-468.

41. Idem: Schlosser, op.cit., no. 744.

The enforcement of a foreign award differs from the enforcement of a foreign judgment. A court is supposed to have some deference and comity towards a foreign court, but none towards a foreign private person, who happens to act as an arbitrator. Moreover, where a foreign judgment always reflects the wisdom of the foreign court, only a few foreign awards, of which enforcement is sought, have been controlled by their "national" courts. Consequently, the control, which preceeds the enforcement of a foreign award, is generally more thorough than the control preceeding the enforcement of a foreign judgment. If no convention governs the enforcement, the criteria for enforcement of foreign awards are often quite similar to the standards for the enforcement of domestic awards.[42] The detailed criteria differ, however, from country to country. Consequently, it is not excluded that an award, which is enforceable by the "domestic" court, is declared unenforceable by a foreign judge who uses different standards to control the arbitral proceedings. The New York Convention on the Recognition and Enforeement of Foreign Arbitral Awards (1958) and the European Convention on International Commercial Arbitration (1961) try to align the controlling jurisdiction of foreign courts, where enforcement is sought, to the jurisdiction of the court where the arbitration has its seat.[43] Yet they do not preclude that enforcement, which would be granted by a domestic court, can be refused by courts of another country. An important stumbling-block is the public policy of the court, where the enforcement of a –for this court – foreign award is sought. This public policy can be compared to the public policy which prevents the enforcement of some foreign judgments, and is even less strict than the public policy which prevents the application of foreign law.[44] In fact, however, courts sometimes appear more sympathetic towards foreign judgments than towards foreign awards. Some Belgian court decisions illustrate this point. The Belgian statute on the termination of exclusive distribution contracts (1961) states that this statute is applicable when the distributor covers Belgian territory and that Belgian courts have exclusive jurisdiction over ques-

42. See, e.g., Belgium: CJud., Artt. 1719-1723, of which Art. 1723 indicates that foreign awards can only be enforced when they respect the criteria for the validity of domestic awards. In France and England, the courts enforce foreign awards as they enforce domestic awards: French Cass. 27 July 1937, Dall. 1938, J. 25 – enforcement analogous to old CPrC Artt. 1020-1021, although the courts introduced less strict standards for the "arbitrage international" (see, *supra*, n.1), New CPrCCom, Artt. 1498-1507); Gill, "United Kingdom Report" *Yearbook Commercial Arbitration* II (1977) p. 90, at p. 113.

43. New York Convention, Art. V; European Convention, Art. IX. The setting aside of the award by its "domestic" court makes the award unenforceable in other countries: New York Convention, Art. V.1, e; only if the award is set aside for specific reasons: European Convention, Art. IX, 1 and 2. If the domestic court considers that the arbitration agreement is invalid, the foreign courts are bound by this statement: European Convention, Art. IX, 1, a. The foreign court probably will come to the same conclusion as the domestic court as to the validity of the arbitration agreement because both courts have to apply the proper law, and not the *lex fori* to decide this question: New York Convention, Art. V, 1, a.

44. See, e.g., Batiffol, op.cit., Vol. 2, no. 727; Cheshire, op.cit., p. 661; Schlosser, op.cit., no. 744.

tions of terminations. However, in spite of these strict provisions, Belgian courts have accepted the enforcement of French and German judgments on the termination of a Belgian distribution, although these judgments did not apply the Belgian statute.[45] On the other hand, however, Belgian courts have refused enforcement of a Swiss award on an identical matter which did not apply the Belgian statute.[46] Consequently, the Belgian judge has measured public policy by two standards. In analogous circumstances he has refused enforcement of a foreign award but enforced comparable foreign judgments.

Can anational or quasi-international awards be enforced by national courts? The New York Convention appears inapplicable as it only regulates the enforcement of foreign awards, namely, awards with a foreign nationality.[47] Consequently, each court can only refer to its domestic law to know whether it may enforce anational or quasi-international awards. At first glance, the text of the Belgian arbitration statute which deals with "awards rendered abroad" should not preclude the Belgian judge from enforcing anational awards as long as they are indeed rendered abroad. However, at all events the enforcement of such awards would be delicate as the arbitration was not monitored by any other court. Therefore, the enforcing judge should always control the proceedings of anational or quasi-international arbitrations thoroughly before granting leave for enforcement.

Truly international arbitrations – in principle – cannot be enforced by national courts. However, the national judge can indirectly help the enforcement of international awards. He could for example, grant an attachment on the basis of the international award.[48] State immunity of the attached defendant, however, may reduce this possibility substantially. The awards governed by the World Bank Convention, form an exception to the principle that international awards cannot be enforced by national courts. Indeed. Article 54 of the Convention states that the obligations, imposed by such awards, have to be enforced by the national courts of each Contracting State as if they were imposed by

45. Trib. Brussels, 6 March 1970, *Journal des Tribunaux,* (1970) p. 298; Cour d'Appel Brussels 14 February 1973, *Pasicrisie* (1973) II, p. 100. The statutory exclusive jurisdiction of the Belgian courts was rendered out of date by the EEC Convention on the Recognition and Enforcement of Judgments in Civil and Commercial Matters 1968.

46. Cour d'Appel Liège, 12 May 1977, *Journal des Tribunaux* (1977) p. 710 refused the enforcement on two grounds: (a) the arbitration clause in exclusive distribution contracts are null and void; (b) the award violated public policy. Cass. 28 June 1979, *Journal des Tribunaux* (1979) p. 625 confirmed the appeal decision on the second motivation.

47. See, Dutch Hoge Raad, 7 November 1975, Rev.Arb. (1978) p. 397. overruling its decision of 27 October 1973, NYIL (1974) pp. 290-297, Société Européenne d'Etudes et d'Entreprises (S.E.E.E.) *v.* Federal Republic of Yugoslavia. The preparatory works of the Convention confirm that the Convention does not apply to anational or quasi-international awards: see, Wetzmuller, *Der "internationale" Schiedsspruch im UN Ubereinkommen* (Munchen, 1966) p. 44.

48. The Brussels court decision of 30 April 1951, Rev.crit., (1952) 111, Socobel *v.* Greece stated that the levying of an attachment on the ground of a judgment of the Permanent Court of International Justice of 15 June 1939, (Series A/B no. 78) was technically possible, although it was not granted for procedural reasons. Consequently, the attachment on the basis of an international award remains a possibility.

domestic courts on the simple presentation of a copy of the award certified by the Secretary-General. However, as the Convention confirms that States may invoke their immunity to bar the enforcement (Art. 55), enforced execution of the award is not always secured.[49]

4. INFLUENCE OF TRANSNATIONAL ARBITRATION ON JUDICIAL LAWMAKING

Arbitrators often have more freedom than judges to interprete a contract, to apply trade customs or to make law.[50] Article VII of the European Convention on International Commercial Arbitration confirms that arbitrators consider the contract and trade usages as separate yardsticks alongside national law, while the national judge primarily has to refer to his national law, which may require him to apply these contract terms and trade usages.[51] Hence, commercial arbitration may venture into rather experimental lawmaking. If some new rules, formulated by arbitrators, are proved sound, they may be taken over by the national judges. However, awards seldom become judicial precedents. As arbitration is usually secret, the award remains unknown to the public at large. Publication and discussion of the awards are often restricted to a rather small group of experts. Most law practitioners ignore awards as valuable precedents.

Under French and English law, arbitration can have more influence upon judicial lawmaking. French law provides for the possibility of judicial appeal against the award.[52] If the court confirms the award on appeal, its decision, which takes over the arbitral motivation, becomes a published judicial precedent. Consequently, the judicial appeal against the award could be a way to provide arbitral lawmaking with access to the judicial world. In fact, however, parties generally waive their right of judicial appeal against the award and only on a few occasions has the court on appeal confirmed the arbitral lawmaking in a judicial precedent. Not surprisingly, therefore, this lawmaking influence of arbitration on the courts is ignored by French writers.[53] A more intense influence of arbitral lawmaking on the courts exists in England. Eng-

49. Broches, loc.cit., at pp. 402-404.

50. See, e.g., the arbitral decisions of the ICC commented by Derains in *Journal de Droit International* (1974) p. 876 et seq.; (1975) p. 916 et seq.; (1976) p. 968 et seq.; (1977) p. 931 et seq.; (1978) p. 976 et seq.; (1979) p. 982 et seq., and the awards published in *Yearbook Commercial Arbitration* since 1976. Furthermore, the more comprehensive studies in Lew op.cit.,; van Houtte, *Rechtsvinding bij Transnationale Handelarbitrage,* (Louvain 1977).

51. E.g., France & Belgium: CC, Art. 1134; "Les conventions légalement formées tiennent lieu de loi à ceux qui les ont faites . . ."; Art. 1135; "Les conventions obligent non seulement à ce qui est exprimé, mais encore à toutes les suites que l'équité, l'usage ou le loi donnent à l'obligation."

52. New CPrCCom, Art. 1482 et seq.

53. See, e.g., Robert, *Arbitrage civil et commercial* (Paris 1967) no. 26.

lish arbitration had the "special case" which allowed an arbitrator to "state any question of law in the course of the reference . . . for the decision of the High Court." [54] Through the "special case" a close relationship and cooperation developed between the arbitrators and the court. The arbitrator referred difficult questions of law to the judge, who had to state the law. More than half of the work of the commercial courts arose from arbitration.[55] In fact, the arbitrators often did not only state the case, but as experts in the trade, they seized the opportunity to propose the court's answers to the questions of law they raised. In this way, many English judgments merely confirmed the arbitrator's lawmaking. The special case was a frequent phenomenon. It was particularly important for the court to remain in touch with the problems of business communities, such as the maritime world, which preferred arbitration to court jurisdiction. Through the special case, important questions of law concerning charterparties, which were almost exclusively submitted to the London Maritime Arbitration, nevertheless reached the courtroom. As the court decisions were often publicized, the answer to a "special case" became a judicial precedent for lawyers, courts and arbitrations. For example, the well-known cases on frustration, which arose from the closure of the Suez Canal in 1956, entered English contract law through the special case.[56] The special case was one of the attractions of English arbitration which tempted foreigners.[57] It guaranteed to the parties that arbitrators would correctly administer the law. It was a support for the arbitrators and an opportunity for the judges to attain uniform application of the law.[58] However, the special case brought with it a supplementary, expensive and time-consuming court procedure. This disadvantage often outweighed its advantage. By the 1979 Arbitration Act the procedure of the special case was abolished and replaced by a more limited right of appeal to the court on questions of law.[59] The appeal cannot be abused to gain time or to delay the enforcement of the award. Parties can even contract out of such appeal. In brief, the possibility for interaction between English courts and arbitrators with regard to lawmaking, although still important, is not so elaborate as it was with the "special case."

54. Arbitration Act 1950, s. 21.

55. Kerr, "The English Courts and Arbitration", *International Commercial Arbitration* (New York 1974) pp. 199-237, 214-226; Kahn-Freund, "La notion anglaise de la "proper law of the contract" devant les juges et les arbitres", Rev.Crit. (1973), p. 607, at p. 621, ***Russell on the Law of Arbitration,*** (London 1970) pp. 244-260.

56. Cheshire, *Law of Contract,* (London 1976) pp. 551-552.

57. Ellenbogen, "Commercial Arbitration" 1 *Business Law Review* (1954) p. 247, at p. 265.

58. The special case had to prevent that "in time codes of law would come to be administered in various trades differing substantially from the English mercantile law": Chaznikow & Co. *v.* Roth, Smidt & Co. (1922) 2 KB 478, at p. 491.

59. Text: XVIII ILM (1979) p. 1249.

5. CONCLUSION

The relationship between transnational arbitration and national adjudication is as intricate as the relationship between a dynamic youngster and more established adults. The comparison could be made: the arbitration has the initiative and freedom of the youngster, while the judge, as with some adults, often belongs to a stagnant world of procedure, formalism and authority. Just as some adults could profit from the reasoning of youngsters, who are more exposed to the actual currents of society, so the judge could profit from his exposure to the sometimes innovative reasoning of arbitrators who, as under English law, may even directly ask him for advice. Just as adults may be blind to the values of youngsters, so judges often ignore the input that arbitration could give. Moreover, as a youngster may only grow up satisfactorily, when he receives help from the adult world if he is in trouble, transnational arbitration may only be effective if it may rely in emergencies on the help and authority of the national judge. This judge could monitor the arbitral proceeding or enforce the award. However, just as adults who are asked for help do not align their decisions to each other, so the national judges, who may thus intervene in the transnational arbitration, have no aligned decisions either.

ANNEX

ILLUSTRATIVE BELGIAN AND DUTCH CASE LAW

1. Cass. (1re ch.), 28 juin 1979 * *(Audi-NSU c. s.a. Adelain Petit et crts.)*

I. – *La signification de l'arrêt à l'étranger, à la requête de la société défenderesse qui connaissait, par l'acte d'appel, le domicile élu de la demanderesse en Belgique, est non avenue et n'a pas fait courir contre la demanderesse le délai de pourvoi en cassation.*

II. – *La reconnaissance des sentences arbitrales étrangères par le juge belge est, en principe, soumise à la condition qu'au regard de la loi belge, le litige soit susceptible d'être réglé par voie d'arbitrage et puisse donc être soustrait à la juridiction des tribunaux.*

La Convention entre la Belgique et la Suisse sur la reconnaissance et l'exécution des décisions judiciaires et de sentences arbitrales, signée à Berne le 29 avril 1959 et approuvée par la loi du 21 mai 1962, ne déroge par à cette règle qui est d'application même si elle n'est pas expressément formulée par les conventions internationales.

III. – *Le litige relatif à la résiliation par le concédant d'un contrat de concession de vente exclusive produisant ses effets dans tout ou partie du territoire belge n'est pas susceptible d'être réglé par la voie d'un arbitrage convenu avant la fin du contrat et qui a pour but et pour effet d'entraîner l'application d'une loi étrangère.*

IV. – *Dans un litige portant sur les conseqûences de la violation par le concédant d'un contrat de concession de vente exclusive, telles que le paiement de dommages et intérêts ou la résolution du contrat, l'obligation à laquelle il faut se référer aux fins de l'application de l'article 5, 1o de la Convention de Bruxelles du 27 septembre 1968 entre les Etats membres de la Communauté économique européenne concernant la compétence judiciaire et l'exécution des décisions en matière civile et commerciale, est celle qui découle du contrat à charge du concédant et dont l'inexécution est invoquée pour justifier la demande de dommages et intérêts ou de résolution du contrat de la part du concessionnaire.*

En conséquence, l'obligation de payer l'indemnité de résiliation prévue par l'article 2 de la loi du 27 juillet 1961 n'est pas une obligation contractuelle autonome, mais une obligation remplaçant l'obligation contractuelle inexécutée de donner un préavis raisonnable.

Cette dernière obligation s'analyse pour le concédant en la continuation, pendant la durée du préavis, de l'exécution de son obligation principale, celle de respecter l'exclusivité du concessionnaire sur le territoire concédé et doit dès lors s'exécuter en l'espèce, en Belgique, comme l'obligation principale de la demanderesse.

---

* *Journal des Tribunaux* (1979) p. 625.

Ouï M. de conseiller Meeùs en son rapport et sur les conclusions de M. Krings, avocat général;

Vu l'arrêt attaqué, rendu le 12 mai 1977 par la cour d'appel de Liège;

Sur la fin de non-recevoir opposée au pourvoi par la défenderesse et déduite de ce qu'il est tardif pour avoir été formé le 18 novembre 1977, soit plus de trois mois après la signification de l'arrêt attaqué par la transmission de l'exploit de signification par le procureur du Roi de Liège au président de l'Amtsgericht d'Ingolstadt, en République fédérale d'Allemagne, qui l'aurait reçu au plus tard le 12 août 1977, sans que la demanderesse puisse se prévaloir de l'augmentation de délai de quinze jours prévue par les articles 55, 1°, et 1073 du Code judiciaire, ayant, dans son acte d'appel, élu domicile en Belgique:

Attendu qu'il apparaît des pièces de la procédure que la demanderesse a, dans son acte d'appel, élu domicile en Belgique et que la défenderesse a fait signifier l'arrêt rendu sur cet appel au domicile de la demanderesse en République fédérale d'Allemagne;

Attendu qu'aux termes de l'article 40, alinéa 4 du Code judiciaire, la signification à l'étranger ou au procureur de Roi est non avenue si la partie à la requête de laquelle elle a été accomplie connaissant le domicile ou la résidence ou le domicile élu en Belgique ou le cas échéant, à l'étranger du signifié;

Attendu que, par application de cette disposition, la signification de l'arrêt à l'étranger, à la requête de la défenderesse qui connaissait, par l'acte d'appel, le domicile élu de la demanderesse en Belgique, est non avenue et n'a pas fait courir contre la demanderesse le délai de pourvoi; que celui-ci n'est pas tardif;

Que la fin de non-recevoir ne peut être accueillie;

Sur le premier et le deuxième moyens, pris, le premier, de la violation des articles 3, 6, 1133 du Code civil, 1er, 2, 3, 6 de la loi du 27 juillet 1961 relative à la résiliation unilatérale des concessions de vente exclusive à durée indéterminée, respectivement modifiés par les articles 1er, 2, 3 et 6 de la loi du 13 avil 1971, et, pour autant que de besoin, de la violation desdits articles; des articles 4 de ladite loi du 27 juillet 1961, 23 à 28, 1723 du Code judiciaire, 1er, 9-1 et 12-2 de la Convention entre la Belgique et la Suisse sur la reconnaissance et l'exécution de décisions judiciaires et de sentences arbitrales, signées à Berne le 29 avil 1959 et approuvée par la loi du 21 mai 1962, et, pour autant que le besoin, de la violation de ladite loi; de l'article 7-1 de la Convention pour la reconnaissance et l'exécution des sentences arbitrales étrangères faite à New York le 10 juin 1958 et approuvé par la loi du 5 juin 1975 et, pour autant que de besoin de la violation de ladite loi; de l'article 9 de la Convention européenne en matière d'arbitrage faite à Strasbourg le 20 janvier 1966 et approuvée par l'article 1er de la loi du 4 juillet 1972, et, pour autant que de besoin, de la violation dudit article et de l'article 97 de la Constitution,

en ce que, pour rejeter le moyen par lequel la demanderesse invoquait, dans ses conclusions régulièrement prises en degré d'appel, en se fondant sur les articles 1er et 9-1 de la Convention belgo-suisse signée à Berne le 29 avril 1959 et approuvée par la loi du 21 mai 1962, l'autorité de chose jugée attachée aux sentences arbitrales des 30 mars 1974 et 6 décembre 1975, ainsi qu'à la décision du 1er juillet 1974 du Tribunal Supérieur du canton de Zürich, et, par voie de conséquence, l'irrecevabilité de l'action mue par la défenderesse devant les tribunaux belges, l'arrêt décide: ≪ que la Convention entre la Belgique et la Suisse sur la reconnaissance et l'exécution de décisions judiciaires et de sentences arbitrales, signée à Berne le 29 avril 1959 et approuvée par la loi du 21 mai 1962, publiée au *Moniteur* du 11 septembre 1962 et entrée en vigueur le 15 octobre 1962, prévoit que "les sentences arbitrales prononcées dans l'un des deux Etats seront reconnues dans l'autre et y seront rendues exécutoires" à condition que "le reconnaissance de la décision ne soit par incompatible avec l'ordre public de l'Etat où elle est invoquée" (art. 9-1 et 1er 1, *a*), mais n'exclut par l'application d'autres conventions ou accords auxquels les deux Etats sont ou seront parties et qui règlent ou règleront la reconnaissance et l'exécution des décisions judiciares ou des sentences arbitrales (art. 12-2) ≫,

alors que, *première branche*, l'arrêt laisse ainsi incertain s'il a refusée de reconnaître l'autorité de chose jugée des sentences arbitrales susdites parce qu'il a estimé que l'une des conditions requises à cet effet par la Convention belgo-suisse du 29 avril 1959, à savoir la compatibilité de la reconnaissance de la sentence avec l'ordre public de l'Etat où elle est invoquée, n'était pas remplie en l'espèce ou s'il a considéré que la reconnaissance des sentences arbitrales ne pouvait être accordée parce que le litige n'était pas susceptible d'arbitrage; d'où il suit que l'arrêt est fondé sur des motifs dont l'imprécision ne permet pas à la Cour d'exercer son contrôle sur la légalité de son dispositif et que, partant, il n'est pas régulièrement motivé (violation des dispositions visées au moyen et spécialement de l'article 97 de la Constitution);

deuxième branche, l'arrêt ne répond pas au soutènement par lequel la demanderesse démontrait, de manière circonstanciée, dans ses conclusions additionnelles régulièrement prises en degré d'appel que les sentences arbitrales précitées n'étaient incompatibles ni avec l'ordre public international belge ni avec l'ordre public interne belge, étant celui de l'Etat où elles étaient invoquées; d'où il suit que, si l'arrêt devait être interprété comme ayant refusé la reconnaissance desdites décisions arbitrales en raison de leur incompatibilité avec l'ordre public belge, interne ou international, l'arrêt ne serait par régulièrement motivé: 1° à défaut d'avoir répondu auxdites conclusions (violation de l'article 97 de la Constitution), 2° en ce qu'il laisse à tout le moins incertain en quoi aurait consisté cette incompatiblité avec l'ordre public belge ou international (violation de l'article 97 de la Constitution);

troisième branche, les dispositions de la loi du 27 juillet 1961 relative à la résiliation unilatérale des concessions de vente exclusive à durée indéterminée, telle qu'elle a été modifiée par la loi du 13 avril 1971, ne revêtent pas un caractère d'ordre public international ni même d'ordre public interne, mais constituent uniquement des dispositions impératives; que la Convention belgo-suisse ne vise, en ses articles 9-1 et 1er-1, *a*, que le cas où la reconnaissance de la sentence arbitrale serait contraire à l'ordre public et même à l'ordre public international; que, si l'arrêt doit être interprété comme ayant refusé la reconnaissance des sentences arbitrales litigieuses sur la base de la Convention belgo-suisse du 29 avil 1959 au motif que cette reconnaissance serait contraire à l'ordre public interne ou internationale, il méconnaît le caractère simplement impératif de la loi du 27 juillet 1961 (violation des dispositions visées au moyen et spécialement des articles 3, 6, 1133 du Code civil, 1er, 2, 3, 4 et 6 de la loi du 27 juillet 1961);

quatrième branche, dut-on même admettre, *quod non*, que la loi du 27 juillet 1961, telle qu'elle a été modifiée par celle du 13 avril 1971, aurait un caractère d'ordre public, encore ne s'agirait-il que de dispositions d'ordre public interne belge, et non d'ordre public international; la Convention belgo-suisse du 29 avril 1959 à laquelle se réfère l'arrêt n'exclut la reconnaissance que des sentences arbitrales incompatibles avec l'ordre public international du pays où elles sont invoquées; que, dès lors, s'il devait être interprété comme ayant refusé la reconnaissance des décisions arbitrales susdites en raison de leur incompatibilité avec l'ordre public international belge, l'arrêt aurait, à toute le moins, conféré à tort aux dispositions de la loi du 27 juillet 1961 visées au moyen le caractère de dispositions d'ordre public international (violation des dispositions visées au moyen et spécialement des articles 3, 6, 1133 du Code civil, 1er, 2, 3, 4 et 6 de la loi du 27 juillet 1961);

cinquième branche, l'arbitrabilité du litige ne figure pas parmi les conditions auxquelles la Convention belgo-suisse du 29 avril 1959 subordonne la reconnaissance des sentences arbitrales rendues dans l'un des Etats contractants; que l'article 12-2 de cette Convention visé par l'arrêt n'a pas pour effet d'en restreindre la portée et de permettre aux tribunaux des Etats contractants de refuser la reconnaissance d'une sentence arbitrale rendue sur le territoire de l'un de ceux-ci en invoquant des conditions qui seraient posées par d'autres Conventions internationales auxquelles ils seraient parties, et qui ne figureraient pas dans ladite Convention belgo-suisse; que, l'article 12-2 dut-il même être interprété en ce sens, *quod non*, encore faut-il constater que les autres Conventions internationales en matière de reconnaissance de sentences arbitrales auxquelles la Belgique et la Suisse sont parties, à savoir la Convention de New York du 10 juin 1958 pour la reconnaissance et l'exécution des sentences arbitrales étrangères et la Convention européenne portant loi uniforme en matière d'arbitrage faite à Strasbourg le 20 janvier 1966, prévoient respectivement en leurs articles 7-1 et 9 qu'elles ne portent pas attainte à l'application des conventions bilatérales ou multilatérales conclues ou qui viendraient à être conlues entre parties contractantes et que, par conséquent, elles ne portent notamment pas atteinte à la Convention belgo-suisse; d'où il suit que s'il fallait l'interpréter comme ayant refusée la reconnaissance des sentences arbitrales précitées au motif que le litige n'était pas susceptible d'arbitrage, l'arrêt aurait ajouté à la Convention belgo-suisse une condition qu'elle ne prévoit pas et partant, ne serait pas légalement justifié (violation des dispositions visées au moyen et spécialement des articles 1er, 9-1, 12-2 de la Convention belgo-suisse du 29 avril 1959, 7-1 de la Convention de New York du 10 juin 1958, 9 de la Convention de Strasbourg du 20 janvier 1966 et 1723 du Code judiciaire):

le deuxième, de la violation des articles 1134 du Code civil, 1676, spécialement alinéa 1er, 1703 du Code judiciaire, 1-1 de la Convention belgo-suisse sur la reconnaissance et l'exécution de décisions judiciaires et de sentences arbitrales, signée à Berne le 29 avril 1959 et approuvée par la loi du 21 mai 1962 et, pour autant que de besoin, de la violation de ladite loi, 5, spécialement 2, de la Convention pour la reconnaissance et l'exécution des sentences arbitrales étrangères faite à New York le 10 juin 1958 et approuvée par la loi du 5 juin 1975 et, pour autant que de besoin, de la violation de ladite loi, VI, spécialement 2, de la Convention européenne sur l'arbitrage commercial international faite à Genève le 21 avril 1961 et approuvé par la loi du 19 juillet 1975 et, pour autant que de besoin, de la violation de ladite loi, 24 de la loi uniforme annexée à la Convention européenne en matière d'arbitrage faite à Strasbourg le 20 janvier 1966 et approuvée par la loi du 4 juillet 1972 et, pour autant que de besoin, de la violation de ladite loi, 1er, 2, 3 et 6 de la loi du 27 juillet 1961 relative à la résiliation unilatérale des concessions de vente exclusive à durée indéterminée, respectivement modifiés par les articles 1er, 2, 3 et 6 de la loi du 13 avril 1971 et, pour autant que le besoin, de la violation desdits articles, et des articles 4 de ladite loi du 27 juillet 1961 et 97 de la Constitution,

en ce que l'arrêt décide que ≪ la loi du 27 juillet 1961, en son article 6, prive d'effets toutes conventions que le concessionnaire aurait conclues avant la fin du contrat au sujet de ses droits quant à la nature de concession à durée indéterminée, comme au préavis et aux diverses indemnités résultant de la résiliation unilatérale de la concession; qu'en l'espèce, la clause compromissoire stipulée avant la fin du contrat et supposant la possibilité d'une transaction était une disposition prohibée; que le litige, portant à titre principal sur la nature du contrat et sur les conséquences de sa résiliation unilatérale par le concédant, comme les demandes qui lui sont accessoires et, partant, nécessairement connexes, n'était, dès lors, pas susceptible d'être réglé par voie d'arbitrage; que la loi de police du 27 juillet 1961 fait donc obstacle à ce que soient reconnues et acquièrent autorité de chose jugée en Belgique tant la sentence arbitrale et la décision du Tribunal Supérieur de Zürich sur la compétence que la sentence arbitrale sur le fond≫, considérant ainsi que les litiges en matière de concessions exclusives de vente à durée indéterminée ne sont pas susceptibles d'arbitrage et écartant pour ce motif le déclinatoire de juridiction soulevé par le demanderesse dans ses conclusions d'appel principales et additionnelles ainsi que l'exception de chose jugée qu'elle invoquait également dans les mêmes conclusions, à tout le moins, en ce qui concerne cette seconde exception, si l'arrêt doit être interprété comme l'ayant rejetée en raison du caractère non arbitrable du litige,

alors qu'aucune disposition de la loi du 27 juillet 1961, telle qu'elle a été modifiée par celle du 13 avril 1971, n'interdit aux parties de prévoir une clause compromissoire dans leur contrat de concession de vente exclusive à durée indéterminée et que le recours à l'arbitrage n'est par conséquent pas incompatible avec les dispositions de cette loi et en particulier avec son article 6 visé par l'arrêt; qu'il en est ainsi, même si la clause compromissoire prévoit l'application au litige d'une loi autre que la loi belge; que les Conventions internationales existantes en matière d'arbitrage, et en particulier la Convention belgo-suisse du 29 avril 1959, la Convention de New York du 10 juin 1958, la Convention européenne de Genève du 21 avril 1961 sur l'arbitrage commercial international et la Convention européenne de Strasbourg du 20 janvier 1966 portant loi uniforme en matière d'arbitrage ne restreignent pas la validité ou la reconnaissance des clauses compromissoires et des sentences rendues sur la base de celles-ci en fonction de la loi déclarée applicable au litige; que la Convention de Genève du 21 avril 1961 prévoit au contraire en son article VII que les parties sont libres de déterminer le droit que les arbitres devront appliquer au fond du litige; d'où il suit qu'en décidant que le litige n'était, en l'espèce, pas susceptible d'arbitrage, l'arrêt viole toutes les dispositions visées au moyen:

Quant à la *première branche* du premier moyen:

Attendu que, se fondant sur l'analyse de la Convention entre la Belgique et la Suisse sur la reconnaissance et l'exécution de décisions judiciaires et de sentences arbitrales et de différentes autres Conventions internationales en matière d'arbitrage auxquelles la Belgique est partie, l'arrêt énonce ≪ qu'ainsi, il apparaît que les Conventions internationales et, en termes explicites, la Convention européenne portant loi uniforme du 20 janvier 1966, autorisent expressément le juge du pays où la sentence arbitrale est invoquée à rejeter celle qui règle un différend dont la solution est, en vertu de son propre droit, soustraite à l'arbitrage; qu'en tout cas, la sentence arbitrale ne doit être reconnue que si elle n'est pas contraire à l'ordre public de l'Etat où elle est invoquée, notamment aux lois de police et de sûreté, en l'espèce la loi du 27 juillet 1961≫; que, dans le dispositif de l'arrêt, la cour d'appel dit n'y avoir lieu à la reconnaissance des sentences arbitrales visées au moyen, ces décisions ayant été rendues à la suite d'un compromis ou d'une clause compromissoire non valables d'après la loi belge qui leur est applicable et l'objet desdites sentences n'étant pas susceptible d'être réglé par la voie de l'arbitrage selon la même loi, et au surplus la reconnaissance de ces décisions étant contraire à l'ordre public international belge en vertu de la loi de police et de sûreté du 27 juillet 1961;

Attendu qu'il ressort des considérations et du dispositif de l'arrêt que celui-ci fonde sa décision, sans ambiguité, sur deux motifs distincts;

Qu'en cette branche, le moyen manque en fait;

Quant à la *cinquième branche* du premier moyen et quant au deuxième moyen:

Attendu qu'en sa *cinquième branche,* le premier moyen soutient qu'en fondant sa décision sur le motif que le litige n'était pas susceptible d'être réglé par voie d'arbitrage, l'arrêt viole les Conventions internationales en matière d'arbitrage qu'il cite et en particulier la Convention belgo-suisse;

Attendu que la reconnaissance des sentences arbitrales étrangères par le juge belge est, en principe, soumise à la condition qu'au regard de la loi belge, le litige soit susceptible d'être réglé par voie d'arbitrage et puisse donc être soustrait à la juridiction des tribunaux;

Attendu que la Convention entre la Belgique et la Suisse sur la reconnaissance et l'exécution de décisions judiciaires et de sentences arbitrales, signée à Berne le 29 avril 1959 et approuvée par la loi du 21 mai 1962, ne déroge pas à cette règle qui est d'application même si elle n'est pas expressément formulée par les Conventions internationales;

Que cette règle est confirmée par la Convention pour la reconnaissance et l'exécution des sentences arbitrales étrangères, faite à New York le 10 juin 1958 et approuvée par la loi du 5 juin 1975, qui dispose en son article 5-2, *a*, que la reconnaissance et l'exécution d'une sentence pourront être refusées si l'autorité compétente du pays où la reconnaissance et l'exécution sont requises constate que d'après la loi de ce pays, l'objet du différent n'est pas susceptible d'être réglé par voie d'arbitrage; que cette Convention a été ratifiée par la Suisse;

Qu'en cette branche, le moyen manque en droit;

Attendu que le deuxième moyen soutient qu'en décidant que le litige n'était pas en l'espèce, susceptible d'arbitrage, l'arrêt viole toutes les dispositions visées au moyen;

Attendu que la loi du 27 juillet 1961 relative à la résiliation unilatérale des concessions de vente exclusive à durée indéterminée, modifiée par la loi du 13 avril 1971, dispose en son article 4 que le concessionnaire lésé, lors d'une résiliation d'une concession de vente produisant ses effets dans tout ou partie du territoire belge, peut en tout cas assigner le concédant en Belgique, soit devant le juge de son propre domicile, soit devant le juge du domicile ou du siège du concédant, et que dans le cas où le litige est porté devant un tribunal belge, celui-ci appliquera exclusivement la loi belge;

Qu'en vertu de l'article 6 de la même loi, les dispositions de celle-ci sont applicables nonobstant toutes conventions contraires conclues avant la fin du contrat accordant la concession;

Attendu que ces dispositions impératives ont pour but d'assurer, dans tous les cas, au concessionnaire le droit d'invoquer la protection de la loi belge, sauf s'il y a renoncé par une convention conclue après la fin du contrat accordant la concession;

Attendu qu'un litige relatif à la résiliation par le concédant d'un contrat de concession de vente exclusive produisant ses effets dans tout ou partie du territoire belge n'est, dès lors, pas susceptible d'être réglé par la voie d'un arbitrage convenu avant la fin du contrat et qui a pour but et pour effet d'entraîner l'application d'une loi étrangère;

Attendu qu'en l'espèce, l'arrêt constate que le contrat de concession de vente exclusive liant les parties contient en son article 16 une clause compromissoire donnant compétence à un collège arbitral siégeant à Zürich et que l'article 15 du contrat prévoit l'application du droit de la République fédérale d'Allemagne;

Que l'arrêt relève, en outre, que le même article 15 du contrat stipule que le lieu d'exécution de l'obligation est au siège social de la demanderesse, en Allemagne; que l'arrêt considère, à cet égard, que cette clause est en opposition avec la nature des choses, la concession devant s'exécuter sur le territoire belge, qu'elle n'est qu'un artifice inspiré par la volonté d'échapper à l'application de la loi belge, ainsi qu'il résulte notamment des termes d'une lettre de la demanderesse, et décide, en conséquence, que ladite clause ne peut être interprétée que comme constitutive de fraude à la loi;

Attendu qu'il résulte des considérations qui précèdent qu'en refusant la reconnaissance des sentences arbitrales visées au moyen et en leur déniant l'autorité de la chose jugée pour le motif que le litige n'était pas susceptible en l'espèce, au regard de la loi belge, d'être réglé par la voie de l'arbitrage, l'arrêt justifie légalement sa décision;

Que le deuxième moyen ne peut être accueilli;

Quant aux *deuxième, troisième et quatrième branches* du premier moyen:

Attendu que l'arrêt ayant légalement, ainsi qu'il ressort des considérations qui précèdent, refusé l'autorité de la chose jugée aux sentences arbitrales invoquées, le premier moyen, fût-il fondé en ses *deuxième, troisième et quatrième branches,* ne pourrait entraîner la cassation de la décision attaquée;

Qu'en ces branches, il est irrecevable à défaut d'intérêt;

Sur le troisième moyen, pris de la violation des articles 6, 1133, 1134, 1167, 1321, 1382, 1383 du Code civil, 2 et 5, spécialement 1°, de la Convention entre les Etats membres de la Communauté économique européenne concernant la compétence judiciaire et l'exécution des décisions en matière civile et commerciale, signée à Bruxelles le 27 septembre 1968 et approuvée par la loi du 13 janvier 1971 et, pour autant que de besoin, de la violation de ladite loi et de l'article 97 de la Constitution,

en ce que, pour rejeter le déclinatoire de compétence opposé par la demanderesse dans ses conclusions d'appel, l'arrêt décide que les tribunaux belges sont compétents sur la base de l'article 5, 1° de la Convention de Bruxelles du 27 septembre 1968, le lieu d'exécution de l'obligation litigieuse étant la Belgique et écarte ainsi l'article 1er (lire 15) du contrat de concession de vente exclusive du 24 août 1961 (lire 1971) prévoyant que le lieu d'exécution dudit contrat était Neckarsulm, au motif que «le choix d'une ville allemande comme lieu d'exécution d'une convention de concession de vente sur un territoire étranger à la République fédérale d'Allemagne (provinces belges et Grand-Duché de Luxembourg) est en opposition avec la nature des choses et n'est qu'un artifice inspiré par la volonté d'échapper à l'application de la loi belge sur la concession à durée indéterminée et ne peut être interprété que comme constitutif de fraude qui, à elle seule, entraîne la nullité de l'article 15 du contrat» et décide en conséquence «que le lieu d'exécution des obligations de l'appelante vis-à-vis de l'intimée était en Belgique», et non en Allemagne comme le prévoyait le contrat de concession et qu' «en vertu de l'article 5, 1°, de la Convention C.E.E., tel qu'il est interprété par la Cour de justice, le premier juge était territorialement compétent »; que l'arrêt écarte et annule ainsi l'article 15 du contrat de concession au motif que celui-ci constituerait une fraude à la loi belge,

alors que les Conventions légalement formées ont force obligatoire, que la théorie de la fraude à la loi n'est pas admise en droit interne hors le cas, étranger à l'espèce, de la fraude aux droits des tiers; d'où il suit que l'arrêt, en refusant de donner effet à l'article 15 du contrat de concession, en a méconnu la force obligatoire (violation de l'article 1134 du Code civil) et n'a en tout cas pas légalement justifié ce refus (violation de toutes les dispositions visées au moyen):

Attendu qu'il ressort des motifs de l'arrêt reproduits dans la réponse au deuxième moyen, que la cour d'appel a considéré que la clause contenue dans l'article 15 du contrat de concession de vente exclusive et déterminant le lieu d'exécution de l'obligation, avait pour objet de simuler un élément d'extranéité contraire à la réalité des choses et que la demanderesse avait ainsi eu pour but d'ècarter par un artifice la loi belge normalement applicable, au profit d'une loi étrangère;

Que l'arrêt décide que cette clause, constitutive de fraude à la loi, est nulle;

Qu'ainsi l'arrêt justifie légalement sa décision;

Que le moyen ne peut être accueilli;

Sur le quatrième moyen, pris de la violation des articles 1247, spécialement alinéa 2 du Code civil, 2, 5, 1° et 5°, de la Convention entre les Etats membres de la Communauté économique européenne concernant la compétence judiciaire et l'exécution des décisions en matière civile et commerciale, signée à Bruxelles le 27 septembre 1968 et approuvée par la loi du 13 janvier 1971, et, pour autant que de besoin, de la violation de ladite loi, et des articles 1er, 2, 3 et 6 de la loi du 27 juillet 1961 relative à la résiliation unilatérale des concessions de vente exclusive à durée indéterminée, respectivement modifiés par les articles 1er, 2, 3 et 6 de la loi du 13 avril 1971 et, pour autant que le besoin, de la violatiron desdits articles et des articles 4 de ladite loi du 27 juillet 1961 et 97 de la Constitution,

en ce que l'arrêt décide qu' ≪en vain l'appelante (ici demanderesse) invoque le caractère alternatif de son obligation – préavis ou indemnité – alors que le paiement de cette dernière constitue l'exécution par équivalent de l'obligation non exécutée, ou mal exécutée, de donner un préavis raisonnable qui dont s'exécuter en Belgique et ne peut lui-même par conséquent être exécuté ailleurs qu'en Belgique; que le principe de la quérabilité de la dette est inapplicable aux obligations qui, spécifiques de la concession exclusive, s'exécutent nécessairement au lieu où s'exploite la concession ≫, que par conséquent le lieu d'exécution de l'obligation litigieuse, à savoir le paiement de l'indemnité prévue par l'article 2 de la loi du 27 juillet 1961, est la Belgique, que les tribunaux belges sont compétents pour connaitre du litige et écarte pour ce motif le déclinatoire de compétence soulevé par la demanderesse,

alors que, *première branche,* comme le soutenait la demanderesse dans ses conclusions d'appel, l'obligation de payer l'indemnité prévue par l'article 2 de la loi du 27 juillet 1961, tel qu'il a été modifié par celle du 13 avril 1971, constitue une obligation autonome de celle de donner un préavis raisonnable prévu par le même article et ne revêt pas le caractère compensatoire que lui attribue l'arrêt; que par conséquent c'est le lieu d'exécution de l'obligation de payer cette indemnité qui détermine la compétence des tribunaux sur la base de l'article 5, 1° de la Convention de Bruxelles; d'où il suit qu'en décidant que l'obligation de payer l'indemnité due en vertu de l'article 2 de la loi du 27 juillet 1961 est compensatoire par rapport à celle qui est prévue par le même article de donner un préavis raisonnable et en prenant pour ce motif en considération cette dernière obligation pour fonder la compétence des tribunaux belges, l'arrêt viole les dispositions visées au moyen et spécialement les articles 5, 1° de la Convention de Bruxelles du 27 septembre 1968 et 2 de la loi du 27 juillet 1961;

deuxième branche, comme le soutenait également la demanderesse dans ses conclusions d'appel, l'obligation de payer une indemnité constitue un paiement qui, en vertu de l'article 1247, alinéa 2 du Code civil, doit être fait au domicile du débiteur; qu'en effet, ledit article 1247, alinéa 2 est applicable à toutes les obligations de paiement, en ce compris celles qui naissent dans le cadre de la rupture d'un contrat de concession de vente exclusive à durée indéterminée; qu'aucune disposition de la loi du 27 juillet 1961, telle qu'elle a été modifiée par celle du 13 avril 1971, ne déroge audit article 1247 en ce qui concerne les paiements d'indemnitées dues en vertu de cette loi; que, dès lors, en l'espèce, l'obligation autonome de payer l'indemnité doit s'exécuter au siège social de la demanderesse, à savoir en Allemagne, et que seuls les tribunaux allemands étaient en conséquence compétents comme le soutenait la demanderesse; d'où il suit qu'en rejetant le déclinatoire de compétence opposé par la demanderesse, dans ses conclusions d'appel au motif que l'obligation de payer l'indemnité prévue par l'article 2 de la loi du 27 juillet 1961 doit s'exécuter au lieu où la concession était exploitée, à savoir en Belgique, l'arrêt viole les dispositions visées au moyen et spécialement les articles 1247 du Code civil et 2 de la loi du 27 juillet 1961:

Attendu que la demanderesse, qui ne critique pas, en ce moyen, la décision de l'arrêt suivant laquelle la loi belge est applicable, soutient que, l'obligation de payer l'indemnité prévue par l'article 2 de la loi du 27 juillet 1961 relative à la résiliation unilatérale des concessions de vente exclusive à durée indéterminée devant en vertu des dispositions de cette loi et de l'article 1247 du Code civil s'exécuter au siège social de la demanderesse en Allemagne, seuls les tribunaux allemands et non les tribunaux belges sont compétents, au regard de l'article 5, 1° de la Convention de Bruxelles du 27 septembre 1968 entre les Etats membres de la Communauté économique européenne concernant la compétence judiciaire et l'exécution des décisions en matière civile et commerciale, approuvée par la loi du 13 janvier 1971, pour connaître de l'action en paiement de cette indemnité;

Attendu que l'article 5, 1° de la Convention de Bruxelles dispose que «le défendeur domicilié sur le territoire d'un Etat contractant peut être attrait dans un autre Etat contractant: 1° en matière contractuelle, devant le tribunal du lieu où l'obligation a été ou doit être exécutée»;

Attendu que, ainsi que la Cour de justice des Communautés européennes l'a décidé par son arrêt n° 14/76 du 6 octobre 1976, dans un litige opposant le bénéficiaire d'une concession exclusive de vente à son concédant à qui il reproche d'avoir violé la concession exclusive, le terme «obligation» qui se trouve inscrit audit article 5, 1° se réfère à l'obligation contractuelle servant de base à l'action judiciaire, c'est-à-dire à l'obligation du concédant correspondant au droit contractuel qui est invoqué pour justifier la demande du concessionnaire;

Que, dans un litige portant sur les conséquences de la violation par le concédant d'un contrat de concession de vente exclusive, telles que le paiement de dommages-intérêts ou la résolution du contrat, l'obligation à laquelle il faut se référer aux fins de l'application de l'article 5, 1° de la Convention est celle qui découle du contrat à charge du concédant et dont l'inexécution est invoquée pour justifier la demande de dommages-intérêts ou de résolution du contrat de la part du concessionnaire;

Attendu que, dans le système de la loi du 27 juillet 1961, ainsi que cela est confirmé par les travaux préparatoires de cette loi et par ceux de la loi du 13 avril 1971, lorsqu'il est mis fin par une des parties à une concession de vente exclusive à durée indéterminée, l'octroi d'un préavis raisonnable constitue la règle et ce n'est qu'à défaut de préavis qu'une indemnité compensant les avantages d'un préavis et calculée en fonction de ces avantages doit être accordée;

Que l'obligation de payer l'indemnité de résiliation prévue par l'article 2 de la loi n'est donc pas une obligation contractuelle autonome, mais une obligation remplaçant l'obligation contractuelle inexécutée de donner un préavis raisonnable;

Que cette dernière obligation s'analyse pour le concédant en la continuation, pendant la durée du préavis, de l'exécution de son obligation principale, celle de respecter l'exclusivité du concessionnaire sur le territoire concédé, et doit, dès lors, s'exécuter en l'espèce en Belgique, comme l'obligation principale de la demanderesse;

Que l'arrêt décide, sans violer les dispositions invoquées au moyen, que l'obligation de payer l'indemnité prévue par l'article 2 de la loi du 27 juillet 1961 doit s'exécuter en Belgique;

Que le moyen manque en droit;

Par ces motifs:

La Cour,

Rejette le pourvoi.

2. Société Européenne d'Etudes et d'Entreprises (Paris) v. Socialist Federal Republic of Yugoslavia *

History of the case

In 1932 a contract was concluded between S.E.E.E. and the Yugoslav Government for the construction of a railway from Veles to Prilep (Yugoslavia). During the years 1932 to 1937 these works were carried out to satisfaction of the Yugoslav Government. Because of the Second World War payments were suspended. After the war, in 1950, a settlement was reached between the Yugoslav Government and the French Government, acting on behalf of S.E.E.E. (diplomatic protection). The residual debt, determined by this settlement, was paid off by the Yugoslav Government and received by S.E.E.E. without reservations. Thereafter S.E.E.E. asked for additional payments because of the devaluation of the French franc.

As the Yugoslav Government refused these payments, S.E.E.E. invoked the arbitration clause contained in the original 1932 contract. This clause provided for the appointment by each of the parties of an arbitrator and, in case these two arbitrators could not reach agreement a third arbitrator (tiers arbitre) would be appointed by the President of the Tribunal Civil of Lausanne. The arbitrators would have to decide as 'amiables compositeurs'. As the Yugoslav Government did not appoint an arbitrator (a.o. on the ground that the arbitration agreement had become null and void as a result of the 1950 agreement between the two Governments) the above-mentioned President appointed André Panchaud as arbitrator, whilst S.E.E.E. appointed Georges Ripert as arbitrator. The two arbitrators rendered an *ex parte*-award in favour of S.E.E.E. on July 2, 1956, the Yugoslav Government not taking part in the proceedings (Publication in French and English in Journal du Droit International 1959, p. 1074 seq.).

The Yugoslav Government introduced an action for setting-aside of the award. On February 12, 1957 the Tribunal Cantonal of Vaud decided, without setting aside the award, that the Ripert-Panchaud decision was not an arbitral award in the sense of Article 516 of the Code of Civil Procedure and that consequently this decision, filed at the Court, should be given back to the party who had deposited it. The Tribunal Fédéral confirmed this judgment on September 18, 1957. Both judgments are published in the Revue Critique de Droit International Privé (1958),

* *Yearbook Commercial Arbitration* (1976) Vol. 1, p. 195.

p. 358 seq., with note Aubert (in French). The federal judgment may also be found in the Revue de l'Arbitrage (1957) p. 100.

Since then, S.E.E.E. has tried on several occasions and in several countries, to get the 1956 award enforced. In these court proceedings many interesting questions were raised. We are concerned here only with those questions which concern the application of the New York Convention 1958 as dealt with by the Dutch courts.

Dutch Judgments
In the Netherlands the *President of the Rotterdam Court* (of first instance) November 9, 1971, refused for other reasons than the existence of the New York Convention enforcement of the award. This decision, refusing leave for enforcement (exequatur) for reasons of State immunity, has only been published in Netherlands Yearbook of International Law (NYIL), 1972, p. 294. An extract of this rather short decision may also be found in the article written by A.M. Stuyt (in English) in the Neth. Yearbook of International Law 1974 p. 35-58, entitled 'Misconceptions about International (commercial) Arbitration'. This article gives a complete survey of the S.E.E.E.-Yugoslavian case up to the Supreme Court (Hoge Raad) October 26, 1973, with extensive commentary.

A. The Hague Court of Appeal September 8, 1972, reversed the decision of the President Rotterdam. At this stage S.E.E.E. for the first time introduced arguments based on the New York Convention, ratified by the Netherlands in 1964 and by Switzerland in 1965 (Yugoslavia has not acceded to this Convention). The Court's judgment has been reported in full in Revue de l'Arbitrage (1972) p. 313 et seq., in French translation. A summary in English has been published in NYIL (1973) p. 390-391. Some extracts (in English) may be found in Stuyt's article. The Court annulled the President's decision, but refused the exequatur as well (see infra).

B. The Supreme Court (Hoge Raad) 26 October 1973 reversed the decision of the Hague Court of Appeal and remitted the case to this Court. This decision is published in full in Nederlandse Jurisprudentie (Netherlands Law Reports) 1974 no. 361 in Dutch. A French translation of the Supreme Court's decision is published in Revue de l'Arbitrage 1974, p. 318 seq. An English translation is published in NYIL (1974), p. 290-297.

C. The Hague Court of Appeal on October 25, 1974, dealing for the second time with this case, again refused enforcement. Until now this judgment has only been published (in French) in Revue de l'Arbitrage 1974, p. 322 seq.

The publication of the three judgments, A, B and C in the Revue de l'Arbitrage 1974 is followed by a note by Batiffol, p. 326-330.

D. The Supreme Court (Hoge Raad) 7 November 1975 brought the case to an end. Although the Supreme Court did not follow the reasoning of the Court of Appeal, it did not remit the case to this Court again but decided the case itself in favour of Yugoslavia. (Provisionally published in Dutch in 'Court decisions of the Week' (1975, no. 91).

Extracts of the decisions of the Court of Appeal (2 x) and the Supreme Court (2 x) are given below in chronological order.

A. Hague Court of Appeal, September 8, 1972
Article I, para. I, of the Convention does not make any exception on behalf of States or other legal persons of public law. On the contrary, it follows from the preparatory works (travaux préparatoires) of the Convention that States are also

included under the term 'differences between persons, whether physical or legal' at least when they act *iure gestionis.* The conclusion of a contract for the construction of a railway with delivery of material is not an act *iure imperii* even if the railway was constructed for military or strategic purposes, which intention was not expressed in the contract or in another manner brought to the knowledge of S.E.E.E. The Rotterdam President was wrong in accepting the exception of State immunity.

Nor can the fact be accepted as defence that Yugoslavia did not adhere to the Convention. This fact does not entail that the Convention could not be applied in cases in which Yugoslavia is a party to an arbitration agreement.

However the defence that the decision of Ripert and Panchard is not an arbitral award in the sense of Article I, para. I, is justified. In spite of the liberty left to the parties as to the composition of the arbitral tribunal and the arbitral procedure (Article V, para. I, sub *d*), the Convention is based on the fact that some national law will be applicable to the arbitral award. This follows both from Art. V, para. I, sub *e* and from Art. I, para. 3: the law of the State where the award was made. According to the judgment of the Tribunal Cantonal de Vaud of February 12, 1957, which has been confirmed by the Tribunal Fédéral (see history supra) the Ripert/Panchaud decision does not constitute an arbitral award in the sense of Art. 516 of the Code of Civil Procedure of Vaud. Consequently, this document is not an arbitral award in the sense of the Convention, made on the territory of a State other than the Netherlands.

The Court declares itself competent to deal with the case but rejects the request for exequatur (leave for enforcement).

B. Supreme Court (Hoge Raad) 26 October 1973

There is an international tendency to restrict the cases in which a State can invoke in a foreign court its immunity. This immunity cannot be claimed in the present case where the State entered, on an equal footing, into a contract of private law with S.E.E.E. There is also no reason to deny the applicability of the Convention to arbitral awards in which Yugoslavia was a party on the ground that this State did not adhere to the Convention. These points of the judgment of the Hague Court of Appeal were therefore confirmed.

However, the Supreme Court did not follow the Court of Appeal where it decided that enforcement should be refused because the Tribunal Cantonal de Vaud decided that the Ripert/Panchaud decision was not an arbitral award in the sense of Art. 516 C.P.C. of Vaud, from which decision the conclusion was drawn that this document was also not an arbitral award in the sense of the Convention. Only in connection with the grounds for refusal mentioned in Article V, para. I, and more particularly in connection with the grounds *a, d* and *e,* questions arise which must be answered on the basis of a specific national law. Only in those cases does the Convention contain rules referring to the law of a specific country. The refusal of the exequatur by the Court of Appeal on the ground of non-recognition by the Tribunal Cantonal de Vaud of the decision as an arbitral award was, therefore, based on incorrect grounds. The case was remitted to the Hague Court of Appeal.

C. Hague Court of Appeal 25 October 1974

The Court, after the judgment of the Supreme Court, has now to decide on the original request of S.E.E.E. for an *exequatur* (leave for enforcement), taking into account the observations of the Supreme Court. Against this request the Yugoslav Government has also opposed that such an exequatur would be contrary to the public policy of the Netherlands.

The agreement reached in 1950 between the French and the Yugoslavian delegation (see history of the case supra) must be regarded as an agreement of international law. The arbitral award in question is in contravention of the said agreement because Yugoslavia has been condemned to pay an additional amount. The enforcement of the award would be contrary to Dutch public policy as this could lead – in violation of an agreement of international law entered into by Yugoslavia – to a seizure of Yugoslavian property in the Netherlands. Leave for enforcement must therefore, as against public policy, be refused.[1]

D. Supreme Court (Hoge Raad) 7 November 1975

The Supreme Court held that the Court of Appeal, in giving an interpretation of the 1950 agreement different from the earlier one of the arbitrators, exceeded the task of a judge who has to decide on a request for *exequatur*. The *exequatur* judge has to accept the facts as determined by the arbitrators, his task not being to examine the facts *de novo*. The Court of Appeal violated this rule when, basing itself on its own interpretation of the 1950 agreement between the French and the Yugoslavian governments, it arrived at the conclusion that the enforcement of the arbitral award would be against Dutch public policy (see under C). The task of the exequatur judge is restricted to an investigation as to whether there exist legal grounds for refusal of enforcement, including those contained in international conventions. He is not allowed to go into the merits of the case itself again.

Nevertheless, in exceptional cases, the Court could refuse enforcement as being contrary to 'public policy' when the arbitrators would have given, in their award, an interpretation of the parties' contract which no reasonable arbitrator would ever give. This was not the case and had not even been argued on behalf of the Federal Republic of Yugoslavia.

The Supreme Court did not remit the case to the Court of Appeal for a second time, but decided the case itself. It referred first of all to Article V para. 1 under *e*. Although the Swiss Court did not set aside the award because they did not regard the arbitral decision as an award under their national law, nonetheless the consequence of this court decision was that 'the decision of Messrs. Ripert and Panchaud was deprived, by a competent authority of the country where the decision was made, of the possibility to be enforced in that country as an arbitral award'. This has to be equated to the setting-aside of the arbitral award as mentioned under *e*.

The Supreme Court added that it would come to the same result in a case where on the basis of para. 1 under *d* it would be accepted as the intention of the Convention to recognize as arbitral awards also those which 'in consequence of the procedure agreed upon by the parties, cannot be deemed to be connected with the law of any specific country and of which the enforceability is thus based exclusively on the Convention and not as well on the national law of any country with which the award is connected'. In the present case there can be no question of such an

1. Compare, between the same parties (S.E.E.E. v. Yugoslavia) the French decision of President Tribunal de grande instance, Paris, 8 July 1970, Semaine Juridique 1971, Jurisprudence 16810; also published in Journal du Droit international 1970, p. 131. Also in France the exequatur was refused, not because of the immunity of the Yugoslavian State (which argument was rejected on the same grounds as under A and B of the Dutch judgments) but because enforcement of the Ripert/Panchaud award which deviated from the settlement made between Yugoslavia and France in 1950 (which also settled S.E.E.E.'s claim, sponsored by the French Government) would be against French public policy (see C above). This decision is not reported here as neither the New York Convention 1958 (nor the Geneva Convention 1927) were considered.

award as the agreement between the parties, from which the arbitrators derive their competence, was concluded (in 1932) long before the date of the Convention (1958). Consequently, it could not have been their intention to obtain such an (extranational) award.

With this judgment of the Supreme Court the case reached its end. S.E.E.E.'s request for an exequatur was rejected as far as the Netherlands are concerned.

ARBITRATION: DISCUSSIONS

The Chair was taken by Professor Clive M. Schmitthoff who proposed that the ensuing discussion should be focused on the issues that had been emphasised in the report of Professor Van Houtte.

In the oral presentation of his report Professor Van Houtte paid special attention to the definition of the concept of internationality in commercial arbitration, as well as to that of "nationality", or seat *c.q.* place of arbitration. Professor Goldstajn's report was introduced by Miss Rosabel Everard,* a senior research officer in the T.M.C. Asser Instituut. In her oral presentation Miss Everard elaborated on what could be considered the main theme of Professor Goldstajn's paper: the need for co-operation between arbitrators and domestic courts in international adjudication.

1. THE CONCEPT OF INTERNATIONALITY

The notion of "international" in such expressions as private international law and international commercial arbitration, presupposes the existence of standards by which to distinguish between international and purely domestic cases in view of the law to be applied or the process of adjudication to be followed. Searching for such standards, it was submitted, is by no means a mere academic exercise. If it is true to say that private international law and international commercial arbitration constitute legal disciplines separate from their domestic counterparts – and in many respects this is indeed true, – there is every practical reason to try and define the dividing line between the international and the domestic areas within the broader system of substantive private law and private law of procedure. And if it is to be assumed that domestic courts should be inclined to allow for a more liberal approach and to "internationalize" standards of domestic law whenever such standards are to be applied to international rather than to purely domestic cases, it would seem of the greatest importance to bring about some certainty as to where that dividing line should be drawn. Here, the doctrine of "international public policy" provides a good illustration.

It is often maintained that on the international level standards of domestic public policy do not necessarily apply. The tendency, clearly noticable in court practice, to qualify public policy requirements when judging cases that are not of a purely domestic nature and accordingly to redress the negative effects of applying domestic public policy standards, is widely applauded: "International public policy, according to a generally accepted doctrine, is confined to violation of really fundamental conceptions of legal order in the country concerned. For the sake of international commercial arbitration the distinction between domestic and inter-

* Most regrettably, Professor Goldstajn was prevented from attending duc to intervening personal reasons.

national public policy is of great importance." (P. Sanders, "Trends in the field of international commercial arbitration", *Recueil des Cours* (1975) II, p. 224.)

However generally accepted the doctrine of international public policy may be, the circumstances under which that doctrine should prevail are very hard to define. The question whether in a given case rules of international law apply, is essentially a question of the relevance of foreign – c.q., non-domestic – elements in the case for it to be subjected to standards of international law including internationalized standards of municipal law. In answering that question in respect of international commercial arbitration, one would have to differentiate between the various stages of arbitral intervention: the agreement to arbitrate, the arbitral intervention proper and the enforcement of the arbitral award.

Assuming that for the purpose of indicating a dividing line one succeeded in listing the relevant elements, the time factor would still have to be included. If, for instance, in respect of the contractual, first stage in arbitration, the domicile of the parties were to be deemed a relevant element for deciding on the internationality of the case, the precise moment at which this criterion would effectively apply, would have to be defined and one would have to assess the effects that would result from changes of domicile during the arbitration process. On the other hand, one would have to take into account that in practice the effects of internationality are not necessarily unique and unambiguous. It may well be so, that courts are inclined to confine international public policy to a means by which to redress violation of fundamental conceptions of legal order, but it is similarly true that the readiness to liberalize domestic standards depends to a considerable extent on the degree to which a case, however international in nature, affects the domestic legal order.

The fringe area between domestic and international cases or arbitration is a region not easy to mark and one that should be navigated with care and a good deal of "local knowledge", both on the part of the national judiciaries and on that of the arbitrators and more particularly the international arbitration institutions. Much of the local knowledge required comes down in fact to this; that each of these partners in adjudication be fully aware of the course steered by the other and in being prepared to adjust his course so as to avoid unnessary hindrance to the other. This is where Professor Goldstajn's plea for co-operation between courts and arbitrators finds its place, a plea in which the latter joined so many other experienced arbitrators and writers on international commercial arbitration.

The fringe area indicated is of course not completely unmarked. Through legislation and particularly through international conventions some very important beacons have been placed. In this connection mention was made of the New York Convention of 1958, which in delimiting its field of application, steers clear of the criterion of the nationality of the parties, avoids any definition of "internationality" and simply accommodates its scope to the territorial demarcation provided by the State boundaries. The Convention does, admittedly, deviate slightly from this clear and straight course where, in the same provision, it states, that it shall also apply *"to arbitral awards not considered as domestic awards in the State where their recognition and enforcement are sought."* However, legal practice concerning international commercial arbitration does not seem to have been affected by this additional provision. In his study of the New York Convention, Dr. Albert Jan van den Berg calls the criterion contained in the latter provision, a "discretionary" one: "The (second) criterion will be applicable only if a court *"considers"* an award as non-domestic. It means that a court has the discretion whether or not to apply the (second) criterion, and hence the Convention, to an award made within its own territory." (A.J. van den Berg, *The New York Arbitration Convention of 1958,* The Hague/Deventer 1981, p. 25.)

It was suggested, however, that this explanation does not seem quite correct. The Convention does not really attribute discretionary powers to courts either to apply the Convention or to leave it aside. In the present provision it introduces an *interpretatio lege fori* in respect of the notion of "domestic". Provisions of this kind are not at all uncommon. Reference was made, in this connection, to the European Judgments Convention, which was concluded in the same year as the New York Arbitration Convention: 1958. When placed in the general legal framework of a convention, notions like "domestic" and "international" are hard to define so as to make them really fit the great variety of cases to which courts may have to apply them. Attempts at listing standards by which precisely to distinguish between "domestic" and "international" are likely to end up in a search for the key to that mental exercise which is in the very nature of adjudication: the amalgamating of fact and law – the chemistry of justice.

2. THE SEAT OF ARBITRATION

As the issue of "internationality" was discussed, questions connected with the "nationality", *c.q.* seat or place of arbitration were gradually introduced into the discussion.

Arbitration is essentially a contractual institution and party autonomy is, consequently, a major factor in the functioning of this particular form of adjudication. The fundamental role played by the will of the parties explains, on the one hand, the vast opportunities arbitration offers to the business world in terms of efficiently settling disputes in accordance with the requirements of the particular trade involved. On the other hand, it is due to that same contractual nature of arbitration that arbitrators – and the parties themselves – are faced with serious limitations when the arbitral intervention comes to a point where the kind of authority and the powers, to which private parties will not normally have access other than through the State controlled mechanism of checks and balances, have to be exercised: the combined forces of the Judiciary and the Administration, for which only States bear responsibility.

The ambivalent nature of (international) arbitration – embedded, as it is, in the contractual freedom of individual parties and embraced, as it may often find itself, at the same time, by the restrictive practices of individual States or State organs – is particularly apparent in such issues as the "nationality" or the "seat" of arbitration and the choice of the *lex arbitralis* by the parties.

There is little doubt that the arbitrators will be bound by the agreement of the parties as to the place where the arbitration should (formally) be held and the domestic legal system that should apply and to which the arbitrators will have to accommodate the conduct of the arbitration. There is little doubt, either, that, generally speaking, parties may choose to have arbitration conducted under a legal system other than that of the State where the arbitrators are supposed to actually prepare and make the arbitral award. It is precisely with a view to a situation of this kind that the above mentioned second criterion of Article 1, paragraph 1, of the New York Convention, pertaining to *"arbitral awards not being considered as domestic awards"* was included in that Convention. It was submitted, moreover, that the choice made by the arbitrators as to the place where they will actually have their conferences will not affect the place of arbitration or the lex arbitralis as formally agreed upon by the parties. Whenever arbitrators, it was maintained, would choose to conduct their investigations and prepare their award in States other than that indicated by the parties, they would have to make sure that, formally, their arbitration would be in full accordance with the requirements set forth by the law of the State to which the parties have chosen to link their case. Arbitrators who would act otherwise, would risk making themselves liable to damages.

There appeared to be far less certainty as to the answers to be given to such questions as whether parties are entitled to "internationalize" an otherwise predominantly – or even purely – domestic arbitration. If it were only a matter for the arbitrators to act upon such intentions of the parties, the fact that the internationality of the arbitration would merely rest upon their agreement would hardly pose a problem. In the background there is, however, always the possibility that, in the event, the administrative machinery of a sovereign State may have to be engaged and that the intervention of a national judiciary may have to be sought, either for the arbitration to be effectively conducted or for the arbitral award to be enforced. Party autonomy might then be regarded as too meagre a connection for the arbitration to be handled as an international arbitration.

3. TRANSNATIONAL ARBITRATION

In case parties have agreed to disengage the arbitration from every national jurisdiction so as to make sure that no particular arbitration law will have to complied with, the resulting arbitration will be a "floating", or "de-nationalized" one, a third form of arbitration, to be distinguished from the purely domestic, as well as from the international arbitration. There was some recognition of the advantages such de-nationalized arbitrations could offer, particularly in respect of disputes in which sovereign States are involved and where arbitration might be a more attractive mode of settlement if the domestic legislation of whatever sovereign State could be disregarded.

In actual practice, the de-nationalized arbitration has so far played a very modest role. The case of the *General National Maritime Transport Co.* v. *Götaverken Avendal AB* was the obvious example to refer to in this connection. In this case the arbitration had actually taken place in France. Exequatur was sought in Sweden where the Svea Court of Appeal issued an enforcement order in spite of the award being challenged before a court in France. The Swedish Supreme Court upheld the decision of the Court of Appeal. In a commentary (J. Paulsson, "The Role of Swedish Courts in transnational commercial arbitration", *Virginia Journal of International Law* (1981) p. 239) the Swedish scholar of international law, Professor Jan Paulsson states: "The Supreme Court's reasoning reaffirmed one of the fundamental objectives of the New York Convention's elimination of the "double exequatur" principle of the Geneva Convention. Adoption of the word *binding* in Article V(1)(e) of the New York Convention was intended to make an award enforceable as soon as ordinary means of recourse are no longer available." Paulsson continued by pointing out that the Supreme Court has, indeed, viewed the distinction between ordinary and extra-ordinary challenges to awards as critical: "When the parties had accepted arbitration as constituting *final* disposition of their dispute, however, the award becomes, as the Court held, binding 'as of the moment and by virtue of the very fact that it was rendered';"etc.

Whatever the advantages may be of severing all links with national jurisdictions and the affilliated arbitration laws, the disadvantages of so de-nationalizing an arbitration may turn out to be quite considerable. And however commendable it may be under circumstances for domestic courts engaged in an exequatur-procedure, to disregard delaying tactics applied by one of the parties in the State where the award was made, for the parties themselves expressly to dissociate their arbitration from whatever national jurisdiction, might well prove a risky course to take. Assistance by a domestic court may often be required, either for the appointment of arbitrator in case parties fail to agree at this point, or for the taking of (coercive) *interim* measures, or possibly, for the taking of evidence from witnesses under oath.

4. THE ISSUE OF PUBLIC POLICY

There was general agreement on the need to distinguish between three classes of public policy: the domestic standards of public policy, international public policy as a form of domestic public policy liberalized in view of the international nature of a given case, and, thirdly, the internationally recognized, generally binding, principles of law.

In this connection, the view was expressed that disclosure to the parties of the names of the arbitrators might well be regarded as a fundamental requirement of due process in international commercial arbitration. Parties are fully entitled to know the names of those who judge their case so as to be able to check on each arbitrator's personal position in relation to the opposing party and to make sure of impartiality.

It is not an easy task for an arbitrator to anticipate, in the conduct of the arbitration as well as in the making of the final award, the various standards of public policy by which his work may be judged by the variety of national courts that will be engaged for enforcement. It was strongly felt, that arbitrators should put emphasis on heeding the general principles of international law and on the standards of the *lex arbitralis* rather than to try and comply with the law of the – possibly unspecified – countries where enforcement could eventually be sought.

Particularly with regard to exequator procedures before domestic courts, arbitrators, and the parties involved, should confidently rely upon a willingness on the part of domestic courts liberally to internationalize standards of public policy as contained in their *lex fori*. In this, arbitration may greatly benefit from relying upon the widely recognized authority of the international arbitration institutions from whose standards valuable guidance can be derived. Finally, parties might contribute greatly by avoiding to complicate unnecessarily the arbitral interventions they may agree upon. Unnecessary complications might well result from a de-nationalization of the arbitration, as explained earlier.

Returning to the position of the arbitrator and the desirability of his intervention being conducted in such a way as to make it as solid and "challenge-proof" as possible, the discussion then switched to the conditions that should ideally be met for an arbitration to secure a definitive settlement.

It was strongly felt that as a requirement of due process there should be the possibility of having an award reviewed and that awards should be keenly motivated. The former requirement is common in arbitration clauses of standard contract forms, such as contract forms currently used in marine insurance and by commodity associations. In this connection mention was made of the review of arbitral awards by courts of justice, as provided for under English law by the Arbitration Act of 1979. This Act replaces the case stated procedure which tended to produce frequent and long reviews in the courts, with a relatively simple procedure aimed at reviewing arbitral interventions on points of law.

Having discussed the arbitral intervention in the light of public policy requirements and in connection with the possiblity, *c.q.* the need for appeal in arbitration procedures, attention was finally focused on the initial stage of the arbitration: the contract to arbitrate.

5. THE CONTRACT TO ARBITRATE

The Chairman invited the participants to comment upon the following question: Should international arbitrators be competent to decide on their own competence, and should the arbitral agreement contained in the contract be regarded as separate from the contract itself?

It was submitted that the UNCITRAL rules of 1976 as well as the I.C.C. rules grant the so-called competence-competence to arbitrators and express themselves in favour of separability. English law, however, presents a somewhat different picture in that parties may directly apply to the courts to have the competence of the arbitrators decided upon. In as far as separability is concerned, English law does not leave room for the contract to be split up for this purpose.

As to the question of competence-competence the situation in Yugoslavia appears slightly different from that under English law. Parties in Yugoslavia may require arbitrators to speak out on their competence. In that event the arbitral tribunal will be enlarged so as to comprise five arbitrators: the three initial arbitrators, the President and the Vice President of the Permanent Court of Arbitration (Belgrade Arbitration Commission). In case the arbitrators would be deemed to have surpassed their competence, it is up to the parties to apply for anullment of the decision. There is no automatism in this competence-procedure. It all depends on a party making an application for the competence to be investigated and decided upon.

The position under Dutch law, it was maintained, is very similar, although the competance of arbitrators would not be judged in a kind of review procedure. Like in Yugoslavia, parties would normally seek the intervention of a court to have the competence of the arbitrators definitively decided. On the other hand, courts in The Netherlands are not likely to judge the competence of arbitrators without having regard to the opinion of the arbitrators involved. Normally, when this issue is raised in court proceedings, courts will stay proceedings in anticipation of the findings of the arbitrators on the question of competence. The same policy is followed when (conservatory) attachment is levied in a case that is to be judged by arbitration. Validation of an attachment will only be decided once the arbitrators have spoken out on the merits of the case. In anticipation of the arbitral award the validation procedure will normally be stayed.

Norwegian practice, it was understood, comes close to that followed in Yugoslavia.

Finally the issue of separability was raised. The Chairman formulated the issue as follows: Suppose one has a contract which contains an arbitration clause. It is alleged that this contract is null and void *ab initio*. Would the arbitrators have jurisdiction to decide this question?

From the answers given it was clear that the attitude in West Germany, the Netherlands and Yugoslavia was in favour of separability, while that prevailing in England and Norway was opposed.

APPENDIX

STUDENT REPORTS ON A NATIONALIZATION CASE

THE CASE

A natural gas exploitation company (Gasexco), established in Rijeka, Yugoslavia or Rotterdam, the Netherlands and carrying on exploitation in various parts of the world, starts business on its own account (without creating a subsidiary) in the developing country Pulentia. Encouraged by promising exploration results and by good cooperation with the local authorities, Gasexco orders in 1976 a drilling platform ("HZ 80") at a cost of $ 5 million from a shipyard in the Federal Republic of Germany for operation in Pulentian territorial waters. The contract contains a choice of forum clause bestowing competence on the court in Rijeka (Rotterdam) but no choice of law clause. Delivery is to take place in Rijeka (Rotterdam), Gasexco to arrange for transportation to the coast of Pulentia. For assistance at another exploitation site, on the high seas (nearest coast Pulentia, but not in any economic zone nor on any continental shelf), where Gasexco is also operating, the Company has hired a team of specialized workers from the Government of Pulentia for the last two months of 1978, under a contract concluded in Pulentia with the Pulentian Mining Department (PMD). No choice of law or choice of forum clause is inserted in this contract.

On 18 October 1978 a *coup d'état* occurs in Pulentia and a Revolutionary Council assumes power. On 1 November 1978 the Council issues a Decree declaring that,

"any and all movable or immovable goods, which are in the possession of foreign natural or legal persons and which are used or destined to be used for the exploitation of natural resources situated on the Pulentian teritory, and any rights or claims relating to such exploitation, are part of the inalienable property of the people of Pulentia."

As of the same date PMD is designated as administrator of the property concerned. On 5 November compensation in the sum of $ 750,000 is fixed for Gasexco's assets (without right of appeal), but refused by the latter which estimates the value of its assets in Pulentia at $ 12,000,000. Meanwhile, on 21 October 1978, the Council had revoked the travel permission previously granted to the workers employed by Gasexco at its exploitation site on the high seas, since the workers were, "indispensable for the democratic development of the country."

The shipyard transports the platform "HZ 80" by tug to Rijeka (Rotterdam), arriving on 10 November. Prior to the contemplated delivery to Gasexco, a delegation of PMD executives succeeds in obtaining possession of the platform from the shipyard's personnel. The next day an attachment is levied on it on behalf of Gasexco which claims the ownership of the "HX 80" by virtue of the contract with the shipyard, all terms of which have been complied with. Litigation follows in the court in Rijeka (Rotterdam) between Gasexco as claimant and PMD and the shipyard as defendants. Against PMD Gasexco claims validation of the attachment and an order of the court that the "HZ 80" be relinquished to it. Gasexco argues that the Decree of 1 November 1978 is an unlawful act under international law which has no effect upon the transfer of title between the shipyard and Gasexco. Moreover, Gasexco brings an additional claim for damages in the amount of $ 12 million for unlawful taking of its property in Pulentia. Finally, Gasexco alleges breach of the contract for the engagement of personnel at its site on the high seas, and claims damages in the amount of $ 800,000 for costs occasioned by delay and engagement of other personnel.

Against all these claims, the State of Pulentia, through its agency PMD, primarily invokes immunity of jurisdiction. Subsidiarlly, it pleads that the Decree in dispute is a lawful exercise of the sovereign right to its natural resources.

The court, having heard arguments from counsel for Gasexco, the State of Pulentia and the shipyard, decides to seek your expert opinion on certain questions. In order to be informed on all the options open to it, the court requests you to answer all the questions although the answer to some of them, if accepted by the court, would render others irrelevant.

1. Is the State of Pulentia entitled to immunity of jurisdiction in respect of Gasexco's claims:
   (a) as to the ownership of the "HZ 80";
   (b) as to the taking of its property in Pulentia;
   (c) as to breach of the personnel engagement contract?
2. Is the Decree of 1 November 1978 to be regarded as an unlawful act under international law?
3. What law governs the action by Gasexco against the shipyard?
4. In connection with your answer to question 2, what is the effect, if any, of the Decree on the ownership of the "HZ 80" at the date of its attachment in Rijeka (Rotterdam)?
5. Irrespective of your answer to question 1(c), would the court have international jurisdiction to hear the action for breach of the personnel engagement contract?
6. Supposing that question 5 is answered in the affirmative, what law would govern that action?

STUDENT REPORT

by V. Crnić and V. Tomljenović

1. JURISDICTIONAL IMMUNITY

Regarding all of Gasexco's claims, the State of Pulentia invokes jurisdictional immunity, claiming that no foreign court has the right to question its acts.

In order to solve the problem of immunity and the invocation of immunity we must first explain the concept of immunity.

Jurisdictional immunity means the right or the privilege of a foreign State to be exempt from the jurisdiction of the courts of any other State. Basically, there are two theories of sovereign immunity.

According to the first theory, i.e., the absolute theory of immunity, also called the classical theory, a State is always entitled to immunity. To the representatives of this theory, it makes no difference in which capacity a State acts, whether it acts in its capacity as a sovereign power or as a private legal person.

"The real principle on which the exemption of every sovereign from jurisdiction of every court has been deduced, is that the exercise of jurisdiction would be incompatible with his regal dignity, that is to say, with his absolute independence of every superior authority." [1]

The fundamental facts and reasons that support absolute jurisdictional immunity are, among others: [2]

1. A State jealously protects its sovereignty;
2. It is difficult to distinguish between the capacity of *ente politico* and *ente civile;*
3. In most cases it is not possible to enforce judgments against a foreign State; and
4. Judicial proceedings against a foreign State could bring about a conflict in the good relations between the States.

Among the States which in principle recognize jurisdictional immunity, even if *acta gestionis* of private law are concerned, are Germany, England (The Parlement Belge, 1830), the USA (*The Shooner Exchange* v. *McFaddon*), Czechoslovakia, Poland, Portugal. As for the Soviet doctrine, it also views the principle of immunity as being absolute: "If one takes that immunity is based on the principle of sovereignty, then it must follow that every state may enjoy it, so long as it remains independent and sovereign." [3] The classical theory, however, is now being applied less and less. One of the main reasons for its abandonment is that modern States are developing their commercial activities to an ever greater extent as private legal persons. Of course, the interests of domestic commercial life as well as justice require that the citizens of the State in question are given legal protection in disputes arising from contracts concluded

1. Brett, L.J., in the Parliament Belge Case, cited in, Friedman, Lissitizyn and Pugh, *International Law – Cases and Materials,* (St. Paul, Minn. 1969), p. 653.

2. Morelli, Eckstein, cited in, Eisner, *Medjunarodno privatno pravo II* (Zagreb 1956), p. 275.

3. Boguslavski, "State Immunity", in Friedman, Lissitzyn and Pugh, op.cit., p. 657.

with foreign States. A change can indeed be detected today; namely, both in legislation and caselaw the viewpoint prevails that a State is entitled to immunity only if it acts in the capacity of a legal person under private law and is, therefore, subject to the rules of private law. This point of view is supported by the followers of the restrictive theory of sovereign immunity. According to their opinion, the statement that States are always entitled to immunity cannot be taken as a rule of international customary law because facts exist that deny this statement. Above, all, there is a permanent body of caselaw in Italy, Belgium, Switzerland and Austria.[4]

Moreover, there is the tendency for the restrictive theory of immunity to be recognized in the legislation of some States. For example, the Argentinian Civil Code explicitly states that foreign States acting as private legal persons are subject to domestic jurisdiction. (Art. 34).[5]

The principle that *acta jure gestionis* of States are exempt from the jurisdiction of another State is also expressed in several international agreements, e.g., The Treaty of St. Germain, the Paris Air Navigation Convention of 1919 and the Warsaw Convention for the Unification of Certain Rules Regarding Air Transport of 1929.

As for the Yugoslav legislation on jurisdictional immunity, a provision of the Code of Civil Procedure states that Yugoslav courts are not competent to hear cases in which the defendant is a foreign person who is entitled to immunity in Yugoslavia. The contents and extent of this privilege are determined by the rules of international law. (Art. 26). Among those entitled to immunity are also foreign States; however, according to some theorists [6], it is disputable whether the rule of immunity applies absolutely to foreign States. Namely, the tendency exists for foreign States to waive immunity in cases where they appear as equal subjects in an economic legal relation. In addition to this exception, the Yugoslav Code of Civil Procedure contains still another connected with real rights concerning immovables in Yugoslavia and problems related to the possession on these immovables. Namely, in such cases actions can be brought even against a person who, otherwise, would have been exempt (Art. 56).

This provision is in accordance with the Vienna Convention on Diplomatic Relations of 1961. Article 31(1) provides that a diplomatic agent shall enjoy immunity from the criminal, civil and administrative jurisdiction of the receiving State,

"except in the case of: (a) a real action relating to private immovable property situated in the territory of the receiving State, unless he holds it on behalf of the sending State for the purposes of the mission." [7]

4. Austria: Dralle *v.* Czechoslovakia, in, Friedman, Lissitzyn and Pugh, op.cit., p. 657.

5. Eisner, *Medjunarodno privatno pravo* (Zagreb 1956), p. 271.

6. Triva, *Gradjansko parnično procesno pravo* (Zagreb 1978), p. 49; Andrassy, *Medjunarodno pravo* (Zagreb 1976), p. 290.

7. See also, North, *Cheshire and North's Private International Law* (London 1974), p. 112.

Therefore, it can be said that the relations between modern States and, furthermore, the tendency of these States to enter to an ever greater extent into economic relations not in their capacity as sovereign but as private legal persons, has made the restrictive theory of immunity more acceptable than the absolute one, which today has lost much of its meaning. Finally, in our opinion, it would not be in accordance with the basic principles of law to prevent one of the parties to the contract from protecting its rights because the other party, i.e., the State, has invoked immunity.

Immunity, the privilege of certain aliens and States to be exempt from local jurisdiction, is a question of a procedural character. Procedural questions in proceedings before Yugoslav courts are solved in accordance with the rules of the domestic procedural law, *lex fori.*[8] *Lex fori* also applies in those cases in which the parties are foreign and the governing law of the action is foreign material law.

According to Article 26 of the Yugoslav Code of Civil Procedure, Yugoslav courts are not competent in actions in which the defendant is a foreign person who is entitled to immunity in Yugoslavia. On the other hand, as an exception to the general rule, Yugoslav courts are competent to hear actions against exempt persons in cases involving real rights to immovables in Yugoslavia (Art. 56).

Gasexco sues Pulentia for real rights to the ownership of platform "HZ 80". In Article 6, paragraph 9 of the Law on Sea and Inland Navigation, we see that the drilling platform is equated with a maritime ship. A ship is, according to provisions of the same law, a movable (Art. 189) since it is intended constantly to change its position. One view, however, which is supported by doctrine, allows for an exception to the rule in cases involving ways of securing, conveying or releasing real rights. Namely, in these cases the ship is regarded as an immovable.[9]

Thus, we come to the conclusion that the platform "HZ 80" would be regarded as an immovable in regard to real rights since it is equated with a maritime ship. In view of the fact that Gasexco files a claim alleging real rights to an immovable, i.e., the platform "HZ 80", which is situated on Yugoslav territory, in our opinion this would be an exception to Article 56 of the Code of Civil Procedure according to which an exemption from immunity exists in cases involving claims of real rights to immovables situated in Yugoslavia. This means that Pulentia would not be entitled to immunity of jurisdiction regarding Gasexco's claims to the ownership of "HZ 80".

Recognition of the privilege of immunity in this case would be in opposition to the principles of sovereignty and independence, according to which every State has its own exclusive or internal competence with which no one can interfere.

2. Answering the second part of the question relating to invocation of immunity of Pulentia, concerning the claim of Gasexco as to the taking of its property

8. Triva, op.cit., p. 48.
9. Jakaša, *Udzbenik plovidbenog prava* (Zagreb 1979), p. 84.

in Pulentia, we can start with the principles of sovereignty and independence. According to these principles of international law, every State has its own exclusive or domestic competence.[10]

The Decree of 1 November 1978 can be identified as an act of State that a State brings in its capacity as a sovereign power on the territory where it has absolute right to exclusive jurisdiction. In pursuance with the restrictive theory of immunity, which is generally accepted today, a State is entitled to exemption from jurisdiction when it exercises its sovereign rights. Since Pulentia acts as a sovereign power when issuing its Decree, this means that there is no possibility for another State to question the legality of nationalization relating to property within its territory at the time of the Decree and therefore, Pulentia is entitled to immunity.

3. Pulentia, furthermore, invokes immunity regarding Gasexco's claims for breach of contract concerning engaged personnel. In this contract, concluded in Pulentia between Gasexco and PMD, Pulentia does not appear in its capacity as a sovereign power but as an equal party in a private legal relation with the same rights and obligations as Gasexco.

With regard to the fact that all of the questions concerning immunity were answered in accordance with the restrictive theory of immunity we shall, therefore, apply this theory to this problem too. Therefore, since the theory makes a distinction between acts of State as a sovereign power and a private person, and with regard to that acknowledges or denies the privilege of immunity, it is our opinion that in the breach of personnel engagement contract case, Pulentia has no right to invoke immunity.

2. NATIONALIZATION

The next problem is whether the Decree of 1 November 1978 can be regarded as an unlawful act according to international law.

In order to answer this question, it is necessary to differentiate two aspects of that Decree since it can refer to property within the territory of Pulentia as well as to property outside its territory.

First of all, we must attempt to define the term nationalization. There are many opinions and viewpoints on this problem depending on the nature of the social and economic structure of the individual country.

According to some theorists (Blagojević, Batiffol), it is necessary to differentiate between two types of nationalization: nationalization of property and nationalization of legal persons, i.e., enterprises.[11] In the case of nationalized property, an ownership relation is involved and therefore, the conflict of laws provisions relating to ownership are to be applied, i.e., *lex rei sitae.* On the other hand, if

10. Andrassy, op.cit., p. 85.
11. Jezdić, *Medjunarodno privatno pravo III* (Belgrad 1978), p. 85.

an enterprise has been nationalized the status relation is that of a legal person and its personal law is to be applied.

According to a second point of view, nationalization is considered a sovereign act of a State carried out on its territory. According to this act of State doctrine, courts of one State cannot judge the governmental acts of another State which are executed within the limits of its sovereignty. This viewpoint has been applied in judgments of American and British courts, e.g., in *Banco National de Cuba* v. *Sabbatino, Princess Palay* v. *Veiss,* etc.[12]

A third group of theorists regards nationalization as a penal or political law. Since the principles of international law do not provide the extraterritorial effect of penal or political law, these theorists are of the opinion that nationalization cannot be recognized outside the territory of the State in question. The penal character of nationalization served American courts as justification for not recognizing the effects of Soviet nationalization in the following cases: *James et. Co.* v. *Second Russian Insurance,* and *Salimoff et Co.* v. *Standard Oil Company of New York.*[13] In the French doctrine, the political nature of the act of nationalization was expressed by Armignon. In England, foreign expropriatory legislation is recognized when it is directed not against a particular person but against national property in general.[14]

In order to answer the above question we must determine the effects of nationalization, i.e., the effects of the Decree in dispute. As we have already stated, the Decree of 1 November can have two kinds of effects depending on whether the property is located inside or outside Pulentian territory. First we shall attempt to outline the effects of nationalization within Pulentian territory.

The principle of permanent sovereignty over natural resources is affirmed today in international law. According to this principle:

"Each State has the right:

(c) To nationalize, expropriate or transfer ownership of foreign property, in which case appropriate compensation should be paid by the State adopting such measures, taking into account its relevant laws and regulations and all circumstances that the State considers pertinent. In any case where the question of compensation gives rise to a controversy, it shall be settled under the domestic law of the nationalizing State and by its tribunals, unless it is freely and mutually agreed by all States concerned that other peaceful means be sought on the basis of the sovereign equality of States and in accordance with the princple of free choice of means."[15]

The principle of permanent sovereignty over natural resources includes the right of a State to use all its economic and natural resources for its development

12. Ibid., p. 86.
13. Ibid., p. 87.
14. North, op.cit., p. 139.
15. Charter of Economic Rights and Duties of States, GA Res. 3281 (XXIX), adopted 12 December 1974, Art. 2.

without any restriction. Two pacts on human rights [16] also contain this principle, slightly restricted, however, in the sense that the free usage of natural resources must not be at the expense of obligations arising from international economic cooperation. The essential document on this subject-matter, the Bolivian Resolution, was adopted in 1952 by the UN. It affirms that it is a sovereign right of every State freely to use its natural resources.[17]

Therefore, we can say that the Decree of 1 November is to be recognized and that it is lawful under international law; but only the part relating to property that was on Pulentian territory at the time of the Decree. In this and other similar cases it follows that, "any act of a sovereign State on its territory has absolute power and therefore it must be recognized by another State." [18] In accordance with this point of view, it is our opinion that the property that was nationalized within Pulentian territory is now the inalienable property of Pulentia, regardless whether that property was owned by some organization or natural alien or subject.

In this case we can identify the Decree with an act of sovereign power. In view of the "act of state" doctrine, it is our opinion that the courts of one State cannot judge the acts of another State that are exercised within the territory of its sovereignty. For example, we can point to the above-mentioned *Banco National de Cuba* v. *Sabbatino* (1964), where the American Supreme Court refused to recognize the decision of the court of first instance, i.e., its legality under international law, thus explaining that an American court is not competent to examine the legality of nationalization in a foreign country.

"The act of state doctrine in American law is closely related to the principle of sovereign immunity. Both stemmed, initially, from conceptions of absolute territorial sovereignty and the relationship between those conceptions and a power-oriented theory of jurisdiction which equated physical power over parties with the right to decide their disputes and lack of such power with the lack of jurisdiction." [19]

Also in English law we can find that the courts recognize the legality of nationalization that is exercised within the territory of the nationalizing State [20]:

"The English courts recognize that the ownership of property is conclusively and finally determined by the terms of the foreign Decree of expropriation if the property is situated within the jurisdiction of the sovereign at the time of the decree notwithstanding that it is later brought to England, and is still there at the time of the action."

16. International Covenant on Civil and Political Rights; International Covenant on Economic, Social and Cultural Rights, Resolution No. 2200 (UN 1966).

17. Jezdić, op.cit., p. 80.

18. Eisner, *Medjunarodno privatno pravo I* (Zagreb 1953), p. 197.

19. Rees and Rosenberg, *Conflict of Laws, Cases and Materials,* (Mineola, N.A. 1971), p. 764.

20. North, op.cit., 10th ed. (1979), p. 141.

As an example, we can cite *Luther* v. *Sagor.* According to Warrington, L.J., who presided in this case, no sovereign State must sit in judgment upon the acts of another foreign State affecting property within its territory.

"It is well settled that the validity of the act of one independent sovereign Government in relation to property and persons within its jurisdiction cannot be questioned in the courts of this country." [21]

In the opinion of Cheshire and North, one of the main reasons for making such decisions is the territorial principle:

"the simple and decisive justification of the decision is the rule that a title to movables, valid according to the *lex situs* at the time of its acquisition, is recognized by English law. The law of the *situs* must prevail in such circumstances unless the rule of that law under which that title has been acquired is so immoral or so alien to the principles of justice as understood in England that it must be disregarded as being contrary to public policy." [22]

The final confirmation of the legality of the Decree in its reference to property within Pulentian territory, is contained in the principles of the "New Economic Order" which were affirmed at the Sixth Conference of Non-Aligned Countries in Havana. In addition, the non-aligned countries initiated a proposal in the United Nations that all countries should have equal rights to a uniform development. This proposal was confirmed by a majority vote of the General Assembly on 16 December 1979.

Thus we come to the next problem, whether to recognize the legality of the part of the decree concerning the nationalization of property outside of the nationalizing State. This deals with the question of the extraterritorial effect of nationalization.

The theory and the practice of some States, e.g., England, differentiate between two situations:

1. when the property belongs to its own citizens;
2. when the property belongs to aliens.

Ad 1. According to Cheshire, historical authority is not lacking for the view that the right to expropriate property may be based upon allegiance of its owner as well as upon its situs. But then an additional claim is demanded, i.e., the State that exercised nationalization has to obtain possession or control of the property at the time the nationalization act is passed. English courts based their decision on this reasoning in the case of Spanish ships nationalized by the Spanish Republican Government in 1938.[23]

21. Ibid., pp. 138-139.

22. Ibid.

23. The Christina Case: the Spanish Republican Government requisitioned all ships registered in Bilbao. The Christina was berthed at Cardiff. The Spanish Consul boarded her, disclosed the requisitioning decree and put a new master in command. The House of Lords held that jurisdiction must be declined since the ship was in the possession of a foreign State.

Ad 2. If an alien's property in question is located outside the jurisdiction of the nationalizing State and there is neither allegiance of its owner nor its *situs* as a reason for nationalization, the decree itself is not sufficient for obtaining ownership. Such a view is generally accepted for two reasons. On the one hand, a decree of nationalization is considered a political act and therefore has no effect outside the country that issues the decree.[24] On the other hand, nationalization with extraterritorial effect refutes the principle of sovereignty in the State where the property is located because in this case it would encroach on the so-called "domain reservé" to which every State has absolute right. In the *Jupiter* (1927) and the *Russian Bank for Foreign Trade Case* (1933), English courts held that Soviet decrees could not have effect on property situated outside the Soviet Union.

In view of the generally accepted point of view expressed in court decisions it is our opinion that the Decree of 1 November 1978, i.e., the part referring to aliens' property not within Pulentia, has no lawful basis under international law and, therefore, is not effective outside Pulentian territory.

3. GOVERNING LAW

The next question concerns the law that governs the action by Gasexco against the shipyard.

As mentioned above, the contract concluded between Gasexco and the German shipyard contained a choice of forum clause, bestowing competence on the court in Rijeka, but no choice of law clause. Since competence has been bestowed on the court at Rijeka, *lex fori,* namely, Yugoslav law will be applied.

The object of this contract is a platform for the exploitation of oil, "HZ 80", which according to our Law on Sea and Inland Navigation is a maritime ship (Art. 6, para. 9). This means that we have to deal with a contract for building a ship. This kind of contract is governed by Article 1008 of that same law: "Relations connected with a contract for the building, rebuilding or reparation of a ship are to be governed by the shipyard's residence law, when there is no choosen law, or the choosen law is not applicable." This provision is in accordance with the principle that has been created for contracts in which one of the parties is a large organisation and the other a number of persons from various contries. The governing law for such contracts is the law of the residence of the party which appears in all these contracts. Since this, to a certain extent, is the case when shipyards are concerned, it is advisable to recommend the application of the law of their residence.[25]

Thus the governing law for the action by Gasexco against the shipyard is German law.

24. Eisner, op.cit., p. 127.
25. Katicić, *Novi ogledi* (Zagreb 1977), p. 106.

4. EFFECT OF THE DECREE ON THE OWNERSHIP OF "HZ 80"

The day before the attachment was levied on behalf of Gasexco, executives of the Pulentian Mining Dept. succeeded in obtaining possession of the platform from the shipyard's personnel by showing their Decree of nationalization that applied also to the platform.

The question to be answered concerns the effect of the Decree, if any, on the ownership of the platform on the day of its attachment in Rijeka, with regard to its legality or illegality under international law.

Answering question 1 (a) we stated that the platform is considered to be a maritime ship in accordance with Article 6, paragraph 9 of the Yugoslav law on Sea and Inland Navigation. Considering the fact that the problem is connected with the ownership of the platform, i.e., with a right *in rem*, we shall therefore apply a conflict of laws provision of the Law on Sea and Inland Navigation relating to rights *in rem* over maritime ships. According to this provision (Art. 996, para. 2) the governing law for the right *in rem* to the ship is the law of the nationality of the ship. The nationality of the ship has been accepted by a majority of States as a connecting factor for determining the governing law for real claims relating to registered ships.[26] The law of the ship's nationality is accepted among others, by the Montevideo Convention on International law (Art. 27), by the *Codigo Bustamente* (Art. 275), by the German *Schiffsrechte G.* (Para. 1/II) and by the Italian *Codice della navigazione* (Art. 6).[27]

From the given text we were not able to determine whether the platform was registered or not. In our opinion, it is, therefore, necessary to present a few of the possiblities and solutions that could be relevant.

One of the possibilities is that the platform was not registered at all. In this case it could not be regarded as a maritime ship, but rather as an ordinary movable and thus *lex rei sitae* would be applicable for the rights *in rem.*[28] Since the platform is located in the Port of Rijeka, the governing law would be Yugoslav law. According to theorists of civil law[29], in order to secure rights *in rem* to movables, it is necessary to present a valid legal title in addition to the ownership of the previous owner, and delivery. Pulentia obtained possession of the platform from the shipyard on the grounds of the nationalization decree that we consider unlawful in the part referring to extraterritoriality. This means that the title used to gain possession of the platform is unlawful and therefore it follows that Pulentian possession of the platform is also unlawful. In a case of unlawful possession it is impossible to secure rights. Therefore, we would conclude that the decree has no effect on the ownership of "HZ 80" on the day of its attachment in Rijeka.

26. Mitrović, *Pomorsko pravo (Jugoslavenski leksikon imovinskog prava* (Belgrad 1979), p. 41.
27. Eisner, op.cit., p. 65.
28. Jakaša, op.cit., p. 84. Eisner, ibid., p. 65.
29. Rajačić, *Stvarno pravo* (Zagreb 1956), p. 13.

The next possibility is that the platform could be registered in Germany. The conflict of laws provision of the Law on Sea and Inland Navigation (Art. 996, para. 2) directs us to the law of the nationality of the ship when real rights to the ship are concerned. Thus, we must turn to German law. According to Paragraph 1/II of the *Schiffrechte Gesetzbuch*, procurement and suspension of ownership rights to a ship registered in Germany is governed by German law.[30] In accordance with the provisions of German law, the existence of a clear express will is sufficient in order to transfer the ownership of registered ships; it is not necessary to deliver the ship.[31] In view of the fact that Gasexco and the shipyard signed a contract for the building and delivery of the platform, the will to transfer the ownership of the platform was expressly declared and thus Gasexco became owner on the grounds of the contract itself.

As for the effects of the nationalization decree concerning ownership of the platform "HZ 80" we stated, in our answer to the second question, that the part of the decree refering to property outside Pulentia is unlawful under international law and can therefore produce no effects on the ownership.

The last possibility which we shall attempt to explain, presupposes that the platform was registered in Yugoslavia and has Yugoslav nationality (Art. 166, Law on Sea and Inland Navigation). In this case the rights *in rem* would be governed by Yugoslav Law in accordance with Article 996, paragraph 2 of our Law on Sea and Inland Navigation which states: "The real rights to a ship are to be governed by the law of the nationality of the ship." This law contains no provision specifying the character of registration of ownership. Hence it follows that ownership is transferred on the grounds of a written contract and the registration is of a purely declaratory character [32], as far as the contract parties are concerned. According, however, to Article 248 it can be concluded that the registration of such rights is constitutive when a third party is involved.

In our case, Pulentia does not obtain possession of the platform from the owner since Gasexco became the owner on the grounds of the registration and the contract for building the platform. This fact makes Pulentian possession of the platform unlawful as well as the fact that the nationalization decree is unlawful under international law, i.e., the part relating to property outside Pulentian territory. Since the Pulentian delegates obtained possession of the platform on the grounds of an unlawful decree, their possession of the platform is also unlawful. As a result they have no rights of ownership because no legal rights can be obtained on the basis of unlawful possession.[33]

Thus we can draw the conclusion that the nationalization Decree of 1 November 1978 has no effect whatsoever on the ownership of the platform "HZ 80" on the day of its attachment in Rijeka.

30. Kegel, *Internationales Privatrecht* (Munich 1977), p. 333.
31. Palandt, *Udžbenik plovidbenog prava* (Zagreb 1979), p. 94.
32. Jakaša, op.cit., p. 94.
33. Rajačić, op.cit., p. 13.

5. JURISDICTION

The court furthermore seeks our opinion whether it would be competent to hear the action by Gasexco for breach of the personnel engagement contract. The contract that has been concluded between Gasexco and the government of Pulentia in Pulentia, contains no choice of forum or choice of law clauses.

First of all, we must emphasize that this dispute contains a foreign element. Provisions on international jurisdiction give us the answer to the question whether a domestic or foreign court is competent to hear an action. Since this is a procedural question, it has to be solved by the *lex fori.*

According to the Yugoslav Code of Civil Procedure (Art. 27 on the jurisdiction of the courts in proceedings with a foreign element), Yugoslav courts have an absolute jurisdiction whenever this is expressly stated by federal law or by international agreement, or whenever that jurisdiction is stated in federal law provisions about local jurisdiction. Since a Yugoslav court does not have absolute jurisdiction in this case, the parties could have agreed on the competent court in accordance with Article 70, paragraph 5: "Parties can bestow competence on a foreign court if one of the parties is a foreign natural or legal person whenever there is no exclusive competence of Yugoslav courts." As we know, Pulentia and Gasexco had no choice of forum clause in their contract. Therefore, we must examine the remaining provisions on competence in the Code of Civil Procedure.

First of all, we must consider Article 46 on general forum: "If there is no exclusive local competence of some other court, the court of general forum is competent." This provision is in accordance with the general principles of jurisdiction and is accepted by practically all legislations.[34] The definition of general forum is given in Article 47: "The court of the defendant's residence is generally competent for hearing actions." In our case, the defendant is Pulentia, which means that the Yugoslav courts have no general forum.

As we have seen, it is not possible to bestow competence on the Yugoslav cour either by the agreement to submit to jurisdiction or by general forum. Thus we have to examine Article 58, paragraph 1 to see if it is possible to bestow competence on the Yugoslav court by forum *rei sitae:* the Yugoslav court would be competent if there is any property of the defendant on its territory." At the time the action was brought, Pulentia had no property on the territory of the court in Rijeka. In view of this the Yugoslav court has no jurisdiction. However, if the court decides to recognize the ownership of the platform "HZ 80" in favour of Pulentia, Pulentia would then have had property on the court's territory and accordingly, the court would then be competent.

34. Katičić, *Medjunarodno privatno pravo* (Zagreb 1977), p. 80.

6. LABOUR CONTRACT

If the Yugoslav court had competence for the action for breach of the personnel engagement contract, what law would govern that action?

The primary connection factor in individual labour contracts in most countries is the autonomy of the parties. However, as we have seen, the parties to this contract, Pulentia and Gasexco, did not establish the choice of law. In such a case, the law to be applied is determined by subsidiary connecting factors, which vary from country to country, which, however, usually include the place where the work is done, employer's residence, or the nationality, i.e., domicile, of the parties.[35]

According to German caselaw and literature, these factors include the business seat of a corporation and the place where the work is done, i.e., the place where the corporation is located or the place where a corporation's dominant activities are performed.[36] If the activities are carried out in territories of different jurisdictions, the governing law is that of the place where the domicile of the employer is situated.[37] In the German Democratic Republic, the Code of the International Private Law of 1976 recognizes the law of the employer's domicile as the governing law for labour relations.

According to Czechoslovak law, relations that arise from labour contracts are governed by the law of the place where the work is done, *lex loci laboris.* If, however, the place where the work is done and the employer's domicile are in different countries, *lex loci delegationis* is applicable, except in cases when the worker's domicile is in the State of the place where the work is done.[38]

In 1937, the Institute de droit international issued a resolution on the Conflict of Laws and the Object of Labour Contracts, according to which *lex autonomiae* is the primary appropriate law and *lex loci laboris* the subordinate one. In cases in which it is not possible to determine the *lex loci laboris,* the resolution differentiates two groups of cases: [39]

1(a) when the place where the work is done is in two or more States; or

1(b) when the place where the work is done is not subject to the law of any State, then the law of the State where the employer's domicile is situated is applicable;

2. when the labour relation involves maritime, river or air navigation, the law of the nationality of the ship or plane governs.

The view represented in the Yugoslav Draft Law on International Private Law and Proceedings of 1974 should also be mentioned. According to the Draft, the governing law for labour contracts is *lex loci laboris.* If the work,

35. Sajko, *Radni odnosi (Imovinsko pravni leksikon)* Vol. II, para. 637.
36. Gamillscheg, *Internationales Arbeitsrecht* (Berlin 1959), p. 127.
37. Vuković, *Mjerodavno pravo zu radne odnose* (Zagreb 1979), p. 7.
38. International Private and Procedural Law, Art. 16/1.
39. Sajko, *Mjerodavno pravo za radne odnose* (Zagreb 1979), p. 5.

however, is temporarily conducted in one State and the domicile of the employer is situated in another, the applicable law is that of the place of his domicile, i.e., *lex loci delegationis* (Art. 31, para. 2).[40]

Returning to the case in question, we have already pointed out that *lex autonomiae* cannot be applied since Gasexco and Pulentia did not agree on the governing law. According to the contract the work is to be done on the high seas, off the "nearest coast of Pulentia, but not in any economic zone nor on any continental shelf". In such cases where the working site is subject to the law of no State at all, e.g., on the high seas, the connecting factor is the employer's domicile. The governing law is thus *lex loci delegationis.*

Therefore, if the Yugoslav court were competent for the action for breach of the personnel engagement contract, it would apply Yugoslav law since Gasexco is situated in Rijeka, Yugoslavia.

7. CONCLUSION

1. The question regarding invocation of immunity we answered in accordance with the restrictive theory of immunity, which is accepted today by most countries.

Pulentia would not be entitled to immunity regarding Gasexco's claim to the ownership of "HZ 80" situated in Yugoslavia, because recognition of invocation of immunity would be incompatible with Yugoslav sovereignty. When issuing its decree Pulentia acts as a sovereign power within the territory of its jurisdiction and is, therefore, entitled to immunity with regard to Gasexco's claims against seizure of its property in Pulentia.

2. In the personnel engagement contract Pulentia appears as an ordinary legal personality and has, therefore, no right to invoke immunity.

3. As to the legality of the nationalization decree under international law, we differentiated two aspects of it. The first aspect of this decree is related to property within Pulentian territory and it is in accordance with the principle of permanent sovereignty over natural resources. Therefore, it is our opinion that it is lawful under international law. On the other hand, this is not the case with the part meant to be extraterritorial, which we regard as unlawful under international law.

4. The governing law for Gasexco's action against the German shipyard is, according to our Law on Sea and Inland Navigation, German law.

As we have already stated, answering the second question, the Decree of 1 November 1978 is unlawful under international law in its part relating to property outside Pulentia. It can, therefore, have no effect on ownership of the platform "HZ 80", no matter whether the platform was registered or not.

40. Nacrt zakona o MPP-u i postupku (Zagreb 1974).

5. According to the Yugoslav Code of Civil Procedure it is not possible to bestow competence on the Yugoslav court for the action for breach of the personnel engagement contract, neither by agreement to submit to jurisdiction nor by general forum. The Yugoslav court would be competent only if Pulentia had any property on the court's territory.

If the Yugoslav court had competence for the action for breach of the personnel engagement contract, the governing law for this action would be Yugoslav law, with regard to the fact that since the place where the work had to be done was on the high seas, we could not apply *lex loci laboris,* but *lex loci delegationis.*

Reijka 1980

STUDENT REPORT

by E.C.H. de Léon and T.Th. Sternfeld

INTRODUCTION

The Court of Rotterdam has asked our opinion on certain questions which have arisen in the case between a gas exploitation company (Gasexco), the State of Pulentia/its Mining Department PMD and a German shipyard.

Before we come to the answers to these questions we would like to make some remarks.

1. For the integral text of the case, as it was laid before us by the Court of Rotterdam, we refer to [Appendix I].
2. Though the text of the case is not clear on this point, we assume that the State of Pulentia is party to the suit, as the PMD, being a State organ, is to be identified with the State of Pulentia.
3. Neither can it be concluded from the case where and when the delegation of the PMD executives obtained possession of the platform. We presume it was after the tenth of November in the harbour of Rotterdam.
4. Further lack of clarity in the text of the case relates to a descrepancy in the given facts: on the one hand, the case speaks of a contemplated delivery by the shipyard to Gasexco, on the other hand, it is said that all the terms of the contract between Gasexco and the shipyard have been complied with, which, in our opinion, would also include delivery.
5. When we use the word 'summons' we mean *dagvaarding/dagvaarden.*
6. We will not answer all the questions in the order in which the Court has put them. We will deal with question four after and in connection with question two. The same procedure will be followed as to questions three and six.

ADVICE

The first question, which is sub-divided, deals with immunity of jurisdiction. First we will give a survey on immunity of jurisdiction, after which we will answer the questions, about which we will give our opinion now: as to question 1a and 1b our advice is denial of immunity of jurisdiction and as to 1c immunity is to be granted.

In our survey on immunity of jurisdiction we will discuss the following aspects:

1. the principle of State Immunity;
2. The extent of State Immunity,
   2.1. the absolute theory,
   2.2. The relative or restrictive theory;
3. The European Treaty on State Immunity.

1. In international law there exists the principle of State Immunity, which rests on two ideas.

One is expressed in the maxim: *par in parem non habet jurisdictionem,* which is based on the concept that no sovereign State against its will can be subject to the jurisdiction of the courts of another State.[1] This maxim is a corollary of the status of equality attached to the independent sovereign State: legal persons of equal standing cannot have their disputes settled in the courts of one of them.[2]

The second idea is that of non-intervention in the internal affairs of other States.[3] It is to be noted that this immunity is a prerogative of States and States only. This privilege is not to be attributed to lower corporations of the state-authorities.

2. Considering now the extent of State Immunity we see that a State is limited in its claims to immunity and also that it is not entitled to immunity under certain circumstances. With the latter we have in mind the so-called waiver of immunity: immunity can be waived by the State concerned either expressly, for instance by contract or treaty, or by conduct, which is to be seen in the actual submission to the proceedings in the local court. And when we say 'limited' we allude to the doctrine of restrictive or relative immunity.

In caselaw we can see that there is a development in the approach to the principle of immunity of jurisdiction by the courts.

2.1. Formerly the quality of 'State' was sufficient to achieve immunity: the character of the act was of no importance. This wide principle of immunity is often called the doctrine of absolute immunity. An example of the doctrine of absolute immunity is given by the Court of The Hague.[4]

However, in the course of the nineteenth century, States went into commercial, industrial and financial businesses on equal terms with their subjects on quite a large scale. Because of this extension of State activity it became neces-

1. Voskuil, *De Nederlandse Rechtspraak betreffende de Staatsimmuniteit,* Preadvies Nederlandse Vereniging voor Internationaal Recht No. 68 (The Hague 1973), p. 9.
2. Brownlie, *Principles of Public International Law,* 2nd ed., (Oxford 1973), p. 316.
3. Brownlie, op.cit., p. 317.
4. Rb. The Hague, 1 March 1917, NJ 1917, 389: Immunity of the German State, based on the general principles of international law according to which two sovereign States are equal and independent and so one State has no jurisdiction over the other. The same goes for the judicature of a State, because this organ of a State can have no more power than the State itself.

sary to diminish the exceptional legal position, which the State used to have according to the doctrine of absolute immunity. The underlying thought was that a State, coming down from its sovereign height and mixing with the common people in the market place could no longer claim this special protection, which was based on the principles mentioned above.[5]

2.2. This brings us to the doctrine of restrictive or relative immunity. The doctrine makes a distinction between acts of government, *acta iure imperii*, and acts of a commercial nature, *acta iure gestionis*, and denies immunity of jurisdiction in the latter case.[6]

When we look at Dutch caselaw we see that the criteria for drawing the distinction between *acta iure imperii* and *acta iure gestionis* were not easy to find. This problem was caused by the question: is it the purpose or rather the character of the act which determines whether it is *iure imperii* or *iure gestionis*.

A very well-known illustration of this problem is given in the situation where the government purchases, e.g., boots for its army. If we look at the purpose of this contract we see that the underlying motives are of a military nature and so this act, which serves the well-being of the State is to be considered as a typical governmental act, for which the State is entitled to immunity. If this doctrine were to be applied, not much would be left of the 'restrictiveness' of immunity, because acts of a government always serve the public well-being in one way or another. But considering the character of this act, we notice that it is just a transaction which might as well have been made between two individuals. It is this criterion which does justice to the doctrine of restrictive immunity.[7]

We can say that nowadays the doctrine of restrictive immunity is the ruling one in all western countries.

3. This has been reflected in the European Treaty on State Immunity, of 16th May 1972 by the Council of Europe.

The set-up of this Treaty is based on the absolute theory. The cases in which a State is not entitled to immunity are listed (in the Artt. 1-15); in all other cases immunity exists (Art. 15). But the exceptions to immunity are so broadly formulated, that they cover most of the *acta iure gestionis*. We can conclude that this Treaty is an example of the doctrine of restrictive immunity.

We would like to remark that for Dutch law this principle of immunity of jurisdiction, which is a principle of public international law, is applicable because of the existence of Article 13a Wet A.B., which states that "the courts' juris-

5. Tammes, *International Publiekrecht*, 2nd ed., (Amsterdam 1973), p. 156.

6. Brownlie, op.cit., p. 320.

7. HR, 26 October 1973, NJ 1974, 361 note Panhuys; HR applies the criterion of the character of the act and denies immunity. It is also interesting to mention the criterion of the quality of the acting institution, which was supposed to determine the character of the act. It did not loosen the concept of immunity, because it always led to immunity, e.g., Rb. Utrecht 14 January 1969, NYIL (1970), p. 229; Brinkhof NV *v.* NV Nederlandse Spoorwegen and the Deutsche Bundesbahn: Railway exploitation is a task of the German State: therefore, immunity can be claimed.

diction . . . is limited by the exceptions, recognized by the Law of Nations."

Now we have reached the point where we come to the answers to the questions about which the Court of Rotterdam has asked our opinion.

1a. Is the State of Pulentia entitled to immunity of jurisdiction in respect of Gasexco's claim as to the ownership on the "HZ 80"?

In our opinion the State of Pulentia has no right to immunity. The delegation of the PMD obtained possession of the platform. The act was based on the Decree of 1st November 1978 and in this case the PMD acted in the capacity of administrator of property that was theirs, according to the Decree. It is clear that the PMD was acting on the territory of another State when it obtained possession of the platform in the harbour of Rotterdam. It is a general principle of international law that a State cannot exercise its power in any form on the territory of another State. This is based on the principle of exclusive territorial sovereignty of a State.[8] There are examples of activities carried on in the territory of a State by organs of another State, acting on behalf of the latter and so encroaching upon the sovereignty mentioned above: for instance, the activities of diplomatic or consular officials. It is to be noted that these organs act with the consent of the sovereign State and so immunity can be claimed for their acts. In this case there is no question of consent having been given to the PMD by the Dutch government to act as officials within the Dutch borders. And by acting as it did, the PMD encroached upon the exclusive territorial sovereignty of the Netherlands. This we consider an international wrong. As an international wrong cannot give rise to an international right, the State of Pulentia is not entitled to immunity of jurisdiction before the Court of Rotterdam.

1b. As to the second question: Is the State of Pulentia entitled to immunity of jurisdiction in respect of Gasexco's claim as to the taking of its property in Pulentia?

It is our opinion that this should be answered in the affirmative. We consider the taking of the property according to the Decree as an act of nationalization.[9] The right to nationalize is the consequence of the exclusive territorial sovereignty of a State, which means that is has supreme power over all persons and things within its territorial jurisdiction, which includes foreigners.[10] Nationalization is

8. *Lotus Case* PCIJ Series A no. 10 p. 18: "Now the first and foremost restriction imposed by international law upon a State is that – failing the existence of a permissive rule to the contrary – it may not exercise its power in any form in the territory of another State. In this sense jurisdiction is certainly territorial; it cannot be exercised by any State outside its territory except by virtue of a permissive rule derived from international custom or from a convention".

9. White, *Nationalization of Foreign Property* (London 1961), p. 41. Nationalization is the term used to describe the process whereby property and rights and interests in property are transferred from private to public ownership by agents of the State, acting on the authority of a legislative or executive measure.

10. Kronfol, *Protection of Foreign Investment: A Study in International Law* (Leyden 1972), p. 22.

to be considered as an exclusively sovereign act; this means it can only be performed by a State.[11] In other words, here we are dealing with an act purely *"iure imperii"* and as we said above, according to the doctrine of restrictive immunity, a State is entitled to immunity for acts done *"iure imperii"*.

1c. Considering now Pulentia's claim to immunity in respect of the breach of the personnel engagement contract, here we advise denial of immunity.

The contract involved is a contract of a purely commercial nature, which can also be concluded by private persons. The fact that specialized workers, hired from the government of Pulentia, were involved, is of no importance, because, as we said above, according to Dutch caselaw on the doctrine of relative immunity, we do not look at the quality of the persons involved, but only at the nature of the act, *in casu* a purely private personnel engagement contract.

Another question the Court asks us to answer concerns the lawfulness under international law of the Decree of 1st November 1978.

This Decree is to be considered as a Nationalization Decree. In order to be able to answer the question as to its lawfulness under international law, which according to our opinion will be an answer in the affirmative, it is necessary to give a survey on:

1. the contents of nationalization.
2. the existence of a State's right to nationalize.
3. the requirements for a lawful nationalization under international law.

1. Many authors have given a definition of nationalization, which is in fact a form of expropriation. We will quote that given by White:

"Nationalization is the term used to describe the process whereby property and rights and interests in property are transferred from private to public ownership by agents of the State, acting on the authority of a legislative or executive measure."

Nationalization is to be distinguished from other kinds of expropriation by its economic motivation and the fact that the nationalized property should be used for the public benefit.

2. The right to nationalize is generally accepted in international law. It is a consequence of the sovereignty of a State over all persons and things within its jurisdiction, including foreigners.[13] In 1952 the General Assembly of the United Nations affirmed this right implicitly in its Resolution of December 2nd, 1952.

11. Victory Transport *v.* Comisaria General, Supreme Court ILR 35, p. 110.
12. White, op.cit., p. 41.
13. Kronfol, op.cit., p. 22.

(Resolution 626 (VII)) (Annex I). It was said that, "the right of peoples freely to use and exploit their natural wealth and resources is inherent in their sovereignty. . ." [14]

The right of a State to nationalize foreign property was more explicitly recognized in the Resolution of the General Assembly of the United Nations of 1962: Resolution 1803 (XVII) (Annex 2). The Resolution refers to, "the sovereign and inalienable right of all states freely to dispose of their natural wealth and resources in accordance with their natural interests and the economic independence of states." It emphasized the national sovereignty with its fundamental corollary: the right to nationalize foreign property.

3. The requirements for a lawful nationalization under international law are the following:
(a) Lawful government
(b) Public purpose
(c) Non-discrimination
(d) Compensation.

(a) According to international law the fact of revolution is *non-obstant* to the lawfulness of a government.

(b) The requirement of public purpose means that the nationalization should promote the public welfare of the nationalizing State. Article 4 of Resolution 1803 (XVII) uses the term 'public utility'.

Many authorities consider this requirement not to be a proper one, since the definition of nationalization presupposes the taking of property to be in the public interest, which leads to the conclusion that any nationalization will automatically satisfy this requirement.[15] The only limitation international law can impose is that the nationalization must be in *bona fides.*

(c) According to international law the principle of non-discrimination demands that no discrimination may be made,
(i) between foreigners and nationals, and
(ii) foreigners as between themselves.
This principle has been modified.
(i) *Non discrimination between foreigners and nationals*

It is not forbidden in international law to nationalize foreign interests in a field where nationals have no interests of the same kind. Nationalization, which takes

14. This Resolution was invoked by Guatemala in support of the nationalization of the United Fruit Company in 1953. In 1954 the Rome Court considered the Iranian Oil Nationalization Law to be internationally legal, citing the Resolution of 1952. James Hyde, "Permanent Sovereignty over Natural Wealth and Resources" AJIL 1956, p. 854.

15. White, op.cit., p. 149.

place in order to obtain sovereignty over natural resources, does not automatically imply that the State should want to expropriate its own nationals too.[16]

(ii) *Non-discrimination between foreign nationalities*

Some authorities demand strict application of this principle; others think that exceptions to this rule can be made. This conflict can be illustrated by the Indonesian nationalizations. The Dutch Appellate Court thought the nationalization to be discriminatory.[17] The German Court took a different view.[18] Here we are particularly concerned with discrimination that takes place in a 'colonial relation', but in general we can state that in cases of nationalization, practice makes it impossible, because of financial, economic and technical reasons, not to discriminate.

In our opinion all that can be insisted on, is that the intention to take over individual property of foreigners should be in good faith and must have a reasonable relation to the various proportions of property owned or business done in the country by the different nationalities.

(d) The fourth limitation according to international law is that compensation for the nationalized property should be paid.

State practice shows that almost all nationalizing countries admit the existence of a duty to compensate: nationalizations are accompanied by the granting of compensation.[19] The problem is when and how compensation must be paid. The classic formula was that it should be "prompt and effective."[20] This rule, which originated from former small scale expropriations, proved to be financially and economically incompatible with the position of the developing countries, nationalizing on a large scale. This resulted in payments being spaced and calculated with reference to the general economic position of the State concerned.[21] This practice

16. Hartmann, *Nationalisierung und Enteignung im Völkerrecht* (Berlin 1977), pp. 108-110: "The only goal of the nationalization is often to shake off the economic and political dependence upon foreign states".

17. Hof Amsterdam, 4 June 1959, NJ 1959, 350, Bank Indonesia *v.* Senembah Maatschappij NV. The nationalization was contrary to international law, because it was directed solely against Dutch enterprises. Moreover, these measures were used as instruments of political pressure.

18. NV Verenigde Deli Maatschappijen en NV Senembah Maatschappij *v.* Deutsch Indonesische Tabak Handelsgesellschaft mbH. Domke, "Indonesian Nationalization Measures before Foreign Courts" AJIL 1960, p. 315. The Bremen Court of Appeals stated that: "the equality concept means only that equals must be treated equally and that the different treatment of unequals is admissible . . . The attitude of former colonial people toward its former colonial masters is of course different from that toward other foreigners".

19. "Almost all countries", e.g., Russia stated that international law could not possibly impose the duty to pay compensation.

20. Kronfol Z.A., op.cit., pp. 28-29: "prompt": the compensation should be paid before the taking of the property or within a short time thereafter. "adequate": meant that compensation should correspond fully to the value of the taken property. "effective": meant and still means that when compensation is paid, it should be of real economic value to the alien recipient. The question of effectiveness usually turns on the currency.

21. State practice shows a variety of ways in which compensation is paid, e.g., lump sum settlements are very frequent. A striking example of compensation is found in the Chilean Copper Nationalizations. In the calculation of the amount of compensation 'excess profits' were taken into account: "Decree concerning excess profits of Copper Companies", ILM 1973, pp. 983-988.

was affirmed by Resolution 1803 (XVII), which states in Article 4 that, " in case of nationalization . . . *appropriate* compensation shall be paid in accordance with the rules in force in the State taking such measures in the exercise of its sovereignty and in accordance with international law".

It seems that for a considerable time the States, which nationalized in order to get permanent sovereignty over their natural wealth and resources and so try to become economic and politically independent, held the view that it is not international law that obliges them to pay compensation, but that it is their own national law which will say whether this duty exists and in what way.[22] This opinion is reflected in the UN Resolution 3281 (XXIX) of 12th December 1974, called the Charter of Economic Rights and Duties of States, which speaks of the State's "right to nationalize . . . foreign property, in which case appropriate compensation should be paid by the State adopting such measures, taking into account its relevant laws and regulations and all circumstances that the State considers pertinent." No more reference is made to international law nor to the requirement of public utility. Irrespective of the international legal value of this Resolution, we think that the industrial countries, which insist on the application of Resolution 1803 (XVII) in case of nationalization, do wrong to the developing countries. While they acknowledge a State's sovereign right over natural wealth and resources, they should also accept the right of a State to determine the amount of compensation in accordance with its financial and economic position as a developing State.[23]

In view of the preceding, we advise the Court to consider the Decree as lawful under international law.

In this Decree the State of Pulentia puts its sovereign right over its natural wealth and resources into effect. As we said above, each State has the right to nationalize. It is to be noted that this Decree is the basis for a series of nationalizations. The contents of the Decree are perfectly lawful: first, we will consider the Revolutionary Council to be the lawful government of the State of Pulentia, as international law does not turn against revolution and we do not see anything from the case that might give us another opinion in this matter; secondly, we assume that the nationalization is of 'public utility' as the terms of the Decree do not lead us to think differently. Moreover, the revoking of the travel permission (previously granted to the workers) because of their 'indispensability for the *democratic development of the country*' is an indication of 'public utility'. Thirdly, we see that all foreign nationalities will be affected by the nationalizations: the Decree does not mention a particular group. So, we conclude that the principle of non-discrimination has been properly applied. The fact that the Decree does not extend to its own nationals does not make it discriminatory. As

22. Brehme, *Souveränität der jungen Nationalstaaten über Naturreichtümer* (Berlin 1967), p. 153.

23. As to the international value of this Resolution: Kokkini-Iatridou, "Naar Aanleiding van een Leidse Oratie" WPNR 1978, 5448, p. 558: "This Resolution cannot be considered to be generally accepted in international law, as the rich industrial countries voted against the Resolution or abstained".

we said above, it is nowadays an accepted fact that nationals of the nationalizing country do not have to be affected by the measure. Fourthly, as to the compensation, we see that it is granted. The fact that the Decree itself does not mention compensation does not make it unlawful in our opinion. So we conclude that the Decree is lawful under international law.

We would like to make another remark concerning the lawfulness of the nationalization in question, which is based on the Decree. We can imagine, that Gasexco, representing the opinion of the Western industrial countries, thinks that the nationalization is unlawful because of the "manifest insufficiency" of the indemnities: there is a considerable difference between the amount fixed by Pulentia ($750,000) and the amount assessed by Gasexco ($12,000,000). Beyond doubt Gasexco will demand the full application of Resolution 1803 (XVII), i.e., "appropiate compensation . . . according to international law." Pulentia, however, will refer to its status of developing country and will appeal to its right to determine the amount of compensation itself according to its financial and economic position. As we do not know what this position is, we do not consider ourselves competent to give a judgment as to this matter.

Now we will answer the question as to the effect of the Decree on the ownership of the platform.

Here we are dealing with the question of the existence and extent of the territorial limitation of the exercise of the State's right to nationalize. A State's right to nationalize is derived from its sovereignty, i.e., the territorial supremacy of the State. The following situations may occur:

1. The property is situated within the territory of the nationalizing State. Inside its territory a State is free to act as it likes; so it is entitled to nationalize any property within its borders.

2. The property is situated outside the territory of the nationalizing State. Here we will make a distinction:

(a) Legislation of a State may extend to persons, acts or property outside the State's own territory, i.e., 'extra-territoriality.' [24] This is a logical consequence of the sovereignty of a State within its own territory.

(b) But an attempt, actual and practical, made by the nationalizing State, to exercise its jurisdiction within the territory of another State is unlawful, unless, of course, the other State should consent.[25] Therefore, this exercise of authority of a foreign State will conflict with the territorial sovereignty of the other.[26] The case at hand is an example of the situation described in II. First,the property is situated *outside* the territory of the nationalizing State. The terms of the

24. E.g., Kronfol, op.cit., pp. 23-24. The Egyptian Decree on the Nationalization of the Suez Canal Company provided for extra-territorial nationalization. This issue was forestalled by the Suez Canal Settlement Agreement of 14 June 1958.

25. Schwarzenberger, *International Law, Vol. I, International Courts,* 3rd ed., (London 1957), p. 185. White, op.cit., pp. 105-106.

26. Adriaanse, *Confiscation in Private International Law* (The Hague 1956), p. 158.

Decree are so widely formulated that one could assume that it might have the intention to have an extraterritorial effect. As we said above, it is generally accepted in international law that legislation, *in casu* the Decree, may extend extraterritorially. Secondly, from the fact that a delegation of PMD executives obtained possession of the platform outside Pulentian territory, we conclude that an actual attempt was made by Pulentia to impose the Decree on property situated abroad.

In spite of the fact that the Decree is lawful under international law, this activity of the PMD, based on the Decree, is to be considered as an excess of jurisdiction and is contrary to international law. This Decree cannot be executed but within the Pulentian territory, so it cannot give title to ownership of the "HZ 80" as it was situated in Rotterdam.

Therefore, we advise the Court to consider the Decree of 1st November 1978 of no importance with regard to the ownership of the platform.

After having given our expert opinion on the preceding three questions, which all concerned public international law, we now enter the field of private international law.

First, we will decide upon the law that governs the action by Gasexco against the German shipyard.

The facts are as follows: In 1976 Gasexco concluded a contract with a German shipyard: the shipyard was to build a drilling platform ("HZ 80") at a cost of $ 5 million and its delivery by the shipyard was to take place in Rotterdam. The contract contained a choice of forum clause bestowing competence on the Court in Rotterdam. No choice of law clause was made.

Is is clear that because of interference by the PMD delegation the German shipyard did not fulfil its part of the contract: it did not deliver the "HZ 80" to Gasexco. This non-fulfilment of the contract is the reason why the shipyard is summoned by Gasexco before the Court of Rotterdam.

In our opinion the law of the Federal Republic of Germany governs the action of Gasexco against the shipyard.

We came to this conclusion after having considered the steps necessary according to private international law. These are the following:

1. The question whether a choice of forum clause implies a choice of law.
2. The problem of the qualification of the legal relation between Gasexco and the shipyard.
3. The existence of relevant treaties.
4. The conflict rules applicable to this specific legal relation.

1. According to Dutch case law the fact that a choice of forum clause has been made, does not imply that the parties concerned have also agreed upon a choice of law.[27] However, a choice of forum clause can, of course, in combination

27. Hof The Hague, 13 April 1960, NJ 1961, 172, Schellen, Scheepvaart en Bevrachting *v.* La Baloise Transport. Hof The Hague, 3 December 1960, S&S 1964, 26, Pan Europa de Comercio SA *v.* Schuitema.

with other relevant facts pertaining to the contract, contribute to the determination of the applicable law.[28] This means that though a Dutch court, *in casu* the Court of Rotterdam, has competence according to the contract between Gasexco and the shipyard, this does not imply that Dutch law automatically governs the action.

2. Now we come to the qualification of the legal relation between the parties concerned, i.e., the determination of the character of the matter in question. According to Dutch doctrine a court has to qualify according to its own system of private international law. In our case this means that the Court of Rotterdam has to qualify in accordance with Dutch law.[29] As can be seen from the case, Gasexco has concluded a contract with the German shipyard according to which the latter was obliged to build and deliver a platform for which Gasexco would pay $ 5 million. Thus, the legal relation can be qualified as belonging to the law of contract. The fact that the HZ 80 had to be built makes us decide that in this case there is no question of the contract being a contract of sale, but that it is to be considered as a contract for the undertaking of work (*aanneming van werk*) with a delivery clause.

3. Relevant to this contract is the Convention relating to a Uniform Law on the International Sale of Goods, The Hague, 1 July 1964 (Trb. 1964, 117 and 1968, 13), which was incorporated into Dutch law by the Law of 15 December 1971, (S. 780), the so-called LUVI. Both Germany and the Netherlands are parties to this Convention.

The law refers to contracts of sale (Art. 1). However, in Article 6 an extension has been made to the scope of application of LUVI: a contract, concerning delivery of goods to be produced, is to be identified with a contract of sale. This might lead to the conclusion that the LUVI has to be applied to our case. But considering Article 5.1.b. we conclude for non-application of the LUVI: as to the sale of ships that have to be registered in a public register, LUVI is not to be applied. We agree with Pabbruwe, where he says that a platform is to be considered as a ship.[30] As the platform is destined for use at sea, we regard it as a seaship. According to the Dutch Merchant Law (Art. 314) a ship over 20 m3 has to be registered. Presumably the "HZ 80" will be over 20 m3, so it should be registered. In this case the LUVI is not to be applied. We would come to the

28. Deelen, *Rechtskeuze in het Internationaal Contractenrecht: Een jurisprudentie-onderzoek* (Amsterdam 1965), p. 126, p. 134; also Rb. Rotterdam, 13 February 1970, AK 6333, Penning *v.* van der Heyden; Rb. The Hague, 1 December 1970, AK 6386, Broekhuyzen & Zn *v.* Hemken.

29. Sauveplanne, *Elementair Internationaal Privaatrecht,* 6th ed. (Deventer 1977), pp. 62-63.

30. Pabbruwe, "Is een Booreiland een (Zee)Schip? " WPNR 1966, 4904, pp. 206-208. In its decision of 8 June 1956, NJ 1957, 67, the Hoge Raad decided that in order to consider a vessel a ship it is not necessary that its primary destination is to sail. This leads Pabbruwe to conclude that a platform is to be considered a ship, because it has the capacity to sail. Also, Dorhout Mees, *Nederlands Handels- en Faillissementsrecht,* Vol. III (Amsterdam 1974), 6th ed. p. 237. (He considers a platform to be a ship, because, though the destination might be to remain in a certain place, it always keeps its capacity to sail).

same conclusion if we were to consider a platform to be an immovable good, since LUVI refers to the sale of movable goods.

4. As no treaties appear to be applicable to this case, we will have to find the law that governs the action between Gasexco and the shipyard according to the conflict rules of Dutch private international law.

As we said above, the parties included no choice of law clause in their contract. Furthermore, the case gives us no facts from which the parties' wish to submit their contract to a specific legal system can be deduced. This means, that we will have to determine the applicable law by objective conflict rules, i.e., rules, which determine the applicable law by means of factors, that exist irrespective of the will of parties.

From of old it was said that, as to international contract law, it was the *lex loci contractus* that determined the applicable law: the law of the place where the contract was concluded was decisive. The present means of communication and the existence of world trade centres make the *locus contractus* an insufficient connecting factor. Another solution was sought in the application of the *lex loci solutionis:* the law of the country, where the obligation has to be executed. This theory proved to be of no use, since most contracts create more than one obligation. This means that, as to the international contract, not one, but various *'leges solutionis'* might be found. A third possibility was said to be found in the presumed will of the parties as to the applicable law. This theory is based on a fiction and does not serve legal certainty.

The prevailing conflict rule concerning international contract law is given in the proper law theory. According to this theory that system of law is applicable with which the contract has its 'closest and most real' connection. To find the applicable law one has to sort out the relevant elements of the contract and to connect these elements with the system of law to which they are related. After weighing the relevant connecting factors one specific system of law will often turn the scales. This 'proper law' theory is to be considered more as an approach than as a rule according to which the applicable law can be found. The difficulty in the 'proper law' doctrine can be the determination of what is to be considered as the most relevant factor, especially when the connecting factors are in balance. This brings us to the doctrine of the characteristic obligation.

According to this doctrine the law to be applied is the one of the country in which the party that has to fulfil the 'characteristic obligation' has its residence or is established. The characteristic obligation is that obligation which determines the specific nature of the contract.

Vischer distinguishes six categories of contracts, for each of which he indicates that obligation which is to be considered as the 'characteristic' one.[31] In the opin-

31. Vischer, *Internationales Vertragsrecht* (Bern 1962), p. 114 et seq. As for our case the contract belongs to category 3: 'Verträge auf ein Tätigwerden'. The charactheristic obligation is performed by the shipyard (i.e., building of the platform).

ion of some Dutch authors it is this doctrine that determines the proper law of the contract.[32] In this opinion the proper law is found, when the characteristic obligation and the law to which it is related have been traced; there is hardly any space left for other connecting factors.[33] The theory of the characteristic obligation applied this way created, as to international contracts, a specific rule giving a substantive connecting factor (the characteristic obligation), which might serve legal certainty, but encroaches upon justice in certain cases. Therefore, we prefer the opinion of others, who regard the characteristic obligation as one of the relevant connecting factors that determine the proper law of the contract, thus leaving the proper law the broad formula it is. According to this view the characteristic obligation is the connecting factor that settles the matter when all relevant factors are in balance.[34]

The importance of the characteristic obligation can be illustrated by the Preliminary Draft Convention of the European Communities on the Law applicable to Contractual and non-Contractual Obligations. Article 4 of this draft Convention says that a contract is governed by the law of the country with which it has its closest connection (i.e., the proper law of the contract which, according to Article 4.2. is supposed to be the law of the country where the party that has to fulfil the characteristic obligation is established or has its residence. In Article 4.4., however, an exception is made in case the contract has a closer connection with another legal sphere.

It is this conception that can be found also in Dutch case law: in international contracts the proper law is to be ascertained by the relevant connecting factors of the contract in question. In the total range of connecting factors the characteristic obligation plays an important part, but not a decisive one: if the contract is considered to belong to another legal sphere than the one indicated by the characteristic obligation, the law of that country is to be applied.[35]

Now we will explain our advice to the Court to apply German law to the action of Gasexco against the German shipyard.

According to the proper law theory the relevant factors pointing to German law are:

32. De Winter, "Enige Beschouwingen over de Wet van de Karakteristieke Prestatie", in, *Met eerbiedigende Werking,* Festschrift Hijmans van den Bergh (Deventer 1971), p. 367 et seq.

33. Hof Amsterdam, 1 April 1970, NJ 1971, 115, NAP NV *v.* Christophery GmbH. The proper law was determined by the characteristic obligation. No other relevant factors were mentioned.

34. De Boer, "Objectieve Verwijzing in het Internationale Overeenkomstenrecht", WPNR 1974, 5244, 5245, p. 7 et seq.

35. HR, 27 October 1972, NJ 1973, 121, Neska *v.* De Beijer. The characteristic obligation is one of the relevant factors that leads to application of Dutch law. Also, HR 6 April 1973, NJ 1973, 371, Topsøe *v.* del Prado. The contract was governed by the law of the country in which the party that fulfilled the characteristic obligation was established. The Hoge Raad, however, did not use the term 'characteristic obligation'. Reference was made to the possibility of application of another law, if more relevant factors would have pointed in that direction. In the same line: HR, 8 June 1973, NJ 1973, 400, Mackay *v.* American Express Company Inc.

(a) the place of business of the shipyard in Germany;
(b) the building of the drilling platform in Germany;
(c) the transportation of the platform by Germans.
The building and transportation we consider to be the characteristic obligation.
The factors that point to Dutch law are:
(a) the place of business of Gasexco in the Netherlands;
(b) the existence of the forum clause bestowing competence on a Dutch court.
The fact that delivery was to take place in Rotterdam we do not consider to be a relevant factor, because the platform was not destined to be used in the Netherlands. It was to be transported to Pulentia.

After weighing all these factors, we find the contract to have its most real and closest connection with the German legal sphere: the characteristic obligation has to be performed by a German shipyard, established in Germany. The facts that point to Dutch law are not sufficient to make the contract belong to the Dutch legal sphere.

We consider it useful to answer the question as to the law that governs the action for the breach of the personel engagement contract now, because we are dealing again with a contract.[36]

The facts are as follows: Gasexco has hired a team of specialized workers from the Government of Pulentia for the last two months of 1978; they were to assist at an exploitation site on the high seas. The contract was concluded in Pulentia with the Pulentian Mining Department. No choice of law or choice of forum was inserted in the contract. On 21st October 1978 the Revolutionary Council revoked the travel permission granted to the workers.

Because of the revoking of the travel permission the PMD committed a breach of contract: it did not place the specialized workers at Gasexco's disposal at the exploitation site.

We would advise the Court to apply Pulentian law to the action by Gasexco against the PMD.

We can be brief in explaining how and why we came to this advice: we followed the same steps taken in the preceding question.

1. This problem did not need to be considered, since neither a choice of law, nor a choice of forum clause was made.

2. The legal relation between Gasexco and the PMD is obviously to be qualified as belonging to the law of contract, i.e., a personnel engagement contract.

3. There exist no relevant treaties relating to this matter.

4. As the foregoing steps did not give us any indication as to a specific law to be applied, we fully depend, here as well, on the conflict rules given by Dutch private international law by means of which the applicable law will be traced. We will have to find the prpper law of the contract.

36. Notwithstanding the fact that here a contract concluded with the *State* is involved, we will apply to this matter the rules given by private international law, for here the PMD did not act in its capacity as State organ but as a 'private person'.

The contract has connections with both the Dutch and Pulentian legal spheres; the only relevant factor pointing to Dutch law is:
(a) The place of business of Gasexco in the Netherlands.

All other relevant factors point to Pulentian law, namely:
(a) the fact that the contract was concluded in Pulentia;
(b) the seat of the PMD in Pulentia;
(c) the fact that it is the PMD that has to place the workers at Gasexco's disposal;
(d) the fact that the workers involved are specialized workers of the Government of Pulentia.

When we take the 'characteristic obligation' into consideration we see that it is to be fulfilled by the Pulentian Mining Department: it has to place the personnel, engaged by Gasexco, at the latter's disposal. The fact that the PMD has its seat in Pulentia makes, according to the doctrine of the 'characteristic obligation', Pulentian law applicable. This and other connecting factors clearly show that the personnel engagement contract between Gasexco and the PMD has its most real and closest connection with the Pulentian legal sphere; we therefore advise the Court to apply Pulentian law to the action in question.

Now we will have to consider the question, whether the Court has international jurisdiction to hear the action for breach of the personnel engagement contracts.

In our opinion the Court of Rotterdam has international jurisdiction as to this action.

To come to this conclusion we took the following into consideration:
1. The existence of relevant treaties relating to this matter.
2. The rules given by Dutch law relating to the international jurisdiction of the Dutch Courts.

1. A relevant treaty regulating jurisdiction is the EEC Convention on Jurisdiction and the Enforcement of Judgments in Civil and Commercial Matters, Brussels 27 September 1968 (Trb. 1969, 101).

Pulentia not being a member of the EEC, is obviously no party to this Convention.

This Convention is to be applied when the defendant party, irrespective of its nationality, is domiciled in a contracting State: Article 4 of the EEC Convention says that in case the defendant has no domicil in the territory of a contracting State, the jurisdiction of each Contracting State is to be determined by the law of that State, except for the cases mentioned in Article 16 ('exclusive jurisdiction'). The action between Gasexco and the PMD does not fall in any of the categories listed in Article 16.

This makes us conclude, that the EEC Convention is not to be applied here since the PMD is established in Pulentia and not in one of the Contracting States.

2. Since there appear to be no relevant treaties relating to this matter , we will have to look for the rules given by Dutch law to determine whether the Court has international jurisdiction.

The international jurisdiction of the Dutch Courts is based on the rules given by the Dutch Code of Civil Procedure.[37] In cases that start with a summons (*dagvaarding*) jurisdiction is mainly based on the rules given in Article 126 of this Code. When a case is started with a request (*verzoekschrift*) the jurisdiction is based on Article 429c BW. Since in our case there is contentious litigation between Gasexco and the PMD we will not further discuss this Article; Article 126 BW is the relevant one.

We base the international jurisdiction of the Court to hear the action for breach of the personnel engagement contract on Article 126 of the Code of Civil Procedure. This principal rule is that in cases relating to purely personal matters [38], the defendant will be summoned before the judge of his domicil (Art. 126.1) or before the judge of his actual residence (Art. 126.2). This is in accordance with the principle *'actor sequitur forum rei'.* As the PMD has neither domicil nor actual residence in the Netherlands, jurisdiction of the Court cannot be based on this principle. However, Article 126.3 states that when the defendant has no domicil or actual residence in the Netherlands he can be summoned before the Dutch court, provided that the plaintiff has his domicil or actual residence in the Netherlands; the competent Court is that of the domicil or actual residence (*forum actoris*).

Since the plaintiff (Gasexco) is established in Rotterdam, this means that the competent Court is to be found in Rotterdam. Thus, it is clear that there exists a competent judge. Another question relates to adjudicatory jurisdiction. According to Articles 38.1 jo 53 of the Law on the Judicial Organisation, the District Court is the competent tribunal, since the claim of Gasexco amounts to over fl. 3.000,--, namely $ 800,000.

So we may conclude that the Court of Rotterdam has international jurisdiction to hear the action of Gasexco against the PMD.[39]

This is our advice concerning the questions the Court of Rotterdam has asked us to answer. We hope it may be of use to the Court.

One further matter we would bring to the Court's attention is to ask for some more details; lack of facts, at times even contradictory facts, have sometimes obliged us to proceed from assumptions when we answered a question. Other solutions might be possible if these assumptions prove to be wrong.

Amsterdam/Zandvoort 1980

37. Sauveplanne, op.cit., p. 84.

38. 'Purely personal matters': Art. 129.1 BW gives a definition of the term personal claim, i.e., a claim relating to the fulfilment of a personal obligation resulting from contract or the law. The action for breach of the personnel engagement contract is such a personal claim.

39. Stein, *Compendium van het Burgerlijk Procesrecht*, 4th ed. (Deventer 1977) pp. 71-72.

ANNEX 1

Resolution 626 (VII) Right to exploit freely natural wealth and resources.

The General Assembly,

Bearing in mind the need for encouraging the under-developed countries in the proper use and exploitation of their natural wealth and resources.

Considering that the economic development of the under-developed countries is one of the fundamental requisites for the strengthening of universal peace.

Remembering that the right of peoples freely to use and exploit their natural wealth and resources is inherent in their sovereignty and is in accordance with the Purposes and Principles of the Charter of the United Nations.

(1) Recommends all Member States, in the exercise of their right freely to use and exploit their natural wealth and resources wherever deemed desirable by them for their own progress and economic development, to have due regard consistently with their sovereignty, to the need for maintaining the flow of capital in conditions of security, mutual confidence and economic co-operation among nations;

(2) Further recommends all Member States to refrain from acts, direct or indirect, designed to impede the exercise of the sovereignty of any State over its natural resources.

ANNEX 2

Resolution 1803 (XVII) Permanent sovereignty over natural resources.

The General Assembly,

Declares that:

(1) The right of peoples and nations to permanent sovereignty over their natural wealth and resources must be exercised in the interest of their national development and of the well-being of the people of the State concerned.

(2) The exploration, development and disposition of such resources, as well as the import of the foreign capital required for these purposes, should be in conformity with the rules and conditions which the peoples and nations freely consider to be necessary or desirable with regard to the authorization, restriction or prohibition of such activities.

(3) In cases where authorization is granted, the capital imported and the earnings on that capital shall be governed by the terms thereof, by the national legislation in force, and by international law. The profits derived must be shared in the proportions freely agreed upon, in each case, between the investors and the recipient State, due care being taken to ensure that there is no impairment, for any reason, of that State's sovereignty over its natural wealth and resources.

(4) Nationalization, expropriation or requisitioning shall be based on grounds or reasons of public utility, security or the national interest which are recognized as overriding purely individual or private interests, both domestic and foreign. In such cases the owner shall be paid appropriate compensation in accordance with the rules in force in the State taking such measures in the exercise of its sovereignty and in accordance with international law. In any case where the question of compensation gives rise to a controversy, the national jurisdiction of the State taking such measures shall be exhausted. However, upon agreement by sovereign States and other parties concerned, settlement of the dispute should be made through arbitration or international adjudication.

(5) The free and beneficial exercise of the sovereignty of peoples and nations over their natural resources must be furthered by the mutual respect of States based on their sovereign equality.

(6) International co-operation for the economic development of developing countries, whether in the form of public or private capital investments, exchange of goods and services, technical assistance, or exchange of scientific information, shall be such as to further their sovereignty over their natural wealth and resources.

(7) Violation of the rights of peoples and nations to sovereignty over their natural wealth and resources is contrary to the spirit and principles of the Charter of the United Nations and hinders the development of international co-operation and the maintenance of peace.

(8) Foreign investment agreements freely entered into by or between sovereign States shall be observed in good faith; States and international organizations shall strictly and conscientiously respect the sovereignty of peoples and nations over their natural wealth and resources in accordance with the Charter and the principles set forth in the present resolution.

ADDRESS OF WELCOME AND PRESENTATION OF STUDENT AWARDS BY THE MAYOR OF FRANEKER, MR. J.J.H. POP

I would like to extend a welcome to you all, especially to you, Mr. Sumonja, Ambassador of the Socialist Republic of Yugoslavia in The Netherlands. It is an honour that you are present in our town on this occasion, and may I therefore present you with this gift, the collection of the Professors of the University of Franeker.

(The presentation to His Excellency took place)

Ladies and Gentlemen, we would have liked this session to have taken place in the old town hall here in Franeker, but much to our regret it is not possible due to restoration of the building at this time. The reception of the Mayor and Aldermen can also not take place there, but we have a good alternative; we will go to our museum after this meeting here. At the end of the meeting I will have the opportunity to tell you something about our former university and about Franeker. I wish you a successful conference. Thank you.

(A discussion, under the Chairmanship of Dr. Voskuil, took place)

Today Franeker is in a sense once again a university town. By your presence the old tradition of the Academy of Franeker is being revived. We had here a college for adult education for more than 250 years from 1585 till 1811. In that period our town played an important role in the Frisean *(Frieslandse)*, the Dutch and international cultural life. The Franeker Academy enjoyed an international reputation. In those times Franeker was populated by students from many countries. One of the reasons was that penniless students were totally, while poor students were partly, financed by the local authority. They did not have to pay lecture fees so a lot of students from countries at war used this opportunity. Some of them later became Professors, like the Pole Makovius. There was great freedom at the Franeker university, there was no censorship and the professors were not checked by inspectors or visitors. When there was a transfer of the rectorship the professors and their wives were invited to a banquet by the local authority. For the rest there was not much amusement for the students in the city, so Franeker gained the reputation of a vicious college life, a dissolute college life; there were quarrels between international student corps, fights frequently took place, (you can see it in the booklet on page 26, you can see such a fight). The Senatus Judiciadus maintained that it was the heyday of the students pub and one of them still exists, de "bocht van quinee", (you can see that on page 15 and also in the other documentation. There is an English translation with it). Some of the students did not complete their studies, but travelled from one European university to the other. It is a bit like today, because you are only here for one afternoon.

And now the Professors. Between 1585 and 1843, 196 Professors lectured at Franeker, some of them more than 50 years and others only for a few months. France, Poland, Sweden, Britain and Switzerland supplied us with many professors. I would like to mention one of them especially, Ulricus Huber, (you can see his portrait on page 13), who in 1675 at the age of 21 was appointed professor in Elocuencia, Historia and Politices. In 1665 he accepted a professorship in law with the *Oratio Exibens Historium Juris Romani et Ues Argumentatio Continuam.* Huber started there with public law, which he built on a new foundation and developed to an independent scholarship. He wrote about it: *De Jure Civitatis Novam Juris Publici Universalis Disciplinam Continentes.* The University of Leyden tried twice to get Professor Huber to Leyden; however, he became a judge at the Court of Leeuwarden. He did not like that and after three years he became Professor in Franeker once more; Leyden was left out in the cold for a time. Huber also did other things for the Academy. Sometime in 1675, when there was talk of moving the Academy to Leeuwarden, Huber wrote a protest dialogue between a Leeuwarder and a Franeker citizen. According to the text of the dialogue the Leeuwarder commoner put forward that the nobility of Leeuwarden was so underdeveloped that the arrival of the University would be a present from heaven. The Franeker citizen, however, got the final word and gained the victory; after that the Academy held out till 1811. Then the University of Franeker was closed down as a result of the concentration of university education by Napoleon and after the defeat of Napoleon a new institute of higher education opened in Franeker in 1815, the State Atheneum, which, however, was not allowed to confer academic degrees. This Institute never flourished and was therefore closed in 1843. You will understand that on this particular afternoon we should think back to the days of our Academy.

Ladies and gentlemen, I have also been asked to present the awards to the winning teams. I feel honoured to do this and I would like to congratulate the winners. In the days of the Academy they also used to present prizes to students. As there were sometimes medals I also offer you, on behalf of the local authority, a commemorative medal.

(The presentation to the student teams took place)

Ladies and gentlemen, I also would like to present our edition of portraits of the Franeker Professors to the Praesidium, Professor Matic and Dr. Voskuil.

(The presentation to the Praesidium took place)

GPSR Compliance

The European Union's (EU) General Product Safety Regulation (GPSR) is a set of rules that requires consumer products to be safe and our obligations to ensure this.

If you have any concerns about our products, you can contact us on ProductSafety@springernature.com

In case Publisher is established outside the EU, the EU authorized representative is:

Springer Nature Customer Service Center GmbH
Europaplatz 3
69115 Heidelberg, Germany

Batch number: 10830943

Printed by Printforce, the Netherlands